Database Transaction Models for Advanced Applications

THE MORGAN KAUFMANN SERIES IN DATA MANAGEMENT SYSTEMS

Series Editor, Jim Gray

Database Transaction Models for Advanced Applications
Edited by Ahmed K. Elmagarmid (Purdue University)

A Guide to Developing Client/Server SQL Applications
Setrag Khoshafian (Portfolio Technologies, Inc.),
Arvola Chan (Versant Object Technology),
Anna Wong (CLaM Associates), and
Harry K. T. Wong (Nomadic Systems)

The Benchmark Handbook for Database and Transaction Processing Systems
Edited by Jim Gray (Digital Equipment Corporation)

Camelot and Avalon: A Distributed Transaction Facility
Edited by Jeffrey L. Eppinger (Transarc Corporation),
Lily B. Mummert (Carnegie Mellon University),
and Alfred Z. Spector (Transarc Corporation)

Database Modeling and Design: The Entity-Relationship Approach
Toby J. Teorey (University of Michigan)

Readings in Object-Oriented Database Systems
Edited by Stanley B. Zdonik (Brown University) and
David Maier (Oregon Graduate Center)

Readings in Database Systems
Edited by Michael Stonebraker (University of California at Berkeley)

Deductive Databases and Logic Programming
Jack Minker (University of Maryland)

Database Transaction Models for Advanced Applications

Edited by

Ahmed K. Elmagarmid

MORGAN KAUFMANN PUBLISHERS

San Mateo, California

Editor: *Bruce M. Spatz*
Production Manager: *Yonie Overton*
Cover Mechanical Artist: *Patty King*
Indexing/Electronic Output: *Superscript Typography*

Morgan Kaufmann Publishers, Inc.
Editorial Office:
2929 Campus Drive, Suite 260
San Mateo, CA 94403

95 94 93 92 5 4 3 2 1

Library of Congress Cataloging in Publication Data is available for this book.

ISBN 1-55860-214-3
ISSN 1046-1698

To beautiful little
Najd Mohammed Elmagarmid,
April 7, 1988–December 15, 1990

Contents

Contents

Foreword

The transaction concept has emerged as the key structuring technique for distributed data and distributed computations. Originally developed and applied to database applications, the transaction model is now being used in new application areas ranging from process control to cooperative work. Not surprisingly, these more sophisticated applications require a refined and generalized transaction model. The concept must be made recursive, it must deal with concurrency within a transaction, it must relax the strict isolation among transactions, and it must deal more gracefully with failures.

This book collects, for the first time, the many generalizations of the basic transaction model. Taken together it represents the latest and best thinking on how to structure distributed and heterogeneous computations. The authors represent the spectrum from research universities to industry. The applications they discuss encompass planning, design, engineering, manufacturing, and commerce. Their approaches range from theoretical models to practical tool kits. In sum, this book covers the entire spectrum of thought on the topic of generalized transaction models and transaction processing.

This book stands as a milestone, collecting the many intellectual threads developed over the decade of the 1980s. Researchers are now working to merge these many approaches into a new unified transaction concept able to handle all applications. This new emerging concept will likely be one of the major contributions to Computer Science in the coming decade.

Jim Gray
Digital Equipment Corporation

Preface

What constitutes a transaction model? This innocent question from an uninformed colleague of mine stopped me, for the first time in ten years, to really think about this issue. It is easy to understand that a data model describes the structure of the database, i.e., data types and the constraints related to the data. But what components one should find in a transaction model? After mumbling something about how to specify the correctness of the database, and the type and structure of the logical operations to manipulate it, I quickly realized that giving a satisfactory answer is not as easy I thought. Several more hours of pondering upon the topic gave more refined, but equally unsatisfactory answers - especially in the light of the new developments in the transaction processing research. All my attempts to give a definition centered not only on the description of properties of the notion of a transaction, but also on the external mechanisms that guarantee such properties. This is exactly what the different chapters of this book are all about.

Active research on database transaction processing dates back to the early '70s, and many theoretical and pragmatic issues of the "traditional transactions" have been explored. The key properties such as atomicity of transaction execution, isolation of intermediate results and a universal correctness criteria (serializability) have been discovered and studied intensively. However, as pointed out by many early researchers, much of this discussion was intended to be relevant for business oriented database applications, where transactions were assumed to be simple, short-lived and non-hierarchical in structure. Attempts to blindly apply this work to other contexts has almost in every case that I know of, produced impractical and sometimes even disastrous results. Indeed, one-by-one each one of the fundamental "ACID" properties has been challenged in various environments, in spite of the appeal of the theoretical elegance of such concepts as serializability or atomic commitment.

So what are the new issues that need to be addressed by these new transaction models? This many faceted question is best answered by reading the various chapter in this book; my attempt here is only to illustrate how a single modification in the assumptions gives rise to several major questions to be answered.

Let's look at one simple (realistic) modification that the transactions are long-lived, their duration is not seconds but minutes, hours or weeks. This type of transactions are especially natural in Computer Aided Design (CAD) or cooperative environments (e.g., in Groupware). The most common commercially used concurrency control method, blocking the data via locks, becomes totally impractical as one would exclude all the access to data for hours. Actually this single modification severely challenges the principles of guaranteeing isolation and atomicity of the traditional transactions, and introduces naturally the notion of compensation used in S-transactions, Sagas, Open Nested transactions and transactions on Active Objects. Secondly, as such environments are decentralized in nature, it is natural to extend the traditional flat transaction control structure to a hierarchical one, i.e., introduce the notion of transaction nesting with subtransactions executing at various sites. Finally, for such long-living transactions it is also typical to allow several alternative execution threads which leads to incorporating multiple acceptable final states into the correctness criteria (e.g., Flex transactions).

The different chapters of this book provide an excellent snapshot of the various questions raised by the new application areas, where transaction processing is needed, but where the underlying assumptions make it impossible to apply the traditional models and algorithms. The book acts both as a reference for the state of the art in advanced transaction models, as well as a good starting point for anybody interested in addressing the important open questions in the area. Since the chapters are written by different authors, the book has unique value in collecting to a single volume various alternative views on the topics, fact that made the book especially appealing to me personally.

Henry Tirri
University of Helsinki

Acknowledgements

This book would not have come about without the contributions and dedication of the many authors involved. This book is an acknowledgement of their many and valuable contributions to the field.

The contributions have endured a roller coaster that lasted for over two years. What was promised to be a fast and painless task took five times longer than promised and went through far too many revisions. We all are indebted to the over 100 reviewers who did the hard job. I was pleased at the level of professionalism and desire for the highest levels of perfection exhibited by the contributors and reviewers.

This book would not have been possible without the help of many of the InterBase team at Purdue. A special mention goes to Sue Barton, Omran Bukhres, Jiansan Chen, Yungho Leu, James Mullen, and Aidong Zhang.

A great amount of input was provided by so many of my good friends. I will not list them all, but a special mention is given to Amit Sheth and M. Tamer Özsu. Special thanks are due to Henry Tirri for writing a preface to the book and to Jim Gray, the series editor, for writing the Foreword to the book.

Special thanks go to the staff at Morgan Kaufmann. Their dedication to this project has been unyielding. Special thanks go to my Production Manager Yonie Overton. She has put up with a tight and often unpredictable schedule. No amount of thanks or appreciation is enough for the force behind the project, Bruce Spatz, the Senior Editor for this book. Indeed he is solely responsible for the inception of the idea of writing the book on transaction models and receives all the credit for seeing the project through thick and thin. He has been gracious, friendly and accommodating at times when I may have been unreasonable. Thanks are due also to Elizabeth Essex, Associate Product Manager.

The push for writing a book started at a meeting with Mike Morgan in my office at Purdue in the Autumn of 1988. A lot has happened in the field since that time, and we hope we have captured some of it in these pages.

This book does not particularly cover heterogeneous databases, as that is the topic of an upcoming book by myself, Amit Sheth and Marek Rusinkiewicz.

This book would not have been possible without the financial support I receive from the Purdue Research Foundation, The Indiana Business Modernization and Technology, The National Science Foundation, The Software Engineering Research Center, Bell Northern Research, and NASA.

Ahmed K. Elmagarmid
Associate Professor and Executive Director
Indiana Center for Database Systems
Department of Computer Sciences
Purdue University

1

Transaction Management in Database Systems

D. Agrawal

A. El Abbadi

1.1 Introduction

Database systems are among the most important applications of computer technology. They provide versatile methods for storing and dealing with large volumes of data. Database systems encompass a large range of applications, such as banking systems, airline reservation systems, and organizational information systems. Database systems provide an organized and uniform method for handling an enormous volume of information in the real world. One of the primary goals of a database system is to allow several users to interact with the database simultaneously while preserving the illusion that each user is executing alone. Users interact with the database through special application programs called transactions. In this chapter, we present a brief description of standard models for transaction management in traditional database systems. Additional information about this topic from different points of view is readily available in several books on database systems including [Gra78, CP84, Bha86, Pap86, BHG87, Mul89, OV91]. More recently the scope of database systems has expanded to nonstandard applications such as CAD/CAM environments, software engineering applications, and multi-media applications. The following chapters in this book present extended models for transaction management in nonstandard database applications.

A database is a collection of objects which satisfy a set of integrity constraints. For example, in a bank, an integrity constraint may be that no account can have a negative balance. Users interact with the database by executing programs that perform the functions desired by the users. The execution of such programs results in a partially ordered set of read and write operations. This set of operations is called *a transaction.* For example, a user wishing to withdraw $50 from an account x may write the program shown in Figure 1.1. This program's execution may result in the following transaction:

$$read_1[x, 100]write_1[x, 50]commit_1$$

We use $read_1[x, v]$ to refer to a read operation executed by transaction 1, where the read value is v; $write_1[x, v]$ refers to a write operation executed by transaction 1 with value v. A transaction terminates by either executing a *commit* or an *abort* operation. A commit operation implies that the transaction was successful, and hence all its updates should be incorporated into the database. An abort operation indicates that the transaction has failed, and hence requires the database management system to cancel or abolish all

```
k ← read(x)
if k ≥ 50 then
    k ← k − 50
    write(x, k)
else
    print("insufficient funds")
endif
```

FIGURE 1.1
A user program for withdrawing $50 from a bank account

its effects on the database system. (For clarity, we sometimes do not include commit or abort operations in executions.)

A transaction that updates the objects of the database must preserve the integrity constraints of the database. In general, two different approaches may be used. The first approach assumes that each user is fully aware of all the constraints and only writes programs that are correct. The second approach makes no assumption about the correctness of the individual transactions, but requires the database to validate statically or dynamically that no transaction violates the integrity constraints. The latter approach is attractive since it relieves the user from the responsibility of knowing and maintaining these constraints. However, this approach results in substantial overhead on the database system. Furthermore, to dynamically ensure the consistency of the database, the state of the database needs to be quiescent after each transaction; this reduces the database availability to the users. For these and other reasons, database management systems have traditionally required users to write correct programs. The standard assumption is that a transaction, if executed alone in a database that is consistent, will leave the database in another consistent state. Note that a transaction may (or by necessity must) violate some of the integrity constraints during its execution. However, once it terminates (commits), it must restore the database to a consistent state.

Traditionally, transactions are expected to satisfy the following four conditions, affectionately known as the ACIDity properties [Gra81, HR83, OV91]. *Atomicity*, or the *all-or-nothing* property, refers to the fact that all the operations of a transaction must be treated as a single unit; hence, either all the operations are executed, or none. *Consistency* requires a transaction to be correct, i.e., if executed alone, the transaction takes the database from one consistent state to another. When transactions are executed concurrently, the database management system must ensure that the execution of a set of concurrent and correct transactions also maintains the consistency of the database. *Isolation* requires each transaction to observe a consistent database, i.e., not to read the intermediate results of other transactions. Finally, *durability* requires the results of a committed transaction to be made permanent in the database in spite of failures.

The ACIDity properties of transactions are usually ensured using two different sets of algorithms or protocols. These protocols are divided into ones that ensure *execution atomicity*, and those that ensure *failure atomicity* [Mos85]. Execution atomicity refers to the problem of ensuring the overall consistency of the database, and hence the consistency property of transactions, even when they are executed concurrently. Protocols that ensure execution atomicity are called *concurrency control* protocols. Failure atomicity, on the other hand, ensures the all-or-nothing as well as isolation and durability properties. Protocols that ensure failure atomicity are usually referred to as *recovery* protocols.

This chapter is organized as follows. In the next section, we discuss the problem of ensuring execution atomicity of transactions. Failure atomicity is dealt with in Section 1.3. In Section 1.4, we discuss transaction management in distributed databases. We then discuss several extensions to the traditional transaction model and conclude the chapter.

1.2 Execution atomicity

One of the main objectives of a database management system is controlling and coordinating the execution of a set of concurrent transactions accessing a shared database. This may also be stated as requiring different transactions to access shared data without interfering with each other and still preserving the integrity constraints of the database. We refer to this property as *execution atomicity*. It has also been referred to simply as *atomicity*, *consistency*, or *concurrency atomicity* [Mos85, PKH88, LP91]. We will now motivate some of the problems that arise when a set of correct transactions are allowed to execute concurrently, and then define the correctness criterion.

1.2.1 Motivation

Consider a bank account s, and two transactions, each withdrawing \$200 when the account has an initial balance of \$300. We assume that a withdraw transaction is executed by first reading the value of account s, and then writing it with the new value. Assume that the interleaved execution of the two withdraw transactions is as shown in Figure 1.2.

User Program 1	**User Program 2**
withdraw(\$200)	withdraw(\$200)
$temp1 \leftarrow read(s)$	
$temp1 \leftarrow temp1 - \$200$	
	$temp2 \leftarrow read(s)$
	$temp2 \leftarrow temp2 - \$200$
	$write(s, temp2)$
$write(s, temp1)$	

FIGURE 1.2
Lost Update

In the execution shown in Figure 1.2, let the withdraw transaction on the left be labeled as 1 and the other as 2. The interleaved execution of the two transactions in Figure 1.2 then can be summarized as follows:

$$read_1[s, 300]read_2[s, 300]write_2[s, 100]write_1[s, 100]$$

In this execution, both transactions read the same initial value, and then update the account with the new value \$100. Note that as far as each transaction is concerned, the integrity constraint of non-negative accounts is not violated. However, in the interleaved execution, the overall result does not reflect the correct execution of two withdraw transactions. In particular, if the two transactions were not interleaved, the second of the two transactions would have violated the integrity constraints, and hence would not have been executed. Alternatively, if in the above interleaved execution the withdraw transactions are replaced with transactions that deposit \$200, both transactions would have written \$500. In this case, \$200 would have disappeared. Again this is not acceptable. This problem is known as the *missing* or *lost* update problem.

Consider another type of transaction which transfers \$100 from a savings account s to a checking account c. Assume that both accounts start with an initial balance of \$200. Further, assume that a transfer transaction was executed concurrently with a balance transaction that computes the total amount in both accounts as shown in Figure 1.3.

User Program 1	**User Program 2**
transfer(\$100)	balance()
$temp1 \leftarrow read(s)$	
$temp2 \leftarrow read(c)$	
$write(s, temp1 - \$100)$	
	$temp3 \leftarrow read(s)$
	$temp4 \leftarrow read(c)$
$write(c, temp2 + \$100)$	
	$print(temp3 + temp4)$

FIGURE 1.3
Inconsistent Retrieval

Let the transfer transaction be transaction 1 and the balance transaction be transaction 2 in Figure 1.3. The above execution is summarized in terms of database operations as follows:

$$read_1[s, 200]read_1[c, 200]write_1[s, 100]read_2[s, 100]read_2[c, 200]write_1[c, 300]$$

In this execution the balance operation returns a sum of \$300, which is incorrect since the two accounts actually have \$400. Again note that if the two transactions were executed one at a time (in either order), the balance transaction would have returned the correct total of \$400. It is also interesting to note that in this case, no integrity constraints were ever violated, even after both transactions have completed. The problem has to do with the balance transaction observing an inconsistent state (this cannot be detected by any mechanism that simply preserves integrity constraints). This problem is referred to as the *inconsistent retrieval* problem.

1.2.2 Serializability

The examples above illustrate that simply requiring each transaction to be individually correct does not guarantee that the interleaved execution of a set of transactions will be correct. One possible restriction that could be imposed by the database management system is to execute transactions one at a time or *serially.* In this case we are guaranteed that the database will always remain in a consistent state, and that transactions always observe consistent states. However, this approach is too restrictive. In general, since transactions often require access to objects that are stored in secondary storage, transactions will be generally I/O bound. In such an environment, serial execution will result in extremely poor CPU utilization. Furthermore, if a pair of transactions do not share a common data item, it is clear that interleaving their operations can not violate any integrity constraints. Such transactions can be executed concurrently, resulting in better CPU utilization. Finally, even if a pair of transactions share some data items, interleaving the execution of their operations may be acceptable as the following example illustrates. Consider again a transfer operation that is interleaved with a balance operation as follows:

$$read_1[s,200]write_1[s,100]read_2[s,100]read_1[c,200]write_1[c,300]read_2[c,300]$$

In this case, the balance operation returns the correct total of \$400. Such an execution is acceptable, and two users could not have distinguished this execution from one in which first the transfer transaction was executed, followed by the balance transaction.

We are now in a position to introduce the main notion of correctness for the execution of a set of transactions. Note that since a serial execution is correct, we would like to allow any interleaved execution whose behavior cannot be distinguished from a serial execution as far as the users of the database are concerned. We therefore can accept an interleaved execution if there is a possible serial execution of the same set of transactions, such that in both executions, each transaction reads the same values and the final values of the database objects are the same. Such executions are referred to as *view serializable* [BSW79, Pap79], since each transaction has the same view of the database in both executions.

In the above example, the execution is serializable and has the same effects as the serial execution of the transfer transaction followed by the balance transaction. In both executions, the transfer reads the values \$200 and the balance reads the values written by the transfer transaction, i.e., \$100 and \$300. In contrast, in the example illustrated in Figure 1.2 there is no possible serial execution with the transactions reading the same values. In particular, both withdraw transactions read the same initial value of the account, which is impossible in any serial execution of the two transactions.

1.2.3 Conflict Serializability

Unfortunately, the intuitively simple definition of correctness described above turns out to be quite difficult to implement; i.e., recognizing view serializable histories is NP-complete [Pap79]. The basic reasoning behind this result is fairly simple and quite instructive for providing ways to modify our definition of correctness to make the problem polynomially tractable. Given an interleaved execution, the definition of view serializability requires us to find a serial execution in which transactions read the same values. This implies that if some transaction T_j reads a value of an object x written by another transaction T_i, then the order of these two transactions is determined in the serial execution: all the operations of T_i followed by all the operations of T_j. However, the definition imposes less strict constraints on other transactions that write the same object. In particular, all we can say is that any transaction T_k that writes x must be either ordered before T_i or after T_j (otherwise, T_j should have read the value written by T_k). Hence for every such pair of transactions T_i and T_j, and every third transaction as T_k, we have two choices. The multiplicity of these choices may give the reader an intuitively simple explanation behind the NP-completeness of recognizing view serializable executions.

The above reasoning also implies that one way of reducing the complexity of the problem is to require the order between write operations and both read and write operations to be determined in some manner. One such approach would be to enforce an ordering between transactions not only when a transaction reads a value from another transaction but also when two transactions perform concurrent write operations and read and write operations irrespective of the order. These ideas are also related to the notion of conflict or commutativity between operations. We now explore such relations between pairs of read and write operations and then provide a practical definition for the correctness of an interleaved execution of transactions.

A pair of operations is said to *conflict* if when considered in isolation the order of execution may effect either: (a) the results returned by one of them (as in the case of read operations), or (b) the final value of the objects of the database (as a result of write operations). Consider any two operations executed by two different transactions. There are five cases to consider depending on the type and order of the operations. First, if the two operations are executed on different objects, then obviously the order of execution is irrelevant, and the two operations do not conflict. Second, if the two operations are read operations on the same object, again the order is irrelevant since the value of the object doesn't change, and the values read are the same irrespective of the order. Hence two read operations on the same object do not conflict. Third, when a write precedes a read operation on the same object. In this case the order is relevant since otherwise the read operation may return a different value. Fourth, a read operation precedes a write on the same object. Again if the order is reversed the read operation may return a different value. Finally, the case of two write operations on the same object. Here again the order of execution is important since the value of the object after the execution of the two write operations depends on which write was executed last.

Read	Write	
No	Yes	Read
Yes	Yes	Write

FIGURE 1.4
Conflict Relation between Read and Write Operations

In summary, two operations conflict if both of them are on the same object and at least one of them is a write operation. Figure 1.4 illustrates the conflict relation between read and write operations on a single object. A "No" entry in the table indicates that the two operations do not conflict whereas a "Yes" entry indicates that the two operations conflict. We can now characterize a correct execution of a set of transactions as one for which a serial execution exists with the same set of transactions such that in both executions the order of conflicting operations is the same. Such executions are referred to as being *conflict serializable* [EGLT76, BSW79, Pap79]. It is clear that any conflict serializable execution must also be view serializable, but the converse is not true. In particular, the following view serializable execution is not conflict serializable:

$$write_1[x,1]write_2[x,2]write_3[x,3]write_2[y,1]read_1[y,1]$$

This execution is view serializable and is equivalent to the following serial execution:

$$write_2[x,2]write_2[y,1]write_1[x,1]read_1[y,1]write_3[x,3]$$

In both executions T_1 reads the value of y written by T_2, and the final value of x is written by T_3 and the final value of y is written by T_2. However, the execution is not conflict serializable since in any equivalent serial execution T_1 must precede T_2 as a result of the conflict between $write_1[x,1]$ and $write_2[x,2]$, and at the same time T_2 must precede T_1 as a result of the conflict between $write_2[y,1]$ and $read_1[y,1]$.

We now discuss a pragmatic restriction to the class of correct executions. This restriction results in a class of executions which is especially useful for a wide range of applications. We start by noting that the above definitions of serializability only mention the relative order between operations of different transactions. No mention is made of the relative order between transactions. In particular, the order between some transactions may be completely reversed in all equivalent serial orders as the following example shows:

$$write_1[x,1]read_2[x,1]commit_2write_3[y,1]commit_3write_1[y,2]commit_1$$

This execution is conflict serializable since it corresponds to a serial execution where transaction 3 is followed by transaction 1, and finally transaction 2. Note that in the actual execution, transaction 2 executed its operation and terminated before transaction 3 had even started executing. However, in the equivalent serial history the order is reversed. Such behavior may be unacceptable for certain applications where the temporal relationship between non-interleaved transactions is relevant. For example, a single user may issue several transactions serially and the user would like to ensure that the relative order of these transactions is preserved in at least some serialization. An execution is said to be *order-preserving conflict serializable* if it is conflict serializable, and where all non-interleaved transactions have the same order in both the original execution and some corresponding serial execution [BSW79, BBG89a, Wei88]. The above example is not order-preserving conflict serializable although it is conflict serializable. It is fairly easy to show that all order-preserving conflict serializable executions are conflict serializable but not vice-versa.

A *concurrency control* protocol is used to ensure the serializable execution of transactions in a database system. A simple way to recognize conflict serializable executions is to construct (online if necessary) a directed graph called a *serialization graph* [BHG87]. This graph has a node for each transaction and an edge $T_i \rightarrow T_j$ if T_i executes an operation which conflicts and precedes some operation executed by T_j. An execution is conflict serializable if and only if its serialization graph is acyclic [BHG87]. Several efficient concurrency control protocols have been proposed including two-phase locking [EGLT76], timestamp ordering [Ree78, BG81], optimistic [KR81], and serialization graph testing [Bad79, Cas81].

The protocols based on locking delay the execution of conflicting operations by using shared and exclusive locks for read and write operations. Shared locks allow several read operations to execute concurrently whereas exclusive locks ensure that a write operation is executed in isolation. The two-phase locking restriction requires a transaction to acquire all locks before releasing any lock. The two-phase locking protocol is vulnerable to deadlocks [Obe82, Elm86, Kna87, Sin89]. Timestamp ordering protocols associate a timestamp with each transaction and associate with each object the timestamps of the latest transactions that read and wrote the object. The protocol permits conflicting accesses only in increasing order of timestamps. A transaction is aborted if it tries to execute an operation out of timestamp order. That is, if the timestamp of a transaction reading an object is smaller than the timestamp of the latest writer on that object, the transaction is aborted. Similarly, if the timestamp of a transaction writing an object is smaller that the timestamps of the latest reader or writer on that object, the transaction is aborted (in special cases an out of order write operation may not result in aborting the issuing transaction [Tho79]). Optimistic protocols allow a transaction to execute with unrestricted read access to the data and later subjecting the transaction to a validation phase to ensure correctness. Timestamp and optimistic protocols do not suffer from deadlocks. Protocols based on serialization graph testing explicitly maintain an online serialization graph and execute the operations of transactions as long as the graph remains acyclic. Otherwise, the transaction that causes a cycle in the graph is aborted. Most commercially used concurrency control protocols are order preserving, and recently a locking based protocol was proposed that recognizes the entire class of order-preserving conflict serializable executions [AE90a]. Several simulation studies such as [Car83, ACL87] have been conducted for evaluating the performance of concurrency control protocols. These performance studies have shown that locking protocols exhibit superior performance than other types of concurrency control mechanisms under a wide variety of database workloads and system configurations. Several researchers, for example [GM83, Lyn83, KS88a, FO89, DE89], have argued that serializability is too strong a notion of correctness and have proposed various relaxation of serializability to improve performance in database systems.

1.3 Failure Atomicity

The transaction model used in multi-user database systems must provide the all-or-nothing property of transactions even in the presence of various types of failures. This property is referred to as *failure atomicity.* The execution of a transaction can be aborted by its initiator, e.g., if the withdrawal of two bank accounts would result in a negative balance in one of them then the transaction may be aborted. Aborts may also occur as a result of other system related faults such as divide-by-zero, memory fault, or deadlock. There can be other kinds of more drastic failures that may occur in a system, e.g., crash failures, disk or media failure, etc. In such situations the operations executed by interrupted transactions must be "undone". That is, the effect of aborted transactions should be as if those transactions were never executed. Similarly, when a system failure occurs we must ensure that the effects of committed transactions are not lost. In this section, we describe the theory and techniques used to ensure failure atomicity of transactions in the presence of transaction and system failures. Media failures, in general, require manual intervention and are therefore not dealt with in this chapter [HR83, OV91].

1.3.1 Transaction Failures

We now discuss how failure atomicity of transactions can be guaranteed when transactions abort as a result of faults. Note that a user initiated abort can also be modeled as a fault in the system. Consider, for example, the following execution of a transaction:

$$read_1[x,1]write_1[x,5]write_1[y,25]$$

If the next operation of transaction 1 is $abort_1$ due to a fault, then the above operations should be undone. That is, the partial effects of transaction 1 on the database state must be eliminated. Note that there is no need to perform any undo action for read operations since they do not modify the state of the database. On the other hand, write operations must be undone to restore the database to the correct state. In particular, operation $write_1[x, 5]$ should be undone by restoring the value of object x that existed before $write_1[x, 5]$. Similarly, the value of y before $write_1[y, 25]$ should be restored.

Failure atomicity of transactions in the absence of concurrency can be easily accomplished by using a simple bookkeeping technique. Read operations do not require any undo action whereas write operations require restoration of the *before-image* of the data objects involved in the write operations [Ver78, HR83, BHG87]. This can be accomplished by requiring that transactions save the before-image of each object on nonvolatile storage before performing a write operation on that object. Before-images are usually stored in a structure called *log* on nonvolatile storage.

However, guaranteeing failure atomicity of transactions in a concurrent environment becomes more cumbersome and complex. In such an environment, when a transaction aborts, all its effects on the database as well as other concurrently executing transactions should be eliminated. Consider, for example, the following execution of two transactions:

$$read_1[x, 1]write_1[x, 5]read_2[x, 5]write_2[z, 20]commit_2$$

In the above execution, if transaction 1 aborts, then we have the following problem. Since the effects of transaction 1 must be eliminated from the database, transaction 2 through its read action $read_2[x]$ observes a value of x that did not exist. The only alternative left now is to withdraw the commitment of transaction 2. However, this approach of guaranteeing failure atomicity violates the property of *durability* that states that once a transaction commits, all its effects become permanent. In order to circumvent this problem, the concurrent execution of transactions is constrained. The constraint requires that if a transaction T reads a value of an object written by transaction T' then the commit action of T can be executed only after T' has committed. Executions that satisfy this property are referred to as *recoverable* executions [Had88].

We can now summarize a protocol for guaranteeing failure atomicity. When a transaction aborts, its effects on the database are eliminated by restoring the before-image of the objects written by the transaction, and its effects on other transactions are eliminated by aborting all transactions that read values written by the aborted transaction. Note that this may lead to further abortions of other transactions and so on. This phenomenon is referred to as *cascading aborts* and can be illustrated with the following example:

$$write_1[x, 5]read_2[x, 5]write_2[z, 20]read_3[z, 20] \ldots$$

In the above execution, if transaction 1 aborts, it will induce an abort of transaction 2 since the latter read uncommitted values from transaction 1. Furthermore, abortion of transaction 2 will trigger the abort of transaction 3. Although this approach is correct from a theoretical point of view, the phenomenon of cascading aborts is undesirable in practice. In many transaction models and database systems, this phenomenon is prevented by introducing another property for transactions called *isolation*. Transactions are isolated from each other by requiring that transactions read only committed data. Thus, concurrent execution of transactions is further constrained by requiring that a transaction T can read a value of an object written by another transaction T' only if T' has committed. Such executions are referred to as executions that *avoid cascading aborts* [Had88].

In this restricted execution model, failure atomicity of transactions can be ensured by simply eliminating the effects of aborted transactions from the database. Note that the issue of the effects of aborted transactions on other concurrent transactions does not arise as a result of the isolation property. However, as the following example illustrates, the simple approach of restoring before-image is not sufficient.

$$write_1[x, 1]write_2[x, 2]$$

Suppose the initial value of x is zero and if transaction 2's commit action is followed by the abortion of transaction 1, restoring the initial value will result in the effects of transaction 2 on x being lost. (This is analogous to the lost update problem due to transaction aborts instead of transaction commit.) On the other hand, if transactions 1 and 2 abort in that order, restoring the before-image of x by transaction 2 will result in x having an incorrect value of 1 instead of zero.

In order to use the simple recovery mechanism of restoring the before-images of aborted transactions, an additional constraint is imposed on the concurrent execution of transactions. This new constraint requires that if a transaction T performs a write operation on an object x, then other transactions are not permitted to write x until T has either committed or aborted.

This constraint, in conjunction with the constraint for avoiding cascading aborts, can be stated as follows:

> If a transaction T writes an object, then that object can be read or written by other transactions only after T has either committed or aborted.

Executions that satisfy the above constraints are referred to as *strict* executions [Had88]. Strict executions can be realized by using a two-phase locking protocol in which write locks held by transactions are released at commit time. This protocol is commonly known as *strict* two-phase locking.

In an execution model that permits only strict executions, an aborted transaction is undone by simply restoring the before-images corresponding to the write operations executed by the aborted transaction. Strict executions greatly simplify the task of ensuring failure atomicity; however, it is at the expense of reduced concurrency.

1.3.2 System Failures

In this section, we consider the problem of ensuring failure atomicity of transactions in the presence of system failures. Database systems usually use two types of memory, volatile, which is usually small but has fast access time, and nonvolatile, such as a disk, which has slower access time, but has much larger capacity. The entire database is stored in nonvolatile memory, and part of the database is cached or buffered in the volatile memory, usually referred to as the *database cache.* A transaction usually executes by reading and updating the database cache. Ideally, when a transaction commits, all its changes should be incorporated into the database on nonvolatile memory. Since disk accesses are generally slower, coherency between the database cache and the database itself is not strictly maintained. Hence, the database may contain data written by uncommitted transactions (which may potentially abort) and the cache may contain data, which has not yet been incorporated into the database, but that was written by committed transactions. A system failure is modeled by assuming that the state of the system in the volatile memory is lost, but the state in the nonvolatile memory survives following the system failure. The recovery from system failure involves the following:

1. The effects of transactions that were in committed state at the time of the system failure must be incorporated into the database.

2. The effects of transactions that were aborted or were active at the time of the system failure must be eliminated from the database. Note that

transactions that were active when the failure occurs are deemed to be aborted since their internal state is lost due to the failure.

Recovery from system failures can be categorized into two processes [HR83, BHG87, MHL+89]:

Redo Process: For each committed transaction, redo the write operations that are not incorporated into the database.

Undo Process: For each active and aborted transaction, undo the write operations that were incorporated into the database.

In order to successfully recover from system failures, additional bookkeeping needs to be performed which is also kept in the log. In particular, the log maintains a list of committed transactions, a list of aborted transactions, and a log of write operations performed on each object in the database. A restart procedure is invoked when the system recovers after a system failure and the procedure recovers the database state by using the two lists and the log.

Note that the need for redoing a committed transaction arises due to the absence of committed data in the database. Similarly, undo processes for aborted transactions are needed due to the presence of uncommitted data in the database. In general, there are two main approaches for synchronizing the updating of the database with the execution of the transaction. The *update-in-place policy* [GMB+81, HR83] where transactions immediately write uncommitted values into the database and the *deferred-update policy* [GMB+81, HR83] where active transactions do not modify the database until the time that they commit. The former approach has the advantage of not requiring any undo process executions, while the later avoids any redo processes. Several performance studies have established that in-place updating is superior to other strategies such as deferred-update in database systems [AD85]. A comprehensive treatment for recovery from system failures in database systems can be found in [Ver78, HR83, BHG87].

1.4 Distributed Databases

In this section, we explore some of the issues that arise for transaction management when the database is distributed over a set of sites connected by a communication network. A *distributed database* is a database where different objects may be stored at different sites and where the users may issue transactions at any site in the system [CP84, Bha86, OV91]. In a database system, sites are assumed to be *fail-stop* [SS82]; i.e., the site simply fails by crashing in a benign manner. Communication links may fail to deliver messages. Combinations of such failures may lead to *partitioning failures* [DGMS85], where sites in a *partition* may communicate with each other, but no communication can occur between sites in different partitions. It is usually assumed that the network provides a routing protocol, which ensures that a message can be delivered between two sites if there is a communication path between them. However, the system is asynchronous; i.e., messages may take arbitrary long periods of time to deliver messages.

The site at which a transaction is initiated is called its *home site*. The home site executes the operations of a transaction by exchanging messages with the sites where the objects are stored. As in centralized databases, we must address the issues of execution and failure atomicity in a distributed environment. However, in a distributed system the possibility of failures gives rise to new problems, especially relating to fault-tolerance and the overhead resulting from the message passing. We start this section by discussing execution and failure atomicity and then address the issue of replicating data to improve the performance and availability of the database.

Execution atomicity requires the execution of a set of transactions to be equivalent to a serial execution. This requirement is the same irrespective of whether the database is distributed or not. Hence from a consistency point of view, the definition of serializability is general enough to encompass distributed databases. It is, however, instructive to discuss some of the issues that arise when designing concurrency control protocols for distributed databases. In particular, we note that ensuring serializability at each site in isolation does not guarantee overall serializability. Consider for example a distributed database with two sites s_1 and s_2, with object x residing at site s_1 and object y residing at site s_2. Two transactions T_1 and T_2 may both write both objects and due to the asynchrony of the system, T_1 may be serialized before T_2 on object x and vice-versa on object y. Each site has a correct serialization order, but the overall execution is not correct. Hence concurrency control protocols must synchronize the global execution of transactions.

The execution atomicity of transactions in a distributed environment can be ensured by extending the centralized protocols for concurrency control. For example, if serialization graph testing is used, the local serialization graphs at all sites are merged to construct a global serialization graph. The test for acyclicity is performed on this global graph. Distributed two-phase locking can be implemented by requiring a transaction to release a lock only after it has acquired all of its locks on all necessary database sites. This restriction can be easily enforced by using the strict two-phase locking protocol. Similar approaches can be used for distributed timestamp ordering [BG81] and distributed optimistic concurrency control protocol [CO82].

Failure atomicity requires that database systems provide the all-or-nothing property of transaction executions. In a centralized database this is usually achieved by executing an atomic commit operation. Unfortunately, in a distributed system this atomic operation must be executed over all the sites where the transaction executed any operations. This may cause several complications, especially as some sites may not agree to commit the transaction. This may arise for example due to recoverability considerations. Another significant concern is the distributed nature of failures in a distributed system. Unlike centralized databases where failure is a local event to the sole site of interest, in a distributed database some site may fail while others may remain functional. Several protocols have been proposed to solve the distributed commitment problem. The most important is the *two-phase commit* [Gra78] and the *three-phase commit* protocols [Ske82, SS83]. Several optimizations have been proposed [MLO86] to reduce the communication costs in the two-phase commit protocol and more recently an optimistic commit protocol [LKS91] has been proposed to reduce the number of phases for atomic commitment.

Data replication is traditionally used for increasing data availability and fault-tolerance in distributed systems. When a data object is replicated on several sites, the object may still be available for reading or writing even after failures have occurred. Thus, data replication may increase data availability and increase the fault-tolerance of the database. On the other hand, replication also holds the promise of reducing communication costs incurred when a transaction can access locally stored data. If data is stored at the site where a transaction is initiated, operations can be executed locally, thus reducing both communication costs and the response time. In a replicated database, copies of an object may be stored at several sites in the network. Multiple copies of an object must appear as a single logical object to the transactions. This is termed as *one-copy equivalence* [BG87] and is enforced by a *replica control* protocol. The correctness criterion for replicated databases is *one-copy serializability* [BG87], which ensures both one-copy equivalence and the serializable execution of transactions.

A simple protocol for ensuring correct execution in a replicated database is to require a transaction to execute every write operation by writing all copies of the object and a read operation to read any copy. Although simple, this protocol fails to execute any write operations once a single copy of an object fails. A fault-tolerant extension [Gif79, Tho79] to ensure one-copy serializability allows a replicated object x to be read by reading a *read quorum* of copies, and it may be written by writing a *write quorum* of copies. The following restriction is placed on the choice of quorum assignments:

> Quorum Intersection Property: For any two operations $o[x]$ and $o'[x]$ on an object x, where at least one of them is a write, the quorums must have a nonempty intersection.

Version numbers or timestamps are used to identify the current copy in a quorum. When timestamps are used, intersection of write quorums is not necessary [Her86]. The notion of intersecting quorums is closely related to *coteries* [GMB85]. Several other replica control protocol have been proposed such as [Sto79, ES83, BG84, ESC85, DB85, JM87, Her87, PL88, ET89, BGMS89, AB91, AE90b]. Some of these protocols emphasize fault-tolerance to site or partitioning failures while others emphasize reduction of communication costs.

1.5 Extensions to the Transaction Model

In this section, we describe three extensions to the traditional transaction model used in database systems. We start by extending the single version database model to a multiversion database model, which is useful for query dominant environments. The generalization of the flat transaction model to nested transactions is described next. Finally, the simple read/write model is generalized to a semantically rich abstract data type model.

1.5.1 Multiversion Databases

Multiple versions of data are used in database systems to support transaction and system recovery. Recall that in Section 1.3, the before-images for each write operation on each object are maintained in the log. These multiple versions of data can also be exploited to improve the degree of concurrency that is achievable in the system. The higher concurrency is realized since out-of-order read requests can be serviced by reading appropriate, older versions of data. Thus, *read-only* transactions, which do not have any write operations, are executed almost unhindered in most multiversion concurrency control schemes. Specifically, the adverse effects of concurrent *read-write* transactions on read-only transactions are minimized.

In a multiversion database, each write operation on an object x produces a new *version* of x. Thus, for each object x in the database, there is a list of associated versions. A read operation on x is performed by returning the value of x from an appropriate version in the list. The existence of multiple versions is visible only to the scheduler implementing the protocol, and not to the user transactions which refer to the object as x. A multiversion history is *one-version serializable* if as far as the users can tell its behavior is the same as a serial history over the same set of transactions executed over a single version database. One-version serializability is a commonly accepted correctness criterion for multiversion databases [BHG87].

Several concurrency control algorithms have been developed for multiversion databases [Ree78, SR81, BG81, CFL+82, CG85, Wei87, AS89]. Multiversion timestamp ordering was introduced by Reed [Ree78]. This approach has the advantage that read requests are never rejected, and hence transactions consisting entirely of read operations are never aborted. Multiversion two-phase locking was originally proposed by Chan et al. [CFL+82]. This protocol makes a distinction between read-only and read-write transactions before transactions begin execution. Read-write transactions are executed as in any other two-phase locking scheme, with some minor changes. Read-only transactions, on the other hand, are never delayed or blocked. Weihl proposed several protocols to implement read-only transactions and to manage multiversion databases [Wei87]. In particular, he describes several techniques to discard old versions of the data. In [AS89], a technique is proposed to decouple the version control mechanism from the concurrency control protocol. Read-only transactions, in this scheme, do not have any concurrency control related overhead.

1.5.2 Nested Transaction Model

The traditional transaction model, although suitable for conventional database applications such as banking and airlines reservations systems, does not provide much flexibility and high performance when used for complex applications such as object oriented systems, long-lived transactions, or distributed systems. *Nested* transactions have been proposed [Mos85] to overcome these limitations of the *flat* transaction model. Nested transactions extend the notion that transactions are flat entities by allowing a transaction to invoke atomic transactions as well as atomic operations. Nested transactions exhibit at least two important advantages over flat transactions. First, they allow the potential internal parallelism to be exploited and offer an appropriate control structure to support their execution. Second, they provide finer control over failures by limiting the effects of failures to a small part of the transaction. This property is achieved by allowing transactions within a given transaction to fail independently of their invoking transaction.

In the traditional transaction model, a transaction consists of a set of partially ordered atomic read and write operations. A nested transaction, on the other hand, is a set of partially ordered atomic read and write operations as well as atomic transactions. This model of execution permits modular and concurrent composition of transaction programs. For example, in the traditional model the programs for writing deposit, withdrawal, and transfer operations are developed independently. In the nested transaction model, however, a transfer transaction can be composed by using the existing deposit and withdraw transaction programs. Furthermore, since the deposit and withdraw transactions will operate on different objects, they can be executed concurrently. Even if the internal transactions conflict with each other, the execution atomicity of these transactions will be ensured by the synchronization algorithms used to implement nested transaction execution. Nested transactions, therefore, provide a modular approach to realize both intra-transaction and inter-transaction parallelism.

The other benefit of nested transactions is that they can be used to localize the effects of failures and faults in the system. In the traditional transactional model, if part of a transaction fails due to faults in the system, the entire transaction is undone to ensure failure atomicity. In nested transactions, on the other hand, the failure-prone part of a transaction can be modeled as an internal transaction and if this component of the transaction fails, the user has the flexibility to retry the failed component or to abort the entire transaction. It is this property of the nested transaction model that makes them highly desirable for distributed applications, and applications with long-running activities where the likelihood of failures and faults is high.

Several protocols exist to synchronize the execution of nested transactions. Moss proposed a two-phase locking protocol for nested transactions [Mos85]. Reed developed a timestamp based technique for nested transactions [Ree78]. Several models have been proposed to prove the correctness of protocols implementing nested transactions [LM86, FLMW88, HH91, BBG89a, FLW90]. In fact, all proposed models are able to establish the correctness of the nested two-phase locking protocol in a straightforward manner. Other models have also been proposed for restricted types of nested transactions called multilayered systems [Wei91, Mar87] and for object-oriented database systems [RGN90].

1.5.3 Transaction Models for Abstract Objects

Traditionally, database systems are modeled as a collection of objects which can only be read or written by transactions. More recently, a number of researchers have considered placing more structure on data objects and have shown how this structure can be used to permit more concurrency [Kor83, SS84, Her86, BR87, KS88b, Ng89, Wei89a, Wei89b]. Atomic data types are especially useful for distributed applications, complex design environments, and object oriented databases. The database is modeled as a collection of objects with abstract data type specifications. Synchronization algorithms for concurrency control and recovery are designed to exploit the semantics of data types. In this section, we summarize some of the results in this area.

Korth [Kor83] uses the notion of commutativity of operations on abstract data types to reduce conflicts in the system. For example, even though an increment operation modifies the state of the object, by using the semantics of the operation, the conflict between two increment operations can be ignored. Schwarz and Spector [SS84] extend this approach by incorporating the instance specific data specified in the operations on abstract data types. For example, an insert operation of a key value k does not conflict with other insert and delete operations with a different key value k'. Several researchers [WL85, Her86] extended the notion of commutativity between operations to exploit the operation types as well as input and output values. For example, by examining the results of a withdraw operation, an unsuccessful withdraw operation can be treated as a read operation. Weihl [Wei89b] has shown that different notions of commutativity are determined by the choice of the recovery mechanism. However, these different notions collapse into one in the read/write model explaining why different approaches for ensuring failure atomicity do not influence the concurrency control protocols in the read/write model. These notions of commutativity can be easily incorporated into two phase locking protocol for concurrency control [Wei89b]. Badrinath and Ramamritham [BR87] have introduced a notion called recoverability, which goes beyond commutativity, to further increase concurrency in databases.

Most of the work referenced above has not been used in commercial database systems. The abstract data type model seems appropriate for transaction management in object oriented databases, however, its utility for other database models needs to be investigated. Although these protocols are theoretically superior to the ones developed for the read/write model, extensive performance analysis is needed to demonstrate their usefulness in practice.

1.6 Concluding Remarks

The transaction model was originally designed for business oriented database applications, where transactions are generally short and atomicity of transactions is of paramount importance. As the scope of databases extends to a large variety of applications, it is important to reevaluate the assumptions and properties of the traditional model of transactions. In particular, different applications may weaken the restrictions on the transaction model. The following chapters address and illustrate some of these applications and propose new models for such environments.

Acknowledgements

We would like to acknowledge the work of all the researchers in the databases community who have contributed significantly to the work described in this chapter. We apologize for any unintended omissions. We also thank the referees for their comments and criticisms. This work is partially supported by the NSF under grant number IRI-9004998.

Bibliography

[AB91] D. Agrawal and A. J. Bernstein. A Non-blocking Quorum Consensus Protocol for Replicated Data. *IEEE Transactions on Parallel and Distributed Systems*, 2(2):171–179, April 1991.

[ACL87] R. Agrawal, M. J. Carey, and M. Livny. Concurrency Control Performance Modeling: Alternatives and Implications. *ACM Transactions on Database Systems*, 12(4):609–654, December 1987.

[AD85] R. Agrawal and D. J. Dewitt. Integrated concurrency control and recovery mechanisms: Design and performance evaluation. *ACM Transactions on Database Systems*, 10(4):529–564, December 1985.

[AE90a] D. Agrawal and A. El Abbadi. Constrained Shared Locks for Increasing Concurrency in Databases. *Journal of Computer and System Sciences.* To appear. A preliminary version appeared in the Proceedings of the Ninth ACM Symposium on Principles of Database Systems, April 1990.

[AE90b] D. Agrawal and A. El Abbadi. The Generalized Tree Quorum Protocol: An Efficient Approach for Managing Replicated Data. *ACM Transaction on Database Systems.* To appear. A preliminary version appeared in the Proceedings of the Sixteenth International Conference on Very Large Data Bases, August 1990.

[AS89] D. Agrawal and S. Sengupta. Modular Synchronization in Multiversion Databases: Version Control and Concurrency Control. In *Proceedings of the ACM SIGMOD International Conference on Management of Data*, pages 408–417, May 1989. To appear in the IEEE Transactions on Knowledge and Data Engineering.

[Bad79] D. Z. Badal. Correctness of Concurrency Control and Implications in Distributed Databases. In *IEEE Proceedings of COMPSAC Conference*, pages 588–593, November 1979.

[BBG89a] C. Beeri, P. A. Bernstein, and N. Goodman. A Model for Concurrency in Nested Transactions Systems. *Journal of the ACM*, 36(2):230–269, April 1989.

[BG81] P. A. Bernstein and N. Goodman. Concurrency Control in Distributed Database Systems. *ACM Computing Surveys*, 13(2):185–221, June 1981.

[BG84] P. A. Bernstein and N. Goodman. An Algorithm for Concurrency Control and Recovery in Replicated Distributed Databases. *ACM Transactions on Database Systems*, 9(4):596–615, December 1984.

[BG87] P. A. Bernstein and N. Goodman. A Proof Technique for Concurrency Control and Recovery Algorithms for Replicated

Databases. *Distributed Computing, Springer-Verlag*, 2(1):32–44, January 1987.

[BGMS89] D. Barbara, H. Garcia-Molina, and A. Spauster. Increasing Availability Under Mutual Exclusion Constraints with Dynamic Vote Reassignment. *ACM Transactions on Computer Systems*, 7(4):394–426, November 1989.

[Bha86] B. K. Bhargava, editor. *Concurrency Control and Reliability in Distributed Systems.* Van Nostrand Reinhold, 1986.

[BHG87] P. A. Bernstein, V. Hadzilacos, and N. Goodman. *Concurrency Control and Recovery in Database Systems.* Addison Wesley, Reading, Massachusetts, 1987.

[BR87] B. Badrinath and K. Ramamritham. Semantics Based Concurrency Control: Beyond Commutativity. In *Proceedings of the International Conference on Data Engineering*, pages 304–311, February 1987. To appear in the ACM Transactions on Database Systems.

[BSW79] P. A. Bernstein, D. W. Shipman, and W. S. Wong. Formal aspects of serializability in database concurrency control. *IEEE Transactions on Software Engineering*, 5(5):203–216, May 1979.

[Car83] M. J. Carey. *Modeling and Evaluation of Database Concurrency Control Algorithms.* PhD thesis, Electronics Research Library, College of Engineering, University of California, Berkeley, September 1983.

[Cas81] M. A. Casanova. *The Concurrency Control Problem of Database Systems*, volume 116 of *Lecture Notes in Computer Science.* Springer-Verlag, Berlin, 1981.

[CFL+82] A. Chan, S. Fox, W. K. Lin, A. Nori, and D. R. Ries. The Implementation of an Integrated Concurrency Control and Recovery Scheme. In *Proceedings of the ACM SIGMOD International Conference on Management of Data*, pages 184–191, July 1982.

[CG85] A. Chan and R. Gray. Implementing Distributed Read-Only Transactions. *IEEE Transactions on Software Engineering*, 11(2):205–212, February 1985.

[CO82] S. Ceri and S. Owicki. On the use of optimistic methods for concurrency control in distributed databases. In *Proceedings of the 6th Berkeley Workshop in Distributed Data Management & Computer Networks*, pages 117–129, February 1982.

[CP84] S. Ceri and G. Pelagatti. *Distributed Databases: Principles and Systems.* McGraw-Hill Book Company, 1984.

[DB85] D. Davcev and W. Burkhard. Consistency and Recovery Control for Replicated Files. In *Proceedings of the Tenth ACM Symposium on Operating Systems Principles*, pages 87–96, December 1985.

[DE89] W. Du and A. Elmagarmid. Quasi Serializability: A Correctness Criterion for Global Concurrency Control in InterBase. In *Proceedings of Fifteenth International Conference on Very Large Data Bases*, pages 347–355, August 1989.

[DGMS85] S. B. Davidson, H. Garcia-Molina, and D. Skeen. Consistency in partitioned networks. *ACM Computing Surveys*, 17(3):341–370, September 1985.

[EGLT76] K. P. Eswaran, J. N. Gray, R. A. Lorie, and I. L. Traiger. The Notion of Consistency and Predicate Locks in Database System. *Communications of the ACM*, 19(11):624–633, November 1976.

[Elm86] Ahmed K. Elmagarmid. A Survey of Distributed Deadlock Detection Algorithms. *SIGMOD Record*, 15(3):37–45, September 1986.

[ES83] D. Eager and K. Sevcik. Achieving Robustness in Distributed Database Systems. *ACM Transactions on Database Systems*, 8(3):354–381, September 1983.

[ESC85] A. El Abbadi, D. Skeen, and F. Cristian. An Efficient Fault-Tolerant Protocol for Replicated Data Management. In *Proceedings of the Fourth ACM Symposium on Principles of Database Systems*, pages 215–228, March 1985.

[ET89] A. El Abbadi and S. Toueg. Maintaining Availability in Partitioned Replicated Databases. *ACM Transaction on Database Systems*, 14(2):264–290, June 1989.

[FLMW88] A. Fekete, N. Lynch, M. Merrit, and W. Weihl. Commutativity-based Locking for Nested Transactions. Technical Report MIT-LCS-TR-367, Massachusetts Institute of Technology, Cambridge, Massachusetts, August 1988.

[FLW90] A. Fekete, N. Lynch, and W. Weihl. A Serialization Graph Construction for Nested Transactions. In *Proceedings of the Ninth ACM Symposium on Principles of Database Systems*, pages 94–108, April 1990.

[FO89] A. A. Farrag and M. T. Özsu. Using Semantic Knowledge of Transactions to Increase Concurrency. *ACM Transactions on Database Systems*, 14(4):503–525, December 1989.

[Gif79] D. K. Gifford. Weighted Voting for Replicated Data. In *Proceedings of the Seventh ACM Symposium on Operating Systems Principles*, pages 150–159, December 1979.

[GM83] H. Garcia-Molina. Using semantic knowledge for transaction processing in a distributed database. *ACM Transactions on Database Systems*, 8(2):186–213, June 1983.

[GMB+81] J. Gray, P. McJones, M. Blasgen, N. Lindsay, R. Lorie, T. Price, F. Putzolu, and I. Traiger. The Recovery Manager of the system R Database Manager. *ACM Computing Surveys*, 13(2), June 1981.

[GMB85] H. Garcia-Molina and D. Barbara. How to assign votes in a distributed system. *Journal of the Association of the Computing Machinery*, 32(4):841–860, October 1985.

[Gra78] J. N. Gray. Notes on database systems. In R. Bayer, R. M. Graham, and G. Seegmuller, editors, *Operating Systems: An Advanced Course*, volume 60 of *Lecture Notes in Computer Science*, pages 393–481. Springer-Verlag, 1978.

[Gra81] J. N. Gray. The transaction concept: Virtues and limitations. In *Proceedings of the 7th International Conference on Very Large Data Bases*, pages 144–154, September 1981.

[Had88] V. Hadzilacos. A Theory of Reliability in Database Systems. *Journal of the ACM*, 35(1):121–145, January 1988.

[Her86] M. Herlihy. A quorum-consensus replication method for abstract data types. *ACM Transactions on Computer Systems*, 4(1):32–53, February 1986.

[Her87] M. Herlihy. Dynamic Quorum Adjustments for Partitioned Data. *ACM Transactions on Database Systems*, 12(2):170–194, June 1987.

[HH91] T. Hadzilacos and V. Hadzilacos. Transaction Synchronization in Object Bases. *Journal of Computer and System Sciences*, 43(1):2–24, August 1991.

[HR83] T. Haerder and A. Reuter. Principles of Transaction-Oriented Database Recovery. *ACM Computing Surveys*, 15(4):287–317, December 1983.

[JM87] S. Jajodia and D. Mutchler. Dynamic Voting. In *Proceedings of the ACM SIGMOD International Conference on Management of Data*, pages 227–238, June 1987.

[Kna87] E. Knapp. Deadlock Detection in Distributed Databases. *ACM Computing Surveys*, 19(4):303–328, December 1987.

[Kor83] H. F. Korth. Locking primitives in a database system. *Journal of the ACM*, 30(1):55–79, January 1983.

[KR81] H. T. Kung and J. T. Robinson. On Optimistic Methods for Concurrency Control. *ACM Transactions on Database Systems*, 6(2):213–226, June 1981.

[KS88a] H. F. Korth and G. D. Speegle. Formal Model of Correctness without Serializability. In *Proceedings of ACM SIGMOD International Conference on Management of Data*, pages 397–386, June 1988.

[KS88b] A. Kumar and M. Stonebraker. Semantics Based Transaction Management Techniques for Replicated Data. In *Proceedings of the ACM SIGMOD International Conference on Management of Data*, pages 117–125, June 1988.

[LKS91] E. Levy, H. F. Korth, and A. Silberschatz. An Optimistic Commit Protocol for Distributed Transaction Management. In *Proceedings* of the *ACM SIGMOD International Conference on Management of Data*, pages 88–97, May 1991.

[LM86] N. A. Lynch and M. Merritt. Introduction to the theory of nested transactions. Technical Report MIT-LCS-TR-367, Massachusetts Institute of Technology, Cambridge, Massachusetts, 1986.

[LP91] A. Leff and C. Pu. A Classification of Transaction Processing Systems. *IEEE Computer*, 24(6):63–76, June 1991.

[Lyn83] N. A. Lynch. Multilevel Atomicity – A New Correctness Criterion for Database Concurrency Control. *ACM Transactions on Database Systems*, 8(4):485–502, December 1983.

[Mar87] B. Martin. Modeling concurrent activities with nested objects. In *Proceedings of the 7th International Conference on Distributed Computing Systems*, 1987.

[MHL+89] C. Mohan, D. Haderle, B. Lindsay, H. Pirahesh, and P. Schwarz. ARIES: A Transaction Recovery Method supporting fine-granularity Locking and Partial Rollbacks using Write-ahead Logging. Technical Report RJ 6649R, IBM Almaden Research Center, 1989. To appear in the ACM Transactions on Database Systems.

[MLO86] C. Mohan, B. Lindsay, and R. Obermarck. Transaction Management in the R* Distributed Database Management System. *ACM Transactions on Database Systems*, 11(4):378–396, December 1986.

[Mos85] J. E. B. Moss. *Nested Transactions: An Approach to Reliable Distributed Computing.* MIT Press, Cambridge, Massachusetts, 1985.

[Mul89] S. Mullender, editor. *Distributed Systems.* ACM Press, Frontier Series. Addison Wesley, 1989.

[Ng89] T. P. Ng. Using Histories to implement Atomic Objects. *ACM Transactions on Computer Systems*, 7(4):360–393, November 1989.

[Obe82] R. Obermarck. Distributed deadlock detection algorithms. *ACM Transactions on Database Systems*, 7(2):187–210, June 1982.

[OV91] M. T. Özsu and P. Valduriez. *Principles of Distributed Database Systems.* Prentice Hall, Englewood Cliffs, New Jersey, 1991.

[Pap79] C. H. Papadimitriou. The Serializability of Concurrent Database Updates. *Journal of the ACM*, 26(4):631–653, October 1979.

[Pap86] C. H. Papadimitriou. *The Theory of Database Concurrency Control.* Computer Science Press, 1986.

[PKH88] C. Pu, G. Kaiser, and N. Hutchinson. Split-Transactions for Open-Ended Activities. In *Proceedings of the Fourteenth International Conference on Very Large Data Bases*, pages 26–37, August 1988.

[PL88] J. F. Pâris and D. E. Long. Efficient Dynamic Voting Algorithms. In *Proceedings of the Fourth IEEE International Conference on Data Engineering*, pages 268–275, February 1988.

[Ree78] D. P. Reed. Naming and Synchronization in a Decentralized Computer System. Technical Report MIT-LCS-TR-205, Massachusetts Institute of Technology, Cambridge, Massachusetts, September 1978.

[RGN90] T. C. Rakow, J. Gu, and E. J. Neuhold. Serializability in Object-Oriented Database Systems, In *Proceedings of the Sixth IEEE International Conference on Data Engineering*, pages 112–120, February 1990.

[Sin89] M. Singhal. Deadlock Detection in Distributed Systems. *IEEE Computer*, 22(11):37–48, November 1989.

[Ske82] D. Skeen. Non-blocking commit protocols. In *Proceedings of the ACM SIGMOD Conference on Management of Data*, pages 133–147, June 1982.

[SR81] R. E. Stearns and D. J. Rosenkrantz. Distributed database concurrency control using before-values. In *Proceedings of the ACM SIGMOD Conference on Management of Data*, pages 74–83, June 1981.

[SS82] R. Schlichting and F. B. Schneider. Fail-Stop Processors: An Approach to Designing Fault-Tolerant Computing Systems. *ACM Transactions on Computer Systems*, 1(3):222–238, August 1982.

[SS83] D. Skeen and M. Stonebraker. A Formal Model of Crash Recovery in a Distributed Systems. *IEEE Transactions on Software Engineering*, 9(3):219–228, May 1983.

[SS84] P. M. Schwarz and A. Z. Spector. Synchronizing shared abstract types. *ACM Transactions on Computer Systems*, 2(3):223–250, August 1984.

[Sto79] M. Stonebraker. Concurrency Control and Consistency in Multiple Copies of Data in Distributed INGRES. *IEEE Transactions on Software Engineering*, 3(3):188–194, May 1979.

[Tho79] R. H. Thomas. A Majority Consensus Approach to Concurrency Control for Multiple Copy Databases. *ACM Transaction on Database Systems*, 4(2):180–209, June 1979.

[Ver78] J. S. M. Verhofstad. Recovery Techniques for Database Systems. *ACM Computing Surveys*, 10(2):167–196, 1978.

[Wei87] W. E. Weihl. Distributed Version Management of Read-only Actions. *IEEE Transactions on Software Engineering*, 13(2):55–64, January 1987.

[Wei88] G. Weikum. Complete Serializability. In *Proceedings of the 1988 Extending Data Base Technology.* LNCS 359, Springer Verlag, March 1988.

[Wei89a] W. E. Weihl. Local Atomicity Properties: Modular Concurrency Control for Abstract Data Types. *ACM Transactions on Programming Languages and Systems*, 11(2):249–283, April 1989.

[Wei89b] W. E. Weihl. The Impact of Recovery on Concurrency Control. In *Proceedings of the Eighth ACM Symposium on Principles of Database Systems*, pages 259–269, March 1989.

[Wei91] G. Weikum. Principles and Realization Strategies of Multilevel Transaction Management. *ACM Transactions on Database Systems*, 16(1):132–180, March 1991.

[WL85] W. E. Weihl and B. Liskov. Implementation of resilient, atomic data types. *ACM Transactions on Programming Languages and Systems*, 7(2):244–269, 1985.

2

Introduction to Advanced Transaction Models

Ahmed K. Elmagarmid

Yungho Leu

James G. Mullen

Omran Bukhres

2.1 Introduction

As discussed in Chapter 1, the traditional transaction concept is very useful because it hides the effects of failures and concurrent processing from the programmer. It has been very effective in areas such as airline reservations, car rentals and electronic funds transfer. Transactions for these applications are generally simple, and are characterized by short duration in the sense that they will generally finish within minutes (most probably within seconds).

Recently, however, there has been widespread use of databases in advanced (non-traditional) applications. It has been found that the traditional transaction concept has limited applicability in many of these advanced applications. For example, in CAD/CAM, office automation, publication environments and software development environments, transactions are usually very complex, need to access many data items and reside in the system for a long duration. Transactions of this kind are usually called *long-lived* transactions [Gra81, GMS87]. Long-lived transactions pose a formidable challenge to the traditional transaction technology. First, a long-lived transaction is more easily interrupted by failures because of its long execution time. Because of the failure atomicity requirement, when a failure occurs, a traditional transaction has to be rolled back, that is, its effects on the database must be undone. This might be reasonable for short transactions; however, this is not acceptable for long-lived transactions due to the fact that much work might have been done and will be lost if the transaction aborts. Second, a long-lived transaction may access many data items in the course of its execution. Due to the isolation requirement, these data items cannot be released until the transaction commits. If a short transaction accesses some data items held by a long-lived transaction, it will end up waiting — perhaps for hours or even days — for the long-lived transaction to commit. Moreover, a long-lived transaction can easily cause deadlocks. According to [Gra81], the frequency of deadlock increases with the fourth power of the transaction size.

Another limitation of the traditional transaction model is that it does not allow much cooperation between activities. In many environments, there is a specific need for cooperation among activities. For example, a CAD project [KKB88] is usually performed jointly by a group of people; each person is responsible for a part of the design project. People of the same group have to cooperate in order to achieve a good design. One means of cooperating is by exchanging information through shared data items. To do this, people (or their corresponding transactions) need to access the shared data items alternately. The traditional transaction concept severely restricts this type of cooperation by requiring the isolation of uncommited transaction results.

Another problem with the traditional transaction model is that it may be too strict for certain environments. That is, all of the traditional transaction properties may not be needed, or it may not be possible to support them. For example, recently there has been a strong demand for systems that integrate existing database systems to support applications that need to access multiple databases [TTC+90]. Systems of this type are called multidatabase systems [Lit86]. An important requirement of multidatabase systems is that local system autonomy is preserved [VPZ86]. The traditional transaction concept is very difficult to maintain in multidatabase systems. First, due to local autonomy, it is very difficult for the multidatabase system to detect conflicts between global transactions. This makes maintaining the serializability requirement of the traditional transaction model very difficult [DELO89, DE89]. Moreover, due to local autonomy, a local database system is entitled to delay or reject the execution of a global transaction. A global transaction might become long-lived and error prone, which makes it very difficult to maintain the atomicity and isolation properties of the traditional transaction model [LER89].

The transaction models presented in this book attempt to overcome the limitations of the traditional transaction model. The remainder of this chapter summarizes theses transaction models, as well as ACTA, a framework for formally specifying transaction models.

2.2 Advanced Transaction Models

In this section we will summarize the transactions models presented in this book. First, however, we will discuss two important early non-traditional transaction models: Nested Transactions, and Sagas.

Nested Transactions. The *nested transaction model* was introduced by Moss in [Mos81]. As described in [Mos81], a transaction in this model may contain any number of *subtransactions*, and each subtransaction, in turn, may contain any number of subtransactions. The whole transaction therefore forms a tree, called a *transaction tree*, of (sub)transactions. The root of the transaction tree is called the *root* or *top-level transaction*. In the following, we use the term "transaction" to denote both top-level transactions and subtransactions. Transactions having subtransactions are called *parents*, and their subtransactions are their *children*. The transactions on the path from a transaction to the root of the transaction tree are called the *superiors* of the transaction. A child transaction must start after its parent transaction and terminate before it.

Top-level transactions have all the properties of traditional transactions, that is, atomicity, consistency, isolation and durability. Therefore, top-level transactions must be isolated from each other, and, in case of failure, they must be rolled back without side-effects to other transactions or to the database. Subtransactions appear atomic to the surrounding transactions and may commit or abort independently. A transaction is not allowed to commit until all its children have terminated. However, if a child fails, its parent is not required to abort. Instead, the parent is allowed to perform its own recovery. In order to meet its goal, the parent may:

- ignore the condition (in which case the child transaction is considered to be *non-vital*).
- choose to retry the subtransaction.
- initiate another subtransaction (a *contingency subtransaction*) that implements an alternative action.
- abort (when its goal cannot be accomplished within a reasonable amount of time).

The commit of a subtransaction is conditionally subject to the commit or abort of its superiors. Even if a subtransaction commits, aborting one of its superiors will undo its effects. Updates of a subtransaction become permanent only when the enclosing top-level transaction commits.

A concurrency control algorithm for nested transactions was proposed by Moss in [Mos81]. The proposed protocol is based on the strict two-phase locking protocol in which a transaction cannot release any locks until the transaction commits. The children of a parent transaction are synchronized as if they were separate transactions. When a child commits, its locks are *inherited* by its parent. When a parent holds a lock, it does not interfere with its children, only with the transactions that are not descendants of the transaction. A transaction is allowed to hold a lock if any other transaction that holds a conflicting lock is the parent of the transaction. In inheriting a lock, the parent chooses to hold a lock in a more exclusive mode if both the parent and the child hold a lock on the same data item. This protocol allows concurrent access to shared data within a transaction to be performed safely (i.e., serializably). Because of lock inheritance, the whole transaction tree is isolated against (or serializable with) other transaction trees.

The main advantages of the nested transaction model are the support of *modularity*, *failure handling* and *intra-transaction parallelism.* For modularity, nested transactions provide a framework for decomposing a transaction hierarchically. For failure handling, nested transactions allow a user to define more graceful units of recovery (namely subtransactions). In contrast to the traditional transaction model where an UNDO operation necessarily rolls back the transaction to the state of "begin of transaction", nested transactions allow the UNDO operation at the granularity of a subtransaction. Such flexibility has been used in developing more powerful recovery mechanisms [HR87, RM89]. Finally, nested transactions allow a higher degree of intra-transaction parallelism, since subtransactions can be executed concurrently.

The nested transaction model is important in the development of advanced transaction models because it introduces the idea of structuring a transaction into a tree (or hierarchy) of subtransactions, and because it introduces the idea of contingency subtransactions and non-vital subtransactions. Most advanced transaction models use the same structure as nested transactions or a specific instance of it (e.g. a 2-level hierarchy, or a balanced hierarchy). Also, many advanced transaction models incorporate the idea of contingency and non-vital subtransactions.

Sagas. The concept of *Sagas* [GMS87] is based on the *compensating transactions* in [Gra81]. For a transaction T, a compensating transaction C is a transaction that can *semantically undo* the effects of T after T has been committed. Sagas were proposed by Garcia-Molina and Salem [GMS87] to deal with the problem of long-lived transactions. A Saga is a long-lived transaction that consists of a set of relatively independent steps (for uniformity, we call them subtransactions hereafter), $T_1, T_2, \cdots, T_n$. Associated with subtransactions $T_1, T_2, \cdots, T_n$ are compensating subtransactions $C_1, C_2, \cdots, C_n$. To execute a Saga, the system must guarantee that either the sequence

$$T_1, T_2, \cdots, T_n$$

(preferably) or the sequence

$$T_1, T_2, \cdots, T_j, C_j, \cdots, C_2, C_1$$

for some $1 \leq j < n$ will be executed. That is, either all of the subtransactions in a Saga are complete or any partial execution is undone with compensating subtransactions. Each subtransaction in a Saga need not observe the same consistent database state. Therefore, once a subtransaction is complete, it can be committed without waiting for other subtransactions of the same Saga, and thereby releases its results to the rest of the concurrent transactions. If interrupted (i.e., some constituent subtransaction fails), a Saga may try to proceed by executing the missing subtransactions (forward recovery). In case forward recovery is not possible, the transaction must abort by executing the compensating transactions for the already committed subtransactions (backward recovery).

Compared to the traditional transaction model, Sagas relax the property of *isolation* by allowing a Saga to reveal its partial results to other transactions before it is complete. Since a Saga can interleave its subtransactions in any order with the subtransactions of other Sagas, consistency (or more specifically serializability) may be compromised. However, a Saga still requires that either all subtransactions successfully complete or none of them complete, and the results of a Saga, once it has completed, must persist despite subsequent failures. In this sense, the Sagas preserve the *atomicity* and *durability* properties of traditional transactions.

By allowing transactions to release partial results (and therefore the objects accessed) before they complete, Sagas help to alleviate the problems caused by long-lived transactions. Sagas are useful only when the subtransactions in a Saga are relatively independent (because of the consistency problem) and each subtransaction can be successfully compensated. In real life, however, there are transactions that are not compensatable. For example, a transaction that fires a missile is not compensatable (without losing the missile). A transaction that dispenses cash from an automatic teller machine (ATM) may not be compensatable. Consider a customer who withdrew some money from an ATM and spent all of it. In these cases, Sagas are inapplicable.

The main contribution of Sagas to advanced transaction models is the idea of incorporating compensating transactions into the transaction model.

2.2.1 Cooperative Transaction Hierarchy

The *cooperative transaction hierarchy* concept was introduced by Nodine and Zdonik for supporting cooperative applications like CAD [NZ84], and is presented in Chapter 3. Serializability in the traditional transaction model restricts cooperation between transactions by not allowing the transactions to exchange information through accessing (i.e., reading and writing) common data. This is because serializability requires that conflicting operations be executed in a strictly sequential way. To overcome this problem, Nodine and Zdonik proposed to structure a cooperative application as a rooted tree called a *cooperative transaction hierarchy*. The *external nodes* of the hierarchy represent the transactions associated with the individual designers. An internal node is called a *transaction group*, and contains a set of members (i.e., children) that cooperate to perform a single task. The term *cooperative transactions* in this model refers to the transactions with the same parent in the transaction tree. Cooperative transactions need not be serializable; instead, the transaction group (i.e., parent) of the cooperative transactions defines a set of rules that regulate the way the cooperative transactions should interact with each other. The rules are defined in terms of a set of finite-state automata. A finite-state automaton specifies, for a set of objects, the operations allowable for each cooperative transaction, and the allowable ways of interleaving the operations of related cooperative transactions.

The main contribution of cooperative transaction hierarchies is the substitution of a notion of user-defined correctness for the notion of correctness defined by serializability. The notion of user-defined correctness criteria allows different parts of a shared task to use different correctness criteria that are suitable for their own purposes. Because isolation is not required, the cooperative transaction hierarchies allow close cooperation between transactions and also help to alleviate the problems caused by long-lived transactions.

2.2.2 Cooperative SEE Transactions

A transaction model to support cooperative work in SEEs (software engineering environments) is presented in Chapter 4. In software engineering environments, support is needed for long-lived transactions and cooperative transactions. It is also desirable to be able to support various levels of cooperation dependent on the particular environment.

The model presented uses nested active transactions with user-definable correctness conditions. Since user-definable correctness conditions are used, semantic-based concurrency control can be used to increase the level of concurrency. It is also possible to allow a higher degree of cooperation between different transactions, and to allow various levels of cooperation. This also helps to support long-lived transactions. However, correctness in the traditional database sense is not supported; that is, the ACID properties of transactions are not supported.

Users can define appropriate correctness conditions based on the following:

- **Conflicts**: Operations that are not allowed to execute concurrently.

- **Patterns**: Sequences of functions that must occur. For example, a pattern of edit — compile — link — test may be required when editing a source code file.
- **Triggers**: Actions that are taken when a request begins or ends.
- **Commit or Abort Semantics**: Actions to be taken when a transaction ends.

2.2.3 DOM Transactions

The DOM Transaction Model was developed for the DOM (Distributed Object Management) project at GTE Laboratories and is covered in Chapter 5. The goal of this project is to support application development in a distributed object-oriented environment that integrates various component systems. The systems being integrated may be autonomous and heterogeneous, and may be non-database systems (such as file systems) as well as database systems.

The DOM Transaction Model allows *closed nested* and *open nested* transactions and combinations of the two. Closed nested transactions are the same as traditional nested transactions as presented in [Mos85]. Open nested transactions do not provide the top-level atomicity of closed nested transactions, so the partial results of the transaction may be viewed by other transactions. *Compensating transactions* can be specified that undo the effects of a commited transaction, and *contingency transactions* can be specified that are executed if a given transaction fails. Subtransactions can be specified as *vital* or *non-vital*. If a vital subtransaction aborts, its parent transaction must abort. However, if a non-vital subtransaction aborts, the parent may continue. Generally, subtransactions may be executed concurrently, however, dependencies may be specified, causing the subtransactions to be executed (or committed) in a specific order.

The correctness theory for the DOM model has not yet been developed. Since the component systems that are integrated may be non-database systems that may not support the ACID properties of transactions, and since the autonomy of the component systems is preserved, clearly it will not be possible, in general, to support the ACID properties for global transactions. Even for database systems, it is difficult to support correctness when component system autonomy is preserved [DELO89]. In addition, the preservation of component system autonomy may make the implementation of compensation difficult, since the global transaction manager will not be able to prevent local transactions from viewing the results of global transactions that will be compensated later.

2.2.4 A Transaction Model for an Open Publication Environment

Chapter 6 presents a transaction model used for an open distributed publication environment[1] (see also [MRKN91]). The publication environment described is a distributed system that combines various component systems, including databases, knowledge bases, and active system components. The transactions in the environment include ones that range from short to long duration, and the level of cooperation between transactions ranges from low to high.

In this environment, three different kinds of components are distinguished: *assistants*, *agents*, and *tools*. Assistants provide users with a homogeneous interface to local tools, such as text editors or information systems. Agents offer direct access to non-local tools, originally available only to the assistants of other users. In order to support transaction properties for users' applications, an open nested transaction model with the following characteristics is proposed: reduced conflict rate between user operations by the use of semantic information for conflict definition, easy integration of existing tools, and guarantee of ACID properties by assistants and agents if tools supporting ACID transactions are accessed.

The open nested transaction model does not provide the top-level atomicity of (closed) nested transactions, which implies that the results of commited subtransactions may be viewed by other transactions. However, to maintain consistency, only those transactions (or subtransactions) that commute with a committed subtransaction are allowed to see the results of the committed subtransaction. If two transactions (or subtransactions) commute it means that the result of the execution of both transactions is independent of their execution order. This enables compensation to be performed. For a further discussion of the open nested transaction model see Chapter 13.

2.2.5 ConTract Model

The *ConTract model* was first proposed by Reuter [Reu89] for defining and controlling long-lived, complex computations in non-standard applications like office automation, CAD and manufacturing control. The ConTract

[1]This environment is currently under development at the Integrated Publication and Information Systems Institute of the German national research institution GMD.

model is discussed in Chapter 7. In [RW91], a ConTract is defined as a set of predefined actions (called steps) with an explicit specification of control flow among them. The main emphasis of the ConTract model is that the execution of a ConTract must be *forward-recoverable.* This means that when an execution of a ConTract is interrupted by failures, it must be re-instantiated and continued from where it was interrupted after the system is recovered. To be able to do so, all state information, including database state, program variables of each step, and the global state of the ConTract, must be made recoverable. Similar to Sagas, a ConTract is allowed to externalize its partial results before the whole ConTract is complete. Compensating transactions are used to obliterate the results of committed steps that are not needed. Similar to the NT/PV model [KS90], the ConTract model uses invariants (i.e., consistency constraints) defined on the database for concurrency control. Finally, ConTract allows one to resolve conflicts in a more flexible way by specifying what to do when conflicts occur.

2.2.6 Split-Transactions

Split-transactions were proposed by Pu et al. in [PKH88]. They were proposed mainly for supporting *open-ended* applications. Split-transactions are discussed in Chapter 8. Some examples of open-ended applications are CAD/CAM projects, VLSI design and software development. Open-ended applications are characterized by (1) uncertain duration (from hours to months), (2) uncertain developments (actions cannot be foreseen at the beginning) and (3) interaction with other concurrent activities. The combination of the above factors may also render the transactions long-lived. The principle of split-transactions is to split an ongoing transaction into two serializable transactions and divide its resources among the resulting transactions.

To split a transaction T into two transactions A and B such that A is serialized before B, the following properties must hold:

1. $AWriteSet \cap BWriteSet \subseteq BWriteLast$
2. $AReadSet \cap BWriteSet = \emptyset$
3. $BReadSet \cap AWriteSet = ShareSet$

Property 1 states that if both A and B write into the same object, B's write operation must follows A's write operation. In other words, A cannot overwrite B's outputs, but B can overwrite A's outputs. Property 2 says that A cannot see any of the results from B. Property 3 says that B may see the results from A. The properties 1, 2, and 3 together guarantee that A is serialized before B. If both $ShareSet$ and $BWriteLast$ are empty (called the *independent case*), then A and B can be serialized in either order and both of them can be committed independently. If either $ShareSet$ or $BWriteSet$ is not empty (called the *serial case*), then A is serialized before B because of data access dependencies. In this case, the objects in the $ShareSet$ must remain unchanged in A, otherwise, B will end up using uncommitted data from A. Furthermore, if A aborts, B must also abort because B read data written by A.

The main purpose of split-transactions is to commit one of the split transactions (A in the above case) and release useful results from the original transaction. The other split transaction (B in the above case) continues. Two advantages of split-transactions are

1. **Adaptive recovery**: committing part of the work done by a transaction which then will not be affected by subsequent failures.
2. **Reducing isolation**: releasing resources by committing part of a transaction.

2.2.7 Flex Transaction Model

Chapter 9 describes the Flex Transaction model [ELLR90], which was designed to allow more flexibility in transaction processing. Consider a transaction that is composed of a set of tasks. For each task, the Flex Transaction model allows the user to specify a set of *functionally equivalent* subtransactions, each of which when completed will accomplish the task. The execution of a Flex Transaction succeeds if all of its tasks are accomplished. A Flex Transaction is resilient to failures in the sense that it may proceed and commit even if some of its subtransactions fail. The Flex Transaction model also allows the specification of dependencies on the subtransactions of a Flex Transaction. Some useful dependencies defined in the Flex model are *failure-dependencies*, *success-dependencies* and *external-dependencies*. Among them, failure-dependencies and success-dependencies define the execution order on the subtransactions, whereas the external-dependencies define the dependencies of the subtransaction execution on the events that do not belong to the transaction. Finally, the Flex Transaction model allows the user to control the isolation granularity of a transaction through the use of compensating subtransactions. All of the above-listed features contribute to the flexibility of the Flex Transaction model, which is useful for transaction processing in multidatabase systems.

The Flex Transaction model has been implemented in the Vienna Parallel Logic (VPL) language [KPE91]. The VPL programming language has explicit parallelism. The design of the VPL language has been influenced mainly by the idea of compensate-actions of the Flex Transaction model [KPE91]. The VPL language is a suitable environment for Flex Transactions for the following reasons: (1) VPL is a superset of Prolog; (2) committed computations can be automatically compensated with the convenient option of compensate-actions; and (3) the programmer can easily specify the OR-AND parallelism, which facilitates the execution of goals and subgoals (transactions and subtransactions) sequentially or in parallel.

The Flex Transaction model is implemented in the VPL environment in the following manner. Transactions of type "C" (compensatable transaction) are specified by the VPL construct with commit operators and corresponding compensate-actions. Transactions of type "NC" (non-compensatable transactions) are specified by the non-committing VPL construct. The success dependencies are expressed by the use of the sequential AND operator "&" instead of the parallel one "&&". Failure dependencies, on the other hand, are expressed by the adequate use of sequential and parallel procedures. Finally, the acceptability function is mapped into the AND/OR structure of the VPL search tree for the goal (transaction). A VPL solution corresponds to an acceptable state of the Flex Transaction. For detailed examples of the VPL implementation, see Chapter 9.

2.2.8 ACTA

ACTA [CR90] is a framework that allows one to specify the effects of transactions on other transactions and also their effects on objects. ACTA is presented in Chapter 10, and is used to formally specify atomic transactions, Sagas, and a number of extensions to Sagas that follow from the specification of Sagas. The main extensions are:

1. Sagas that can commit if a non-vital subset of the components of a Saga abort.

2. Sagas that may contain subtransactions that are not compensatable.

3. Sagas that may have nested Sagas within them.

4. Sagas that may contain alternative and contingency subtransactions.

ACTA is used to show correctness properties of the Saga model and can also be used to show correctness properties of the Saga extensions presented.

2.2.9 Transaction Tool Kits

The *tool kit approach* proposed by Unland and Schlageter [US91] represents an attempt to model and control transactions that have conflict requirements on their subtransactions. To accomplish this, the notion of an *application-specific transaction manager* was proposed. This model is discussed in Chapter 11. An application-specific transaction manager provides the user with a number of *transaction types*, each of which is especially designed for one kind of application. The user is then allowed to arbitrarily structure different types of subtransactions in a nested transaction to form a heterogeneous transaction tree.

To allow different types of transactions to coexist in the same transaction tree, some fundamental rules must be followed. The first rule is that a child in a transaction tree can only request an object that is held by its parent. If a requested object is not held by its parent, a *stepwise transfer* is performed, which requires that the parent request the object from its parent on behalf of its child. This operation is continued until the designated object is found in one of the superiors of the child. The second rule is that a parent transaction is only responsible for the correct coordination and execution of the work on its level. In other words, the environment (such as the concurrency control protocol, for example) set up by a transaction only applies to the children of the transaction. The children, in turn, may establish a different environment for their own children. This rule is called the *two stage control-sphere* and is essential for supporting a heterogeneous transaction tree.

To implement this approach, the tool kit system supports a set of basic components. These basic components can be assembled in different ways to form different transaction types. A transaction in a transaction tree can be assigned with any transaction type that is suitable for its application.

2.2.10 S Transactions

The *S-transaction model* [EVT88] was introduced to support cooperation of the international banking system and is discussed in Chapter 12. In this environment, *local autonomy* is of major concern. An S-transaction is a nested transaction in form, however, it is different from the nested transaction in other important respects. First, due to the autonomy requirement and confidentiality, a component system issuing an S-transaction cannot dictate to other systems which further systems should participate in the execution of the S-transaction. A component system is entitled to execute a subtransaction of an S-transaction in any way it wishes. In case of failures, a component system can issue an equivalent request to an *alternative system.* Consequently, the exact execution tree of an S-transaction is indeterminate and may vary from one execution to another. Second, like Sagas, S-transactions use compensating transactions for recovery. Each subtransaction will commit when it completes. Therefore, the isolation of S-transactions is only supported at the subtransaction level (by the component systems). No concurrency control or commitment control at the S-transaction level is required. The success or failure of a subtransaction depends on the successes or failures of its children, and is described as an algebraic expression called a *semantic constraint.*

2.2.11 Multilevel and Open Nested Transactions

The *Multilevel transaction model* [WS91, Wei91] and its generalization, the *open nested transaction model*, are presented in Chapter 13. Multilevel transactions are a specialization of open nested transactions where the tree of subtransactions is balanced. Nodes at the same depth of a tree correspond to operations of the same level of abstraction in a database management system. The edges in a transaction tree represent the implementation of an operation by a sequence of operations at the next lower level. The levels of an n-level transaction are denoted by $L0, \cdots, Ln$ in bottom-up order. An Li action $(0 < i < n)$ can be viewed as an Li subtransaction from the underlying implementation level $L(i-1)$. The key idea of multilevel transactions is to exploit the *level-specific semantics* for concurrency control. Due to the level-specific semantics, two Li operations may not conflict (if they commute) even though their implementations at level $L(i-1)$ do conflict (i.e., two implementations contain $L(i-1)$ operations that conflict). In this case, the conflict at level $L(i-1)$ becomes a *pseudo-conflict* at level Li. Therefore, an execution that is non-serializable at level $L(i-1)$ may be serializable at level Li. By taking advantage of the level-specific conflict information, multilevel transactions allow a degree of concurrency that is higher than traditional transactions.

2.2.12 Polytransactions

Chapter 14 presents polytransactions [RS91], which were developed with the goal of finding a transaction model that would facilitate the support of interdependent data in multidatabase environments. Interdependent data is defined to be two or more data items stored in different databases that are related to each other through an integrity constraint. The integrity constraint specifies the data dependency and the consistency requirements between the data items. For example, one might have data items X and X' stored in different databases, where X' is supposed to be a copy of X that is at most 15 minutes out of date.

In the polytransaction model, it is *not* assumed that for a given transaction all of the subtransactions and execution dependencies between them are known in advance. Instead, it is assumed that there exists an IDS (Interdatabase Dependency Schema) that contains a set of Data Dependency Descriptors (D^3) that specify the interdatabase dependencies. The D^3s contain information indicating the conditions when the data dependency is to be considered violated, and the action to take to maintain the data dependency. A polytransaction (T^+) is a "transitive closure" of a transaction T with respect to the IDS. That is, when a transaction T is executed, the Data Dependency Descriptors are checked to see if actions need to be taken to maintain the consistency of the database. The appropriate actions (if any) are taken, which may in turn cause other actions to be taken, which may cause other actions, and so on. In effect, the transaction T is considered the root transaction of polytransaction T^+ and the actions generated by T are considered to be the subtransactions of T. The actions generated by actions are considered to be subtransactions of subtransactions.

Just as the traditional transaction model frees the programmer from having to worry about concurrency and failure issues, the polytransaction model frees the programmer from having to worry about maintaining global data dependencies. In addition, having data dependencies explicitly specified in the IDS makes the task of identifying the data dependencies easier than in systems where one must extract the dependencies from application code. And, using an IDS implies that changes in data dependencies do not require application programs to be rewritten.

2.3 Summary of Transaction Models

Figure 2.1 summarizes the transaction models presented in this book. ACTA is not presented in this table as it is a framework for formally specifying transaction models, and not a specific transaction model. The models are listed in order of the chapter in which they first appear.

Transaction Structure. For transaction structure, *subtransaction hierarchy* implies that arbitrary tree structures are allowed. *Subtransactions* implies a set of subtransactions.

Model	Transaction Structure	Subtransaction Types	Transaction Correctness	Comments
Traditional	—	—	ACID	
Nested	Subtransaction Hierarchy	Contingency, Non-Vital	ACID	
Sagas	Subtransactions	Compensating	$ACID^C$	
Cooperative (Ch. 3)	Subtransaction Hierarchy	Compensating	User-Defined	For cooperative environments, e.g. design databases
Coop. SEE (Ch. 4)	Subtransaction Hierarchy	Trigger	User-Defined	Cooperative work, e.g. engineering environments
DOM (Ch. 5)	Subtransaction Hierarchy	Compensating, Contingency, Non-Vital	Component System Dependent	For active MDBSs with long-lived transactions
Open Nested (Ch. 6 & 13)	Subtransaction Hierarchy	Compensating, Contingency, Non-Vital	$ACID^C$	For a publication environment in Ch. 6
ConTract (Ch. 7)	Subtransactions	Compensating, Contingency, Non-Vital	$ACID^C$	Supports long-lived and cooperating transactions
Split (Ch. 8)	Dynamic Restructuring (Split and Join)	—	Original Semantics Preserved	Supports long-lived and cooperating transactions
Flex (Ch. 9)	Subtransaction Hierarchy	Compensating, Contingency, Non-Vital	$ACID^C$	Supports long-lived and cooperating transactions
Tool Kit (Ch. 11)	Subtransaction Hierarchy	Contingency, Non-Vital	User-Defined	Supports long-lived and cooperating transactions
S (Ch. 12)	Subtransaction Hierarchy	Compensating, Contingency, Non-Vital	CD to $ACID^{AC}$	For international banking and general MDBSs
Multi-Level (Ch. 13)	Balanced Subtr. Hiearchy	Compensating, Contingency, Non-Vital	$ACID^C$	Supports long-lived and cooperating transactions
Polytrans. (Ch. 14)	Dynamic Transaction Hierarchy	—	User-Defined	Supports interdependent data

^{C} For transactions where subtransactions are compensatable.
^{A} Depending on the degree of component system autonomy.

FIGURE 2.1
Characteristics of Advanced Transaction Models

When a transaction is executed in the polytransaction model, an *Interdatabase Dependency Schema* is checked to see if any transactions need to be triggered to keep the database system consistent. The triggered (or child) transactions may be *coupled or decoupled* from the triggering (or parent) transaction. Coupled means that the parent transaction must wait for the child transaction to finish before proceeding, and decoupled means that the parent transaction is free to continue executing. In addition, *non-vital* child transactions are allowed that do not have to succeed in order for the parent transaction to succeed.

Subtransaction Types. This column lists the special types of subtransactions that are allowed in the transaction model. Contingency subtransactions are subtransactions that can be executed in place of another subtransaction, in case it fails, that will act as a substitute for the failed subtransaction. Non-vital subtransactions are subtransactions whose failure will not cause the transaction that owns them to abort.

Transaction Correctness. Transaction correctness describes the level of transaction correctness provided by the model.

In the open nested chapter, component systems are not guaranteed to provide ACID properties, but when they do, the overall system should provide the ACID properties also.

In the DOM transaction model it is not required that the component systems provide the ACID properties, so it is clearly impossible to provide this for global transactions in general.

Split transactions may commit a different set of transaction than the set of transactions submitted because of restructuring, however, the original semantics of the submitted transactions are preserved, So, for example, if the original transactions have the ACID properties, the (possibly restructured) commited transaction will have the ACID properties also.

Comments. In the comments, note that MDBS stands for multidatabase system. Also note that "supports cooperating transactions" may only mean that a transaction model has features which facilitate cooperation (generally they allow non-commited results to be visible), not necessarily that the model is a model of cooperative work.

The open nested transaction model is presented in both Chapters 6 and 13. In Chapter 6 the open nested model is used in a distributed open publication environment, and in Chapter 13 it is presented as a generalization of the multi-level transaction model.

Bibliography

[CR90] P. K. Chrysanthis and K. Ramamtitham. Acta: A framework for specifying and reasoning about transaction structure and behavior. In *Proceedings of ACM-SIGMOD International Conference on Management of Data*, pages 194–203, 1990.

[DE89] W. Du and A. Elmagarmid. Quasi serializability: a correctness criterion for global concurrency control in interbase. In *Proceedings of the International Conference on Very Large Data Bases*, pages 347–355, Amsterdam, The Netherlands, August 1989.

[DELO89] W. Du, A. Elmagarmid, Y. Leu, and S. Ostermann. Effects of autonomy on global concurrency control in heterogeneous distributed database systems. In *Proceedings of the Second International Conference on Data and Knowledge Systems for Manufacturing and Engineering*, pages 113–120, Gaithersburg, Maryland, October 1989.

[ELLR90] A. Elmagarmid, Y. Leu, W. Litwin, and M. Rusinkiewicz. A multidatabase transaction model for interbase. In *Proceedings of the International Conference on Very Large Data Bases*, Brisbane, Australia, August 1990.

[EVT88] F. Eliassen, J. Veijalainen, and H. Tirri. Aspects of transaction modelling for interoperable information systems. In *Interim Report of the COST 11ter Project*, pages 39–55, 1988.

[GMS87] H. Garcia-Molina and K. Salem. Sagas. In *Proceedings of the ACM Conference on Management of Data*, pages 249–259, May 1987.

[Gra81] J. Gray. The transaction concept: Virtues and limitations. In *Proceedings of the International Conference on Very Large Data Bases*, pages 144–154, Cannes, France, September 1981.

[HR87] T. Haerder and K. Rothermel. Concepts for transaction recovery in nested transactions. In *Proceedings of the ACM Conference on Management of Data*, pages 239–248, May 1987.

[KKB88] H. Korth, W. Kim, and F. Bancilhon. On long-duration cad transaction. *Information Sciences*, 46(1-2):73–108, 1988.

[KPE91] E. Kuehn, F. Puntigam, and A. Elmagarmid. Transaction specification in multidatabase systems based on parallel logic programming. In *Proceedings of the First International Workshop on Interoperability in Multidatabase Systems, IMS91*, Japan, April 1991.

[KS90] H. Korth and G. Speegle. Long-duration transactions in software design projects. In *Proceedings of the Sixth International Conference on Data Engineering*, pages 568–574, February 1990.

[LER89] Y. Leu, A. Elmagarmid, and M. Rusinkiewicz. An extended transaction model for multidatabase systems. Technical Report CSD-TR-925, Department of Computer Science, Purdue University, 1989.

[Lit86] W. Litwin. A multidatabase interoperability. *IEEE Computer*, 19(12):10–18, December 1986.

[Mos81] J. E. Moss. *Nested Transactions: An Approach to Reliable Distributed Computing.* PhD thesis, Department of Electrical Engineering and Computer Science, MIT, 1981.

[Mos85] E. Moss. *Nested Transactions, an Approach to Reliable Distributed Computing.* The MIT Press, 1985.

[MRKN91] P. Muth, T.C. Rakow, W. Klas, and E.J. Neuhold. A transaction model for an open publication environment. *IEEE Data Engineering Bulletin*, 14(1), March 1991.

[NZ84] M. Nodine and S. Zdonik. Cooperative transaction hierarchies: A transaction model to support design applications. In *Proceedings of the International Conference on Very Large Data Bases*, pages 83–94, 1984.

[PKH88] C. Pu, G. Kaiser, and N. Hutchinson. Split-transactions for open-ended activities. In *Proceedings of the 14th VLDB Conference*, 1988.

[Reu89] A. Reuter. Contract: A means for extending control beyond transaction boundaries. In *Proceedings of the 2nd International Workshop on High Performance Transaction Systems*, September 1989.

[RM89] K. Rothermel and C. Mohan. Aries/NT: A recovery method based on write-ahead logging for nested transactions. In *Proceedings of the International Conference on Very Large Data Bases*, August 1989.

[RS91] Marek Rusinkiewicz and Amit Sheth. Polytransactions for managing interdepndent data. *IEEE Data Engineering Bulletin*, 14(1), March 1991.

[RW91] A. Reuter and H. Wachter. The contract model. *IEEE Data Engineering Bulletin*, 14(1), March 1991.

[TTC+90] Gomer Thomas, Glenn R. Thompson, Chin-Wan Chung, Edward Barkmeyer, Fred Carter, Marjorie Templeton, Stephen Fox, and Berl Hartman. Heterogeneous distributed database systems for production use. *ACM Computing Surveys*, 22(3), September 1990.

[US91] R. Unland and G. Schlageter. A flexible and adaptable tool kit approach for transaction management in non-standard database systems. *IEEE Data Engineering Bulletin*, March 1991.

[VPZ86] J. Veijalainen and R. Popescu-Zeletin. On multi-database transactions in a cooperative, autonomous environment. Manuscript, Hahn-Meitner Institute, Berlin, FRG, December 1986.

[Wei91] Gerhard Weikum. Principles and realization strategies of multilevel transaction management. *ACM Transactions on Database Systems*, 16(1):132–180, March 1991.

[WS91] G. Weikum and H. Schek. Multi-level transactions and open nested transactions. *IEEE Data Engineering Bulletin*, March 1991.

3

A Cooperative Transaction Model for Design Databases

Marian H. Nodine

Sridhar Ramaswamy

Stanley B. Zdonik

3.1 Introduction

Serializability has long been held as the definitive notion of correctness of transaction execution in databases. This is because transactions that run in most "traditional" databases such as those for banking and airline reservation systems satisfy certain criteria implicitly.

If we assume that all transactions are carefully designed to preserve the consistency of the data that they access, and that transactions have no need to interact during their execution, then the notion of serializability serves as a good correctness criterion for transaction execution. Serializability makes it easier to reason about programs because they appear to execute in isolation. Serializable transactions are expected to be short, and therefore unlikely to be disrupted by a failure in the underlying computer system. Thus, since the transactions run independently of one another, the cost of aborting a particular transaction and rerunning it is not very high. If a transaction aborts in the middle of its execution, we simply "wipe out" its effects. The effect is that transactions are atomic – either they run completely, or all their effects on the database are removed.

Design applications that require shared persistent data tend to have different requirements for transaction management. Examples of these applications include CAD/CASE tools, office information systems and interactive programming environments. They manipulate data that is often huge, complex and interrelated by numerous consistency constraints. This is very different from banking databases, where the data is relatively uniform and only loosely interrelated.

We give an example in computer-aided design. Suppose that a car company wants to design a new car. The design is subdivided into three major parts, namely, designing the engine, designing the body and designing the interior. Designing the engine (given the constraints imposed on it by the design of the rest of the car) is once again divided into designing the engine block and designing the Carburetor. Verification procedures are run to ensure that the engine conforms to federal regulations. Natural subdivisions also occur in the design of the body and the interior. What is to be noted here is that the natural subdivisions do not separate the problem into independent subproblems. Numerous constraints will still persist across the subdivisions. Figure 3.1 gives an example of a breakdown for the car design transaction.

We now can make some observations about the properties of design transactions and the impact they have on the transaction control system of the

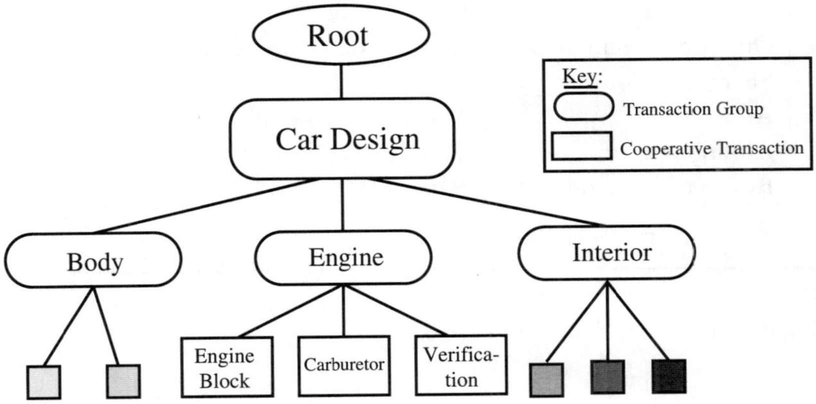

FIGURE 3.1
A Hierarchy

database that they use. We contrast these properties of design transactions with the properties of traditional transactions in Figure 3.2.

Firstly, they manipulate data that is often complex and intricately connected by numerous consistency constraints. Because of the underlying complexity, object-oriented databases are often chosen for these applications.

Secondly, transactions tend to be very long. Designing a car can take a significant amount of time. Previously, failure of transactions and machines was handled by removing all effects of unfinished transactions (failure atomicity). Here, the long duration of the transactions implies that there is a heavy price to be paid for enforcing this property. A significant amount of work has to be redone, which may not always be possible. Failure of transactions and machines has to be handled differently. This implies that the recovery mechanism has to be powerful and versatile enough to partially undo transactions while preserving the consistency of the database.

Thirdly, design tasks often subdivide naturally into hierarchies. However, unlike traditional nested transactions [Mos85], siblings at a given level may constrain each others' behavior and/or interact with each other. This is illustrated in Figure 3.1, where the size and shape of the car body constrains the size and shape of the engine. We expect a design transaction system to support cooperative nesting of transactions; that is, where sibling subtransactions in the hierarchy are allowed to interact. Further, such nesting would

Traditional	Cooperative
Operate on simple data	Operate on complex data
Short duration	Long duration
Atomic	May be non-atomic
Atomic nesting	Cooperative nesting
Recovery by undo	Partial undo capability helpful

FIGURE 3.2
Traditional and cooperative transactions

also help increase concurrency while helping to keep recovery under control.

Transactions in this environment may need to cooperate with each other. This means that the different concurrent transactions involved in a single design may need to share the data associated with the design. In these cases, serializability is not an appropriate correctness criterion. Correctness tends to be inherently application dependent. Therefore, we would like to provide the designers with a way of controlling the interaction between these transactions. Serializability could be one of the possible choices for control, as it may be useful in cases where cooperation is not necessary. This control mechanism should be flexible enough to allow the designers to specify their sharing patterns easily. It should also be possible to enforce these specifications efficiently while doing concurrency control. As we shall see, the expressiveness of the specification mechanism heavily influences the cost of doing concurrency control. In spite of all this, we should still be able to manage recovery as automatically as possible.

In this section, we looked at how design environments differ from traditional transaction environments. This helped identify the characteristics of design transactions. The rest of this paper is organized as follows: Section 3.2 explains some desirable characteristics of a model for design transactions. Section 3.3 describes our cooperative transaction model. Section 3.4 explains how we define correctness in our model. Section 3.6 describes procedures for synchronization, and section 3.7 describes requirements for recovery. We give an example in Section 3.5 and use it to illustrate the synchronization process. In Section 3.8, we describe related research. We conclude with a brief summary.

3.2
Characteristics of the Transaction Model

In this section, we examine the requirements that we stated previously in more detail to determine how they impact the design of the transaction model.

3.2.1 Hierarchical Organization of Transactions

There are compelling reasons why design transactions should be organized hierarchically. First of all, such a nesting will reflect a natural breakdown of work common in most design environments. Details of a subtask can be isolated from its parents and siblings. Tasks can be abstracted away in subtransactions, facilitating overall management. Secondly, the hierarchical structure can be exploited to allow subtransactions of the same parent transaction to run concurrently, shortening the perceived execution time of the transaction. Thirdly, nested transactions help keep recovery under control. When a subtransaction fails, we only have to undo its effects. This effectively shields its siblings. A flat organization would impact all work, related or unrelated.

In general, it is not possible to determine a priori the maximum nesting a problem can have. Therefore, it is logical to allow arbitrary nesting. Also, we cannot always determine the clustering of transactions beforehand. Hence, we would like to allow subtransactions to be added to or removed from the hierarchy as the need arises. This need may arise after some parts of a transaction have already done some work. In this respect, the hierarchy that we support should be dynamic.

We use the terminology of [Ska89] and say that a *Cooperative Transaction (CT)* is a program that issues a stream of operations to the underlying database. It is a leaf in the transaction hierarchy. A *Transaction Group (TG)* corresponds to an internal node in the hierarchy and is a collection of CT's or other TG's. This collection of children cooperate to perform a specific task.

Figure 3.1 represents a possible initial breakdown of the example design task. We see that the hierarchy facilitates abstraction and task control. However, since the structure of most design tasks evolves as the work progresses, a dynamic hierarchy is essential. For instance, the designers could decide to make the *Engine Block* transaction a transaction group with several members doing different subtasks. We would then need the ability to abort the *Engine Block* cooperative transaction and create a transaction group instead.

3.2.2 Correctness Criteria

In the domain of cooperative applications, there is no single correctness criterion like global consistency and atomicity that supports cooperation. Rather, the notion of what is correct may vary from application to application and from task to task. Hence, we have to allow user-specified correctness criteria.

A TG's correctness criteria describe its valid histories. A history is a sequence of operation invocations issued by its member CT's. A TG's history in turn is reflected in its parent's history.

We also want the correctness criteria pertaining to the members of a TG to be localized. For instance, we do not want a TG to decide correctness directly for its grandchildren. Rather, we want it to decide correctness for its children, which in turn decide it for their children. With localized specifications, we can call a history of a TG *correct* if it satisfies its own criteria and the histories are respectively correct for each of its children.

We now see that concurrency control among members of the transaction hierarchy requires that each TG enforce its localized, user-specified correctness criteria. Thus, we can define the correctness of a TG in terms of a *language*. The alphabet of the language consists of operation invocations issued by the members of the TG. We use *grammars* to define how the operations can be ordered to form correct sentences, or *histories*.

We face an inherent trade-off in choosing an appropriate specification mechanism for TGs. If the specification mechanism is very restrictive—for example, we allow only regular expressions in our specifications— correctness can be efficiently enforced. If we allow arbitrary programs, we gain flexibility, but enforcing the specifications can be very hard. A good specification mechanism should allow the user flexibility in defining how transactions behave and interact. Simultaneously, it should be efficiently enforceable.

Enforcing a specification can be done in two ways. In the optimistic way, the members of the TG issue their entire sequence of operations. We then check this sequence against its specifications. This could lead to a lot of wasted work in an environment where iteration and mistakes are inherently part of the development process. It would be much better if we could enforce the criteria *online.* That is, we inform the member (TG or CT) immediately when it submits an invalid operation. This means that the algorithm that we use to enforce the criteria should not only be able to recognize correct histories but should also be able to able to recognize *valid prefixes* of correct histories. To a great extent, our ability to do this is dominated by the freedom allowed in the specification mechanism. We will say that a specification has the *viable prefix property* if we can recognize all valid prefixes of its members online.

3.2.3 Multi-copy versus Single-copy system

We now discuss an issue that is orthogonal to the way we allow correctness criteria to be specified and the way we implement them. This is the issue of object copies at different points in the hierarchy.

We can take a simple approach and decide that every object will have only one copy in the entire database. We then don't have to keep track of where the multiple copies are, or how they relate to each other. Merging and garbage collection can be completely avoided.

On the other hand, having only a single copy has its disadvantages. Since many members may be accessing this copy simultaneously, the copy must be kept at the root of the hierarchy where it is visible to all the transactions. Therefore, we have to validate every operation all the way up to the root at the time an operation is issued. That is, each time an operation is issued, it must be examined against the correctness criteria of each ancestor of the member that issued it. We see that this violates our intuitive notion of abstraction that each CT and TG is supposed to enforce.

Also, it is hard to control the visibility of an object with a single copy. With multiple copies, the hierarchy naturally defines a notion of visibility. The disadvantage is that of having to manage versions, i.e., creating new ones when transactions are created, merging them when there are commits and deleting them when there are aborts. However, we feel that it is well worth the extra effort to allow each TG to maintain private copies of the objects that it accesses because of the reasons mentioned above.

To elaborate, each TG has its own private copies of the objects being used by its members. The TG acquires its copy of an object the first time one of its members accesses the object. Thus, the TG projects a complete environment, a virtual database, to each of its children. The TG's object copies are accessed and modified by its members' operations, and are in turn presented to the TG's parent when the TG wants to commit. At this point, they subsume the copies that the TG's parent maintains. When the entire design transaction commits, its changes to the database are made by the *Root* TG at the top of the hierarchy.

3.2.4 Operation-Based Recovery

The process of design inherently involves iteration and mistakes. After a designer has completed a part of a task, he might decide that part of what has been done is not right. It is essential for any design transaction system to provide for undoing changes made to the database.

Undoing changes in a design database is fraught with complications. The underlying transactions are long, open-ended, and interact with each other. Undoing a whole transaction implies potentially undoing a lot of work, some of which the designer may in fact wish to preserve. Furthermore, the abort can cascade to other transactions as well—we allow the transactions to interact. Thus, it is more appropriate to manage undo and restoration at an *operation* level; we remove the effects of the invalid operations as well as the operations that depend on them. This may affect many transactions, but each transaction is impacted as little as possible.

This type of recovery scheme implies that we need to be able to compute correctly which operations are affected by the failure of an operation (dependencies). We need to maintain these dependencies in the log for potential use later during recovery.

Sometimes, a transaction may not want the effects of an invalidated operation to be removed completely from the database. For example, certain parts of an operation may still be valid, even though others are not. For example, a large edit may still be partially correct, even though a piece of it depends on some operation that is no longer valid. Therefore, instead of completely deleting the effects of the invalid operations, it is better to allow the designers to sort out the changes, deleting those that definitely should be deleted and modifying files that have been affected by the invalidation. Operations associated with work that should be preserved can then be requested again in a correct manner.

3.3 The Model

A cooperative transaction hierarchy is a structured set of cooperative transactions, whose interactions are structured to reflect the underlying hierarchical decomposition of the task they are working on together. The internal nodes are the *transaction groups (TGs)*, and the leaves are *cooperative transactions (CTs)*[1]. The *Root* transaction group, which is at the top of the hierarchy, always exists. Each transaction group contains a set of *members* that cooperate to do a single task. It actively controls the interaction of its cooperating members. A member may be either an individual CT or another

[1] For an earlier reference to this type of transaction hierarchy, see [FZ89].

Transaction Group	• Is not atomic. • Corresponds to some task that is done by its members. • Enforces its own correctness criteria. • Mediates communication among its members. • Operates on its own object copies. • Is a unit of recovery. • Makes own guarantees about the recoverability of its object copies.
Cooperative Transaction	• Is not atomic. • Is the collection of operations by a single member.
Operation	• Is atomic. • Is specified by a tuple $<M, o, O>$, where M is a member. o is an operation specifier. O is an object identifier.

FIGURE 3.3
Basic Features.

TG. Figure 3.1 shows an example of a cooperative transaction hierarchy. In this figure, *Car Design*, *Body*, *Engine*, and *Interior* are all TGs. *Engine Block*, *Carburetor*, and *Verification* are all examples of CTs.

This section describes the basic cooperative transaction hierarchy model, including definitions of transaction groups, cooperative transactions, and operations. The features of each are summarized in Figure 3.3.

3.3.1 Transaction Groups

A transaction group (TG) is a set of members that are directly cooperating on a specific task. Because of the cooperative nature of the members, we do not assume that the sequence of operations by a single member necessarily leaves the database in a correct state. Instead, each TG has its own *correctness specification*. For specifying correctness, we use the notion of *patterns* and *conflicts* first used by Skarra [Ska89, Ska91]. Each subtask in the design process must execute according to some form. We use the notion of patterns to define that form — the patterns in the TG state ways that the members' operations must be ordered to complete the task. However, since subtasks executing concurrently may interact with each other in undesirable ways, we also need a way for the transaction group to enforce that its members are adequately isolated from each other. Conflicts specify how the members' operations cannot be ordered, to prevent unwanted side-effects. The TG ensures that the members interact only in the ways allowable by its correctness specification, and in that way guarantees that the operations by its members as a group leave the database in a correct state.

Each transaction group has a local set of object versions. Thus, there may be many versions of an object scattered throughout the transaction hierarchy. For a specific object, the version at the *Root* TG is the oldest version, and the ones further down are more recent. Visibility is defined naturally according to the hierarchy. That is, the version of an object in a group's object set is accessible to any of its descendants in the transaction hierarchy. For example, say the *Car Design* TG has made a copy of the *carb* object. If the *Engine* TG has made a copy of it and modified the copy, then the new version is the one the *Verification* CT would read.

Each TG makes its own guarantees about how resilient its copies are to different kinds of failure (*permanence*). Thus, a TG may have its own backing store from which it can recover its copies of its objects after a system failure. The *Root* TG at the top of the hierarchy contains the most stable version of each object, and makes the strongest guarantees about the permanence of its copies.

An object version is copied automatically into a member TG's set from that of its parent when the member initiates a read operation on that object. A new version of the object is written back to the parent TG's set when the member indicates that it has finished modifying the object and the write operation is acceptable. All operations must conform to the TG's correctness specification.

We allow the individual members to commit or undo parts of their work as it progresses. When some subtask is complete, we allow the member to *checkpoint*. A member checkpoint causes all of its operations that previously have been neither checkpointed nor aborted to be checkpointed. The checkpoint propagates the effects of the operations to the group's parent by mapping sequences of operations by the group's member(s) into shorter, equivalent sequences of operations initiated in its parent by the transaction group. By "equivalent sequence", we mean one that accesses the same objects and has the same net effect on those objects.

The mapping of sequences to equivalent sequences is specific to the object type and the operations it supports. For example, several write operations on a single object version in the TG's object set may be collapsed into a single write operation on the object version in its parent's set. A sequence of equal numbers of increment and decrement operations has no effect, so nothing is propagated to the parent in this case.

We allow a member to selectively undo certain parts of its work by aborting individual uncheckpointed operations. Aborting an operation may mean that other operations need to be aborted as well, either because they read the effects of the aborted operation, or because the abort caused the history to become incorrect in some way.

Because we cannot determine the transaction groups a priori, the transaction hierarchy can be modified dynamically. The *Root* TG, whose task is to maintain the database, always exists. Other TGs and CTs may join and leave the hierarchy as the overall task progresses.

3.3.2 Cooperative Transactions

Cooperative transactions (CTs) represent designers or intelligent design applications. We assume that CTs are long-lived and open-ended, and that they can interact with other CTs in their TG both externally and through the objects in the database. Thus, they may have a reasonable notion of what the other members in their TG are doing.

During its lifetime, a CT issues operations on object versions in its TG. These operations are executed by the TG once it determines that they conform to its correctness specification. Operations may be rejected by the TG if they do not conform to the correctness specification. As with TGs, as the design task progresses, operations may be either aborted individually or be checkpointed when the CT has completed some subtask.

3.3.3 Operations

Members access and update their local object versions using *operations*. An operation defines an atomic action on a single object by a single member of a transaction group. Eventually, the effects of an operation are either propagated towards the *Root* TG or undone by one of the members of the group.

An operation is a tuple $\mathcal{O}=<M, o, O>$, where M is a member, o is an operation name, and O is an object identifier. We ignore any arguments, e.g. the version written in a *write* operation.

In our example, we support two kinds of objects. *Files* support the two operations *read* and *write*. *Counters* support the operations *read*, *increment*, and *decrement*. Our scheme could support other operations and operation types as well, provided that all operations are not nested; that is, no operation invokes another operation on some other object internally.

When a member submits an operation to its parent transaction group, it must be accepted as correct according to the group's correctness criteria before it can be executed. If the member that did the operation decides later that it is incorrect in some way, it can abort the individual operation. Otherwise, the operation checkpoints the next time the member checkpoints, and the process begins of making more permanent any changes resulting from the operation. However, checkpointing an operation does not guarantee that its effects on the database are permanent. It still may be undone if some other member aborts some operation that the checkpointed operation depends on. Once an operation cannot be undone for any reason, and thus its effects on the database are permanent, it is called *complete*.

3.3.4 Histories

The history of a transaction group is a partially-ordered sequence containing the operations executed on the group's object versions. The history of a transaction group is kept in the group's *log*.

3.4 Correctness

In Section 3.2, we argued that global correctness criteria such as atomicity were inapplicable in a domain that supports cooperation. This prompted us to look for user-supplied, programmable correctness criteria. Further, we elaborated on the desirable features that correctness criteria for cooperative transactions should have. In this section, we examine a specification mechanism for correctness.

3.4.1 Patterns and Conflicts

Patterns and conflicts naturally reflect the requirements of correctness criteria for cooperative transactions. The user makes use of the semantic knowledge that he has about the design transactions in a TG in defining correctness criteria appropriate to the group's task. These correctness criteria constrain the order in which operations are submitted to the transaction group to ensure that they maintain some form of consistency in the database.

Patterns specify the interleavings of operations that *must* happen for the execution in a transaction group to be correct. For example, a pattern for the *Engine* TG may state, "if the Carburetor design is changed, the engine must be tested to check that it still fits within the federal guidelines for fuel efficiency". In traditional atomic transactions, all pattern information is encoded within the transaction itself.

Conflicts specify interleavings that are forbidden. A conflict might state that, if you have not seen the latest version of the carburetor, you cannot modify it because you may be overwriting someone else's changes. With atomic transactions, locks are the principal conflict mechanism. For example, a write lock guarantees that no other transaction can access an object for the duration of the lock. The use of two-phase locks guarantees that conflict among whole transactions is enforced.

Each transaction group has an *active set* of pattern and conflict specifications. These specifications as a whole restrict the allowable ordering of operations in the transaction group's history. Intuitively, we define a history to be *correct* when it conforms to all of the pattern specifications and contains no conflicts.

We view the problem of recognizing correct histories as a language problem, where user-definable grammars are used to specify what histories are correct in the language. In [RZ91], we analyzed various classes of grammar for their suitability in specifying correctness. We attempted to maximize the underlying flexibility and expressiveness of the grammar, while at the same time retaining the following desirable properties for synchronization and recovery:

1. The *viable prefix property*, that allows us to do efficient online recognition of correct histories.

2. The ability to compute and maintain operation dependencies for efficient operation-level recovery.

One class of grammar that is not very restrictive but still maintains these properties is the LR(0) grammars. LR(0) grammars are also more expressive than the operation machines used in our earlier cooperative transaction hierarchy work [NZ90], which were equivalent to regular expressions. With LR(0) grammars, it is also efficient to decide whether or not a history is correct; it can be done in linear time. All deterministic context-free grammars can be written in LR(0) form. LR(0) stands for "left-to-right scan of the input using 0 symbols of lookahead."

3.4.2 LR(0) Grammars and DPDAs

An LR(0) grammar is a special kind of context-free grammar (CFG)[2]. A grammar is defined by a set of *productions*, where each production has a variable on the left, and a string of terminal symbols and/or variables on the right. An *ϵ-production* specifies an empty string on the right.

A string in the grammar is generated by a *derivation*. A derivation starts with a special variable called the *start symbol*. It uses the productions to replace variables with their associated strings, and continues until the string only contains terminal symbols. A *rightmost* derivation is a derivation in which the rightmost variable is replaced at each step.

Dots are used to keep track of the current position in a rule during a derivation. An *item* for a given CFG is a production with a dot anywhere on the right side, including the beginning or end. In the case of an ϵ-production, $B \rightarrow \epsilon$, $B \rightarrow .$ is an item. An item is *complete* if the dot is its rightmost symbol.

A *sentential form* is a string of variables and terminal symbols that is derivable from the start symbol. A *right sentential form* is a sentential form derivable using a rightmost derivation.

In an LR(0) grammar, there is only one valid item in each situation and therefore we can apply it. This results in the production of a rightmost derivation of the string. Intuitively, what this means is that at any point in the recognition of the input string, we can determine the correct action to be done without looking ahead at any symbol. Thus, LR(0) grammars have the viable prefix property. The actual method of recognition works by computing the set of valid items and constructing a table of actions to be taken when a particular symbol is encountered at some particular point in the derivation. More details can be found in [ASU88].

A Deterministic Push Down Automaton (DPDA) is a finite state machine augmented with a *stack*. In addition to changing state after reading an input symbol, the DPDA has the option to push a symbol onto the stack or pop a symbol from the stack or do nothing to the stack. A DPDA accepts a string when its finite control is in a final state and the stack is empty.

[2]See [HU79] for more details regarding grammars.

It is an elementary result of language theory that every DPDA has an equivalent LR(0) grammar [HU79] and vice-versa.

3.4.3 Correct Transaction Group Histories

A transaction group's correctness specification consists of an active set of pattern and conflict grammars. This set varies over time as members are added to and removed from a transaction group, as different members interact with different objects, and as an understanding of the underlying task evolves. Examples of this are given in later sections.

Intuitively, a TG's history is correct if it conforms to all of the patterns in the TG's correctness specification, and to none of the conflicts. That is, a correct history looks like an interleaving of patterns. Operations in the history that participate in a pattern are called *relevant* to that pattern. Also, no sentential form for any conflict grammar can be extracted from a correct history by eliminating operations irrelevant to that conflict. More formally:

Definition 3.4.1 (Correct History) *A history is* correct *if each pattern that was active during the history satisfies the* pattern criterion, *and each conflict that was active during the history satisfies the* conflict criterion.

Pattern criterion
For the pattern grammar P_i, call the portion of the history that was generated while the grammar was active in the transaction group H_i. Call S_i the sequence of operations that constitute the projection from H_i of the operations relevant to the grammar P_i. If the sequence S_i is a sentential form in the grammar P_i, then P_i satisfies the pattern criterion.

Conflict criterion
For the conflict grammar C_j, define H_j and S_j analogously to the definitions for the pattern criterion. If the sequence S_j is not *a sentential form in the grammar C_j, then C_j satisfies the conflict criterion.*

3.5 Example

This section contains an example of a correctness specification for a TG, and a history that is correct for that TG. We use this example as an illustration in the remainder of the paper.

The example grammars define the correctness specification for the *Engine* TG (see the hierarchy in Figure 3.1). In this example, *carb* is the Carburetor object and *spec* is the report to the EPA concerning fuel efficiency. These are both of type *File*. *Prob_count* is the count of reported problems, and is of type *Counter*. The cooperative transaction *Carburetor* is the one responsible for the carburetor design, and the group *Verify* is responsible for testing the engine.

We present each grammar in the correctness specification for the *Engine* TG in two ways. The first is as a set of rules, which describe the grammar concisely in LR(0) form. In these rules, we represent the nonterminals as script letters, e.g. $\mathcal{A}, \mathcal{B}$, with $\mathcal{S}$ reserved as the start symbol. The terminals are operations of the form $<M, o, O>$, as defined in Figure 3.3. The second representation is as an automaton (either regular or pushdown). In this form, the start state (indicated by a $>$) represents the beginning of the pattern or conflict grammar. The final state (represented by a $\bullet$ in the state) indicates a point at which a string in the grammar is complete. The transitions are annotated by the operations that cause them. In a pushdown automaton, a string is complete when the automaton is in a final state and its stack is empty.

One constraint that is present with respect to the car design is that it has to conform to federal limitations on fuel efficiency. This might be specified within the database in the form "If someone changes the carburetor, it must be verified that the MPG on the car is still acceptable, and the verification spec must be updated." Thus, if the *carb* object is written, the *Verify* group must read it and update the *spec* object accordingly so that we know the appropriate tests have been done. The pattern grammar P_1 and conflict grammar C_1 that together enforce this constraint are shown in Figure 3.4.

For engineering purposes, the group may also want to ensure that all reported problems concerning the various engine parts are solved before the engine design is finally released. This can be done by keeping a problem count, and enforcing constraints on it, as shown in the pattern grammar P_2 in Figure 3.4. From the pushdown automaton representation, we see that only histories that that have an equal number of increments and decrements to the *prob_count* counter are complete for this grammar.

The group itself also may wish to enforce some protocol on the interactions between the members and the objects to ensure that these interactions maintain some sort of consistency in the data. This notion of consistency could be serializability, or it could be something else. We can enforce this

P_1:

$S \leftarrow {<}any, w, carb{>}A \mid \epsilon$

$A \leftarrow {<}any, w, carb{>}A \mid {<}verify, r, carb{>}B$

$B \leftarrow {<}verify, w, spec{>}S$

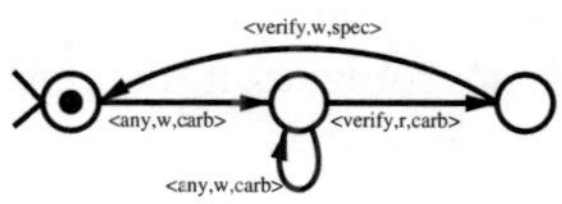

C_1:

$S \leftarrow {<}any, w, carb{>}A$

$A \leftarrow {<}any, w, carb{>}A \mid {<}verify, r, carb{>}B$

$B \leftarrow {<}any, w, carb{>} \mid {<}verify, w, spec{>}S$

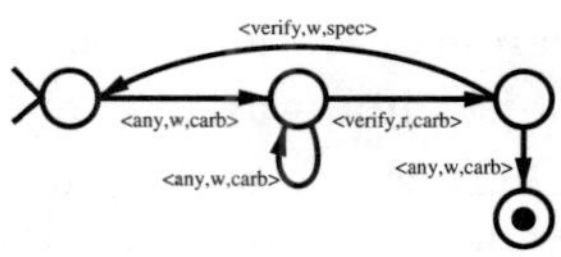

P_2:

$S \leftarrow B$

$B \leftarrow AB \mid A$

$A \leftarrow {<}any, inc, prob\_count{>}B{<}any, dec, prob\_count{>} \mid$
$\quad {<}any, inc, prob\_count{>}{<}any, dec, prob\_count{>}$

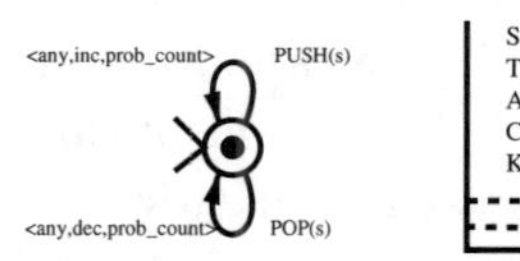

P_3:

$S \leftarrow {<}M, r, o{>}A \mid \epsilon$

$A \leftarrow {<}\bar{M}, w, o{>}S \mid {<}M, r/w, o{>}A \mid \epsilon$

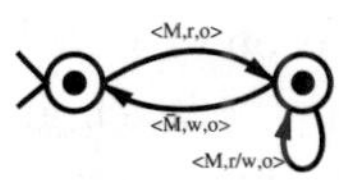

C_2:

$S \leftarrow {<}M, w, o{>} \mid {<}M, r, o{>}A$

$A \leftarrow {<}\bar{M}, w, o{>}S \mid {<}M, r/w, o{>}A$

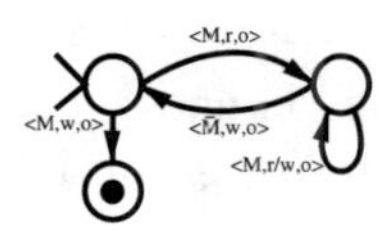

FIGURE 3 4
Pattern and conflict grammar examples, as productions and as automata.

P_3:	$\mathcal{S} \leftarrow\ <Carburetor,r,carb>\ \mathcal{A} \mid \epsilon$ $\mathcal{A} \leftarrow\ <\overline{Carburetor},w,carb>\ \mathcal{S} \mid\ <Carburetor,r/w,carb>\ \mathcal{A} \mid \epsilon$
C_3:	$\mathcal{S} \leftarrow\ <Carburetor,w,carb> \mid\ <Carburetor,r,carb>\ \mathcal{A}$ $\mathcal{A} \leftarrow\ <\overline{Carburetor},w,carb>\ \mathcal{S} \mid\ <Carburetor,r/w,carb>\ \mathcal{A}$

FIGURE 3.5
Synchronization pattern and conflict grammars, with M=*Carburetor* and O=*carb*.

using a special set of grammars called *synchronization grammars.* Each synchronization grammar ensures that a single member interacts with a single object in a way that preserves the TG's notion of consistency for the object. There is one such grammar in place for each <*Member, Object*> pair where *Member* is a member of the TG and *Object* is an object that it is interacting with. All of these grammars have an identical underlying structure, because the TG has a uniform notion of consistency for all of its objects.

We implement this by defining for each TG a template to use in generating a synchronization grammar, with the variables M and O kept as slots for the member and object identifiers, respectively. When a member first reads an object in its group's set, the pattern and conflict grammars for the group's synchronization protocol are instantiated for that interaction. This is done by making a copy of each grammar template, replacing M with the member's ID and O with the object's ID, and adding the two new grammars to the set of grammars that together are being used to define the correctness of the group.

In this case, we want the members of the *Engine* group not to overwrite each other's changes. Figure 3.4 shows the synchronization grammar templates (pattern P_S and conflict C_S) for the *Engine* group. Figure 3.5 shows P_3 and C_3, the synchronization grammars for the interactions the *Carburetor* CT has on the object *carb*. Examining the grammar P_3 closely, we see that once the *Carburetor* CT reads the *carb* object, it can do anything it wants to the object until someone else writes a new version. At that point, the *Carburetor* CT must read the new version before it can continue to work on it.

In our example, we also define P_4 and C_4 to be the pattern and conflict grammars for synchronization with M= *Verify* and O=*carb*, instantiated from the synchronization grammar templates P_S and C_S, respectively. Similarly, P_5 and C_5 are the pattern and conflict synchronization grammars with M= *Verify*

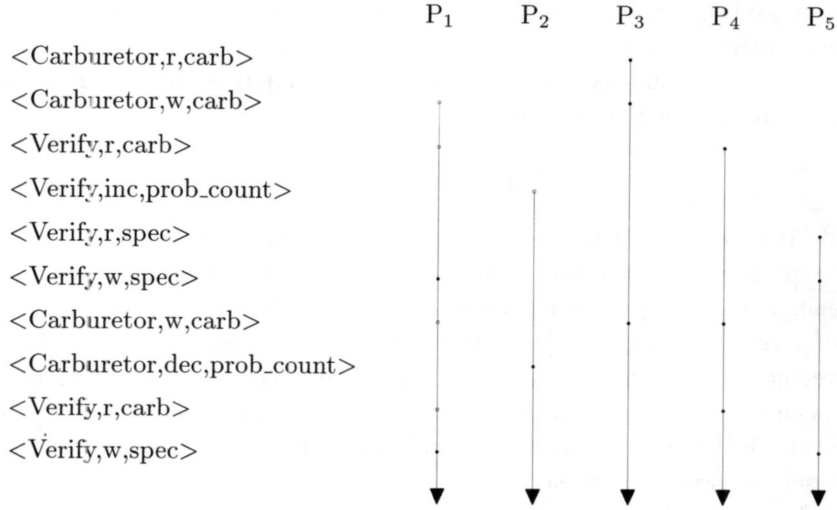

FIGURE 3.6
Example history showing operations relevant to each pattern grammar in *Engine* TG's correctness specification.

and *O=spec*.

In Figure 3.6 we show a correct history for the *Engine* transaction group, given the example correctness specification. In this figure, we indicate which operations in the history are relevant to which pattern grammars using dots. Filled dots indicate that the relevant operation also completes a sentential form in the grammar. Note that, while the first *<Verify,w,spec>* operation completes a sentential form in pattern grammar P_1, the task is not complete because the *Verify* CT detected a problem and incremented *prob_count*. The problem with *carb* needs to be fixed and the result verified again before the task is complete.

3.6 Synchronization

At any given time, we use the active set of pattern and conflict grammars to determine what operations are allowed at that time in a transaction group history. When a grammar is added to the active set, we use standard compiler techniques to develop an SLR parsing table for that grammar. As the operations are submitted, we use shift-reduce parsing techniques to determine whether or not they are allowed.

3.6.1 Algorithm

At a given point in the execution of a transaction group, the synchronization mechanism has allowed some of the operations in its input operation stream to be executed, and rejected others. Call the sequence of operations that have been executed the *history prefix*. Each grammar defined in the correctness specification is in the middle of some rightmost derivation based on (some of) the operations in the history prefix. Also, the synchronization mechanism is examining a single submitted operation to determine whether it should be accepted or rejected.

Let us consider the action that should be taken now. This process is easier to visualize in terms of DPDAs. Therefore, we will consider the action that should be taken when an operation is submitted to a DPDA.

If the DPDA corresponds to a pattern grammar, and the operation causes the transition to a dead state in the finite state control, we should *reject* the operation. On the other hand, if the operation causes a transition to a state from which a final state is reachable, we should *accept* the operation. If the current state in the DPDA has no outgoing arc labeled with the operation, that operation does not affect the DPDA and we *ignore* it. Presumably, this operation is causing some other DPDA to take some action.

The case when the DPDA corresponds to a conflict grammar is handled in analogous fashion. If the operation causes a transition to a final state, *reject* the operation. If the operation causes a transition to a state from which a non-final state is reachable, *accept* the operation. If there is no outgoing arc labeled with the operation, *ignore* the operation.

We call an operation *relevant* when it causes the DPDA to accept or reject an operation. We call a history *complete* with respect to a set of DPDA's if the following criterion holds: after the operations in the history are submitted in sequence to the DPDA's, all the pattern DPDA's are in a final state with the stack empty, and all the conflict DPDA's are in non-accepting configurations.

Parsing with grammars closely corresponds to parsing with the DPDA's. The actions taken are the same. That is, an operation can be rejected, accepted, or ignored by a grammar. The acceptance or rejection of an operation, which causes a transition in the DPDA, causes a change in parse state of the corresponding LR(0) grammar.

We can now state the synchronization algorithm very simply. When an operation is submitted, we accept it only when none of the grammars rejects it. We reject an operation when any of the grammars rejects it. If an operation is accepted, we also update the parsing information for each grammar.

3.6.2 Example

Figures 3.7 through 3.9 illustrate how synchronization works. The example shows a sequence of operations submitted to the *Engine* TG. In this example, we use the correctness specification described in Section 3.5 for the *Engine* TG. The history accepted by the synchronization mechanism given this correctness specification and the defined input sequence is shown in Figure 3.6.

The operations that are submitted to the group are submitted chronologically from top to bottom in each table. For each operation, we specify whether the operation was *rejected* or *accepted.* We also show the current parse states of the grammars relevant to a particular operation. For each relevant grammar, we specify the current items in the parsing process. A period between two tokens indicates the current place in the parse. If the operation was rejected, we indicate in this column only the parse that caused the rejection. If the operation was accepted, we indicate the progress of the parse in the relevant grammars. For conciseness, we also elide non-critical parts of long parse rules.

The subset of the history prefix relevant to each grammar can be inferred from the parse by reading the items from top to bottom, reading only the parts in the item that precede the dot.

3.6.3 Checkpointing

When a member checkpoints and terminates, it indicates that it believes it has successfully completed its task. A member can checkpoint (and terminate) only when all of the grammars relevant to some operation that it has submitted are complete. This indicates that the subtasks that the member is involved in leave the objects in the TG's cache in a consistent state, according to the correctness specification.

Figure 3.10 shows the pattern and conflict grammars when the *Carburetor* and *Verify* CTs checkpoint after our example operation sequence. As

OPERATION	DECISION	RELEVANT GRAMMAR PARSE
<Carburetor,w,carb>	rejected	C_3: $\mathcal{S} \leftarrow <Carburetor,w,carb>$.
<Carburetor,r,carb>	accepted	C_3: $\mathcal{S} \leftarrow <Carburetor,r,carb>$. A P_3: $\mathcal{S} \leftarrow <Carburetor,r,carb>$. A
<Carburetor,w,carb>	accepted	C_1: $\mathcal{S} \leftarrow <any,w,carb>$. A C_3: $\mathcal{S} \leftarrow <Carburetor,r,carb>$. $\mathcal{A}$ $\mathcal{A} \leftarrow <Carburetor,w,carb>$. $\mathcal{A}$ P_1: $\mathcal{S} \leftarrow <any,w,carb>$. $\mathcal{A}$ P_3: $\mathcal{S} \leftarrow <Carburetor,r,carb>$. $\mathcal{A}$ $\mathcal{A} \leftarrow <Carburetor,w,carb>$. $\mathcal{A}$
<Verify,r,carb>	accepted	C_1: $\mathcal{S} \leftarrow <any,w,carb>$. $\mathcal{A}$ $\mathcal{A} \leftarrow <Verify,r,carb>$ $\mathcal{B}$ C_4: $\mathcal{S} \leftarrow <Verify,r,carb>$. $\mathcal{A}$ P_1: $\mathcal{S} \leftarrow <any,w,carb>$. $\mathcal{A}$ $\mathcal{A} \leftarrow <Verify,r,carb>$. $\mathcal{B}$ P_4: $\mathcal{S} \leftarrow <Verify,r,carb>$. $\mathcal{A}$
<Verify,inc, prob_count>	accepted	P_2: $\mathcal{S} \leftarrow$. $\mathcal{B}$ $\mathcal{B} \leftarrow$. $\mathcal{A} \cdots$ $\mathcal{A} \leftarrow <any,inc,prob\_count>$ . . . .
<Verify,r,spec>	accepted	C_5: $\mathcal{S} \leftarrow <Verify,r,spec>$. $\mathcal{A}$ P_5: $\mathcal{S} \leftarrow <Verify,r,spec>$. $\mathcal{A}$
<Verify,w,spec>	accepted	C_1: $\mathcal{S} \leftarrow <any,w,carb>$. $\mathcal{A}$ $\mathcal{A} \leftarrow <Verify,r,carb>$. $\mathcal{B}$ $\mathcal{B} \leftarrow <Verify,w,spec>$. $\mathcal{S}$ C_5: $\mathcal{S} \leftarrow <Verify,r,spec>$. $\mathcal{A}$ $\mathcal{A} \leftarrow <Verify,w,spec>$. $\mathcal{A}$ P_1: $\mathcal{S} \leftarrow <any,w,carb>$. $\mathcal{A}$ $\mathcal{A} \leftarrow <Verify,r,carb>$. $\mathcal{B}$ $\mathcal{B} \leftarrow <Verify,w,spec>$. $\mathcal{S}$ P_5: $\mathcal{S} \leftarrow <Verify,r,spec>$. $\mathcal{A}$ $\mathcal{A} \leftarrow <Verify,w,spec>$. $\mathcal{A}$

FIGURE 3.7
Example operation sequence for the *Engine* transaction group (page 1/3).

OPERATION	DECISION	RELEVANT GRAMMAR PARSE
$<\mathit{Carburetor,w,carb}>$	accepted	C_1: $\mathcal{S} \leftarrow <\mathit{any,w,carb}> . \mathcal{A}$ $\mathcal{A} \leftarrow <\mathit{Verify,r,carb}> . \mathcal{B}$ $\mathcal{B} \leftarrow <\mathit{Verify,w,spec}> . \mathcal{S}$ $\mathcal{S} \leftarrow <\mathit{any,w,carb}> . \mathcal{A}$ C_3: $\mathcal{S} \leftarrow <\mathit{Carburetor,r,carb}> . \mathcal{A}$ $\mathcal{A} \leftarrow <\mathit{Carburetor,w,carb}> . \mathcal{A}$ $\mathcal{A} \leftarrow <\mathit{Carburetor,w,carb}> . \mathcal{A}$ C_4: $\mathcal{S} \leftarrow <\mathit{Verify,r,carb}> . \mathcal{A}$ $\mathcal{A} \leftarrow <\overline{\mathit{Verify}},\mathit{w,carb}> . \mathcal{S}$ P_1: $\mathcal{S} \leftarrow <\mathit{any,w,carb}> . \mathcal{A}$ $\mathcal{A} \leftarrow <\mathit{Verify,r,carb}> . \mathcal{B}$ $\mathcal{B} \leftarrow <\mathit{Verify,w,spec}> . \mathcal{S}$ $\mathcal{S} \leftarrow <\mathit{any,w,carb}> . \mathcal{A}$ P_3: $\mathcal{S} \leftarrow <\mathit{Carburetor,r,carb}> . \mathcal{A}$ $\mathcal{A} \leftarrow <\mathit{Carburetor,w,carb}> . \mathcal{A}$ $\mathcal{A} \leftarrow <\mathit{Carburetor,w,carb}> . \mathcal{A}$ P_4: $\mathcal{S} \leftarrow <\mathit{Verify,r,carb}> . \mathcal{A}$ $\mathcal{A} \leftarrow <\overline{\mathit{Verify}},\mathit{w,carb}> . \mathcal{S}$
$<\mathit{Carburetor,dec,}$ $\mathit{prob\_count}>$	accepted	P_2: $\mathcal{S} \leftarrow . \mathcal{B}$ $\mathcal{B} \leftarrow \mathcal{A} . \cdots$ $\mathcal{A} \leftarrow <\mathit{any,inc,prob\_count}>$ $<\mathit{any,dec,prob\_count}> .$
$<\mathit{Verify,r,carb}>$	accepted	C_1: $\mathcal{S} \leftarrow <\mathit{any,w,carb}> . \mathcal{A}$ $\mathcal{A} \leftarrow <\mathit{Verify,r,carb}> . \mathcal{B}$ $\mathcal{B} \leftarrow <\mathit{Verify,w,spec}> . \mathcal{S}$ $\mathcal{S} \leftarrow <\mathit{any,w,carb}> . \mathcal{A}$ $\mathcal{A} \leftarrow <\mathit{Verify,r,carb}> . \mathcal{B}$ C_4: $\mathcal{S} \leftarrow <\mathit{Verify,r,carb}> . \mathcal{A}$ $\mathcal{A} \leftarrow <\overline{\mathit{Verify}},\mathit{w,carb}> . \mathcal{S}$ $\mathcal{S} \leftarrow <\mathit{Verify,r,carb}> . \mathcal{A}$

FIGURE 3.8
Example operation sequence for the *Engine* transaction group (page 2/3).

OPERATION	DECISION	RELEVANT GRAMMAR PARSE
$<\mathit{Verify,r,carb}>$ cont'd	accepted	P_1: $\mathcal{S} \leftarrow <\mathit{any,w,carb}> \,.\, \mathcal{A}$ $\mathcal{A} \leftarrow <\mathit{Verify,r,carb}> \,.\, \mathcal{B}$ $\mathcal{B} \leftarrow <\mathit{Verify,w,spec}> \,.\, \mathcal{S}$ $\mathcal{S} \leftarrow <\mathit{any,w,carb}> \,.\, \mathcal{A}$ $\mathcal{A} \leftarrow <\mathit{Verify,r,carb}> \,.\, \mathcal{B}$ P_4: $\mathcal{S} \leftarrow <\mathit{Verify,r,carb}> \,.\, \mathcal{A}$ $\mathcal{A} \leftarrow <\mathit{Verify,w,carb}> \,.\, \mathcal{S}$ $\mathcal{S} \leftarrow <\mathit{Verify,r,carb}> \,.\, \mathcal{A}$
$<\mathit{Verify,w,spec}>$	accepted	C_1: $\mathcal{S} \leftarrow <\mathit{any,w,carb}> \,.\, \mathcal{A}$ $\mathcal{A} \leftarrow <\mathit{Verify,r,carb}> \,.\, \mathcal{B}$ $\mathcal{B} \leftarrow <\mathit{Verify,w,spec}> \,.\, \mathcal{S}$ $\mathcal{S} \leftarrow <\mathit{any,w,carb}> \,.\, \mathcal{A}$ $\mathcal{A} \leftarrow <\mathit{Verify,r,carb}> \,.\, \mathcal{B}$ $\mathcal{B} \leftarrow <\mathit{Verify,w,spec}> \,.\, \mathcal{S}$ C_5: $\mathcal{S} \leftarrow <\mathit{Verify,r,spec}> \,.\, \mathcal{A}$ $\mathcal{A} \leftarrow <\mathit{Verify,w,spec}> \,.\, \mathcal{A}$ $\mathcal{A} \leftarrow <\mathit{Verify,w,spec}> \,.\, \mathcal{A}$ P_1: $\mathcal{S} \leftarrow <\mathit{any,w,carb}> \,.\, \mathcal{A}$ $\mathcal{A} \leftarrow <\mathit{Verify,r,carb}> \,.\, \mathcal{B}$ $\mathcal{B} \leftarrow <\mathit{Verify,w,spec}> \,.\, \mathcal{S}$ $\mathcal{S} \leftarrow <\mathit{any,w,carb}> \,.\, \mathcal{A}$ $\mathcal{A} \leftarrow <\mathit{Verify,r,carb}> \,.\, \mathcal{B}$ $\mathcal{B} \leftarrow <\mathit{Verify,w,spec}> \,.\, \mathcal{S}$ P_5: $\mathcal{S} \leftarrow <\mathit{Verify,r,spec}> \,.\, \mathcal{A}$ $\mathcal{A} \leftarrow <\mathit{Verify,w,spec}> \,.\, \mathcal{A}$ $\mathcal{A} \leftarrow <\mathit{Verify,w,spec}> \,.\, \mathcal{A}$

FIGURE 3.9
Example operation sequence for the *Engine* transaction group (page 3/3).

P_1: $\mathcal{S} \leftarrow <any, w, carb>\ \mathcal{A}$. $\mathcal{A} \leftarrow <Verify, r, carb>\ \mathcal{B}$. $\mathcal{B} \leftarrow <Verify, w, spec>\ \mathcal{S}$. $\mathcal{S} \leftarrow <any, w, carb>\ \mathcal{A}$. $\mathcal{A} \leftarrow <Verify, r, carb>\ \mathcal{B}$. $\mathcal{B} \leftarrow <Verify, w, spec>\ \mathcal{S}$. $\mathcal{S} \leftarrow \epsilon$. P_2: $\mathcal{S} \leftarrow \mathcal{B}$. $\mathcal{B} \leftarrow \mathcal{A}$. $\mathcal{A} \leftarrow <any, inc, prob\_count>$ $<any, dec, prob\_count>$. P_3: $\mathcal{S} \leftarrow <Carburetor, r, carb>\ \mathcal{A}$. $\mathcal{A} \leftarrow <Carburetor, w, carb>\ \mathcal{A}$. $\mathcal{A} \leftarrow <Carburetor, w, carb>\ \mathcal{A}$. $\mathcal{A} \leftarrow \epsilon$.	P_4: $\mathcal{S} \leftarrow <Verify, r, carb>\ \mathcal{A}$. $\mathcal{A} \leftarrow <\overline{Verify}, w, carb>\ \mathcal{S}$. $\mathcal{S} \leftarrow <Verify, r, carb>\ \mathcal{A}$. $\mathcal{A} \leftarrow \epsilon$. P_5: $\mathcal{S} \leftarrow <Verify, r, spec>\ \mathcal{A}$. $\mathcal{A} \leftarrow <Verify, w, spec>\ \mathcal{A}$. $\mathcal{A} \leftarrow <Verify, w, spec>\ \mathcal{A}$. $\mathcal{A} \leftarrow \epsilon$.

FIGURE 3.10
Pattern grammars at the time *Carburetor* and *Verify* checkpoint.

we stated in Section 3.3.1, the checkpoint causes the effects of this operation sequence to be propagated to the group's parent; in this case, the *Car Design* TG. Figure 3.11 shows what operations are propagated up as a result of the checkpoint, and how they relate to the history in the *Engine* TG.

3.7 Recovery

In this section, we discuss the requirements for recovery. We also describe a recovery algorithm that can be used when an operation aborts or a member fails.

3.7.1 Dependency Maintenance and Logging

As we explained in Section 3.2.4, we would like to preserve as much work as possible when changes are aborted. Consequently, we only purge the database of the effects of all *operations* that are directly or transitively

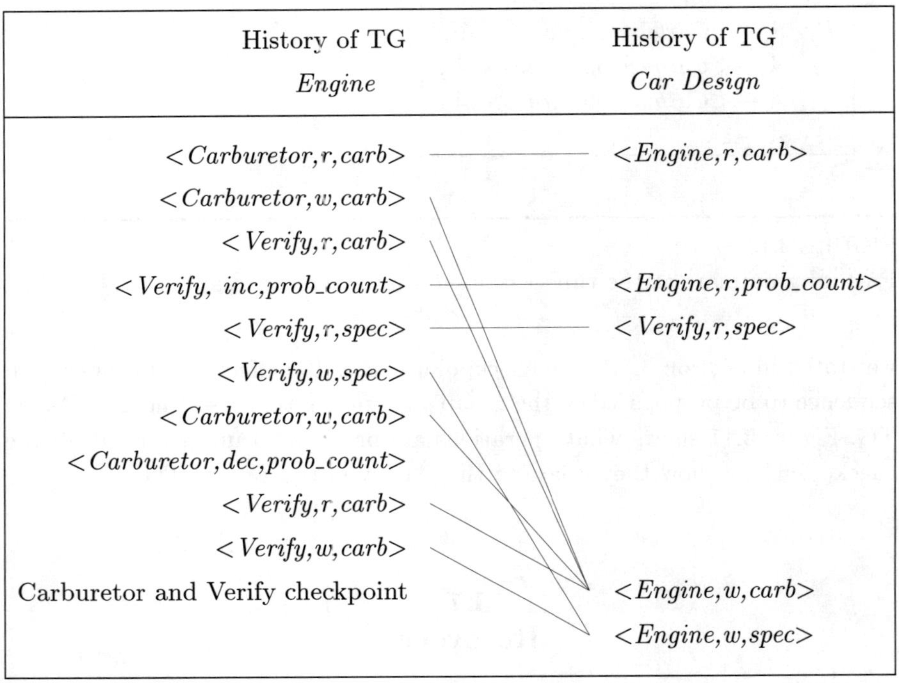

FIGURE 3.11
Relationships between histories.

affected by the operation's abort, instead of aborting whole transactions. To do this, we need to log not only the history of a transaction group, but also the *dependencies* among operations in the history.

For each defined pattern in a transaction group, *pattern dependencies* are formed among operations that participate in that pattern. Since patterns define required orderings of operations, each operation in the sequence relevant to some pattern depends on the correctness of the previous operations in that sequence. However, since the sequence of operations associated with a pattern is fully ordered in the history, the definition of a pattern dependency can be simplified to say that each operation *op* is pattern-dependent on the previous operation in each pattern in which *op* participates.

Reads-from dependencies occur because a read of an object version by member M is only correct if the operation that wrote that version is also correct. If the write operation later becomes invalid, then M's read operation read incorrect information, and is also invalid.

Parent-child dependencies occur among operations at adjacent levels of the transaction hierarchy. For example, when a member M of a transaction group TG reads an object, TG must already have a copy of the object to pass to M. M's read is correct only if TG read a correct version. If that version is later invalidated as a result of some abort, then M's read is also invalid. A similar situation exists with writes; when TG writes a version to its parent, the validity of that write is based on the validity of the most recent write operation by one of its members.

The dependencies for each operation are maintained in its log entry. Pattern and read-write dependencies are easily computed as a transaction group executes operations. Pattern dependencies are computed for each pattern grammar relevant to the operation being executed. Read-write dependencies can be computed by keeping in each object version an indicator of the log entry for the operation that wrote the version, and including that information in the log entry for any operation that reads the version. Parent-child dependencies point to entries in other logs. For example, a read operation points to an entry in the parent's log.

Figure 3.12 shows the log for our *Engine* TG example. The log includes a record of the operation sequences and the pattern and reads-from dependencies for each operation. Each operation is represented by a row in the diagram. In the first five columns of bullets, we represent the dependencies associated with patterns P_1 to P_5. For a pattern, a bullet in the row indicates that that operation is relevant to that pattern. An arrow between two bullets

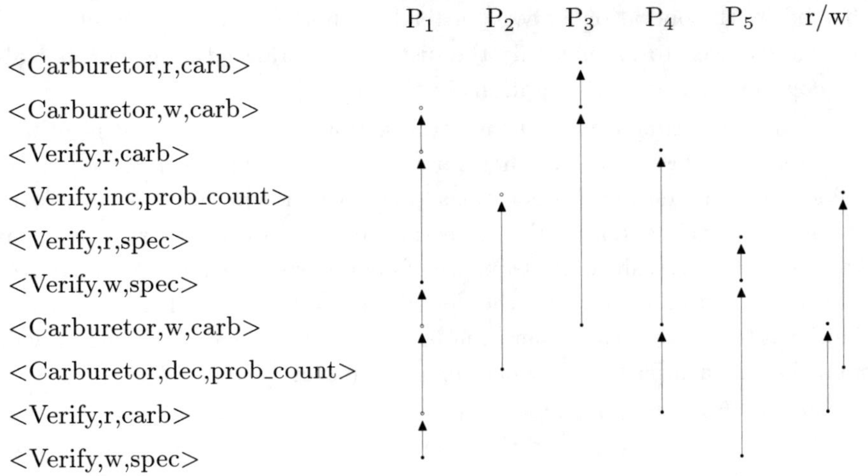

FIGURE 3.12
A log, and an abort example.

indicates that the operation at the tail of the arrow depends on the operation at the head of the arrow. Similarly, the last column indicates the various reads-from dependencies.

3.7.2 Algorithm

When an operation is aborted, the database enters an *invalidation* phase where it purges all the effects of that operation from the database. This phase processes the log chronologically, beginning at the aborted operation, and invalidating any operation that fits any of the following criteria:

1. It was aborted directly by the member.
2. It is dependent on some invalid operation, either because of a pattern dependency, a reads-from dependency, or a parent-child dependency.
3. It now conflicts. That is, because of the differences between the new history and the old history, it now completes some conflict grammar.

In Figure 3.12, we have a log. Suppose the *Carburetor* member decides that it wants to try a different fix to the Carburetor and aborts the operations

<*Carburetor,w,carb*> and <*Carburetor,dec,prob_count*>. Then the operation <*Verify,r,carb*> must also be invalidated, because of the pattern dependency from P_4 and a reads-from dependency on the operation <*Carburetor,w,carb*>. Also, the operation <*Verify,w,spec*> must be aborted because of the pattern dependency from P_1.

Once the invalid operations have been computed, all object versions written by invalid write operations are purged from the database. Also, the parse state of each affected grammar is reset to reflect the state of the parse in the new history. Thus, in our example, P_1 is reset to the parse state it was in just after it recognized the operation <*Verify,w,spec*>. P_2 is reset to the parse state just after it recognized the operation <*Verify,inc,prob_count*>. A similar process also takes place for the other pattern and conflict grammars in the correctness specification.

At the end of the invalidation phase, each member that has had some operation invalidated is sent an *invalidation message*, stating which of their operations have been invalidated. In the *recovery phase*, these members use the invalidation messages as a starting point in working towards recovering their work.

During the recovery phase, the members that have had operations invalidated are allowed to do any of the following things to recover their work:

1. Reread invalid versions to determine exactly what work was invalidated and to determine whether or not any of it should be preserved. This helps the member to determine which compensating operations it needs to submit, if any. The rereading of invalid versions is not arbitrated by the synchronization mechanism. It is indistinguishable from the case where the member maintains the invalid version in its own private store.
2. Submit compensating operations. Compensating operations must be accepted by the synchronization mechanism, given the current parse state of the pattern and conflict grammars. Compensating operations allow the member to maintain changes that may have been valid, while removing invalid changes. For example, the *Carburetor* TG may wish to keep any changes it made to the *carb* object that were not related to the problem detected by the *Verify* TG.
3. Abort any uncheckpointed operations, initiating further recovery actions. This option is useful in emulating a more traditional abort procedure.

3.8 Related Research

We have seen various approaches to making transactions more flexible, to better support long-lived and interactive transactions.

Skarra [Ska89, Ska91] defines a transaction hierarchy for a general object-oriented system. Her scheme is the first one that uses *patterns* and *conflicts* for specifying correctness. Her model differs from ours in that it uses a more complex, Turing-complete grammar to define patterns and conflicts in a transaction group, and also in that it uses a one-copy strategy and a static transaction hierarchy. Much of her work addresses the problem of correct interleaving of nested operations, and does not address issues of recovery.

In nested transactions [Mos85], a transaction may be decomposed hierarchically. However, since nested transactions preserve serializability among their subtransactions, they can neither cooperate nor share data. Nested transactions can be viewed as the first step in the development of a more general transaction model than that of short, atomic, flat transactions. They embody important ideas for increasing concurrency, and allow fine-tuning of recovery by protecting parts of the hierarchy that are not involved in a failure.

Sagas [GS87] break up long transactions into sequences of shorter transactions. Sagas have recently been extended to provide nesting [GGK$^+$90], but there is no mechanism for controlling interleavings between two distinct sagas. Also, sagas must be defined in advance and are consequently not open-ended.

The constraint-based models, for example NT/PV [KKB87, KS88], allow more cooperation by relaxing serializability at the lower levels of the transaction hierarchy. At these levels, transactions can cooperate as long as each transaction preserves its specified consistency constraint. The constraints are defined implicitly; the users cannot tailor them to the task at hand. This work was later extended to define a weaker notion of correctness called *entity-wise serializability* [KLS90]. Current work in this model includes developing a notion of recovery based on compensation.

Multilevel atomicity [Lyn83] allows the specification of a hierarchy of breakpoints within the operation sequence of a transaction that states how other transactions can interleave their operations. Thus, sharing of intermediate results among different transactions in a controlled fashion is supported. However, it is not clear how to specify the breakpoint hierarchy for open-ended transaction before it has executed.

Other approaches to increasing the flexibility of design transactions that are unrelated to the approach in this paper include operation transformation for groupware systems [EG89] and the flexible transaction model [Kai90].

A weakness of many of these approaches is the failure to discuss recovery. Of the examples mentioned above, [GS87] and [GGK+90] discuss forward recovery using compensating transactions. [Mos85] and [KKB87] discuss how long transactions can be restarted when a short transaction fails or is aborted. Also, [KLS90] presents a formal analysis for the use of compensation during recovery in schemes related to those proposed in [KKB87, KS88].

3.9 Summary

In this paper, we have examined the requirements that design applications place on databases and have determined several useful properties for a transaction model for these applications. These properties include the following:

1. Allowing a transaction to be decomposed hierarchically according to the structure of the task the transaction is trying to accomplish.
2. Keeping multiple versions of objects to encapsulate sets of related changes and to localize synchronization.
3. Providing a programmable correctness criterion that supports cooperation among transactions or subtransactions. The model should be flexible enough to allow the designer to tailor the correctness criterion to the needs of the application, including serializability if that is what is needed.
4. Allowing specific parts of a transaction to be aborted without causing the whole transaction to abort. This mandates recovery at the *operation* level as opposed to the *transaction* level.

We have described a transaction model for design databases, called a *cooperative transaction hierarchy*. A cooperative transaction hierarchy is a tree structure that reflects the structure of the underlying design task. Each node in the tree is responsible for some specific subtask, and has its own private set of versions of the objects it is currently using in accomplishing that subtask. The internal nodes (*transaction groups*) accomplish their tasks through the cooperation of their children (*members*). The leaf nodes (*cooperative transactions*) represent individual designers or individual design applications.

We have defined a programmable correctness criterion for cooperative transaction hierarchies that structures the interactions among cooperative transactions and allows for controlled data sharing. Each transaction group has a set of active *patterns* and *conflicts* that defines its current notion of correctness. Conflicts are like locks in the sense that they specify when certain operations cannot occur. Patterns specify operation sequences that must occur in a history for it to be correct. We use LR(0) grammars to specify patterns and conflicts in a transaction group.

We have defined a synchronization algorithm that uses a transaction group's programmed correctness criteria to ensure that the operations accepted by the group are ordered correctly. We have provided an extended example to show how the synchronization algorithm works to accomplish a specific subtask. We have also discussed recovery when specific operations are aborted, to ensure that all effects of those operations on its history and on the database are purged, and that the history remains correct.

Acknowledgments

Support for this research is provided in part by an IBM Graduate Fellowship, and in part by IBM under contract No. 559716, by DEC under award No. DEC686, and by ONR under Contract N00014-83-K-0146.

Bibliography

[ASU88] A. Aho, R. Sethi, and J. Ullman. *Compilers: Principles, Techniques, and Tools.* Addison-Wesley, 1988.

[EG89] C. A. Ellis and S. J. Gibbs. Concurrency control in groupware systems. In *ACM SIGMOD Proceedings.* ACM, 1989.

[FZ89] Mary Fernandez and Stanley Zdonik. Transaction groups: A model for controlling cooperative transactions. In *Third International Workshop On Persistent Object Systems*, January 1989.

[GGK+90] Hector Garcia-Molina, Dieter Gawlick, Johannes Klein, Karl Kleissner, and Kenneth Salem. Coordinating multi-transaction activities. Technical Report CS-TR-247-90, Princeton University Department of Computer Science, February 1990.

[GS87] Hector Garcia-Molina and Kenneth Salem. Sagas. In *ACM SIGMOD Proceedings*, pages 249–259. ACM, 1987.

[HU79] J. Hopcroft and J. Ullman. *Introduction to Automata Theory, Languages, and Computation.* Addison-Wesley, 1979.

[Kai90] Gail E. Kaiser. A flexible transaction model for software engineering. In *Proceedings of the 6th International Conference on Data Engineering*, pages 560–567, 1990.

[KKB87] Henry F. Korth, Won Kim, and Francois Bancihon. On long-duration CAD transactions. *Information Systems*, 13, 1987.

[KLS90] Henry F. Korth, Eliezer Levy, and Abraham Silberschatz. A formal approach to recovery by compensating transactions. In *VLDB Proceedings*, pages 95–106, 1990.

[KS88] Henry F. Korth and Gregory D. Speegle. Formal model of correctness without serializability. In *ACM SIGMOD Proceedings*, pages 379–386, 1988.

[Lyn83] Nancy A. Lynch. Multilevel atomicity – a new correctness criterion for database concurrency control. *ACM Transactions on Database Systems*, 8(4):484–502, December 1983.

[Mos85] J. Eliot B. Moss. *Nested Transactions: An Approach to Reliable Distributed Computing.* MIT Press, Cambridge, Massachusetts, 1985.

[NZ90] Marian H. Nodine and Stanley B. Zdonik. Cooperative transaction hierarchies: A transaction model to support design applications. In *VLDB Proceedings*, pages 83–94, 1990.

[RZ91] Sridhar Ramaswamy and Stanley B. Zdonik. Transaction control for cooperative applications. Technical Report CS-91-25, Brown University Department of Computer Science, 1991.

[Ska89] Andrea H. Skarra. Concurrency control for cooperating transactions in an object-oriented database. *SIGPLAN Notices*, 24(4), April 1989.

[Ska91] Andrea Skarra. Localized correctness specifications for cooperating transactions in an object-oriented database. *Office Knowledge Engineering*, 4(1):79–106, 1991.

4

A Flexible Framework for Transaction Management in Engineering Environments

Sandra Heiler

Sara Haradhvala

Stanley Zdonik

Barbara Blaustein

Arnon Rosenthal

4.1 Introduction

We describe a framework for a transaction management system to support cooperative work, such as is needed in engineering environments.[1] The framework includes structural and operational models and a system architecture. The structural model will often mirror the group structure of an organization. The operational model enforces different protocols for collaboration and sharing among members of different groups or among different sub-groups. This framework provides for increased parallelism and enforcement of flexible, application-specific procedural constraints and policies, in order to support concurrent engineering and advanced development methodologies.

The strengths of our approach lie in:

1. a hierarchical structure to organize and modularize methodologies and enforce policies based on the organization's group structure;

2. accommodating multiple notions of correctness that can range from serializability to much weaker conditions appropriate to the specific objects and operations of the application, as well as each group's mode of cooperation;

3. integration with an Object Management System to obtain a uniform and general notion of "request", for resolution of high-level references to appropriate copies and versions, and to allow protocols to exploit the abstraction/representation hierarchy to support multi-level transactions.

The contribution of our work, then, is a *framework* for developing transaction management systems that enforce appropriate protocols, rather than specific protocols that define various notions of correctness. The framework is incomplete without protocols that are appropriate for engineering applications. These protocols will often be found in libraries delivered with Software Engineering Environments (SEE's).

The paper is divided into four sections. Section 4.1 presents the motivation and goals for our work, illustrates the kind of transaction management we wish to provide, and identifies related work. Our work builds principally on [Ska90], which pursued issues 1-2 above. Section 4.2 describes the proposed

[1] This research was sponsored as part of the STARS Breakthrough Initiative by the Defense Advanced Research Projects Agency and IBM under IBM Contract No. 308356-PJ.

framework for transaction management. Section 4.3 describes approaches to building groups' protocols for a software engineering environment. Section 4.4 summarizes our results and the status of our work, and identifies future directions.

4.1.1 Motivation

Concurrent Engineering has been proposed as the solution to many of the problems that plague product development [WPBS88]. Rapid prototyping and concurrent design for development, test, and maintenance have been shown to greatly enhance productivity in many engineering domains. They can provide similar benefits to software engineering. Already, software engineers are aware of the benefits of prototyping. However, concurrent engineering will require far more than just the ability to prototype. It will need support for *collaboration* among workers from all parts of the development organization. It will require greatly increased cooperation and parallelism in software engineering processes, and safety in sharing objects that span stages of the product life cycle.

Integrated Software Engineering Environments (SEEs) often improve productivity and provide needed controls [DEFH87]. But the methodologies they support tend to isolate workers from one another in order to reduce the possibility of interference or premature release of changes. The methodologies encourage ownership of objects (e.g., source code), serial processing, and independent operation. When workers do share objects, the process is encumbered by myriad administrative locks and checks. This severely limits concurrency and practically eliminates the possibility of collaboration, except by arrangements outside the purview of the SEE.

Ideally, in a large organization, tasks and products are divided so that each group of workers is assigned to some functional subtask or subset of products. Multiple people *cooperate* in groups to perform some overall function or to produce the larger product. By dividing the work in this way, the organization often can achieve a high degree of concurrency. Group members cooperate on their component, sharing both the responsibility for execution of the task and the results of the members' activities. Similarly, each group's results are shared with other groups as the overall product emerges from the results of the sub-products and the subtasks.

We have all seen how the collaborative efforts and streamlined processes of small, clever teams who don't necessarily obey all the "rules" can sometimes lead to higher quality products and shortened delivery times. Organizations need to be able to exploit these "pockets of competence" and allow for variations in methodology based on group size, expertise, role, and style. However, current practice in large organizations is to apply a uniform methodology based on locking of objects or strict versioning and configuration management schemes. This "lowest-common-denominator" approach produces an ultra-conservative structure that limits concurrency, since not all groups can be trusted to collaborate effectively.

Different groups need to be able to share data and to collaborate in different ways. This means that they need to be able to tailor policies to support the specific interactions among members of their groups. More importantly, the way groups interact with each other is different from the way that individuals within groups interact with one another [PK91]. The model must look at the hierarchy of groups, mediating conflicts and promoting sharing among members of individual groups and among groups at each level of the hierarchy. Each group needs to be able to enforce its own policies for interaction among its members, whether they are individuals or subgroups.

We define a model of transaction management that attempts to provide the needed structure and flexibility to support concurrent engineering and to exploit increased opportunities for concurrency. Our model allows different "protocols" that enforce methodologies and policies for different groups or subgroups of workers, to accommodate their individual strengths and weaknesses and modes of collaboration, as well as group size and composition. It benefits SEEs (and other engineering environments) by supporting collaboration and increased parallelism to improve productivity, while enforcing domain-specific methodologies to improve quality. Specifically, the model can:

- **increase concurrency and collaboration** among individuals and among groups. This can increase productivity, reduce products' lead times, and support concurrent engineering methodologies by involving multiple disciplines throughout the entire design process.

- **enforce application-specific methodologies, constraints, and procedures** expressed in terms of objects and actions that are natural to the application. Powerful mechanisms for coordinating and controlling individual and group actions reduce the likelihood of errors and thus foster improved product quality.

- **allow organizations to exploit different policies and methodologies for different groups and individuals**. By accommodating the style of work that is most effective for each group, the model can enhance both control and flexibility. By allowing protocols to be developed independently and modularly, it facilitates implementation.

4.1.2 Summary of the Approach

Our model exposes the fact that the user is working within a group and sub-group structure with a shared database, instead of providing the user with the illusion of operating independently with a private database. All objects can be accessible to every user (within the constraints of security and access controls) regardless of what other group members are doing. The user can *share* the results of everyone else's work in the common database, unless explicitly prevented by the protocols that apply to the groups to which each worker belongs.

Protocols can enforce limits or provide notifications of this sharing and concurrency, in order to protect the objects from unintended interference. They define conditions under which requests to perform specific operations (or types of operations) on specific objects (or types of objects) should be accepted, rejected, or queued for later consideration. The operations and objects in the protocols are those of the applications, for example, *compile(program_unit_p)* or *edit(chapter_q)*. Moreover, the object model includes a "resolution" step that selects an appropriate copy or version of each operation and argument. The model also enables requests to reference objects and operations at different levels of abstraction to provide the effects of multilevel transactions as in [Weik91].

Often, protocols will mediate requests by specifying that between the beginning and ending of a particular task, requests to perform some other tasks are to be rejected or queued; for example, a protocol might indicate that simultaneous editing of the same file is prohibited and that the second edit request must be queued until the first finishes. In addition, protocols can require that users perform some set pattern of operations to ensure correctness; for example, a protocol might require that after editing source code and before releasing it, the user must compile and successfully test it. Finally, protocols can trigger actions automatically; for example, a protocol might trigger notification of active users when a new version of a design is released. In essence, protocols enforce procedural constraints and trigger operations that ensure correctness based on local software engineering methodologies and policies.

In our model, workers (users and application programs) operate in the context of a group structure – a hierarchy of groups. The top-most node of the hierarchy represents the whole organization. Each lower node has smaller sub-groups as members. The leaves represent the lowest-level sub-groups, whose members are the individual users and application programs.

A group's protocol regulates the sharing of objects and concurrent operations by the immediate members of that group, whether they are users or application programs or sub-groups. For example, imagine an organization that is divided into two main divisions, D1 and D2. The top level protocol might indicate that all operations on a system s from D1 are to be rejected while s is being tested by D2, and vice versa. At the next lower level, the protocol for D1 might allow two different members of D1 to test the system concurrently, but not to modify the system while it is being tested. The protocol for D2 might enforce different policies for interactions among its members.

Each group in the hierarchy has a (local) transaction manager, which has two main parts: 1) a group-specific protocol, and 2) a uniform capability (over all groups) for coordinating with neighboring transaction managers. This division of responsibilities keeps the protocols independent of each other and allows each protocol-writer to focus on interactions within one group.

4.1.3 An Example of Transaction Management in a Simple Organization

Imagine a Software Product organization which is divided into three divisions: Documentation, Software Engineering, and Maintenance. Software Engineering has two sub-divisions: Development and Prototyping as shown in Figure 4.1.

We will give a narrative description of the desired transaction management. This narrative maps directly to easily-implemented protocols for each of the groups.

In our example organization, Software Engineering releases documents to Documentation and code modules to Maintenance. If Software Engineering subsequently modifies a document, it must notify Documentation. Software Engineering cannot modify a code module once it has been released to Maintenance. These policies are expressed in the top-level protocol (for the whole organization), which includes the following rules:

- At the end of an operation by Software Engineering to modify a document d, e-mail Documentation that d has been modified.

- After the end of an operation by Software Engineering to release a module m, reject any subsequent operation to modify m by Software Engineering.

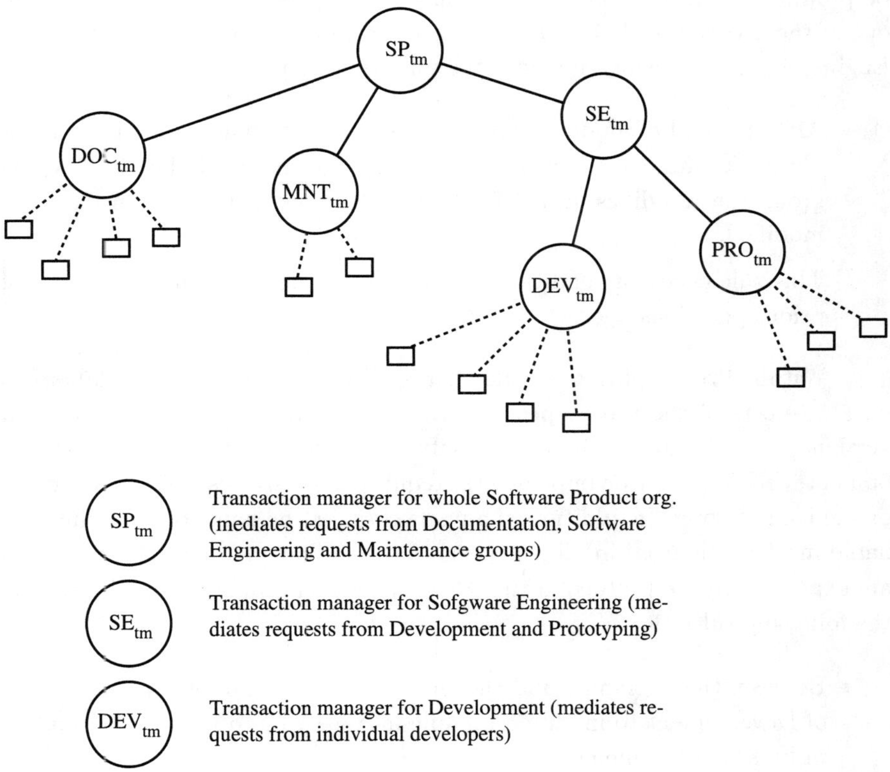

FIGURE 4.1
A Hierarchy of Transaction Managers

Note that the first rule triggers a new request (e-mail), and the second rule references the history of prior operations to see if it contains the event "release operation ends normally".

Within Software Engineering, Prototyping provides the Development group with prototyped versions of many of the software modules which are to be produced by Development and notifies Development when it has modified one of these versions. This policy is expressed in the protocol of the Software Engineering group, which includes the following rule:

- After the end of an operation by Prototyping to make available a module m, at the end of each operation by a member of the Prototyping group that modifies m, notify the Development group that m has been modified.

  This rule checks a condition involving multiple events in the history of prior operations.

Within Prototyping everyone shares all objects; everyone collaborates on all aspects of the prototypes, and anyone can test or release prototyped versions. No rules are required to specify this policy. However, within Development, each designer or implementer requires exclusive use of any object he or she is modifying. In addition, if anyone changes the name of a module, the name must be changed in all programs that use that module. These policies are expressed in the protocol of the Development group, which might include the following rules:

- Between the beginning and the end of any operation by any member D of Development to modify a module m, reject any operation on module m by any other member of Development.

- Between the beginning and the end of any operation by any member D' of Development on module m, reject any operation by any other member of Development that modifies m.

- At the end of the rename operation to rename a module m, trigger a request to edit all modules that *use* m to modify their calls to m.

In general, requests for concurrent modification of an object can be queued or rejected or they can trigger the creation of a copy of the object for the requester, or some other action to make concurrent modification safe. For example, a different company's protocol might have specified that if two members of Development want to edit the same module, the transaction manager should trigger copying of the module for each of them and that when both are finished with their modifications, the transaction manager should trigger a merge of their updates to produce a single copy. Yet another protocol might specify that if a member of Development wants to test the module while someone in Maintenance is modifying the module, Development's request is to be rejected and a message that the module is unavailable is to be triggered.

4.1.4 Related Work

This section describes the base technologies for our work and how each has been applied or extended.

Classical Transactions

Database Management Systems (DBMSs) have developed a mature body of theory and implementation techniques in the area of concurrency control and recovery. Traditional DBMS concurrency control and recovery (as described in [BHG87]) are based on transactions that are characterized by *atomicity* (which ensures that a transaction is run in its entirety or not at all), *serializability* (which guarantees that concurrently executing transactions do not interfere with each other, by controlling the interleaving of operations among them), and *permanence* (which guarantees that effects of completed transactions do not disappear as a result of later failures). Each transaction is isolated from intermediate results or the success or failure of other transactions running concurrently.

The natures of software engineering and of the software life cycle inherently require more cooperation among transactions than is possible using the conventional criteria for correctness. In an SEE a transaction may extend over a much longer time than the usual database transaction. The usual locking and recovery protocols could cause some users to be unable to access needed data or programs for days or weeks, and would cause an entire transaction's work to be lost in case of a complete rollback after a failure. Several proposals, such as [DE89, Ban85, GS87], have suggested retreating from serializability, but in small increments. We believe that even these may be too restrictive for many groups.

Nested Transactions

Nested transactions [Mos85] extend traditional, atomic transactions by applying concurrency control and recovery concepts within transactions as well as among them. This permits safe concurrency within transactions and allows transactions to fail partially, in a controlled manner. Any transaction can have child transactions nested within it. Nested transactions can, in turn, have their own child transactions. Therefore, there can be a whole hierarchy of transactions associated with a given transaction.

Multilevel transactions [Moh90, Weik91], e.g., in OS2/EE's ARIES system, impose additional assumptions in order to lower the overhead of supporting access methods. Our model differs substantially from the nested transaction model - our transactions are flat, and groups are allowed to define and enforce their own procedural notions of correctness.

Transaction Groups

[Ska90] proposes extensions to the nested transaction model to address the needs of collaboration and cooperative work. Her model is based on a hierarchy of nested *transaction groups*, where each group operates with respect to its own notion of correctness. This approach allows more collaboration by allowing weaker notions of correctness than atomicity and serializability. Intermediate results may be made visible to a transaction's siblings, and the effects of an aborted transaction are not necessarily rolled all the way back to the last consistent state. In addition, the approach allows different notions of correctness at different nodes in the hierarchy.

[Ska90] allows for arbitrary abstract operators on abstract objects, as our model does. Earlier work described in [EIS89] applied the ideas in [Ska90] to the domain of VLSI engineering, and added operational support, including abort and recovery semantics, for long-lived VLSI design transactions. [NZ90] adds recoveries, but considers only traditional DBMS *read* and *write* operators.

Our model extends [Ska90], adding both detail and flexibility. We handle concurrent execution of individual functions, and sub-requests generated by individual functions. We allow protocols to generate requests (e.g., to produce copies to support concurrent operations) that are not part of the original transaction, and define an operational model that allows requests to be queued, and an architecture that exploits facilities of an Object Management System.

4.2 The Model

This section describes our proposed model for transaction management. Section 4.2.1 gives an overview of the transaction management model and of the object model that provides much of the basic terminology. 4.2.2 describes how a request is processed, as seen from the outside, i.e.,the global behavior of transaction management; 4.2.3 describes how this behavior can be implemented as a hierarchy of local transaction managers. 4.3 will then describe how the model might be used by an organization building a customized (global) transaction manager through specification of protocols.

4.2.1 Overview

Overview of Transaction Management

A transaction manager has two jobs – to *mediate* the execution of individual requests, and to support specific transaction management functions, such as commit or abort. *Mediation* means determining which requests will be allowed to execute, and triggering actions that make the execution safer (e.g., notification of concurrent users, creation of private copies).

For a large organization, it would be nearly impossible to produce a single, integrated transaction management protocol that accommodates the needs of all subgroups. The only possible solution is modularization. *Our contribution is to simplify this task.* We provide a *framework* – an algorithm and software interfaces for coordinating the groups in a hierarchy – so that the SEE-customizer need only provide local protocols for individual groups.

Transaction management in our model is implemented modularly as a *Transaction Manager Hierarchy (TMH)* – a set of *local transaction managers (local TMs)*, plus a global (but decentralized) algorithm to coordinate them. Diversity is accommodated by diverse protocols at the local TMs; the global coordination algorithm is fixed, and is delivered with the framework. Requests originated by lower-level groups do not bypass the safeguards imposed by higher levels – the effects are additive. Our experience indicates that useful global protocols can be implemented in this fashion. Unlike classical transactions, our model has no simple "correctness" criterion. Each group decides what is correct behavior within the group; global "correctness" must be relative to these individual protocols. We have not formalized this relation.

A long term goal of this research is the ability to provide a toolkit for building customized transaction managers. The toolkit would contain implementations of 1) the framework algorithms, and 2) commonly-useful protocols. Organizations would describe their group structure to the framework, and select, write, or customize a protocol for each group.

Basic Terminology of the Object Model

Our transaction management scheme is based on an object-oriented (OO) model and is integrated with the facilities of an Object Management System. The notion of an object from OO programming languages and OO databases provides a way to describe all of the complex data that is required by the various stages of the software life cycle. It is sufficiently powerful to describe things as diverse as program modules, test cases, compilation, specifications, and documentation, so it provides a natural, uniform way of describing the artifacts and processes of software engineering.

Object: An *object* is an abstraction that has an identity that is independent of the values of any of its properties or relationships to other objects. This identity is captured by a unique, immutable object identifier (OID). Everything in the SEE, no matter what its granularity, can be defined as an object. Software tools (e.g. compilers, editors), program units, designs, documents, network nodes, databases, integers, and strings are all objects. Objects are associated with types, which describe the operations that may be applied.

Function: A *function* is a mapping from some input objects to output objects. Typically, functions will be software engineering operations, e.g., compiling, or data access operations, e.g., querying. The mapping is performed in response to a *request* which specifies a particular function and the input objects. A request is equivalent to sending a "message" in other object models. However, it does not imply a particular order for arguments or that one argument is distinguished, as is usually implied by the term "message" in other object models.

A function may be applied to an object or objects to yield the object's properties (attributes) or related objects, to compute results, to test constraints, or to cause side effects. For example, one might apply the *uses* function to a program unit object to yield its nested program units; one might apply the *edit* function to the program unit to modify it; or one might apply the *compile* function to the program unit to validate its syntax and produce an object file. It is requests to apply functions to objects that are synchronized and recovered, based on knowledge of which functions conflict if applied concurrently and which function application patterns are required to ensure correctness.

Each function that can be applied to an object must have a "body" (implementation), which is a procedure, written in some programming language, that is executed when the function is applied. (It may, in fact, have multiple bodies, one of which will be selected by the Resolution step below). This procedure, which can access or modify the state of the object, performs the mapping from inputs to outputs, and may have side effects, e.g., update some value or produce other outputs. (Notice that our "functions" are not true functions in the mathematical sense, since they do not necessarily return anything and they can have side effects and can be updated.)

Transactions, functions, protocols, and transaction managers can all be objects in the model, and changes to them can be implemented as functions. Such requests to modify the TMH and its protocols are subject to transaction management. For example, a protocol that mediates requests to modify objects of type Protocol might prohibit modification while the protocol's group has transactions that have begun but not ended.

Representation: Each object has a *representation* (or implementation) that captures its state. For example, a program unit might be represented by a file (which may itself be an object). Notice that the representations may also be objects that are described by types and have representations of their own. For example, a file might be represented by a set_of_records. An arbitrary number of levels of abstraction and representation can be defined. The body of a function (i.e., its implementation) is a representation of the function. The transaction management system controls access both to object abstractions and to object representations (i.e., logical and physical access) in the same way.

Resolution: Request resolution maps the specified function and arguments to their implementations, so that the required procedure can be invoked and references to the arguments can be passed as parameters. The process maps references to objects into references to their representations. Both function resolution and argument resolution selects an appropriate copy of each argument, as described later.

Transactions Transactions provide a convenient means of grouping requests into a larger unit suitable for enforcing consistency and permanence. Several different notions of transaction might be supported simultaneously in an SEE. In this paper, we briefly address one issue – how transaction semantics may be structured using the hierarchy of groups.

A *transaction* is a partially ordered set of requests, where the partial order is expressed by programs' control structures, or induced by the order in which requests are individually submitted to the system. All requests are submitted in the context of some transaction. In the simplest case, each request can define its own transaction. A transaction is created when some group member issues *begin_transaction*. The end of a transaction is signalled by a transaction management command, either *commit* or *abort*. Commit signals a normal termination and abort signals an abnormal termination of the transaction.

To the model, these functions have only rudimentary built in semantics. Each protocol can add more semantics by triggering additional requests. In such a way, for example, we might get a group-specific notion of "commit".

4.2.2 Semantics of Request Processing

This section describes how transaction management looks from the outside. Section 4.2.3 will describe how a request is processed within the TMH.

Requests

Group members (users and applications) submit requests in the context of an Object Management System. Each request asks the system to apply a function to (a list of) argument objects. The requests are submitted to the Request Handler of an Object Management System, as shown in Figure 4.2.

The requests originate from end users and application programs, from the bodies of requested functions (*sub-requests*), from transaction managers themselves (*triggered requests*), and from system administrators, who add users or groups or otherwise modify the TMH. Thus, both execution of the requested function body and testing of the request by the TMH can cause other requests to be submitted to the Request Handler. The additional requests are processed in exactly the same way as the original request. Sub-requests are part of the original transaction; a triggered request comprises a new transaction.

The basic steps in processing a request (and the agent who performs each step) are: receipt by the OMS's Request Handler (OMS); mediation of the beginning of the request (TMH); resolution and execution (OMS); mediation of the end of the request (TMH); return results (OMS). This is illustrated in Figure 4.3.

Events within Request Processing

Each request r has three associated events: *begin(r)* when r is submitted, *execute(r)* when the TMH approves r for execution, and *end(r)* when r completes or is rejected. IDs of the request's originator and the associated

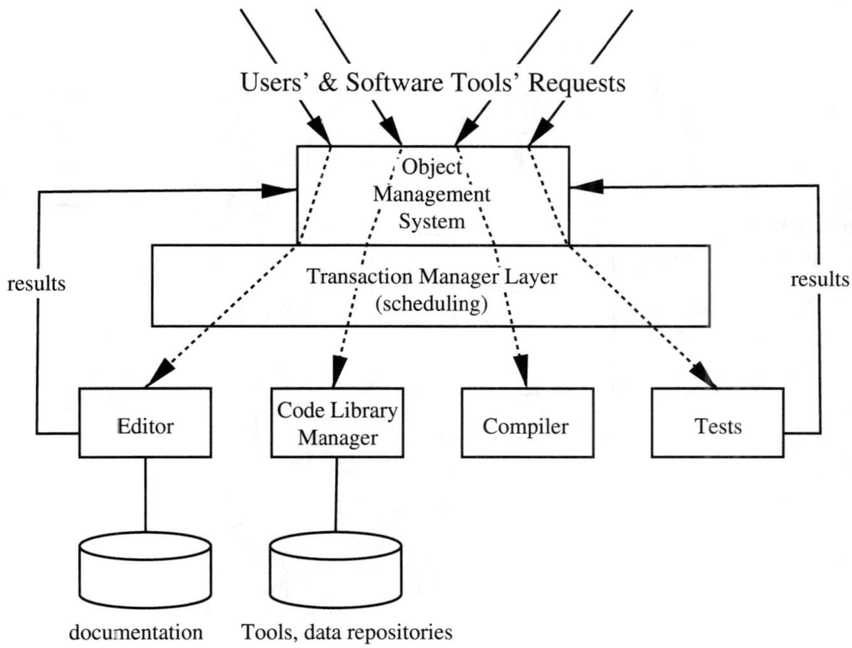

FIGURE 4.2
SEE Architecture

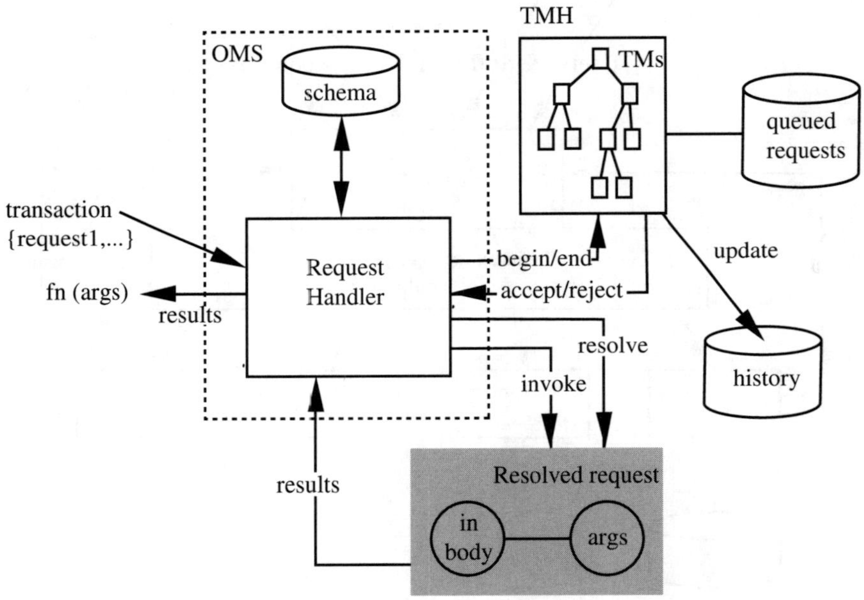

FIGURE 4.3
Request Processing

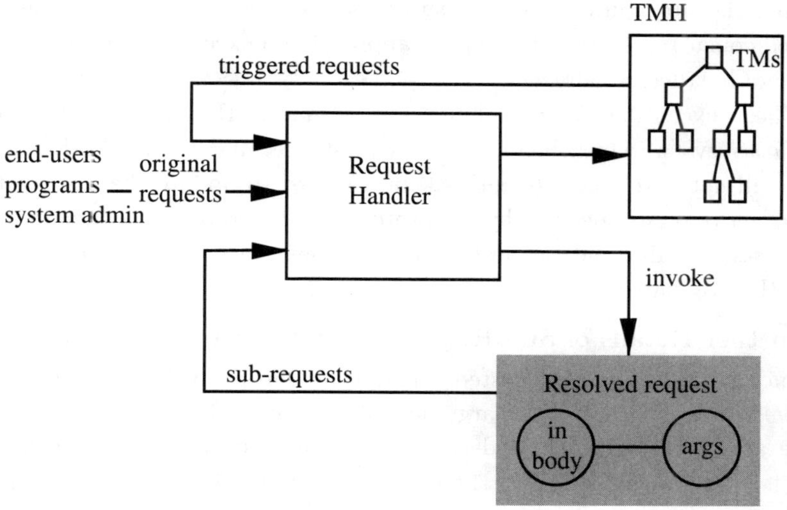

FIGURE 4.4
Sources of Requests

transaction are attached to each event, and after execution *end(r)* includes the results of r. The Request Handler asks the TMH to mediate these events, i.e., to run protocols that may trigger further requests, and to approve *begin* events so that the request may be executed[2].

For each *begin(request)* event that it receives, the TMH responds with "accept" or "reject" or queues the request. If the request is queued, the TMH does not respond to the Request Handler until the request is dequeued and re-processed and the TMH can respond with "accept" or "reject". (This queuing does not block the TMH from considering other requests). If the TMH rejects the request, the Request Handler passes the "reject" response back to the originator. If the TMH accepts the request, the Request Handler resolves the request, converts the input argument references to data structures and invokes the procedure, passing the data structures as parameters. During

[2]The protocol governing a *begin(request)* event controls not only the requested use of the input objects (i.e applying the requested function to them) but also the use of the requested function (i.e. execution). Execution of a function might be rejected or queued based on concurrent uses of the body (e.g., modification of the code) or if the code needs exclusive control of some other resource (e.g., the terminal's screen).

execution, the procedure may issue sub-requests. Separate requests can be processed concurrently, but the steps of approval and execution for any single request are handled serially.

When execution is complete, the Request Handler submits an *end(request)* event (which includes the request's results) to the TMH. This request will not be rejected or queued, but is used to update the history, to trigger other requests specified by the protocol, and possibly to dequeue waiting requests. Finally, the Request Handler passes the results or error codes back to the originator.

Further Details of Sub-Requests and Triggered Requests

Once the body of a requested function has been invoked, it can issue *sub-requests* that operate on the arguments to the invocation, representations of these arguments, or objects derived from these arguments, as shown in Figure 4.4. Sub-requests run in the context of the transaction in which the original request is running and are submitted to the system and synchronized in the same way as the original request. The placement of controls at the sub-request level can increase concurrency by allowing the queuing of requests to be limited to the duration of the sub-requests, and copying to be limited to objects of smaller granularity than the arguments of the original request.

Triggered Requests: As a protocol executes, it can submit *triggered requests.* As with any request, the submitting program can await the result. Therefore begin-triggered requests are usually evaluated and executed prior to execution of the remainder of the protocol, and of the original request whose *begin* event caused the protocol to execute. The originator of a triggered request is the TM whose protocol did the triggering. Results of a triggered request go directly to the protocol that submitted it. Results of triggered requests are noted in the history, and may be detected by subsequent steps in the protocol. For example, suppose a request to copy a particular object is triggered so that the object can be safely updated by an edit request. If the copy fails, the protocol may reject the edit request.

End-triggered requests are processed after the original request has completed execution, so queuing or rejecting them occurs too late to affect acceptance of the original request. However, the transaction manager may trigger actions to invalidate the original request or to prohibit acceptance of further requests as part of the transaction (e.g., reject checkpoint requests).

Hidden Sub-Requests: Large, off-the-shelf components (e.g., compilers, editors) often act on shared information via program mechanisms (e.g., #include files) that are not visible to the Request Handler or to the TMH.

As a result, needed controls are bypassed. For example, when a transaction requests the compilation of a particular program unit p, the compiler might automatically compile nested program units, say q and r, upon encountering their use in the program. In this case, the sub-requests, *Compile(q) and Compile(r)*, are called *hidden* in the execution of the body of the compile function when it compiles p.

As a palliative, we provide a mechanism to declare to the transaction management system that the body of a request f(x) acts "as if" it included hidden sub-requests {g1(x), g2(x), ...}. For purposes of transaction management, *begin* events for these sub-requests are generated as soon as f(x) is accepted for execution. *End* events for the sub-requests are generated as soon as the *end* event for the request is received. For example, such a history might look like:

begin(req) begin(s1), begin(s2), {events from non-hidden sub-requests of req}, end(s2), end(s1), end(req)

A procedure that returns the set of hidden sub-requests must be associated with each function's implementation. A request may have both hidden and non-hidden sub-requests. Both may have hidden sub-sub-requests, but only the non-hidden ones are *executed* by the Request Handler.

The palliative makes some strong assumptions – that all sub-requests can be determined without actually executing the request, and that the hidden sub-requests occur in the order shown (or at least, that mediation in the indicated sequence will give a correct result). But the simple capability was useful in our prototype.

4.2.3 Request Processing by the TMH

Transaction management is provided by a hierarchy of local TMs corresponding to the hierarchy of groups. This section describes how the efforts of local TMs are coordinated. In brief, each event from the Request Handler is processed by the TMs between the root and the *originator's TM* (i.e., the lowest-level group to which the originator belongs). *Begin* events travel top-down, while *end* and *execute* events travel upward. In addition, appropriate information about accepted events is written into the TMs' histories, and appropriate notifications are sent to other TMs and to the Request Handler.

We now specify the rules for each of the three types of events, for a request r.

begin(r): Each TM in the path from the root to the originator's TM will process *begin(r)*, in sequence. The TM's protocol may trigger additional requests, but eventually returns a decision about whether *this group's* criteria would allow r to execute. The decision is based on r and on the *local* history. Now let TMi denote any TM in the path.

When TMi decides to "accept", the event is written in TMi's history. If TMi was not the originator's TM, the event is passed to the child along the downward path. If TMi does represent the originator's group, then all relevant TMs have agreed to accept. To notify these other TMs, TMi creates an *execute(r)* event whose processing is described below. It then notifies the Request Handler than the TMH accepts r for processing.

When TMi decides to "reject", the process is shortcut – children of TMi will not receive this *begin(r)* event. If TMi is not the root, it generates an *end(r)* event that it submits to its parent. Processing of *end* events is described below. If TMi is the root, it sends the "reject" answer back to the Request Handler.

When TMi decides to "queue", the process resembles treatment of reject. An *end(r)* event is sent to inform ancestors, but the root does not inform the Request Handler. r is queued here at TMi, and it is TMi's responsibility to maintain the list of waiting events. Release of queued events (not necessarily FIFO) is described under *end* processing.

Note that "reject" and "queue" both generate *end(r)* events that will be sent to TMi's ancestors. Some ancestors' protocols may regard the *begin(r)* acceptance in their histories as an obligation to block certain other requests; in effect, the protocols are holding locks on behalf of r. Frequently the obligation will be removed by the matching *end(r)*.

As an example of *begin* processing, imagine an organization divided into two groups A and B. As shown in Figure 4.5, group A consists of subgroups A1 and A2, plus an individual user who issues requests as a part of a transaction T3. A1 has members whose requests are part of transactions identified as T1 and T2. The transactions associated with the groups A, B, A1 and A2 are called, respectively, TA TB, TA1, and TA2. Requests from members of group A are part of transaction TA; requests from members of group A1 are part of transaction TA1, etc.

Suppose that a request f(x) is submitted by a member of subgroup A1 (as part of transaction T1). Evaluation of the *begin(request)* event in the TMH will proceed by making the following tests:

- Can a request that is part of transaction TA apply function f to object x, according to the root node's transaction manager (protocol that governs requests by groups A and B) and history?

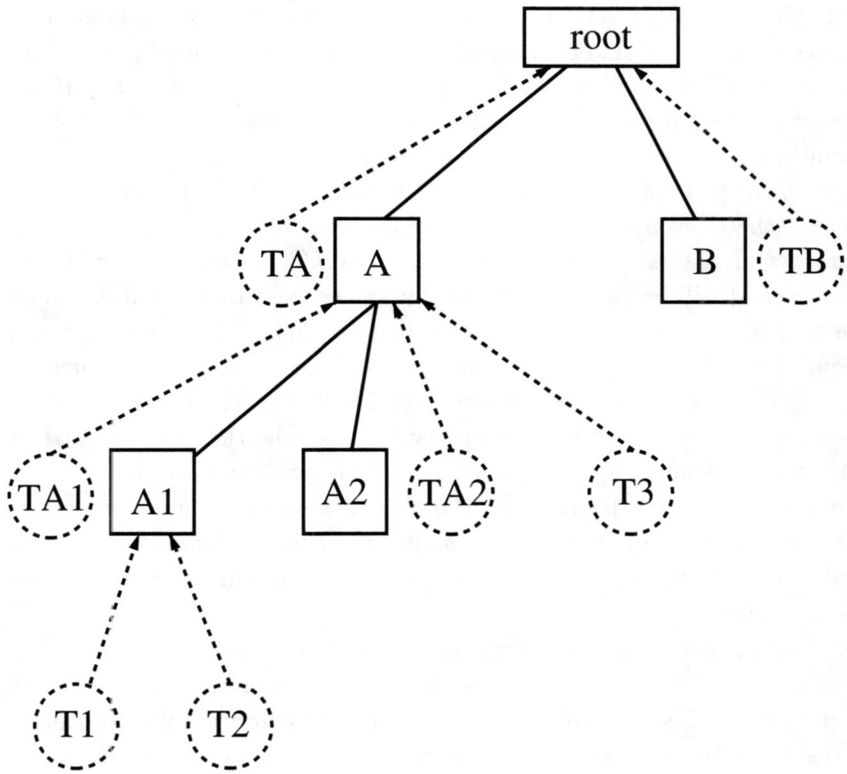

FIGURE 4.5

- If so, can a request that is part of transaction TA1 apply f to x, according to group A's transaction manager (protocol that governs requests by groups A1, A2 and T3) and history?

- If so, can a request that is part of transaction T1 apply f to x, according to group A1's transaction manager (protocol that governs T1 and its sibling transaction T2)?

Each TM considers the requester to be a member of its own group, rather than of the originator's group, which may be a distant descendent. For example, in the organization described above, A1's protocol mediates between requests from individual members of A1, whereas the top-level protocol mediates between requests from group A versus those coming from group B. Thus, the scope of each group's protocol is limited to requests from its immediate members.

end(r): These events are processed in the TMH in the reverse order of *begin(request)* events, passing from the lowest node that manages the originator's transaction to the root node. *End* events are entered into the TM's history, and will be passed to the parent. Since execution has already ended, the *end* request cannot be rejected or queued by a TM's protocol; however, requests triggered by processing that protocol can be rejected or queued.

As part of processing an *end* event, a TM's protocol may choose to release any of *its own* waiting requests; for example, the protocol might test whether all conflicting requests have now ended. Such dequeued requests are resubmitted to the Request Handler as requests from their originator (rather than from the transaction manager). This resubmission allows other nodes to rerun their protocols in the context of their histories at the time of resubmission.

execute(r): *execute* events indicate to ancestors that the request has been accepted for execution. The processing resembles *end* – it proceeds bottom-up, and is recorded in each TM's history. Our example protocols used *execute* events in histories to distinguish between accepted requests versus rejected or queued requests, and to react differently in the two cases.

Transaction Management Requests:

Each TM must deal with requests to *begin_transaction*, which creates a new "transaction" instance, and returns its identifier. The programming language and environment may associate later requests with this transaction.

Transactions terminate normally by issuing a *commit* request. The lowest-level TM associated with the transaction provides a Commit procedure that removes the transaction. This procedure may invoke Commit functions provided by higher level groups. Transactions terminate abnormally by issuing an *abort* request. The TMs may provide customized Abort procedures that, as far as possible, remove the transaction's modifications. A request to abort a transaction can never be rejected, although it may be queued. In other ways, the processing is analogous to Commit. After Commit or Abort ends, the transaction is removed and further requests associated with this transaction will be rejected.

4.2.4 Framework Services and Their Interfaces

Our goal is to make it possible to deliver software for the TMH framework as part of a Software Engineering Environment, and to allow organizations to plug in customized components. The *framework* (i.e., *model*) specifies the semantics of a TMH and its interfaces – it describes the part of our transaction management approach that individual groups need not implement, and do not modify. There are three kinds of interfaces – outward to the Request Handler (to which the TMH supplies a service), between TMs, and within a TM to customized components (groups' protocols, histories, and queues) that are invoked by the TMs.

The code that implements the framework is principally concerned with *coordination*, i.e., with ensuring that each event and decision is sent to the appropriate sequence of TMs, as specified in previous sections. Other capabilities include providing a single *conceptual recipient* to which the Request Handler sends *begin* and *end* events[3]; and *inclusion of context information*, such as IDs for the originator, requester (i.e., member of the current group that contains the originator), and transaction.

A natural implementation strategy for the framework is to distribute its intelligence among the TMs. A layer at the top of each TM handles coordination (with parents, children, and the Request Handler) and other framework services. This layer also interfaces to group-specific protocols, history mechanisms, membership lists, and so forth.

Each group has a protocol that embodies the group's way of protecting objects and functions from unintended interference by other members of the group. Protocols' interfaces are fixed by the model, though each group's

[3]The Request Handler will be insulated from the details of transaction management; for example, it should not need to know whether there is a single integrated TM or a TMH. It simply submits requests to the framework and awaits a decision.

protocol may implement different semantics. A protocol's inputs are: the request event and the history of previous events at this transaction manager up until the time when the request is received. The output (i.e., the decision) must be "accept", "reject", or "queue". In each case, the protocol's decision is returned to the framework software that coordinates TMs.

Histories

Each transaction manager maintains a history, for reference by its protocol. Conceptually, the history contains the *begin(request)* and the *end(request)* events for all requests *accepted* by this local TM, and an *execute(request)* event for each request that was accepted both by this TM and globally by the other relevant TMs. *End(r)* includes the result of r. The identities of the requester and associated transaction are included with each request.

Request events appear in the order in which they were processed, with *begin, execute*, and *end* events interleaved in order of occurrence. *Begin* events for requests triggered by processing *begin(r)* will appear in a history *before* the beginning of r, and *begin* and *end* events for requests triggered by processing of *end(r)* will appear after *end(r)*. Note that a group member's *begin, execute*, and *end* event entries in the history will be interleaved with entries from siblings in the group, identified by their own requester and transaction IDs. Begin events for sub-requests will also be nested in the history in the order in which they are received.

The actual contents of histories may become somewhat more complicated, since each group is likely to have different needs. Some groups may choose to include additional information in their histories, e.g., for use by locally-defined transaction management functions such as Commit, Abort, or Recover functions. Other protocols depend on only a small fraction of the history; for protocols that accept a finite-state language [Ska90], only the final state need be remembered. And although most events will be processed by multiple TMs, they need not be *physically* repeated in each history.

4.3 Protocols for Software Engineering Environments – Approaches and Idioms

We first survey constructs that are often used in specifying protocols. Next, we show that if protocols are sufficiently well-behaved, deadlocks are detectable by a single TM. The final sections discuss protocols for limiting sharing.

4.3.1 Specifying Protocols

In our model, transaction management is based on each organization's specification of 1) how concurrent functions can interleave; and 2) required procedural patterns. In other words, the model supports a scheme in which the transaction manager does not have a single, built-in notion of correctness, but rather is programmed to accept its own application-specific protocols, which enforce appropriate methodologies and policies in the SEE. Our goal is to accommodate the variety of protocols that prove useful in an SEE, such as described in [KH83, KP87].

As in [Ska90], protocols can be used to describe:

- **Conflicts**: Requests that are not allowed to execute concurrently because the functions, the arguments, or both conflict. For example, no member of group G1 may test a code module m while a member of G2 is editing m. Once the member of G2 is finished editing, the member of G1 may be allowed to proceed.

- **Patterns**: Sequences of requests that must occur before a transaction may commit, or before a request can be accepted. For example, immediately after linking a system, a test suite must be executed to determine if that system still works. If the system were linked, and the test suite were not executed, then other requests, including the request to end the transaction (commit) would be rejected.

- **Triggers**: Additional requests that are submitted when a request begins or ends. For example, before an update is performed to a system module, a copy is made to a separate directory to isolate the released system from the experimental version; or after a modification has been made and tested, the new code is merged back into the release directory.

The transaction manager at each node, and thus its protocol, is independent of all other transaction managers. Each TM mediates requests from its own immediate members. As a request traverses a path, at each stage it is treated as coming from the appropriate member of the TM's immediate group. A group's protocol defines correctness with respect to the actions and interactions of its group members, and there are no dependencies across protocols. Hence protocols (or transaction managers) are modular – changes to one have no effect on the others. There is no requirement to ensure that the protocols of different transaction managers are consistent with one another. In addition, each potential deadlock situation can be detected at a single node.

The language for specifying protocols need not be uniform across all transaction managers, but can be selected for each protocol. We have developed numerous protocols, some of which were specified in the Ada code of our prototype's transaction manager, some as condition/action rules, and some as state machines similar to those described in [Ska90, FZ89]. Finite State Automata are often a good specification choice since they minimize the amount of history information that needs to be actually maintained, and allow very fast decisions [Ska90]. Other examples of useful languages include Context-Free and LR(0) grammars [NZ90].

The full power of protocols carries substantial danger, so protocol-writers will need guidelines to promote understandability, correct operation and modularity. For example, in the interests of modularity, a group's protocol should avoid knowledge of the membership or internal structure of subgroups [FZ89]. And each protocol should be aware that it may receive the *begin* event multiple times for the same request – every time the request is removed from a queue and resubmitted.

4.3.2 Deadlock Prevention/Detection

The TMH's processing algorithm attempts to insulate each node from the effects of queuing at other nodes. As a result, if protocols are well-behaved, potential deadlocks are detectable by individual TMs, without needing global checking. Furthermore, resolution of the deadlock can be directed by the protocol at that node.

Deadlock is caused by a cycle of "wait-for" among requests. In the simplest case, deadlock occurs when a request r1 has exclusive access to (a lock on) an object o1 and is blocked because a sub-request awaits exclusive use of another object o2; at the same time another request r2 has exclusive access to o2 and is blocked because a sub-request awaits exclusive use of o1. Neither transaction can release its lock so that the other transaction can be dequeued, and the two remain deadlocked. Of course, the situation may be far more complex.

Conflicts and locks are not explicit in our model. Instead, queuing occurs whenever a TM's protocol decides to queue a request due to events in its history. Conceptually, the TM considers dequeuing each time it receives an event. This decision to dequeue is internal to the protocol, and may depend on any information in the queued request, the received event, and the TM's history. Deadlock localization depends on an assumption that each group's protocol will be "well-behaved," in the sense that no TM queues a group member's request to await completion of a request by the *same* group member.

A potential deadlock (i.e., a necessary condition for deadlock) is detectable at the lowest common transaction manager for the transactions involved. Queuing occurs at the same node at which locks are granted, i.e., where usage would be tested in the history. This can only be at the node that controls the requests of both transactions involved in deadlock. It is at this node that queuing is performed and analyzed and potential deadlock is detected and dealt with, using the local policies specified in that node's protocol.

The potential deadlock, then, is visible to a single node, which can autonomously determine what response to take. Notice that the contention between siblings is never noticed except at their immediate parent. This node uses its own criteria – distinct from those at any other node – to determine how to grant or restrict access by its members. Thus, the protocol of a transaction manager can prevent deadlock by rejecting the request that would cause it. In general, traditional deadlock detection/prevention mechanisms (as in [RB88], for example) can be utilized locally within a transaction manager.

The condition is robust. It applies regardless of whether the group is composed solely of individuals, solely of subgroups, or a mixture; it does not depend on whether deadlocking was caused by waits for access to the master copy of an object, or for a copy of a copy, or for a mixture of copied and uncopied objects; and it holds whether the requests in the deadlock are original requests, sub-requests, or triggered requests.

4.3.3 Limiting Sharing

This section illustrates protocols that limit sharing. We show how the user of our model might implement two styles for protocols that restrict sharing – copying and locking. Unlike [NZ90], our system allows these modes to coexist with each other and with notification protocols.

Accomodating Diverse Organizational Styles

Transaction management is often regarded as restricting allowable sequences to provide some sort of guarantee that concurrent operations do not interfere with each other. On the other hand, cooperation often requires freer interaction. Therefore, our model emphasizes the following paradigm: Users are aware that they are sharing objects as members of a group, and expect that effects of operations on objects are immediately visible to other users, unless explicitly prevented by a protocol.

Transaction management hierarchies often mirror organizational units, decomposition of the product, or decomposition of the development process. Often, there will be influences that suggest greater freedom nearer the bottom (smaller groups, smaller or less final products, etc.) As an example, suppose the largest group (e.g., the whole organization) is represented by the top level. Its protocol controls interactions among the major divisions. Presumably these processes require the tightest controls. Successively lower levels representing smaller groups (e.g., two and three member design teams) can assume more knowledge of internal processes and more sharing (e.g., viewing intermediate results). For example, simultaneous editing of a file may constitute conflict across high-level groups, but once edit rights have been granted to a group, it can allow simultaneous edits among its members (who may be aware of each other and may be sharing the editing responsibilities).

The model also can support departure from traditional tight controls in yet another direction – *gradual safety improvements.* In this mode, on top of a system mediated by informal mechanisms and providing no guarantees, one gradually adds controls and notifications to provide greater safety. This gradual approach avoids suddenly imposing tight, uniform, automatically-enforced controls that may hobble the engineering process.

Copying versus Locking

The transaction manager makes the objects accessible and yet restricts requests from other member transactions that may interfere. Protocols accomplish this by ensuring that some *controlled copy* of the object is accessed by the procedures referenced in the transactions. (Notice that we'll refer to these as "copies" but they might be called "versions" to reflect that they may not remain identical and that changes to individual "copies" may require merging.)

As an example, an object may have just one copy, shared by all users and groups in the system (and, therefore, controlled by the root node). This approach is often associated with protocols that use histories to obtain the effect of locking. Alternatively, a protocol may produce copies of objects for its children to share, thus providing "less public" copies whose modifications are not seen by members of the larger group until made available by the user's "checkpointing" those objects. Copies may exist at only *some* lower levels in the hierarchy (e.g., each transaction manager may have access to a different copy, with this copy in turn being made accessible to its group's members). Our model makes it easy to define protocols where different groups use different modes.

The "locking" approach avoids dangerous concurrent operations on the same copy of an object. It queues or rejects requests that conflict with some request that is currently being performed; the blocked request may be scheduled at a later time when it is no longer dangerous. This approach eliminates the need to make multiple copies at the cost of making transactions wait. There are cases in which the waiting (i.e., pessimistic) approach is desirable, particularly where there is no way to merge changes from multiple copies or where very large objects are involved and therefore copying and merging is too costly.

The "copy" approach avoids dangerous concurrent operations on the same object by replicating the state of the object (its representation) for each group member who accesses the object. This approach is optimistic since it allows requests that are logically conflicting to proceed simultaneously on their respective copies. It requires reconciliation of changes to the locally cached copies with the next higher copy, e.g., replace, merge, append, etc., when each group member "checkpoints" the object (or commits) or otherwise indicates that his or her modifications are complete.

The transaction manager hierarchy can correspond to a similar hierarchy of shared object copies. Corresponding to the root node is the "workspace" containing all of the shared objects in the database. Lower level nodes may cache copies of some of those shared objects for sharing among their children. The hierarchy of copies allows objects to be shared at lower and lower levels, as shown in Figure 4.6. In this figure, the rectangles represent workspaces containing copies that are shared among the members of the transaction manager's group, the small dark circles represent objects, and the lines between pairs of objects indicate that the lower object is a copy of the higher one.

The outputs of a request may be new objects, which become part of the workspace of the transaction manager for the group that originates the request, accessible only by that member's siblings (other members of the group). When the originator "checkpoints" the new object (or the transaction commits), the object may become part of the group's parent's workspace, ultimately becoming part of the shared object base as the checkpoint is processed though the transaction manager hierarchy. Checkpointing of new objects should be treated similarly to the handling of copies, except that the contents need not be merged with other representations of the object (copies).

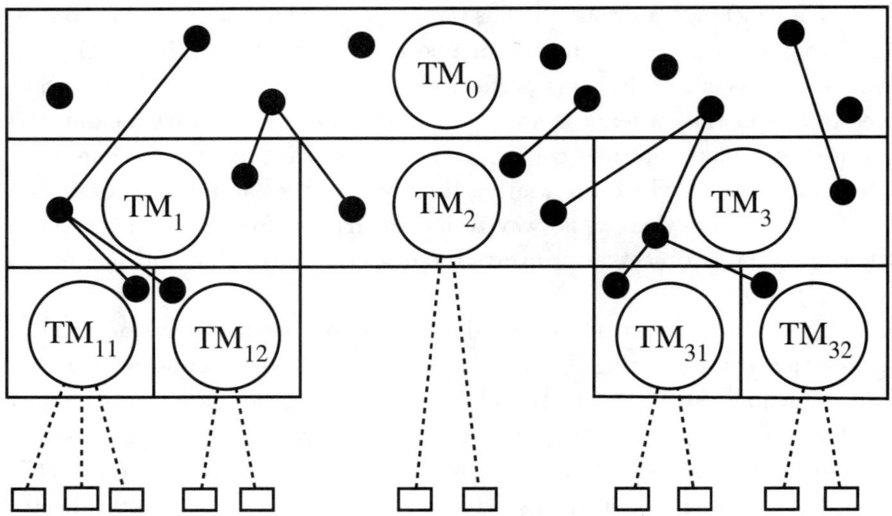

FIGURE 4.6
TMs may create private copies

4.3.4 Triggering Copies and Merges

When a *begin(request)* is processed by a transaction manager, the protocol might indicate that it is safe to begin (i.e., that the request can be accepted) only if the requester (the request's originator or an ancestor of the originator) has its own copy of the argument objects or of the function body. Copying is provided by a type-specific function, which takes an abstract object as input, and creates a new *representation* of that object for its requester. The copy function links the new representation to the abstract object it represents, and also establishes the contents of the representation to match the one that is being copied.

Since the request was triggered in the transaction manager, the requester is not aware that a copy has been made for its exclusive use. However, the resolution procedure will select this copy (rather than the master copy or some higher-level copy) when it resolves the request. Processing at the various nodes may result in the creation of multiple copies (i.e., copies of copies). For example, using the TMH structure in Figure 4.5, a request by T2 to *edit(source_code_x)* might cause the following process:

1. Root's protocol triggers a *copy(source_code_x)* request – makes a new representation of source_code_x for group A by copying root's representation.
2. Group A's protocol triggers a *copy(source_code_x)* request – makes a new representation of source_code_x for group A1 by copying group A's copy.

Resolution of the function and argument objects includes selection of a particular *copy* of the implementation or representation. If transaction managers have triggered the creation of copies, then resolution must select the copy of the "nearest" group of which the requester is a member. For example, resolution of the *edit(source_code_x)* request will select the copy produced for group A1 from above. In contrast, resolution of the *copy(source_code_x)* which is triggered by group A's protocol for its member TA1 will select the copy produced for group A in order to produce the new copy.

CHECKPOINTING

To *checkpoint* an object or a set of objects is to make the effects of a transaction's operations on those objects permanent before they are committed. TMs can provide "checkpoint" functions that guarantee that in the case of the subsequent failure of the transaction, those effects can be recovered (if Recover functions have been provided). A request to checkpoint objects is processed like any other request through the transaction manager hierarchy.

The protocol for a group determines how the group reacts when one of the objects shared by its members is checkpointed. For example, if the protocol has triggered creation of a private copy for the requester, it might trigger an update to its master copy with the updated values of the group's private (locally cached copy), in order to share that value with other groups. Likewise, checkpointing may trigger messages to notify others that the requester has completed modifications or tests, etc. Typically, an *end(checkpoint)* event will cause the removal of private copies (as they are no longer needed) by triggering requests to merge the requester's private representations of objects into the representations shared by higher-level groups. After the merge, the private representations are destroyed. In general, the same transaction manager that triggered *copy* requests will trigger the corresponding *merge* requests.

Like the Copy function, the Merge function is object-type specific (i.e., the semantics of Merge for each type of object can be different), as in [Hardwick]. For example, one type's representations might be merged by appending one representation to the other, whereas for another type one might interleave the contents of two representations.

4.4 Results and Status

We have produced a framework for transaction management systems that helps to support software and other engineering environments. As described in Section 4.1, the approach can lead to important benefits for engineering organizations – promoting increased productivity, fostering improved product quality, and enhancing control and flexibility.

The main contribution of our model is to provide a structure to *modularize* the protocols that govern transaction management, to support group- and application-specific protocols. The framework handles inter-group coordination. We have shown how this structure can accommodate versioning and the concept of copies and merging as part of a scheduling algorithm, and how the versioning methodology can be integrated with the resolution facilities of an object model.

Each protocol can be written in any convenient specification language, e.g., either a programming language or a formal grammar that defines acceptable histories. Different protocols can use different languages. In addition, the group-specific scope of protocols ensures that potential deadlocks can be detected within one group's transaction manager.

We have developed a prototype implementation of the transaction management facilities and inserted them into a simple Ada software engineering environment. This prototype was used to demonstrate the power and flexibility of the model by building a sample group structure with protocols that provide, in some cases, for very conservative sharing policies, and in other cases, for very liberal policies. For example, one group requires exclusive locking of source code objects that are being modified, whereas another allows simultaneous editing of the same source code objects by multiple members of the group.

Our model was designed to be implemented over existing environments. The interface to the Request Handler is narrow, requiring only *begin* and *end* events, plus the use of resolution functions. We do not require that the components be object-oriented, or conform to any particular standard – existing software can easily be encapsulated. In addition, the approach does not require that engineering tools communicate with the transaction manager. Facilities are provided to specify sub-requests that would otherwise be hidden in the code of existing tools and data managers, so the sub-requests can be mediated by transaction management.

These strengths were illustrated in the prototype, which provides the transaction management facilities in a separate layer. Off-the-shelf commercial packages – tools and data repositories of the SEE – were used without modification.

Future Work: Our future work will focus on two areas. First, we will work to characterize "well-behaved" protocols. This will concentrate mainly on extending the characteristics of protocols that allow them to be independent from one another and yet provide the desired global behavior, including lack of node-spanning deadlocks.

Second, we will incorporate more sophisticated protocols into the prototype. The protocols developed as part of the demonstration were extremely simple and reflects only the most basic needs of "real" software development environments. We intend to codify much more complex methodologies and protocols, (as in [CRR91, Kru90]) and to incorporate them in the prototype. This will allow us to determine how difficult it is to specify protocols to meet the requirements of the framework.

Acknowledgements

The authors wish to thank Frank Manola, Matthew Morgenstern, and Ahmed Elmagarmid for their helpful comments and reviews, and Mary Spollen and Claudia Arango for patiently preparing the manuscript. David Goldhirsch and Sy Danberg produced the implementation and demonstration of the prototype system.

Bibliography

[Ban85] Bancilhon, F. et al. A Model of CAD Transactions. *Proceedings of the Eleventh Intl. Conference on Very Large Databases*, Stockholm, Sweden, 1985.

[BHG87] Bernstein, P.A., Hadzilacos, V. and Goodman, N. *Concurrency Control and Recovery in Database Systems*, Addison-Wesley, Reading, MA, 1987.

[CRR91] Chrysanthis, P.K., Raghuram, S., and Ramimritham, K. Extracting Concurrency from Objects: A Methodology. *Proceedings of the ACM-SIGMOD Intl. Conference on Management of Data*, Denver, 1991.

[DEFH87] Dart, S. A., Ellison, R. J., Feiler, P. H. and Huberman, A. N. Software Development Environments, *Computer*, Vol. 20, No. 11, November, 1987.

[DE89] Du, W. and Elmagarmid, A. Quasi serializability: a correctness criterion for global concurrency control in InterBase. *Proceedings of the Fifteenth Intl. Conference on Very Large Databases*, Amsterdam, Netherlands, 1989.

[EIS89] Honeywell, XAIT, TRW. Engineering Information Systems: Organization and Concepts, Vol. 1, Honeywell Systems and Research Center, Minneapolis MN, 1989.

[FZ89] Fernandez, M. and Zdonik, S. Transaction Groups: A Model for Controlling Cooperative Transactions. *Proceedings of the Workshop on Persistent Object Systems*, Springer-Verlag, Newcastle, Australia, 1989.

[FLMW89] Feteke, A., Lynch, N., Merritt, M. and Weihl, W. Commutativity-Based Locking for Nested Transactions. *Proceedings of the Workshop on Persistent Object Systems*, Springer-Verlag, Newcastle, Australia, 1989.

[GS87] Garcia-Molina, H. and Salem, K. Sagas. *Proceedings of the ACM-SIGMOD Intl. Conference on Management of Data*, San Francisco, 1987.

[KH83] Kaiser, G. E. and Hubermann, A. N. An Environment for System Version Control. *Proceedings of the Twenty-sixth IEEE Computer Society Intl. Conference*, San Francisco, CA, 1983.

[KP87] Kaiser, G. E. and Perry D. E. Workspaces and Experimental Databases: Automated Support for Software Maintenance and Evolution. *Proceedings of the Conference on Software Maintenance*, Austin, TX, 1987.

[Kru90] Krueger, C. W. Persistent Long-term Transactions for Software Development. Carnegie Mellon University report CMU-CS-90-188, Pittsburgh, 1990.

[Moh90] Mohan, C. ARIES/KVL: A Key-Value Locking Method for Concurrency Control of Multiaction Transactions Operating on B-Tree Indexes. *Proceedings of the Sixteenth Intl. Conference on Very Large Databases*, Brisbane, Australia, 1990.

[Mos85] Moss, E. Nested transactions: an approach to reliable, distributed computing. MIT Press, Cambridge, MA, 1985.

[NZ90] Nodine, M.H. and Zdonik, S.B. Cooperative transaction hierarchies: a transaction model to support design applications. *Proceedings of the Sixteenth Intl. Conference on Very Large Databases*, Brisbane, Australia, 1990.

[PK91] Perry, D. E. and Kaiser, G. Models of Software Development Environments, *Transactions of Software Engineering*, March 1991.

[RB88] Roesler, M., and Berkhard, W. A. Deadlock Resolution and Semantic Lock Models in Object-Oriented Distributed Systems. *Proceedings of the ACM SIGMOD Conference*, Chicago, IL, 1988.

[Ska90] Skarra, A. A model of concurrency control for cooperating transactions, PhD Thesis, Department of Computer Science, Brown University, 1990.

[Weih89] Weihl, W. Local Atomicity Properties: Modular Concurrency Control for Abstract Data Types, *ACM TOPLAS II*, 1989.

[Weik91] Weikum, G. Principles and realization strategies of multilevel transaction management. *ACM Transactions on Database Systems*, March 1991.

[WPBS88] Winner, R., Pennell, J., Bertram, H., Slusarczuk, M. The role of concurrent engineering in weapons system acquisition. Institute for Defense Analysis, Alexandria, VA, 1988.

5

A Transaction Model for Active Distributed Object Systems

Alejandro Buchmann

M. Tamer Özsu

Mark Hornick

Dimitrios Georgakopoulos

Frank A. Manola

5.1 Introduction

Two recent developments in data management are the emergence of database systems with extended functionality [ABDM89, SRLGCB90], and the integration of multiple, heterogeneous database systems [Lit88, Gup89, SL90]. An even more ambitious goal is the integration of autonomous, heterogeneous database and non-database systems into a distributed computing environment. The DOM (Distributed Object Management) project at GTE Laboratories addresses precisely these issues. The DOM project has as its goal the development of a distributed, object-oriented environment in which new (non-traditional) applications can be developed, and in which autonomous, heterogeneous systems can be integrated [Man88, Man89, MB90, Buc90].

A DOM system (Figure 5.1) consists both of *native* objects that are fully implemented by Distributed Object Management components of the system, and of objects that are wholly or partially implemented in heterogeneous attached systems. These attached systems are not limited to database systems, but may be conventional file systems, hypermedia systems, application programs, etc. Interaction with an attached system is through objects defined in a DOM's Local Application Interface (LAI). Objects from the attached systems have placeholders defined within the DOM object space. These placeholders are used for materialization of external data within DOM, data transfer, the invocation of an application's functionality on external data, and for global concurrency control. The LAI objects, when used for concurrency control purposes, can be treated like any other DOM object. The LAI objects act as guards for accesses that cross a DOM/attached system boundary. If they are defined as *active objects*, they can enforce cross-boundary consistency concepts.

The same data or functionality may be available at more than one node, either in exact duplication or in a form that could be considered equivalent for some purposes. For example, a set of employee records in an employee database might be equivalent to a corresponding set of employee cards in a Hypercard stack, if the relevant information can be derived from both). Similarly, the ability to make a reservation via the attached airline reservation systems of two airlines might be considered equivalent functionality (if the flights involved were equally acceptable).

A DOM system creates an environment in which complete applications can be developed in what appears to be a homogeneous, distributed object system, in which all objects are expressed in a common object model, even

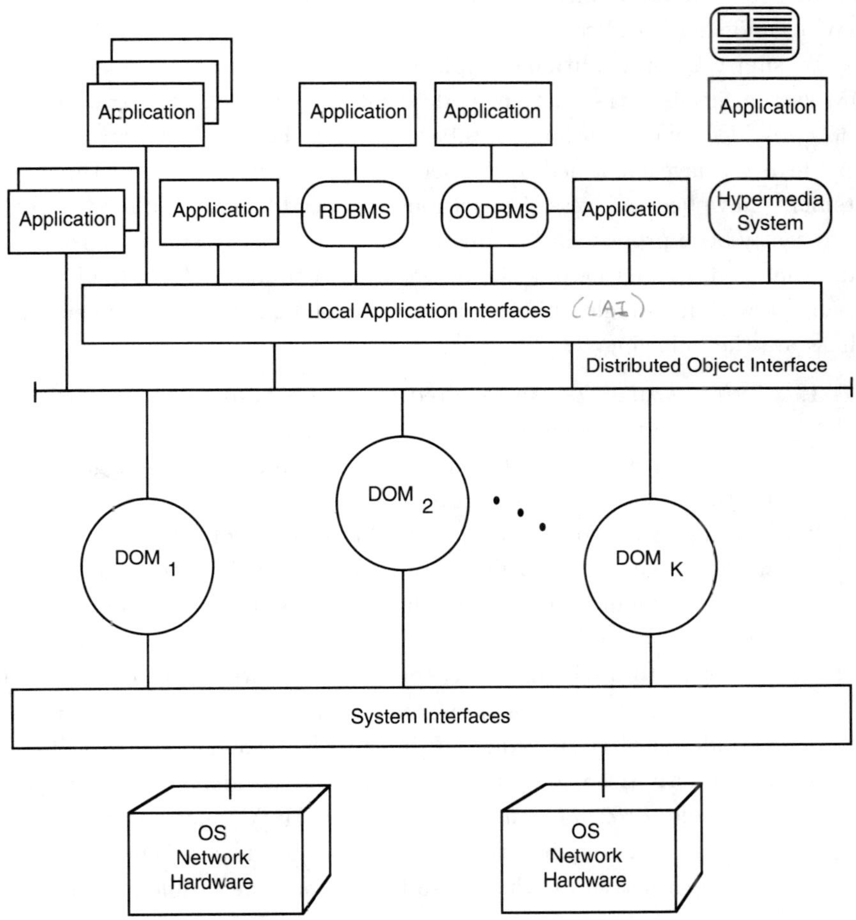

FIGURE 5.1
Schematic representation of a DOM system.

though some of the objects actually represent data and functionality of attached heterogeneous systems. In its role of integrator, DOM ensures that the attached systems retain a high degree of autonomy by maintaining their behavior, and their local control.

To support non-traditional applications in such an environment, the DOM system needs a transaction model that is richer than the transaction models provided by conventional database systems. For the DOM transaction mechanism we have identified a number of requirements. Some of these requirements have been addressed by various advanced transaction models that have recently been proposed. The main contribution of the DOM transaction model that is described here is the integration of solutions to individual requirements within a single uniform transaction model. The requirements we address are the following:

1. *Active capabilities* are required for timely response to events and changes in the environment. This new database paradigm requires the monitoring of events and the execution of system-triggered activities within running transactions.
2. The support of *long-running activities* spanning hours, days or even weeks is part of the DOM objectives. Therefore, the transaction mechanism must support the sharing of partial results. Further, to avoid the failure of a partial task jeopardizing a long activity, it is necessary to distinguish between those activities that are essential for the completion of a transaction and those that are not, and to provide for alternative actions in case the primary activity fails.
3. DOM activities will require interaction with *heterogeneous and autonomous external systems* over which DOM may not exert any control. This requires that the transaction mechanism be able to deal with activities whose results may become visible and permanent (i.e., committed) before the DOM transaction that spawns them commits. It also means that the transaction mechanism must support the execution of compensating actions to undo the effects of committed subtasks.
4. Since DOM is an object-oriented system, the transaction mechanism must be able to deal with *abstract operations*. It may even be possible to improve concurrency by utilizing semantic knowledge about the objects and their abstract operations.

We review briefly a few typical applications which illustrate the need for the capabilities discussed above.

Computer Aided Design (CAD) is an application domain that requires many of the features envisioned by a DOM system. Existing CAD tools have evolved as stand-alone systems. DOM acts as the integrator among the systems, and must provide the necessary mapping mechanisms between the various representations of an application object. DOM also ensures that the consistency among multiple representations is kept. This is best done through the execution of rules [BP85, Kot88] Since CAD databases are slowly populated as parts of the design become available, it is often necessary to delay consistency checks. Further, two or more designers often cooperate in producing a design. Therefore, the system has to allow certain users to see preliminary design data [BKK85, BP85, Kat85]. An integrated CAD system usually provides for the production of bills of materials and project control information. The generation of bills of materials and stock control is a typical database application that requires access to complex objects that consist of many smaller objects, resulting in the implicit nesting of data accesses [RH87]. The project control system, on the other hand, can benefit from triggers or alerters that signal conditions that arise and automatically produce appropriate actions or alerts.

Another example is a bank's stock brokerage system that receives trading information over a wire and updates the database. The same system receives buy and sell orders, which are pegged to stock prices and have expiration dates. One of the critical aspects of such a system is the timeliness with which it can respond to fluctuations in the market. Active databases provide for monitoring of changes in the database and activation of the appropriate buy and sell orders. What to monitor and how to respond can be expressed as rules. The same brokerage system, however, may have to access the customer's bank account to check for availability of funds. In many cases, that information is kept on a different system. This introduces heterogeneity with transactions that may have to be split and executed on different systems.

Most transactions in a banking environment, however, are of short duration. In many business applications in which an agent has to interact with a client and perform operations on the user's behalf this is not the case. Consider a travel agency in which an agent is trying to book a trip for a customer. The travel agent has to set up the trip in the agency's machine but has to access a variety of external systems, such as an airline's or a hotel chain's database. Setting up the trip is a long-running activity which may span from minutes to several days. The external databases accessed by the travel agent, however, do not allow the travel agent to block anything for long time. Instead, they accept a request, process it, and make the effects visible to everybody. If the long transaction at the travel agency must be aborted because the customer decides not to travel, the only way to back out is to execute a compensating transaction that undoes the effects of the completed part of the transaction. In this case, a cancellation will undo the effects of a reservation. In this setting, it is unacceptable to cancel the whole trip just because a subtransaction failed. A travel agent typically deals with contingency plans, i.e., if a flight is not available, an alternate flight is booked. The transaction mechanism has to reflect the typical way of doing business; in the case of the travel agency, by providing for alternative transactions.

To facilitate the development of a transaction model that combines the required features, we organize previous research on transactions according to a working taxonomy presented in Section 5.2. In that section we also show where a transaction model with the features we identified above fits. In Section 5.3, we describe the DOM transaction model, illustrate it with an example, and relate it to the taxonomy. To eliminate ambiguities and to allow reasoning about a transaction model, it is necessary to express it in a formal and unambiguous manner. Therefore, in Section 5.4 we provide a formal specification using a transaction metamodel. Section 5.5 concludes and points out future work.

5.2 A Characterization of Transaction Schemes

The need for more general and powerful transaction models has been recognized for some time and significant work has been done in extending the original transaction concept (e.g., [BBG89, ELLR90, Her90, GS87, Mos85, PKH88, Wei89]). Many of the notions encompassed in these extensions are useful in defining the DOM transaction model, but, at the same time, they have resulted in a wealth of new concepts, some of which overlap, leave gaps, or hide incompatibilities that arise from incomparable criteria. Hence, the combination of existing results into a single transaction model is problematic, making it difficult to determine whether different transaction mechanisms used by attached systems (in a DOM setting) are compatible.

In order to identify the various models that have been proposed, establish their relationships, and highlight which of the functionalities a DOM

Transaction Management System (TMS) has to provide, we have developed a taxonomy of transaction mechanisms. This taxonomy characterizes a transaction mechanism according to its *transaction model*, and its *correctness criterion*. A transaction model, in turn, is characterized by its *transaction structure* (the structure of the individual transactions allowed in the model) and *object structure* (the structure of objects on which the transactions can operate).

Transaction models, in one sense, specify the user interface to the TMS. The user is required to write the transactions according to the model restrictions. In another sense, the transaction model determines the capabilities of the TMS.

The correctness criterion, on the other hand, indicates the notion of correctness that is employed to achieve a certain degree of *concurrency transparency* in the system. Full concurrency transparency means that each user transaction seemingly executes alone in the system, without interference from other transactions. The implication is that the result of concurrent execution of transactions should not compromise database consistency. In this context, the correctness criterion employed by a transaction management system determines the "acceptable" concurrent transaction histories. It is the responsibility of the scheduler to employ the necessary protocols to ensure that the histories are acceptable with respect to the chosen correctness criterion.

The separation of the transaction model and the correctness criterion allows us to identify a large number of alternative transaction management schemes, many of which have not yet been studied. The remainder of this section concentrates on these two aspects in more detail.

5.2.1 Correctness Criteria

The typical correctness criterion that is used in concurrency control is serializability. However, there is a need for less restrictive non-serializable correctness criteria for complex application domains. We briefly review both types of correctness criteria in this section.

Serializability-Based Correctness Criteria

Serializability requires that any history of concurrent execution of a set of transactions be equivalent (in some sense) to a serial execution represented by a serial history. Since (by hypothesis) a serial history does not violate database consistency, any concurrent execution history that is "equivalent" to a serial history (i.e., a *serializable history*) would also maintain database consistency and enforce concurrency transparency.

A first differentiation among serializability-based correctness criteria is introduced by variations in the definition of "equivalence" between histories. Two types of history equivalence that have been proposed are *view equivalence*, leading to *view serializability*, and *conflict equivalence*, leading to *conflict serializability*. Since determining whether a history is view serializable has been shown to be NP-complete [Pap86], for practical reasons we are only concerned with conflict equivalence. Two histories are conflict equivalent if the relative order of conflicting operations is the same in the two histories. A history is said to be *conflict serializable* if it is conflict equivalent to a serial history.

There are a number of serializability-based correctness criteria that basically differ in how they define a *conflict*. We concentrate on three criteria discussed in the literature: *commutativity* [Wei88, Wei89, FLMW89], *invalidation* [Her90], and *recoverability*[1].

Commutativity states that two operations conflict if the results of the serial executions of these operations are not equivalent. Consider the simple operations **Read** and **Write**. If nothing is known about the abstract semantics of the read and write operations or the object x that they operate on, it has to be accepted that a **Read** on x following a **Write** on x does not retrieve the same value as it would prior to the **Write**. Therefore, a **Write** operation always conflicts with other **Read** or **Write** operations. The conflict tables for **Read** and **Write** operations are, in fact, derived from the commutativity relationship between these two operations. Since this type of commutativity relies only on syntactic information about operations (i.e., that they are **Read** and **Write**), we call this *syntactic commutativity*.

If the semantics of the operations are taken into account, however, it may be possible to provide a more relaxed definition of conflict. Specifically, some concurrent executions of **Write-Write** and **Read-Write** may be considered non-conflicting. Consider, for example, a set object and three operations defined on it: **Insert** and **Delete**, which correspond to a **Write**, and **Member**, which tests for membership and corresponds to a **Read**. Due to the semantics of of these operations, two **Insert** operations would commute, allowing them to be executed concurrently. The commutativity of **Insert** with **Member** and the commutativity of **Delete** with **Member** depends upon whether or not they reference the same argument and their results[2]. *Semantic commu-*

[1]Recoverability as used in [BR87] is different from the notion of recoverability found in [BHG87, Had88, BR87]

[2]Depending upon the operation, the result may either be a flag that indicates whether the

tativity (e.g., [Wei88, Wei89]) makes use of the semantics of operations and their termination conditions. It is also possible to define commutativity with reference to the database state. In this case, it is usually possible to permit more operations to commute. For example, we indicated that an **Insert** and a **Member** would commute if they do not refer to the same argument. However, if the set already contains the referred element, then these two operations would commute even if their arguments are the same.

Invalidation [Her90] defines a conflict between two operations not on the basis of whether they commute or not, but according to whether the execution of one invalidates the other or not. An operation p invalidates another operation q if there are two histories H_1 and H_2 such that $H_1 \bullet p \bullet H_2$ and $H_1 \bullet H_2 \bullet q$ are legal, but $H_1 \bullet p \bullet H_2 \bullet q$ is not. In this context, a legal history represents a correct history for the set object and is determined according to its semantics. Accordingly, an *invalidated-by* relation is defined consisting of all operation pairs (p, q) such that p invalidates q. The invalidated-by relation establishes the conflict relation that forms the basis of establishing serializability. Considering the same example as above, an **Insert** cannot be invalidated by any other operation, but a **Delete** can be invalidated by an Insert if their arguments are the same.

Recoverability [BR87] is another conflict relation that has been defined to determine serializable histories. Intuitively, an operation p is said to be *recoverable with respect to* operation q if the value returned by p is independent of whether q executed before p or not. The conflict relation established on the basis of recoverability seems to be identical to that established by invalidation. However, this observation is based on a few examples and there is no formal proof of this equivalence. As we indicate in Section 5.5, the relationship of these criteria has to be established more precisely.

Non-Serializable Correctness Criteria

Serializability requires that the execution of each transaction must appear to every other transaction as a single atomic step. This requirement may be unnecessarily strong for many applications. The semantic information about transactions and the objects that they operate on can be used to weaken serializability and achieve a higher level of concurrency.

There have been a number of proposals along these lines. All depend upon establishing how transactions can interfere with each other between

---

operation was successful (for example, the result of **Insert** may be "OK") or the value that the operation returns (as in the case of a **Read**).

steps, which may consist of a single operation or a collection of operations. In [Gar83] transactions are grouped into disjoint classes such that the transactions that belong to the same class are *compatible* and can interleave arbitrarily, whereas transactions that belong to different classes are *incompatible* and cannot interleave at all. Early use of the concept of transaction classes can be found in SDD-1 [BSR80].

The concept of compatibility is refined in [Lyn83] and several levels of compatibility among transactions are defined. These levels are structured hierarchically so that interleavings at higher levels include those at lower levels. Furthermore, [Lyn83] introduces the concept of *breakpoints* within transactions which represent points at which other transactions can interleave. This is an alternative to the use of compatibility sets.

Another work along these lines is [FÖ89] which uses breakpoints to indicate the interleaving points, but does not require that the interleavings be hierarchical. A transaction is modeled as consisting of a number of steps. Each step consists of a sequence of atomic operations and a breakpoint at the end of these operations. For each breakpoint in a transaction the set of transaction types that are allowed to interleave at that breakpoint is specified. A correctness criterion called *relative consistency* is defined based on the correct interleavings among transactions. Intuitively, a relatively consistent history is equivalent to a history that is stepwise serial (i.e., the operations and breakpoint of each step appear without interleaving), and in which a step (T_{ik}) of transaction T_i interleaves two consecutive steps (T_{jm} and T_{jm+1}) of transaction T_j only if transactions of T_i's type are allowed to interleave T_{jm} at its breakpoint. It can be shown that [FÖ89] some of the relatively consistent histories are not serializable, but are still "correct."

Another class of non-serializable correctness criteria has been defined in the context of multidatabase systems. In these systems there are two classes of transactions: *local* transactions are accepted directly by the individual, autonomous component DBMSs, and *global* transactions access multiple databases. This requires a two-level transaction mechanism. Each individual DBMS manages its local transactions together with the *subtransactions* of global transactions that are submitted to it, and the multidatabase software maintains the correctness of the global transactions. There has been some suggestion that the serializability theory may be inappropriate for multidatabase transactions since it does not differentiate between global and local transactions, thereby restricting the set of acceptable histories. Consequently, *quasi-serializability* [DE89] and *multidatabase serializability* [BÖ90] have been proposed as non-serializable correctness criteria for multidatabase environments. Both of these are equivalent and, in effect, require that all of the local histories be serializable and the global history be conflict-equivalent to a serial one. It has been shown that the set of quasi-serializable (or multidatabase serializable) histories is a superset of conflict-serializable histories.

The notion of serializability and other correctness criteria have proven useful to describe the behavior of transactions. However, they encapsulate a variety of behaviors and only allow us to state whether a transaction system does guarantee a certain behavior as a package, i.e., the schedules produced by a system are either serializable or not. In many situations it is useful to look "under the covers" and distinguish the various aspects that influence the behavior of a transaction system[3]. Such an attempt is the characterization of transactions by the so-called ACID properties, which stand for *atomicity*, *consistency*, *isolation*, and *durability* [HR83]. A similar categorization, using as the four basic dimensions *visibility*, *failure atomicity*, *permanence*, and *consistency* is used in [CR90] as the basis of the ACTA transaction metamodel. We use that metamodel to describe our transaction model in Section 5.4, where we also summarize the metamodel.

Most of the correctness criteria that have been proposed as alternatives to serializability relax the isolation or visibility restrictions. This results in side-effects on failure atomicity. In heterogeneous and autonomous systems, we submit, the notion of consistency will also have to be revised to consider such issues as the locality of consistency (i.e., for which (sub)systems consistency must be enforced), the level of consistency supported by the (sub)systems, and the timeliness of enforcement. However, we do not address those issues here.

5.2.2 Transaction Models

As we discussed in Section 5.1, the requirements of new application domains demand richer transaction models. These richer transaction models have to be connected to some correctness criterion to derive a concurrency control algorithm. Furthermore, transaction management design decisions have to be made to develop full-fledged transaction management sys-

[3]An analogy between the relational calculus and the relational algebra may illustrate this. Although the calculus is powerful as an abstract notation, it must be mapped into algebraic expressions as the basis for actual operation. In the same way, an operational specification of a transaction mechanism's behavior in terms of the properties that actually can be relaxed is more practical than a closed correctness criterion when deriving new correctness notions and when integrating existing systems.

tems. These design decisions are related to systems issues such as distributed versus centralized control, optimistic versus pessimistic concurrency control schemes, update scheme (deferred/immediate, in-place/private copy), the recovery methods, etc. In this section we do not address all these issues, but restrict our discussion to the model aspects.

There have been many advanced transaction model proposals in the literature, which we classify along two dimensions: the transaction structure and the structure of objects that they operate on. A few representative alternatives are depicted in Figure 5.2. We discuss the basic ideas behind those approaches and the classification in the remainder of this section. As noted earlier, not all of the possible alternatives have been studied. Most of the existing work has been concentrated on models located close to one of the two axes. The requirements for DOM indicate a need for a transaction model that resides at the upper right hand corner.

Object Structure

Along the object structure dimension, we identify *simple objects* (e.g., files, pages, records), objects as instances of *abstract data types* (ADTs), *complex objects*, and *active objects* in increasing complexity.

Current transaction management systems operate on simple objects, mostly on physical pages. There have been suggestions for providing concurrency at the record level, but the overhead involved is high. The characterizing feature of this class is that the operations on simple objects do not take into account the semantics of the objects. For example, an update of a page is considered a write on the page, without considering what logical object is stored on the page.

Abstract data types are programming language constructs that encapsulate the representations of a set of objects and a set of operations on these objects. The operations are the only means of accessing and manipulating the objects. From the perspective of transaction processing, ADTs introduce a need to deal with abstract operations. The operations of transactions that execute on ADTs are not simple reads and writes, but are more abstract, such as **Insert**, **Delete**, and **Member** for a set object. The execution of transactions on ADTs require a multi-level mechanism [BSW88, Wei91]. In such systems, individual transactions represent the highest level of abstraction. The abstract operations constitute a lower level of abstraction and are further decomposed into simple reads and writes at the lowest level. The correctness criterion, whatever it is, has to be applied to each level individually. In addition, abstract operations lend themselves nicely to the incorporation of

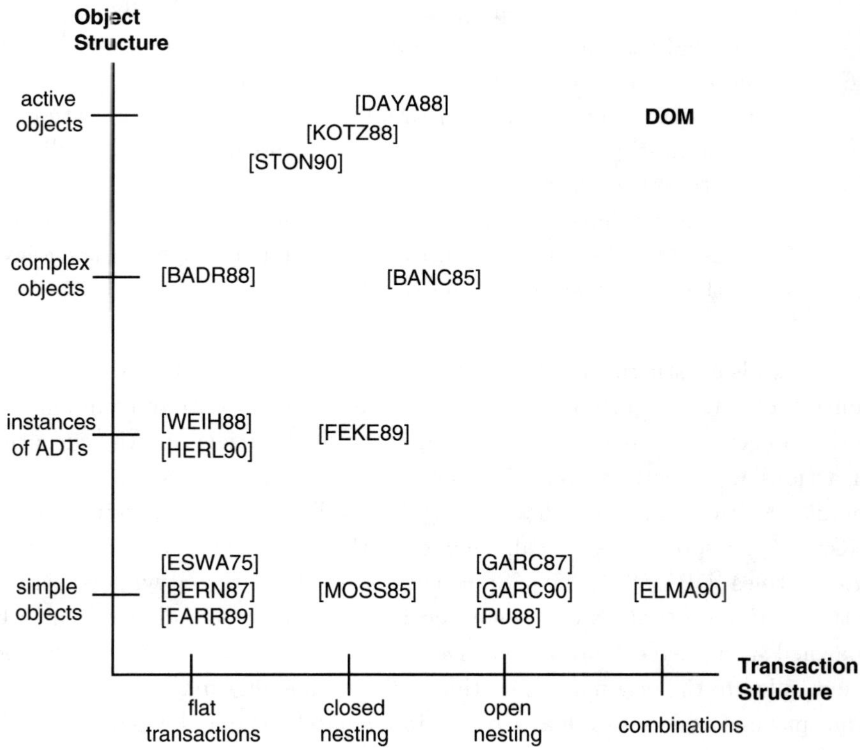

FIGURE 5.2
Representation of transaction model space and examples. The labels for the references are given following each citation in the Bibliography.

their semantics into the definition of the correctness criterion, as we discussed above.

We make the distinction between objects as instances of abstract data types and complex objects to note that the latter have a complex structure (i.e., contain other objects) and their types participate in an inheritance lattice[4]. These are objects as found in object-oriented systems. They need to be treated separately due to of a number of considerations:

1. Running a transaction against one object may actually spawn additional transactions on component objects. This forces an *implicit nesting* [BR88] on the transaction itself (as opposed to explicit nesting that we discuss below). More importantly, the operations in these nestings are themselves abstract and need to be handled as multilevel transactions.
2. Inheritance involves sharing of state and/or behavior among objects. Therefore, the semantics of accessing an object at some level in the lattice has to account for this.

We also distinguish between *passive* and *active* objects. Although the concept of active objects is just emerging, all proposals have in common that active objects are capable of responding to events by triggering the execution of actions when certain conditions are satisfied. The events that are to be monitored, the conditions that have to be fulfilled, and the actions that are executed in response are typically defined in the form of event-condition-action (ECA) rules [DBM88, Kot88]. Since events may be detected while executing a transaction on that object, the execution of the corresponding rule may be spawned as a nested transaction. Depending on the manner in which rules are coupled to the original transaction, different nestings may occur [HLM88]. The spawned transaction may execute immediately, it may be deferred to the end of the transaction, or it may execute in a separate transaction. Since additional rules may fire within a rule execution, nestings of arbitrary depth are possible.

Transaction Structure

[4]Strictly speaking, abstract data types can have complex structures. However, the transaction work on abstract data types has consistently assumed a "simple" ADT structure. Our reference to "objects as instances of ADTs" should be understood within this context and with this qualification.

Along the transaction structure dimension, we distinguish *flat transactions*, *closed nested transactions* as in [Mos85], and *open nested transactions* such as sagas [GS87], and *combinations* of these forms, in increasing order of complexity.

Flat transactions [EGLT76] are those that have a single start point (**Begin_transaction**) and a single termination point (**End_transaction**). Most of the transaction management work in databases has concentrated on flat transactions that operate on simple objects and use serializability as their correctness criterion. [BHG87] is an excellent discussion of this work. [HW88, Her90, Wei88, Wei89] involve flat transaction models operating on ADTs and [BR87, BR88] deal with flat transactions on complex objects. All of these use serializability-based correctness criteria, but differ in the way they define the conflict relation. On the other hand, [Gar83, Lyn83, FÖ89] discuss the application of flat transactions to simple objects using non-serializable correctness criteria. All represent studies that go along the vertical axis in Figure 5.2.

A nested transaction includes other transactions with their own beginning and termination points. In this taxonomy, we differentiate between *closed* and *open* nesting because of their termination characteristics. Closed nested transactions [Mos85] commit in a bottom-up fashion through the root. The semantics of these transactions enforce atomicity at the top-most level. Significant work has been done in establishing the concurrency control aspects of closed nested transactions which use a serializable correctness criterion [BBG89]. Closed nesting for ADTs was reported in [FLMW89]. A variant of closed nesting with the possibility of making partial results selectively available to other transactions that are tightly structured into a transaction type hierarchy of transactions is discussed in [BKK85]. Closed nesting derived from the firing of rules occurs in active database systems. Representative approaches are [HLM88, Kot88, SJGP90]. They appear staggered in Figure 5.2, because Postgres [SJGP90] provides only for immediate evaluation of a single rule. The triggering transaction is halted until the triggered transaction completes execution. This is a very primitive type of nesting that has the behavior of a flat transaction. The most general approach is that taken by HiPAC [HLM88], which allows for arbitrarily deep nesting with immediate evaluation, evaluation at the end of the triggering transaction, or as a separate transaction, thus providing a form of execution outside the closed nesting. In all cases, serializability is the underlying correctness criterion.

Open nesting relaxes the top-level atomicity restriction of closed nested transactions. Therefore, an open nested transaction allows its partial results to be observed outside the transaction. Sagas [GS87, GGKKS90] and split transactions [PKH88] are examples of open nesting.

Finally, we identify those transaction models that incorporate both open and closed nesting [ELLR90, NZ90]. The model proposed in [ELLR90] allows for combination of compensatable and non-compensatable transactions on simple objects in a multidatabase environment. It also includes the notion of alternative transactions, and factors time into its correctness criterion. DOM's transaction model [MB90, BHMC90] is a model that combines closed and open nesting with contingency transactions and executes on complex and active objects. In the remainder we describe it in more detail.

5.3
The DOM Transaction Model

The DOM transaction model consists of building blocks from which more complex transactions can be constructed. Depending on the requirements of the applications, the transaction model can behave as a conventional flat transaction model, it can behave like a transaction model that allows for closed nesting and the execution of triggered processes, or it can be used in its most powerful and flexible form by defining combinations of closed and open nestings.

In this chapter we address the behavior of the DOM transaction model as it applies to a homogeneous, distributed object space. The local application interface (LAI) objects which act as gateways to the attached systems are part of this homogeneous object space, and the transaction model with all its features applies to them. However, we do not address in this chapter the coordination with external systems, other than by issuing subtransactions in an open nested fashion. This is an aspect that requires further research.

In DOM, we call the closed nested transactions *toptransactions*. Flat transactions are a degenerate case of toptransactions. A toptransaction is any transaction that makes its results visible to the entire system when it commits. Toptransactions can be combined into *multitransactions* that have some global transaction semantics but permit partial results to be visible outside the multitransaction. The component transactions of a multitransaction may be either *vital* or *non-vital* [GGKKS90]. If a vital transaction aborts, its parent must abort.

These basic building blocks can be used further to define specialized subtransactions. As soon as the visibility rules are relaxed and partial results become visible before the multitransaction commits, it becomes necessary to define *compensating transactions*. Compensating transactions are the logical equivalent of a rollback in a multitransaction and are defined to undo already committed partial results. *Contingency transactions* are transactions that are executed if the primary transaction fails. They provide alternatives that may be equivalent but potentially of lesser quality or less desirable.

5.3.1 Example of a DOM Transaction

With the basic building blocks introduced, we examine an example before describing in more detail the components of the DOM transaction model and their semantics. The example is presented using a graphical notation meant for interactive construction and visualization of complex transactions. We will be using a variation of the travel reservation example [ELLR90], which is rapidly becoming the example of choice.

Figure 5.3 shows a DOM transaction designed to access an internal database as well as various external databases. It shows a trip plan that is set up as a multitransaction (denoted by a rectangle) and has as its first action a component transaction for opening a new account and defining the itinerary. This initial toptransaction (marked by a rounded rectangle) triggers the rules for preferences the customer might have, as well as his credit card information. The preferences are retrieved as triggered subtransactions (marked as ovals) of the first toptransaction.

Next, two toptransactions are shown, to get a flight on United as the first option, and to get an equivalent flight on American, as the second option. Consider the transaction that makes a reservation on a United flight. It automatically triggers the rule for the frequent flyer information as a nested subtransaction. Because a flight reservation becomes visible once the toptransaction commits it requires a compensating transaction to cancel the reservation in case the multitransaction aborts. If the reservation on United fails, a contingency transaction is invoked to attempt a reservation on American. It is only invoked if the primary option fails. If the contingency transaction also fails, the multitransaction should abort, since the flight-reservation is a vital transaction (marked by the double outline). Notice that the transaction to rent a car is not vital, since one might always use a taxi instead. It is only executed in case the first choice fails. Precedence dependencies may be specified between components of a multitransaction. For example, the flight reservation should always precede the car and hotel reservations.

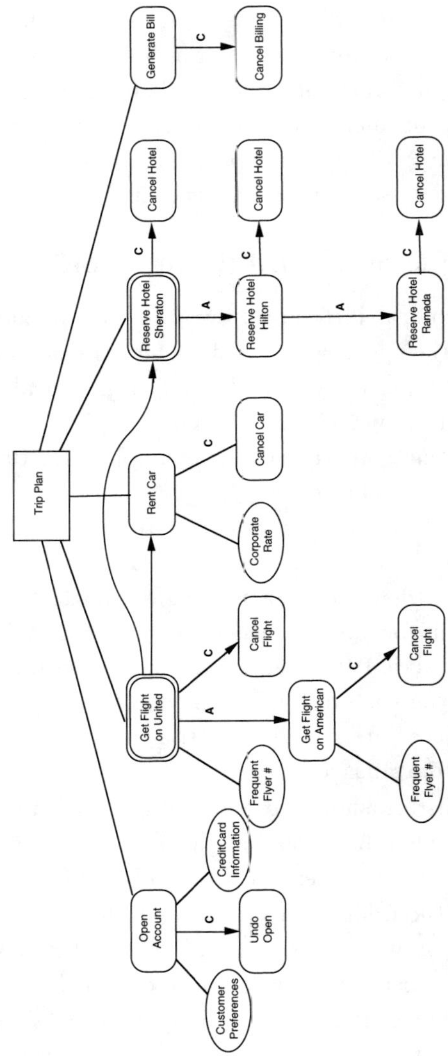

FIGURE 5.3
Transaction visualization.

5.3.2 Multitransactions

Multitransactions are defined for long-running activities and access to external databases over which the DOM cannot exert full control. Multitransactions have the abort and commit properties of a transaction, but different visibility rules. Transactions within a multitransaction are allowed to commit individually, and to make their results visible outside the scope of the multitransaction. The transactions within a multitransaction are either other multitransactions or nested toptransactions. Any toptransaction in a multitransaction must have a compensating transaction defined for it. In our example, the **Trip Plan** is a multitransaction with five toptransactions (**Open Account**, **Get Flight**, **Rent Car**, **Reserve Hotel**, and **Generate Bill**).

When a multitransaction aborts, it causes all its component transactions to abort. If a component transaction has already committed, a compensating transaction is invoked. Conversely, if a component transaction aborts, the multitransaction must abort if the component transaction is vital, or it may continue execution if the component transaction is not vital. This is explained in Section 5.3.6.

Transactions within a DOM multitransaction are assumed to be executable in parallel, unless specified otherwise through a precedence constraint (for example, between **Get Flight** and **Reserve Car**). Precedence constraints are viewed as a user-level mechanism for specifying sequential behavior.

Precedence constraints can have different meanings. The first interpretation is that the subsequent cannot start execution before the precedent commits (begin precedence used in sagas). Another possible interpretation is that the subsequent cannot commit until the precedent commits (commit precedence used in HiPAC's causally dependent transactions).

Both interpretations can be expressed through rules if the rule mechanism provides for event composition. To express the serial, non-parallelizable case the triggering event for the second transaction has to contain the commit of the precedent.

If the flow of execution is specified without the help of rules and no strict begin dependencies have to be enforced, then commit precedence will provide the same effect as begin precedence. In the case where transactions ordered by a precedence constraint perform no accesses to common data, they are indistinguishable. In case of common data accesses, commit dependence will delay the subsequent's commit and abort/reexecute it if there is a conflict over data with the precedent. Given the distributed, heterogeneous nature of a full-fledged DOM it is possible that individual component transactions of a multitransaction may be delayed for considerable time. An approach that calls for sequential execution of component transactions could result in unnecessary delays. Therefore we opted for commit precedence as the default with begin precedence specifiable through rules.

5.3.3 Nested Transactions

A toptransaction is the root of a tree of closed nested transactions through which the whole tree commits. If no confusion is possible within a context, we refer to the whole nested transaction tree by the name of the corresponding toptransaction. Nested transactions can be defined either explicitly by the user, or they can result from the firing of rules while executing another transaction (for example, the firing of rules specifying customer preferences and credit information while executing **Open Account**). The structure of a nested transaction that results from the firing of a rule within another transaction depends on the *coupling mode* defined for the rule. The valid coupling modes are *immediate*, *deferred*, *detached*, or *causally dependent detached* [HLM88, CBBCD89].

Immediate and *deferred* rule execution results in a nested transaction. In the case of immediate coupling, the subtransaction is executed at the point of the spawning transaction where the event was detected. Deferred coupling causes execution of the subtransaction at the end of the transaction but prior to commit.

Detached execution of the condition and/or action part of a rule results in another transaction that is parallelizable without any commit dependencies.

Causally dependent detached execution results in a parallelizable subtransaction (called CDTop in [CBBCD89]) with a commit dependency on the spawning transaction. CDTop transactions are serialized like independent transactions that can see only the latest committed state of the database, i.e., they cannot see changes made by the spawning transaction. If they can proceed in their evaluation in parallel with the spawning transaction, that is an optimization. If they acquire locks later required by the spawning transaction, the CDTop transaction is always the victim and the visibility semantics are preserved.

5.3.4 Compensating Transactions

Each toptransaction within a multitransaction has a compensating transaction defined for it, e.g. **Cancel Car** is the compensating transaction for

Rent Car. A compensating transaction is a transaction with the opposite effect of an already committed transaction. It is intended to undo the visible effects of a previously committed transaction. Open nesting should be used only if it is possible to define an appropriate compensating transaction for each toptransaction in a multitransaction.

When a multitransaction must be aborted, the currently active transactions within the multitransaction are aborted, while the committed transactions are compensated. Compensation order is the inverse of the commit order[5]. There exists a begin dependency between a toptransaction and its compensating transaction. This begin dependency is comparable to the strict precedence constraint discussed above. A compensating transaction may never start unless the transaction that has to be compensated has previously committed.

Rules complicate the definition of compensating transactions. In the DOM model, rules are "attached" to objects. Therefore, any transaction may fire an arbitrary number of rules. Since the user is not aware of all the rules that might have fired, we define compensation in a system with rules strictly as the semantic inverse of the user-specified transaction. If any rules were triggered by the initial action, for example, constraint or security rules, the proper rules will also fire when executing the compensating transaction. We part from the assumption that in a correctly designed objectspace each rule that modifies the state of the objectspace also has a compensation defined for it[6].

5.3.5 Contingency Transactions

Transactions within DOM can also have contingency transactions associated with them. In our example, **Reserve Hotel Hilton** is the contingency transaction for **Reserve Hotel Sheraton**. A contingency transaction is invoked upon the occurrence of some failure condition and before commit of the transaction for which it is an alternative. It is intended to accomplish a similar

[5]We have to investigate conditions under which it is safe to relax the requirement of having compensation in reverse commit order, i.e. to compensate in some other order.

[6]There exists a strong relationship between the rule- and the execution models. If rules are introduced and new couplings between the user-submitted transactions and system-triggered tasks are introduced, the execution model has to be extended to account for it, as demonstrated by HiPAC. Similarly, if the execution model is extended to account for new processing strategies, such as externally visible subtransactions and compensation, then the rule system has to be extended to accommodate the added flexibility of the transaction model.

goal as the original transaction, as opposed to the compensating transaction which is intended to undo a committed (sub)transaction. The DOM transaction model makes a clear distinction between compensating transactions and contingency transactions. While compensating transactions can be viewed as a special case of contingency transactions, their semantics are sufficiently different to warrant their distinction in the model. One of the main differences is that contingency transactions may abort like any other transaction. Failure of a compensating transaction requires special exception handling, the default being human intervention.

The notion of failure condition is difficult to define. It could range from the abort of a transaction to its termination but without accomplishing its intended task. For example, a reservation transaction may execute correctly but it cannot book a seat because none is available, or even more subtly, because none is available in the desired class or fare-category. Therefore, each transaction that defines a contingency transaction must also define its failure condition(s), and the contingency transaction has to include the definition of the proper triggering event.

Two possible ways of modeling the notion of "contingency plans" as transactions are possible. A simple structure requires just one contingency transaction for a toptransaction. If the toptransaction fails, the contingency transaction is invoked, which may in turn have its own contingency transaction.

In the more general case, a transaction can have multiple contingency transactions associated with it. The order in which the contingency transactions are executed is determined by the definition of the triggering events. For example, a transaction could have one contingency transaction defined for the case that a resource is not available (if Sheraton has no rooms make a reservation with Hyatt), and another in case the deadline for execution is missed.

It is left to the user to model contingency transactions in the manner most natural to the user or the application's semantics. A contingency transaction always takes the place of the failed transaction in any transaction structure and inherits its properties, such as being vital.

5.3.6 Vital and Non-vital Transactions

Transactions that are specified as component transactions of another transaction may be either *vital* or *non-vital*. This distinction was first introduced in [GGKKS90]. A vital transaction must be executed successfully (i.e.

it has to commit) for its parent transaction to commit. A non-vital transaction may abort without preventing the parent transaction from committing. In the example, **Get Flight** and **Reserve Hotel** are vital, while **Rent Car** is not.

5.4 Formal Specification of the Model

To eliminate ambiguities, to allow analysis and further reasoning about our transaction model, and to facilitate its comparison with other models, it is necessary to express the model in a formal manner. In this section, we define the operational semantics of the DOM transaction model, using the ACTA transaction metamodel. We present first in Section 5.4.1 a brief summary of the formalism, but refer to [CR90] for detail. The specification of our transaction model is then presented in four parts: the specification of the semantics of multitransactions and their component transactions (open nesting) in Section 5.4.2, the nested structure of the component transactions (closed nesting) in Section 5.4.3, the semantics of contingency transactions in Section 5.4.4, and compensating transactions in Section 5.4.5. For each part of the specification, we present the formal notation followed by a brief textual explanation of the formalism.

5.4.1 Summary of the ACTA Formalism

The ACTA framework is a notation for formal specification and analysis of transaction models. The basic concepts of this framework are:

- A transaction model is characterized by the interactions of objects and transactions. Each object has a state and a status. The state represents an object's value; the status contains concurrency control information.

- Each transaction T has a *view set* (denoted as $ViewSet_T$) which is the set of objects potentially visible to it, and an *access set* (denoted as $AccessSet_T$), which is the set of all objects accessed by a transaction. No distinction is made in the access set between read and write accesses.

- Transactions may relinquish objects that belong to their access set via *delegation*. A transaction may delegate the state or the status of objects in its access set. In delegation of state, partial results become visible to other transactions. In delegation of status, the modifications of the delegator are undone before the objects are added to the access set of the delegate.

- Transactions interact with each other through *commit* and *abort dependencies*:

  Commit dependencies: If $A \rightsquigarrow B$ (A develops a commit dependency on B) then transaction A cannot commit until transaction B either commits or aborts.

  Abort dependencies: If $A \rightarrow B$ (A develops an abort dependency on B) and transaction B aborts, then transaction A also must abort.

  Abort/compensation dependencies: If $A \Rightarrow B$ (A develops an abort or compensation dependency on B) and transaction B aborts, then transaction A must abort or be compensated. For the sake of clarity we make the distinction between abort and abort/compensation dependencies, although this is not part of the original ACTA model[7].
  The above dependencies can be restricted by making them exclusive (e.g., $\xrightarrow{x}$) meaning that the dependency can only be established with one transaction, thus representing a hierarchical structure of dependencies, or they may be transitive (e.g., $\xrightarrow{*}$) meaning that the dependency, in this case an abort dependency, is on the transitive closure of that particular type of dependency starting at A.

- The *compatibility table* of an object specifies the dependencies formed by the interactions of an object's operations and encodes its synchronization properties. An (O_i, O_j) entry may be a condition involving completion dependencies, operation arguments and results. Example entries might be wait, abort, notify, form_x_dependency, etc.

5.4.2 Multitransactions

The following specifications formally describe the semantics of multitransactions.

[7] We later introduce another extension, exclusion dependencies, which are needed for modeling contingency transactions.

Commit Dependencies for Multitransactions:

$$M \leadsto T$$

This means that the multitransaction M has a commit dependency on all its active component transactions T. An active component transaction has neither committed nor aborted. This specification applies between two levels in the transaction structure, but can be applied recursively in the case of nested multitransactions. Among the possible contingency transactions for any given component transaction, only the first for which the triggering condition is true will be executed. Contingency transactions are not active unless the primary transaction failed.

Abort Dependencies for Multitransactions:

$$\forall T \in V \quad M \xrightarrow{x} T$$

This means that the multitransaction M aborts if any of the vital component transactions aborts.

$$\forall T \in (V \cup NV) \quad T \Rightarrow M$$

This abort/compensation dependency means that all vital and non-vital transactions of a multitransaction M are aborted or compensated if M aborts. The dependencies of the compensating transactions are specified below. Note that independent transactions are not affected. The exclusive property reflects the fact that each component transaction can only belong to one multitransaction M.

Compensation is understood as in sagas. If M aborts while executing T_i then the compensation order is $C_{i-1}, \ldots, C_1$. Given the more general notion of commit dependencies in DOM versus begin dependencies in sagas, the compensation order is also specified as the inverse of the commit order.

A transaction T may be nested. If the nesting is due to user definition, it is the user's responsibility to define the compensating transaction such that the nesting is considered. If the nesting is due to rule firing and the fired rules are compensatable, then the system will fire the corresponding compensation rules.

Visibility Rules for Multitransactions:

$$\forall T \in M \quad ViewSet_T = DB$$

This means that the view set for each component transaction of a multitransaction M is the whole database.

5.4.3 Nested Transactions

Each component transaction of a multitransaction M can itself be a multitransaction or a nested toptransaction. Nested multi-transactions are defined recursively as above. Nested toptransactions are defined below.

Commit Dependencies for Nested Toptransactions:

$$\forall C \quad T \leadsto C$$

This means that T (the top level of a nested transaction) cannot commit until all its children C commit or abort. The set of transactions C is composed of all transactions that are coupled via an immediate or deferred coupling mode.

$$\forall CDTop \quad CDTop \leadsto T$$

This means that the causally dependent transactions that were spawned by a transaction T cannot commit until T commits or aborts (this case is restricted further through the abort dependency specified below to ensure that T commits before any $CDTop$ can commit).

Abort Dependencies:

$$\forall C \xrightarrow{x} T$$

This means that all the children C (i.e., immediately and deferred-coupled subtransactions) should be aborted if the parent transaction T aborts.

$$\forall CDTop \xrightarrow{x} T$$

This means that all causally dependent top transactions should abort if the parent (or spawning) transaction aborts. It also specifies that each $CDTop$ transaction depends exclusively on one spawning transaction.

Visibility Rules:

The visibility rules are expressed via the $ViewSet$:

$$\forall C \quad ViewSet_C = \{\cup AccessSet_P \mid C \overset{*}{\rightarrow} P\} \cup DB$$

where $\cup$ is an ordered union that has the effect that a child transaction gets to see the latest version accessible to its parent rather than the original version. This is the classic rule of visibility in nested transactions. The children can view the partial results of their ancestors, the partial results of their committed siblings, plus any results from committed detached transactions.

Delegation Specification:

The delegation specification for the nested subtransactions is:

$$\forall C \quad DelegateSet_{state}(C, P) = AccessSet_C$$

The delegation specification states that, at commit, the child transaction's objects are delegated to the parent transaction. This delegation makes the effects of committing child transactions selectively visible to the parent and the parent's other descendants.

5.4.4 Contingency Transactions

Commit Dependencies for Contingency Transactions:

The commit dependency between a transaction and its contingency transaction K is one of exclusion. We introduce the notion of an *exclusion dependency*:

DEFINITION

A transaction B has an exclusion dependency *on A, $A \not\hookrightarrow B$, if B may not commit in the case that A has already committed.*

For all transactions T in DOM for which a contingency transaction is specified the commit dependencies are:

$$\forall T \not\hookrightarrow K$$

If T and K execute in a common environment, i.e. under the control of the same transaction manager so that K can be aborted at any time, a commit dependency is enough. If K executes under the control of a separate transaction manager, for example in an external repository, then the dependency has to be a begin dependency.

The commit dependency between K and its multitransaction is the same as for any other transaction.

Abort Dependencies for Contingency Transactions:

There are no abort dependencies between the original transaction T and its contingency transaction K. The abort dependencies between the transaction K and the multitransaction it executes in are the same as between any member transaction.

Visibility Rules for Contingency Transaction:

The view set of a contingency transaction is exactly the same as that of the transaction it replaces.

Delegation for Contingency Transactions:

No delegation occurs between a transaction and its contingency transaction[8].

5.4.5 Compensating Transactions

The semantics of the compensating transactions is defined by the following specifications.

Commit Dependencies for Compensating Transactions:

Compensating transactions cannot begin executing unless the transaction they are compensating has committed. This is a strictly serial begin dependency.

Compensating transactions also have an exclusion dependency on the multitransaction of which the transaction to be compensated is a part.

$$\forall CT \quad M \not\rightsquigarrow CT$$

This means that a compensating transaction CT cannot execute if the multitransaction committed.

[8] In case we want to change this specification, it would have to be a delegation of status, namely, the passing of objects from T's access set to K's access set after undoing all changes to the transferred objects, given that we consider that T failed.

Abort Dependencies for Compensating Transactions:

$$\forall T \in M \quad CT \Rightarrow T$$

This means that any compensating transaction has meaning only if T, the transaction that is to be compensated, commits. If T aborts, then CT is never enabled.

Visibility Rules for Contingency Transaction:

The view set of a contingency transaction is the latest committed state of the database.

Delegation for Contingency Transactions:

No delegation occurs among a compensating transaction and other transactions.

5.5 Conclusions and Future Work

We described the transaction model for the DOM system. DOM is a distributed active object system that promotes interoperability among heterogeneous systems, and provides object management support for complex applications. Because of the variety and complexity of the applications DOM intends to support, the transaction model needs to be powerful. We illustrated this by means of a few examples in Section 5.1. The relative power of our transaction model vis a vis other models can easily be seen from the taxonomy we present in Section 5.2. The development of this framework, even though preliminary, is an additional contribution of this chapter.

The main points of the DOM transaction model are:

- It is a complete, distributed, object-oriented transaction model that combines in a single model the capability of handling open nesting, closed nesting, both explicitly and as a result of handling active objects, and contingency transactions.

- It is tailorable and can provide as much flexibility as is required by the applications.

- It can use the LAI objects as concurrency control placeholders for external repositories.

There are many issues of the DOM transaction model that require further investigation. Some of the more important are:

- Even though we formulated our model in terms of the ACTA formalization, a correctness theory for it is yet to be developed. The execution semantics of the transactions certainly points to a non-serializable correctness criterion, but the formalization has not yet been attempted.

- Our transaction model has yet to deal with many of the recovery ramifications. This is closely related to the determination of the correctness criterion, as pointed out by [Wei88, Wei89]. We are currently examining architectural issues, such as update policy, to determine their impact on the whole transaction system.

- We have, so far, not relaxed the notion of consistency beyond what results from relaxed visibility constraints among transactions. For the full heterogeneous system, new notions of consistency must be defined. Relaxations along the lines of locality or timeliness of consistency enforcement must be formalized.

- Transactions in the DOM model are first-class objects. We started expressing the transaction model in terms of the ECA rules that are an integral part of the DOM object model. If successful, we expect to have a system that uses the same rule mechanism to enforce consistency and transaction execution.

- Temporal dependencies among transactions are not currently captured by the DOM transaction model. In order to satisfy such dependencies, new correctness criteria and mechanisms for enforcing them have to be developed.

In addition to the DOM transaction model per se, there are a number of issues that need to be worked out. The first issue is to determine whether the framework of our taxonomy is complete and minimal. In our view, an equally important issue concerns the correctness criteria classification, especially the relationship between the various serializability-based definitions. Each of the proposals claim to provide "more concurrency" than some other criterion. However, there is no formal and comparable definition of "level of concurrency." It is not clear how to incorporate the ultimate measure of performance, throughput, into these formal models. Furthermore, our initial attempt to establish a "containment" relationship between conflict relations has not proven successful. Such a containment relationship is necessary to be able to assert the compatibility of schedules based on different conflict relationships. Conflicting results exist. On the one hand, the set of serializable schedules obtained using recoverability and invalidation under certain conditions seem to be equivalent. On the other hand, invalidation (as in [Her90]) and semantic commutativity (as in [Wei89]) appear to be incomparable. This contradicts the claims in [BR88] that all commutative schedules as defined in [Wei89] are recoverable. The available results suggest a lattice of correctness criteria rather than a linear containment.

Acknowledgments

Special thanks are due to Evangelos Markatos and Catherine Chronaki who worked on the first implementation. We would like to acknowledge the interaction with members of the DOM project, Michael Brodie, Vivek Virmani, and Dinesh Desai, and helpful comments from Umeshwar Dayal, Panos Chrysanthis, Krithi Ramamritham, and Renato Barrera. Prasad Sistla contributed valuable insight and comments.

Bibliography

[ABDM89] M. Atkinson, F. Bancilhon, D.J. DeWitt, K. Dittrich, D. Maier, and S. Zdonik. The Object Oriented Database System Manifesto. In *Proceedings of 1st International Conference on Deductive and Object-oriented Databases*, pages 40–57, 1989.

[BR87] B.R. Badrinath and K. Ramamritham. Semantics-Based Concurrency Control: Beyond Commutativity. In *Proceedings of 3rd International Conference on Data Engineering*, pages 304–311, 1987.

[BR88] B.R. Badrinath and K. Ramamritham. Synchronizing Transactions On Objects. *IEEE Transactions on Computers*, 37(5): 541–547, May 1988.

[BKK85] F. Bancilhon, W. Kim, H. Korth. A Model of CAD Transactions. In *Proceedings of the 11th International Conference on Very Large Databases*, pages 25–33, 1985.

[BÖ90] K. Barker and M.T. Özsu. Concurrent Transaction Execution in Multidatabase Systems. In *Proceedings of COMPSAC'90*, pages 282–288, 1990.

[BBG89] C. Beeri, P.A. Bernstein, and N. Goodman. A Model for Concurrency in Nested Transaction Systems. *Journal of ACM*, 36(2): 230–269, April 1989.

[BSW88] C. Beeri, H.J. Schek, and G. Weikum. Multi-Level Transaction Management, Theoretical Art or Practical Need? In J.W. Schmidt, S. Ceri, and M. Missikoff, editors, *Advances in Database Technology – EDBT '88*, Springer-Verlag, pages 134–154, 1988.

[BSR80] P.A. Bernstein, D.W. Shipman, and J.B. Rothnie. Concurrency Control in a System for Distributed Databases (SDD-1). *ACM Transactions on Database Systems*, 5(1): 18–51, March 1980.

[BHG87] P.A. Bernstein, V. Hadzilacos, and N. Goodman. *Concurrency Control and Recovery in Database Systems*. Addison-Wesley, Reading, Massachusetts, 1987.

[BP85] A.P. Buchmann and C. Perez de Celis. An Architecture and Data Model for CAD Databases. In *Proceedings of the 11th International Conference on Very Large Databases*, pages 105–114, 1985.

[BD88] A.P. Buchmann and U. Dayal. Constraint and Exception Handling for Design, Reliability and Maintainability. In *Proceedings of the ASME Computers in Engineering Conference, Managing Engineering Data: Emerging Issues*, pages 95–100, 1988.

[BHMC90] A.P. Buchmann, M. Hornick, E. Markatos, C. Chronaki. Specification of a Transaction System for a Distributed, Active Object System. In *Proceedings of the Workshop on Transactions for Object Oriented Systems held in conjuntion with OOPSLA '90*, Ottawa, Canada, Oct. 1990.

[Buc90] A. Buchmann. Modeling Heterogeneous Systems as a Space of Active Objects. In *Proceedings of the 4th International Workshop on Persistent Object Systems*, pages 279–290, 1990.

[CBBCD89] S. Chakravarthy, B. Blaustein, A. Buchmann, M. Carey, U. Dayal, D. Goldhirsch, M. Hsu, R. Jauhari, R. Ladin, M. Livny,

D. McCarthy, R. Mckee, and A. Rosenthal. HiPAC: A Research Project in Active, Time-Constrained Database Management. Final Technical Report, Xerox Advanced Information Technology, July 1989.

[CR90] P.K. Chrysanthis and K. Ramamritham. ACTA: A Framework for Specifying and Reasoning About Transaction Structure and Behavior. In *Proceedings of ACM SIGMOD International Conference on Management of Data*, pages 194–203, 1990.

[DBM88] U. Dayal, A. Buchmann, and D. McCarthy. Rules Are Objects Too: A Knowledge Model For An Active Object-Oriented Database System. In *Proceedings of the 2nd International Workshop on Object Oriented Database Systems*, pages 129–143, 1988.

[DE89] W. Du and A. Elmagarmid. Quasi-Serializability: A Correctness Criterion For Global Concurrency Control in InterBase. In *Proceedings of the 15th International Conference on Very Large Data Bases*, pages 347–355, 1989.

[ELLR90] A. Elmagarmid, Y. Leu, W. Litwin, and M. Rusinkiewicz. A Multidatabase Transaction Model for InterBase. In *Proceedings of the 16th International Conference on Very Large Data Bases*, pages 507–518, 1990.

[EGLT76] K.P. Eswaran, J.N. Gray, R.A. Lorie, and I.L. Traiger. The Notions of Consistency and Predicate Locks in a Database System. *Communications of ACM*, 19(11): 624–633, November 1976.

[FÖ89] A.A. Farrag and M.T. Özsu. Using Semantic Knowledge of Transactions to Increase Concurrency. *ACM Transactions on Database Systems*, 14(4): 503–525, December 1989.

[FLMW89] A. Fekete, N. Lynch, M. Merritt, and W. Weihl. Commutativity-Based Locking for Nested Transactions. Technical Report MIT/LCS/TM-370.b, Massachusetts Institute of Technology, Laboratory for Computer Science, July 1989.

[Gar83] H. Garcia-Molina. Using Semantic Knowledge for Transaction Processing in a Distributed Database. *ACM Transactions on Database Systems*, 8(2): 186–213, June 1983.

[GS87] H. Garcia-Molina and K. Salem. Sagas. In *Proceedings ACM SIGMOD International Conference on Management of Data*, pages 249–259, 1987.

[GGKKS90] H. Garcia-Molina, D. Gawlick, J. Klein, K. Kleissner, and K. Salem. Coordinating Multi-Transaction Activities. Technical Report CS-TR-247-90, Princeton University, Department of Computer Science, February 1990.

[Gup89] A. Gupta, editor. *Integration of Information Systems: Bridging Heterogeneous Databases*. IEEE Press, 1989.

[Had88] V. Hadzilacos. A Theory of Reliability in Database systems. *Journal of ACM*, 35(1): 121–145. January 1988.

[HR83] T. Härder and A. Reuter. Principles of Transaction-Oriented Database Recovery. *ACM Computing Surveys*, 15(4): 287–317, December 1983.

[HW88] M. Herlihy and W. Weihl. Hybrid Concurrency Control for Abstract Data Types. In *Proceedings of the 7th ACM SIGACT-SIGMOD Symposium on Principles of Database Systems*, pages 201–210, 1988.

[Her90] M. Herlihy. Apologizing Versus Asking Permission: Optimistic Concurrency Control for Abstract Data Types. *ACM Transactions Database Systems*, 15(1): 96–124, March 1990.

[HLM88] M. Hsu, R. Ladin, and D. McCarthy. An Execution Model for Active Database Management Systems. In *Proceedings of the 3rd International Conference on Data and Knowledge Bases*, pages 171–179, 1988.

[Kat85] R. Katz. *Information Management for Engineering Design Applications*. Springer Verlag, 1985.

[Kot88] A.M. Kotz, K.R. Dittrich, and J.A. Mulle. Supporting Semantic Rules by a Generalized Event/Trigger Mechanism. In J.W. Schmidt, S. Ceri, and M. Missikoff, editors, *Advances in Database Technology – EDBT '88*, Springer-Verlag, pages 76–91, 1988.

[Lit88] W. Litwin. From Database Systems to Multidatabase Systems: Why and How. In *Proceedings of the British National Conference on Databases (BNCOD 6)*, pages 161–188, 1988.

[Lyn83] N. Lynch. Multilevel Atomicity: A New Correctness Criterion for Database Concurrency Control. *ACM Transactions on Database Systems*, 8(4): 484–502, December 1983.

[Man88] F. Manola. Distributed Object Management Technology. Technical Memorandum TM-0014-06-88-165, GTE Laboratories Incorporated, June 1988.

[Man89] F. Manola. Object Model Capabilities for Distributed Object Management. Technical Memorandum TM-0149-06-89-165, GTE Laboratories Incorporated, June 1989.

[MB90] F. Manola and A. Buchmann. A Functional/Relational Object-Oriented Model for Distributed Object Management, Preliminary Description. Technical Memorandum TM-0331-11-90-165, GTE Laboratories Incorporated, December 1990.

[Mos85] E. Moss. *Nested Transactions*. MIT Press, Cambridge, Massachusetts, 1985.

[NZ90] M. Nodine and S. Zdonik. Cooperative Transaction Hierarchies: A Transaction Model to Support Design Applications. In *Proceedings of the 16th International Conference on Very Large Data Bases*, pages 83–94, 1990.

[Pap86] C.H. Papadimitriou. *The Theory of Concurrency Control*. Computer Science Press, 1986.

[PKH88] C. Pu, G. Kaiser, and N. Hutchinson. Split-Transactions for Open-Ended Activities. In *Proceedings of the 14th International Conference on Very Large Databases*, pages 26–37, 1988.

[RH87] A. Rosenthal, and S. Heiler. Querying Part Hierarchies, A Knowledge-Based Approach. In *Proceedings of the 23rd ACM/IEEE Design Automation Conference*, 1987.

[SL90] A. Sheth and J.L. Larson. Federated Databases: Architectures and Integration. *ACM Computing Surveys*, 22(3): 183–236, September 1990.

[SRLGCB90] M. Stonebraker, L.A. Rowe, B. Lindsay, J. Gray, M. Carey, M. Brodie, P.A. Bernstein, and D. Beech. Third Generation Database Systems Manifesto. *SIGMOD Record*, 19(3): 31–44, September 1990.

[SJGP90] M. Stonebraker, A. Jhingran, J. Goh, and S. Potamianos. On Rules, Procedures, Caching and Views in Data Base Systems. In *Proceedings of the ACM SIGMOD International Conference on Management of Data*, pages 281–290, 1990.

[Wei88] W. Weihl. Commutativity-Based Concurrency Control for Abstract Data Types. *IEEE Transactions on Computers*, 37(12): 1488–1505, December 1988.

[Wei89] W. Weihl. Local Atomicity Properties: Modular Concurrency Control for Abstract Data Types. *ACM Transactions on Programming Languages and Systems*, 11(2): 249–281, April 1989.

[Wei91] G. Weikum. Principles and Realization Strategies of Multilevel Transaction Management. *ACM Transactions on Database Systems*, 16(1): 132–180, March 1991.

[WF90] J. Widom and S. Finkelstein. Set-Oriented Production Rules in Relational Database Systems. In *Proceedings of the ACM SIGMOD International Conference on Management of Data*, pages 259–270, 1990.

6

A Transaction Model for an Open Publication Environment

Peter Muth

Thomas C. Rakow

Wolfgang Klas

Erich J. Neuhold

6.1 Overview

Producing publications is a complex process consisting of many different tasks and involving a variety of specialist contributors. A publication process includes authoring, editing, composition and ends with the distribution of the publication. In the past, the publication process allowed only a limited cooperation between the participants, and only a small number of revision cycles were feasible.

Today increasingly sophisticated tools result in a new level of requirements. The publication process must be faster, the quality improved, and new media provide for innovative forms of presentation and distribution. As an answer to these requirements we propose an open, distributed publication environment, used by the different specialist contributors, e.g. authors, editors, layout designers, typesetters, jointly producing and distributing a publication.

We distinguish three different kinds of components in such an environment: assistants, agents, and tools. Assistants provide users with a homogeneous access to local tools, such as text editors or information systems. In addition, they support user cooperation. Agents offer direct access to non-local tools, originally available only to the assistants of other users. In order to support transaction properties for the user's applications, we propose a transaction model with the following characteristics: reduced conflict rate between user operations by the use of semantic information for conflict definition, easy integration of existing tools and guaranty of ACID properties by assistants and agents if tools supporting ACID transactions are accessed.

6.2 Introduction

In conventional publishing, the tasks in a publication process were performed separately and lacked cooperation support. Revisions caused considerable delays, and therefore only a limited number of revision cycles were acceptable. The final product was distributed on paper.

To satisfy the growing need for rapid and encompassing information and to reduce the cost of producing this sometimes short-lived information it is evident that the publication process has to be optimized. In order to ensure the quality of such publications, a large amount of information sources have to be explored, and the relevant information has to be filtered. In order to reach as many people as possible, new media have to be used for distribution.

As a first step towards these goals, the wide availability of desktop publishing systems may have suggested that new ways and processes for publishing will replace the traditional complex multi-person publishing activities. However, it turned out that in most cases an author is not capable of maintaining the quality of a publication ensured by the different specialists in traditional publishing. Now multi-media document types which include sound, voice and video require even broader expertise, e.g., sound engineers, script writers, cutters. In addition, in the authoring phase cooperation between authors and co-authors is needed to achieve high quality of contents. As a consequence, supporting the traditional publishing process electronically by an open distributed publication system now is a major research and development topic.

The Publication Environment

At GMD-IPSI, we investigate an open distributed publication environment for multi-media products. It has to support a multi-user publishing process, where individuals or groups play specialist roles, but want to cooperate and use the system concurrently. To have confidence in such a system, they all require durability for the results of their effort. Powerful versioning and undo-facilities are also needed, if different versions and variants of documents are to be explored or changes are subject to discussion and possibly rejection. Database systems play a crucial role within such an environment. However, it turns out that conventional database systems cannot provide sufficient functionality to support the needs of applications in the publication field:

- The publication environment consists of many different components. New components may be added at any point of time. Users of the system do not only need an integrated system interface, but a homogeneous system behavior. They may not know which components are activated by their operations, how these components behave, and where they are located in a computer network.
- The various users need to utilize existing information sources – databases, knowledge bases, even active system components.
- Publication activities consist of many subactivities, some of them taking place during a short time span, others for a longer period. Some of them are quite independent from each other, others are heavily dependent on each other.

- User cooperation needs to be supported by the system, where synchronous and asynchronous tasks performed by the different users and system components may occur.

A publication environment meeting the above requirements is currently under development at GMD-IPSI. Our research activities focus on developing an individualizable scientific newspaper: *is-News.* This electronic newspaper contains multi-media information and is embedded in an environment supporting all publication activities. The architecture of our publication environment is defined by three basic types of components: assistants, agents and tools. Each user of the publication environment owns a personalized assistant. The assistant reflects the user's knowledge about his specific role in the publication process. The user's tasks are performed by accessing specific tools, e.g., writing, drawing or layout tools. If the user's knowledge is not sufficient to perform a task, and/or his assistant does not provide access to corresponding tools, the user will need to get the knowledge and tool access through other users. Two strategies exist: Contact the assistant of another user, or purchase an agent from the other user. In the first case, the task is performed by the assistant of the other user which in turn may involve his human "master". In the second case, the purchased agent is used as an independent system component. The agent offers the desired functionality for the task without further communication with the assistant of the other user and its "master". The agent remains available to perform similar tasks in the future.

The Concept of Open Nested Transactions

User operations in the publication environment are relatively long and typically require interaction. In order to maintain consistency for concurrent operations of different users, some concurrency control scheme is required. From the user's point of view, the goal of concurrency control is to minimize waits on objects that are concurrently accessed by other users. The concurrency control will be little appreciated if a wait is not caused by possible consistency violations on the users view, but is due to conflicts below the user's level of abstraction, e.g. at the level of complex operations on document structures, or simply on indexes in a database. Concurrency control performs well if only the semantics at the user level determine the necessity to wait. For example, consider two users who concurrently create different versions of the same document. There is no need for them to wait on each other. Even though, conventional concurrency control schemes would block one transaction if at some point a single page is written by one transaction and read or written by another.

The most commonly used correctness criterion for concurrent transaction execution is serializability. Conventional concurrency control schemes ensure serializability on the page level and thereby cause many delays due to page conflicts, especially for long duration transactions. One solution to this problem is to use a different correctness criterion. For example, it is possible to explicitly define valid interleaving sequences for concurrent operations. We propose another solution: ensuring serializability at the user's level of abstraction, not at the page level. This requires the conflict definition to be made with respect to the semantics of operations. Waits will be caused by conflicts based on the application semantics, and will occur less frequently. For a considerable amount of applications, the reduced conflict rate will make serializability a preferable solution. An additional benefit of serializability is that most protocols guarantee recoverability (e.g. strict two phase locking). Non-serializable execution may cause transaction abort to be impossible. In general, this will not be acceptable in the publication environment.

The concept of open nested transactions fits well with the concurrency control requirements for the publication environment. Open nested transactions constitute hierarchies of subtransactions on different levels of abstraction and commutativity relations define conflicts between operations [BBG89, FLMW88, Lyn83, RGN90, Wei86, Wei91]. This kind of conflict definition reduces the number of conflicts to those of semantic relevance. On each level of abstraction, conflicts of lower levels that were only caused by the lack of semantic knowledge are filtered out. Serializability is achieved without the drawback of conventional approaches, i.e., long transaction delays due to pseudo-conflicts that are caused by the implementation of the system, not by the application.

The enhanced concurrency however requires a more complex recovery scheme. Undo of transactions can no longer be managed by simply restoring before-images of objects. This is due to the fact that before-images do not reflect the changes of parallel updates on the same object. Instead of restoring before-images, a compensating operation has to be executed for each change that is to be undone. Similar to normal operations, compensating operations will call subtransactions on lower levels of abstraction.

The Use of Open Nested Transactions in the Publication Environment

Besides the above requirements caused by the typical usage of the publication environment, the publication system architecture also imposes some additional properties:

- Transaction execution may be distributed, since the publication environment typically will involve several nodes in a computer network.
- Even if some tools have their own, non-changeable transaction management, a consistent transaction behavior of global user transactions is required.
- The system should support global transactions with atomicity, consistency, isolation, and durability (ACID) properties [HR83] if the involved tools provide them. In case they do not, that behavior will have to be reflected in the integrated system only where these tools are involved.

In our open nested model, transactions on different levels of abstraction can be managed relatively independent of each other. The independent management allows the integration of existing tools which provide their own transaction management. It is used to maintain serializability and recoverability on the lowest level of abstraction. If ACID properties are provided on this level, they can be maintained up to the user level.

The proposed transaction model for the is-News publication environment has been developed for the object oriented database system *VODAK* [KNS89, KNS90, KN90]. *VODAK* provides a powerful open data model and uses open nested transactions [MKN90, MR91, MRKN91, Rak91, RMWHB91, RGN90, WHBM90]. This chapter is an extended version of [MRKN91].

Related Work

For the support of non-standard database applications, many other groups investigate advanced transaction models. Multi-level transactions, a special case of open nested transactions, have been implemented in DASDBS [HW91, SPSW90, Wei86, Wei91], are used in a model based on O2 [CF90], by [Mar88], and in an approach for office automation systems [Wal85]. In contrast to open nested transactions, closed nested transactions increase the degree of concurrency for subtransactions that belong to the same father transaction [Mos85]. [RW91] proposes the ConTracts model, which uses petri-net like synchronization mechanisms for intra-transaction parallelism (as suggested in

[ELLR90] also) and persistency for every, even an 'intermediate' transaction state. Sagas [AGS87] provide a transaction model for heterogeneous systems, but global serializability is not guaranteed. Recovery schemes for systems that use type-specific locking are discussed in [NKKN87]. [DE89] introduces a new correctness criterion called quasi-serializability for transactions in heterogeneous database systems by relaxing the serializability definition. This approach illustrates the problems of integrating unchangeable existing transaction managers in presence of local autonomy. A concurrency control algorithm for cooperative editing, discarding serializability, is presented in [EG89].

The paper is organized as follows. After introducing the architecture of the publication environment in section 6.3 we describe the requirements of transaction management in our publication environment. Section 6.4 discusses concurrency control and recovery for open nested transactions. The execution of open nested transactions in the publication environment and requirements caused by distribution and Heterogeneity are described in section 6.5. Section 6.6 concludes the paper.

6.3 The Architecture of the Publication Environment and its Transaction Needs

In this section, we first describe the general architecture that forms the basis for our publication environment. Typically, tasks in the environment will take place at different locations on different nodes of a computer network. Such a large and complex environment cannot be defined as a closed system. Instead, we propose an open architecture, i.e., a system that consists of independently developed modules. This approach allows us to extend the system dynamically with new modules, and replace old ones by modules with richer and improved functionality. In the second part, we discuss the requirements resulting from such an environment with respect to the transaction model.

6.3.1 Architecture

In order to support a high degree of flexibility, we define three major system components: assistants, agents, and tools. At first, we describe the overall architecture at the level of these system components and illustrate the usage of assistants, agents, and tools by a sample scenario. Then we go into more details of the components' structure and describe the communication between them.

Assistants

Assistants are system modules that interactively support users in their fields of expertise by providing integrated access to *tools* such as text editors, information bases, video production environments, etc. Assistants are components which behave like an expert system and which are tailored to the specific needs of a user's task. Each user has his own assistant. If a user's task needs services from tools which are not directly accessible by his assistant, an assistant of another user which has access to these tools can be consulted. This assistant may again consult other assistants for subtasks of the subtask, etc. For some tasks, no appropriate service might be found or exist in the system. In this case, the assistant detecting this lack of functionality will ask its owner for help.

Agents

Because assistants are directly assigned to users, these users may not want their assistant to be consulted frequently by other assistants. Instead, a user may create and offer independent components to perform tasks normally done by him and his assistant. We call such components *agents*. Depending on the functionality offered (and price charged) such agents can access a subset of the tools available to the corresponding assistant. That is, the services provided by an agent are a subset of the services of the assistant, but are independent of the assistant and of interaction with the owner of the assistant. Foreign assistants have to be consulted only if no corresponding agent is available or the available agent is not able to perform the requested task.

In general, assistants will reside on different nodes of a computer network. Agents which were purchased by a user for a specific task will typically reside on the same site as the user's assistant. Hence, consulting an agent instead of the corresponding assistant also saves in communication costs.

Tools

As mentioned previously, tools are used by assistants and agents to perform a user's task. Both, assistants and agents, coordinate and control the execution of the operations offered by these tools as needed to get the desired results. A tool can be used by several assistants and agents. Tools constitute the elementary layer in our architecture. They perform specific tasks like text editing, spell checking, page layout, information retrieval, storing and maintaining information. Most tools existed before integrated publication environments were designed. Those tools have to be incorporated even though they have not been designed for an integrated use. New tools are integrated into the publication environment by extending the functionality of existing assistants. Corresponding extensions in the agent modules offer the facilities of the new tools directly to other assistants.

A Sample Scenario

Figure 6.1 shows an author who uses the publication environment for writing a document. The author's assistant provides an appropriate environment, but during writing, the author may need some additional information about some topic. Let us assume that these facts are stored in an information base which has been integrated into the publication environment, and the

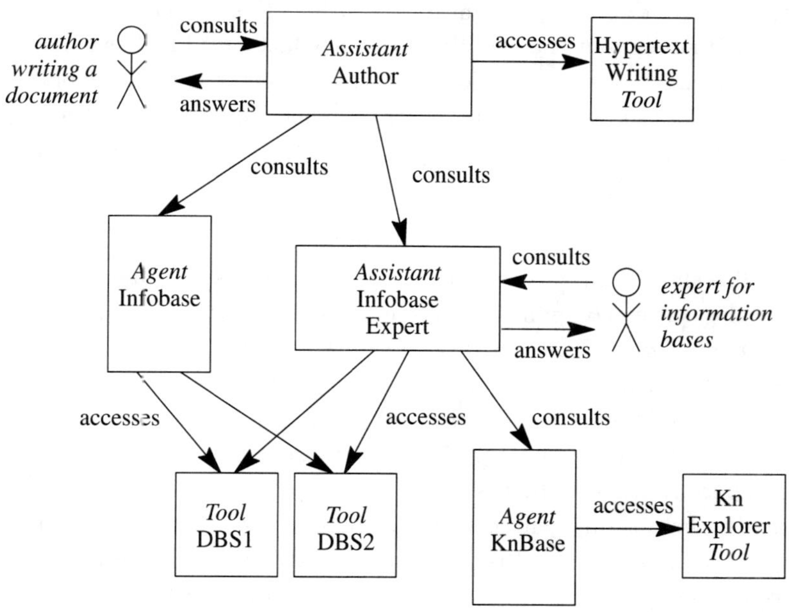

FIGURE 6.1
A Sample Scenario for an Author's Request.

user owns an agent with access to this information base. The assistant will call the agent to execute the appropriate query, i.e., retrieve the additional facts. If the execution succeeds, the author will get the required facts and may continue writing his document. If not, the user's assistant will consult the assistant of the information base expert, who originally offered that agent. The failure of the agent may have been caused by a mismatch between concept names in the query and in the schema specification of the information base. Let us assume that the assistant of the information base expert has access to an agent which knows about the schema of the information base. This agent can use a *Knowledge Explorer* [KN89] to resolve the mismatches. The agent will then be able to transform the query which will in turn be executed by the assistant of the information base expert. The result of the query will be sent to the assistant of the author. If all this fails, the assistant of the information base expert may contact the human information base expert for help.

After the author receives the required facts, he may derive a new document version in order to incorporate those facts. After that, he may check another document which discusses the same topic. During this probably long period of time, the author doesn't want his co-authors to see his changes, e.g., because he is not sure about the validity of the new facts until he has checked the other documents. But he also doesn't want to hinder his co-authors in doing their work on the document, i.e., deriving their own versions, deleting old, obsolete versions, running spelling checkers on their changes, or printing a consistent version of the complete document.

Structure of Assistants and Agents

Figure 6.2 shows the general structure of assistants and agents, and outlines how the system components communicate with each other. Each assistant consists of a *task manager* and several *task experts*. The task manager coordinates the task experts which perform the specific tasks assigned to an assistant. The user is able to tune the task experts provided by his assistant, i.e., the task experts of an assistant reflect (parts of) the user's expert knowledge in performing specific tasks.

Internally, there is one generic interface between the task manager and the task experts of an assistant. Task experts of an assistant can communicate with each other via the task manager. The communications between the user and his assistant, between assistants, and between assistants and tools are based on the following interfaces:

- A user communicates with his assistant via a user-customized interface to the task manager which includes the interfaces provided

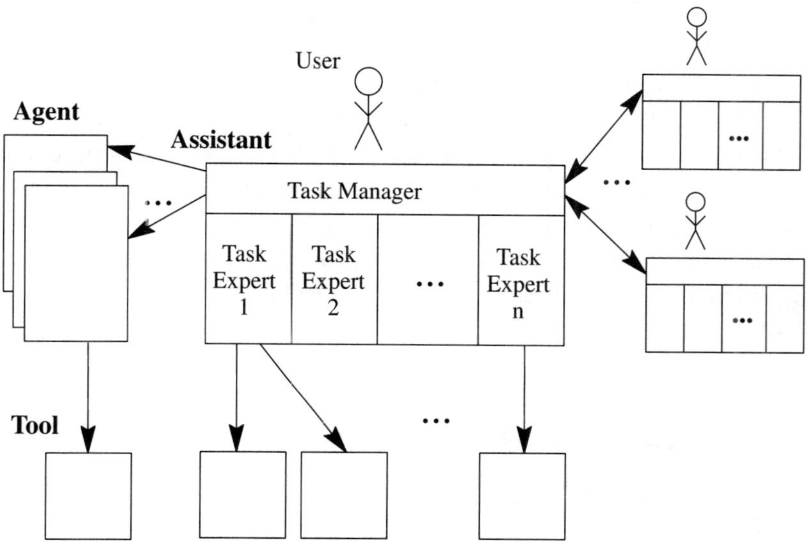

FIGURE 6.2
System Components Assistant, Agent, and Tool.

by the individual task experts. The set of operations constituting this interface contains task dependent operations, but they have a homogenized interface to the user.

- An assistant communicates with other assistants through their task managers. The interface between task managers is of a generic type, i.e., the set of operations of this interface is defined for all task managers and is independent of any specific task. The communication between assistants may cross the network as assistants may be located at different nodes.
- The communication between task experts and tools is based on different interface types. That is, the operations constituting the interfaces between task experts and tools depend on the specific tasks and tools. (In a way these operations reflect the functionality of mediators as described in [Wie90].) The communication again may cross the network as tools and assistants may reside on different nodes.

As described above, an agent provides the expertise for performing a specific task that is also provided by an assistant. An agent is always derived from a single task expert of an assistant. Hence, the functionality of an agent, i.e., the set of operations provided by the agent, is similar to the one of the task expert the agent is derived from. But different to task experts, agents are not part of a user's assistant. Figure 6.3 shows the relationships between an agent and the assistant the agent is derived from, and the agent's use by other assistants. The creation of agents has the additional effect that the tools used by the corresponding task expert will be shared by the agent. The database systems DBS1 and DBS2 shown in Figure 6.1 are examples of such shared tools.

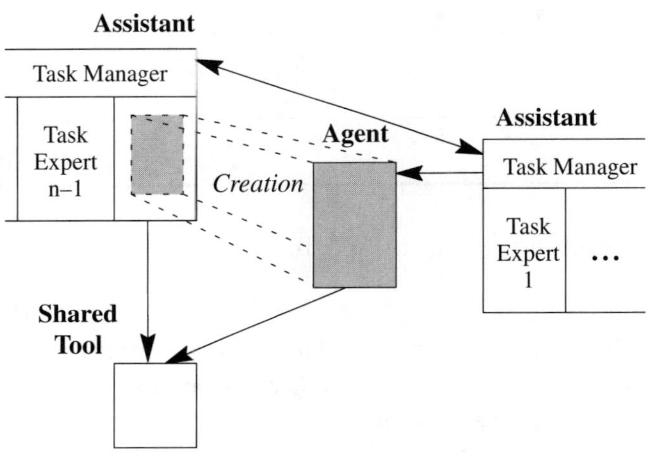

FIGURE 6.3
Relationships between Agents, Assistants, and Tools.

Agents can communicate with assistants and tools, but not with other agents:

- The communication between an agent and any assistant involves the task manager of the assistant and is based on the generic interface, i.e., the operations constituting the interface are independent of a specific task. Although an agent is derived from a task expert this interface slightly differs from the one between the task manager and the task experts within an assistant, because the assistant needs some additional information about the agent, e.g., information about the commands performed by the agent and how these can be employed. Note: As agents and assistants may be located at different nodes communication may cross node boundaries in the network.

It might be useful to restrict the set of operations available with the task manager-agent interface to a subset of the corresponding operations constituting the task manager-task expert interface if a user doesn't want to sell all the facilities provided by his assistant.

- The interfaces between an agent and the tools accessed by the agent are similar to the interfaces between task experts of an assistant and the tools.

6.3.2 Requirements for the Transaction Model

From the above scenario, we can derive the requirements for the underlying transaction model in our publication environment.

User interaction:

Different from the usage of isolated tools for editing, retrieving information from databases, defining the layout, etc., the persons involved in the publication process will interact through assistants. Hence, the user's tasks will typically cause long lasting operations involving many components.

Covering the whole publication process with transaction services:

The transaction model must support the whole publication process and all involved components in the same way. Otherwise, the user would have to deal with different transaction models and interfaces, which is not acceptable as he does not even know which tools, agents, and assistants may be involved in solving his problem. Hence, every operation should be executed under the control of a single, global but distributed transaction management.

Isolation of user's tasks:

As a consequence of the interaction and close cooperation of several users through their assistants, there is a need to control information exchange between these system components in order to avoid unintended visibility of intermediate data. There is also a need to control changes to data, in order to avoid inconsistencies like lost updates and inconsistent reads.

Recoverability of user's tasks:
The system must provide an undo-operation for each user-operation, because complex operations may involve many system components and may cause many changes which are not known to the user. Undoing parts of the work of a user must not affect the whole global transaction, because too much previous work would be lost. Partial abort of user transactions is required.

Limiting contention between tasks to the minimum necessary interdependencies:
Tasks in the publication environment involve long lasting user operations. From the user's point of view any concurrency control should minimize waits on objects that are concurrently accessed by other users. Therefore, the concurrency control should incorporate the semantics on the user level when deciding on the necessity to wait.

Distributed processing:
The tasks of a publication process are performed by using assistants and agents on different network nodes. This means that the transaction model has to reflect a distributed environment.

Integration of other transaction models:
Since our architecture is open for the integration of new tools, the transaction model must be able to support the integration of the transaction models coming with these new tools. Many existing database systems provide ACID transaction properties for their internal transactions. Hence, a transaction model must support the combination of ACID subtransactions into a global ACID user transaction. If it is not allowed or not possible to change a new tool and if it had not been designed to be used in a multi-user environment, this integration will be difficult. For example the newly integrated systems may not provide transaction management at all. In this case, we have to cover this lack of functionality as far as possible in order to provide the required homogeneous interface, but we might not be able to provide full ACID properties for these parts.

Supporting specific correctness criteria:
Some tools in the publication environment may need a different notion of transactions. For example, hypertext writing tools should support

cooperation between authors editing the same document. Hence, a definition for cooperation between transactions of different users is needed. Because of this requirement, such transactions should be designated as *co-transactions* in contrast to ACID transactions. For co-transactions, the isolation property is no longer valid but is violated in a controlled way.

As a consequence, our transaction model has to support the combination of transactions with different correctness criteria into global transactions. The properties of these global transactions depend on the transaction properties of the involved systems. For example, if a user makes changes to data that is stored in a database and to text maintained by a hypertext editor inside of a single transaction, ACID properties should be ensured for the users view of his changes to the database, independent of the non ACID properties for the changes in the hypertext editor.

Incorporating local autonomy of tools:
If autonomous transactions in an existing system component are still to be allowed after the integration into the publication environment, special correctness criteria for the dependencies between the autonomous local transactions and the global transactions of the publication environment have to be considered [DE89].

6.4 Transaction Model

The publication environment integrates system components with varying degrees of heterogenity. Assistants and agents are originally developed for the environment, tools are developed independently of the environment and are "plugged-in" later. We treat this heterogeneous environment in a homogenous way and speak about *objects* and their *operations*. Where applicable, we rely on the object-oriented paradigm and especially on *encapsulation* of objects, i.e. objects are only accessible by a predefined set of operations [KL89]. This is the case for assistant and agent components and for some tools. Where encapsulation is not used we cannot take advantage of it, but we are still able to include such components in our transaction model.

In this section, we introduce our model where concurrency control and recovery are based on *open nested transactions.* A nested transaction consists of subtransactions which in turn call other subtransactions, until the called actions are indivisible. In contrast to closed nested transactions [Mos85], open nested transactions make the changes of a subtransaction visible at the end of the subtransaction, not at the end of the whole transaction. But the changes must not be visible to every other transaction. In order to avoid inconsistent use of the results of committed subtransactions, only those subtransactions which commute with the committed one are allowed to use the results. A potentially higher degree of parallelism is therefore achieved. The behavior of *opening* the access to objects before the end of the transaction gives *open* nested transactions their name [Tra83].

Two principles are utilized by open nested transactions:

(1) *Commutativity is semantically defined.* In conventional concurrency control, only read operations among the operations accessing an object do not conflict, i.e. they *commute.* A semantic definition of commutativity also allows update operations of an object to be defined as commuting. For example, two increment operations of a counter commute because no other operation can determine their execution order. Conventionally these operations are conflicting read and write operations of a disk page. More operations can be specified as commuting by including parameters and return values of operations and by including the states of accessed objects.

(2) *The levels of abstraction are considered.* Operations on a higher level of abstraction are implemented by a sequence of operations on a lower level. For example, assume the increment of a counter at one level is implemented as a read and a write operation of a disk page. An uncontrolled interleaving of the page operations of different transactions may cause parallelism anomalies as lost update and inconsistent read. Hence, an increment must be executed isolated. If this property is guaranteed, the execution order of conflicting page operations on the lower level doesn't matter on the higher level because the increment operations commute. Low-level conflicts can be *"forgotten"* at higher levels of abstraction.

These principles are also utilized by *multi-level transactions* which are a special case of open nested transactions developed for layered systems [BR90, Lyn83, Wei91]. In a layered system each object belongs to exactly one level and actions on one level can only be called from the next higher level. Two adjacent levels build up one layer: the higher level contains transactions, the lower level contains the actions. In an object-oriented environment no restrictions are imposed on the nesting of transactions. The maximum depth of the calling hierarchy is not limited, i.e., application dependent, and an arbitrary calling hierarchy of subtransactions is allowed.

The original contribution of our transaction model is:

(1) The definition of commutativity in an object-oriented environment is discussed and it is shown how commutativity of operations in advanced applications can be specified.
(2) The correctness of a schedule of open nesteds in an object-oriented environment is defined.
(3) A locking protocol for open nested transactions is introduced.
(4) The compensation of open nested transactions in the case of transaction abort and crash recovery is defined.

The definitions of this paper are intended to summarize the concepts and are not formal definitions. Hence, no theorems or proofs are given, but we show that the defined terms fit in our framework. Our related work is cited, but we believe that the description is complete and understandable without knowing those references.

Related work for transactions in advanced applications mostly utilizes structural information on objects. A simple example is the class-instance relationship [KBG89, PS87]. Another example is the usage of composite objects and their part-of-relationship [Her90, KBG89]. However, it should be noted that the usage of structural information is independent of applying open nesteds.

Behavioral information is utilized to a lesser extent, e.g. as extensions to read/write locks [KKB88, PS87, RRD90, US91], or in combination with multi-level transactions [CF90, Mar88, SPSW90, Wal85]. The performance of multi-level transactions has been shown to yield good results [BR90, HW91, Wei91]. Multi-level transactions impose the above described restrictions on the nesting of transactions. Theoretical models of nested transactions are defined in [BBG89, FLMW88] but are not applied to a practical environment.

Several other approaches are partially related to our transaction model. The usage of semantics-based commutativity definition for application-defined data types can be found in [GK85, SS84, Weh89] but nesting of transactions is not applied. The approach of [HW88] goes beyond the symmetric commutativity definition to an unsymmetrical dependency condition, which takes the actual execution order of operations into account. Their approach allows more parallelism than our model but it imposes additional complexity on the corresponding protocols. The protocol of [BR88] is already semantics-based. Granularity of objects and semantic conflict definitions are considered, but parts of objects must be accessed via a root object and cannot be manipulated directly.

This section is organized as follows. In the first part, we show why serializability is used as a correctness criterion and define serializability in the object-oriented environment as object-oriented serializability. In the second part, concurrency control of open nesteds is introduced. The third part handles the impact of concurrency control on recovery.

6.4.1 Object-Oriented Serializability

Serializability defines the correctness of an interleaved execution of the actions of several transactions. A schedule (history) of transactions is serializable if it is equivalent to a serial schedule of the same transactions. Commuting actions of different transactions can occur in any order. Serializability is the one and only correctness criterion of concurrency control in conventional transaction models. Should (or must) serializability be compared to the shoes of growing kids which need to be replaced by larger ones? Or can serializability also be applied to non-standard applications such as our publication environment?

Some approaches of concurrency control for advanced applications abandon serializability. New correctness criterions other than serializability are demanded (e.g. [KS90]). On the one hand, serializability is indicated as being too restrictive: objects which are not yet committed by a transaction should be accessible by other transactions ("uncommitted data"). On the other hand, serializability does not allow synchronization of transactions as a whole, e.g., it should be possible to define an execution order of transactions. Such requirements are already met by statements for *explicit* synchronization in parallel programming languages (Modula-2, Ada, Occam). In database systems, only the interleaving of transactions is synchronized, independently which transactions are executed concurrently. Hence, consistency is guaranteed by *implicit* synchronization.

We favour serializability as the basic correctness criterion because serializability

- is easy to understand and
- offers transparency of parallel execution.

Serializability *with a semantic commutativity definition* fits best in our publication environment. Based on this correctness criterion a model for the cooperation of users can be build (compare [Mos90]). Indeed, cooperating users should not see any temporary state of objects. It depends on the kind of cooperation which state of objects should be visible and which must be isolated [Rak91].

In the following, we clarify the notion of commutativity in an object-oriented environment. Some new aspects are described making a semantic commutativity definition more applicable in advanced applications like our publication environment.

Definition of Commutativity

Commutativity of two operations presumes that their "effect" is the same no matter in which order they are executed. The "effect" of an operation is its *result* (return value) and – if the accessed object is changed – the *state* of the accessed object. In an object-oriented environment, objects are encapsulated and the state of an object can only be accessed as the result of an operation. Hence, commutativity will no longer be defined by the state of the accessed object (e.g. as in [BR90]) but by the return values of operations accessing an object.

DEFINITION 6.1 *(Commutativity and Conflict)*

Two operations a *and* b *commute if*

(i) *the results of the two sequences* (a; b) *and* (b; a) *are the same and*

(ii) *there does not exist any sequence of operations* (s) *such that* ((a; b); s) *and* ((b; a); s) *have different results.*

If two operations do not commute they conflict.

The result of executing a (finite) sequence s of operations (a; b; ...; e) consists of the results of the operations in the sequence. These results are unordered but related to their according operations respectively. In the first part of the definition, we require that the results of two commuting operations must be independent of their execution order. In the second part of the definition, we require that changing the execution order of two commuting operations must not change the result of other operations executed after the commuting operations.

This definition cannot be applied directly to a mechanism testing commutativity dynamically, e.g. for a locking protocol. The results of the operations must be available for the test before execution but are delievered after execution. Instead, commutativity of two operations is specified and the specification is used by the mechanism. In general, the specification can depend on the accessed object and the names, the parameters, and the results of the operations. However, for more complex specifications more overhead occurs. Even if only the comparison operators ($=, \neq, <, >$) are allowed in the specification, the test of commutativity is NP-hard [HR79]. A restriction to simpler specifications which do not cover all possible commuting cases is always possible since only parallelism is reduced but correctness is not violated. An alternative solution is to restrict the time allowed for the commutativity test [BJS86]. If the test is not finished in a defined time a conflict is assumed.

In some advanced models, every operation is mapped to one out of a fixed set of lock modes [KBG89, US91]. Commutativity is defined for the set of lock modes only. Our definition of commutativity implies that commutativity of two operations must be judged against all other operations in a system. To overcome this drawback we take advantage of encapsulation in an object-oriented environment: Only the operations of each object type must be compared among each other. Hence, the definition of a commutativity table for every object type is sufficient. Furthermore, some "related" object types may also be comparable, e.g. object types which can share subobjects [RMWHB91].

The design of a commutativity table for an object type is a creative process like programming. It must be judged whether more parallelism pays for the increased overhead of the conflict test. This task can best be solved by the programmer of the operations, who knows the semantics of the type first hand. Nevertheless, the commutativity definition should be independent of the implementation, because a specific implementation should not change the semantics of object-oriented operations.

Two corollaries can be derived from the definitions which are simple but very helpfully in defining a commutativity table.

COROLLARY 6.1 *(Symmetricity of Commutativity)*

If two operations a *and* b *commute then also* b *and* a *commute.*

Because the commutativity relation is symmetric, only half of the commutativity table must be defined explicitly, the other half can be derived. The second corollary states that two so called *transparent* [FLMW88] operations always commute.

DEFINITION 6.2 *(Transparent Operation)*

An operation a *is called transparent if for any sequence* (s) *the following holds: the result of* (s) *is the same for the sequences* (a; (s)) *and for* (s).

COROLLARY 6.2 *(Commutativity of Transparent Operations)*

If two operations a *and* b *are transparent then they commute.*

Usually, only read operations are transparent because they do not change the state of the accessed object and therefore commute with each other. In an object-oriented environment changing internal effects, which cannot be seen by other operations, also are transparent. For example, a search tree with a specific set of items can be structured differently without any interference of requests. Assume, the tree is dynamically restructured according to an access profile to minimize the search depth. Even though the tree structure is changed through the access of one operation, this operation is transparent for other operations accessing the tree structure.

Let us now give an example which will be used throughout this chapter to illustrate our concepts. We introduce a simplified *version model for documents*. The whole model is explained in detail in [Web91]. A document in this model consists of a sequence of versions with variants and allows for the merge of versions. As a consequence we have to deal with a directed-acyclic graph of versions. A new version of a document can only be derived from another version:

(1) Doc.deriveVersion (V, D): Derive a new version D from the version V in the document Doc.

A variant of a version can be derived by creating a version and a sub-graph containing the new version. Such a sub-graph is called a *task*:

(2) Doc.deriveTask (V, T, D): Derive a new task T in the document Doc, starting with the version D that is derived from version V. The version D is created by this operation, i.e. two tasks cannot start with the same version.

Often the most actual version of a specific task or of the document has to be accessed. Therefore, the following three operations exist:

(3) Doc.readVersion (V): Read the version V of the document Doc.

(4) Doc.readLatestTaskVersion (T): Read the latest version of the task T in the document Doc.

(5) Doc.readLatestVersion: Read the latest version of the document Doc.

In addition, an operation delievers the number of versions of a document:

(6) Doc.getVersionNo: Get the number of versions of the document Doc.

EXAMPLE 6.1 *(Operations in the Version Model)*

In Figure 6.4 the creation of a version graph of a document is shown. Starting with a version A a new version B is derived. One variant of B is derived in a new task T', then another version in the same task T is derived. The operation readLatestTaskVersion (T') returns the version C. The operation readLatestVersion returns the most actually derived version D. At this point, the document consists of four versions as counted by getVersionNo.

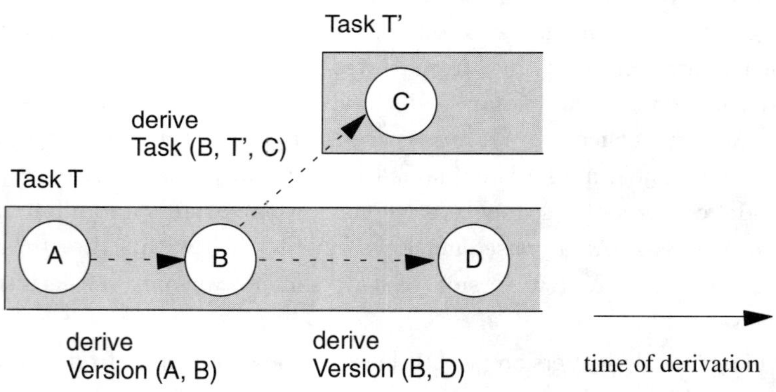

FIGURE 6.4
Example of a Document with Version Graph.

Additional operations are necessary to provide a complete interface, e.g. an operation to delete a version. However, for the sake of simplicity we only include the operations described above in the commutativity table of our example.

Figure 6.5 shows the commutativity table for the version operations. An element (a, b) of the table defines under which condition a commutes with b. A + means that under all conditions the two operations commute, a – means that under no conditions the two operations commute. The parameters of a condition must be seen as formal parameters which are replaced by the actual parameters at runtime.

All the read... operations and getVersionNo commute because they are transparent operations with respect to operations of other transactions, i.e., the sequence s of Corollary 6.2 consists of operations of other transactions only. For the row of the operation deriveVersion we now show how the commutativity table is specified. The derivation of the other table elements is straightforward. Note, the symmetric conditions (Corollary 6.1) and the conditions for transparent operations (Corollary 6.2).

(1) readVersion (V'): The creation of a new version D can be seen if D is read. Therefore, deriveVersion (V, D) and readVersion (V') commute only if the new version D is unequal to the read version V'.

(2) readLatestTaskVersion (T'): The operation readLatestTaskVersion (T') commutes with the derive operation if the derivation does not change the version structure of task T'. This is the case if the newly created version D is not an element of T', i.e., D $\notin$ T'.

(3) readLatestVersion: Because the result of the operation readLatestVersion will always be changed by the derivation of a new version both operations conflict.

(4) getVersionNo: The result of getVersionNo is changed by all operations deriving a new version.

(5) deriveVersion (V', D'): The creations of different versions, i.e. D $\neq$ D', always commute.

(6) DeriveTask (V', T', D'): Due to the semantics of a new task which initially begins with its own derived version the creation of the new task T' and the derivation of a new version D in the current and therefore different task generally commute.

Levels of Abstraction

In the previous example, we implicitly require that the operations are executed indivisibly. Otherwise inconsistencies may occur. Assume, the version operations are implemented by read and write operations on objects. The derive... operations must maintain pointers from the old to the new derived

Object. version Operations	read Version (V')	readLatest TaskVersion (T')	readLatest Version	get VersionNo	deriveVersion (V', D')	deriveTask (V', T', D')
read Version (V)	+	+	+	+	V$\neq$D'	V$\neq$D'
readLatest TaskVersion (T)	+	+	+	+	D'$\notin$T	T$\neq$T'
readLatest Version	+	+	+	+	−	−
get VersionNo	+	+	+	+	−	−
deriveVersion (V, D)	D$\neq$V'	D$\notin$T'	−	−	D$\neq$D'	+
deriveTask (V, T, D)	D$\neq$V'	T$\neq$T'	−	−	+	T$\neq$T'

V, V' Versions
D, D' Derived versions
T, T' Tasks

(shaded) Symmetric condition holds (Corollary 1)

- - - - - Condition for transparent operations holds (Corollary 2)

FIGURE 6.5
Commutativity Table for Version Operations.

version (Figure 6.4). For example, let the operations deriveTask (B, T', C) and deriveVersion (B, D) of Example 6.1 be called by separate transactions, respectively:

$T_1 \rightarrow T_{1.1}$: Doc.deriveTask (B, T', C) $\rightarrow$ {$T_{1.1.1}$: B.read; $T_{1.1.2}$: B.write},

$T_2 \rightarrow T_{2.1}$: Doc.deriveVersion (B, D) $\rightarrow$ {$T_{2.1.1}$: B.read; $T_{2.1.2}$: B.write}.

Because Doc.deriveTask (B, T', C) commutes with Doc.deriveVersion (B, D) both operations can operate in parallel. However, an uncontrolled interleaving of the operations may cause parallelism anomalies like a lost update on version B in the following sequence:

($T_{1.1.1}$: B.read; $T_{2.1.1}$: B.read; $T_{1.1.2}$: B.write $T_{2.1.2}$: B.write).

In general, operations must be executed isolated from other operations on the same object. To define that two operations commute (Definition 6.1) does not mean that these operations may be executed without any control of interleaving. Even operations on different objects, which commute, may access the same object at the next lower level of abstraction and must be isolated.

One way to ensure isolation of operations is an exclusive execution. This solves the problem but reduces parallelism significantly. In case of long-term operations, an interleaving of lower-level operations should therefore be allowed. Operations can be interleaved if they are executed serializable, i.e. as *sub*transactions (Figure 6.6). But the interleaved execution of lower-level

Requirement: Isolation of transactions
Solution: Serializability of top-level-transactions
Requirement: Isolation of subtransactions
Solution: Serializability of subtransactions
Requirement: Isolation of sub-subtransactions
Solution: ...
until actions are indivisible

FIGURE 6.6
How Open Nested Transactions Guarantee Isolation.

operations may cause additional conflicts for the execution of higher-level operations. How about the advantage of using semantic commutativity if more conflicts than for flat transactions may occur?

An answer to this question has to investigate the meaning of the definition of a conflict. A conflict shows that an execution order can be identified. If this can no longer be done, the conflict need not be considered further. Roughly speaking, in the conventional transaction model with higher-level transactions and lower-level actions, a conflict is no longer valid at the end of a transaction. In our model, this property is fulfilled at the end of a calling subtransaction if the commutativity of operations can be utilized. In this case, a conflict on a lower-level can be *"forgotten"* at a higher level.

Definition of Object-Oriented Serializability

In contrast to conventional transaction models, *transactions* are defined as operations. As usual, the dynamically called operations implementing a transaction are called *actions*. Because actions can be divisible and must be executed isolated they serve as transactions at the next lower level of abstraction. A divisible action is therefore called a *subtransaction*. Open nested are defined by using these terms. Figure 6.7 shows an example of an open nested transaction.

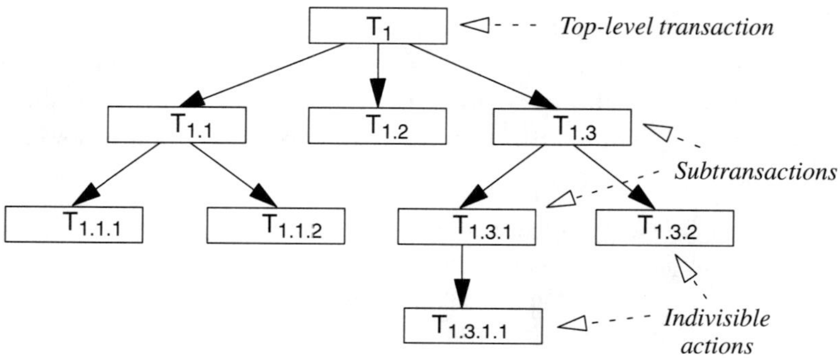

FIGURE 6.7
An Open Nested Transaction.

DEFINITION 6.3 *(Transaction and Action)*

A transaction is the actual execution of an operation t. *The dynamically called operations which implement* t *are the actions of the transaction. Actions and transactions commute/conflict if their corresponding operations commute/conflict.*

DEFINITION 6.4 *(Indivisible Action)*

An action a *accessing an object* O *is indivisible if for all actions* c *accessing* O *either* a *is executed* before c *or* c *is executed* after a.

DEFINITION 6.5 *(Subtransaction)*

If an action is not indivisible it must be executed as a transaction. Such a transaction is called subtransaction.

DEFINITION 6.6 *(Open Nested Transaction)*

An open nested is a tree with the following properties:

- *(i)* *the root node is the user-defined transaction, also called top-level transaction, (ii)* *the inner nodes are subtransactions,*

(iii) *the leaves are Indivisible Actions,*

(iv) *an arc from one node to another node is created if a transaction calls an action.*

The question to be answered by the definition of *object-oriented serializability* (oo-serializability) is the following: Which conflicts of actions must be considered for which (sub-)transactions?

First of all, we consider at single objects. From the point of view of an object the nested structure of object-oriented operations is mapped to a flat two-level structure: operations accessing the object are mapped to actions and direct and indirect calling operations are mapped to calling transactions. Hence, it makes no difference whether a transaction calls an action directly or indirectly. A transaction depends on another transaction if they both access the same object and the accessing actions are in conflict. Thess dependencies are recorded in a *transaction dependency relation* $\ll$. An *object schedule* – i.e., the interleaved execution of actions of an object – is oo-serializable if the transaction dependency relation is acyclic, i.e. equivalent to a serial schedule.

OO-Serializability of an object schedule assumes that a schedule of actions is given. Two actions of an object O may be transactions of another object P, i.e. actions accessing O call directly or indirectly actions accessing P. We must not allow different dependencies for the same subtransactions in the object schedules of O and P. Therefore, the transaction dependencies of the object P are inherited by the object O and result in *action dependencies* $<$. The Indivisible Actions which are not transactions of any other object must fulfil a bootstrap condition: their dependencies, i.e. their execution order, must be given. Because actions of an object may be transactions of two or more other objects contradicting action dependencies are possible. Contradicting dependencies signify that actions have been executed inconsistently. In addition to the condition for the transaction dependency relation, contradicting action dependencies are not allowed in an oo-serializable object schedule.

The inheritance process between objects may cause some dependencies to be lost. A transaction dependency for two subtransactions, which access different objects, may exist. In this case no common object exists which inherits the transaction dependency as an action dependency. The dependency may be recorded at some control object, by one selected object or by both objects redundantly. We record the information at both objects. We add an *added action dependency relation* $<+$ to the action dependency relation of an object. Then, a schedule is oo-serializable if all object schedules are oo-serializable and the added action dependency relation contains no contradictions, i.e. is acyclic.

A formal definition of object-oriented serializability is given in [RGN90].

EXAMPLE 6.2 *(Dependencies in the Version Model Example)*
The version graph of Example 6.1 is used (Figure 6.4). Assume, before the derivation of C another transaction requests the latest version of the task T, and after the derivation a third transaction requests the latest version of the document, i.e. of all tasks (Figure 6.8). The version operations are implemented by operations on objects, which in turn are implemented as operations on pages. The page operations are not shown, i.e., no interleaving is assumed. In the following, the action and transaction dependency relations are shown. Added action dependencies do not occur in the schedules but would be possible, e.g., if the same version is shared by two documents.

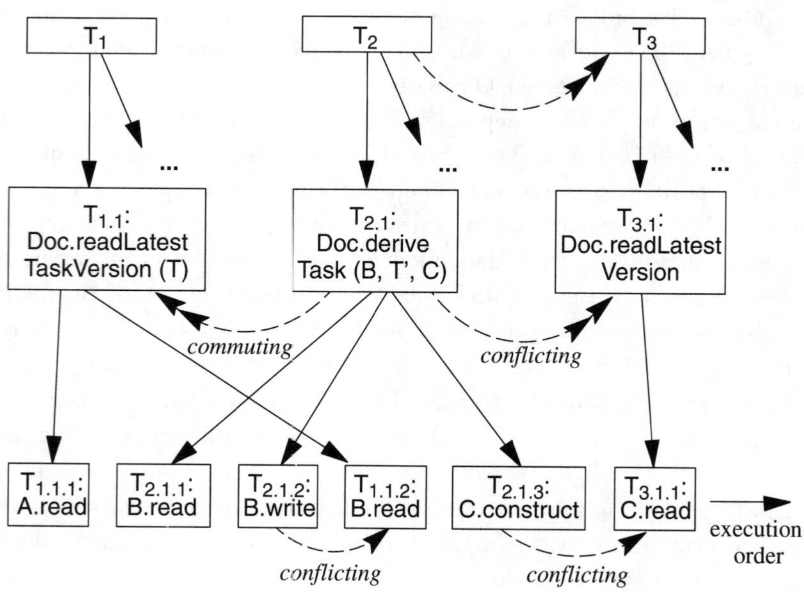

FIGURE 6.8
Schedule and Dependencies for the Example.

The object schedule of B has the following dependency relations:

- actions: $T_{2.1.2} < T_{1.1.2}$.
- transactions: $T_{2.1} \ll T_{1.1}$.

The object schedule of C has the following dependencies:

- actions: $T_{2.1.3} < T_{3.1.1}$.
- transactions: $T_{2.1} \ll T_{3.1}$, $T_2 \ll T_3$ (due to the conflict of $T_{2.1}$ and $T_{3.1}$).

The transaction dependencies of the objects schedule of B and of C which are actions of Doc must be inherited by the object schedule of Doc as action dependencies:

- actions: $T_{2.1} < T_{1.1}$, $T_{2.1} < T_{3.1}$.
- transactions: $T_2 \ll T_3$.

The schedule is oo-serializable and equivalent to the serial schedule $T_2 \ll T_3$. The schedule is also (conventional) serializable but equivalent to $T_2 \ll T_1 \ll T_3$. This imposes an unnecessary dependency for T_1 in contrast to the oo-serializable schedule.

6.4.2 Object-Oriented Concurrency Control

Object-oriented concurrency control implements object-oriented serializability. It has to be designed according to the above principles: (1) semantic conflict definition by the use of commutativity between actions and (2) execution of actions by separate subtransactions on lower levels of abstraction.

Because commutativity only extends the conventional conflict definition originally defined between read and write actions, the basic design of conventional schedulers can be used. The test for read/write conflicts is substituted by a lookup of the commutativity tables. If a locking scheme is used, a lock is granted if and only if the requesting action commutes with every other action executed at that time. Note that multiple transactions may now concurrently hold a lock for an update on a single object.

The execution of actions as subtransactions cannot be modeled by simply extending existing concurrency control schemes. This is due to the fact that subtransactions must be executed isolated (Definition 6.5). Our goal is to design a scheme able to control each level of abstraction separately. At best, independent concurrency control modules could be used at each level of abstraction. In this case, a concurrency control module for each level, providing the commutativity extension described above, would be sufficient to implement object-oriented serializability.

In fact, such an approach can be used for multi-level transactions, a special case of open nested. In contrast to open nested transactions, multi-level transactions only model a layered transaction execution:

DEFINITION 6.7 *(Layer Requirement)*

A system is layered if each object belongs to exactly one level and actions on one level can only be called from the next higher level.

There are two essential differences between open nested in general, and multi-level transactions:

(1) In the open nested model, the maximum depth of the calling hierarchy is not limited, i.e., the depth is application dependent. For multi-level transactions, there is a fixed number of layers defined by the system, common to all applications.

(2) Open nested transactions allow an arbitrary calling hierarchy of subtransactions, whereas multi-level transactions only allow subtransaction to be called on the next lower system layer (Definition 6.7). Skipping layers is not allowed.

For multi-level transactions, it has been shown that serializability can be ensured level-by-level under a reasonable assumption: A conflict on one level is always caused by a conflict at the adjacent lower level. If the schedules on all levels are serializable, the complete schedule is serializable [Wei86, Wei91]. This allows the usage of independent concurrency control modules, every module ensuring serializability on its level.

For open nesteds in the object-oriented model, no layers can be identified. Even though, we may implement each divisible operation as a subtransaction. One may hope that a serializable execution is achieved if two phase locking is used for all the subtransactions. As shown by the following example, this is not the case:

EXAMPLE 6.3 *(Non-serializable Schedule)*

The schedule of Figure 6.9 is not a multi-level schedule, since transaction T_2 skips the version layer. T_2 directly constructs a new object D_2, representing the new version, and directly increments VCount, a counter that counts the number of Versions for document Doc. T_2 may have decided to skip the version layer because no deriveVersion operation for constructing D_2 was available that uses the operation construct' instead of the operation construct.

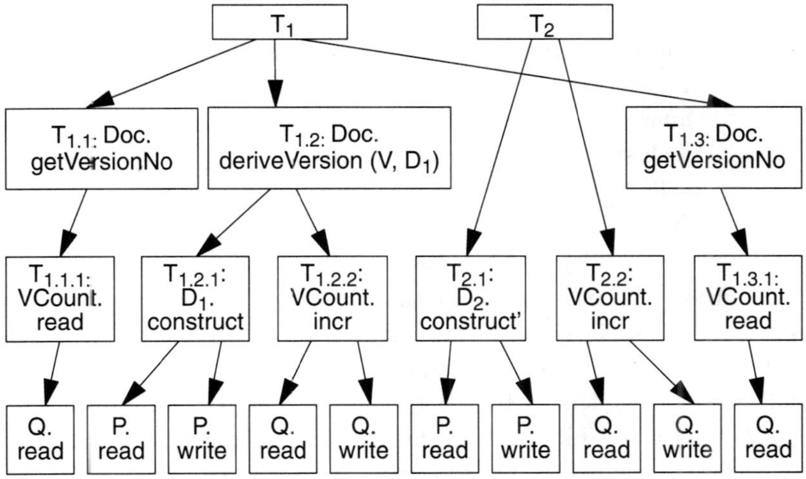

FIGURE 6.9
Non-serializable Execution of T_1 and T_2.

Obviously, the schedule of Figure 6.9 is a correct two phase locking schedule, since all accesses to D_1 and D_2, VCount, and P, Q are executed in a serial order and document Doc is only accessed by T_1. But here an inconsistency occurred due to a violation of the isolation property: Even though T_1 derived only one version of Doc, the version counter VCount is incremented by two during the execution of T_1. This is visible to T_1 by executing the getVersionNo operations, which return the total number of versions derived from Doc.

We give a short outline of the solution for the "skipped layer problem". The idea is to prevent the execution of $T_{2.2}$: VCount.incr before T_1 is finished, since $T_{2.2}$: VCount.incr conflicts with $T_{1.1.1}$: VCount.read. Up to now, our concurrency control algorithm cannot detect this conflict, since the conflict becomes invalid after the end of $T_{1.1}$: Doc.getVersionNo, the transaction which called $T_{1.1.1}$: VCount.read.

If a locking scheme uses a new kind of locks which are not released at the end of a subtransaction but at the end of the corresponding top-level transaction the problem is solved. We call these locks *retained locks.* Retained locks are acquired in addition to normal locks and are granted iff the normal lock is granted. Normal locks conflict with retained locks iff the following conditions hold:

(i) The subtransaction that requires the normal lock and the subtransaction which currently holds the retained lock belong to different top-level transactions.

(ii) Both subtransactions were started by transactions that are controlled by different concurrency control modules.

(iii) There is no pair of actions in the hierarchically list of callers of the considered subtransactions that actually commute.

Conditions (ii) and (iii) ensure that the degree of concurrency is not reduced to the one achieved with conventional locks. Using retained locks, the schedule shown in Figure 6.9 would not have been allowed by the concurrency control. Since the callers of $\mathsf{T}_{1.1.1}$: VCount.read and $\mathsf{T}_{2.2}$: VCount.incr, $\mathsf{T}_{1.1}$: Doc.getVersionNo and T_2, are controlled by different concurrency control modules, i.e., the do not belong to the same level of abstraction (condition (ii)), the retained lock $\mathsf{T}_{1.1.1}$: VCount.read would have prevented the execution of $\mathsf{T}_{2.2}$: VCount.incr until T_1 finished.

Condition (iii) provides a chance to grant a lock even in the presence of a conflicting retained lock if the commutativity of the callers allows to do so. The correctness of condition (iii), together with a discussion of the resulting concurrency control overhead, is given in [RMWHB91]. Note that retained locks only affect transactions that actually cause problems when skipping layers. Otherwise, condition (ii) simply states the compatibility of all retained locks.

Another problem special to open nesteds in the object-oriented model is the access of shared subobjects. An object is shared if it is part of more than one other object, i.e., a change of a subobject also results in a change of the (super-)objects which own the shared subobject. Conflicts on the shared subobject have no counterpart in the calling objects, since this requires the notion of conflicts between operations on different objects. The added action dependency relation contains such dependencies (section 6.4.1).

Concurrency control algorithms solving the problem of skipped layers based on the sketched solution and the problem of shared subobjects are discussed in detail in [RMWHB91].

6.4.3 Recovery

Recovery for open nested transactions introduces a new concept: compensating operations. Transactions are no longer aborted by simply restoring before-values. Instead, operations are executed which compensate all previous changes. In this section, we show why conventional state-based undo is no longer feasible in the open nested model. We discuss both transaction abort and crash recovery.

The Impact of Concurrency Control on Recovery

The enhanced concurrency control allows updates on a single object to occur in parallel. This causes the need for aborting transactions by executing compensating operations rather than restoring before-values, as shown by the following example.

EXAMPLE 6.4

Consider the concurrent execution of $\mathsf{T_1}$ and $\mathsf{T_2}$ in Figure 6.10. Both transactions derive new versions of document Doc. Since the derived versions and the constructed objects are different and the increment operations commute, both transactions are allowed to do this in parallel. Assume that after the commit of $\mathsf{T_2}$, $\mathsf{T_1}$ has to be aborted.

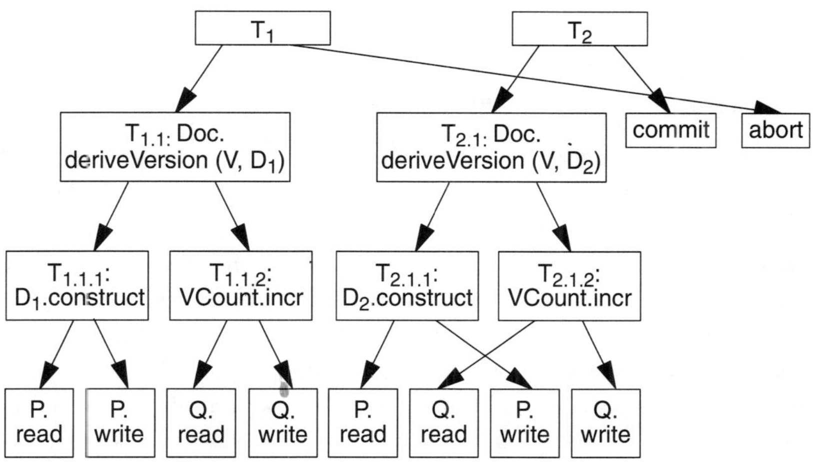

FIGURE 6.10
Abort of Open Nested Transactions.

As a first approach, we consider restoring the before-images of pages in order to handle the abort. It is easy too see that the result is incorrect: By restoring the before-images of P and Q, the version derived by the committed transaction T_2 would also disappear, since both new versions are stored on page P. The same is true for the increment of VCount performed by T_2.

Another way is to restore before-values on higher levels of abstraction. In order to undo the construction of Object D_1, this approach is sufficient. Assume the construction of D_1 is undone by just restoring a NIL entry in the corresponding object table. This would not affect the entry of D_2. But if parallel updates on the same object are allowed, the approach is also not feasible. In the above example, VCount would be restored to the value before T_1 started. The increment of T_2 would again be lost.

The only correct way to abort an open nested is to apply compensating operations for all previously executed operations [KLS90, Wei86, Wei91]. In order to abort transaction T_1 of Example 6.4, the operation Doc.deriveVersion (V, D1) is compensated by executing operation Doc.deleteVersion (D1). This operation has to delete D_1, maintain the references to D_1, and decrement VCount. The changes of T2 will not be affected by these operations, but all the changes of T_1 are undone.

Transaction Abort

We will now discuss the correct abort of a single transaction. An abort may occur for every (sub-)transaction in the system at any time. Aborting a single transaction has no direct influence on the outcome of other transactions, in particular, a transaction need not be aborted if one of its subtransactions is aborted [Mos85]. An abort just signals an error to the calling transaction. This error is interpreted as a failure of the corresponding action. Only the calling transaction decides how to continue, e.g., repeat the action, try another, or abort. Hence, when dealing with transaction aborts, we need not consider the whole transaction tree. Only the node that is to be aborted and the nodes below are affected. In terms of Figure 6.10, a failure of $T_{1.1}$ indicates an unsuccessful execution of the Doc.deriveVersion (V, D1) operation of T_1. T_1 may now abort, repeat the derive operation, or continue by executing an alternative operation [ELLR90].

Because we have to abort a transaction by executing compensating operations, a transaction is not stopped in case of an abort. Instead, from the concurrency control point of view, the compensating operations are executed as normal actions inside of the transaction that is to be aborted [Wei91]. They are implemented as subtransactions on the next lower level of abstraction (Definition 6.5). After the execution of all necessary compensating operations, the abort is finished. In the subsequent discussions, we will rely on the following definitions:

DEFINITION 6.8 *(Primary Action)*

An operation a that is executed during normal transaction execution is called Primary Action.

DEFINITION 6.9 *(Inverse Action)*

An operation a^{-1} *which compensates the changes of the corresponding primary action* a *is called Inverse Action.*

DEFINITION 6.10 *(Relationship Primary and Inverse Actions)*

- *(i) Each Inverse Action belongs to exactly one Primary Action.*
- *(ii) The schedule* (a; a^{-1}) *must be transparent (Definition 6.2).*
- *(iii) Inverse actions are repeated until they successfully finish.*

Conditions (i) and (ii) establish a 1:1 mapping between primary and inverse actions. Condition (iii) ensures a successful compensation of operations, since changes are compensated only if the execution of the corresponding inverse action is successful.

Up to now, we have not considered how an Inverse Action is specified. An inverse action is determined by an operation and a number of parameters. The operation is the compensating operation to the operation of the Primary Action. In general, if one defines an operation, e.g., deriveVersion or increment, the corresponding compensating operation must also be defined, i.e., deleteVersion or decrement. These definitions are static and do not change until the definition of the original operation changes.

The actual parameters of Inverse Actions must be determined during runtime of the primary actions. In the simplest case, only the object on which the operation is executed has to be known, e.g., Counter.incrByOne is compensated by Counter.decrByOne. Sometimes the parameters can be derived directly from the parameters of the primary action, e.g., Counter.incrBy (Value) is compensated by Counter.decrBy (Value).

For some operations, the parameters for an inverse action have to be determined by retrieving information from the database:

EXAMPLE 6.5

In order to compensate a deleteVersion action, the corresponding inverse deriveVersion action must be supplied with two parameters: The old contents of the deleted version and the version the deleted version was derived from. In this case, an additional readVersion operation and an additional getFather operation must be executed before reallyDelete is started (we disregard optimized implementations such as using a delete flag instead of real deletion). This is shown in Figure 6.11. The old contents of V is saved in SaveVersion and SaveFather before reallyDelete is executed. SaveVersion and SaveFather are supplied later as parameters for the inverse action deriveVersion.

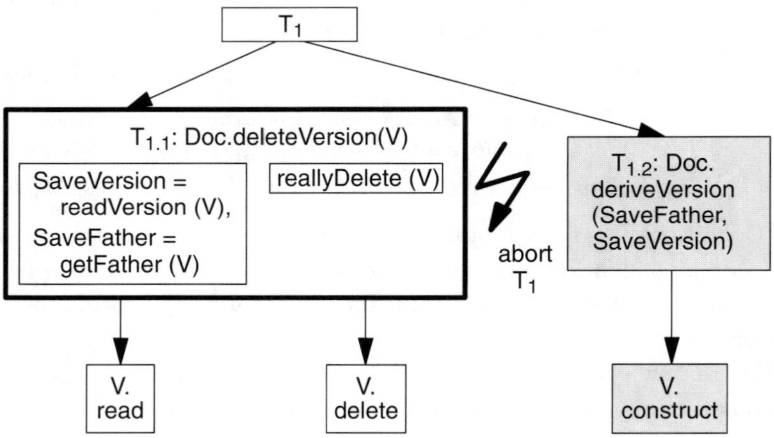

FIGURE 6.11
Parameters for Inverse Actions.

Note that the retrieve and store of before-images in conventional, flat transaction models is a special case of our scheme. The conventional before-image serves as a parameter for a write operation that is executed during transaction abort.

In general, additional operations may be needed before and after the execution of a Primary Action. Most of the times, the additional operations will be read-only. But this is not required by our scheme. The execution of additional actions is not different to the execution of other actions. Both concurrency control and recovery can treat them as normal Primary Actions.

How to help the designer of operations to define the corresponding compensating operations and how to define a scheme for getting the actual parameters of inverse actions is subject of further studies. However, in an object-oriented world the interface of an object often already contains operations and the corresponding compensating operations. Sometimes, the compensating operations are complex and are not part of the interface. Even though, it is almost always possible to design them by using less complex operations that are part of the interface. Otherwise, even without considering recovery for open nesteds, the object would be of little value. A user always wants to be able to undo erroneous changes in his work, which is impossible if the interface is incomplete in this respect.

We now define how a complete transaction abort is performed:

DEFINITION 6.11 *(Transaction Abort)*

A transaction is aborted if the following conditions hold:

- *(i)* *After the transaction decided to abort, no Primary Action is executed any more.*
- *(ii)* *For each executed Primary Action, the corresponding inverse action is executed.*
- *(iii)* *Inverse actions are executed in reverse order compared to the execution of the primary actions.*

Figure 6.12 shows the complete execution of transaction T_1 of Figure 6.10, including the inverse actions. The subtransactions of T_2 are omitted. T_1 is aborted after the new versions are derived and T_2 is committed. End of transaction is marked by EOT and shown for T_1 and T_2 only. The inverse actions of T_1 and the subtransactions executed by these Inverse Actions are drawn in grey boxes. It is interesting to note that for both transactions the same EOT operation is used. In fact, the commit operation is directly mapped to the EOT operation. The abort operation is mapped to the execution of the Inverse Actions and a final EOT. This is correct since only the execution of primary and inverse actions as part of the complete transaction execution is transparent according to Definition 6.2.

System Crash

A crash causes the system to loose all the non-persistent information and data. During restart, a transaction consistent state which reflects all the changes of transactions that have been committed before the crash has to be recovered. For the sake of simplicity, we assume that all transactions which were not finished before the crash have to be aborted since their execution

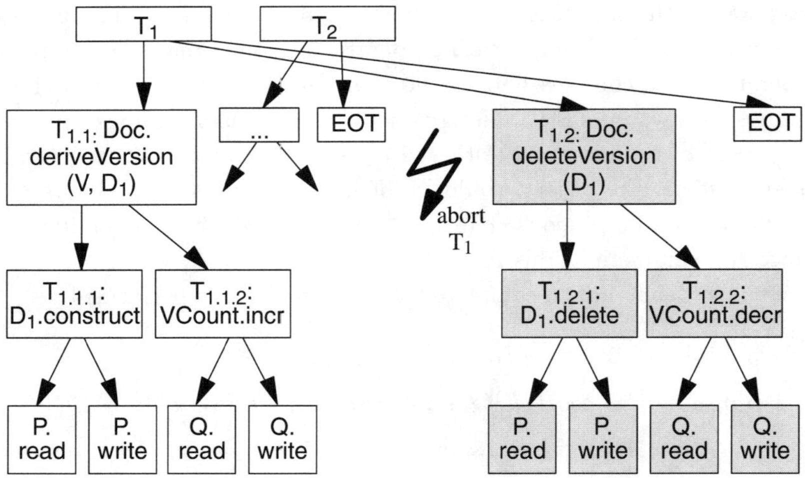

FIGURE 6.12
Complete Abort of T_1.

cannot be resumed. Hence, we have to consider both: transaction redo and transaction undo. A prerequisite for a successful redo is persistence of changes.

Persistence

Persistence is generally required for all changes of user transactions. In flat transaction models, no other than user transactions exist, i.e., persistence is required for all committed transactions in the system [BHG87]. This is not necessarily the case for open nesteds. In order to achieve persistence for user transactions in the open nested model, all direct or indirect subtransactions of a user transaction must be persistent at commit time of the user transaction. Hence, as first approach we could require subtransactions to become persistent at the commit time of the corresponding user transaction, not at their own commit time.

However, generally delaying the point of time a subtransaction is made persistent until the corresponding user transaction commits is wrong [WHBM90]. Consider two subtransactions T_i and T_j which belong to different user transactions. Assume, they made changes on the page level and their write-sets have page P in common. If the user transaction of T_i is committed, the changes of T_i are made persistent. If the smallest write granularity is a page, the change of $\mathsf{T_j}$ on page P has also become persistent. Atomicity requires that all other changes of $\mathsf{T_j}$ have to become persistent, too. Hence, $\mathsf{T_j}$ must be made persistent before the corresponding user transaction commits.

In order to simplify the following discussions, we assume that all (sub-) transactions are made persistent at their commit times.

DEFINITION 6.12 *(Persistence)*

All transactions are made persistent at their commit time.

Note that according to Definition 6.12 even aborted transactions consist of persistent actions. However, on the level of the aborted transaction, no changes ever become visible since they are all compensated. Changes of subtransactions may still become visible on lower levels of abstraction. Assume a transaction which deleted a version of a document is aborted by re-inserting the version. Between deletion and re-insertion, the corresponding pages on the disk may have been reused by other transactions. The re-inserted version has to be located on different pages. This is not visible on the level of the aborted transaction, but it is visible on the page level.

Redo

Definition 6.12 requires durability for all changes of transactions that were finished before the crash. In general, this is achieved by repeating the execution of all actions of a transaction that is to be recovered. The repetition, i.e., redo of transactions, can take place at different levels of abstraction. In general, three rules must be obeyed:

(1) If a transaction is redone, none of its direct or indirect subtransactions must be redone, since this would result in a multiple redo.

In particular, if a user transaction is redone by repeating its actions, redo on lower levels of abstraction is not needed and not allowed. The repetition of actions is performed by executing subtransactions on lower levels of abstraction. These subtransactions perform the necessary changes and can be regarded as a substitution for the redo of actions on lower levels of abstraction.

(2) If a subtransaction has been redone, the calling transaction must not redo the corresponding action.

This is the opposite situation compared to (1) and would also lead to multiple redo.

(3) Redo can be performed in a state-based fashion if it takes place at one level of abstraction only and if the sequence of the original schedule is not changed.

In other words, state-based redo is correct if it is not done on a per-transaction basis, but on the basis of the original interleaving of different transactions. Exactly repeating the history of actions that were executed before the crash restores the database to the state it had before the crash.

In the following, we will assume that redo is done for leaf-transactions only. Obviously, this is correct since all transactions in the system consist directly or indirectly of leaf-transactions (rule (2)), they have no subtransactions themselves (rule (1)), and the redo can be done according to the original sequence of log-writes (rule (3)). This scheme is efficient, since leaf-transactions are executed at the page level. Only simple page-writes are required to perform the redo. Another advantage is the abstraction from redo management problems for all non-leaf transactions. Redo at higher levels of the transaction tree would require relatively complex computations to satisfy the above rules.

DEFINITION 6.13 *(Redo of Leaf-Transactions)*

Redo of transactions is provided on the leaf-level of the transaction tree only.

Note that some of the transactions that were redone have to be undone later. This is an inherent property caused by the enhanced concurrency of open nesteds. For example, consider again a transaction which has deleted a version, but could not commit before a system crash occurred. If another transaction has reused the space of the deleted version and committed before the crash, the version must be re-inserted on other pages. Only the redo of the original delete operation followed by the compensation ensures correct management of free-pages and versions.

Undo

We are now able to describe how the undo part of the crash recovery is performed. Different to the redo part, we have no option where to start the undo recovery, as stated by the first undo rule:

(1) The undo recovery of a transaction must not be started before the undo recovery of all its subtransactions is finished.

If the undo recovery of a subtransaction is not finished, some parts of its changes may be reflected in the current database state, some may not. In other words, the state of the transaction that called this subtransaction is not action consistent. Hence, the calling transaction cannot be undone at that time, since this would require the execution of actions in a non-action consistent state.

Undo rule (1) implies the usage of a bottom-up undo scheme. The scheme has to start with the leaf transactions, since these are the only transactions that cannot violate the rule. All uncommitted leaf-transactions are undone.

The following undo rules ensure a correct undo of transactions at higher levels of abstraction. They are similar to the redo rules (2) and (3) above:

(2) If a subtransaction has been undone, the calling transaction must not undo the corresponding action.

If all changes of the subtransactions have been undone, nothing is left to undo at the level of abstraction of the calling transaction.

(3) Undo cannot be performed in a state-based fashion.

This is due to the same reasons as described for transaction abort.

In order to obey the undo rules (1), (2) and (3), we need an algorithm which starts the undo of transactions in the right order and avoids the undo of transactions that have previously been undone. The following gives a brief outline of such an algorithm:

> According to rule (1), the algorithm first determines all transactions which have not been committed before the crash. For each transaction in this set it has to be checked if there exists a subtransaction of the considered transaction which is also in the set.
>
> *If such a subtransaction exists:*
>
> > The undo has to be delayed according to undo rule (1) and another transaction in the set is selected.
>
> *If such a subtransaction doesn't exist:*
>
> > The abort of the transaction is performed. Since inverse actions are executed instead of performing a state-based undo, the requirement of undo rule (3) is met. The algorithm executes inverse actions for all primary actions that do not belong to previously undone subtransactions (rule (2)). It starts with the inverse action belonging to the last subtransaction which has not previously been undone.
>
> The undo-recovery stops when the set is empty.

After the algorithm has terminated, all transactions that were not committed before the crash, including non-committed user transactions, have been undone. A consistent database state is recovered.

In general, idempotence of compensating operations is required. To achieve idempotence for state-based recovery is relatively simple. Writing before- or after-images is idempotent. This is generally not true for complex compensating operations, e.g., a decrement operation. For such operations the recovery algorithm has to make sure that they are only applied to a database state which reflects the original operation.

Strategies for undo and redo during crash recovery have been analyzed in [HR83]. An optimized implementation is described in [Moh89, MP91]. A discussion considering especially multi-level transactions can be found in [WHBM90].

Optimizations

The recovery of open nested transactions is relatively complex and expensive compared to flat transaction models. The price of the concurrency gain is paid by the recovery. Even though, optimizations addressing both runtime-overhead and the overhead that occurs during transaction abort and recovery are possible. [WHBM90] addresses the reduction of I/O amount and I/O costs. By relaxing Definition 6.12, it is no longer needed to make the changes of each subtransaction persistent at subtransaction commit time. For the special case of two-level transactions, it has been shown that the I/O amount can be reduced to the amount of a flat transaction scheme if the increased concurrency is actually not used, i.e., if no concurrent updates on a single object actually occur. In fact, for specific workloads the I/O amount can be reduced below the amount needed by conventional systems. [HW91] gives detailed performance results of these algorithms.

6.5 Transactions in the Publication Environment

In this section, we map the transaction model discussed in section 6.4 to the architecture of assistants, agents and tools presented in section 6.3.1. At first, we define transaction execution in our environment. The integration of existing tools that were not designed to be part of the publication environment causes additional problems. We discuss the impact of these problems on the management of transactions.

6.5.1 Transaction Execution

If a user of the publication environment has to perform a specific task, he will start a top-level transaction. The transaction consists of user actions and is managed by the task manager of the user's assistant. The task manager decides how to execute the actions. For each action that can be executed locally by a task expert of the user's assistant, a subtransaction in the corresponding task expert is started. In order to implement the subtransaction, a task expert may start subtransactions in some of the accessible tools, which will finally call Indivisible Actions. User actions that can not be executed locally are given to agents of the assistant – if applicable – or to other assistants. An agent again calls subtransactions on tools. An assistant acts like the requesting assistant i.e., calls subtransactions on task experts, its agents or other assistants. Recursive calls are allowed, but must not lead to an ultimate calling loop, i.e., an infinite depth of the transaction tree.

The sample scenario of section 6.3.1 can now be discussed in terms of transaction execution. For the sake of simplicity, we only present the part of the user's task that is concerned with getting additional facts (getFacts) for composing the document:

EXAMPLE 6.6

In order to execute the user action getFacts, the task manager of the author's assistant executes a subtransaction in an Infobase agent, which is directly available to the assistant (Figure 6.13). The agent starts subtransactions in DBS1 and DBS2. These subtransactions are implemented by Indivisible Actions inside of DBS1 and DBS2. Since both subtransactions could not provide the desired answer, the agent gives back an error-information to the task manager of the user's assistant. The task manager decides to directly call the Infobase assistant. An appropriate subtransaction is executed by the task manager of the Infobase assistant. This results in subtransactions executed by a knowledge base agent and the task expert which is responsible for DBS1. The subtransactions of the task expert are implemented by Indivisible Actions of DBS1. Finally the result is given to the user by the following chain: DBS1; Infobase assistant-task expert for DBS1; Infobase assistant-task manager; author's assistant.

Transactions executed by task managers, task experts, agents and tools may again be implemented as open nesteds. According to section 6.4.1, these transactions must be atomic and isolated, but a restriction on how to achieve these properties is not imposed. In fact, the increased parallelism makes open nested transactions a good choice for the usage inside of the publication environment components.

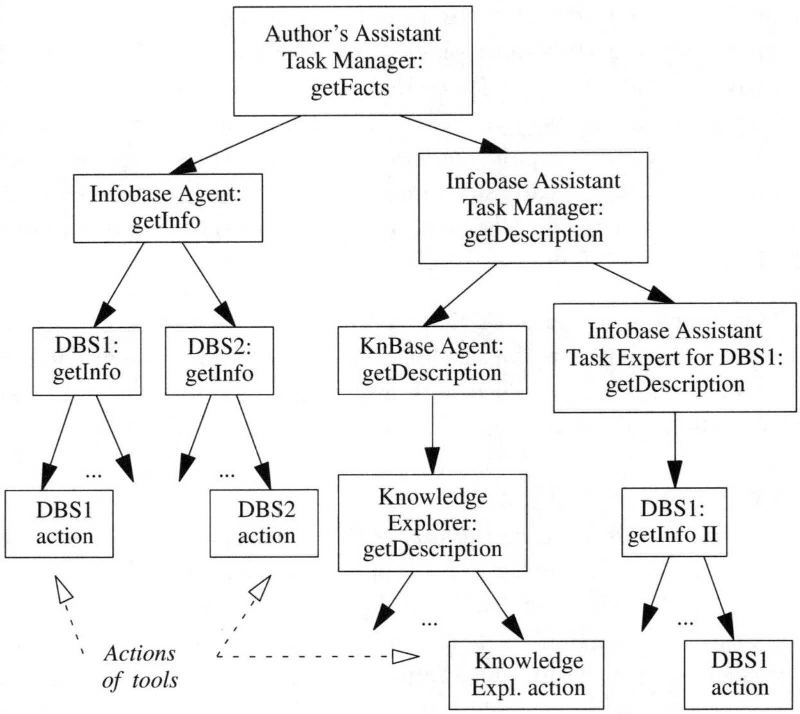

FIGURE 6.13
Transaction for the Sample Scenario.

6.5.2 The Impact of Distribution

As described in section 6.3.1, the publication environment is a distributed system. We will show how a distributed execution of open nested transactions can be managed.

The most commonly used approach to model transaction execution in a distributed system is to split a global transaction into several local subtransactions. Each subtransaction represents a subset of the read/write actions of the global transaction. The subtransactions are executed on different nodes of the distributed system, and the local results are combined into a global transaction result. The previous section gave a mapping of the open nested model to the architecture of the publication environment. In contrast to the conventional model, our mapping does not define the split of a global transaction into local ones. Instead, we define operations to be executed on remote nodes. It is up to a remote node to implement the operation in terms of read/write actions. In other words, a remote subtransaction is an execution of one global operation, not a subset of read/write actions of the global transaction.

As a consequence, transactions in our environment are not allowed to directly access objects on remote nodes. The only way to access remote objects is to start a subtransaction on the remote node by means of a global operation. The concurrency control scheme given in section 6.4.2 can be applied, since no restrictions were imposed on the location of subtransaction executions. However, synchronization between operations that represent subtransactions on different nodes is necessary to ensure serializability for distributed open nested transactions in general. In this section, we assume that all the components of the publication environment are designed to fulfil our needs. The integration of existing tools that must not be modified according to these needs is discussed in the next section. In the following, we investigate the reduction of information flow between transaction managers on different nodes.

Due to the interface definition of section 6.3.1, the publication environment imposes several restrictions on the calling structure between different components. Disregarding the transaction structure inside of components, the transaction structure for subtransaction calls between components is relatively simple. In particular, the following conditions for remote subtransaction calls hold (Figure 6.14):

(1) A task manager may call subtransactions on remote task managers.
(2) A task manager may call subtransactions on remote agents.
(3) A task expert may call subtransactions on remote tools.
(4) An agent may call subtransactions on remote tools.
(5) Agents can only be called by the task manager of the assistant they belong to.

These restrictions simplify the concurrency control and recovery problems for distributed transactions in the publication environment. Except for calling-type (1), we find a hierarchical structure, as shown by Figure 6.14.

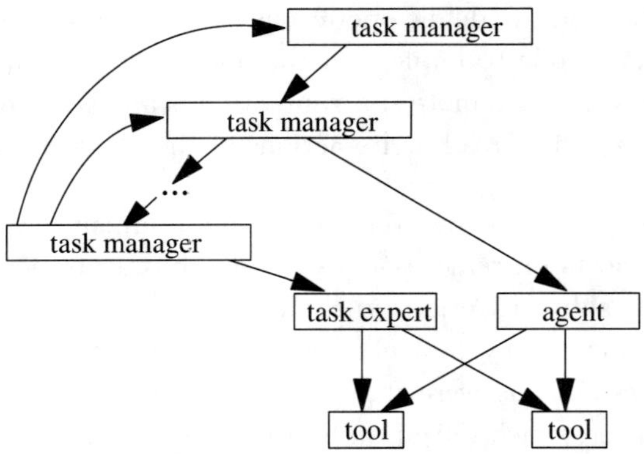

FIGURE 6.14
Calling Structure between Components.

Concurrency Control

For a layered structure, i.e. balanced transaction trees of a fixed depth, it has been shown that each layer may run its own, independent transaction manager [Wei91]. Applying such a layered structure for a distributed system allows the usage of independent transaction managers on different nodes. A remote subtransaction is just called, and the outcome is signalled to the caller.

In the publication environment, two exceptions cause transactions not to be layered:

(1) The calling structure of task managers may be of arbitrary depth, and it may even contain a cycle, since there is no restriction on the call of task managers by other task managers.

(2) A tool may be called by different task experts and agents.

Exception (1) requires the exchange of concurrency control and recovery information between task managers of different nodes. Exception (2) requires information exchange between different task experts and/or agents on different nodes if they access the same tool.

In order to manage the access of tools from different, independent components we use retained locks as described in section 6.4.2 and in [RMWHB91]. Retained locks ensure serializability for higher levels of abstraction even if the calling operations on the higher levels were not checked for commutativity. Such a situation may occur for multiple reasons. In the publication environment, transactions of a single tool may be called by transactions of different agents and task experts. These callers are not controlled by a common concurrency control module, because a commutativity check between all actions which are controlled by independent concurrency control modules is too expensive.

Using retained locks in our system means that tool transactions no longer release all their locks at commit/abort time, but convert them into retained locks. These locks are held until the end of the user transaction. Even though, retained locks do not decrease the potential degree of concurrency to the level of systems which use a flat transaction management. This is due to the fact that according to their definition, retained locks do not cause as many conflicts as normal locks. In the following, we show how the conflict test for retained locks can be performed by the corresponding components of the publication environment. We reconsider conditions (i)-(iii) for the conflict test of retained locks given in section 6.4.2.

Conditions (i) and (ii) can easily be checked inside the tool. In order to check condition (iii), the commutativity tables of the calling transactions have to be used. The list of callers of a tool transaction consists of the task expert or agent transaction which executed the tool transaction, and at least one task manager transaction. According to Figure 6.14, task managers can call other task managers and therefore the number of task managers that occur in the calling list is not limited.

Note that the conflict test required by condition (iii) only involves transactions that actually have accessed the same data in a tool. Compared to commutativity checks for all actions before the subtransactions are executed, this is a substantial reduction of concurrency control overhead. However, if the necessary computations are still too expensive, only a subset of the calling actions may be checked or condition (iii) may be be assumed to be true without any checking. In the latter case no concurrency gain can be achieved compared to a global locking scheme, since all the tool locks are held until the end of the user transaction. Even though, global serializability is achieved.

Assume, a task expert and an agent that was derived from this task expert and sold to another user execute concurrent subtransactions in a single tool. Since both offer similar functionality, the probability for a conflict of tool transactions is high. In this case, condition (iii) should at least be checked up to the level of task experts and agents, because, dependent on the type of operation, it is likely that the operations in the task expert and agent commute.

Recovery

We now discuss the recovery for distributed transactions in our environment. Without considering node failures, the transaction will be executed regardless of distribution. Transaction abort also makes no difference:

(1) Aborting a transaction which called subtransactions on remote nodes is realized by executing compensating operations as normal actions inside of the transaction that is to be aborted.
Consider again the sample scenario of Figure 6.1. Assume, the knowledge base and the hypertext-writing tool are located on different, remote network nodes. If the example transaction aborts after deriving a new version, a deleteVersion operation is sent to the hypertext-writing tool in order to compensate the changes. The direct call of a hypertext-writing tool command for the non-distributed case is substituted by a remote call. Nothing else has to be changed.

(2) Transaction aborts of subtransactions on remote nodes are also handled according to the scheme given in section 6.4.3. The remote subtransaction may be repeated, another subtransaction, possibly on a different node, may be executed, or the calling transaction aborts.

The problem is how to make such distributed transactions atomic in presence of node failures. For conventional distributed systems, this reduces the problem to the question of how to either commit or abort all the subtransactions. A commonly used algorithm to ensure this is two-phase commit [BHG87]. In our model, two-phase commit is not applicable, since subtransactions are allowed to commit before the global transaction is finished. Instead, we compensate the changes of a subtransaction if the calling transaction is to be aborted. Hence, atomic commitment in our model considers the following two cases:

(1) Commit: all Primary Actions of all subtransactions on all involved nodes are made persistent.

(2) Abort: all finished Primary Actions and the corresponding Inverse Actions of all subtransactions on all involved nodes are made persistent.

We have to consider node failures for the nodes of the subtransactions and for the node of the calling transaction. In both cases, a transaction consistent state is achieved by the recovery of the failed node according to the description of crash recovery in section 6.4.3. This can be assumed since all the participating components are designed as parts of the publication environment and provide the necessary crash recovery.

Transactions which called subtransactions on a failed node have to wait until the remote node recovered in order to determine the outcome of the subtransactions. After that, the decision how to continue is made by the calling transaction. If all subtransactions committed before the crash, the calling transaction is committed. If one or more subtransactions aborted, the calling transaction may either decide to repeat them, call another, or may abort, too. An abort is possible since the calling transaction maintains the corresponding log-information and the concurrency control on its level of abstraction. Like transaction abort described in section 6.4.3, the Inverse Actions are repeated until the compensation of all subtransactions is successful. One may consider this as a continuation of the crash recovery of the failed node. It is important to notice that this continuation will occur during normal transaction execution, because subtransaction repetition and the execution of Inverse Actions do not require specific concurrency control or recovery modes (section 6.4.3, Transaction Abort). Hence, the 'continued crash recovery' is executed with a minimum of delay for other transactions.

A failure of the node that runs the user transaction also needs no additional recovery techniques. During crash recovery, the outcome of all remote transactions has to be determined. From the point of view of the crashed node, committed remote subtransactions can be considered as subtransactions that survived the node crash, aborted ones can be considered to be killed by the crash.

An algorithm for atomic commitment of multi-level transactions following the scheme presented above is given in [MR91]. It can easily be extended to the non-layered transaction structure of the publication environment.

6.5.3 The Impact of Heterogeneity

The integration of existing tools is important since not all the tools used by the publication environment can be newly developed. Instead, existing tools are made available. In general, we assume that existing tools cannot be modified in order to be integrated in the publication environment. Even though, they must provide some basic functionality to allow integration. For the subsequent discussions, we define four prerequisites of integration:

(i) The existing tool must provide concurrency control if used by different users on the same objects concurrently.

(ii) If the existing tool may be used by different users on the same objects concurrently, local users which are not globally controlled must no longer be allowed to use the tool on these objects concurrently.

(iii) The existing tool must provide recovery. All the changes that were made inside of a transaction must be persistent. In addition, it must be possible to undo all changes that were made inside of a transaction until the transaction commits.

(iv) It must be possible to determine the outcome of every transaction executed by the existing tool, even after the tool recovered from a crash.

If tools are only known to fulfil the above prerequisites, we consider their transaction management modules as black boxes. These black boxes will manage the leaf-transaction in our transaction tree, because a tool is not allowed to start transactions on assistants, agents, or other tools. A tool simply executes its transactions and reports the results.

Different concurrency control algorithms may be used for the transaction management of tools. If serializability and recoverability is provided by a transaction manager, these properties can be preserved by the transaction management of the assistants and agents. In the following, we will show that guaranteeing the prerequisites (i)-(iv) is sufficient to ensure full serializability and recoverability for transactions in the publication environment.

Concurrency Control

Obviously, global serializability cannot be achieved if tools provide access to shared data without concurrency control (prerequisite (i)). But the integration of existing tools has another impact on concurrency control:

At first, we cannot assume that an existing tool supports retained locks. Hence, if a tool provides access to shared data for different task experts or agents, another scheme has to be found. A correct solution is to hold the locks of the tool transactions until the corresponding user transaction is finished. This also implies that a user transaction must not execute more than one subtransaction in each accessed tool. The achievable concurrency for actions accessing an existing tool decreases to the level of global locking. A better solution that allows a higher degree of concurrency is subject of further research.

In addition, existing tools may also execute autonomous local transactions. These transactions are not controlled by the transaction management of the publication environment.

EXAMPLE 6.7

Consider the example shown in Figure 6.15. Assume, after T1 derived a new version D_1 from version V of document Doc, a local transaction T_L deletes V. If T1 now tries to derive another version from V, this will cause the transaction to fail since it detects a consistency violation. We can consider the execution of tool transactions which are not under global control as an action on the next level of abstraction that is not visible to the open nested concurrency control. In this case, the isolation of transactions is violated. Obviously, T_L must not be scheduled between actions of T1. If T_L was known to the concurrency control of the publication environment, this could not happen, since deriveVersion (V, D) and deleteVersion (V) do not commute.

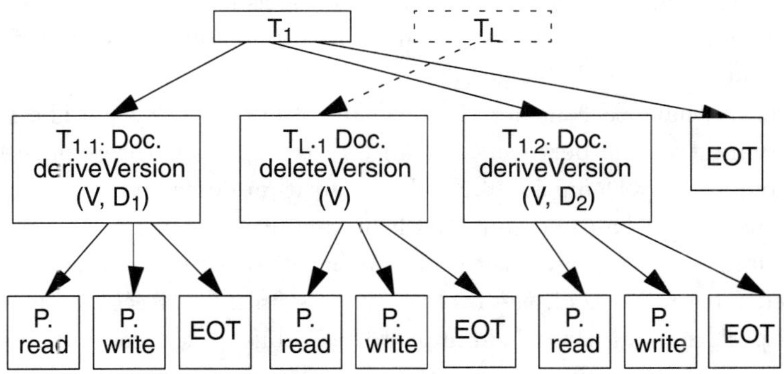

FIGURE 6.15
Autonomous Tool Transactions.

A safe way to completely avoid such problems is to disallow concurrent local transactions which are not controlled by the publication environment. This is ensured by prerequisite (ii). A specific correctness criterion called quasi-serializability has been proposed for heterogeneous database system which do not fulfil prerequisite (ii) [DE89]. In the future, we will work on a relaxation of prerequisite (ii) in order to allow a higher degree of autonomy for the integrated tools.

Recovery

The recovery scheme for transaction abort described in section 6.4.3 can also be applied for the heterogeneous case. An abort of a leaf-transaction is handled by the tool recovery autonomously. We only require such a mechanism to exist (prerequisite (iii)). The calling transaction has to be informed of the abort (prerequisite (iv)). It will decide how to continue. If prerequisite (iv) is not fulfilled by the system, inserting the transaction into the database will help. A transaction is committed if and only if its transaction identifier had been successfully inserted. See also [WV90]. Since the undo-logs for compensating leaf-transactions are managed by the callers of leaf-transactions, the logs are maintained by the recovery components of the publication environment. Heterogeneity has no impact on these logs. For a correct scheduling of recovery operations we need again prerequisites (i) and (ii). No additional prerequisites are needed with respect to concurrency control. This is due to the fact that from the concurrency control point of view Inverse Actions are treated the same as Primary Actions. Prerequisite (i) allows us to run primary and inverse actions of higher levels of abstraction as isolated tool transactions. Prerequisite (ii) ensures that no autonomous local transactions will violate a correct compensation of changes.

We also have to consider the problem of crash recovery. The tool recovery guarantees the persistence of all tool transactions (prerequisite (iii)). This is required by Definition 6.12. The algorithm described in section 6.4.3 requires an undo of all uncommitted leaf-transactions during recovery. This is also guaranteed by prerequisite (iii). After a transaction consistent state is recovered for a failed tool, the tool recovery is finished. Recovery for higher levels is performed afterwards in order to reestablish a transaction consistent state for the whole publication environment. Those transactions which called subtransactions in the failed tool and have not committed before the crash of the tool must be aware of the outcome of its subtransactions. Prerequisite (iv) ensures that the required information is available.

Similar to the previous discussion of a homogeneous distributed system, the algorithm of [MR91] will guarantee atomic commitment. Note that, different to two-phase commit, a specific crash recovery on remote nodes is not necessary. Two-phase commit requires that the crash recovery restores a 'ready' state for transactions which waited for a global commit or abort decision before the crash occurred. Specific termination protocols are used to determine how to continue. Because our algorithm does not require additional transaction states, the tool recovery need not provide such a specific facility.

We just need transaction consistent states for all transactions on the failed node after recovery, and it must be possible for the calling transactions to determine those states after the tool recovery is finished.

If no autonomous local transactions are allowed, the required prerequisites (i)-(iv) are fulfilled by all systems that provide ACID transactions. Hence, providing ACID transaction properties is a sufficient condition if an existing tool is to be integrated in our publication environment. It would be interesting to consider which concurrency control and recovery optimizations could be applied to the general scheme even in presence of Heterogeneity. Most recovery optimizations described in [WHBM90] are not applicable in an heterogeneous environment, because they are based on the exchange of concurrency control and recovery information between leaf-transactions and their callers. Even though, optimizations seem to be possible if more than the four prerequisites of integration is known about an existing tool. For example, this could be knowledge about the scheduling algorithm.

6.6 Conclusion

In this paper, we discussed an architecture for an open, distributed publication environment. Each user owns a personalized assistant supporting him to do specific tasks in the publication process. A user may communicate with other users in order to perform tasks that require foreign knowledge or facilities. A user may also buy foreign facilities by purchasing agents from other users. Agents work independently of the user who sold them.

As the underlying transaction model, we propose the use of open nesteds for the publication environment. Our transaction model provides a reduced conflict rate compared to flat models without violating serializability. This is achieved by using the semantics of operations, i.e. the commutativity between operations. An operation is always executed as a subtransaction on the next lower level of abstraction, except for operations on the lowest level, which are defined to be indivisible. Executing operations as transactions makes them atomic and isolated from others, which is required for a correct concurrent execution of commutative operations. In addition, this scheme has two advantages:

(1) Conflict definitions between operations on lower levels can again be based on commutativity.

(2) The scope of conflicts is restricted to the scope of subtransactions.

If subtransactions commute, the validity of conflicts is reduced to the lifetime of subtransactions, i.e. to the execution of a single operation.

Both advantages together significantly increase the potential degree of concurrency on all levels of abstraction. The reduced conflict rate makes the model applicable even for applications that require relaxed isolation if only read/write conflicts are considered.

Recovery in our model requires the execution of compensating operations instead of state-based undo. This is due to the fact that commutative updates are allowed on a single object in parallel. Restoring before-values of objects for transactions that performed such parallel updates would also affect the changes of other parallel updating transactions. Partial abortion of transactions is handled by aborting subtransactions which are relatively short compared to whole user transactions. A complete recovery scheme for transaction abort and crash recovery was discussed.

As another major achievement, our model allows the integration of new tools into the publication environment without changing the overall architecture. The transaction managers of the new tools are simply plugged into the global transaction management. If all the connected systems provide ACID properties for their transactions, the user transactions of the publication environment will also have these properties.

The proposed transaction model is currently under implementation within the *VODAK* project. The goal of VODAK is the development of an open object-oriented and distributed database system as a part of our publication environment.

Acknowledgement

We are indebted to Hannelore Eisner for her technical support.

Bibliography

[AGS87] R. Alonso, H. Garcia-Molina, K. Salem: Concurrency Control and Recovery for Global Procedures in Federated Database Systems. *IEEE Data Engineering* 10(3), Special Issue on Federated Database Systems, 1987.

[BR88] B.R. Badrinath, K. Ramamritham: Synchronizing Transactions on Objects. *IEEE Transactions on Computers* 37(5), 541-547, May 1988.

[BR90] B.R. Badrinath, K. Ramamritham: Performance Evaluation of Semantics-based Multilevel Concurrency Control Protocols. *Proc. SIGMOD 90*, 1990. In: *SIGMOD Record* 19(2), 163-172, 1990.

[BBG89] C. Beeri, P.A. Berstein, N. Goodman: A Model for Concurrency Control in Nested Transaction Systems. *JACM* 36(2), 1989.

[BHG87] P.A. Bernstein, V. Hadzilacos, N. Goodman: *Concurrency Control and Recovery in Database Systems.* Addison-Wesley, Reading, Mass., 1987.

[BJS86] St. Böttcher, M. Jarke, J.W. Schmidt: Adaptive Predicate Managers in Database Systems. *Proc. VLDB 86*, 21-29, 1986.

[BSW88] C. Beeri, H.-J. Schek, G. Weikum: Multi-Level Transaction Management, Theoretical Art or Practical Need? *Proc. EDBT '88*, 143-154, 1988.

[CF90] M. Cart, J. Ferrié: Integrating Concurrency Control into an Object-Oriented Database System. *Proc. EDBT'90.* In: *LNCS* 416, Springer, Berlin, 1990.

[DE89] W. Du, A.K. Elmagarmid: Quasi Serializability: a Correctness Criterion for Global Concurrency Control in InterBase. *Proc. VLDB*, 1989.

[EG89] C.A. Ellis, S.J. Gibbs: Concurrency Control in Groupware Systems. *Proc. SIGMOD*, 1989.

[ELLR90] A.K. Elmagarmid, Y. Leu, W. Litwin, M. Rusinkiewicz: A Multidatabase Transaction Model for InterBase. *Proc. VLDB*, 1990.

[FLMW88] A. Fekete, N. Lynch, M. Merritt, W. Weihl: *Commutativity-Based Locking for Nested Transactions.* MIT/LCS/TM-370, Cambridge, Mass., 1988.

[GK85] D. Gawlick, D. Kinkade: Varieties of Concurrency Control in IMS/VS Fast Path. *IEEE Database Engineering* 8(2), 3-10, 1985.

[Her90] U. Herrmann, P. Dadam, K. Küspert, E.A. Roman, G. Schlageter: A Lock Technique for Disjoint and Non-Disjoint Complex Objects. *Proc. EDBT'90.* In: *LNCS* 416, Springer, Berlin, 1990.

[HR79] A. Harry, B. Hunt, D.J. Rosenkrantz: The Complexity of Testing Predicate Locks. *Proc. SIGMOD 79*, 127-133, May 1979.

[HR83] T. Härder, A. Reuter: Principles of Transaction-Oriented Database Recovery. *ACM Computing Surveys* 15(4), 1983.

[HW88] M.P. Herlihy, W.E. Weihl: Hybrid Concurrency Control for Abstract Data Types. *Proc. PODS 88*, 201-210, March 1988.

[HW91] C. Hasse, G. Weikum: *Multi-Level Transaction Management for Complex Objects: Implementation, Performance, Parallelism.* Manuscript, accepted for Proc. VLDB, 1991.

[KBG89] W. Kim, E. Bertino, J.F. Garza: Composite Objects Revisted. *Proc. SIGMOD 89.* In: *SIGMOD Record* 18(2), 337-347, 1989.

[KKB88] H.F. Korth, W. Kim, F. Bancilhon: On Long-Duration CAD Transactions. *Information Sciences* 46, 73-107, 1988.

[KL89] W. Kim, F.H. Lochovsky (eds.): *Object-Oriented Concepts, Databases and Applications.* Addison-Wesley, Reading, 1989.

[KLS90] H.F. Korth, E. Levy, A. Silberschatz: Compensating Transactions: A New Recovery Paradigm, *Proc. VLDB*, 1990.

[KN89] M. Kracker, E.J. Neuhold: Schema Independent Query Formulation. *Proc. Conf. on Entity-Relationship Approach*, 1989.

[KN90] W. Klas, E.J. Neuhold: Designing Intelligent Hypertext Systems using an Open Object-Oriented Database Model. *Arbeitspapiere der GMD* 489, St. Augustin, Sept. 1990.

[KNS89] W. Klas, E.J. Neuhold, M. Schrefl: Tailoring Object-Oriented Data Models through Metaclasses, *Proc. of the Advanced Database Systems Symposium*, Kyoto, Japan, 1989.

[KNS90] W. Klas, E.J. Neuhold, M. Schrefl: Using an Object-Oriented Approach to Model Multimedia Data, *Computer Communications, Special Issue on Multimedia Systems* 13(4), 1990.

[KS90] H.F. Korth, G.D. Speegle: Long-Duration Transactions in Software Design Projects. *Proc. Conf. on Data Engineering*, 568-574 ,1990.

[Lyn83] N.A. Lynch: Multilevel Atomicity - A New Correctness Criterion for Database Concurrency Control. *ACM TODS* 8(4), 484-502, Dec. 1983.

[Mar88] B. Martin: *Concurrent Nested Object Computations.* PhD thesis, University of California at San Diego, La Jolla, Ca., June 1988.

[Mos85] J.E.B. Moss: *Nested Transactions - An Approach to Reliable Distributed Computing.* MIT Press, Cambridge, Mass., 1985.

[Mos90] J.E.B. Moss: Design of the Mneme Persistent Object Store. *ACM TOIS* 8(2): 103-139, April 1990.

[Moh89] C. Mohan, D. Haderle, B. Lindsay, H. Pirahesh, P. Schwarz: ARIES: A Transaction Recovery Method Supporting Fine-Granularity Locking and Partial Rollbacks Using Write-Ahead Logging *IBM Research Report* RJ6649, San Jose, 1989, to appear in: *ACM TODS.*

[MGG86] J.E.B. Moss, N. Griffeth, M. Graham: Abstraction in Recovery Management. *Proc. SIGMOD*, 72-83, 1986.

[MKN90] P. Muth, W. Klas, E.J. Neuhold: How to Handle Global Transactions in Heterogeneous Database Systems. *Workshop on Multidatabases and Semantic Interoperability*, Tulsa, Oklahoma, USA, Nov. 3-4, 1990.

[MP91] C. Mohan, H. Pirahesh: ARIES-RRH: Restricted Repeating of History in the ARIES Transaction Recovery Method. *Proc. Conf. on Data Engineering*, 1991.

[MR91] P. Muth, T.C. Rakow: Atomic Commitment for Integrated Database Systems. *Proc. Conf. on Data Engineering*, 296-304, 1991.

[MRKN91] P. Muth, T.C. Rakow, W. Klas, E.J. Neuhold: A Transaction Model for an Open Publication Environment. *IEEE Data Engineering Bulletin*14(1), Special Issue on Unconventional Transaction Management, March 1991.

[NKKN87] J.D. Noe, J. Kaiser, R. Kröger, E. Nett: The Commit/ Abort Problem in Type-Specific Locking. *Arbeitspapiere der GMD* 267, St. Augustin, Sept. 1987.

[O'N86] P.E. O'Neil: The Escrow Transaction Method. *ACM TODS* 11 (4), 405-430, Dec. 1986.

[PS87] D.J. Penney, J. Stein: Class Modification in the GemStone Object-Oriented DBMS. *Proc. OOPSLA 87.* In: *SIGPLAN Notices* 22(12), 111-117, 1987.

[Rak91] T.C. Rakow: Aspects of Concurrency Control in Object-Oriented Database Systems (*in german*). In H.-J. Appelrath (Ed.): *Datenbanksysteme in Büro, Technik und Wissenschaft*, Proc., 485-492. In: IFB 270, Springer, Berlin, 1991.

[RMWHB91] T.C. Rakow, P. Muth, G. Weikum, C. Hasse, P. Broesler: *Semantic Concurrency Control in Object-Oriented Database Systems.* Manuscript, 1991.

[RGN90] T.C. Rakow, J. Gu, E.J. Neuhold: Serializability in Object-Oriented Database Systems. *Proc. Conf. on Data Engineering,* 1990.

[RRD90] M.A. Ranft, S. Rehm, K. R. Dittrich: How to Share Work on Shared Objects in Design Databases. *Proc. Conf. on Data Engineering,* 575-583, 1990.

[RW91] A. Reuter, H. Wächter: The ConTract Model. *Data Engineering Bulletin* 14(1), Special Issue on Unconventional Transaction Management, 1991.

[SPSW90] H.J. Schek, H. B. Paul, M. H. Scholl, G. Weikum: The DASDBS Project: Objectives, Experiences, and Future Prospects. *IEEE Transactions on Knowledge and Data Engineering* 2(1), 1990.

[SS84] P.M. Schwarz, A.Z. Spector: Synchronizing Shared Abstract Types. *ACM TOCS* 2(3), 223-250, 1984.

[Tra83] I.L. Traiger: Trends in System Aspects of Database Management. *Proc. 2nd Int. Conf. on Databases*, Wiley & Sons, 1983.

[US91] R. Unland, G. Schlageter: A Flexible and Adaptable Tool Kit Approach for Transaction Management in Non Standard Database Systems. *Data Engineering Bulletin*14(1), Special Issue on Unconventional Transaction Management, 1991.

[Wal85] B. Walter: Multi-level Synchronization and Nested Transactions in Advanced Information Systems. *Proc. BTW '85*, 336-355. In: *IFB* 94, Springer, Berlin, 1985.

[Web91] A. Weber: Publishing Tools Need Both: State-Oriented and Task-Oriented Version Support. *Arbeitspapiere der GMD* 526, St. Augustin, 1991. Accepted for COMPSAC '91, Tokyo.

[Wei86] G. Weikum: A Theoretical Foundation of Multi-Level Concurrency Control. *Proc. PODS*, 1986.

[Wei91] G. Weikum: Principles and Realization Strategies of Multi-Level Transaction Management, *ACM TODS* 16(1), 1991.

[Weh89] W.E. Weihl: Local Atomicity Properties: Modular Concurrency Control for Abstract Data Types. *ACM TOPLAS* 11(2), 249-282, 1989.

[WHBM90] G. Weikum, C. Hasse, P. Broessler, P. Muth: Multi-Level Recovery. *Proc. PODS*, 1990.

[Wie90] G. Wiederhold, et. al.: A Mediator Architecture for Abstract Data Access. Technical Report No. STAN-CS-90-1303, Dept. of Computer Science, Stanford University, CA, 1990.

[WV90] A. Wolski, J. Veijalainen: 2PC Agent Method: Achieving Serializability in Presence of Failures in a Heterogeneous Multidatabase. *Proceedings PARBASE*, 1990.

7

The ConTract Model

Helmut Wächter

Andreas Reuter

7.1 Introduction and Overview

The limitations of classical ACID transactions have been discussed extensively in the literature [Gra81]. Developed in the context of database systems, they perform well only when the controlled units of work are small, access only a few data items, and therefore have a short system residence time. Given this assumption, transactions could be made atomic state transitions. But atomicity, taken verbally, means that there is no structure whatsoever that can be perceived and referred to from the outside. Another way of putting this is the following: If there is a unit of work that has a structure, say, in terms of control flow, which needs to be maintained by the system, it cannot be modelled as a transaction – and current database systems, operating systems, etc. have no other means for dealing with that.

Now in distributed systems and in so-called non-standard applications like office automation, CAD, manufacturing control, etc. one frequently finds units of work that are very long compared to classical transactions, touch many objects and have a complex control flow which may include migrations of (partial) activities across the nodes of a network [KR88]. Because the lack of appropriate system mechanisms to support this processing characteristics, controlling such activities requires organizational means or enforces the application itself to take care of, e.g. recovering the activity from a crash. But even simple examples like the mini-batch [GR91] demonstrate that the resulting code contains large portions that are not application-specific, but have to do with flow control.

The ConTract-model, first proposed in [Reu89], tries to provide the formal basis for defining and controlling long-lived, complex computations, just like transactions control short computations. It was inspired by the concept of spheres of control [Dav78], and by the mechanisms for managing flow that are provided by some TP-monitors, like queues, context databases, etc. [GR91].

Since ConTracts introduce a unit of work and control that consists of the whole application instead of individual database state transitions, they define a control mechanism above ACID transactions. It is not an extension of the transaction concept like those suggested in, e.g., [Mos81, Lyn83, KLMP84, Wei86, GS87, HHMM88, ELLR90] in the sense that a more powerful but still structurally limited framework denotes. It rather is a programming model that — in contrast to conventional programming languages — includes persistence, consistency, recovery, synchronization and cooperation.

This chapter starts by illustrating the problem domain (section 2) and then proposes mechanisms to meet the identified requirements of managing long-lived activities in distributed systems. After the presentation of the ConTract model (section 3), issues concerning the implementation of ConTracts as a consistent and reliable execution environment are discussed as well as considerations how to extend existing database and operating systems for this task (section 4). Then a comparison to other work follows (section 5) before the paper concludes with a summary of results and a brief sketch of the current status as well as future work on the ConTract Model (section 6).

7.2 Transaction Support for Large Distributed Applications

Classical transactions are the first application–independent control mechanism that supports the units of work of a database application with the following well known properties: *A*tomicity, *C*onsistency, *I*solation and *D*urability. These properties are used widely to the advantage of many applications, especially for reservation systems, banking or inventory control. In other database applications, however, several aspects of the transaction concept limit its use. The main reason for this is that some of its implicit assumptions are no longer valid in so-called non-standard applications:

> Transactions model short and concurrent computation steps which operate on small amounts of simply structured shared objects existing solely as data in a computer system.

The most fundamental drawback of traditional transaction systems in the context of long-lived applications is their notion of transactions being concurrent and completely unrelated units of work. As a consequence, any existing interrelations between individual transactions, like control flow dependencies and other semantic connections, cannot be implemented by the system, but have to be handled by the application (Fig. 7.1).

As an example, it is not possible to run the following sequence of transactions according to the specification given below solely within the control sphere of a database transaction manager without further application programming:

Specification of a simple transaction sequence:
Run transaction T1. Then execute transactions T2, T3, T4 in

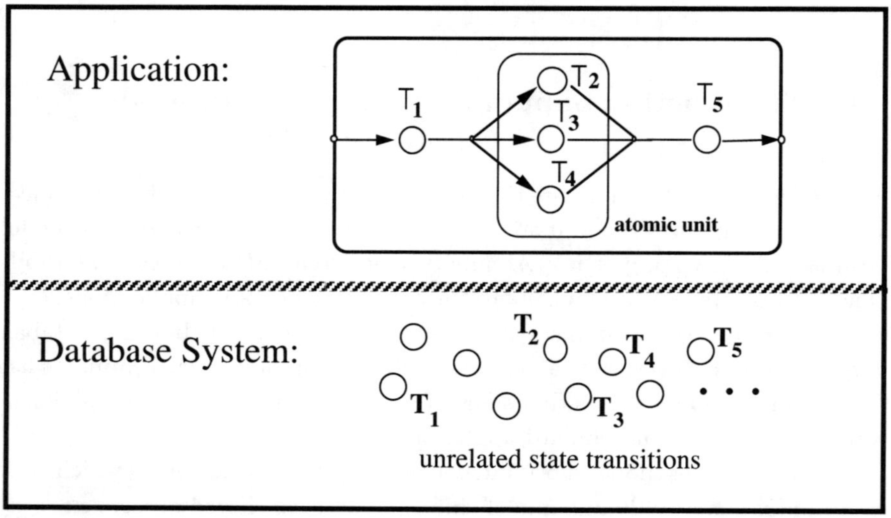

FIGURE 7.1
Control flow and other inter-transaction dependencies at the application level are mapped to unrelated and therefore isolated database state transitions.

parallel. Immediately after their successful completion start T5. But if one of (T2, T3, T4) fails, then abort the other two. In this case the effects of T1 have to be cancelled as well.

In the cooperation of a current DBMS with programming languages and operating systems there is no system mechanism to achieve a concatenation of transactions that is robust against system failures. And there is no means to control global concurrency concerning the synchronization of, e.g., T1 and T5 against other applications.[1]

This simple example hints at several major requirements, which need to be addressed by a mechanism for the reliable and correct execution of large distributed applications:

1. *Programming model*:
   Large applications are usually defined by combining existent (trans-) actions. Therefore, an appropriate programming model has to support code reusability.
2. *Flow control for non-atomic computations*:
   Most long-lived activities show an internal structure that has to be maintained by the system. This requires a means to describe and manage control flow between transactions in both static and dynamic terms. A typical requirement is the ability to suspend, migrate and resume an application on another node in the network.
3. *Failure and recovery model*:
   Because failure handling according to the "all-or-nothing" principle is unacceptable or sometimes impossible, the language used for control flow description needs an explicitly and precisely defined failure model. Three central requirements are the following:
   - Building a large activity from several smaller actions needs a flexible mechanism for defining and managing atomic units of work.
   - A system failure may not destroy or extinguish an entire computation.
   - In contrast to short transactions, an application as a whole has to be forward recoverable, e.g., by re-instantiating and continuing it according to its control flow specification.

[1]Combining all actions into one long transaction is not a satisfactory solution, neither conceptually nor under performance considerations.

4. *Context management for related actions*:
Roll-forward requires the ability not only to reconstruct the database but also the local state of the application (-program).
5. *Referencing the execution history*:
Applications running during a long period of time sometimes need to remember their history and execution path, for example, when the decision what to do next depends on previous computation steps. Though, there must be a way to reference this history as well as local state produced in the past.
6. *Externalization of preliminary results*:
Long computations will have to externalize results before they are completely done. This implies that unilateral roll-back is no longer possible [GS87]; one rather needs to specify compensating actions as part of the control flow description.
7. *Concurrency and consistency control*:
For the same reason, consistency definitions can no longer be based on serializability; rather they have to allow for application oriented policies of synchronizing access to shared objects.
8. *Conflict handling*:
In general, it is neither feasible to let some activity wait in case of a resource conflict until a long-duration activity has completed. Nor is it acceptable to roll it back to its beginning. Therefore, part of the control flow description has to specify what should be done, if a resource conflict occurs, how it can be resolved, etc.

Essentially, the key requirement of controlling long-lived activities demands that the computation itself must be a recoverable object, and not just the state manipulated by it, as is the case with classical transactions. To realize this feature, the concept of classical transactions has to be generalized substantially.

The next sections refine this list of control problems and present the respective ConTract mechanisms to meet the identified requirements. The term *ConTract* is used throughout the rest of the article to indicate a unit of work with the above listed features and qualities. The term *ConTract manager* denotes a system service that implements the requirements listed above for all kinds of applications.

7.3 ConTracts

The basic idea of the ConTract model is to build large applications from short ACID transactions and to provide an application independent system service, which exercises control over them. As a main contribution, ConTracts provide the computation as a whole with reliability and correctness properties:

> *A* **ConTract** *is a consistent and fault tolerant execution of an arbitrary sequence of predefined actions (called steps) according to an explicitly specified control flow description (called script).*

In other words, a ConTract is a program that has control flow like any parallel programming environment, that has persistent local variables, accesses shared objects with application oriented synchronization mechanisms, and which has a precise error semantics.

The design rationale behind the ConTract model is the objective to capture system failures by the system and to present the user or application programmer with an arbitrarily reliable execution platform. By a similar argument all burdening tasks which result from controlling parallel or concurrent computations, scheduling (distributed) executions etc. should be removed from the application programmer and accomplished by the ConTract manager.

In the following sections the basic mechanisms of the ConTract model are explained by (parts of) a travel planning activity. Fig. 7.2 illustrates a simplified version of this commonly used example [Gra81, KR88, ELLR90]:

Making flight, hotel and car reservations for a business trip is a typical activity that can last a long time and sometimes needs more than one session to be completed. It is therefore not possible to do the whole reservation procedure within one transaction.

To keep things simple there are only three airlines to be consulted for a flight and only two hotel resp. car rental companies. These give an exclusive discount to each other (in this example) and therefore are only booked in combinations (Cathedral Hill Hotel, Avis) or (Holiday Inn, Hertz). We assume this application to be run on a terminal of a travel agency connected to a worldwide network of heterogeneous computers running the various database servers.

Focusing basically on logical aspects of transaction processing we omit considerations of physical aspects like communication, authentication and other problems concerning the interrelations of advanced transaction management with an operating system [Gra78, Spe87, CCF89].

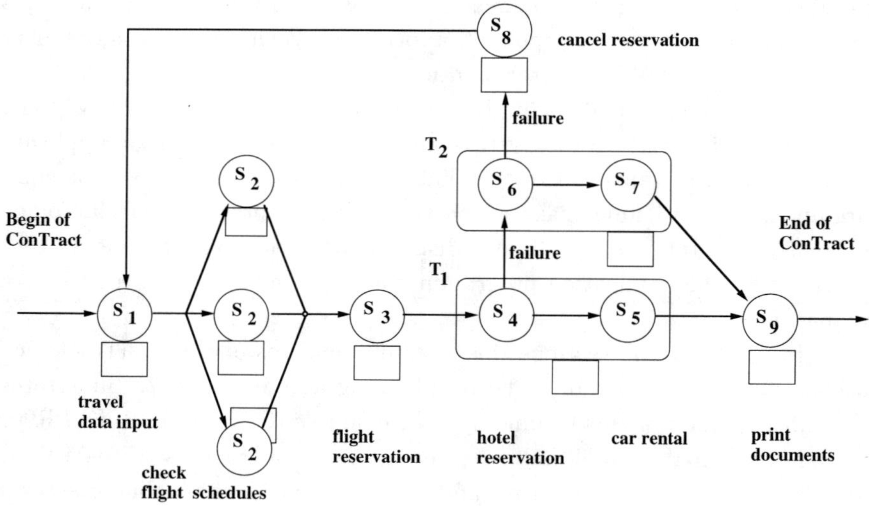

FIGURE 7.2
A sample script "Business Trip Reservations" — graphical representation

7.3.1 Modelling Control Flow: Scripts and Steps

A **script**[2] describes the control flow and other execution strategies of a long-lived activity (Fig. 7.3).

Control flow between related steps can be modelled by the usual elements: sequence, branch, loop and some parallel constructors. It is also possible to specify a loop over a tuple set forming, e.g., a query result. In the travel planning activity the *PAR_FOREACH(airline ...)* statement consults n dynamically computed airline timetables in parallel.

Steps are the elementary units of work in the ConTract model. Each step implements one basic computation of an application, e.g., booking a flight, cancelling a reservation and so on (Fig. 7.4). There is no internal parallelism in a step and therefore it can be coded in an arbitrary sequential programming language. Its size is determined by the amount of work an application can tolerate to be lost after a system failure.

This paper does not want to define yet another language for parallel and distributed computing systems [BST89], since the focus of the ConTract model is not on activity *specification* (like in the script mechanism described in [BMW84]), but on activity *control*. And for the same reason the expressive power of the script language is not the primary concern here. It could be extended by adding recursion, nesting, generic steps with late code binding and other features if this seems useful to model special kinds of applications. The point here is to have a means for explicitly specifying control flow for operations on shared persistent objects (i.e. the database). A central issue in extending control beyond transaction boundaries is to use this activity specification for reliable flow control.

The basic idea is that scripts describe the structure (the control flow) of a complex activity, while steps implement its algorithmic parts. All aspects concerning execution control at run time, however, have to be done by the ConTract manager.

The ConTract manager internally implements an event oriented flow management by using some sort of predicate transition net to specify activation and termination conditions for a step. The execution of a step is started if

[2] A graphical editor would be the optimal choice for a user-friendly script definition. Since we are not concerned with such aspects in this approach, a Concurrent Pascal like textual language is used (see Appendix A for a complete version of the sample script). Of course, there are other syntactic means for specifying control flow, but this is not the point of this paper.

```
CONTRACT  Business_Trip_Reservations

CONTEXT_DECLARATION
  cost_limit, ticket_price:     dollar;
  from, to:                     city;
  date:                         date_type;
  ok:                           boolean;
   :
CONTROL_FLOW_SCRIPT
  S1: Travel_Data_Input(in_context: ;
                        out_context: date, from, to, seats, cost_limit);
  PAR_FOREACH( airline: EXECSQL select airline from  ...  ENDSQL )
    S2: Check_Flight_Schedule(in_context: airline, date, from, to, seats;
                              out_context: flight_no, ticket_price );
  END_PARFOREACH

  S3: Flight_Reservation(in_context: airline, flight_no, date, seats,..);
  S4: Hotel_Reservation( in_context:  "Cathedral Hill Hotel";
                         out_context:  ok, hotel_reservation );
  IF ( ok[S4] ) THEN  S5: Car_Rental(  ... "Avis" ... );
  ELSE BEGIN
          S6: Hotel_Reservation( ... "Holiday Inn"  ... );
          IF ( ok[S6] )
             THEN      S7:  Car_Rental( ... "Hertz"  ... );
          ELSE  S8: Cancel_Flight_Reservation_&_Try_Another_One( .. );
       END
  S9: Print_Documents( ... );

END_CONTROL_FLOW_SCRIPT
  :
  :      /* further specifications as shown below  */
  :
END_CONTRACT  Business_Trip_Reservations
```

FIGURE 7.3
Sample script “Business Trip Reservations” — textual representation

```
STEP Flight_Reservation

   DESCRIPTION: Reserve n seats of a flight and pay for them ...
   IN           airline:        STRING;
                flight_no:      STRING;
                date:           DATE;
                seats:          INTEGER;
                ticket_price:   DOLLAR;
   OUT          status:         INTEGER;

flight_reservation()
{  char*  flight_no;
   long   date;
   int    seats;
     :
   EXEC SQL
        UPDATE  Reservations
        SET     seats_taken =  seats_taken + :seats
        WHERE   flight      =  :flight_no     AND
                date        =  :date          ...
   END SQL
     :
}
```

FIGURE 7.4
Code fragment of a sample step "Flight Reservation"

the event predicate for its activation becomes true and the required execution resources are available. For example, step S_3 in Fig. 7.2 is triggered when all three parallel activations of step S_2 are finished. An interactive step (e.g. S_1) additionally needs the responsible user to be ready for input etc.

The triggering of events after step termination can be controlled by a set of conditions. Each condition which evaluates to be true triggers one or more events. These in turn trigger the subsequent steps.

The idea behind this simple internal language is to use it as an intermediate language onto which higher-level programming languages [BST89] can be compiled.

7.3.2 ConTract Programming Model

In the ConTract programming model, the coding of steps is separated from defining an application's control flow script. As a consequence, the programming of a reservation step and the concatenation of steps to form the business trip script of Fig. 7.3 are two different tasks, which even may be performed by different people.

The idea behind this separation is to keep the programming environment for the actual application programmer as simple as possible: Steps are coded without worrying about things like managing asynchronous or parallel computations, communication, resource distribution (localization), synchronization and failure recovery. In particular, the programmer of a step does not have to consider where in the network a step is executed and whether a step or a set of steps (for instance (S_4, S_5) or (S_6, S_7)) is combined to one ACID transaction. The latter decision, for example, is made at the script level in the *TRANSACTIONS* part of the specification, see below (7.3.3).

The consequence, though, is that there exist at least two "levels" of programming. Actually, each dimension of the ConTract model is decoupled from the remaining control aspects and can be defined separately. The hypothesis is that a layered programming model will be inevitable when specifying and implementing long–lived, complex applications, no matter which framework one uses.

From the programmer's view, steps will be run on a virtual machine (resource manager) which is arbitrarily reliable and executes in single user mode. How to achieve this is discussed in the next sections.

7.3.3 Transaction Model

ConTracts offer a sophisticated set of transaction control mechanisms at the script level. They are designed to support the following requirements:

a) to provide flexible transaction mechanisms for the structuring of large distributed applications;

b) to provide the script (transaction) programmer with control mechanisms which are still easy to understand and manageable.

The approach is to define a small set of basic mechanisms with reasonable default strategies while providing powerful transaction control parameters as a feature for the experienced transaction programmer.

Transaction Properties for Scripts and Steps

Each step is implemented by embedding it into a traditional ACID transaction, if nothing else is specified in the *TRANSACTIONS* part of the script (see below). Steps, thereby, have all of the ACID properties, but they preserve only local consistency for the manipulated objects.

Since not being a transaction, a whole ConTract is not an ACID unit of work; here are the differences to the standard definition:

Atomicity: The fundamental deviation from classical transactions is that ConTracts give up atomicity at the script level because this property is incompatible with the needs of long duration activities. A ConTract can be interrupted explicitly and continued by the user after an arbitrary delay.

And more important, a crash along the way does not initiate rollback. Rather the system initiates roll forward recovery, maybe along a different path than the one taken before.

Consistency: ConTracts maintain system integrity, and they do this on a much larger scale than single transactions.

Isolation: A ConTract typically is a long-lived activity, and therefore isolating the shared data it accesses by standard means of locking would be detrimental for system performance. ConTracts rather rely on semantic isolation, which is based on application specific invariants (predicates on shared state) that have to be maintained by the system for the duration of a ConTract.

Durability: A ConTract's global effects installed at the end of its steps are durable and can be undone only by running another ConTract (step).

Defining Atomic Units of Work

Steps are coded without considering their concatenation and combination into larger units later on. This is done by the script programmer. He can define atomic units of work consisting of more than one step by arbitrarily grouping them into sets. In Fig.7.2 the dotted lines around (S_4, S_5) and (S_6, S_7), respectively, reflect the decision that these pairs should be executed as an atomic unit of work to model the application semantics correctly. In the textual notation this definition looks like that:

```
TRANSACTIONS
        T1 ( S4, S5 )
```

```
    T2 ( S6, S7 )
END_TRANSACTIONS
```
[3]

In addition to this quite simple atomic concatenation the resulting groups can be nested into a tree like hierarchical structure. In the textual notation this could be indicated by writing:

```
T3 ( T1, T2 )
```

Furthermore, the transaction programmer may specify events depending on the outcome (resp. activation) of steps and/or transactions. These events are controlled by the ConTract run time system.

A very common usage is to set up the ConTract system to supervise the outcome of a transaction. In case of its failure the script programmer perhaps wants it to start another step, which could be a functional alternative to this step or could try to correct an error in order to enable the continuation of the executing activity.

Trying another (hotel, car company) pair in the business trip ConTract is an example of this kind of transaction control. The textual notation for that is:

```
DEPENDENCY( T1 abort ↦ begin T2 )
```

The semantics of this dependency is defined as:

If T_1 aborts, then T_2 must be started.[4]

Note, that there exists some interrelation between the control flow part of a script and the transaction dependencies. What is written out in full detail with S_4, S_5, S_6, S_7 in Figure 7.2 could just be achieved without S_6, S_7 and T_2 through the following dependency declarations:

```
T1 ( S4, S5 )
DEPENDENCY( T1 abort[1] ↦ begin T1 ) /* 1st abort of T1 */
DEPENDENCY( T1 abort[2] ↦ begin S8 ) /* 2nd abort of T1 */
```

Comparing this specification with Figure 7.2 shows the latter to be more adequate for a simple and predefined control flow structure (like a small number of alternatives) because it lists the possible control flow paths explicitly.

[3] T_1,T_2, ... are logical identifiers to reference the specified atomic units.

[4] This dependency declaration is similar to the so-called failure (or negative) dependency defined in [ELLR90]. However, since there is no distinction between transactions and steps, the dependency declaration mechanism of the ConTract model seems to be more flexible.

But this detailed and illustrative notation gets lengthy and expensive for more complex flow structures as can be seen by looking at the following specification of a "very reliable" transaction T in a shorthand notation:

$$\mathtt{T\ b{\mapsto}b\ T_1\ \ldots a{\mapsto}b\ T_k\ a{\mapsto}a\ T} \quad \mathtt{/*}\ k\ \mathtt{alternatives\ for\ T\ */}$$

$$\mathtt{T_i\ c{\mapsto}c\ T}$$

$$\mathtt{T\ a[1]{\mapsto}b\ T\ \ldots T\ a[n]{\mapsto}b\ T_{rescue}} \quad \mathtt{/*\ retry\ T}\ n\ \mathtt{times\ */}$$

As a negative "side effect", this compact and flexible notation, however, leads programmers to lose track of *global* control flow aspects. Therefore it is useful to have both possibilities for control flow specification and to choose the appropriate one in accordance with the given activity.

Shifting the implementation of dependency declarations into the ConTract system allows the script programmer to exercise flow control even in case of failures or system crashes. Besides that, the declarative style of transaction and flow control avoids a complicated and error-prone procedural style of exception programming. This is difficult enough in today's systems anyway, since DBMS *do*, but most programming languages *do not* know about the semantics of aborts.

How to manage transactions with dependencies efficiently and correctly is beyond the scope of this paper, since this is still an open question of current research. First steps to the required concepts and techniques can be found in [Dav78, CR91, Kle91, HGK91]

7.3.4 User Interface for Controlling Large Distributed Applications

Since ConTracts maintain the structure of an activity, they consequently need a means for administering the flow of control. The following paragraphs exemplify three important mechanisms for controlling a whole application as a unit of work.

Controlling Long–Lived Computations

The first mechanism allows to suspend the execution of a ConTract. It can then be resumed after an arbitrary period. In the meantime the complete processing context is kept on stable storage and protected in a way to ensure the suspended ConTract's continuation.

In the sample ConTract it may happen that a customer makes a flight reservation, but then interrupts the reservation procedure in order to book hotel and car just before the trip.

Controlling Distributed Computations

Controlling distributed computations sometimes requires to migrate an application's execution from one node to another in the network [KR88]. This is necessary, for example, if one node fails forever and the user has to tell the system from which node he wants to continue the interrupted ConTract. Or assume a travel agency where one agent does the flight reservation, and a colleague at another terminal is responsible for car and hotel reservations.

Just migrating the executing operating system process is not sufficient, since portions of the context of the database application may be kept in different processes. Migrating a ConTract involves at least two ConTract managers running a reliable protocol to transfer all required state information and to continue the application properly.

Monitoring Distributed Computations

Other available user commands for managing long–lived ConTracts in distributed systems include facilities to show the current computation state, to determine a ConTract's location and to trace its execution. Figure 7.5 gives some examples how to access a ConTract's execution history.

The consistency and reliability qualities coming with the ConTract execution model are explained in the next two sections.

7.3.5 Forward Recovery and Context Management

System reconfiguration, communication failures, node crashes and other failures should not cause an application to turn undefined or, even worse, vanish without a trace. But that is what normal transactions would do for you without further application programming:

- An ordinary operating system process running application code is gone after a crash. The user has to know which application was affected, what the state of the activity was, and how to recover it manually.

- A transaction system restores only a consistent database by rolling back all uncommitted operations. This does not matter for short transactions but is unacceptable for long lived activities.

A reliable system, on the other hand, would resume (automatically after system restart or on user demand, if a node goes down permanently) all ongoing computations and try to minimize the loss of work. In case a local

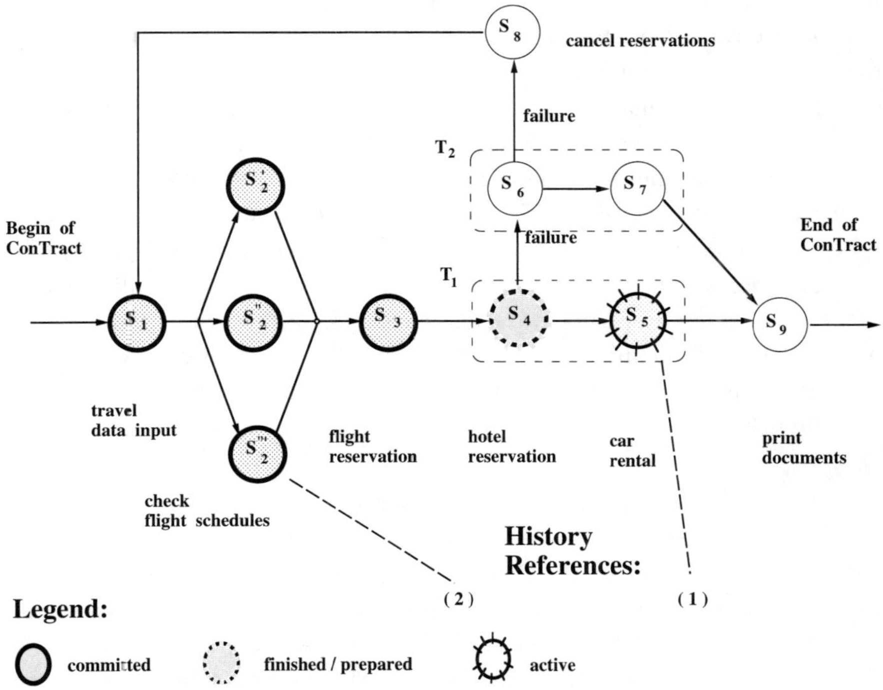

(1) "How far is the execution of my ConTract *Business Trip Reservations* ?"	
ConTract	Business Trip Reservations, *cid 123456*
currently active step	S_5
running on node	int_rentals_db_server@avis-frankfurt.de
activation time	17:15
:	:

(2) "Which flight offered Lufthansa ($S_2^{''}$) ?"			
$S_2^{''}$	IN	airline	Lufthansa
	OUT	flight_no	LH136
		from	Stuttgart
		to	Paris
		date	5/17/1991
		seats free	9

FIGURE 7.5

Referencing the sample ConTract's execution history.

computer fails during the sample ConTract, the agent would like just to turn to another terminal and to continue the suspended reservation procedure right from the last valid ConTract state.

The ConTract manager therefore tries to overcome resource failures and re-instantiates an interrupted ConTract by restoring the recent step consistent state and then continues its execution according to the specified script. Only a non–recoverable failure outside the scope of the system causes a ConTract to be continued along a path that cancels all externalized effects (see 7.3.7).

The realization of this forward oriented recovery scheme implies that all state information a step's computation relies upon has to be recoverable. This set of private data defining an application specific computation state is called *Context*. To re-instantiate an interrupted ConTract the following information is required to be recoverable:

1. the global system state seen by all applications, i.e. the involved databases;
2. the local state of the ConTract, e.g., the program variables, sessions, windows, file descriptors, cursors etc. used by more than one step;[5]
3. the global computation state of the affected application. This means a stable bookkeeping in the ConTract system of which event has been triggered, which step has (or has not yet) been executed etc.

This list gives evidence that taking a savepoint or checkpointing the database part of an application is not sufficient to guarantee continuation of an interrupted ConTract after a system failure. Beside that, context contains data that is not captured by any existing data model, like sessions or windows.

Context Management

In principle, there are three different ways to manage context reliably:
(a) keeping it in the global database;
(b) transferring it explicitly from one step to another, e.g., through a reliable queue mechanism [Gar91, GGKKS91, BHM90];
(c) setting up a special context database with a private interface for each ConTract.

[5]These global variables or intermediate results are usually not kept in the database. Nevertheless, this information is absolutely necessary to implement forward recovery.

The first possibility would require the step programmer to know about the public context database, its structure and how to access the needed context elements. Apart from complicating the step code considerably, in this case the application programmer would have to deal with problems that are not application specific. This consideration rules out proposal (a), since ConTracts try to resolve exactly this problem.

The second approach (b) turns out to be very inflexible and expensive, especially for large amounts of context elements. The most significant disadvantage, however, is the effect, that steps transferring the whole accumulated computation context explicitly can no longer be re-used in other scripts with different context elements. Beside that, mechanism (b) causes quite some problems with respect to branching, parallel or distributed control flow.

For these reasons, the ConTract model introduces the notion of a private context database to keep all the relevant local state of a long-lived application stable. Context management is characterized by a binding mechanism that keeps the existence and details of parameter assignment from context elements to step parameters (and vice versa) transparent to the step application programmer.

Fig. 7.6 shows the principles of context management in a ConTract system. Each ConTract has a private context database for the global script variables its steps create (output parameters) or use (input parameters). The script programmer declares these variables and their types in the context declaration section at the beginning of a script. Context elements can be accessed at the script level by their name, just like ordinary program variables. Not shown are additional mechanisms to reference context by time and date of its creation. All tasks to keep the specified context stable and to resolve context references are in the ConTract manager's responsibility.

Context Binding

According to the multi-level ConTract programming model, a coherent context binding concept is defined as follows:

1. *Step coding*:

The step programmer chooses arbitrary variable names for the input and output parameters he uses, without any knowledge about the step's future execution environment, i.e. whether their values come from an input message, whether they are passed through usual programming language mechanisms, or whether they reference context elements of a ConTract using this step code. Hiding the notion of context from step programming and binding context transparently on the script level is essential for step code reusability.

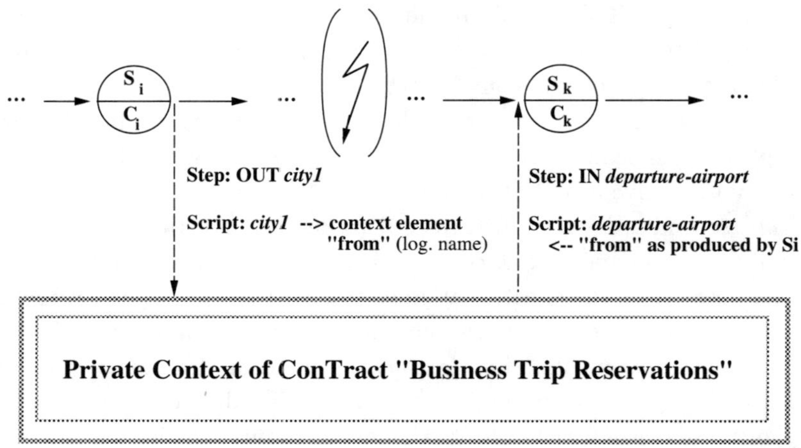

FIGURE 7.6
Robust Context Management for Related Steps

2. *Script definition*:
The script programmer introduces logical names to reference context elements. For each step he specifies which context elements have to be bound to its input/output parameters. A parameter could also be bound to a constant or to a global object by specifying its value or address (i.e. a SQL select statement referencing a tuple or relation in the database).

Without introducing logical names for context elements, all step programmers would have to use the same name for the same thing throughout all ConTracts. Obviously, this is not practicable. As a concrete example it could be the case in the business trip ConTract, that the programmer of step S_1 used a variable named *city1* (e.g. in a function `input( IN city1, city2, ... OUT airlines, ... ); )`. In the sample script the variable *city1* takes the value that S_3 wants to access as an input parameter, but under the name *departure-airport*. This mapping is established by a logical context identifier "from" which may be indexed by the producing step S_1 for a unique reference:

```
S1( out-context:  city → from )
S3( in-context:  departure-airport ← from[S1] ).
```

3. *ConTract runtime system*:
Because a step can be activated more than once (e.g., in a loop), the unique

identification of context elements at run time requires further (key) attributes besides its logical name:

- a ConTract identifier
- a step identifier
- time and date of creation
- a version counter to differentiate multiple activations of the same step
- a counter for parallel activations of a step, e.g., S_2 in the parallel loop *PAR_FOREACH(airline)*.

Execution History and Context Management

For two reasons update in place is not applicable for managing context elements:

1. Managing long-lived applications has to deal with time dependent queries to the context, e.g.,
   - Show all airlines which have already been tried for a flight.
   - Compute the average value a frequently modified context element had yesterday.
2. During compensation (see below) the execution of the respective counter steps requires the values of the original parameters and other context elements of a step. Therefore, update in place would corrupt compensation. [6]

Instead of overwriting old values, the ConTract model creates a new version for each updated (output) context element. This version can be referenced uniquely throughout the lifetime of a ConTract by the above specified attributes. An addressing scheme using versioning makes any synchronization of context updates superfluous, since no read/write conflicts occur.

As a result, the context database contains the complete execution history of a ConTract. After the termination of a ConTract its context database is discarded, which means that only steps within the same ConTract can access it. More precisely, steps can get context values indirectly via their IN/OUT interface. But they have no direct access to the complete execution history, since the notion of context is transparent at the step level. The

[6] This problem is not considered in other approaches to compensation, like [GS87, KS88].

hypothesis is that the described separation of context naming and binding makes application programming (steps and scripts) much easier.

The naming scheme proposed for context variables is perfectly suited for "flat" ConTracts, which refers to those consisting of elementary steps only. If nesting is allowed, things get more complicated, for instance, if a step can be another ConTract, or if the ConTract type can be activated recursively. Take as an example a flight reservation script iteratively calling itself in case there exists no direct flight connection and a multi-hop flight is tried by recursively searching the airline timetables. Passing context elements explicitly to and from a step containing a whole script can be achieved easily by extending the IN/OUT parameter list to the script level. But to name and reference nested context elements and histories needs improved scoping and versioning rules, which have not yet been developed.

Note that unlike persistent programming languages not each and every update is made stable, but only the relevant ones, i.e. the output context elements at the end of a step. Since writing into the context database is part of the commit of the enclosing step or sphere of control, this allows for similar optimizations as are applied to the system log. Nevertheless, managing context reliably causes some costs in terms of performance.

In essence, the need for robust context comes in as soon as one wants to have guaranteed stability for long-lived activities covering a set of related (trans)actions and finally ending up with the computation itself becoming a recoverable object.

7.3.6 Consistency Control and Resource Conflict Resolution

ACID transactions control concurrency by isolating atomic state transitions against each other in order to create a serializable schedule. To achieve this, nearly all concurrency control methods [BHG87] delay updates until the commit of a transaction.

However, this is not feasible for long lived transactions: first of all, it results in a tremendous performance degradation because holding long locks could block other activities, which also hold resources blocking others and so on. Secondly, this leads to a high rate of transaction aborts due to conflict and deadlock resolution. According to [Gra81b] the probability of deadlock increases with the fourth power of transaction size. And moreover, serializability is a sufficient condition, but not a necessary one for isolated execution [Gar83, PRS88, KS88].

ConTracts are neither atomic nor short. They externalize[7] some of their updates as they go, e.g., by releasing locks after step completion. But there is still a chance that these updates will be rolled back later on. Consequently, a ConTract might operate using data that have been externalized early by other ConTracts.

This creates two kinds of consistency problems, which have to be dealt with correctly:

a) In case a ConTract has to be cancelled, its global effects cannot be undone by simply restoring before images [HR83]; rather they have to be compensated for by semantical undo, i.e. compensating actions [Gra81, GS87, KLS90]. Under certain circumstances other ConTract steps may be affected by this compensation. This situation must be handled adequately.

b) Releasing locks early without any further concurrency control mechanism beyond transaction boundaries, like in the Saga model [GS87], could lead to severe inconsistencies. Because of that risk, there must be a way for a ConTract step to specify and get its isolation requirements.

The techniques used in the ConTract model for dealing with compensation and semantic synchronization are discussed in the following sections.

7.3.7 Compensation

Since updates can be externalized at the end of each step, unilateral roll-back of a ConTract is not possible. If, nevertheless, a ConTract has to be cancelled, it is necessary to undo its global effects explicitly. For this reason a so-called compensating action [GS87] has to be provided for each step in the script (rectangular boxes in Fig. 7.2), which semantically undoes the updates of global (database etc.) objects. To compensate, for example, for the flight reservation (step S_5), it is necessary to perform the reverse operation and to add the previously booked seats instead of simply restoring the before image of the reservation database. Compensation steps are specified in a separate part of the script as shown in Figure 7.7.

It is important to note, that compensation of a ConTract takes place only on the explicit demand of the user (by issuing *cancel_contract(cid)*) and not as an implicit means of recovery or conflict resolution by the system.

[7] The term "commitment" should be avoided, because there are two aspects to it: updates are externalized and the right to revoke them is waived.

```
CONTRACT  Business_Trip_Reservations
   :
END_CONTROL_FLOW_SCRIPT
   :
COMPENSATIONS
   C1: Do_Nothing_Step();
   C2: Do_Nothing_Step();
   C3: Cancel_Flight_Reservation( ... );
   C4: Cancel_Hotel_Reservation( ... );
   C5: Cancel_Car_Reservation( ... );
   C6: Cancel_Hotel_Reservation( ... );
   C7: Cancel_Car_Reservation( ... );
   C8: Do_Nothing_Step();
   C9: Invalidate_Tickets( ... );
END_COMPENSATIONS
   :
   :
END_CONTRACT  Business_Trip_Reservations
```

FIGURE 7.7
Specifying compensation steps in the script.

The problems and correctness requirements coming with the concept of compensation can be illustrated by looking again at the business trip sample ConTract of Fig. 7.2. The customer at the travel agency can decide for any reason to cancel the whole activity just until he has got the final acknowledgement of the ConTract's termination. This implies to compensate for all global effects by running the counter actions C_1 to C_9: After the confiscation and invalidation of all issued travel documents and tickets, the cancellation of the car, hotel and flight reservation can be done in parallel. S_2 (checking flight schedules) and S_1 (asking for travel data input) need no compensating action. Therefore, they could have an "empty" compensation step. After C_9 through C_1 are finished, a termination message tells the user of the compensated ConTract.

This scenario illustrates several aspects of the ConTract compensation model:

(a) Somewhat surprising is the observation that the degree of parallelism is much higher than during execution in forward direction. In the example given it might be even possible to perform all compensations at the same time. On one hand, this is due to the fact that coincidentally there are no control flow dependencies between compensating steps resulting from updates to global objects. On the other hand, dependencies between normal steps caused by creating and using context elements no longer exist at the time of compensation, because the context history is fully available to all C_i's: Although in the sample script S_4 has to wait for the completion of S_3 to get his input context, C_3 depends in no way on out-context of C_4. The context it needs is already available, thus C_4 and C_3 could run in parallel.

(b) The example emphasizes the importance of time for compensation: Depending on the dates of the reservation, the cancellation and the planned flight, different counter actions have to be performed (amount of the refund – if any, etc.). This gives another reason for saving the execution date of each step (implicitly) as part of the context.

(c) Another result from this discussion shows that compensating a step (e.g. a flight reservation) can be a complex task with several branches in its control flow. This suggests to allow (sub-)scripts as compensations rather than simple steps only. Just as well there are situations where the script programmer may not want to use the compensations coded by the step programmer, but decides to compensate for a sequence of steps with one single action. This can be achieved by re-defining a step's compensation action in the script, e.g., by a compensation on a higher level of abstraction.

(d) Specifying compensations is not as big a problem as it seems at first glance. By careful observation one will discover compensations being part of the applications anyway: For example, a debit corresponds to a credit operation, a reservation to a cancellation, and so on. This also shows that the same step code can be used as a normal action, or as a compensation, depending on the script context it is used in. This is the case with C_3 and S_8 in the sample ConTract (Figures 7.2, 7.7).

(e) Compensating for drilled holes, issued tickets and other real world actions may cause some difficulties, which cannot be discussed in this paper. See [RS91] for an approach to this problem by sophisticated protocols between the transaction system and the outside world, for example physical devices in a manufacturing application.

Correctness Criteria For Compensation

For the compensation mechanism to work correctly, the ConTract system has to satisfy the following consistency criteria:

- For each step in the script, there must exist exactly one valid compensating step.
- After the completion of a step all the input data for the compensating step must be computed. If the exact current values of some global objects are required for the compensation, they must be saved in the context, too.
- All of the global objects a step has used and which are relevant for its compensation have to exist until the ConTract's termination without interruption. Accessed database relations (tuples), e.g., must be protected by "existence locks", which prevent nothing but deletion. If this is not guaranteed, it may happen that between completing a step and starting its compensation an updated relation is dropped and created again with the same name and structure but with a completely different meaning. This is a consistency violation and performing the compensating action makes no sense.
- After the decision to compensate a ConTract, the termination of remote executing steps may not trigger any further steps; they rather must be aborted or compensated, in case the remote ConTract system learns about compensation after some delay. Obviously, a ConTract cannot be completed without all remote compensations being finished.
- For each previously completed step S_i with a "committed" entry in the log, the corresponding C_i has to be executed. All these compensation steps are required to commit eventually. This means not, that a compensation may not abort. In this case it is correct to retry an aborted C_i k times until it is committed once. By this way a legal history may look like that:

  ... committed(S_i) ... (compensation request) ... aborted(C_i) ... aborted(C_i) ... committed(C_i) ...

- If, nevertheless, the system does not manage to complete a compensating step successfully (due to a permanent failure of C_i or after a limited number of retries) this has no effect on the ongoing compensation (as opposed to the normal execution in forward direction). In other words, there is no compensation of the compensation, because this could produce infinite loops.

In case of such a failure the ConTract manager's compensation strategy is to notify a human system administrator and to provide him with a "snapshot" (i.e. the complete state and context) of the compensating ConTract in trouble. An administrator can be nominated for each ConTract and for each involved resource class. If neither automatic nor manual correction does help, compensation continues with an error message, but without any further recovery actions by the system. Thereby, a ConTract reaches a syntactically correct termination within finite time, no matter what.

Though, the guarantee of termination within finite time has to be taken with a grain of thought: One cannot rule out the case where a ConTract terminates without having established a consistent state, because the underlying database has changed in a way that the ConTract has not been designed to cope with. This is somewhat like trying to navigate using an out-dated map — an effect one has to take into consideration when talking about long-lived activities. To somebody concerned about semantic correctness this may seem an unacceptable, at least an unsatisfactory solution. However, it simply reflects the fact there might be inconsistencies caused by the application or by its operational environment.

The ConTract mechanism for compensation provides the necessary information and control mechanisms for automatic or manual recovery which helps to overcome at least a considerable number of failures, including permanent node crashes.

Conditional Cascading Compensations and Backtracking

After compensating a ConTract CT_1 the value of some object O could have changed because it was updated by a compensation step of CT_1, say C_i. This compensation could affect another ConTract, say CT_2, by invalidating the work of S_k, one of its steps. Take for example an account, which was debited some money (by S_k) just after a credit operation (S_i within CT_1) has put some money onto it. Compensating S_i could leave an account with insufficient money to allow the debit operation of S_k. As a result there either exists an overdrawn account or the system decides to invalidate CT_2 from S_k on by compensating for the respective steps S_k, S_{k+1}, etc., and restarting S_k.

To determine which other steps (ConTracts) are affected by the compensation step C_i, the system has to keep track of all steps which have used a compensated object after the update of the original step S_i and before the termination of the compensating ConTract. A step S_k of ConTract CT_2 is under no circumstances affected if its entry invariant still holds after the execution of C_i. If ConTract CT_2 is affected in such a way that S_k became invalid, the system has to backtrack its execution history until S_k and all its successors are aborted or compensated for. Then CT_2 can be redone starting with S_k. See [Dav78] for an extensive discussion of that subject.

7.3.8 Synchronization with Invariants

The synchronization problems caused by the interleaving of multiple ConTract steps can be solved by generalizing an idea that was already proposed for special types of hot spots [PRS88]. Rather than holding locks on objects, one remembers the predicates that should hold on the database in order for the activity to work correctly. Put in a more application oriented style: No program needs serializability or even worries whether or not it is serializable. Its only concern is to keep the database free of unsolicited changes in the parts it works on. If this is guaranteed, this is isolated execution from that program's point of view. Now this observation is more than just another phrase for the same thing. Keeping the database free of unsolicited changes generally means much less than preventing all the attributes, tuples etc. that have been used from being modified at all. In many situations it is sufficient, e.g. to make sure that a certain tuple is not deleted; that a certain attribute value stays within a specified range; that there are no more than x of a certain type of tuples, etc.

To implement synchronization based on the idea of "environmental invariance", ConTract scripts need two things:

1. It must be able to state the invariance predicates on the database defining a ConTract's view of the world after a certain step has been executed. This postcondition defining an isolation requirement of the ConTract is called *exit invariant*. *Establishing* a postcondition means binding the current values of shared objects to variables in a predicate expression.
2. It must be able to specify which of these exit invariants specified before must be fulfilled for a later step to execute correctly. This predicate is called a step's *entry invariant*.

In the example of Fig. 7.2, step S_1 establishes that the travel budget (a tuple in the database) of the department was higher than the cost limit allowed for that trip. To state that this fact is relevant for future synchronization, the script programmer defines an exit invariant containing the following predicate:

"*budget* $>$ *cost_limit*".

Before a flight can be booked (S_3), this must still be true. If S_3 revalidates the above predicate and it holds, then S_3 is synchronized correctly, although other ConTracts could have added or even withdrawn some money from the department's budget in the meantime.

At the end of step S_3 the ticket price has been debited from the budget, and so it only needs to be higher than the cost limit minus the ticket price. This postcondition of S_3 is specified in its exit invariant:

"*budget* $>$ *cost_limit* – *ticket_price*".

The other invariants in the sample script follow the same logic (Fig. 7.8).

Managing Invariants and Resolving Resource Conflicts

Since there are purely declarative specifications, some hints are needed to tell the ConTract manager and the database system how to handle the specified invariants. Fig. 7.9 illustrates three policies, which can be used to manage an invariant on an attribute a: One way to keep things "as they are" is to lock all objects as in today's systems (a). The ConTract manager at the DBMS would then have to manage long locks, i.e. locks that are held beyond transaction boundaries. Instead of locks, the DBMS could use semantic synchronization techniques like escrowing [O'Ne85] if the operations have the necessary properties (b). Or the DBMS could control all operations accessing the objects mentioned in an invariant. If operations that would invalidate it are rejected, then the invariant would never fail. The most liberal approach is to use no locks at all (c); this requires the check/revalidate technique [PRS88]: After establishing an exit invariant, the specified database objects may be updated by other ConTracts without any restrictions. At the time a step with this entry invariant wants to be executed, the invariant predicate simply is revalidated. If it evaluates to true, then the isolation condition for the ConTract in question is fulfilled and synchronization was correct from its point of view. Note that this consistency definition allows non-serializable schedules, but achieves application defined correctness.

Now if one accepts that the world might change while executing a ConTract, one has to cope with the situation of an invariant's database objects

```
CONTRACT  Business_Trip_Reservations
   :
CONTROL_FLOW_SCRIPT    ...   END_CONTROL_FLOW_SCRIPT
   :
SYNCHRONIZATION_INVARIANTS_&_CONFLICT_RESOLUTIONS
   S1: EXIT_INVARIANT( budget > cost_limit ),
       POLICY:         check/revalidate;
   S3: ENTRY_INVARIANT( (budget > cost_limit)  AND
                        (cost_limit > ticket_price) );
       CONFLICT_RESOLUTION: S8: Cancel_Reservation( .. );
       EXIT_INVARIANT( budget > cost_limit - ticket_price );
       POLICY:         check/revalidate;
   S4, S6: ENTRY_INVARIANT( hotel_price < budget ),
       CONFLICT_RESOLUTION: S110: Call_Manager_to_Increase_Budget(...);
   S5, S7: ENTRY_INVARIANT( car_price < budget ),
       CONFLICT_RESOLUTION: S110: Call_Manager_to_Increase_Budget(...);
END_SYNCHRONIZATION_INVARIANTS_&_CONFLICT_RESOLUTIONS
   :
END_OF_CONTRACT  Business_Trip_Reservations
```

FIGURE 7.8
Invariants in the sample script

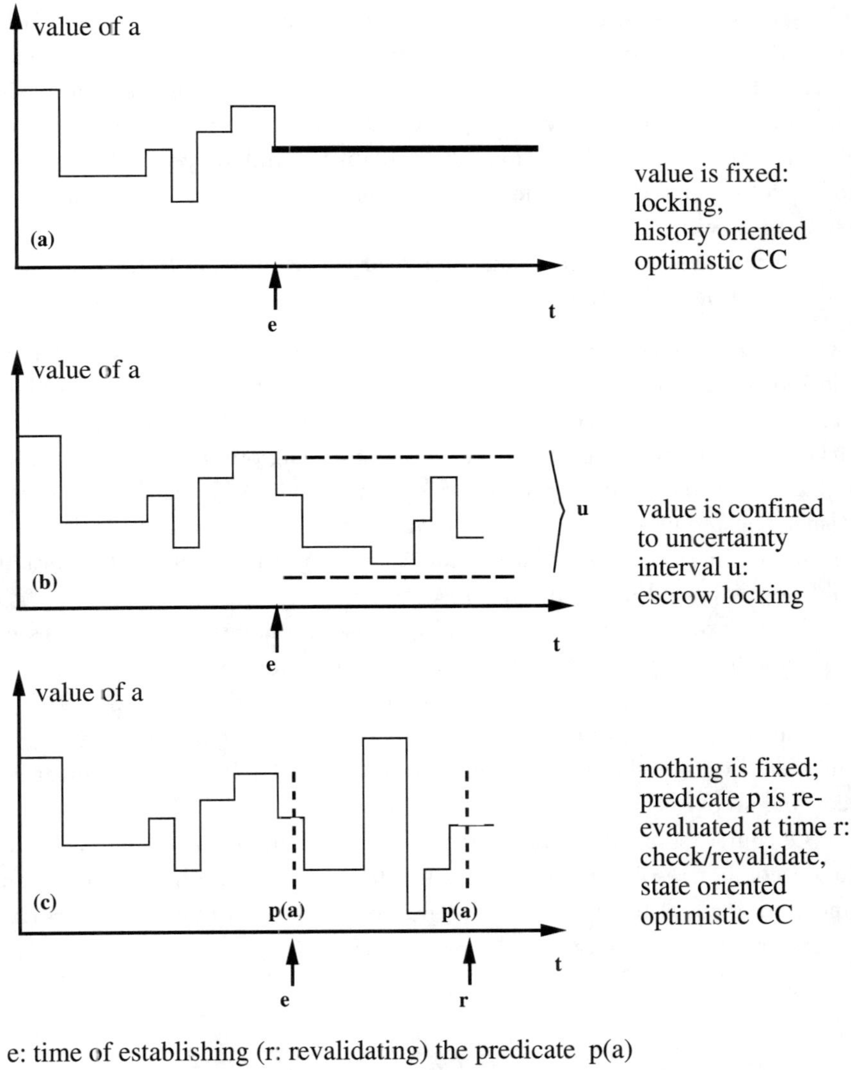

FIGURE 7.9
(a)–(c): Managing invariants on an attribute a.

having changed, such that its revalidation fails and the next step cannot be executed - like the department budget being overdrawn in the example. In ACID transactions, such conflicts are not communicated to the application; rather the system decides whether the transaction is rolled back or just has to wait. Both approaches do not make much sense for long-lived activities. Therefore, ConTracts allow to explicitly talk about conflicts, and to specify actions for conflict resolution. To explain the difference to the standard model, recall that there is one isolation condition for all transactions which reads as follows:

> *During the whole execution the resource state is exactly the same as a transaction has seen it the first time.*

However, the ConTract model allows each application to define less restrictive isolation conditions, as the above sample invariants have shown. This makes it feasible to handle a conflict using other than the standard mechanisms: Rather than manipulating the *caller* of a conflicting operation, one could try to change the requested *resource* state (object value) in such a way that it satisfies the required isolation condition; or the application could decide to wait some time doing other work and then to try it again; or the activity could be performed using another resource, etc.

In the example, somebody could increase the budget in case it does not hold enough money to pay for a ticket, or the whole business trip must be cancelled. These conflict resolution actions are specified together with an entry invariant like normal steps (Figure 7.8). They define a "contingency plan" for the case that this entry invariant should fail when executing the according step.

Of course, some ultimate resort must be built into the system to take over when a conflict resolution repeatedly has failed to re-establish the invariant. Cancellation could be chosen for this purpose, although real life applications rely on this decission only in very few situations.

7.4 Implementation Issues

As was mentioned in the introduction, ConTracts are not another transaction model. They rather try to integrate database techniques with programming languages and operating systems in order to create a reliable execution environment for large distributed applications. This execution environment is characterized by the design objective to push the implementation of control mechanisms from the application layer down to the system level. Therefore, a key requirement for implementing ConTracts is to build an activity control service that is able to capture and to handle all system failures, that controls parallelism, and manages the resources needed for a ConTract execution. The direction for that comes from the declarative style of application control modelling in a script.

This section sketches briefly the implications of this design rationale as well as architectural and functional aspects of a ConTract processing system.

As a main result, implementing ConTracts as an execution environment for long-lived, consistent distributed applications requires some major extensions of existing system components. The following list covers the most important issues.

7.4.1 Flow Management

The script language could be realized by a persistent programming language in which the non-volatile program variables make up a major part of the context. However, the ConTract model does not require to save each and every update *within* a step, but only *at the end* of a context writing step.

The run time system for that language has to implement robust flow management, which imposes three requirements: First of all, neither the event of a step being finished nor the events triggering successing steps may get lost. Secondly, the ConTract manager has to take care that executing steps do not fail without arranging their recovery or migration and restart on a functional alternative computation instance (i.e. another server or node in the network). And thirdly, in case a node fails completely, a secondary ConTract manager on another node has to take over the interrupted ConTract execution.

The first of the above aspects indicates an event based flow management to be an appropriate runtime mechanism. The necessity of a basic system service for event trigger management is confirmed by the requirements of other system components, especially by the interrelations between flow control and transaction management, see below.

7.4.2 Transaction Management

Traditional transaction management has to be improved to a large extent:

- The ConTract run time system needs an interface to the transaction manager for defining (ACID) spheres of control and dependencies between them [Dav78] and additionally for notifications about transaction events, like commit, abort and so on. An interface is necessary because of the functional separation of transaction and flow management. This in turn is motivated by the architectural design goal to have a modular and extensible system architecture with standardized interfaces and which is adjustable to the needs of various distributed transaction processing applications.

- Another implication of robust flow management is to distinguish between system-initiated and step-initiated abort. While the first case requires to abort and restart the affected step, this is not always feasible in the second case. Repeated calls for *roll back work* indicate a severe problem which cannot be resolved by retry but may require to initiate compensation.

- A special kind of global, nested transactions is necessary for structuring the system's work during processing ConTracts. The execution of a step is divided into several subtransactions, for example, to implement the actual step code and the ConTract managers pre- and postprocessing (evaluating invariants, binding context elements etc.). Since a DBMS executing database operations of a step acts as a resource manager, it can not decide about the step's completion. In order to transfer this decision to the ConTract manager, the DBMS has to open its commit protocol and to have a *prepare-to-commit()* call at its application interface [X/Open]. Managing transaction events and dependencies correctly requires this call, too.

- An obvious demand in the context of migrating activities is the necessity to determine the commit coordinator (node) not prior to the end of the activity [KR88]. And one must be able to select a certain trusted node with respect to availability and reliability [RP90] in order to avoid blocking or relocating the commit processing after coordinator failures.

- Beside the states of individual transactions the specified transaction events and dependencies have to be managed correctly and efficiently. This particularly requires more flexible and reliable transaction management protocols, for example a "two phase state transition" instead of an ordinary two phase commit protocol.

7.4.3 Logging

The realization of robust, distributed applications relies heavily on a global, distributed log service, which implements very reliable write once storage. This is due to the requirement that the forward recovery of a ConTract has to be feasible even if one involved node fails forever – and consequently its local log data, too. Therefore, the loss of log information has to be excluded with sufficient probability by using techniques, like

- logging on mirrored disks
- redundant arrays of independent disks (RAID)
- replication of log archives
- disaster and archive recovery protocols etc.

Migrating a ConTract to another node requires to move its log records, too, or at least to transfer a pointer where previous log data could be found.

7.4.4 Synchronization

Synchronizing ConTracts with invariants needs a logical calculus to define and evaluate the specified pre- and postconditions. In the context of database applications, using SQL would provide a workable solution.

Besides that, improved synchronization techniques are required to manage the accesses to global objects:

- There have to be existence locks which prevent nothing than deletion of an object mentioned in an invariant.

- All objects must have a global "eternal" identity.

- Additionally, a synchronization component must notify callers about synchronization conflicts and must support negotiation and other conflict resolution protocols, especially enabling the "repair" of a violated invariant by changing the affected resource values.

Synchronization of ConTracts identifies another disadvantage of classical transactions which has to be removed to support long-lived activities adequately: Since only an active transaction could held locks, it is not possible to exercise access control, e.g., during the suspension of a ConTract. Furthermore, it is neither possible to pass locks from one transaction to another (e.g. the next step), nor to re-acquire locks after a system crash.

In short, long, recoverable locks, which can be hold without an ongoing transaction are a minimal basis for a concurrency control schema to exercise access control beyond transaction boundaries.

7.4.5 Transactional Communication Service

Steps and other computation requests in a ConTract system are defined without considering the actual location of a computation server at programming time or at run time. This requires a generalized remote procedure call mechanism (RPC) that can be used in the same way to call a service within the same address space, on the local site, or on remote systems. Each interaction has to be tagged by the transaction identifier of the requestor issuing the RPC to make the call recoverable. The communication service implementing RPCs must be able to schedule and migrate tasks and processes for requests. Therefore, the used naming service must take into account the load situation and availability of requested resources according to an extended naming scheme, which considers global and local load balancing as follows:

logical global name $\longrightarrow$ [(node-id, log. local name, up/down), ...]

logical local name $\longrightarrow$ [process-id$_1$, pid$_2$, ...]

Note, that on the right hand side of both mappings there are address *lists*, because a service could be available on several nodes, and more than one process could run the same service on one node. Appropriate naming mechanisms can use this redundancy to improve reliability by an application transparent failure handling and retry technique. To implement this addressing schema, the name service must be able to handle value dependent roles.

7.5 Comparison with Other Work

The literature on transactions abandons. Thus a rough classification helps to draw a meaningful comparison with a (necessarily) small number of other approaches.

By and large, the work on transactions can be classified according to one of the following two categories: structural extensions and the embedding of transactions in a special execution environment.

7.5.1 Structural Extensions

The first category contains approaches which try to enrich the classical concept of flat transactions with more internal structure. This is to achieve more flexibility for the other aspects of a transaction, like synchronization, consistency, failure isolation. Among many others, the following approaches belong to this group: [Mos81, Wei86, HR87, PKH88].

Besides that, one finds work with mentionable contributions to special aspects of transaction management or theory, for example synchronization, recovery and so on [BHG87, O'Ne85, KS88, KLS90].

7.5.2 Embedding Transactions in an Execution Environment

This category is made up of (at least) two subclasses.

The first adds some application specific mechanisms to the "pure" transaction model, like domain specific synchronization, object versions, mechanisms for checkin/checkout or cooperative object manipulations. Some well known representatives are [KLMP84, BKK85, KKB88, HHMM88, MRKN91, NRZ91]

The second group is aimed at developing more general control mechanisms around and above transactions. The approaches concerned in particular with long-running activities show an important distinguishing feature in the way they model control flow. This can be done either event oriented [HLM88, DHL90, HGK91, BOHGM91] or script based, as is the case with ConTracts [GS87, KR88, Gar91, Reu89, ELLR90, VEH91].

When comparing ConTracts with other approaches to execution control for long-lived transaction applications two main characteristics of the ConTract model stand out:

1. *Semantic synchronization* is achieved by application defined isolation requirements. Concurrency is controlled beyond transaction boundaries with invariants depending on the situative needs of the activity, rather than by a fixed consistency definition built into the system. And *conflict resolution* is no longer restricted to system enforced blocking or abortion of the transaction issuing a conflicting operation, but is generalized to the possibility to "repair" the actual conflict causing resource state. This results in much more flexibility for constructive conflict resolution and therefore seems to be more appropriate for long-lived activities.

2. *Robust context management*, which is mostly transparent to the application, helps to fulfill a fundamental requirement of long-running applications: guaranteed continuation despite of system failures like node crashes and so on. This aspect is combined with a last original contribution of the ConTract model concerning the reliability of an execution:

Not only the former computation history, but the executing application itself is made a recoverable object.

The other described ConTract mechanisms can be found (with minor variations) in many other approaches, too. Compensation, for example, is also discussed in [Gra81, GS87, KLS90, ELLR90]. Nevertheless, the analysis of these control aspects and their interrelations brought some additional insight in details not investigated so far by other research, like the observation that the ability to compensate depends heavily on the execution history and the context database.

7.6 Conclusions

The main contribution of the ConTract model can be seen in extending traditional transaction concepts to a generalized control mechanism for long-lived activities. ConTracts are designed to meet the requirements which result from dividing large distributed applications into a set of related processing steps and defining appropriate consistency and reliability qualities for the execution of the whole activity.

Analyzing the requirements of large distributed applications has proved transactions to be promising building blocks, but not a complete and sufficient mechanism for reliable and consistent distributed computing. The ConTract model presents some necessary extensions to generalize classical transactions to a control mechanism for large distributed applications. Beside mechanisms concerning inter-transaction synchronization and recovery, the key issue is a reliable flow control layer tying together individual transactions and implementing the required control mechanisms exceeding transaction boundaries.

The ConTract model is characterized by the separation of control aspects into several orthogonal dimensions, which can be exercised independently by an application using declarative techniques. This feature is a key difference to classical transactions, where the *bot* ... *eot* bracket is the one and only syntactical construct with the limited ACID semantics. As shown in the above sections,

- control flow description
- defining spheres of control (transactions)
- dependency declaration

- context management
- step and transaction recovery
- recovering whole applications
- synchronizing basic operations of concurrent steps
- synchronization beyond individual steps at the script level and
- conflict resolution

are (at least partly) independent control aspects, which can and must be treated separately using more flexible mechanisms when managing long-lived and distributed applications.

A PRototype Implementation of a COnTract System (APRICOTS) currently under development shows the feasibility of the proposed mechanisms. The separation of control aspects is reflected by a modular and extensible system architecture. Future experiments with real life office automation and CIM applications [RS91] will help to elaborate the requirements of long–lived distributed applications and the described control mechanisms.

Although there can be seen first hints about the overall shape of future systems for transaction oriented distributed application processing [Reu90], there remains a lot of work concerning the presented dimensions of application control as well as an advanced system architecture for a reliable execution platform. Future research is aimed at working out the design of such a system.

This work was supported in part by the *Deutsche Forschungsgemeinschaft* under contract Re 660–2/2.

7.7 Sample Script "Business Trip Reservations"

```
CONTRACT  Business_Trip_Reservations

CONTEXT_DECLARATION
  cost_limit, ticket_price:    dollar;
  from, to:                    city;
  date:                        date_type;
  ok:                          boolean;
   :

CONTROL_FLOW_SCRIPT
  S1: Travel_Data_Input( in_context: ;
                         out_context: date, from, to, cost_limit );
  PAR_FOREACH( airline: EXECSQL select airline from  ...  ENDSQL )
    S2: Check_Flight_Schedule( in_context:  airline, date, from, to;
                               out_context: flight-no, ticket_price );
  END_PARFOREACH
  S3: Flight_Reservation( in_context:  flight, ticket_price;    ...   );
  S4: Hotel_Reservation( in_context:  "Cathedral Hill Hotel";
                         out_context:  ok, hotel_reservation );
  IF ( ok ) THEN  S5: Car_Rental(  ... "Avis" ... );
  ELSE BEGIN
          S6: Hotel_Reservation( ... "Holiday Inn"  ... );
          IF ( ok )  THEN
               S7:  Car_Rental( ... "Hertz"  ... );
          ELSE  S8: Cancel_Flight_Reservation_&_Try_Another_One( .. );
      END
  S9: Print_Documents( ... );
END_CONTROL_FLOW_SCRIPT

COMPENSATIONS
   C1: Do_Nothing_Step();
   C2: Do_Nothing_Step();
   C3: Cancel_Flight_Reservation( ... );
   C4: Cancel_Hotel_Reservation( ... );
   C5: Cancel_Car_Reservation( ... );
   C6: Cancel_Hotel_Reservation( ... );
   C7: Cancel_Car_Reservation( ... );
   C8: Do_Nothing_Step();
   C9: Invalidate_Tickets( ... );
```

```
END_COMPENSATIONS

TRANSACTIONS
        T1 ( S4, S5 ),  DEPENDENCY( T1:abort |---> begin:T2 );
        T2 ( S6, S7 ),  DEPENDENCY( T2:abort |---> begin:S8 );
END_TRANSACTIONS

SYNCHRONIZATION_INVARIANTS_&_CONFLICT_RESOLUTIONS
   S1: EXIT_INVARIANT( budget > cost_limit ),
       POLICY:         check/revalidate;

   S3: ENTRY_INVARIANT( (budget > cost_limit)  AND
                        (cost_limit > ticket_price) );
       CONFLICT_RESOLUTION: S8: Cancel_Reservation( .. );
       EXIT_INVARIANT( budget > cost_limit - ticket_price );
       POLICY:         check/revalidate;

   S4, S6: ENTRY_INVARIANT( hotel_price < budget ),
       CONFLICT_RESOLUTION: S110: Call_Manager_to_Increase_Budget(..);

   S5, S7: ENTRY_INVARIANT( car_price < budget ),
       CONFLICT_RESOLUTION: S110: Call_Manager_to_Increase_Budget(..);
END_SYNCHRONIZATION_INVARIANTS_&_CONFLICT_RESOLUTIONS

END_CONTRACT  Business_Trip_Reservation
```

Bibliography

[BST89] Bal, H.E., Steiner, J.G., and Tanenbaum, A.S. Programming Languages for Distributed Computing Systems. *ACM Comput. Surveys, Vol. 21, (3)*, 1989.

[BKK85] Bancilhon, F., Kim, W., and Korth, H. A Model of CAD Transactions. *Proc. VLDB*, 1985.

[BHG87] Bernstein, P.A., Hadzilacos, V., and Goodman, N. Concurrency Control and Recovery in Database Systems. *Addison–Wesley*, 1987.

[BHM90] Bernstein, P.A., Hsu, M., and Mann, B. Implementing Recoverable Requests Using Queues. *Proc. ACM SIGMOD*, 1990.

[BMW84] Borgida, A., Mylopoulos, J., and Wong, H.K.T. Generalization/Specialization as a Basis for Software Specification. *In: On Conceptual Modelling, pp. 87-117*, Springer, 1984.

[BOHGM91] Buchmann, Ozsu, Hornick, Georgakopoulas, Manola A Transaction Model for Active Distributed Object Systems. *In: A.K. Elmagarmid (ed.): Transaction Models for Advanced Database Applications*, Morgan Kaufmann Publishers, 1991.

[CCF89] Clay, L., Copeland, G., and Franklin, M. Operating System Support for an Advanced Database System. *MCC Technical Report Number: ACT-ST-140-89*, 1989.

[CR90] Chrysanthis, P.K., and Ramamritham, K. ACTA: A Framework for Specifying and Reasoning about Transaction Structure and Behavior. *Proc. ACM SIGMOD*, 1990.

[CR91] Chrysanthis, P.K., and Ramamritham, K. ACTA: The SAGA Continues. *In: A.K. Elmagarmid (ed.): Transaction Models for Advanced Database Applications*, Morgan Kaufmann Publishers, 1991.

[Dav78] Davies, C.T. Data Processing Spheres of Control. *IBM Systems Journal, Vol. 17(2)*, pp. 179-198, 1978.

[DHL90] Dayal, U., Hsu, M., and Ladin, R. Organizing long-running activities with triggers. *Proc. ACM SIGMOD*, 1990.

[ELLR90] Elmagarmid, A.K., Leu, Y., Litwin, W., and Rusinkiewicz, M. A Multidatabase Transaction Model for InterBase. *Proc. VLDB*, 1990.

[EMS91] Eppinger, J.L., Mummert, L.B., and Spector, A.Z. (eds) Camelot and Avalon - A Distributed Transaction Facility. *Morgan Kaufmann Publishers*, 1991.

[Gar83] Garcia-Molina, H. Using Semantic Knowledge for Transaction Processing in a Distributed Database. *ACM Transactions on Database Systems*, Vol. 8 (2), June 1983.

[Gar91] Garcia-Molina, H. et al. Modelling Long-Running Activities as Nested Sagas. *IEEE Data Engineering Bulletin*, March 1991.

[GGKKS91] Garcia-Molina, H., Gawlik, D., Klein, J., Kleissner, K., and Salem, K. Coordinating Activities Through Extended Sagas. *Proc. IEEE Spring CompCon*, 1991.

[GS87] Garcia–Molina, H., and Salem, K. Sagas. *Proc. ACM SIGMOD*, 1987.

[Gra78] Gray, J. Notes on Database Operating Systems. *LNCS 60*, Springer, New York, 1978.

[Gra81] Gray, J. The Transaction Concept: Virtues and Limitations. *Proc. VLDB, Cannes*, Sept. 1981.

[Gra81b] Gray, J. et al. A Straw Man Analysis of Probability of Waiting and Deadlock. *IBM Research Report RJ3066(38112), San Jose, California*, Feb. 1981.

[GR91] Gray, J., and Reuter, A. Transaction Processing Systems, Concepts and Techniques. Morgan Kaufmann Publishers, to appear 1991.

[HHMM88] Härder, T., Hübel, C., Meyer-Wegener, K., and Mitschang, B. Processing and transaction concepts for cooperation of engineering workstations and a database server. *Data & Knowledge Engineering 3*, pp. 87-107, 1988.

[HR83] Härder, T., and Reuter, A. Principles of Transaction-Oriented Database Recovery. *ACM Computing Surveys*, 15(4), 1983.

[HR87] Härder, T., and Rothermel, K. Concepts for Transaction Recovery in Nested Transactions. *Proc. ACM SIGMOD*, 1987.

[HGK91] Hsu, M., Ghoneimy, A., and Kleissner, C. An Execution Model for an Activity Management System. *Proc. 4th Int. Workshop on High Performance Transaction Systems*, Asilomar, Sept. 1991.

[HLM88] Hsu, M., Ladin, R., and McCarthy, D.R. An Execution Model for Active Data Base Management Systems. *Proc. 3rd Int. Conf. on Data and Knowledge Bases, Jerusalem*, June 1988.

[KLMP84] Kim, W., Lorie, L., McNabb, D., and Plouffe, W. A Transaction Mechanism for Engineering Design Databases. *Proc. VLDB*, 1984.

[Kle91] Klein, J. Advanced Rule Driven Transaction Management. *Proc. IEEE Spring CompCon*, 1991.

[KR88] Klein, J., and Reuter, A. Migrating Transactions. *Proc. IEEE Workshop on the Future Trends of Distributed Computing Systems*, Hong Kong, Sept. 1988.

[KS88] Korth, H.F., and Speegle, G.D. Formal Model of Correctness Without Serializability. *Proc. ACM SIGMOD*, 1988.

[KKB88] Korth, H.F., Kim, W., Bancilhon, F. On Long-Duration CAD Transactions. *Information Sciences 46*, pp. 73-107, October 1988.

[KLS90] Korth, H.F., Levy, E., and Silberschatz, A. A Formal Approach to Recovery by Compensating Transactions. *Proc. VLDB*, pp. 95-106, 1990.

[LU6.2] Format and Protocol Reference Manual: Architecture Logic For LU Type 6.2. *IBM*, Dec. 1985.

[Lyn83] Lynch, N.A. A New Correctness Criterion for Database Concurrency Control. *ACM Transactions on Database Systems, 8 (4)*, Dec. 1983.

[Mos81] Moss, E.J.B. Nested Transactions: An Approach to Reliable Computing. *M.I.T., Report MIT-LCS-TR-260*, 1981.

[MRKN91] Muth, P., Rakow, T.C., Klass, W., and Neuhold, E. A Transaction Model for an Open Publication Environment *In: A.K. Elmagarmid (ed.): Transaction Models for Advanced Database Applications*, Morgan Kaufmann Publishers, 1991.

[NRZ91] Nodine, Ramaswamy, Zdonik A Cooperative Transaction Model for Design Applications. *In: A.K. Elmagarmid (ed.): Transaction Models for Advanced Database Applications*, Morgan Kaufmann Publishers, 1991.

[OSI TP] Information technology – Open Systems Interconnection – Distributed Transaction Processing. *Draft International Standard ISO/IEC DIS 10026-1, International Organization for Standardization*, 1990.

[PRS88] Peinl, P., Reuter, A., and Sammer, H. High Contention in a Stock Trading Database - A Case Study. *Proc. ACM SIGMOD*, 1988.

[PKH88] Pu, C., Kaiser, G., and Hutchinson, N. Split-Transactions for Open-Ended Activities. *Proc. VLDB*, 1988.

[O'Ne85] O'Neil, P.E. The Escrow Transaction Method. *ACM Transactions on Database Systems 11 (4)*, pp. 405-430, Dec. 1986.

[Reu89] Reuter, A. ConTracts: A Means for Extending Control Beyond Transaction Boundaries. *Proc. 3rd Int. Workshop on High Performance Transaction Systems*, Asilomar, Sept. 1989.

[Reu90] Reuter, A. Performance and Reliability Issues in Future DBMSs. *Proc. Int. Syp. Distributed Database Systems in the 90s, LNCS 466*, Springer, Berlin 1990.

[RS91] Reuter, A., Schmidt, U. Transactions in Manufacturing Applications *4th Int. Workshop on High Performance Transaction Systems*, Asilomar, Sept. 1991.

[RP90] Rothermel, K., and Pappe, S. Open Commit Protocols for the Tree of Processes Model. *Proc. 10th Int. Conf. on Distributed Computing Systems*, pp. 236-244, 1990.

[Spe87] Spector, A.Z. et al. High Performance Distributed Transaction Processing in a General Purpose Computing Environment. *Proc. 2nd Int. Workshop on High Performance Transaction Systems*, Asilomar, Sept. 1987.

[VEH91] Veihalainen, Eliassen, Holtkamp, B. The S-Transaction Model. *In: A.K. Elmagarmid (ed.): Transaction Models for Advanced Database Applications*, Morgan Kaufmann Publishers, 1991.

[Wäc91] Wächter, H. ConTracts: A Means for Improving Reliability in Distributed Computing. *Proc. IEEE Spring CompCon*, 1991.

[Wei86] Weikum, G. A Theoretical Foundation of Multi-Level Concurrency Control. *Proc. PODS*, 1986.

[X/Open] X/Open. Distributed Transaction Processing: The XA Specification. *Preliminary Specification XO/PRELIM/90/020, X/Open*, 1990.

8

Dynamic Restructuring of Transactions

Gail E. Kaiser

Calton Pu

Abstract

Open-ended are characterized by uncertain duration, unpredictable developments, and interactions with other concurrent activities. Like other database applications, they require consistent concurrent access and fault-tolerance, but their unconventional characteristics are incompatible with the conventional database mechanisms of concurrency and failure atomicity. We present the split-transaction and join-transaction operations for *restructuring* in-progress transactions, as an approach to consistent concurrent access and fault-tolerance for open-ended. Split-transaction divides an on-going transaction into two or more transactions that are serializable with respect to each other and all other transactions, and each of the new transactions is later committed or aborted independently of the others. Join-transaction merges two or more transactions that are serializable with respect to each other into a single transaction as if they had always been part of the same transaction, and all their work is now committed or aborted together. Split-transaction is useful for committing some work early or dividing on-going work among several co-workers. Join-transaction allows to hand over results to a co-worker to integrate into his or her own ongoing task. The transaction manager enforces that the new transaction(s) will in fact be serializable, and does not permit the split or join otherwise.

8.1 Introduction

Database transactions provide atomicity in two senses: concurrency atomicity, for consistent concurrent access, and failure atomicity, for fault-tolerance. Unfortunately, these atomicity properties restrict the applicability of the transaction concept in *open-ended activities*, such as those that arise in design environments and office automation, even though for these activities we still want consistent concurrent access and fault-tolerance.

Open-ended activities are characterized by:

- *Uncertain duration* – from hours to months;
- *Unpredictable developments* – actions unforeseeable at the beginning; and
- *Interaction with other concurrent activities* – for concerted efforts among database users.

Each one of these characteristics introduces difficulties when constrained by traditional transaction atomicity properties.

Uncertain duration results in *long transactions*[1] with two specific problems. First, work done within a long transaction is vulnerable to crashes because of transaction rollback during recovery. Second, long transactions become concurrency bottlenecks if resources are retained for the duration of the transaction; if resources are released early, this introduces the possibility of cascaded aborts, which are particularly problematic for long transactions. Interaction with other concurrent activities is even more difficult, since resource access from all other transactions must be serialized either before or after the transaction.

Unpredictable developments in open-ended reveal two characteristics intrinsic to traditional transactions. First, sometimes initial activities modify data early in the transaction, which will remain unchanged until commit. Second, some (or all) of the later activities may become independent of the previous activities. In both cases, it may be desirable for the results of the earlier activities to be made available to other concurrent activities before the end of the transaction, but without introducing the possibility of cascaded aborts. But interaction among ongoing concurrent activities is intentionally prohibited by the concurrency atomicity property of transactions.

[1]Informally defined as those transactions that last for at least the same time magnitude as the mean time between failures of the computer system on which they run.

To solve these difficulties, we introduce *transaction restructuring operations*, which dynamically modify the set of concurrent transactions while they are in progress. Our operations preserve serializability among all committed transactions, although the committed set of transactions may not bear any simple relationship to the set of transactions that was initiated. Another way to say this is the concurrency atomicity is violated, but serializability (equivalence to some serial schedule) is not.

The *split-transaction* operation divides an ongoing transaction into two serializable transactions. In particular, resources read and written by the original transaction are divided among the two resulting transactions. Thereafter, each one of the new transactions may proceed independently with its own resources. A special case is to use split-transaction to immediately commit one of the new transactions, for early release of useful results from the original transaction. The other new transaction continues. In the general case, both new transactions continue, and may later commit or abort entirely independently of each other as if they had always been distinct, serializable transactions. The new transactions are thus **not** subtransactions of the original, but instead effectively replace the original transaction.

The inverse operation of split-transaction, called *join-transaction*, can combine results together and release them atomically. In particular, two ongoing serializable transactions are merged into one, as if they had always been a single transaction. Split-transaction and join-transaction can be combined in any formation, so direct transfer of resources from one transaction to another can be achieved by a split where one of the new transactions immediately joins some previously ongoing transaction.

Dynamic restructuring operations thus bring three major advantages to transaction-oriented open-ended activities:

1. Adaptive recovery, committing resources that will not change;
2. Added concurrency, releasing the committed resources or transferring ownership of uncommitted resources; and
3. Serializable access to resources by all activities.

We do not intend to address the debate of whether serializability is too restrictive for open-ended activities [NS89, Row89]. Powerful serializable access is useful even in a system that admits non-serializable operations, and therefore we restrict our discussion to serializable access.

It can be argued that split-transaction and join-transaction do not truly preserve serializability, since the set of committed and aborted transactions may not be the same as the set of originally initiated transactions. Our claim is not that the originally initiated transactions are necessarily serializable, as this would be meaningless in our context where some of the originally initiated transactions are subsumed into other transactions. Instead, our transaction restructuring operations ensure that the operations finally attributed to the committed transactions result in a schedule equivalent to a serial schedule.

The rest of this paper is organized as follows. We first elaborate in section 8.2 on the requirements of open-ended activities. We then define split-transaction and join-transaction, first assuming conventional programmed transactions in section 8.3 and then extending in section 8.4 to our context of user-controlled transactions whose operations are selected by the users as they go along. We give several example scenarios in section 8.5 to demonstrate that our transaction restructuring operations fulfill the requirements of open-ended activities. We discuss some approaches to implementing dynamic restructuring operations in section 8.6. In section 8.7 we compare to other work on extended transaction models that address some or all of the requirements of open-ended activities, and then conclude by summarizing our contributions.

8.2 Requirements

Numerous researchers have studied the nature of concurrent behavior in open-ended activities, and have arrived at new requirements for consistent concurrent access. These requirements are based on three underlying characteristics of open-ended activities, which we term uncertain duration, unpredictable developments, and interaction with other concurrent activities. We discuss these characteristics and mention a few approaches to concurrency control here. In section 8.7 we compare our transaction restructuring approach to many of the other extended transaction models developed to fulfill some or all of these requirements.

Uncertain duration: Operations on data in design environments (such as compiling source code or circuit layout) are often long-lived. If these operations are embedded in transactions, these transactions, unlike traditional ones, will also be long-lived. Long transactions need different support than traditional short transactions. In particular, blocking a transaction until another commits is rarely acceptable for long transactions. The problem of long transactions has also been addressed in traditional data processing applications, bank audit transactions, for example, where most proposed solutions rely on *a priori* static analysis of the transaction code [Lyn83, SGA87].

Consider the following example scenario. Say that a programmer Bob edits and recompiles module F, and then works for several days on other modules. Another programmer Alice would like to test her own changes to module G, but has to wait until the Bob commits his work, in order to be able to read module F's object code to build the system executable. The length of Bob's transaction may effectively prevent Alice from carrying out productive work for an unacceptably long period of time.

Unpredictable developments: In order to support user-controlled tasks that are nondeterministic and interactive in nature, the transaction manager should provide the user with the ability to start a transaction, interactively execute operations within it, dynamically restructure it, if needed, and commit or abort it at any time. The nondeterministic nature of transactions implies that the transaction manager will not be able to determine whether or not the execution of a transaction might violate database consistency, except by actually executing it and enforcing consistency along the way. Thus mechanisms based on static analysis are not applicable. Optimistic concurrency control [KR81] also should not be used, since this might lead to situations in which the user might have invested many hours running a transaction, only to find out later when he wants to commit his work that some of the operations he performed within the transaction violated some consistency constraints. The user would definitely oppose deleting all of his work (by rolling back the transaction). He might, however, be able to perform some operations explicitly to restore consistency, such as manually merging multiple updates to data [AHM89]. Thus, there is a need to support user control over transaction management as well as transaction execution.

For instance, suppose a programmer Charlie is developing two modules, F and G, to be released together in a transaction. Module F has been coded and tested before module G is finished. In this case, transaction abort due to a system failure will cause the loss of module F. Now consider the possibility that module F may have been modified so it does not use module G any more. In this case, module F remains unavailable unnecessarily until transaction commits. In both cases, even though the original plan might have been to commit F and G atomically, the developments lead Charlie to want to commit module F, while continuing with module G.

Interaction with other concurrent activities: Cooperation among users to develop project components has significant implications on consistent concurrent access. In multi-user design environments and office automation systems, several users might have to exchange data (i.e., share it collectively) in order to be able to carry out their work. The activities of two or more users working on shared data may not be serializable. They may pass the shared data items back and forth in a way that cannot be accomplished by a serial schedule. Also, two users might be modifying two parts of the same data item concurrently, with the intent of integrating these parts to create a new version of the item. In this case, they might need to look at each others' work to make sure that they are not modifying the two parts in a way that would make their integration difficult. This kind of sharing and exchanging data was termed *synergistic interaction* by Yeh *et al.* [YEEK87]. To insist on concurrency atomicity in multi-user environments might thus decrease concurrency or, more significantly, actually disallow desirable forms of cooperation among users.

The first example problem above could be solved by maintaining multiple versions of modules [Kat90]. Then Alice could use the object code for an old version of F together with the new version of G in order to build the system executable. But this does not permit the situation where the two programmers Bob and Alice are participating in a concerted effort, where the new version of G is intended to use the new version of F, and in fact will not even compile together with any old versions of F. In this case, Alice is in fact forced to wait, even if Bob has completed all his changes to F and is working on other parts of the system. If the independence of F from Bob's other changes had been known when the work began, he could have initiated a separate transaction to contain only his work on F. But it may be that Bob's situation is like Charlie's, where F and his other modules became independent of each other only because of unforeseen modifications during the transaction. Thus there seems to be no way for Bob and Alice to interact and exchange partial results while their transactions are in progress.

The goal of our transaction restructuring model is to satisfy all three requirements for practical cases of open-ended activities.

8.3 Programmed Transactions

For ease of exposition, we introduce the split-transaction and join-transaction operations in the artificial context where transactions are programmed in advance and statements invoking the split-transaction and join-transactions operation appear directly in the code. This context is unrealistic, since if the need for restructuring transactions was known when the code was written, then the transaction code itself would have been restructured without the need for dynamic restructuring operations. (Perhaps dynamic restructuring might be a useful facility for conditional execution within programmed transactions, but we do not address this.) Then in the following section we present split-transaction and join-transaction in the intended context of open-ended activities with unpredictable developments, where it becomes known only while a set of transactions are in progress that they should be restructured in some manner. Although the possibility of restructuring was anticipated at the start, by definition, the specific restructuring needed could not be foreseen.

8.3.1 Definitions

The operations supported by the transaction manager are:

- Begin-Transaction,
- Commit-Transaction,
- Abort-Transaction,
- Read-Data,
- Write-Data,
- Split-Transaction,
- Join-Transaction.

Begin, Commit, Abort, Read and Write have their usual meaning. We do not distinguish between actually reading or writing a data item as opposed to reserving the item in some way, since any differences depends on the specific implementation mechanisms employed. These issues are postponed until section 8.6. In general, we assume all other operations not on this list that appear in the transaction code have the normal semantics of the underlying programming language and do not impact transaction management.

The Split operation on some transaction T produces two new transactions, A and B, and dissolves the original T. The syntax of split-transaction is as shown below. It is not necessary to mention T explicitly among the arguments, since split-transaction may only be executed within the body of some transaction – which is T, by definition.

```
Split-Transaction(
    A:(AReadSet, AWriteSet, AProcedure),
    B:(BReadSet, BWriteSet, BProcedure))
```

`AReadSet`, `AWriteSet`, `BReadSet`, and `BWriteSet` are sets of data items accessed in A and B. `AProcedure` and `BProcedure` are the starting points of code at which A and B, respectively, will begin execution.

For simplicity of presentation, we describe only the two-way split-transaction. To split a transaction n ways, we can apply the two-way split $n-1$ times in succession. An n-way split-transaction operation may be seen as syntactic sugar for the successive two-way splits.

The Split operation divides all the operations completed in T into two subsets, A and B. The data sets associated with A (respectively, B) are the data items accessed by A (B). From the definition, the union of data sets in A and B must equal the set of data items accessed by T prior to the execution of the split-transaction statement. Without loss of generality, we assume that A precedes B in the following discussion on the intersections of the data sets for A and B:

1. $\texttt{AWriteSet} \cap \texttt{BWriteSet} \subseteq \texttt{BWriteLast}$

2. $\texttt{AReadSet} \cap \texttt{BWriteSet} = \emptyset$

3. $\texttt{BReadSet} \cap \texttt{AWriteSet} = \texttt{ShareSet}$

Property 1 states that data items in `BWriteLast` are written last by B. This property says that A should not clobber B's output, but B is allowed to write over A's output. Property 2 says that A can be serialized before B, since A has not seen any of the results produced by B. Property 3 says that B may see the results from A; in other words, A is the preceding transaction and B is the following transaction.

The above properties 1, 2, and 3 serialize A before B. Since the transaction manager guarantees the serializability of T, if A and B can be serialized with each other then they can be serialized with respect to all other transactions.

If both `ShareSet` and `BWriteLast` are empty, we call this the *independent* case, in which there is no data access conflict between A and B, so they can be serialized in either order. Since A and B are independent, they can both continue without additional restrictions.

If either `ShareSet` or `BWriteLast` is not empty, we call this the *serial* case, in which B follows A because of data access dependencies. In the serial case, each data item in the `ShareSet` must remain unchanged in A after the split. Otherwise, B would be using uncommitted data. In the serial case where `ShareSet` is non-empty, if A aborts at some time, B must also be aborted since otherwise B would be relying on aborted data. B need not be aborted, however, if `BWriteLast` is non-empty but `ShareSet` is empty.

One special case of the serial case is when we divide T into two consecutive subsequences, A and B. We then call A a *prefix* of T relative to B [BHG87]. A prefix can be split and committed, saving its results and releasing its resources.

The more general case of the serial case is when the operations in A and B interleave, but for each data item, A's accesses constitute a prefix of T relative to B. If all information exchange between the interleaved operations is from A's blocks to B's blocks, we can rearrange the blocks to make A a prefix of T with respect to B.

When we discuss user-controlled transaction, we will concentrate on the independent case. As will be shown, although the prefix special case is very useful, the general serial case is inappropriate for open-ended activities.

The `AProcedure` and `BProcedure` given in the split-transaction statement may indicate procedure calls, with arguments, or represent statement labels (i.e., targets of goto statements). The subsequent code executed by A and B are by definition disjoint portions of the original code associated with T. A and B might incidentally invoke the same subroutines; what is intended is that the original computation of T is now divided between A and B.

Neither the previous notion of dividing operations completed in T between A and B nor this notion of "disjoint" portions of code is precisely defined. Since this description of the Split operation within programmed transactions is only to aid intuition when we later discuss user-controlled transactions, and not intended as a practical model, the lack of a formal semantics is not an issue.

The inverse Join operation on some transaction T dissolves T, making its results part of the target transaction S. The syntax of the join-transaction operation is: `Join-Transaction(S:TID)`

Again, it is not necessary to mention T as a parameter, since join-transaction may only be executed within the body of this transaction T.

The join-transaction operation is conceptually simpler than split-transaction. Transaction T joins the target transaction S to commit (or abort) the results of T atomically with S. The sets of data items read and written by T, respectively, are merged into the sets of data items read and written thus far by S. It is not necessary to indicate a point in the code, since by definition join-transaction must be the last statement executed in T; the concurrent (with respect to T) execution of S is interrupted at some safe point, the join-transaction is accomplished, and then S continues where it left off. S may or may not make use of the resources inherited from T, depending on its code, but in any case both the data sets from T as well as those acquired directly by S are committed or aborted atomically as part of a single transaction.

As previously, it is unnecessary to be precise regarding the notion of "safe"; this kind of issue, however, is treated more carefully when we later examine user-controlled transactions.

8.3.2 Nested Transactions

The previous section assumed the simple transaction model where each transaction is composed of a *sequence* of operations that can be abstracted into Reads and Writes [EGLT76], starting with Begin and ending with either Commit or Abort. This sequential model has been extended to include parallelism. Rather than a general concurrent model, where the transaction constitutes a partially ordered set of database operations, some form of *nesting* is employed [Mos82, Pu86].

In the nested transactions model, there is a set of top-level transactions, which may be executed concurrently with respect to each other. A top-level transaction consists of a sequence of steps, where each step is either a primitive operation (Read or Write) or the initiation of a *subtransaction*. A subtransaction may execute concurrently with further steps in the top-level transaction as well as its sibling subtransactions. The subtransactions may themselves be nested.

The nested transactions model has been extended to include *supertransactions* [Pu87]. A supertransaction encloses two or more independent transactions and makes them appear atomic to transactions outside the supertransaction.

The same properties of split-transaction described in section 8.3.1, relating the data sets in A and B, hold for the concurrent model. For the independent case, A and B are subsets of the transaction's operations that access disjoint sets of data items. For the serial case, A and B are subsets of operations such that for each resource, all writes in A precede the first read in B.

The join-transaction operation remains simple in the concurrent transaction model, since the operation can be invoked only at the end of the transaction, when all concurrency has ceased. We will first consider the case corresponding to prefix in the sequential model.

To model the prefix, we describe the set of operations as a directed-acyclic graph (DAG). An arrow represents a dependency between operations. There are no cycles since such a computation would be impossible to carry out. An isolated node in the graph represents an operation independent of other operations on the database. A prefix of computations in the DAG is a subset of nodes such that each node is either a source node (a node without any incoming arrows), or connected to a source node through a path entirely in the subset. In other words, the extended prefix contains only operations that are independent of the rest of the computation. One simple example of this extended definition of prefix is a subset of connected components in the DAG, which corresponds to the independent case. Since the two subsets are disconnected, there is no dependency between them, so they can be serialized either way. The serial case corresponds to a cut in the DAG, with the source part as transaction A and the sink part transaction B. Since A does not depend on B, A can be serialized before B.

For the general case, we really need the log of operations in T for the data flow analysis. Since the log records data access in a serial order, the same algorithms from the sequential model suffice. The same observation applies to the external data access.

It is important to clarify that dynamic restructuring of transactions is not the same as either nested transactions or supertransactions. It is possible to solve Charlie's problem posed in section 8.2, of losing F when his long transaction aborts, by treating the work on F and the work on G as two subtransactions of Charlie's top-level transaction, and making subtransactions rather than top-level transactions the unit of failure atomicity (recovery) [Wal84].

It is also possible to extend the notion of nested supertransactions to allow interaction between Bob and Alice by treating their work on F, G, and the other modules as all transactions of the same supertransaction, and in fact such transaction grouping is the basis of many approaches to open-ended activities [SZ89, FZ89].

But both nested transactions and transaction groups presume that the structure of the set of (sub)transactions is known in advance, when the code is written. In contrast, we require support for unpredictable developments, where the durations and particularly the possible interactions are determined while the transactions are in progress rather than in advance before they start. Thus programmed transactions containing split-transaction and join-transaction really do not make much sense; the real application is to what we call *user-controlled transactions.*

8.4 User-Controlled Transactions

We now present split-transaction and join-transaction in the intended context of open-ended activities with unpredictable developments, where users determine what database operations to execute as they go along.

The user commands supported by the transaction manager should include:

- Begin-Transaction,
- Commit-Transaction,
- Abort-Transaction,
- Split-Transaction,
- Split-Commit-Transaction,
- Join-Transaction
- Accept-Join-Transaction
- Suspend-Transaction,
- Resume-Transaction.

The Begin, Commit and Abort commands operate as expected. The Abort command would be selected by the user to intentionally rollback to before her transaction began, probably to return to a known consistent state after modifying the data into a hopeless mess. (It might be desirable to save the modifications in some way, so the user could retrieve partial work, but we do not address this.)

Instead of Read and Write, the other user commands are specific to the application, e.g., edit and compile for software development. We can abstract these user commands into those that invoke tools that only read, those that read and write, and those that only write. Some commands, such as compile, will invoke tools that read one or more data items (the source code and include files) and write one or more other data items (the object code and symbol table). Thus without loss of generality, we continue in this section to refer to Read and Write operations and Read and Write data sets.

The Split command during some transaction T produces two new transactions, A and B, and dissolves the original T. The user provides six arguments, as shown below.

```
Split-Transaction(
    AReadSet, AWriteSet, AUser,
    BReadSet, BWriteSet, BUser)
```

`AReadSet`, `AWriteSet`, `BReadSet`, and `BWriteSet` are sets of data items accessed or reserved in A and B. `AUser` and `BUser` indicate the users who should take control of A and B, respectively.

The Split command divides all the user commands previously completed in T into two subsets, A and B. The data sets associated with A and B are the data items accessed by the commands in A and B, respectively. The transaction manager permits the Split command only if the following hold:

1. $\texttt{AWriteSet} \cap \texttt{BWriteSet} = \emptyset$

2. $\texttt{AReadSet} \cap \texttt{BWriteSet} = \emptyset$

3. $\texttt{BReadSet} \cap \texttt{AWriteSet} = \emptyset$

This corresponds to the independent case of the previous section, in which there is no data access conflict between A and B, so they can be serialized in either order.

The general serial case discussed in the previous section is not desirable for user-controlled transactions, with unpredictable developments. In that case, execution of A and B would depend on B being serialized after A, unreasonably restricting the commands that could be performed later on in A. Further, if A aborts then B must abort, unreasonably throwing away BUser's work because of some problem detected by AUser – or a crash of AUser's workstation.

Only the prefix special case of the serial case seems to makes sense for user-controlled transactions. To enforce that the newly split A transaction immediately commits, a distinct command is provided. The Split-Commit command takes only five arguments:

```
Split-Transaction(
    AReadSet, AWriteSet,
    BReadSet, BWriteSet, BUser)
```

Split-Commit divides all the user commands previously completed in T into two subsets, A and B. The data sets associated with A and B are the data items accessed by the commands in A and B, respectively. Then A immediately commits, while B may be taken over by BUser.

The following restrictions are placed:

1. $\texttt{AWriteSet} \cap \texttt{BWriteSet} \subseteq \texttt{BWriteLast}$

2. $\texttt{AReadSet} \cap \texttt{BWriteSet} = \emptyset$

3. $\texttt{BReadSet} \cap \texttt{AWriteSet} = \texttt{ShareSet}$

If A can immediately commit, as a subaction of the Split-Commit command, then `ShareSet` and `BWriteLast` need not be empty. Notice that the commit of A should not release any resources in `ShareSet` or `BWriteLast`, since these must continue to be held by B.

For Split or the B transaction of Split-Commit, a user must explicitly take control of a newly split transaction, using the new Resume command. It does not make much sense for a user to suddenly find that her commands are part of some transaction split by another user. Further, it is reasonable that in some cases that AUser and BUser will be the same person, often the same as the person who selected the Split command. But of course this user's commands cannot be part of both A and B, then they would not be split.

The Suspend command provides a means for giving up control of a transaction, in order to Resume another, or to execute commands outside any transaction. (From the transaction managers' point of view, each individual command executed outside any transaction is itself a transaction, and must be serializable with respect to all others.)

The notion of taking control over a transaction requires transaction *naming*, so that a user can indicate which particular transaction to Resume. One apparent way to avoid introducing user-visible transaction names is to restrict each user to exactly one transaction at a time. Then Resume by definition would take control over the user's personal transaction, and would fail if there had not been either a previous Suspend by this user or a previous Split assigning her one of the newly split transactions. Note that this disallows the case discussed above where AUser and BUser are the same person. This approach does not seem very practical, so we need transaction names.

A transaction's name might be assigned by the user as an argument to the Begin command. Newly split transactions would be named by additional arguments to the Split and Split-Commit commands. Perhaps a catalog of active and suspended transactions could be maintained by the design environment, with each associated with a human-intelligible description of the task being undertaken in that transaction. Further discussion of user interface issues is outside the scope of this paper; see [Kai91].

The Join command on some transaction T dissolves T, making its results part of the target transaction S. The user provides one argument, the name of the ongoing transaction to join.

```
Join-Transaction(S:TNAME)
```

Again, transaction T joins the target transaction S to commit (or abort) the results of T atomically with S. The sets of data items read and written by T, respectively, are merged into the sets of data items read and written thus far by S.

But the user controlling S should agree to accept responsibility for T's changes, prior to completing the merge. Thus this user must execute the Accept-Join command in transaction S, with the argument T.

```
Accept-Join-Transaction(T:TNAME)
```

The Accept-Join command might be executed before or after the original user requests the Join command, but the join is not consummated until both users have agreed. The environment might provide additional support, for example, to notify one user that another user had asked to join her transaction.

8.5 Applications

8.5.1 Editing

One of the simplest open-ended activities is the modification of a text file, known as editing. The fundamental problem in enclosing an editing session within a transaction is that if the machine crashes in the middle of the session, all the typing effort would have been lost due to abort rollback. Typical text editors provide the explicit-rollback aspect of transactions with an "undo" facility and the fault-tolerance aspect by periodically saving consistent intermediate results on disk (sometimes called a "checkpoint"). In the editing of a single text file, a consistent state is defined by the completion of all previous editor commands.

To provide the same functionality of saving intermediate results of a single text file, the editor can split to commit after any command. At that point, the consistent version is split into A's writeset and the current state (which happens to be the same) into B's readset. Committing A saves the consistent version on disk, and B continues the editing transaction, as if it has started from the version A has just written to disk.

Note that in this example, the programmed transaction model works, since the points to execute split-commit-transaction are preplanned (e.g., after every N commands). Although conventional "undo" and "checkpoint" is probably a better model for editing of a single text file, transaction restructuring operations become more useful when the user is editing several files that depend on each other for consistency, to coordinate the checkpointing of multiple files.

8.5.2 Design Environments

We mentioned in the introduction that open-ended activities are characterized by uncertain duration, unpredictable developments, and interaction with other concurrent activities. One example of uncertain duration is that an operation in design environments may take arbitrarily long — it may even be set aside by the user for arbitrary periods of time, without committing, while he works on some higher priority task. The problem with traditional transactions is that no information can be released while the design remains in the drawer. The transaction restructuring operations would allow partial results to be published by committing transaction A while the unfinished part stays under wraps in transaction B.

Another example of unpredictable developments arises when a programmer sets out to fix a bug. He normally goes through a cycle where he examines the program's execution in a debugger, reads certain source files that he guesses are related to the bug, modifies some subset of these files, compiles and links, runs test cases, discovers that the patch does not work, backs up to the previous versions of some or all of these files, reads other source files (perhaps overlapping with the first set), modifies some subset, etc., until he's finally satisfied with the results and commits all changes. Transaction restructuring allows the programmer to back up by aborting transaction A while keeping the changes he's currently happy with in the ongoing transaction B. In the case of fixing multiple bugs, he may split to commit some subset of the changes along the way to allow other programmers to take advantage of the code already fixed.

In a traditional transaction, in contrast, the solutions become public only when all the changes are committed. Note also that all source files read would remain unavailable until commit — even if they turn out irrelevant to the bug(s)! The former problem can be avoided by publish each part of the change as soon as it is made, but this might lead to a catastrophic cascading rollback if the programmer decided his solution was incorrect and aborted the transaction. The latter problem can be avoided by using optimistic concurrency control, but then the programmer might discover when it came time to commit (1) that his changes were invalidated by activities of other programmers or (2) if multiple versions are used, then he is faced with a complicated merge.

Although traditional transactions are clearly inappropriate, design environments still need the fault-tolerance associated with transactions. Consider a VLSI layout tool that has been given a specification and is now busy laying out. Such tools often run for several hours, so it is desirable to save intermediate results if (1) it is possible for the tool to continue from the saved results, or (2) the intermediate results include error messages that it would be useful for the human users to see —to correct his specifications— even though the full set of error messages was not generated due to a crash. This applies to make [Fel79] as well, where the appropriate split points are the distinct command lines. However, an individual linking or compilation job can run very long, and reasonable split points are not so obvious — and in fact only (2) applies to most instances of these tools. Atomic transaction would rollback everything in the case of a crash.

8.5.3 Multi-User Design Environments

The class of systems called "design environments" includes both single-user design tools and multi-user environments that support cooperation among multiple users working together on the same large project. The same issues come up in office automation systems and other computer-supported cooperative work [Gre88].

A simple example of cooperation among multiple users is when a programmer has finished a hash-table package that she is going to use in some larger program. Somebody else discovers her package and wants to use it. Even though this has not been planned beforehand, she can split the transaction with the hash-table in transaction A, to be committed and released, while continuing her own work in transaction B. If she had only atomic transactions available, her manager would have had to foresee the usefulness of the hash-table package and therefore assign it as a separate task, and thus a separate transaction.

For a more complex example, consider again a coordinated change to modules F and G, where programmer Bob is responsible for F and programmer Alice for G. Bob needs to use the new version of G and Alice needs to use the new version F. When we treat Bob's work and Alice's work as a pair of traditional transactions, we arrive at a deadlock.

However, most modern programming languages provide language constructs for separating the specification portion of a module from its implementation, and enforce the constraint that one module can depend only on the specification part of another and can in no way depend on the details hidden in another module's implementation part [Sha84]. This works well using transaction restructuring operations: Bob and Alice can modify their specifications at the same time; the transactions are then split making the new specifications public; finally, Bob and Alice can modify their implementations using the new specifications. If we had used simple nested transactions, only the immediately enclosing transaction would be able to see the specification, instead of the public.

This simple division at the specification/implementation level does not work well for changes involving large numbers of programmers — say, more than twenty — because too many programmers could be held up waiting for all the others to finish their specifications so the transactions can split. This problem can be solved by dividing the programmers into groups whose modules most closely depend on each other [KP87]. Only programmers within the same group see the new version of a module, while others initially use the old version; only the members of the same group must split their transactions at the same time. A further set of splits is made later when the groups coordinate to make their new versions public to all the other groups so they can complete the necessary modifications.

Another reason to split an ongoing transaction is management re-organization. For instance, one project transaction may have to be split into two to adjust workload. If the project can be separated into two serializable parts, then a split operation would define the responsibilities clearly. In such cases, it may be desirable for a managerial user to be able to execute transaction restructuring operations externally, to affect in-progress transactions controlled by subordinate users [KP91].

Join-transactions are useful when two open-ended activities turn out to relate to each other through some consistency constraints, *after* the activities have started. For example, modules from two programmers may need to be bundled together in an emergency release for the unexpected development of a demo for a potential customer. If the programmers knew they were bound by the same consistency constraints at the beginning, they could have created two subtransactions nested in a larger one, which maintains the consistency constraints. However, due to unpredictable developments in open-ended transactions, the flexibility to join originally separate transactions is desirable. In our example, the demo may require a set of modules that work with each other and some *ad hoc* utility programs that show off those modules. Join-transaction can group a particular subset of modules that have been tested together and release them to the utility programmers.

8.6 Implementation Issues

When the split-transaction operation is called, the transaction manager checks the external operations on data using an optimistic concurrency control algorithm [KR81] to certify the serializability between A and B. This certification sweeps the external operations recorded on the log or versions to verify the three properties enumerated in section 8.3.1, for programmed transactions, or in section 8.4 for user-controlled transactions, to ensure serializability. Note that optimistic concurrency control is employed only to detect conflicts between A and B *before* rather than *after* they have been split, so there is no possibility of rollback of the long transaction — the worst that can happen is the split is disallowed.

Version-based recovery algorithms record read accesses as well as write accesses. But typical log-based database systems register only the write accesses. For the above automatic checking algorithm to work, we need to record the long-transaction read accesses on the log to verify the three properties. In case the user-specified split is not serializable, the transaction manager might modify the set A or B and calculate some serializable splits, using closure algorithms, as suggestions to the user. In practice, the user may request a split and choose the appropriate split from a menu.

We should recognize that even though external accesses conform to the three properties, rigorously speaking the algorithm in general does not guarantee serializability between A and B. The reason is that as part of the same original transaction, A and B may have exchanged information through shared variables, e.g., clipping from one editor buffer and pasting into another. To guarantee serializability in the rigorous sense, we need to record all data access (as in an undo log for an editing session) in the long-transaction and perform a data flow analysis on the internal operations in T.

We note that even though we have introduced the need for logging of read access and possibly shared variable access, this kind of overhead is imposed only on long-transactions, and is not needed for short transactions executing in the same database. Since long-transactions have low throughput by definition, the additional overhead will not become a bottleneck.

A pessimistic scheme is necessary in the rest of the implementation, to avoid undesired rollback of long transactions. Otherwise, our transaction restructuring operations are independent of any particular concurrency control or failure recovery methods. Any pessimistic implementation technique chosen in a database system, as long as it guarantees serializability, can be employed in conjunction with split-transaction and join-transaction. We will consider the two major techniques: two-phase locking and timestamps.

The general algorithm for split-transaction contains three steps after the transaction manager has validated that the operation is valid. First, the transaction manager creates a new unique transaction, say for B. Second, it adds B's TID to the reader's list of all the data items in `BReadSet`. Third, it reassigns B's TID to be the writer of all the data items in `BWriteSet`. Specifically, for two-phase locking, the transaction manager just adds or assigns B's TID to the appropriate lock owner list. For timestamp-based methods, it updates the timestamps for the data with B's TID. Transaction A retains T's original transaction identifier. Threads of control in A and B are transferred to

AProcedure and BProcedure, respectively, when implementing programmed transactions.

From the concurrency control point of view, the transfer is relatively straightforward. For two-phase locking, the transaction manager simply changes the ownership of the locks in BReadSet and BWriteSet to the new transaction. For timestamps, it needs to assign a new timestamp to B, preferably immediately after A's timestamp. Multidimensional timestamps [LB87] is one of the techniques that provides this capability.

From the crash recovery point of view, the transfer is also simple. For recovery systems based on versions (which is what we have assumed in this discussion), the system simply makes B the creator of the versions in BWriteSet. For systems based on logging, the recovery manager needs to write a special "transaction record" to the log, marking the transition of BWriteSet data from the old transaction to the new transaction. During the log processing for recovery, the transaction record should be read during the backward pass, and then the log records on BWriteSet written by the old transaction will be translated correctly as B's records.

Another important concern is the restricted case of cascaded aborts introduced by the general serial case for programmed transactions (section 8.3.1). If A aborts then B must abort, since B has read data written by A. Fortunately, this restricted case is much easier to handle than general cascaded aborts. Specifically, the database system does not have to maintain the dependencies among all transactions. It is sufficient to remember only the dependency between transactions that have split, given to the transaction manager explicitly by the split-transaction operation. Transactions that have not split are protected by the usual concurrency control mechanism. Consequently, if the "native" concurrency control prevents cascaded aborts (e.g. strict two-phase locking), then the cascaded aborts are restricted exclusively to transactions that have split. Recall that cascaded aborts are explicitly prevented by the properties required for user-controlled transactions (section 8.4).

The implementation of join-transaction is straightforward. Say that the transaction manager is trying to join-transaction T and S. Since a pessimistic concurrency control scheme is used, it is guaranteed that T and S are already serializable with respect to each other, so there is no need to check. The transaction manager then adds TReadSet to SReadSet and TWriteSet to SWriteSet. If S is aware of T's joining, then S can start accessing data read and written by T. This is unlikely to be the case for programmed transactions, but works correctly if S would have tried to access T's data later on in its code anyway, since there are now no conflicts. This general algorithm works for all the concurrency control methods and crash recovery techniques mentioned above for split-transaction.

8.7 Comparison to Related Work

There has been a flurry of research to develop new approaches to transaction management that meet the requirements of open-ended activities given in section 8.2. One of the authors has developed a survey of extended transaction models proposed in the literature and/or evident in existing systems [BK91]. The survey concentrates on concurrency control issues, and does not directly address recovery.

Figure 8.1 summarizes the main models covered in that survey in terms of whether they have been implemented, and their capabilities for supporting uncertain duration, unpredictable developments, and interaction with other concurrent activities. None of the existing models, including our own, provides a fully satisfactory solution to all three problems — but it may be possible to reach such a solution by combining some of the mechanisms that have complementary strengths, for example, participation domains and transaction restructuring. A limited form of participation domains is currently being implemented for the multi-user Marvel environment [BK90, Bar9x], and we are investigating the integration of participation domains with transaction restructuring operations.

It is interesting to note that many of the ideas implemented in the mechanisms surveyed were actually discussed earlier in other contexts. For instance, some of the ideas related to multilevel transactions, long transactions and cooperative transactions were discussed by Davies in 1973 [Dav73]!

Our work was influenced by the brief mention of the terms *split* and *join* in conjunction with transactions in a technical report by Jessop *et al.* [JNJBP82] discussing the Eden Transactional File System.

Chrysanthis and Ramamritham have defined the ACTA formalism for specifying the semantics of various transaction models in terms of commit-dependencies and abort-dependencies among transactions [CR90]. They have used this formalism to model several extended transaction schemes, including our transaction restructuring operations. They also tested the reasoning capabilities of their formalism by combining our model with conventional nested transactions, to verify that the result retained the properties of the two original schemes.

Mechanism	System	Duration	Unpredictable	Interaction
Altruistic Locking[SGA87]	N/A	Yes	No	Limited
Snapshot Validation[PSU86]	N/A	Yes	No	Limited
Order-Preserving Transactions[WS84]	DASDBS	Yes	No	Limited
Entity-State Transactions[KE83]	N/A	Yes	No	Limited
Semantic Atomicity[Gar83]	N/A	Yes	No	Limited
Multilevel Atomicity[Lyn83]	N/A	Yes	No	Yes
Sagas[GS87]	N/A	Yes	No	Limited
Conflict-Based Serializability[KS88]	N/A	Yes	No	Limited
Checkout[Tic85]	RCS	No	No	Limited
Conversational Transactions[LP83]	System R	Limited	Limited	No
Multilevel Coordination[KP87]	Infuse	Yes	Yes	Limited
Domain Relative Addressing[WBMN88]	Cosmos	Yes	No	Limited
Copy/Modify/ Merge[AHM89]	NSE	Yes	Yes	Limited
Multiple Commit Points[Wal84]	N/A	Yes	Yes	Limited
Interactive Notification[EE87]	Gordion	No	Limited	Limited
Visibility Domains[DN89]	N/A	Yes	Limited	Yes
Group-Oriented CAD Transactions[KSUW85]	N/A	Yes	Limited	Yes
Cooperating CAD Transactions[BKK85]	Orion	Yes	Limited	Yes
Transaction Groups[FZ89]	ObServer II	Limited	Limited	Yes
Participation Domains[Kai90]	N/A	Yes	Limited	Yes
Transaction Restructuring	N/A	Yes	Yes	Limited

TABLE 8.1
Comparison Table of Mechanisms

8.8 Conclusions

We have informally introduced the class of open-ended activities, which arise in design environments, office automation systems and other advanced database applications. These activities have become an important application area for which the next generation of databases are aiming [SRLGCBBD90, ABDD90]. The common requirements of these activities include the ability to support consistent concurrent access and fault-tolerance when the activities are of uncertain duration, may include unpredictable developments, and often require interaction with other concurrent activities.

To solve these problems, we have introduced the split-transaction and join-transaction operations for dynamically restructuring ongoing transactions. Split-transaction divides the data in a transaction into two sets of data items contained in two serializable transactions, while join-transaction merges the data in two transactions into a single set containing in one serializable transaction. We have described the syntax of these operations, their semantics, and the properties that they should satisfy. We also outlined the algorithms to implement these operations. We have demonstrated the safe use of our transaction restructuring operations for several real-world problems.

The traditional transaction guarantees consistent concurrent access and fault-tolerance of databases by enforcing concurrency atomicity and failure atomicity, both very desirable properties for conventional data processing, but problematic for open-ended activities. The uncertain duration, unpredictable developments, and interaction with others in open-ended activities are formidable challenges to the traditional transactions. With dynamic transaction restructuring, we maintain the desirable properties of transaction serializability at the same time as we increase flexibility.

Acknowledgments

We first described the split-transaction and join-transaction operations in Calton Pu, Gail E. Kaiser and Norman Hutchinson, Split-Transactions for Open-Ended Activities, *Fourteenth International Conference on Very Large Data Bases*, August 1988, pp. 26-37. This paper expands on our previous ideas, benefitting from discussions with Bob Balzer, Naser Barghouti, Panos Chrysanthis, Dan Duchamp, Bill Harrison, Scott Hudson, Eliot Moss, Dewayne Perry, Ken Salem and Stan Zdonik. We would particularly like to thank Wenwey Hseush for his corrections on a previous version of this paper. We would also like to thank the anonymous reviewers for their comments.

Kaiser is supported by National Science Foundation grants CCR-9000930 and CCR-8858029, by grants from AT&T, BNR, DEC and SRA, by the New York State Center for Advanced Technology on Computer and Information Systems and by the NSF Engineering Research Center for Telecommunications Research. Pu is supported by National Science Foundation grant CDA-8820759, by grants from AT&T, DEC and Sun, and the New York State Center for Advanced Technology on Computer and Information Systems.

Bibliography

[AHM89] Evan W. Adams, Masahiro Honda, and Terrence C. Miller. Object management in a CASE environment. In *11th International Conference on Software Engineering*, pages 154–163, Pittsburgh PA, May 1989.

[ABDD90] Malcolm Atkinson, Francois Bancilhon, David DeWitt, Klaus Dittrich, David Maier, and Stanley Zdonik. *The Object-Oriented Database System Manifesto.* Elsevier Science, 1990.

[BKK85] Francois Bancilhon, Won Kim, and Henry Korth. A model of CAD transactions. In *11th International Conference on Very Large Databases*, pages 25–33, Stockholm, Sweden, August 1985.

[Bar9x] Naser S. Barghouti. *Concurrency Control in Rule-Based Software Development Environments.* PhD thesis, Columbia University, 199x.

[BK90] Naser S. Barghouti and Gail E. Kaiser. Modeling concurrency in rule-based development environments. *IEEE Expert*, 5(6):15–27, December 1990.

[BK91] Naser S. Barghouti and Gail E. Kaiser. Concurrency control in advanced database applications. *ACM Computing Surveys*, 1991. In press. Available as Columbia University Department of Computer Science CUCS-425-89, revised March 1991.

[BHG87] Philip A. Bernstein, Vassos Hadzilacos, and Nathan Goodman. *Concurrency Control and Recovery in Database Systems.* Addison-Wesley, Reading MA, 1987.

[CR90] Panayiotis K. Chrysanthis and Krithi Ramamritham. ACTA: A framework for specifying and reasoning about transaction structure and behavior. In Hector Garcia-Molina and H.V. Jagadish, editors, *1990 ACM SIGMOD International Conference on Management of Data*, pages 194–203, Atlantic City NJ, May 1990. Special issue of *SIGMOD Record*, 19(2), June 1990.

[Dav73] Charles T. Davies, Jr. Recovery semantics for a DB/DC system. In *28th ACM National Conference*, pages 136–141, Atlanta GA, August 1973.

[DN89] Mark Dowson and Brian Nejmeh. Nested transactions and visibility domains. In *1989 ACM SIGMOD Workshop on Software CAD Databases*, pages 36–38, Napa CA, February 1989. Position paper.

[EE87] Aral Ege and Clarence A. Ellis. Design and implementation of Gordion, an object base management system. In *3rd International Conference on Data Engineering*, pages 226–234, Los Angeles CA, February 1987.

[EGLT76] K. P. Eswaran, J. N. Gray, R. A. Lorie, and I. L. Traiger. The notions of consistency and predicate locks in a database system. *Communications of the ACM*, 19(11):624–632, November 1976.

[Fel79] S.I. Feldman. Make — a program for maintaining computer programs. *Software — Practice & Experience*, 9(4):255–265, April 1979.

[FZ89] Mary F. Fernandez and Stanley B. Zdonik. Transaction groups: A model for controlling cooperative work. In *3rd International Workshop on Persistent Object Systems: Their Design, Implementation and Use*, pages 128–138, Queensland, Australia, January 1989.

[Gar83] Hector Garcia-Molina. Using semantic knowledge for transaction processing in a distributed database. *ACM Transactions on Database Systems*, 8(2):186–213, June 1983.

[GS87] Hector Garcia-Molina and Kenneth Salem. Sagas. In Umeshwar Dayal and Irv Traiger, editors, *ACM SIGMOD 1987 Annual*

Conference, pages 249–259, San Francisco CA, May 1987. Special issue of *SIGMOD Record*, 16(3), December 1987.

[Gre88] Irene Greif, editor. *Computer-Supported Cooperative Work: A Book of Readings*. Morgan Kaufmann, San Mateo CA, 1988.

[JNJBP82] W.H. Jessop, J.D. Noe, D.M. Jacobson, J-L. Baer, and C. Pu. An introduction to the Eden transactional file system. Technical Report 82-02-05, Department of Computer Science, University of Washington, February 1982.

[Kai90] Gail E. Kaiser. A flexible transaction model for software engineering. In *6th International Conference on Data Engineering*, pages 560–567, Los Angeles CA, February 1990. IEEE Computer Society.

[Kai91] Gail E. Kaiser. Interfacing cooperative transactions to software development environments. *Office Knowledge Engineering*, 4(1):56–78, February 1991. Invited paper.

[KP87] Gail E. Kaiser and Dewayne E. Perry. Workspaces and experimental databases: Automated support for software maintenance and evolution. In *Conference on Software Maintenance*, pages 108–114, Austin TX, September 1987. IEEE Computer Society Press.

[KP91] Gail E. Kaiser and Dewayne E. Perry. Making progress in cooperative transaction models. *Data Engineering*, 14(1), March 1991. Invited paper.

[Kat90] Randy H. Katz. Toward a unified framework for version modeling in engineering databases. *ACM Computing Surveys*, 22(4):375–408, December 1990.

[KSUW85] P. Klahold, G. Schlageter, R. Unland, and W. Wilkes. A transaction model supporting complex applications in integrated information systems. In *ACM-SIGMOD 1985 International Conference on Management of Data*, pages 388–401, Austin TX, May 1985. ACM.

[KS88] Henry F. Korth and Gregory D. Speegle. Formal model of correctness without serializability. In *SIGMOD International Con-*

ference on the Management of Data, pages 379–386, Chicago IL, June 1988. ACM Press.

[KR81] H. T. Kung and John Robinson. On optimistic methods for concurrency control. *ACM Transactions on Database Systems*, 6(2):213–226, June 1981.

[KE83] Ali R. Kutay and Charles M. Eastman. Transaction management in engineering databases. In *Engineering Design Applications, Annual Meeting Database Week*, pages 73–80, San Jose CA, May 1983. IEEE Computer Society Press.

[LB87] P.J. Leu and B. Bhargava. Multidimensional timestamp protocols for concurrency control. *IEEE Transactions on Software Engineering*, SE-13(12):1238–1253, December 1987.

[LP83] Raymond Lorie and Wilfred Plouffe. Complex objects and their use in design transactions. In *Engineering Design Applications, Annual Meeting Database Week*, pages 115–121, San Jose CA, May 1983. IEEE Computer Society.

[Lyn83] Nancy A. Lynch. Multilevel atomicity — a new correctness criterion for database concurrency control. *ACM Transactions on Database Systems*, 8(4):484–502, December 1983.

[Mos82] J. Eliot B. Moss. Nested transactions and reliable distributed computing. In *2nd Symposium on Reliability in Distributed Software and Database Systems*, pages 33–39, Pittsburgh PA, July 1982. IEEE Computer Society.

[NS89] Erich Neuhold and Michael Stonebraker (editors). Future directions in DBMS research. *SIGMOD Record*, 18(1):17–26, March 1989.

[PSU86] U. Pradel, G. Schlageter, and R. Unland. Redesign of optimistic methods: Improving performance and availability. In *International Conference on Data Engineering*, pages 466–473, Los Angeles CA, February 1986.

[Pu86] Calton Pu. *Replication and Nested Transactions in the Eden Distributed System.* PhD thesis, Department of Computer Science, University of Washington, 1986.

[Pu87] Calton Pu. Supertransactions. In *2nd Workshop on Large Grained Parallelism*, Hidden Valley PA, October 1987.

[Row89] Lawrence A. Rowe. Report on the 1989 Software CAD Databases Workshop. In Gerhard Ritter, editor, *11th World Computer Conference IFIP Congress '89*, pages 719–725, San Francisco CA, August 1989. Elsevier Science Publishers B.V.

[SGA87] Kenneth Salem, Hector Garcia-Molina, and Rafael Alonso. Altruistic locking: A strategy for coping with long lived transactions. In *2nd International Workshop on High Performance Transaction Systems*, Pacific Grove CA, September 1987.

[Sha84] Mary Shaw. Abstraction techniques in modern programming languages. *IEEE Software*, 1(4):10–26, October 1984.

[SZ89] Andrea H. Skarra and Stanley B. Zdonik. *Concurrency Control and Object-Oriented Databases*, pages 395–421. ACM Press, New York, 1989.

[SRLGCBBD90] Michael Stonebraker, Lawrence A. Rowe, Bruce Lindsay, James Gray, Michael Carey, Michael Brodie, Philip Bernstein, and David Beech. Third-generation database system manifesto. *SIGMOD Record*, 19(3):31–44, September 1990.

[Tic85] Walter F. Tichy. RCS — a system for version control. *Software — Practice & Experience*, 15(7):637–654, July 1985.

[WBMN88] J. Walpole, G.S. Blair, J. Malik, and J.R. Nicol. A unifying model for consistent distributed software development environments. In Peter Henderson, editor, *ACM SIGSOFT/SIGPLAN Software Engineering Symposium on Practical Software Development Environments*, pages 183–190, Boston MA, November 1988. Special issue of *SIGPLAN Notices*, 24(2), February 1989 and of *Software Engineering Notes*, 13(5), November 1988.

[Wal84] B. Walter. Nested transactions with multiple commit points: An approach to the structuring of advanced database applications. In Umeshwar Dayal, G. Schlageter, and Lim Huat Seng, editors, *10th International Conference on Very Large Data Bases*, pages 161–171, Singapore, August 1984. Morgan Kaufmann.

[YEEK87] Show way Yeh, Clarence Ellis, Aral Ege, and Henry Korth. Performance analysis of two concurrency control schemas for design environments. Technical Report STP-036-87, MCC, June 1987.

[WS84] Gerhard Weikum and Hans-Jorg Schek. Architectural issues of transaction management in multi-level systems. In Umeshwar Dayal, G. Schlageter, and Lim Huat Seng, editors, *10th International Conference on Very Large Data Bases*, pages 454–465, Singapore, August 1984. Morgan Kaufmann.

9

Multidatabase Transaction and Query Processing in Logic

Eva Kühn

Franz Puntigam

Ahmed K. Elmagarmid

9.1 Introduction

The integration of data is a complex process. In a MultiDataBase System (MDBS), pre-existing Local DataBase Systems (LDBSs) are integrated to support global applications that access data items in more than one local database. For many applications, an MDBS is an attractive alternative to a single integrated database system. An MDBS is different from a set of database systems in that it supports global applications accessing multiple systems simultaneously. It is also differs from traditional homogeneous distributed database systems in that it interconnects LDBSs in a bottom up fashion, thereby allowing existing applications developed on each of the LDBSs to be executable without modification.

An important feature of MDBSs is the autonomy of LDBSs. Local autonomy defines the right of each LDBS to control access to its data by other LDBSs and the right to access and administer its own data independently of other LDBSs. Generally, local autonomy reflects the fact that LDBSs were independently developed and maintained by different organizations.

In this chapter we present a specification for an advanced transaction model, which we term the Flex Transaction model. We also describe transaction management in multidatabase systems and examine the details of query processing in a parallel logic programming environment.

The research work on MDBSs, performed at the University of Technology in Vienna, was influenced by Litwins's work on the Multidatabase SQL (MSQL) [LANV87]. We have implemented a prototype of the MDBS in sequential Prolog, which is the version of the Integrated Prolog MultiDataBase System (VIP-MDBS). Through the VIP-MDBS environment we show how all the features of MSQL can be represented in Prolog and that it can provide more flexibility than MSQL. Furthermore, we show that the VIP-MDBS environment can also support many of the global integration aspects. The goal of this prototype system was to allow the logical integration of heterogeneous schemas while preserving a high degree of local autonomy.

At Purdue University, in the InterBase lab, the representation of the Flex Transaction model through the use of the Vienna Parallel Logic language (VPL) has been demonstrated. This language has been designed as a transaction language for the MDBS environment. The major advantage of using such a language to represent Flex Transaction specifications is its semantic power and suitability. Through the use of the VPL language, a higher degree of parallelism is achieved in the MDBS environment. The properties of the Flex

Transaction model such as compensability, function replication and function dependency are very easily performed in VPL which allows parallel transactions that try to acquire the same goal. We show that the Prolog-based query language used here is a superset of the MSQL. Finally, it is our belief that combining the features of VPL through the interface with MSQL to implement Flex Transactions will greatly enhance the development process of MDBSs.

The rest of the chapter is organized as follows. In Section 9.2, we show how sequential Prolog may serve as the query language for MDBS integration, and we discuss various integration approaches, such as that of global integration (*static*) and that of *dynamic* MDBS languages like MSQL. Subsequently, we present the VIP-MDBS prototype that uses Prolog for MDBS integration, including advanced features of VIP-MDBS that have no counterpart in existing approaches. See references [Küh89, KL88a, KL88b].

In Section 9.3, we discuss the specification of MDBS transactions using the logic programming paradigm, and we give an overview of the Flex Transaction model. We then propose the idea of using a parallel logic language to specify MDBS transactions and give an overview of approaches to incorporating parallelism into Prolog. We explain why existing concurrent Prolog languages are not sufficient for this purpose and formulate the requirements for the design of the VPL language. See references [ELLR90, Leu91, KPE91a] for further details.

Section 9.4 shows how VPL can serve as both query and transaction specification language for MDBSs and presents our proposed MDBS architecture. This is followed by a more detailed introduction to the VPL language, and a comparison of it with other parallel logic languages. We then explain some VPL primitives essential for the MDBS application. These include VPL's control-meta-call primitive that allows exception handling and the remote call primitive that serves as an interface with another software (DBS) system. Finally, we prove that VPL is at least as powerful as the Flex Transaction model, by briefly outlining a mapping algorithm from Flex Transactions into VPL. See references [KP91, KPE91b].

Section 9.5 demonstrates how VPL may extend the power of Flex Transactions.

9.2 Representation of MDBS Queries in Prolog

An MDBS comprises several local database systems (LDBSs) that may differ with respect to aspects including data representation, naming, data model, execution of queries, and communication protocols. In this analysis, each LDBS is autonomous and is maintained and developed independently of any other LDBS.

Different forms of autonomy have been identified [GK88], however, design autonomy seems to be the most important one. Therefore, we briefly describe the impact of design autonomy on the requirements of an MDBS query language.

Each LDBS may use its own data model as well as its own paradigm (e.g., relational, hierarchical, network, deductive, object-oriented). The languages of the LDBSs may differ, and even if all LDBSs use the same data model, the representation of data may differ between any two LDBSs. These differences concern such aspects as the structuring of data, attribute and relation names, semantics, and scaling. For example, in one airline DBS, prices for flights are stored in a table called `fprices` with the attribute names `flno` and `flprice`, whereas in another airline DBS, the price table is called `price` and has the three attributes `start`, `end`, and `price`. In this example, we find different names because the relation and attribute designators are different, and structure differences because in one DBS the price is associated with a unique flightnumber, whereas in the other DBS all flights between two cities have the same price. Further integration problems arise if data in different LDBSs are redundant and perhaps also inconsistent. In the above example there is no redundancy, as flights from different airline DBSs are usually disjoint.

Design autonomy primarily results in problems concerning the integration of data dictionaries. These problems remain the same, whether they arise on one site only, or in a distributed network with many sites. We may provide solutions for the integration of several LDBSs with design autonomy without any concern for transaction control. The main aim is to find a unique way to formulate queries on the heterogeneous data. In the following section we discuss existing approaches to data integration, which we classify as *static* and *dynamic* approaches. We present an overview of our VIP-MDBS system that uses Prolog for integration and provides both kinds of integration within one system—they may even be combined within one query.

9.2.1 Dynamic and Static Integration

An MDBS may be designed on the basis of either existing or entirely new concepts. We believe that the first approach, to take existing technologies that were developed for a centralized DBS or for homogeneous distributed

DBSs and to upgrade them to the MDBS level, may not always be adequate. Autonomy requires completely new criteria.

In the literature we find two approaches for MDBS integration, *static* and *dynamic*. The first approach resembles the attempt to adapt existing DBS technologies; the second approach is based on the observation that an LDBS, in order to participate in the MDBS cannot be changed, substituted or extended by any other software without violating its autonomy. Existing DBS technologies are not designed to deal with autonomy.

The Global Integration Approach

The global integration approach is based on the idea of integrating non-homogeneous data schemas into one uniform schema [Sch87]. A new schema is constructed, and existing application programs must be adapted. We differentiate between *bottom-up* and *top-down* integration.

- **Bottom-up Integration:** The first context in which schema integration occurs is when different user views are used for the generation of a global schema on several databases. The different databases are presented to the user as if they were only one database. This global view forms the interface on which the user puts his queries. A query on the global view automatically is decomposed into several subqueries onto the underlying physical databases. Global schema integration can be seen as a bottom-up strategy because it operates on pre-existing DBSs.

- **Top-down Integration:** The second context in which schema integration occurs is during the logical design of (M)DBSs. A top-down strategy can only be used when designing (M)DBSs from the beginning. [NSE84] differentiates between starting the design by considering individual data items, and by operating with semantic data models, such as the entity-relationship model. In the first case, all functional dependencies must be defined before a fully automatic synthesis can occur; in the second case, redundancies and alternatives have to be considered, and thus only a semi-automatic synthesis can occur.

In [NS88], an object-oriented integration approach is described that allows the user to formulate not-predefined queries by means of *personalized views*. It is also possible to treat not-completely-specified queries. This work was a first step towards incorporating dynamic aspects into the global integration approach.

The Dynamic MDBS Languages Approach

MDBS languages represent a dynamic concept. We object to the approach of the construction of a global schema, in which all users operate as if they are on a single integrated DBS. The concept of *interoperability* has led to the definition of MSQL (Multidatabase SQL) [LANV87] which is an extension of SQL by MDBS features. MSQL provides declarative language constructs which allow the addressing of data in several autonomous relational DBSs within one query. A scope defines which DBSs are involved. A *multiple identifier* is a single identifier that designates identically-named data from several DBSs. *Semantic variables* are provided to map similar names or to define new identifiers that may stand for different names in different DBSs.

One valuable extension is the concept of *dynamic columns* (also termed *dynamic attributes*) [LV86], which generates virtual attributes. A set of pre-defined functions can be used to map data names into data values. As an example, let us assume that one user wishes to see the prices of flights in US dollars, while another one wants to see them in French francs. Modifications and updates are allowed on virtual attributes. For updates on dynamic attributes, the user generally needs to specify an inverse mapping. However, there are some cases where this inverse mapping can be computed automatically, so that no user interference is necessary.

For dealing with incompletely specified queries, MSQL provides *implicit joins*. Two attributes are naturally dependent if they share the same domain and if at least one of them is part of a primary key. The dependencies are computed with the help of a dependency graph. For incomplete queries, this dependency graph is disconnected. A special completion algorithm has been developed for these cases. The problems arising are similar to database update problems in general where incomplete data may occur. Implicit joins permit the avoidance of logical navigation, as in the universal relation model. Implicit natural equi-joins are detected automatically by the system. Unlike the universal relation model, this approach places no extra requirements on data schemas, nor are extra types or objects necessary.

The dynamic integration approach relies on the assumption that data with the same meaning usually have the same or similar names. Data integration is thus based on attribute or relation names. This approach guarantees autonomy at a very high degree; existing schemas and applications remain unchanged.

Comparison

For schema integration in general, the effort to integrate all nonhomogeneous data structures into one view may be very expensive. In public networks, the number of DBSs to which a user has access could be so large that the integration of all of them is not possible. Another problem is that it must be guaranteed that the stored global schema is up to date. Serious problems can arise, especially if the data schemas in LDBSs are modified. The violation of LDBS autonomy may be a consequence.

The dynamic approach has the following disadvantages: MSQL queries always have to be formulated ad hoc. An MSQL query is decomposed into several queries which are passed to the DBSs. The results are produced independently by the DBSs and are returned to the MDBS user in several tables. These tables are not integrated and therefore cannot be processed by subsequent queries. A further criticism of the dynamic approach is that the formulation of dynamic (ad hoc) queries assumes that the user is aware of the data schemas of all DBSs. This assumption can lead to unexpected or erroneous results. For example, the assumption that same or similar data designators always address data with same meaning is dangerous; in a heterogeneous environment, not all names of relations starting with b may designate banks. On the other hand, this criticism also addresses a positive feature of MSQL, that queries may be reused even if data schemas are changed.

The advantage of the static approach is that user queries are simpler than in the dynamic approach. Advantages of the dynamic approach are that it allows for a high degree of local autonomy and a high re-usability of query formulations.

Autonomy necessitates new concepts for MDBSs. Concerning autonomy, the dynamic approach should be preferred, but the static approach is advantageous because of the convenience of writing queries. Probably only the support of *both* integration aspects—dynamic and static—within one system will provide the most flexible solution. We use advanced tools for integration, in particular the logic programming paradigm.

The VIP-MDBS System

The VIP-MDBS (Vienna Integrated Prolog MultiDataBase System [KL88a, KL88b]) is the prototype implementation of an MDBS based on Prolog. The aim of this project was to build a system for the logical integration of data that provides both dynamic and static integration aspects. It was the first MDBS prototype system using Prolog for the integration of heterogeneous data [LZ88]. The MSQL language has influenced the design of VIP-MDBS, mainly in that we started with mapping the features of MSQL into Prolog. (M)SQL and Prolog are related to each other; both are based on first order logic. In addition, Prolog is powerful enough to express all the features of dynamic MDBS languages. On the other hand, an important observation was that (M)SQL queries designate data by names, whereas Prolog addresses data by position. For the SQL user, the ordering of arguments within a relation is irrelevant. MSQL relies even more on the use of names when bridging structural, semantic and other differences between autonomous DBSs. For example, MSQL allows the use of names that are automatically expanded to names within several DBSs. In contrast, Prolog does not support names for arguments; arguments are always addressed by their positions in the relation (procedure). With this approach, Prolog forces the user to provide detailed knowledge about the structure of the data. To overcome this problem, we have introduced a naming concept (explained below) that permits more convenient MDBS queries. Prolog, extended by this naming concept, provides even more flexibility than MSQL. Prolog is a general purpose programming language, and thus the user is not restricted to the use of only predefined features and functions.

To provide the advantages of the static integration approach as well, we have introduced the concept of *semantic relations.* Semantic relations are similar to relational views, because they do not physically store tuples; they describe how data from several DBSs may be derived. They can be considered stored queries. The main differences between relational views and semantic relations are that the latter can also integrate deductive data and can be used to represent recursive data. It it possible to define semantic relations by other semantic relations and compose them into hierarchies.

Usually there exists only one optimal way to formulate a query in MSQL, whereas VIP-MDBS offers many ways to formulate the same task. First, Prolog serves as the MDBS language; second, the user has the choice of using dynamic as well as static integration aspects, combining them to any desired degree. In the remainder of this chapter, we will present examples with several solutions for VIP-MDBS queries; we will also compare them with MSQL queries. We will not explain the MSQL queries in detail; see [LANV87] for a description of MSQL. The comparison with MSQL queries will serve to show the expressiveness of VIP-MDBS. Often, the VIP-MDBS representation of the query is more complex than the MSQL representation, but VIP-MDBS is not intended to be the end user's interface. MSQL can easily be embedded into Prolog as a high-level user-interface.

Prolog serves as the implementation, user interface and data representation language. Semantic relations and other integration information for the MDBS are stored as Prolog facts and rules. In Section 9.4.1, we will discuss the architecture of an MDBS in more detail. For the rest of this section, we will assume that integration data are available in the form of Prolog clauses, and that (relational) local database systems (LDBSs) provide a Prolog interface. This limitation is not a restriction of generality, especially as many feasible approaches to coupling Prolog with relational database systems already exist [CGT90]. We will see that VIP-MDBS already provides more flexibility than existing MDBS approaches, and that these assumptions add even more flexibility. The claim for deductiveness in an MDBS can be argued as follows: if the LDBSs are deductive DBSs, then the MDBS must also be a deductive system to represent intensional data at the MDBS level. VIP-MDBS fulfills these requirements.

Each LDBS that belongs to the MDBS is addressed by its name. (Section 9.4.1 will explain how the integration directory acts as a name server.) To call a query in an LDBS, we have introduced the primitive `remote_call(`*Database*`,`*Query*`)` which sends a Prolog query to the named (database) system. *Query* is a Prolog query that is passed to the LDBS[1], which we assume is able to process Prolog queries. In Section 9.4.2, we will refine this assumption and explain the use of the remote-call primitive in cases where the LDBS provides no Prolog interface.

The rest of this chapter will provide examples using the MDBS of a travel agency, as detailed in the Appendix. We will use the following conventions. We distinguish between Prolog (or VPL) language constructs, written in a `typewriter`-like style, and meta-variables that are used for the language description, written in *italics*. We write function and predicate (viz. relation) symbols as sequences of letters and numbers beginning with a lowercase letter, or as sequences of special characters. Variable names are sequences of letters and numbers beginning with an uppercase letter or _ (underline). The variable _ is the anonymous variable that is different from all other variables. We use infix notation for some binary predicates and prefix or postfix notation for some unary predicates. The predicate *name*(...) with arity n is denoted by *name*/n. Clauses of the form "*Head* :– `true`." can be written as "*Head.*"

[1]More precisely, the query is passed to the multidatabase interface of this LDBS.

EXAMPLE **9.1** *VIP-MDBS Query on one LDBS*

The query "retrieve all flight numbers for flights from Vienna (airportcode is `vie`) to Amsterdam (`ams`) from the `klm` database" can be written in VIP-MDBS as follows:[2]

```
ask((result(Flno) :-
    remote_call(klm,timetable(vie,ams,_,_,Flno))).
```

EXAMPLE **9.2** *Definition of the* `ta` *MDBS*

We want to create a new multidatabase system on the three local airline databases `klm`, `ua` and `twa`. The query is given in MSQL (see "`query`") and in VIP-MDBS (see "`representation in Prolog`"):

```
/* query: */
CREATE MULTIDATABASE ta (klm ua twa)

/* representation in Prolog: */
create_mdb(ta,[klm,ua,twa]).
```

The Dynamic Concept of VIP-MDBS

In the dynamic approach to MDBS integration, as previously discussed, no additional information about relationships between data is stored in the system. Each query has to be posed ad hoc. Data in an LDBS is addressed by means of the logical variable and backtracking.

MSQL does, however, allow the definition of a scope for queries. A scope declares a set of DBSs which will be considered by MDBS queries (also called global queries). Scope definitions remain valid until they are re-defined. In VIP-MDBS, we provide the primitive `use(`*List*`)`, where *List* contains a list of (M)DBS names; MDBS names are then decomposed by the system into its component DBSs. All names that occur in an MDBS query will be automatically expanded according to the actual scope. In this way, `use/1` can serve to let simple designators become multiple identifiers (see below). The syntax of attribute names has four possible formats:

```
Database:Relationname → Attributename
Database:Attributename
Relationname → Attributename
Attributename
```

[2] `result` serves to collect the result tuples and corresponds to the "`SELECT *...`" statement of (M)SQL.

The "→" operator has the same semantics as the "." operator of (M)SQL and serves to select an attribute. These four formats are different with regard to their completeness of specification. All missing components are expanded in the given scope.

As mentioned earlier, we have extended our Prolog system with a naming technique that allows access to attribute values not only by position but also by attribute names. This approach is very useful in a heterogeneous environment; it supports the interoperability of DBSs. We have also introduced the two primitives `allargs(`*RelationName*`,`*ResultList*`)` (`allargs` stands for "all arguments") and `value(`*AttributeName*`,`*AttributeValue*`)`. These primitives require a meta-interpretation. A user may specify several of these primitives in one query, and the system must ensure that these primitives always refer to the same tuple—otherwise consistent semantics cannot be guaranteed. The first argument of `allargs/2` is an identifier that is interpreted as a relation name and is expanded in the corresponding context. The second argument contains a list with the argument values of the retrieved tuples. `value/2` relates an attribute with its value; it can be used with multi-mode arguments[3]. `allargs/2` as well as `value/2` finally result in calls to the remote-call primitive in order to execute LDBS subqueries.

The concept of *multiple identifiers* of MSQL refers to names of relations and attributes that may stand for several data objects from different LDBSs. The user knows (or assumes) that identically named data have the same meaning. We may use relation names and attribute names as multiple identifiers.

EXAMPLE **9.3** *Relation Names as Multiple Identifiers*

Use the MDBS of the travel agency and select all arguments from all `timetable` relations:[4]

```
/* query: */
USE ta
SELECT * FROM timetable

/* representation in Prolog: */
use([ta]) &
ask((result(ResultList) :- allargs(timetable,ResultList))).
```

[3] Depending on which argument is specified, the other one is computed.

[4] "&" denotes Prolog's sequential AND-operator.

MSQL produces three independent tables, which are the `timetables` of the `klm`, `ua`, and the `twa` DBSs. The same solution is produced by the Prolog query. The Prolog query is expanded to three queries that are sent independently to the three DBSs. Each of the three `timetables` has a different structure, of which the user need not be aware. When relation names are used as multiple identifiers, two situations may arise:

1. All relations show the same structure; i.e., they have the same number of arguments, and arguments at the same position semantically correspond to each other. In our example, this is true for the `timetable` relations in the `klm` and the `twa` DBSs but not for the `timetable` relation in the `ua` DBS. With this knowledge, the query of Example 9.3 can be represented in Prolog as follows, when the scope shall be the `klm` and the `twa` DBSs only:[5]

```
use([klm,twa]) &
ask((result(From,To,Dept,Arriv,Flno) :-
    timetable(From,To,Dept,Arriv,Flno))).
```

   `timetable` is specified without an explicit path and therefore is interpreted as a `timetable` in the `klm` and the `twa` DBSs. This specification produces only one result table, which is the integration of both timetables. However, it can be observed that the user needs to provide detailed knowledge about the local data dictionaries in order to achieve correct results. Such queries may be formulated without the use of the naming concept, but they are less powerful, because they require the user's knowledge instead of the system's knowledge.

2. The structures of the addressed relations differ, although the relation names are equal. The task of finding all timetables in the `klm`, `ua`, and `twa` DBSs will now be represented as a dynamic query without the use of the naming concept. This is a bad example of the use of the dynamic approach, as it requires the user to have knowledge about the data schemas, but it does represent the structural differences in the query. The result is one integrated table:[6]

```
ask((result(From,To,Dept,Arriv,Flno) :-
    ( member(DBS,[klm,twa]) &
```

[5]`timetable/5` is expanded to the corresponding remote-calls in each LDBS.

[6]The first argument of `member/2` is a member of the list in the second argument.

```
        DBS:timetable(From,To,Dept,Arriv,Flno) ) or
      ua:timetable(Flno,From,To,Dept,Arriv)).
```

`or` designates the sequential OR operator of Prolog. The navigation over the three DBSs is performed by Prolog's backtracking mechanism. The logic variable `DBS` consequently receives the values `klm` and `twa`. `DBS:timetable` accordingly starts remote-calls in both databases; finally, `ua:timetable` starts the remote-call in the `ua` database.

We will now explain the concept of attribute names as multiple identifiers, where an attribute name may designate attribute names of several relations from several DBSs:

EXAMPLE **9.4** *Attribute Names as Multiple Identifiers*

Retrieve all flight numbers of flights from Vienna to Amsterdam from all `timetables` of the `ta` MDBS:

```
/* query: */
USE ta
SELECT flno WHERE from = vie AND to = ams

/* representation in Prolog: */
use([ta]) &
ask((result(Flno) :-
    value(from,vie) & value(to,ams) & value(flno,Flno))).
```

EXAMPLE **9.5** *Attribute Names as Multiple Identifiers*

Set all flight numbers with value equal to 300 to 3000 in all `timetables` of the `ta` MDBS:

```
/* query: */
USE ta
UPDATE * SET flno = 3000 WHERE flno = 300

/* representation in Prolog: */
use([ta]) &
modify(value(flno,3000),value(flno,300)).
```

In general, when the concept of multiple identifiers is used in ad hoc queries, solutions with the naming concept are preferred. If one integrated table must be produced, then such a query in principle may also be formulated ad hoc but, as we will argue later, the use of the static features of VIP-MDBS is more advantageous in this case.

In addition to multiple identifiers, the concept of *semantic variables* has been introduced by MSQL. Semantic variables provide a single identifier to refer to an arbitrary number of names. Differing names can also be addressed, a capability not possessed by multiple identifiers. In particular, *explicit* and *implicit* semantic variables have been introduced.

For an *explicit semantic variable*, a new name is defined in the domain of several data objects. This mechanism may also serve for aliasing. The MSQL definition is as follows:

```
LET <semantic variable> BE <designator> [<designator>] ...
```

A query that follows such a definition equals a set of queries that can be derived by the substitution of the semantic variable by the specified designators.

Explicit semantic variables can be directly supported by means of Prolog's logical variables. The substitution of the semantic variable occurs automatically on backtracking.

EXAMPLE **9.6** *Explicit Semantic Variable for Attribute Names*

Retrieve all prices for flights from the `ta` MDBS. The problem is that two DBSs store a `price` attribute and the third DBS administrates a `flprice` attribute:[7]

```
/* query: */
USE ta
LET y BE price flprice
SELECT y

/* representation in Prolog: */
use([ta]) &
member(Y,[price,flprice]) &
ask((result(Price) :- value(Y,Price))).
```

EXAMPLE **9.7** *Explicit Semantic Variable for Relation Names*

Retrieve information about seats and flight numbers (stored in relations with name `planes` or `seats`) from the `ta` MDBS of all flights using a Boeing 747:

[7] This example does not deal with the problem of different currencies.

```
/* query: */
USE ta
LET x BE planes seats
SELECT * FROM x WHERE planetype = 'Boeing 747'

/* representation in Prolog: */
use([ta]) &
member(X,[planes,seats]) &
ask((result(Result) :- value(planetype,'Boeing 747') &
    allargs(X,Result))).
```

EXAMPLE **9.8** *Mixed Use of Explicit Semantic Variables*

Mixed use of explicit semantic variables for relation and attribute names is also possible. Retrieve all flight numbers of flights in the `ta` MDBS where planes with more than 120 seats are used:

```
/* query: */
USE ta
LET x.y BE seats.seatnrs planes.nr_seats
SELECT flno FROM x WHERE y > 120

/* representation in Prolog: */
use([ta]) &
member(X,[seats → seatnrs,planes → nr_seats]) &
ask((result(Flno) :-
    value(X,Nr) & Nr > 120 & value(flno,Flno))).
```

Implicit semantic variables refer to relation or attribute names with the same meaning and different but similar names. For example, queries are supported where the user knows that all desired relation names start with a certain letter. The MSQL user has to rely on pre-defined primitives, whereas the VIP-MDBS user may use the general purpose language Prolog, thus considerably more flexibility can be provided.

EXAMPLE **9.9** *Implicit Semantic Variable*

Retrieve all information about flights starting from New York from the `ta` MDBS:

```
/* query: */
USE ta
SELECT * WHERE dep% = jfk
```

```
/* representation in Prolog: */
use([ta]) &
is_attributename(A) & name(A,[d,e,p|_]) &
ask((result(R) :- allargs(_,R) & value(A,jfk))).
```

In MSQL the function "%" serves as a wild card; `name/2` is a Prolog system primitive that relates a name with the list of its characters; `is_attributename/1` serves to retrieve information from the data dictionaries.

The Static Concept of VIP-MDBS

The static integration concept is based on the idea of storing information about relationships and dependencies of data. (The automatic derivation of such knowledge is not discussed in this chapter.) We model such knowledge with *semantic relations* that we have introduced for this purpose. Dynamic queries always can be represented by the static approach, and in the following, we present solutions involving semantic relations for the examples addressed earlier with the dynamic approach.

A semantic relation is a relation that derives data (or knowledge) from one or more LDBSs by means of a unique schema. Semantic relations can be viewed as the axioms of an integration theory. They are related to relational views in the following ways.

- A semantic relation can be viewed as a stored query.
- A semantic relation does not physically store tuples, but it represents a description of how to access data in the DBSs.

Semantic relations also differ from relational views in several ways:

- A semantic relation supports the ideas that different users may be interested in different data, and that different users may require different interpretations of the same data to the MDBS level.
- A semantic relation is able to integrate deductive knowledge.
- Semantic relations can be modeled in a hierarchical way; recursion for data representation is also allowed.

Semantic relations have been called "semantic," in order to express that semantic rules (e.g. Prolog clauses) are used to describe how to deduce knowledge. They have been called "relations" because queries on semantic relations do not differ from queries on normal relations, including retrieval[8], and the definition of data. A semantic relation is defined by the primitive `semantic_relation(SR)`, which defines a new relation name, as well as data mappings. In contrast to the dynamic approach (using the naming concept), a single integrated result table is produced. In the following examples, we mark all statically stored integration information with "`static`" and the user's query with "`representation in Prolog:`"

EXAMPLE **9.10** *(Compare with Example 9.3)*

Retrieve all arguments from all timetable relations in the `ta` MDBS:[9]

```
/* static: */
semantic_relation((ta:timetable(From,To,Dept,Arr,Air,Fno) :-
    ( twa:timetable(From,To,Dep,Arr,Fno) & Air=twa ) or
    ( ua: timetable(Fno,From,To,Dep,Arr) & Air=ua  ) or
    ( klm:timetable(From,To,Dep,Arr,Fno) & Air=klm ))).
  /* representation in Prolog (variant 1): */

ask((result(F,T,D,A,Air,Fno) :-
    ta:timetable(F,T,D,A,Air,Fno))).

/* representation in Prolog (variant 2): */
ask((result(R) :- allargs(ta:timetable,R))).
```

EXAMPLE **9.11** *(Compare with Example 9.4)*

Retrieve all flight numbers of flights from Vienna to Amsterdam from all `timetables` of the `ta` MDBS:

```
/* static: "ta:timetable" as above: */

/* representation in Prolog: */
ask((result(Flno) :- ta:timetable(vie,ams,_,_,_,Flno))).
```

EXAMPLE **9.12** *(Compare With Example 9.6)*

Retrieve all prices for flights from the `ta` MDBS:[10]

---

[8] We have identified cases where safe updates can be performed on semantic relations. This work is based on the assumption that an LDBS may store incomplete knowledge by means of Prolog rules.

[9] ":" is the module operator of our Prolog system and helps to reference the (M)DBS.

[10] The semantic relation `ta:price/4` produces one integrated result table and also performs the conversion between different currencies.

```
/* static: */
semantic_relation((ta:price(From,To,Price,Air) :-
    ( twa:price(From,To,Price) & Air=twa ) or
    ( ua:timetable(Fno,From,To,_,_) &
      ua:fprices(Fno,Price) & Air=ua ) or
    ( klm:price(From,To,Price1) &
      ta:convert_dfl_us(Price1,Price) & Air=klm ))).

/* representation in Prolog: */
ask((result(Price) :- ta:price(_,_,Price,_))).
```

EXAMPLE **9.13** *(Compare with Example 9.7)*

Retrieve information about seats and flight numbers from the ta MDBS of all flights using a Boeing 747:

```
/* static: */
/* static: (we assume that the attribute names
    for ta:planes are ptype,pseats and pflno) */
semantic_relation((ta:planes(Type,Snr,Flno) :-
    klm:seats(Flno,Type,Snr) or
    ( member(DBS,[ua,twa]) & DBS:planes(Type,Snr,Flno) ))).
def_attributenames(ta:planes(ptype,pseats,pflno)).

/* representation in Prolog (variant 1): */
ask((result(R) :- allargs(ta:planes,R) &
    value(ta:planes→ptype,'Boeing 747'))).

/* representation in Prolog (variant 2): no redundant
    column for the plane type is produced */
ask((result(S,F) :- ta:planes('Boeing 747',S,F))).
```

EXAMPLE **9.14** *(Compare with Example 9.8)*

Retrieve all flight numbers of flights in the ta MDBS where planes with more than 120 seats are used:

```
/* static: "ta:planes/3" as defined above */

/* representation in Prolog: */
ask((result(Flno) :- ta:planes(_,Snr,Flno) & Snr > 120)).
```

EXAMPLE **9.15** *(Compare with Example 9.9)*

Retrieve all information about flights originating in New York from the `ta` MDBS:

```
/* static: "ta:timetable/5" as defined above */
def_attributenames(
    ta:timetable(from,to,departure,arrival,airline,flno)).
/* representation in Prolog: */

ask((result(R) :- allargs(ta:timetable,R) &
    value(ta:timetable → departure,jfk))).
```

Reference may be made to [Küh89] for the representation of the concepts of implicit joins and dynamic columns of MSQL in VIP-MDBS.

Advanced Features of VIP-MDBS

Transitive closure is one of the most significant features of deductive databases, whereas recursion in relational DBSs is possible only for data retrieval, if at all. Furthermore, such closure would require complex mechanisms which extend the SQL language with features for which it has not been been designed.

In the context of our travel agency example, Let us consider the problem of finding all possible flight connections between two given cities. The client indicates a number of cities he wishes to visit, as well as a number of conditions, e.g., conditions concerning arrival and departure times. We define the following recursive semantic relation `ta:route/2` in the `ta` MDBS:

```
semantic_relation((ta:route([L1,L2],[FnoL]) :-
    ta:connect(L1,L2,FnoL,[L1]))).
semantic_relation((ta:route([L1,L2|Ls],[FnoL|FnoLs]) :-
    ta:connect(L1,L2,FnoL,[L1]) &
    ta:route([L2|Ls],FnoLs))).
```

This semantic relation generates all possibles routes for a given list of layovers. The information about flights and times is derived from all airline DBSs of the MDBS. The second argument of `ta:route/2` stands for all possible routes. It is a list of all flightnumbers of all connections of which the route is composed. These connections are derived through the use of the semantic relation `ta:connect/4` which is explained below. The first argument of `ta:route/2` contains the list of all desired layovers. It consists of triples `layover(Where,From,Until)`, standing for the unique airportcode, and the planned arrival and departure times. The arguments of both semantic relations are not in first normal form, but as they do not physically store data, the well-known problems of NF2-DBSs do not arise.

The semantic relation `ta:connect/4` is also recursively defined. It calls the semantic relation `ta:timetable/5`, which integrates the knowledge of the timetables of the autonomous airline DBSs. A query on `ta:timetable/5` is automatically decomposed into a correspondingly large number of queries on all LDBSs. The definition of `ta:connect/4` is as follows:

```
semantic_relation((ta:connect(layover(A1,_,DEP1),
                       layover(A2,ARR2,_),[Fno],_) :-
    ta:timetable(A1,A2,DEP1,ARR2,Fno))).
semantic_relation((ta:connect(layover(A1,_,DEP1),
                       layover(A2,ARR2,_),[Fno|Fnos],AXs) :-
    ta:timetable(A1,AX,DEP1,ARRX,Fno) &
    AX \= A2 & not member(AX,AXs) &
    ta:connect(layover(AX,ARRX,_),
        layover(A2,ARR2,_),Fnos,[AX|X]))).
```

This semantic relation generates a part of the route; namely, a connection between two given layovers. The first and the second argument of `ta:connect/4` are triples of the form `layover(Where,From,Until)`. The third argument is a list of flights connecting two cities. The fourth argument[11] serves to avoid cycles[12] in that it does not pass the same city twice within one route, unless such a double passage is explicitly specified by the user. `ta:connect/4` is called by `ta:route/2` as many times as necessary to compute the whole route. A combination of flights from different airline DBSs within one route is possible. If no direct flight exists between two specified layovers, or if on backtracking no other direct flight can be found, then an additional layover is generated, and an additional intermediate landing for the client is provided.

EXAMPLE **9.16** *Recursion in Data Representation*

Retrieve all possible flights from New York (`jfk`) to Los Angeles (`lax`) and back to New York so that the departure from New York is not before 8:30 a.m.:

[11] This argument is redundant; however, it contributes to efficiency.

[12] Prolog provides no mechanism to avoid endless loops.

```
/* static: all three semantic relations from above */

/* representation in Prolog: */
ask((result(Route) :- ta:route([layover(jfk,Dep,_),
    layover(lax,_,_),layover(jfk,_,_)],Route) & Dep>8:30)).
```

EXAMPLE **9.17** *Transitive Closure*

Retrieve all possible flights routes from New York (`jfk`) to any destination:

```
/* static: all three semantic relations from above */

/* representation in Prolog: */
ask((result(Route) :-
    ta:route([layover(jfk,_,_),layover(_,_,_)],Route)).
```

9.3
Transaction Control with Logic Programming

This section deals with the specification of MDBS transactions which use logic programming. Sequential Prolog may serve for the specification of MDBS queries, as well as the logical integration of heterogeneous data schemas, as described in the previous section, but sequential Prolog is not sufficient for the specification of MDBS transactions. A language that allows the parallel execution of subtransactions is needed. Therefore, we have extended sequential Prolog by explicit language constructs to express parallelism; this extension results in the VPL (Vienna Parallel Logic) language. VPL is a transaction-oriented parallel logic programming language.

Transactions usually have the properties of *atomicity, consistency, isolation,* and *durability* (ACID). The autonomy requirements of LDBSs have profound effects on the execution of global transactions [DELO89]. For example, global transactions in MDBSs could be long lived because of the delay of subtransactions. We cannot adapt existing transaction concepts because the requirements of MDBSs are different from those of LDBSs, for example, the throughput of the entire MDBS, including local queries, must be optimized, not just global queries. Thus, an important concern in optimization is to avoid holding locks in LDBSs for a long period.

To this point, we have been concerned with the design autonomy of LDBSs, but in MDBSs execution and communication autonomy also play an important role. Execution autonomy means that each LDBS may decide by itself whether or not it will execute a query, when it executes a query, and which algorithm it uses to execute the query. Because of communication autonomy, an LDBS cannot be forced to communicate with other software systems like the MDBS. Despite these kinds of autonomy, an MDBS must be able to execute a global transaction. Fully relying on the ACID properties of transactions and maintaining a high degree of autonomy, imply a severe loss of efficiency.

In order to overcome some of these problems, it is useful to extend the traditional transaction model by relaxing the atomicity and isolation properties for global transactions. A flexible transaction model is needed in which each application decides to which extent it requires the ACID properties.

9.3.1 The Flex Transaction Model

In [ELLR90, Leu91] a new transaction model (called *Flex Transactions*) was proposed to cope with the autonomy problems of transaction processing in MDBSs. The concept of Flex Transactions is a generalization of traditional transactions. Flex Transactions have the following features:

Function replication: In many multidatabase applications, a specific function can be accomplished by more than one local system. For example, the transaction programmer may leave to the system the choice of renting a car from Hertz or Avis. This property is called function replication and is incorporated in Flex Transactions to allow flexible composition of global transactions.

Mixed transaction: Some actions can be "semantically undone" even after they are completed. For example, a subtransaction reserving a seat on a flight can be compensated by another subtransaction which cancels the reservation. This fact allows subtransactions to commit before the corresponding global transaction has committed. Global transactions consisting of both compensatable and non-compensatable subtransactions are called mixed transactions.

Value function: In Flex Transactions, a value function may be associated with each global transaction and subtransaction. The typical value function is completion time of the transaction. For example, the reservation of a seat for a flight must be made before the trip.

We briefly summarize the formal definition of Flex Transactions:

DEFINITION

A Flex Transaction *T is a 5-tuple* (B, S, F, Π, f) *where*

- $B = \{t_1(type_1), t_2(type_2), \ldots, t_n(type_n)\}$ *is a set of* typed subtransactions. *In particular, B specifies whether a transaction t_i is* compensatable *($type_i$ = "C") or not ($type_i$ = "NC"). A compensatable transaction may commit earlier, but its effects may be later "semantically undone".*
- *S is a partial order of B, called the* success order *of T. $t_i \prec t_j \in S$ means that transaction t_i has to be successfully executed before transaction t_j may be started. S describes* internal dependencies.
- *F is a partial order of B, called the* failure order *of T. F is analogously defined to S. If $t_i \prec t_j \in F$, then transaction t_j depends on the failure of transaction t_i. F also describes internal dependencies.*
- *Π is a set of* external predicates *on B. Π may contain cost functions, time constraints (e.g., when a local transaction may be scheduled), etc.*
- *f is an n-ary boolean function and is called the* acceptability function *of T. f describes all* acceptable states. *E.g.,* $f(x_1, x_2, x_3, x_4) = (x_1 \wedge x_3) \vee (x_2 \wedge x_4)$ *is defined over 4 transactions on local databases and states that the Flex Transaction can be accepted when either transactions 1 and 3 or transactions 2 and 4 are a success. $x_1, \ldots, x_4$ are the execution states of $t_1, \ldots, t_4$. The subset $C \subseteq B$ of all subtransactions which finally are committed is called the* commit-set *of T. C corresponds to one acceptable state.*

EXAMPLE **9.18** *A Simple Flex Transaction*

Consider our MDBS example of a travel agency. The system consists of local databases including two airline databases ($database_1$ = `klm`, $database_2$ = `twa`), a car rental database ($database_3$ = `avis`), and two hotel databases ($database_4$ = `hilton`, $database_5$ = `ramada`). For this example, transactions on hotel databases are compensatable. Assume we wish to book a flight from New York to Chicago in either $database_1$ or $database_2$ (we prefer $database_1$, so we do not try to book in $database_2$ unless it is not possible to book in $database_1$). After booking a flight, we wish to rent a car in $database_3$. This action must be performed during office hours. We need a hotel reservation in Chicago (*database*$_4$ or *database*$_5$); we have no preference between either of the two hotels and thus we can try to reserve a room in these databases in parallel.

We may express the above transaction as a Flex Transaction $T = (B, S, F, \Pi, f)$ (t_i denotes the local subtransaction on *database*$_i$):

$$\begin{aligned}
&B = \{t_1(\mathrm{NC}), t_2(\mathrm{NC}), t_3(\mathrm{NC}), t_4(\mathrm{C}), t_5(\mathrm{C})\}\\
&S = \{t_1 \prec t_3, t_2 \prec t_3\}\\
&F = \{t_1 \prec t_2\}\\
&\Pi = \{8 < \mathrm{time}(t_3) < 17\}\\
&f(x_1, x_2, x_3, x_4, x_5) = (x_1 \wedge x_3 \wedge x_4) \vee (x_2 \wedge x_3 \wedge x_4) \vee\\
&\qquad (x_1 \wedge x_3 \wedge x_5) \vee (x_2 \wedge x_3 \wedge x_5)
\end{aligned}$$

The success dependencies $t_1 \prec t_3$ and $t_2 \prec t_3$ express the fact that t_3 (rent a car) must not be started before either t_1 or t_2 (book a flight) has succeeded. Because of the failure dependency $t_1 \prec t_2$ the subtransaction t_2 must not be started before t_1 has failed. The external predicate in Π requires that the subtransaction t_3 be executed during office hours (between 8 a.m. and 5 p.m.). The acceptability function f describes the set of acceptable states. Note that, because of function replication, each acceptable state contains only one of the subtransactions t_1 and t_2 and one of the subtransactions t_4 and t_5.

Flex Transactions specify MDBS transactions, but they are not executable queries. The Flex Transaction model is defined by a logical notation. Therefore, it is straightforward to use a logic programming language as the transaction specification and execution language.

9.3.2 Parallel Logic Programming

In this section we will present an overview of parallel logic programming languages and discuss why existing languages are not sufficient for our purpose. We will discuss the new requirements posed by the Flex Transaction model and briefly outline the basic concepts of the VPL language. A more detailed language description is provided in Section 9.4.2.

One approach of incorporating parallelism into Prolog is to improve the performance of the Prolog interpreter/compiler by executing goals in parallel (for example, [War87, HJ90]). The programmer writes Prolog programs in the usual way and need not be aware of the parallelism—*implicit parallelism* keeps the sequential semantics of Prolog.

In the Flex Transaction model it is possible to start subtransactions in parallel. Therefore, we need another approach to a parallel logic programming language that allows one to express parallelism explicitly. Some well-known logic programming languages with *explicit parallelism* are GHC (Guarded Horn Clauses), Parlog, and CP (Concurrent Prolog) [Sha89]. The semantics of all these languages differ from the semantics of sequential Prolog and are based on Dijkstra's Guarded Commands [Dij75]. These languages may be characterized by the concepts of *guard, commitment operator,* and *shared variable data synchronization.* A program consists of a finite set of *guarded clauses* of the form:

$$Head \ :- \ Guard \mid Body.$$

Clauses with the same *Head* predicate form a *procedure.* These languages support *committed choice OR-parallelism* and *stream AND-parallelism.* All clauses of a procedure are tried in OR-parallel. The first clause that succeeds in proving its *Guard* (i.e., this clause *commits*) is selected—all other OR-parallel running clauses of the same procedure are killed. Even if this choice does not produce a solution, backtracking is not possible. Stream AND-parallelism means that two or more AND-parallel goals may work on the same solution and may share *stream variables* by which communication and synchronization are possible.

For MDBS transactions, only languages with explicit parallelism are of value, but there are several reasons why existing languages of this class are not yet sufficient for our purpose. The main disadvantages of these languages are:

- For a query, only one search path is possible because of the lack of backtracking. Thus, a potentially existing solution may not be found, and without extra language extensions there is no means of producing several solutions to a problem.

- Compensation of committed computations, as in the Flex Transaction model, is not possible if an entire computation fails.

- The granularity of commitment is exactly one clause; the granularity cannot be chosen arbitrarily. Therefore, delayed commitment, as required for non-compensatable transactions, is not possible.

- Committed-choice OR-parallelism allows the parallel execution of only small pieces of code. A flexible granularity of OR-parallelism would be desirable, especially for the concept of function replication in the Flex Transaction model.

For these reasons, we propose a new logic programming language with explicit parallelism—the VPL (Vienna Parallel Logic) language—for the specification of transactions and queries in MDBSs. The design of the VPL language has been shaped particularly by the idea of compensate-actions found in the Flex Transaction model. We place the following requirements on the VPL language:

- VPL is a superset of Prolog, which includes backtracking. Thus, each existing solution to a problem is eventually found. The results of Section 9.2 concerning MDBS query representation therefore remain valid for VPL.

- Committed computations may be automatically compensated. The programmer must specify a *compensate-action* if he wishes to commit computations before the global transaction has terminated. This compensate-action is automatically executed if the committed computation is not part of the final solution.

- The programmer may choose the granularity of commitment; each clause need not contain a commit operator ("|").

- The programmer may specify the degree of AND-parallelism. The subgoals *Goal*1 and *Goal*2 are executed in sequence (or in parallel) if they are connected by a sequential (or parallel) AND-operator *Goal*1 & *Goal*2 (or *Goal*1 && *Goal*2).

- The programmer may specify the degree of OR-parallelism. A *sequential clause* of the form "*Head* :– *Body*." is tried only if all preceding clauses of the same procedure have failed; procedures with clauses of this form are called *sequential procedures. Parallel clauses* of the form "*Head* ::– *Body*." are tried in parallel (*parallel procedures*).

The relationship between the Flex Transaction model and the VPL language constructs is as follows: Transactions of type "C" (compensatable transactions) are specified by VPL clauses with commit operators and corresponding compensate-actions. Transactions of type "NC" (non-compensatable transactions) are specified by non-committing VPL clauses. Success dependencies are expressed through the use of sequential AND-operators ("&") instead of parallel ones ("&&"). The use of sequential rather than parallel procedures expresses failure dependencies.

The acceptability function can be mapped into the AND/OR-structure of the VPL search tree for the goal (viz. query). An acceptable state corresponds to a VPL solution. All computations that are not part of the solution are aborted or compensated.

EXAMPLE **9.19** *A Simple VPL Transaction*

The Flex Transaction given in Example 9.18 may be represented as a VPL transaction as follows:

$$T \text{ :- } (t_a \;\&\; t_c) \;\&\&\; t_h \mid .$$

The subtransactions t_a, t_c, and t_h denote the local transactions in the airline, car rental, and hotel databases, respectively. Between t_a and t_c there is a sequential AND-operator, so that the success dependencies of T are satisfied. t_h may run in parallel to t_a and t_c. The transaction T is the top-level transaction that must be committed in any event. Since we cannot reject a top-level transaction after commitment, we need not provide a compensate-action; T will never be backtracked or aborted.

$$t_a \text{ :- } t_1.$$
$$t_a \text{ :- } t_2.$$

We use a sequential procedure for t_a because of the failure dependency $t_1 \prec t_2$ in T.

t_c :- `actualtime(TM)` & `TM>8` & `TM<17` & t_3.

Before t_3 may be executed, we must test the external predicate by ensuring that the actual time corresponds to the office hours of the car rental database. The primitive `actualtime/1` binds its argument `TM` to the actual system time.

$$t_h \text{ ::- } t_4.$$
$$t_h \text{ ::- } t_5.$$

We use a parallel procedure for t_h because F contains no failure dependency between t_4 and t_5. The subtransactions may have the following structures:

$$t_1 \text{ :- } \cdots.$$
$$t_2 \text{ :- } \cdots.$$
$$t_3 \text{ :- } \cdots.$$
$$t_4 \text{ :- } \cdots \mid .$$
$$t_5 \text{ :- } \cdots \mid .$$

The hotel subtransactions commit immediately after they have succeeded because they are compensatable. We have to specify compensate-actions for them:

```
compensate(t4) :- ···.
compensate(t5) :- ···.
```

In the next section, we will show how queries are embedded into VPL transactions. After a more precise description of the semantics of the VPL language, it will be seen that each Flex Transaction can be represented as an executable VPL transaction. However, each Flex Transaction cannot necessarily be represented in the nested form seen in Example 9.18.

9.4 Query and Transaction Processing in VPL

From the results of the previous sections we conclude that for transaction specification in a heterogeneous environment we need both "Query + Execution Plan." Furthermore we require that a language which fulfills this requirement should at least be as powerful as MSQL and the Flex Transaction model. We will show how VPL fulfills these requirements. We will now present our MDBS architecture, the VPL language, a comparison with other concurrent logic programming languages, some examples, and an algorithm for automatically mapping Flex specifications into VPL. Then we will show how VPL may extend the Flex Transaction model.

9.4.1 Architecture

In this section we briefly describe the proposed architecture for an MDBS currently being prototyped at the Center for Databases at Purdue University and at the University of Technology in Vienna. An interface showing both features of an MDBS language (e.g., MSQL) and support for powerful transactions (e.g., Flex Transactions) is incorporated on top of an MDBS. The resulting system combines features found in both the DOL (Distributed Operation Language) based architecture [ROEL90] and the VIP-MDBS architecture [KL88b] (see Figure 9.1).

The *integration directory* contains static information used by the *interoperability component* for the integration of heterogeneous systems. In particular, the integration directory consists of two parts: the directory for

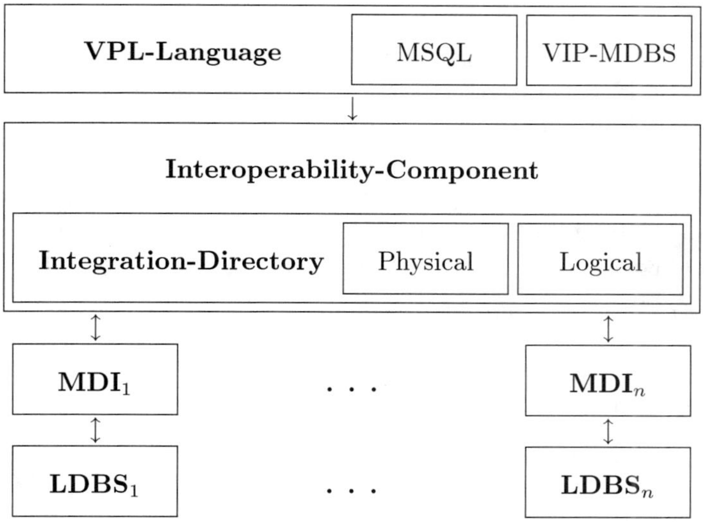

FIGURE 9.1
System Architecture

physical integration and the directory for *logical integration.* the directory for *physical integration* contains information about how to log-in into a local system, which network/protocol to use, which systems are accessible by the MDBS, etc. The directory for *logical integration* contains information about name mappings, semantic relations, descriptions of MDIs' features, etc.

An MDI (MultiDatabase Interface) is a server process that accepts queries by the interoperability component. It is in charge of the execution of the query, and returns the results. Each LDBS that wishes to participate in the MDBS must provide its own MDI server. In this manner, the LDBS remains unchanged, and a high degree of autonomy can be guaranteed. Depending on the MDI and the query, the MDI either passes the query directly to the LDBS or transforms the query into the language of the LDBS. The interoperability component and the MDIs are VPL processes that may be located at different sites.

The interface between an interoperability component and an MDI is the VPL primitive

remote_call(*Database*, *Query*).

Database specifies a database's MDI that is responsible for the execution of the *Query*. *Query* is a VPL clause that will be executed by the MDI. If the LDBS understands VPL, or if its MDI is able to translate VPL queries into queries in the language of the LDBS, then *Query* contains the LDBS query written in VPL. Otherwise, *Query* is of the form `query(`*Input*`,`*Output*`,`*Error*`)`. On execution, the query represented by *Input* is passed to the LDBS, and *Output* and *Error* eventually contain the results and error messages returned by the LDBS.

EXAMPLE **9.20** *Remote-Call*

Assume that the database `twa` understands VPL syntax. To retrieve the price for a flight from Vienna to New York, the following remote-call may be used:

```
remote_call(twa,price(vie,jfk,Price)).
```

Now assume that the database `aua` and its MDI understand only SQL. The same query may be represented as follows:[13]

```
remote_call(aua,query(
    'SELECT price FROM flights
     WHERE from="vie" AND to="jfk"',
    TupleList,Error)).
```

A system controlled by an MDI need not be an LDBS; it may be any kind of software system, such as, for example, a UNIX shell. Assume `sh` denotes the MDI of a UNIX shell. The following remote-call executes the UNIX program `cat` to read the contents of the file `/usr/spool/uucp/myfile`:

```
remote_call(sh,
    query('cat /usr/spool/uucp/myfile',Contents,Error)).
```

9.4.2 Operational Semantics of the VPL Language

The VPL language consists of three layers: the VPL kernel language, VPL language primitives, and VPL procedures defined by programmers. We will first describe the kernel language, then explain some language primitives, and then briefly compare the VPL language with other logic programming languages.

[13]Note that the query is given in SQL and is passed directly to the `aua` DBS by the MDI.

The VPL Kernel Language

The VPL kernel language consists of VPL language constructs executed by the VPL inference machine. These constructs are sequential and parallel procedures, sequential and parallel AND-operators, the cut operator, and the commit operator. Before explaining these constructs, let us define the syntax of VPL programs and goals:

DEFINITION

Term, atom, goal, clause, procedure, and program are defined as follows:

- *A* term *is a variable or a function symbol of arity $n \geq 0$ applied to n terms.*
- *An* atom *is a formula of the form $p(T_1, \ldots, T_n)$, where p is a* predicate *of arity n and $T_1, \ldots, T_n$ are terms.*
- *A* goal *is an atom, called* atomic goal, *or a sequential or parallel conjunction. A* sequential conjunction *is a formula of the form B_1 & $\cdots$ & B_n, and a* parallel conjunction *is a formula of the form B_1 && $\cdots$ && B_n, where $B_1, \ldots, B_n$ are goals. We denote a conjunction with $n = 0$ by* `true`. *"&" is the* sequential AND-operator *and "&&" is the* parallel AND-operator.
- *A* clause *is a formula of the form "A :– B."* (sequential clause) *or "A ::– B."* (parallel clause), *where A is an atom and B is either a goal or of the form "C | D" or "C ! D", where C and D are goals. A is the* head *of the clause and B is its* body; *":–" is the* sequential rule operator *and "::–" is the* parallel rule operator; *"|" is the* commit operator; *"!" is the* cut operator.
- *A* procedure *is a sequence of sequential clauses* (sequential procedure) *or a set of parallel clauses* (parallel procedure) *where the heads of all clauses of a procedure have the same predicate.*
- *A* program *is a finite set of procedures.*

As is generally the case in logic programming, the execution of a VPL program can be viewed as the finding of a proof to a given goal (query). VPL, like Prolog, is based on the principles of resolution and unification [Rob65, Kow79]. A clause is read as: "the head is true if the body is true." In order to prove an atomic goal, the VPL inference machine must select one clause, unify the atomic goal with the head of the selected clause, and prove the body of the clause. `true` is always proven. A goal or body of a clause containing more than one atom is true if all the atoms in the goal or body are true. Thus, all conjunction operators within a goal or body (&, &&, !, and |) have the logical reading "AND." Goals within a parallel conjunction may be executed in parallel (*AND-parallelism*).

If a parallel procedure consists of more than one clause that is unifiable with an atomic goal, then the VPL inference machine selects an arbitrary clause (*nondeterminism*) on the assumption that the clauses of a program are connected by "OR." This selection influences the result because the variable bindings may vary. If a goal cannot be proven with the selected clause, then the inference machine must undo all the variable bindings computed up to that point and select another clause (*backtracking*). The VPL programmer may influence the clause selection through the use of either sequential or parallel rule operators.

In order to prevent the inference machine from performing needless backtracking, the cut and the commit operators are provided. The commit operator is an extended version of the cut operator in that it starts a compensating procedure on backtracking or on abortion, and commits *communication variables*, variables used for the communication between parallel executing VPL processes.

Sequential and Parallel Procedures: Within a parallel procedure there is no ordering on the clauses. The inference machine may select any one of them to prove a goal. Moreover, it may try all the clauses in parallel. If the execution of one of the clauses blocks, then the inference machine *must* try another clause of the parallel procedure, in order to give a chance for any clause [Sha89]. Clauses of a sequential procedure are tried in the specified order. The n-th clause is not tried before the $(n-1)$-th clause has failed.

Sequential and Parallel AND-Operators: Goals within a sequential conjunction are proven in the given lexical order; i.e., from left to right. The cut and commit operators are logically handled as sequential AND-operators. Goals within a parallel conjunction may be executed in any order or in parallel. They must be executed in parallel if they communicate via partially bound communication variables.

Cut and Commit Operators: The cut operator within a sequential clause disallows backtracking over the goals at the left hand side of the cut operator. Since "!" behaves like a sequential AND-operator, on the execution of "!", the goals to the left of it are already proven and the goals to the right of it are not yet tried. The cut operator also disallows trying another clause of the same procedure if one of the goals to the right of it fails. In parallel procedures, the execution of a cut operator aborts all clauses of the procedure running in OR-parallel. We require that all or none of the clauses of a parallel procedure contain a cut or commit operator.

The commit operator behaves like the cut operator but also commits the writing on communication variables (i.e., their bindings). One may consider a communication variable to be a data item in a database. This data item cannot be deleted once it has been written (single assignment property). With the *full unification* primitive "=#=", values can be written to communication variables. More precisely, with " =#= ", only the request to write a value to a communication variable is expressed; the actual writing is delayed. The commit operator in an atomic action actually writes the values into the communication variables as requested during the execution of the goals to the left of the commit operator.

Bindings of communication variables cannot be undone like the bindings of normal variables. Nevertheless, we need a mechanism that allows backtracking over committed clauses. The solution is to *compensate* a committed procedure instead of undoing it. If a computation has been communicated to other processes, it cannot be undone as if it had never happened. For example, in order to compensate a committed procedure that has bound the communication variable X, the compensate-action may bind another communication variable Y to inform each reader of both X and Y that the value bound to X is no longer valid. The sequential procedure `compensate/1` is automatically called by the inference machine whenever a committed procedure must be compensated. The argument of `compensate/1` is the goal, with the same normal variable bindings as when the commit was executed, that called the procedure to be compensated. The programmer provides clauses for the `compensate/1` procedure. If no `compensate/1` clause succeeds, an exception is raised.

Goals to the left of the commit operator may have called procedures that themselves have committed. If a committed clause must be compensated, the inference machine calls the procedure `compensate/1` for the "outermost" committed clause. It is assumed that the compensate-action of the "outermost" clause compensates all the side effects made by the goals to the left of the commit operator, including those made by all "inner" committed clauses.

We have used the notions of backtracking, undoing, compensating, and aborting computations; we will now briefly summarize each of these notions and explain how they are related to each other.

Backtracking: The inference machine starts backtracking whenever a goal fails. It searches for the last *choice point*—i.e., the last procedure with an untried alternative clause—and undoes and compensates all computations done between the choice point and the current point of execution. The inference machine then attempts again to prove the goal with an alternative clause. Backtracking may involve the abortion of calculations. If a goal within a parallel conjunction fails, then all AND-parallel executing goals must be aborted.

Undoing: If an already proven goal is not needed for the final solution, then the bindings of normal variables and the not yet committed requests for communication variable bindings made during its execution are no longer valid. Normal variable bindings must be undone; i.e., they must regain the value they had before the execution was started. This mechanism corresponds to Prolog's mechanism for undoing variable bindings.

Compensating: The commit operator commits communication variable bindings. These bindings stay forever. The programmer knows the semantics of the program and therefore also knows if and how the effects of a committed procedure can be compensated. The programmer may provide clauses for the `compensate/1` procedure that is called whenever a committed procedure must be compensated.

Aborting: If the conditions for the execution of a goal are no longer satisfied, all the computations that have been done must be aborted by undoing and compensating them. An abort is initiated in the following cases: (1) when a cut or commit operator is executed and there exist OR-parallel running processes in the scope of the cut or commit operator; (2) when the backtracking mechanism is used; (3) when an exception occurs that cannot be handled.

The Unification Primitives

VPL provides three unification primitives.

- **Normal Unification:** The *normal unification* primitive "=/2" is used for *goal-head unification,* i.e., to prove an atomic goal *Goal* with the clause "*Head* ::– *Body.*" (or "*Head* :– *Body.*") *Goal*= *Head* is executed and the *Body* of the clause needs to be proven. The normal unification does not bind communication variables; instead of binding a communication variable A, this primitive waits until A has been bound to a non-variable term. This behavior can be used for synchronization. If X and Y are terms that do not contain communication variables, $X=Y$ behaves like Prolog's unification primitive. Let us assume that Y does not contain communication variables, and that X contains such variables but does not contain normal variables. The primitive then performs *matching*[14] instead of unification, with the result that the normal variables in Y become bound. The execution is suspended instead of binding communication variables in X.

- **Full Unification:** The *full unification* primitive "=#=/2" is used for binding communication variables. This primitive requests that communication variables be properly bound on commitment.

- **Test Unification:** The *test unification* primitive "$X == Y$" tests whether two terms X and Y are identical, and suspends execution if the terms can be made identical only by binding communication variables. "$X == Y$" behaves as in Prolog if X and Y do not contain communication variables. "$X == Y$" behaves as in concurrent logic programming languages if X and Y do not contain normal variables.

The three unification primitives described above can be defined by means of VPL procedures:

```
X==Y :- test(X,Y,==) ! .
X==Y :- suspend(X,Y) & X==Y.

X=Y :- test(X,Y,=) ! .
X=Y :- suspend(X,Y) ! X=Y.
X=Y :- bind(X,Y).

X=#=Y :- test(X,Y,=#=) ! .
X=#=Y :- bind(X,Y).
```

[14] In contrast to unification, matching may bind variables in only one argument.

TABLE 9.1
Procedures used to describe the unification primitives

X	Y	test(X,Y,P)	suspend(X,Y)	bind(X,Y)
nvar	nvar	equal(X,Y)	fail	X := Y or Y := X
nvar	cvar	fail	fail	X := Y
nvar	nonvar	fail	fail	X := Y
cvar	cvar	equal(X,Y)	wait([X,Y])	request(X,Y)
cvar	nonvar	fail	wait([X])	request(X,Y)
nonvar	nonvar	look(X,Y,P)	fail	fail
otherwise		test(Y,X,P)	suspend(Y,X)	bind(Y,X)

The procedures `test/3`, `suspend/2` and `bind/2` are defined in Table 9.1 by means of VPL procedures. The headings of the three columns to the right indicate the heads of the procedures, and the columns delineate the bodies depending on the types of the arguments X and Y, listed in the left double-column of the table. The possible types for X and Y are normal variables (nvar), communication variables (cvar), and non-variable terms (nonvar). The primitive `equal/2` is true if its arguments are identical variables. `look/3` is defined as a VPL procedure (list notation, `call/1`, and "=../2" (univ) as in Prolog):

```
look(X,Y,P) :-
    X =.. [F|Xs] & Y =.. [F|Ys] &
    look_call(Xs,Ys,P).

look_call([X|Xs],[Y|Ys],P) :-
    (C =.. [P,X,Y] & call(C)) &&
    look_call(Xs,Ys,P).
look_call([],[],P).
```

If the functors of the non-variable arguments X and Y are equal, then the binary operator P is called in sequence for all arguments of X and Y in the corresponding position.

The primitive `wait/1` suspends computation until at least one communication variable in its argument has been bound; `wait/1` always succeeds eventually. Normal variables are bound as in Prolog; ":=" is used as an assignment operator where bindings can be undone on backtracking or aborting. The `request/2` primitive requests binding a communication variable and binds each free normal variable in Y to a new communication variable. On commitment, requests for communication variable bindings are executed and become visible. The primitives defined by Table 9.1 are symmetrical in their first two arguments because all unification primitives are commutative.

Additional Language Primitives

- **Creation of Communication Variables:** `#/1`

  Newly introduced variables are normal variables by default. Communication variables must be created explicitly, with the prefix operator "#" applied to a term. $\#X$ binds each free normal variable in X to a new communication variable. Other primitives, such as those for opening a file or a connection to another software system (e.g., to a DBS or to another VPL system), also return communication variables as their results. Communication variables are so called because they engender communication when they are shared by several systems. If any one of the systems binds a communication variable, this binding is communicated to the other systems sharing this variable.

- **Variable Testing:** `var/1, nonvar/1, commvar/1`

  The primitive `var/1` succeeds if its argument is an unbound normal variable, and otherwise fails. The primitive `nonvar/1` succeeds if its argument is not a normal free variable. Thus, `nonvar(X)` is the same as `not var(X)`, if the prefix operator `not` is defined as follows:

  ```
  not X :- call(X) ! fail.
  not X.
  ```

  The primitive `commvar/1` succeeds if its argument is an unbound communication variable. It has the additional effect of ensuring that the communication variable remains unbound until the calling clause commits. Thus, all $X = \# = Y$ and `commvar(`Z`)` primitives to the left of a commit operator, and within already executed but not yet committed subgoals of a clause, are treated as an atomic action (i.e., a *VPL transaction*) which is confirmed by the execution of the commit operator of the clause.

  The goal `not commvar(X)` succeeds if `X` is not an unbound communication variable. This goal does not guarantee that `X` remains unbound until commitment (the first clause of `not` always fails). Thus, `not not commvar(X)` is not the same as `commvar(X)`, because `not not commvar(X)` does not guarantee atomicity.

- **Synchronization:** `data/1`

  The primitive `data/1` suspends execution until its argument is bound. `data/1` fails if its argument is a free normal variable. This primitive can be implemented as a VPL procedure:

  ```
  data(X) :- commvar(X) & X=x ! .
  data(X) :- nonvar(X).
  ```

  The first clause waits until the argument—a communication variable—is bound to a non-variable term and compares the term with `x`. If the term is `x`, the first clause succeeds; otherwise, the second clause succeeds. Both clauses fail if the argument is an unbound normal variable. The "!" prevents `data/1` from producing more than one solution.

Control-Meta-Call and Error Handling

The control-meta-call was first introduced in Parlog [Gre87] to allow the programmer to control the execution of a goal. VPL uses a variant of the control-meta-call—`process(`*Goal*`,`*PID*`)`—to isolate parallel executing processes and to handle errors. The first argument of this primitive is the goal to be executed by a new process. The communication variable *PID* is returned as a communication link to the new process. The primitive succeeds immediately without waiting until the goal has succeeded. The new process executes a copy of *Goal* in which all normal variables have been substituted by new normal variables (communication variables are not substituted). The communication variable *PID* is eventually bound to one of the following terms:

`succeeded`	if the computation of the goal has succeeded,
`failed`	if the computation of the goal has failed,
`aborted`	if an exception has occurred that could not be handled.

The process created by `process(`*Goal*`,`*PID*`)` may be controlled by some primitives that use *PID* as argument; e.g., `suspend(`*PID*`)` suspends the execution of the designated process until `continue(`*PID*`)` is executed. Each of these primitives can be called with a free normal variable as argument. In this case the primitive refers to the process from which it was called.

One of these process controlling primitives is `exception(`*PID*`,`*Type*`)`, which raises an exception in the process denoted by *PID*. *Type* is a term specifying the reason for the exception. If an exception occurs in a process, the process suspends execution and tries to handle the exception by calling the *exception handlers* in the process's *exception handler list*—one after another, until one of them succeeds. If the exception is handled, the process continues execution; otherwise, the process stops and *PID* becomes bound to `aborted`. The primitive `exception/2` succeeds in both cases.

Comparison with other Logic Programming Languages

The VPL language is a superset of Prolog.[15] VPL programs that do not use communication variables, the commit operator, the parallel AND operator, and parallel procedures are sequential Prolog programs. The combination of sequential Prolog programs with the parallel AND operator yields a Prolog program with independent AND parallelism. Sequential Prolog combined with parallel procedures results in OR-parallel Prolog. Note that the cut operator within parallel procedures is equivalent to the "commit" operator in OR-parallel Prolog; i.e., in OR-parallel procedures the cut operator does not wait until all preceding clauses of the procedure have failed.

The VPL language is at least as powerful as concurrent logic programming languages [Sha89]. We will see that programs of a language in that class, the Flat Concurrent Prolog variant FCP(:), can be embedded into VPL. Each FCP(:) clause

$$H \quad \leftarrow \quad A_1, \ldots, A_{n_a} : T_1 = T'_1, \ldots, T_{n_t} = T'_{n_t} \mid G_1, \ldots, G_{n_g}.$$

is transformed into the VPL clause

$$\begin{aligned} H \quad ::- \quad & (\#X_1 \;\&\&\; \cdots \;\&\&\; \#X_{n_x}) \;\& \\ & (A_1 \;\&\&\; \cdots \;\&\&\; A_{n_a}) \;\& \\ & (T_1 =\#= T'_1 \;\&\&\; \cdots \;\&\&\; T_{n_t} =\#= T'_{n_t}) \mid \\ & (G_1 \;\&\&\; \cdots \;\&\&\; G_{n_g}). \end{aligned}$$

All variables of FCP(:) have the semantics of communication variables in VPL. New VPL variables are normal variables that must be explicitly bound to communication variables by the primitive "#." On executing the transformation, a "#" operator is inserted into the VPL clause for each variable $X_1, \ldots, X_{n_x}$ occurring in the FCP(:) clause, except the variables occurring in the head H of the clause. All variables in the head of the VPL clause become bound to communication variables by goal-head unification, since all variables in the goal are communication variables. The unification primitives

[15]Note that the VPL syntax is not a real superset of Prolog's syntax (e.g., cut), but a parser for Prolog syntax can easily be provided.

in the FCP(:) clause are replaced by VPL's nonblocking full unification primitives. FCP(:)'s "=" and VPL's "=#=" have identical semantics. The goals in the VPL clause[16] are connected by parallel AND-operators ("&&").

The semantics of VPL's commit operator differ from those in FCP(:) insofar as VPL calls the procedure `compensate/1` if a committed clause fails, whereas in FCP(:) the whole program fails. To simulate the behavior of FCP(:) we must define `compensate/1` as follows:

```
compensate(Goal) :- exception(_,error).
```

Assuming that the exception `error` is not handled, the computation fails.

FCP(:) is a flat[17] concurrent logic programming language. Non-flat variants of these languages can of course also be mapped into VPL, since the VPL language is non-flat.

Implementations of non-flat concurrent programming languages tend to be inefficient because the interpreter must utilize many parallel executing processes, with the result that the resources of the computer are quickly exhausted. Each OR-parallel process must have its own copy of all variables of this branch. Synchronization of shared variables is computationally expensive. The main idea of flat concurrent logic programming languages is to reduce OR-parallelism to a minimum, in order to avoid multiple copies of shared variables. OR-parallelism can be simulated by AND-parallelism, but the implied overhead, in comparison to directly implemented OR-parallelism, is not justified.

OR-parallelism is an essential feature of the VPL language, as OR-parallelism is strongly related to the concept of function replication found in the Flex Transaction model. If we use the VPL language as a transaction and query language for MDBSs, we can take advantage of a high degree of parallelism even on a single processor computer. The execution of each LDBS query will usually take more time than starting the LDBS query. Therefore, the VPL system will frequently have to wait for the result of a local query. This time can be used for starting parallel executing queries on other computers.

The Remote-Call

The primitive `remote_call(`*Database*`,`*Query*`)` executes the database query *Query* at the specified local database. This is a very complex primitive, charged with handling concurrency control, commitment, and recovery.

[16] In VPL, the A_i and $(T_i = T_i')$ are goals.

[17] In flat languages, the guard must not contain user-defined primitives.

All communication with the MDI is accomplished by binding shared communication variables.

The remote-call first reads the database address from the integration-directory, then executes the query on the database. This process is accomplished by the opening of a communication link (i.e., a shared communication variable) to the VPL system representing the MDI and writing the goal to be executed by the MDI to this communication link. Next, the remote call waits until the MDI returns a result and succeeds. The result contains an unbound communication variable that must be bound to `commit` so that the query in the LDBS is committed (in DBS sense). If the clause containing the remote-call is committed, this communication variable is also committed. The implementation of the remote-call primitive contains a subgoal that is committed on execution of the remote-call. If the remote-call is backtracked or aborted, a compensate-action for this subgoal is called. This compensate-action binds the communication variable returned by the MDI to `abort`.

The VPL system at the site of the MDI creates a process for each local subtransaction. The process starts the local subtransaction and waits until the local subtransaction enters its prepare state (we assume two phase commit). After returning the result, the process waits until the communication variable, which is a part of the result, is bound to either `commit` or `abort` and causes the local transaction to proceed accordingly.

This simple commitment protocol can be improved in some ways. That is, it can be extended so that it can handle LDBSs without a two-phase commit. Furthermore, mechanisms for concurrency control and recovery are needed.

9.4.3 Mapping Transactions into VPL Queries

In Section 9.2.1, we have shown that Prolog, and therefore also VPL, are both more expressive than MSQL. In this section, we will prove that the VPL language is at least as powerful as the Flex Transaction model. In [KPE91b], we presented an algorithm which maps Flex Transaction specifications into VPL transactions. In the following, we will give a brief overview of this mapping. Although it is possible to transform Flex Transactions into VPL transactions automatically, we do not argue that a transaction programmer should write transaction specifications in the notation of the Flex Transaction model. VPL transactions allow more flexibility in expressing a problem and allow better control of the execution than the Flex Transaction model (see Section 9.5).

The mapping algorithm between Flex Transactions and VPL transactions operates as follows. For each transaction $t_i, (i = 1, \ldots, n)$ in B, a process p_i is started; all processes run AND-parallel. Each process p_i communicates the execution state x_i of transaction t_i to the other processes. Using this information, each process p_i can test the internal dependencies $t_j \prec t_i$ which must be satisfied in order to start t_i. To test external predicates, no extra information is necessary. Thus, each p_i has enough information to decide when to start t_i. An additional AND-parallel running process p_0 also has information on the execution states $x_1, \ldots, x_n$ of the transactions $t_1, \ldots, t_n$. p_0 tests whether the acceptability function $f(x_1, \ldots, x_n)$ has been fulfilled. The acceptability function describes a commit-set that corresponds to a subset $C = \{t_{i_1}, \ldots, ti_m\} \subseteq \{t_1, \ldots, t_n\}$, where $x_{i_k} = \textit{succeeded}$ for $t_{i_k} \in C, (k = 1, \ldots, m)$. If there is a commit-set C, then p_0 sends messages to the processes $p_{i_1}, \ldots, p_{i_m}$ that allow $p_{i_1}, \ldots, p_{i_m}$ to commit all not yet committed transactions in $\{t_{i_1}, \ldots, t_{i_m}\}$. At the same time, p_0 sends messages to the processes $p_{i_{m+1}}, \ldots, p_{i_n}$ that cause abortion of $p_{i_{m+1}}, \ldots, p_{i_n}$ where $\{t_{i_{m+1}}, \ldots, t_{i_n}\} = B \backslash C$, and each p_{i_k} controls the transaction $t_{i_k}, (k = m + 1, \ldots, n)$.

This mapping of Flex Transactions into the VPL language simulates OR-parallelism by AND-parallelism. It can serve to map any Flex Transaction specification into VPL. Its disadvantages are that it requires extensive communication between processes, with negative effects on the readability of the program and the performance, and that it does not make use of backtracking. One reason for these deficiencies is the flat structure of the above VPL transaction; the ability of the VPL language to represent nested transactions is not used. We have found an algorithm that extracts the nested transaction structure from an acceptability function, whenever the transaction can be represented as a nested transaction. Assuming that each local subtransaction appears only once in the nested transaction, not all Flex Transactions can be represented as an AND/OR-tree without extra communication between the subtransactions. However, all Flex Transactions using the capability of function replication, and many other Flex Transactions, can be at least partly represented as nested VPL transaction. Some of the Flex Transactions that cannot be represented as nested VPL transactions can easily be modified so that they have a nested representation.

EXAMPLE **9.21** *Mapping a Flex into a Nested VPL Transaction*

Again, consider an MDBS of a travel agency. We want to book a flight from Vienna to Tokyo and reserve a hotel room in Tokyo. On two of three days we want to have dinner at a restaurant. There is no preference regarding airline, hotel, or restaurant. All subtransactions can be executed in parallel. We use the following local subtransactions:

t_1	Order a ticket for a flight Vienna-Tokyo from Austrian Airlines
t_2	Order a ticket for a flight Vienna-Singapore from Lufthansa
t_3	Order a ticket for a flight Singapore-Tokyo from Japan Airlines
t_4	Reserve a room at Ramada
t_5	Reserve a room at Hilton
t_6	Reserve a table in a restaurant on 1st April
t_7	Reserve a table in a restaurant on 2nd April
t_8	Reserve a table in a restaurant on 3rd April

The acceptability function f is as follows:

$$\begin{aligned} f(\ldots) = \; & (x_1 \wedge x_4 \wedge x_6 \wedge x_7) \vee (x_2 \wedge x_3 \wedge x_4 \wedge x_6 \wedge x_7) \vee \\ & (x_1 \wedge x_4 \wedge x_6 \wedge x_8) \vee (x_2 \wedge x_3 \wedge x_4 \wedge x_6 \wedge x_8) \vee \\ & (x_1 \wedge x_4 \wedge x_7 \wedge x_8) \vee (x_2 \wedge x_3 \wedge x_4 \wedge x_7 \wedge x_8) \vee \\ & (x_1 \wedge x_5 \wedge x_6 \wedge x_7) \vee (x_2 \wedge x_3 \wedge x_5 \wedge x_6 \wedge x_7) \vee \\ & (x_1 \wedge x_5 \wedge x_6 \wedge x_8) \vee (x_2 \wedge x_3 \wedge x_5 \wedge x_6 \wedge x_8) \vee \\ & (x_1 \wedge x_5 \wedge x_7 \wedge x_8) \vee (x_2 \wedge x_3 \wedge x_5 \wedge x_7 \wedge x_8) \end{aligned}$$

The automatically derived nested representation of the corresponding VPL transaction is as follows:[18]

```
T :- (t1 ;; (t2 && t3)) && (t4 ;; t5) && tr.

X ;; Y ::- call(X).
X ;; Y ::- call(Y).
```

The subtransaction t_r for reserving a table in a restaurant for two days cannot be represented as a nested VPL transaction. The algorithm that maps Flex Transactions into flat VPL transactions produces the following output:

```
tr :- #A6 & #A7 & #A8 & ( control(A6,A7,A8) &&
      (process6(A6) && process7(A7) && process8(A8) ).

process6(A6) :- t6 & A6<=succ(B) & B=ok.
process6(A6) :- A6<=fail.
process6(A6).

process7(A7) :- t7 & A7<=succ(B) & B=ok.
```

[18]The infix operator ;; expresses OR-parallelism and is usually predefined.

```
process7(A7) :- A7<=fail.
process7(A7).

process8(A8) :- t8 & A8<=succ(B) & B=ok.
process8(A8) :- A8<=fail.
process8(A8).

control(succ(B6),succ(B7),A8) ::-
    B6=#=ok & B7=#=ok & interrupt(A8) | .
control(succ(B6),A7,succ(B8)) ::-
    B6=#=ok & B8=#=ok & interrupt(A7) | .
control(A6,succ(B7),succ(B8)) ::-
    B7=#=ok & B8=#=ok & interrupt(A6) | .

interrupt(succ(B)) ::- B=#=not_ok.
interrupt(A)       ::- A=#=fail.

X<=Y :- X=#=Y | .

compensate(control(_,_,_)) :- exception(_,abort).
compensate(_ <= _).
```

It is easy to see the advantage of the nested part of the VPL transaction, compared to the part without nested representation. Of course, by defining appropriate procedures, it is also possible to generate a VPL transaction that is easier to read. This example shows the extra communication needed even for simple transactions. Larger flat VPL transactions with internal dependencies are much more complex.

A transaction programmer who writes VPL transactions without using the notation of the Flex Transactions might have specified t_r as follows:

t_r :- t_6 ! (t_7 ;; t_8).
t_r :- t_7 && t_8.

The first clause of t_r executes t_6. If t_6 succeeds, t_7 and t_8 are started in parallel, and one of them is in the commit-set. Otherwise, t_7 and t_8 are started in parallel by the second clause, and they are both in the commit-set. The cut operator in the first clause prevents the second clause from being executed if t_6 has succeeded. Thus, t_r produces, at most, one solution.

This specification of t_r is not equivalent to the output of the mapping algorithm because t_6 must not run in parallel with t_7 and t_8, but the result is the same; this VPL transaction is easy to understand and does not introduce communication and synchronization overhead. This simple example illustrates that a maximum of parallelism is not always the best solution.

9.5 Extending the Power of Flex Transactions

The Flex Transaction model allows the specification of MDBS transactions, but these specifications are not executable queries. VPL transactions, however, are executable, and they allow the transaction programmer to specify many details regarding transaction control. For example, the Flex Transaction model allows one to specify which local subtransactions may be executed in parallel, but it does not allow the specification of the communication between parallel executing transactions. Communication usually implies synchronization, and thus it may restrict the parallel execution. It is not always possible to represent synchronization by success or failure dependencies, as the Example 9.22 illustrates. Communication variables allow communication between parallel executing transactions and enable synchronization in a manner that cannot be expressed by the Flex Transaction model.

EXAMPLE **9.22** *Communication between two Transactions*

Let us assume that twa and aua interchange prices for their flights from Vienna to New York. Consequently, twa offers its flight at the original price of aua, and aua offers its flight at the original price of twa. The prices may be "swapped" by the following VPL transaction (see the Appendix for relation definitions):[19]

```
swap :- #Q1 & #Q2 &
    ( remote_call(twa,
        delete(price(vie,jfk,P1)) & Q2<=P1 &
        insert(price(vie,jfk,Q1))) &&
      remote_call(aua,
        delete(flights(vie,jfk,P2)) & Q1<=P2 &
        insert(flights(vie,jfk,Q2))) ).
```

This example shows how two subtransactions communicate with each other by binding communication variables. The remote-call primitive is not aware of this communication. The MDIs of the two LDBSs first delete the tuples for flights from Vienna to New York and thereby read the prices into P1 and P2.

[19]The procedure <=/2 is defined in Example 9.21.

Then `<=/2` writes `P1` and `P2` to the communication variables `Q2` and `Q1`, which are shared by the MDIs. Finally, the tuples with the new prices are inserted into the databases. Synchronization is achieved by waiting on insertion until `Q1` (resp. `Q2`) is bound.

Let us now consider what happens if one of the local subtransactions fails, and causes the remote-call to fail. Then `swap/0` will also fail, and the other remote-call will be aborted (due to the " && " between the remote-calls). The communication variables `Q1` and `Q2` are not visible outside `swap/0`, so no harm is done if they are already bound to some invalid terms. An intelligent MDI may automatically restart a local subtransaction that has failed for some reason. Let us assume that a subtransaction has failed and been restarted by the MDI after writing its communication variable. The price read by the restarted subtransaction is either equal to or different from the price read by the failed subtransaction. In the latter case, `<=/2` fails because the old price is not unifiable with the new price, and thus the subtransaction and `swap/0` fail. `<=/2` always fails if two values read from the same data item are not equal, because all data in a database are ground; i.e., they do not contain free variables.

A Flex Transaction specification gives no information about how to compensate subtransactions. In the VPL language, compensate-actions must be explicitly specified. Compensate-actions are VPL transactions that may use all the features of function replication, mixed transactions, value functions, etc. Note that a compensate-action may cause the execution of other compensate-actions.

The granularity of the compensate-action may vary. In nested VPL transactions, either a single subtransaction on one LDBS or a group of subtransactions is compensated by one compensate-action.

The VPL language allows the transaction programmer to control exactly when a subtransaction should be executed, aborted, or compensated. Compare the following VPL transactions:

t_a ::– t_1.
t_a ::– t_2.

t_b ::– t_1 ! .
t_b ::– t_2 ! .

t_c ::– t_3 | .
t_c ::– t_4 | .

Assuming that t_1 and t_2 commit immediately, while t_3 and t_4 propagate their commit to the calling clause, t_a allows backtracking over its committed solutions by using the compensate-actions for t_1 and t_2. t_b does not allow backtracking because of the cut operator. As soon as one of the subtransactions t_1 or t_2 has succeeded, the other subtransaction is aborted. If both t_1 and t_2 succeed, then one of them is chosen randomly and the other is compensated. Otherwise the earlier subtransaction causes the other to abort before it can commit. t_c commits at most one of the subtransactions and aborts the other. Another solution within the same LDBS may be tried, and the previously found solution is undone or compensated.

9.6 Conclusions

Traditionally, query processing and transaction management are studied independently in multidatabase systems (MDBSs). It is our belief that they interact in subtle ways, and that a powerful language can serve to fulfill both tasks. We have chosen the logic programming paradigm to pursue this goal for several reasons. First, logic and SQL have the same mathematical foundation, as both are based on first order logic. SQL language embeddings can therefore be easily provided. Second, transaction specifications in a very flexible model for MDBS transactions, the Flex Transaction model, can easily be formulated in logic. Third, logic programming gives rise to highly declarative and easily understandable programs (queries). Fourth, a specification in a logic language is also an executable program.

We have shown how sequential Prolog may be employed in the logical integration of heterogeneous data. With the VIP-MDBS (Vienna Integrated Prolog MultiDataBase System) prototype, we have proven not only that Prolog as an MDBS query language is powerful enough to express all the features of dynamic MDBS languages like MSQL (Multidatabase SQL), but also that Prolog provides features, such as transitive closure, that do not have a counterpart in MSQL. In addition to its dynamic aspects, the VIP-MDBS system also provides static integration aspects based on the ideas of global integration. Depending on the frequency and complexity of a query, the dynamic and static integration aspects can be combined to various degrees, thus providing a high level of flexibility in query formulation. In particular, the dynamic aspects guarantee a high degree of design autonomy for the local databases.

To apply Prolog to transaction management, we have extended sequential Prolog with the concept of parallelism. This work was influenced mainly by the ideas of the Flex Transaction model, especially the concepts of function replication and compensation of already committed subtransactions. Flex Transactions support local execution and communication autonomies. These ideas have led to the design of the VPL (Vienna Parallel Logic) language, a transaction oriented programming language. The main advantage of VPL is that nested subtransactions may be committed earlier if a compensate-action for them exists (i.e., a semantic undo operation). This may enable a higher degree of parallelism in the MDBS environment, as locks on autonomous database systems may be released before the completion of the entire global MDBS transaction. Flex Transaction specifications can automatically be mapped into runnable VPL queries. In addition, we have shown how the use of VPL can even extend the ideas of the Flex Transaction model. Finally, VPL is both a transformational and reactive programming language and therefore facilitates the support of long-lived and everlasting transactions.

Acknowledgement

This research was supported by the Austrian FWF (Fonds zur Förderung der Wissenschaftlichen Forschung) under project number P7773-PHY , "Interoperability of Autonomous Databases."

We thank Thomas Ludwig for his work on the VIP-MDBS prototype system and Witold Litwin for the many discussions we had with him about his MSQL language. His work influenced our research on MDBSs. We thank Manfred Brockhaus, the department head at the University of Technology, Vienna, who provided continual encouragement. We also thank Ulrich Neumerkel for his comments on this article and Omran Bukhres for checking the English style of the text.

Appendix: Example Databases

To demonstrate our system we will use the MDBS of a travel agency, called `ta`. The autonomous databases are airline, hotel, and car rental databases, all of which show differences in structure, scaling, names, and semantics. In the following, we show the definitions of the relations of these DBSs needed for our examples. We also provide the definition of the semantic relations of the MDBS `ta`. Attribute names are assumed to be defined as the argument names of the following relation definitions:

```
/* klm database */

timetable(from,to,dept,arriv,flno).
price(start,end,price).
seats(flno,planetype,seatnrs).
seat_reservation(flno,date,firstname,lastname).

/* United Airlines (ua) database */

timetable(flno,from,to,dep,arriv).
fprices(flno,flprice).
planes(planetype,nr_seats,flno).
seat_reservation(flno,date,firstname,lastname).

/* twa database */

timetable(from,to,dept,arriv,flno).
price(start,end,price).
planes(planetype,nr_seats,flno).
seat_reservation(flno,date,firstname,lastname).

/* travel information database */

airport(airportcode,airportname,country,
    continentzone,timezone).
convert_dfl_us(dfl,us_dollar).

/* Austrian Airlines (aua) database */

flights(from,to,price).


/* travel agency database:  semantic relations */

timetable(from,to,departure,arrival,airline,flno).
```

```
price(from,to,price,airline).
planes(ptyp,pseats,pflno).
seat_reservation(airline,flno,date,firstname,lastname).
route(layovers,flights).
route_price(route,price).
connect(layover1,layover2,fnolist,cities).
```

Bibliography

[CGT90] S. Ceri, G. Gottlob, and L. Tanca. *Logic Programming and Databases*, Springer Verlag, 1990.

[Dij75] E. W. Dijkstra. Guarded commands, nondeterminacy, and formal derivation of programs. In *Communications of the ACM*, Vol. 18, No. 8, August 1975.

[DELO89] W. Du, A. K. Elmagarmid, Y. Leu, and S. Osterman. Effects of Local Autonomy on Global Concurrency Control in Heterogeneous Distributed Database Systems. In *Proceedings of the 2nd International Conference on Data and Knowledge Systems for Manufacturing and Engineering*, October 1989.

[ELLR90] A. K. Elmagarmid, Y. Leu, W. Litwin, and M. Rusinkiewicz. A Multidatabase Transaction Model for InterBase. In *Proceedings of the 16th International Conference on Very Large Databases*, Australia 1990.

[GK88] H. Garcia-Molina and B. Kogan. Node Autonomy in Distributed Systems. In *Proceedings of the International Symposium on Databases in Parallel and Distributed Systems*, IEEE Computer Society Press, Austin Texas, December 1988.

[Gre87] S. Gregory. *Parallel Logic Programming in PARLOG. The Language and its Implementation*, Addison-Wesley Publishing Company, Reading, 1987.

[HJ90] S. Haridi and S. Janson. Kernel Andorra Prolog and its Computation Model. In *Proceedings of the 7th International Conference on Logic Programming*, June 1990.

[Kow79] Robert Kowalski. *Logic for Problem Solving*, North Holland, New York, 1979.

[Küh89] e. Kühn. *Implementierung von Multi-Datenbanksystemen in Prolog.* Ph.D. Thesis, University of Technology, Vienna, April 1989.

[KL88a] e. Kühn and T. Ludwig. Extending Prolog by Multidatabase Features. In *Proceedings of European Teleinformatics Conference on Research into Networks and Distributed Applications*, North-Holland, R. Speth (ed.), April 1988.

[KL88b] e. Kühn and T. Ludwig. VIP-MDBS: A Logic Multidatabase System. In *Proceedings of International Symposium on Databases in Parallel and Distributed Systems*, IEEE Computer Society Press, Austin Texas, December 1988.

[KP91] e. Kühn and F. Puntigam. The VPL Vienna Parallel Logic Language. Technical Report TR-185-91-1, University of Technology, Vienna, Institute of Computer Languages, January 1991.

[KPE91a] e. Kühn, F. Puntigam, and A. K. Elmagarmid. Transaction Specification in Multidatabase Systems based on Parallel Logic Programming. In *Proceedings of the First International Workshop on Interoperability in Multidatabase Systems*, IEEE CS, Japan, April 1991.

[KPE91b] e. Kühn, F. Puntigam and A. K. Elmagarmid. An Execution Model for Distributed Database Transactions and Its Implementation in VPL. To appear in *Proceedings of the International Conference on Extending Database Technology, EDBT'92*, Vienna, 1992.

[Leu91] Y. Leu. Composing Multidatabase Applications using Flex Transactions. In *IEEE Data Engineering Bulletin*, 14(1), March 1991.

[LANV87] W. Litwin, A. Abdellatif, B. Nicolas, Ph. Vigier, and A. Zerounal. MSQL: A Multidatabase Manipulation Language. In *Information Science, An International Journal*, Special Issue on DBS, June 1987.

[LV86] W. Litwin and Ph. Vigier. Dynamic Attributes in the Multidatabase System MRDSM. In *Proceedings of the International Conference on Data Engineering*, IEEE Computer Society, 1986.

[LZ88] W. Litwin and A. Zeroual. Advances in Multidatabase Systems. In *Proceedings of European Teleinformatics Conference on Research into Networks and Distributed Applications*, North-Holland, R. Speth (ed.), April 1988.

[NSE84] S. B. Navathe, T. Sashidar, and R. Elmasri. Relationship Merging in Schema Integration. In *Proceedings of the 10th International Conference on Very Large Data Bases*, Singapore, 1984.

[NS88] E. Neuhold and M. Schrefl. Dynamic Derivation of Personalized Views. In *Proceedings of the 14th International Conference on Very Large Data Bases*, LA, USA, 1988.

[Rob65] J. A. Robinson. A machine oriented logic based resolution principle. In *Journal of the ACM*, Vol. 12, No. 1, January 1965.

[ROEL90] M. Rusinkiewicz, S. Osterman, A. K. Elmagarmid, and K. Loa. The Distributed Operation Language for Specifying Multi-System Applications. In *Proceedings of the 1st International Conference on Systems Integration*, 1990.

[Sch87] M. Schrefl. A Comparative Analysis of View Integration Methodologies. In *Informatik Fachberichte*, Band 143, Springer Verlag, 1987.

[Sha89] E. Shapiro. The Family of Concurrent Logic Programming Languages. In ACM Computing Surveys, Vol. 21, No. 3, September 1989.

[War87] D. H. D. Warren. Or-Parallel Execution Models of Prolog. In *Proceedings of the International Conference on Theory and Practice of Software Development, TAPSOFT'87*, Pisa, Italy, Springer-Verlag, March 1987.

10

ACTA: The SAGA Continues

Panos K. Chrysanthis

Krithi Ramamritham

10.1 Introduction

Transactions in database systems are defined in terms of several important notions such as: *visibility*, referring to the ability of one transaction to see the results of another transaction *while* it is executing; *consistency*, referring to the correctness of the state of the database that a committed transaction produces; *recovery*, referring to the ability, in the event of failure, to take the database to some state that is considered correct; and *permanence*, referring to the ability of a transaction to record its results in the database. The flexibility of a given transaction model depends on the way these four notions are combined.

Although powerful, the transaction model [EGLT76, Gra81] found in traditional database systems is found lacking in *functionality* and *performance* when used for applications that involve reactive (endless), open-ended (long-lived) and collaborative (interactive) activities. Hence, various extensions to the traditional model have been proposed, referred to herein as *extended transactions* [Mos81, VRS86, BKK85, PKH88, KLS90, GGK+91, BHMC90, FZ89, SZ89, Elm91]. Compared to the traditional transaction model, these models associate "broader" interpretations with the four transaction notions mentioned above to provide enhanced functionality while increasing the potential for improved performance. Upon examining these *ad hoc* extensions to the traditional transaction model, one is prompted to seek answers to the following questions:

- What properties does a model possess *vis a vis* visibility, consistency, recovery, and permanence? (For example, traditional transactions guarantee failure atomicity, serializability, and durability.) What added functionality does a model provide?

- In what respects is a model similar to traditional transactions? In what respects is it dissimilar? More generally, how does one transaction model differ from another? Can two models be used in conjunction?

In attempting to answer these questions, we found a need for a common framework within which one can specify and reason about the nature of interactions between transactions in a particular model. This motivated the development of a comprehensive transaction framework, called *ACTA*[1], which characterizes the effects of transactions as per the taxonomy of Figure 10.1.

[1] ACTA means *actions* in Latin.

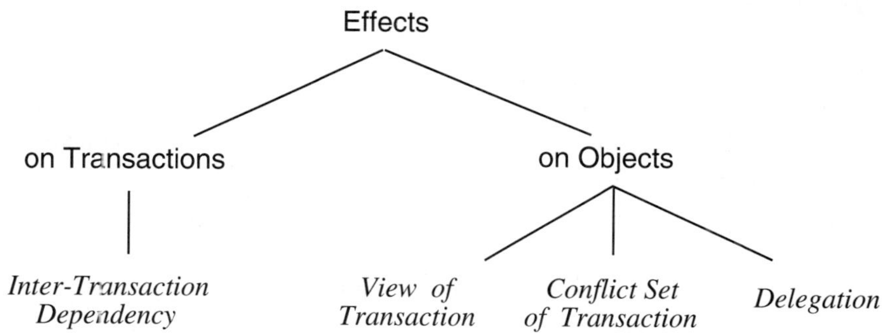

FIGURE 10.1
Dimensions of the ACTA Framework

After giving a brief introduction to the modeling primitives of ACTA, we illustrate its use by giving a complete formal characterization of *Sagas*, an extended transaction model developed to support long-lived activities. A Saga is a set of relatively independent (component) transactions which can interleave in any way with component transactions of other Sagas. Components can commit even before the Saga commits. However, if the Saga subsequently aborts, effects of the committed components are nullified through the invocation of compensating transactions.

The reasoning power of ACTA is shown by proving properties of Sagas. Finally, the flexibility of ACTA is displayed through a series of variations to the original model of Sagas, each variation coming out of changes to the formal characterization of Sagas. This will show the use of ACTA for "inventing" new transaction models by methodically varying the definition of existing models.

10.2 The Formal ACTA Framework

This section attempts to provide a concise yet complete introduction to ACTA. Subsection 10.2.1 provides some of the preliminary concepts underlying the ACTA formalism.

ACTA allows the specification of the effects of transactions on other transactions and also their effect on objects. Inter-transaction dependencies, discussed in Subsection 10.2.2, form the basis for the former while visibility of and conflicts between operations on objects, discussed in Subsection 10.2.3 form the basis for the latter.

We would like to point out that with the evolution of ACTA, some aspects of ACTA introduced in earlier papers have changed. For example, the notion of *view set* introduced in [CR90] has been replaced in the current version by the notions of *view* and *conflict set* (see Subsection 10.2.3).

10.2.1 Preliminaries

Objects Events

A database is the entity that contains all the shared objects in a system. A transaction accesses and manipulates the objects in the database by invoking operations specific to individual objects. The *state* of an object is represented by its contents. Each object has a type, which defines a set of operations that provide the only means to create, change and examine the state of an object of that type. It is assumed that an operation always produces an output (return value), that is, it has an outcome (condition code) or a result. The result of an operation on an object depends on the state of the object. For a given state s of an object, we use $return(s,p)$ to denote the output produced by operation p, and $state(s,p)$ to denote the state produced after the execution of p.

DEFINITION

Invocation of an operation on an object is termed an object event. The type of an object defines the operations and thus, the object events that pertain to it. We use $p_t[ob]$ *to denote the object event corresponding to the invocation of the operation* p *on object* ob *by transaction* t *and* OE_t *to denote the set of object events that can be invoked*[2] *by transaction* t *(i.e.,* $p_t[ob] \in \mathrm{OE}_t$*).*

The effects of an operation on an object are not made permanent at the time of the execution of the operation. They need to be explicitly *committed* or *aborted.*

[2] We will use "invoke an event" to mean "cause an event to occur." One of the meanings of the word "invoke" is "to bring about."

DEFINITION

The effects of an operation p invoked by a transaction t on an object ob are made permanent in the database when $p_t[ob]$ *is committed.*

DEFINITION

The effects of an operation p invoked by a transaction t on an object ob are obliterated when the $p_t[ob]$ *is aborted.*

Depending on the semantics of the operations and on the object's recovery properties, aborting an operation may force the abortion of other operations as well.

Commit and *Abort* operations are defined on every object for every operation. Invoked operations that have neither committed nor aborted are termed *in progress* operations. Typically, an operation is committed only if the invoking transaction commits and it is aborted only if the invoking transaction aborts. However, it is conceivable that an extended transaction may commit only a subset of its operations on an object while aborting the rest. Furthermore, through delegation (see Subsection 10.2.3), a transaction other than the *event-invoker*, i.e., the transaction that invoked an operation, can be granted the responsibility to commit or abort the operation.

Significant Events

In addition to the invocation of operations on objects, transactions invoke transaction management primitives. For example, atomic transactions are associated with three transaction management primitives: Begin, Commit and Abort. The specific primitives and their semantics depend on the specifics of a transaction model. For instance, whereas the Commit by an atomic transaction implies that it is terminating successfully and that all of its effects on the objects should be made permanent in the database, the Commit of a subtransaction of a nested transaction implies that all of its effects on the objects should be made persistent and visible with respect to its parent and sibling subtransactions[3]. Other transaction management primitives include Spawn, found in the nested transaction model, and Split and Join, found in the split transaction model [PKH88].

[3] As shown in Subsection 10.2.3, in ACTA, the ability of a nested subtransaction to make its effect visible to its parent is specified by means of the notion of delegation.

DEFINITION

Invocation of a transaction management primitive is termed a significant event. *A transaction model defines the significant events that pertain to transactions adhering to that model.* SE_t *denotes the set of significant events that is relevant to transaction t.*

ACTA does not *a priori* assume a given set of significant events nor does it associate any semantics with the significant events, but it provides the means by which significant events and their semantics can be specified.

It is useful to distinguish, given the set of significant events associated with a transaction t, between events that are relevant to the initiation of t and those that are relevant to the termination of t.

DEFINITION

Initiation events, *denoted by* IE_t, *is a set of significant events that can be invoked to initiate the execution of transaction t.* $\mathrm{IE}_t \subset \mathrm{SE}_t$.

DEFINITION

Termination events, *denoted by* TE_t, *is a set of significant events that can be invoked to terminate the execution of transaction t.* $\mathrm{TE}_t \subset \mathrm{SE}_t$.

For example, in the split transaction model, Begin and Split are transaction initiation events whereas Commit, Abort and Join are transaction termination events.

A transaction is *in progress* if it has been initiated by some initiation event and it has not yet executed one of the termination events associated with it. A transaction *terminates* when it executes a termination event.

Histories and Conditions on Event Occurrences

Fundamental to ACTA is the notion of *history* [BHG87] which represents the concurrent execution of a set of transactions T. ACTA captures the effects of transactions on other transactions and also their effects on objects through constraints on histories. This leads to definitions of transaction models in terms of a set of *axioms* which are either invariant assertions about the histories generated by the transactions adhering to the particular model or explicit *preconditions* or *postconditions* of operations or transaction management primitives. Also, the correctness properties of different transaction models can be expressed in terms of the properties of the histories produced by these models.

DEFINITION

The execution of a transaction t is a partial order of events E_t with ordering relation $<_t$ where

1. $E_t \subseteq (OE_t \cup SE_t)$; and
2. $<_t$ denotes the temporal order in which the related events invoked by t occur.

In words, E_t contains events which are either object events allowed to be invoked by t or significant events related to t.

DEFINITION

A history H *of the concurrent execution of a set of transactions T contains all the events associated with the transactions in T and indicates the (partial) order in which these events occur. H_{ct} (the current history) is used to denote the history of events that occur until a point in time.*

The partial order of the operations in a history pertaining to T is consistent with the partial order $<_t$ of the events associated with each individual transaction t in T.

The occurrence of an event in a history can be affected in one of three ways: (1) An event ϵ can be constrained to occur *only after* another event ϵ'; (2) An event ϵ can occur *only if* a condition c is true; and (3) a condition c can *require* the occurrence of an event ϵ.

DEFINITION

The predicate $\epsilon \rightarrow \epsilon'$ is true if event ϵ precedes event ϵ' in history H. It is false, otherwise. (Thus, $\epsilon \rightarrow \epsilon'$ implies that $\epsilon \in H$ and $\epsilon' \in H$.)

DEFINITION

$(\epsilon \in H) \Rightarrow Condition_H$, *where* $\Rightarrow$ *denotes* implication, *specifies that the event* ϵ *can belong to history* H only if $Condition_H$ *is satisfied. In other words,* $Condition_H$ *is* necessary *for* ϵ *to be in* H. $Condition_H$ *is a predicate involving the events in* H.

Consider $(\epsilon' \in H) \Rightarrow (\epsilon \rightarrow \epsilon')$. This states that the event ϵ' can belong to the history H *only if* event ϵ occurs before ϵ'.

DEFINITION

$Condition_H \Rightarrow (\epsilon \in H)$ *specifies that if* $Condition_H$ *holds,* ϵ *should be in the history* H. *In other words,* $Condition_H$ *is* sufficient *for* ϵ *to be in* H.

Consider $(\epsilon \rightarrow \epsilon') \Rightarrow (\alpha \in H)$. This states that *if* event ϵ occurs before ϵ' *then* event α belongs to the history.

In specifying conditions over histories, we will find it useful to define the *projection* of a history H according to a given criterion $\wp$, denoted $Projection(H, \wp)$. For instance, $Projection(H, t)$, the projection of a history H on a specific transaction t yields the order of events related to t, denoted by H^t; whereas $Projection(H, ob)$, the projection of the history H on a specific object ob yields the history of operation invocations on the object, denoted by $H^{(ob)}$.

10.2.2 Effects of Transactions on Other Transactions

Dependencies provide a convenient way to specify and reason about the behavior of concurrent transactions and can be precisely expressed in terms of the significant events associated with the transactions.

DEFINITION

Dependency set, *denoted by DepSet, is a set of inter-transaction dependencies developed during the concurrent execution of a set of transactions* T. *Thus, DepSet is relative to a history* H. $DepSet_{ct}$ *(the current dependency set) is used to denote the set of dependencies until a point in time and hence, it is relative to* H_{ct}.

In the rest of this section, after formally specifying different types of dependencies, we identify the source of these dependencies.

Types of Dependencies

Let t_i and t_j be two extended transactions and H be a finite history which contains all the events pertaining to t_i and t_j.

Commit Dependency $(t_j\ \mathcal{CD}\ t_i)$: if both transactions t_i and t_j commit then the commitment of t_i precedes the commitment of t_j; i.e., $(\mathsf{Commit}_{t_j} \in H) \Rightarrow ((\mathsf{Commit}_{t_i} \in H) \Rightarrow (\mathsf{Commit}_{t_i} \rightarrow \mathsf{Commit}_{t_j}))$.

Strong-Commit Dependency $(t_j\ \mathcal{SCD}\ t_i)$: if transaction t_i commits then t_j commits; i.e., $(\mathsf{Commit}_{t_i} \in H) \Rightarrow (\mathsf{Commit}_{t_j} \in H)$.

Abort Dependency $(t_j\ \mathcal{AD}\ t_i)$: if t_i aborts then t_j aborts; i.e., $(\mathsf{Abort}_{t_i} \in H) \Rightarrow (\mathsf{Abort}_{t_j} \in H)$.

Weak-Abort Dependency $(t_j\ \mathcal{WD}\ t_i)$: if t_i aborts and t_j has not yet committed, then t_j aborts. In other words, if t_j commits and t_i aborts then the commitment of t_j precedes the abortion of t_i in a history; i.e., $(\mathsf{Abort}_{t_i} \in H) \Rightarrow (\neg(\mathsf{Commit}_{t_j} \rightarrow \mathsf{Abort}_{t_i}) \Rightarrow (\mathsf{Abort}_{t_j} \in H))$.

Termination Dependency $(t_j\ \mathcal{TD}\ t_i)$: t_j cannot commit or abort until t_i either commits or aborts; i.e., $(\epsilon' \in H) \Rightarrow (\epsilon \rightarrow \epsilon')$ where $\epsilon \in \{\mathsf{Commit}_{t_i}, \mathsf{Abort}_{t_i}\}$, and $\epsilon' \in \{\mathsf{Commit}_{t_j}, \mathsf{Abort}_{t_j}\}$.

Exclusion Dependency $(t_j\ \mathcal{ED}\ t_i)$: if t_i commits and t_j has begun executing, then t_j aborts (both t_i and t_j cannot commit); i.e., $(\mathsf{Commit}_{t_i} \in H) \Rightarrow ((\mathsf{Begin}_{t_j} \in H) \Rightarrow (\mathsf{Abort}_{t_j} \in H))$.

Force-Commit-on-Abort Dependency $(t_j\ \mathcal{CMD}\ t_i)$: if t_i aborts, t_j commits; i.e., $(\mathsf{Abort}_{t_i} \in H) \Rightarrow (\mathsf{Commit}_{t_j} \in H)$.

Begin Dependency $(t_j\ \mathcal{BD}\ t_i)$: transaction t_j cannot begin executing until transaction t_i has begun; i.e., $(\mathsf{Begin}_{t_j} \in H) \Rightarrow (\mathsf{Begin}_{t_i} \rightarrow \mathsf{Begin}_{t_j})$.

Serial Dependency $(t_j\ \mathcal{SD}\ t_i)$: transaction t_j cannot begin executing until t_i either commits or aborts; i.e., $(\mathsf{Begin}_{t_j} \in H) \Rightarrow (\epsilon \rightarrow \mathsf{Begin}_{t_j})$ where $\epsilon \in \{\mathsf{Commit}_{t_i}, \mathsf{Abort}_{t_i}\}$.

Begin-on-Commit Dependency $(t_j\ \mathcal{BCD}\ t_i)$: transaction t_j cannot begin executing until t_i commits; i.e., $(\mathsf{Begin}_{t_j} \in H) \Rightarrow (\mathsf{Commit}_{t_i} \rightarrow \mathsf{Begin}_{t_j})$.

Begin-on-Abort Dependency (t_j $\mathcal{BAD}$ t_i): transaction t_j cannot begin executing until t_i aborts; i.e., $(\mathsf{Begin}_{t_j} \in H) \Rightarrow (\mathsf{Abort}_{t_i} \rightarrow \mathsf{Begin}_{t_j})$.

Weak-begin-on-Commit Dependency (t_j $\mathcal{WCD}$ t_i): if t_i commits, t_j can begin executing after t_i commits; i.e., $(\mathsf{Begin}_{t_j} \in H) \Rightarrow ((\mathsf{Commit}_{t_i} \in H) \Rightarrow (\mathsf{Commit}_{t_i} \rightarrow \mathsf{Begin}_{t_j}))$.

The formal definitions of weak-abort dependency and abort dependency clearly reflect that weak-abort dependency is weaker than abort dependency. Weak-abort dependency is useful, for example, in specifying and reasoning about the properties of nested transactions [Mos81]. Begin-on-commit dependency, begin-on-abort dependency and force-commit-on-abort dependency are useful for compensating transactions [KLS90] and contingency transactions [BHMC90]. Begin-on-commit dependency and begin-on-abort dependency are special cases of serial dependency. The important difference between exclusion dependency and force-commit-on-abort dependency is that exclusion dependency allows both transactions to abort whereas force-commit-on-abort dependency does not.

We would like to note that this list of dependencies is *not* exhaustive. Other dependencies that involve significant events besides the Begin, Commit and Abort events, can be defined. As we will see in Section 10.5.4, when new significant events are associated with extended transactions, new dependencies may be specified in a similar manner. In this sense, ACTA is an open-ended framework.

Source of Dependencies

Dependencies between transactions may be a direct result of the structural properties of transactions, or may indirectly develop as a result of interactions of transactions over shared objects. These are elaborated below.

Dependencies due to Structure

The structure of an extended transaction defines its component transactions and the relationships between them. Dependencies can express these relationships and thus, can specify the links in the structure. For example, in hierarchically-structured nested transactions, the parent/child relationship is established at the time the child is *spawned*. This is expressed by a child transaction t_c establishing a weak-abort dependency on its parent t_p ((t_c $\mathcal{WD}$ t_p)) and a parent establishing a commit dependency on its child ((t_p $\mathcal{CD}$ t_c)).

Specifically, this is specified in terms of the postcondition of the Spawn event ($post(\mathsf{Spawn}_{t_p}[t_c])$):

$$post(\mathsf{Spawn}_{t_p}[t_c]) \Rightarrow (((t_c\ \mathcal{WD}\ t_p) \in DepSet_{ct}) \wedge ((t_p\ \mathcal{CD}\ t_c) \in DepSet_{ct})).$$

The weak-abort dependency guarantees the abortion of an uncommitted child if its parent aborts. Note that this does not prevent the child from committing and making its effects on objects visible to its parent and siblings. (In nested transactions, when a child transaction commits, its effects are not made permanent in the database. They are just made visible to its parent. See [Chr91] for a precise formal definition of nested transactions.) The commit dependency of the parent on its child is preserved if (1) the parent does not commit before its child terminates, or (2) the child aborts in case its parent commits first. The weak-abort dependency together with the commit dependency says that an orphan, i.e., a child transaction whose parent has terminated, will not commit.

Other hierarchically-structured transactions may define various relationships between a parent and its child transactions. For example, in the transaction model proposed in [BHMC90, GGK+91] a parent can commit only if its *vital* children commit, i.e., a parent transaction has an abort dependency on its *vital* children t_v ($t_p\ \mathcal{AD}\ t_v$) (see Section 10.5.2). Child transactions may also have different dependencies with their parents if the transaction model supports various spawning or coupling modes [DHL90]. Sibling transactions may also be interrelated in several ways. For example, components of a *saga* [GS87] can be paired according to a compensated-for/compensating relationship [KLS90]. Relations between a compensated-for and compensating transactions as well as those between them and the saga can be specified via begin-on-commit dependency $\mathcal{BCD}$, begin-on-abort dependency $\mathcal{BAD}$, force-commit-on-abort dependency $\mathcal{CMD}$ and strong-commit dependency $\mathcal{SCD}$ (see Figure 10.5). In a similar fashion dependencies that occur in the presence of alternative transactions and contingency transactions [BHMC90] can also be specified (see Section 10.5.3).

Dependencies due to Behavior

Dependencies formed by the interactions of transactions over a shared object are determined by the object's synchronization properties. Broadly speaking, two operations conflict if the order of their execution matters. For example, in the traditional framework, a compatibility table [BHG87] of an object *ob* expresses simple relations between conflicting operations. A conflict relation has the form

$$(p_{t_i}[ob] \rightarrow q_{t_j}[ob]) \Rightarrow (t_j \ \mathcal{D} \ t_i)$$

indicating that if transaction t_j invokes an operation p and later a transaction t_j invokes an operation q on the same object *ob*, then t_j should develop a dependency of type $\mathcal{D}$ on t_i. As we will see in the next section, ACTA allows conflict relations to be complex expressions involving different types of dependencies, operation arguments, and results, as well as operations on the same or different objects.

10.2.3 Objects and the Effects of Transactions on Objects

In order to better understand the effects of transactions on objects, we need to first understand the effects of the operations invoked by the transactions.

Conflicts between Operations and the Induced Dependencies

A history $H^{(ob)}$ of operation invocations on an object *ob*, $H^{(ob)} = p_1 \circ p_2 \circ ... \circ p_n$, indicates both the order of execution of the operations, (p_i precedes p_{i+1}), as well as the functional composition of operations. Thus, a state s of an object produced by a sequence of operations equals the state produced by applying the history $H^{(ob)}$ corresponding to the sequence of operations on the object's initial state s_0 ($s = state(s_0, H^{(ob)})$). For brevity, we will use $H^{(ob)}$ to denote the state of an object produced by $H^{(ob)}$, implicitly assuming initial state s_0.

DEFINITION

Two operations p and q conflict *in a state produced by* $H^{(ob)}$*, denoted by* $conflict(H^{(ob)}, p, q)$*, iff*

$$\begin{aligned}(state(H^{(ob)} \circ p,\ q) &\neq state(H^{(ob)} \circ q,\ p)) \quad \vee \\ (return(H^{(ob)},\ q) &\neq (return(H^{(ob)} \circ p,\ q)) \ \vee \\ (return(H^{(ob)},\ p) &\neq (return(H^{(ob)} \circ q,\ p)).\end{aligned}$$

Two operations that do not conflict are compatible.

Thus, two operations conflict if their effects on the state of an object or their return values are not independent of their execution order. Since state changes are observed only via return values, the semantics of the return values can be considered in dealing with conflicting operations.

DEFINITION

Given $conflict(H^{(ob)}, p, q)$, $return\text{-}value\text{-}independent(H^{(ob)}, p, q)$ *is true if the return value of q is independent of whether p precedes q, i.e.,* $return(H^{(ob)} \circ p, q) = return(H^{(ob)}, q)$*; otherwise q is* return-value dependent *on p* $(return\text{-}value\text{-}dependent(H^{(ob)}, p, q))$.

Given a history H in which $p_{t_i}[ob]$ and $q_{t_j}[ob]$ occur, the state of ob when p_{t_i} is executed is known from where p_{t_i} occurs in the history. Hence, from now on, we drop the first argument in *conflict*, *return-value-independent*, and *return-value-dependent* when it is implicit from the context.

Interactions between conflicting operations can cause dependencies of different types between the invoking transactions. The type of interactions induced by conflicting operations depends on whether the effects of operations on objects are *immediate* or *deferred*. An operation has an immediate effect on an object only if it changes the state of the object as it executes and the new state is visible to subsequent operations. Thus, an operation p operates on the (most recent) state of the object, i.e., the state produced by the operation immediately preceding p. For example, effects are immediate in objects which perform *in-place updates* and employ logs for recovery. Effects of operations are *deferred* if operations are not allowed to change the state of an object as soon as they occur but, instead, the changes are effected only upon commitment of the operations. In this case, operations performed by a transaction are maintained in *intentions lists*.

In the rest of the paper, we will consider the situation when the effects are immediate. In this case, when an operation q follows operation p and q is return-value dependent on p, the transaction t_j invoking the operation q must abort q if for some reason the transaction t_i aborts p.

$$(return\text{-}value\text{-}dependent(p, q) \wedge (p_{t_i}[ob] \rightarrow q_{t_j}[ob])) \Rightarrow \\ ((Abort_{t_i}[p_{t_i}[ob]] \in H) \Rightarrow (Abort_{t_j}[q_{t_j}[ob]] \in H)).$$

This dependency ensures the correct behavior of objects in the presence of failure.

Motivated by this, in ACTA, the concurrency properties of an object are formally expressed in terms of *conflict relations* of the form:

$$(p_{t_i}[ob] \rightarrow q_{t_j}[ob]) \Rightarrow Condition_H,$$

where $Condition_H$ is typically a dependency relationship involving the transactions t_i and t_j invoking conflicting operations p and q on an object ob. Obviously, the absence of a conflict relation between two operations defined on an object indicates that the operations are compatible and do not induce any dependency[4].

This generality allows ACTA to encompass both object-specific and transaction-specific semantic information. First consider some object-specific semantics. *Commutativity* does not distinguish between return-value dependent and independent conflicts. It treats both the same and uses abort dependency for both:

$$(p_{t_i}[ob] \rightarrow q_{t_j}[ob]) \Rightarrow (t_j \ \mathcal{AD} \ t_i).$$

Recoverability [BR90] avoids the unnecessary development of an abort dependency for return-value independent conflicts. Thus, recoverability induces the following conflict relations:

$$\textit{return-value-independent}(p, q) \wedge (p_{t_i}[ob] \rightarrow q_{t_j}[ob]) \Rightarrow (t_j \ \mathcal{CD} \ t_i);$$

$$\textit{return-value-dependent}(p, q) \wedge (p_{t_i}[ob] \rightarrow q_{t_j}[ob]) \Rightarrow (t_j \ \mathcal{AD} \ t_i).$$

We introduce *transaction-specific* semantics through an example. Consider a *page* object with the standard *read* and *write* operations, where read and write operations conflict. A read is return-value dependent on write, whereas a write is return-value independent of a read or another write. In addition, consider transactions which have the ability to reconcile potential read-write conflicts: When a transaction t_i reads a page x and another transaction t_j subsequently writes x, t_i and t_j can commit in any order. However,

[4] Clearly, when an invoked operation conflicts with an operation in progress, a dependency, e.g., an abort or commit dependency, will be formed if the invoked operation is allowed to execute. That is, this may induce an abortion or a specific commit ordering. One way to avoid this is to force the invoking transaction to (a) wait until the conflicting operation terminates (this is what the traditional "no" entry in a compatibility table means) or (b) abort. In either case, conflict relationships between operations imply that the transaction management system must keep track of in-progress operations and of dependencies that have been induced by the conflict. A commonly used synchronization mechanism for keeping track of in-progress operations and dependencies is based on (logical) *locks*.

if t_j commits before t_i commits, t_i must reread x in order to commit. This is captured by the following conflict relation:

$$(read_{t_i}[x] \dashrightarrow write_{t_j}[x]) \Rightarrow ((\mathsf{Commit}_{t_j} \rightarrow \mathsf{Commit}_{t_i}) \Rightarrow (\mathsf{Commit}_{t_j} \rightarrow read_{t_i}[x]))).$$

This conflict relation cannot be derived solely from the object-specific semantics of the page. Clearly, transaction specific concurrency control might *not* achieve serializability but still preserves consistency.

In the example, t_i has to reread the page x when, subsequent to the first read, the page is written and committed by t_j. In general, t_i may need to invoke an operation on the same or a different object. For instance, instead of x, t_i may have to read a *scratch-pad* object which t_i and t_j use to determine and reconcile potential conflicts. Thus, ACTA allows the specification of operations that need to be controlled to produce correct histories as well as the specification of operations that *have* to occur in correct histories. These correspond to *conflicts* and *patterns* in [Ska91].

The $Condition_H$ in a conflict relation may include other significant events defined by the various transaction models. As an example, consider the significant event *Notify*, related to the notion of *notification* useful in a cooperative environment [FZ89]. For instance, the condition $Notify_{t_j}[(t_i \; \mathcal{CD} \; t_j)]$ will cause a commit dependency to be established from transaction t_i to t_j as well as *notify* t_j about the development of the commit dependency. Such compound conditions can be used to define a recoverability-based table in a cooperative environment. Transaction t_j can use the information about the existence of the commit dependency to postpone the invocation of another operation that causes a commit dependency of t_j on t_i, and thus postpone the formation of a circular commit dependency.

The generality of the conflict relations allows ACTA to capture different types of type-specific concurrency control discussed in the literature [SS84, HW88, Wei88, BR90, CRR91], and even to tailor them for cooperative environments.

Controlling Object Visibility

Visibility and Conflicts

As defined earlier, visibility refers to the ability of one transaction to see the effects of another transaction on objects *while* they are executing. ACTA allows finer control over the visibility of objects by associating two entities, namely, *view* and *conflict set*, with every transaction.

DEFINITION

The view *of a transaction, denoted by $View_t$, specifies the* state *of objects visible to transaction t at a point in time.*

$View_t$ is formally specified to be a subhistory derived by projecting events in H_{ct}:

$$View_t = Projection(H_{ct}, \mathcal{P}redicate(t, H_{ct}, DepSet_{ct})).$$

In other words, the subhistory is constructed by eliminating any events in H_{ct} that do not satisfy the given $\mathcal{P}redicate$. $\mathcal{P}redicate$ depends on t, events in H_{ct} and inter-transaction dependencies $DepSet_{ct}$. For example, the view of a subtransaction t_c in the nested transaction model is defined to be the current history, i.e., $View_{t_c} = H_{ct}$, allowing t_c to view *the* most recent state of objects in the database.

For a more elaborate example, suppose that a subtransaction t_c is restricted to operate only on those objects that have been accessed by its parent t_p and is allowed to notice the changes done to them by its parent. The view of such a subtransaction t_c is defined as following form.

$$View_{t_c} = Projection\{H_{ct}, p_t[ob] \| (t = t_c \vee t = t_p \vee (CommittedTr(t) \wedge \exists q\ (q_{t_p}[ob] \in H_{ct})))\}.$$

The predicate $CommittedTr(t)$ is true if transaction t has committed. Thus, t_c can see the changes done by committed transactions on the objects accessed by its parent.

DEFINITION

The conflict set *of a transaction t, denoted by $ConflictSet_t$, contains those in-progress operations with respect to which conflicts have to be determined.*

The composition of $ConflictSet_t$ is determined by the particular transaction model. It is specified via a predicate which can involve events invoked by t and any other transaction t_i, events in H_{ct}, and dependencies in $DepSet_{ct}$:

$$ConflictSet_t = \{p_{t_i}[ob] \mid \mathcal{P}redicate(t, t_i, H_{ct}, DepSet_{ct})\}.$$

A transaction t_j can invoke an operation on an object without conflicting with another transaction t_i if the operations in progress performed by t_i on the same object are in the view of t_j but are not included in the conflict set of t_j. Let us illustrate this by considering nested transactions. In nested transactions, a subtransaction t_c can access without conflicts any object currently accessed by one of its ancestors t_a. This is captured by

$ConflictSet_{t_c} = \{p_{t_i}[ob] \mid t_i \neq t_c, t_i \notin Ancestor(t_c), \mathcal{I}nprogress(p_{t_i}[ob])\}$;
$Ancestor(t_c)$ is the set of ancestors of t_c.
$\mathcal{I}nprogress(p_{t_i}[ob])$ is *true* with respect to current history H_{ct} if $p_{t_i}[ob]$ has been performed but has neither committed nor aborted yet; i.e.,

$$\mathcal{I}nprogress(p_{t_i}[ob]) \Rightarrow ((p_{t_i}[ob] \in H_{ct}) \wedge ((Commit_{t_i}[p_{t_i}[ob]] \notin H_{ct}) \wedge (Abort_{t_i}[p_{t_i}[ob]] \notin H_{ct}))).$$

This states that any operation invoked by an ancestor of t_c is not contained in $ConflictSet_{t_c}$. For this reason, a transaction t_c can invoke an operation that conflicts with another in progress, invoked by its ancestor t_a, without forming a dependency.

At any given time, the current history H_{ct} and current dependency set $DepSet_{ct}$ exist. The axiomatic definition of a transaction model specifies the $View_t$ and $ConflictSet_t$ of each transaction t in that model. These determine if a new event can be invoked. Specifically, the preconditions of the event derived from the axiomatic definition of its invoking transaction are evaluated with respect to H_{ct} and $DepSet_{ct}$ using the $View_t$ and $ConflictSet_t$. If its preconditions are satisfied, the new event is invoked and appended to the H_{ct} reflecting its occurrence.

The axiomatic definitions also specify how the dependency set is modified when a significant event is invoked. As we saw earlier, if an event is an object event, the operation semantics may also induce new dependencies to be added to $DepSet_{ct}$.

The degree of visibility allowed by a transaction model depends on the *width* of the views of the transactions in the model and on the *size* of their conflict sets. By width we mean the length of the subhistory specifying the view. A larger width makes more operations visible while a smaller size leads to fewer conflicts permitting more operations to be performed without conflicting.

Delegation

DEFINITION

ResponsibleTr$(p_{t_i}[ob])$ *identifies the transaction responsible for committing or aborting the operation* $p_{t_i}[ob]$ *with respect to the current history* H_{ct}.

In general, a transaction may *delegate* some of its responsibilities to another transaction. More precisely,

DEFINITION

$Delegate_{t_i}[t_j, p_{t_i}[ob]]$ *denotes that* t_i *delegates to* t_j *the responsibility for committing or aborting operation* $p_{t_i}[ob]$.

More generally, $Delegate_{t_i}[t_j, DelegateSet]$ *denotes that* t_i *delegates to* t_j *the responsibility for committing or aborting each operation* $p_{t_i}[ob]$ *in the* $DelegateSet$.

Delegation has the following ramifications which are formally stated in [Chr91]:

- $ResponsibleTr(p_{t_i}[ob])$ is t_i, the event-invoker, unless t_i delegates $p_{t_i}[ob]$ to another transaction, say t_j, at which point it will become t_j. If subsequently t_j delegates $p_{t_i}[ob]$ to another transaction, say t_k, $ResponsibleTr(p_{t_i}[ob])$ becomes t_k.

- The precondition for the event $Delegate_{t_j}[t_k, p_{t_i}[ob]]$ is that $ResponsibleTr(p_{t_i}[ob])$ is t_j. The postcondition will imply that $ResponsibleTr(p_{t_i}[ob])$ is t_k.

- A precondition for the event $Abort_{t_j}[p_{t_i}[ob]]$ is that $ResponsibleTr(p_{t_i}[ob])$ is t_j. Similarly, a precondition for the event $Commit_{t_j}[p_{t_i}[ob]]$ is that $ResponsibleTr(p_{t_i}[ob])$ is t_j. Hence, from now on, unless essential, we will drop the suscript, e.g., t_j, associated with the operation abort and commit events.

- Delegation cannot occur in the event that the delegatee has already committed or aborted, and has no effect if the delegated operations have already been committed or aborted.
- Delegation redirects the dependencies induced by delegated operations from the delegator to the delegatee — dependencies are sort of responsibilities.

Note that delegation broadens the visibility of the delegatee and is useful in selectively making tentative or partial results as well as hints, such as, coordination information, accessible to other transactions.

In controlling visibility, we will find it useful to associate each transaction with an *access set.*

DEFINITION

$AccessSet_t = \{p_{t_i}[ob] | ResponsibleTr(p_{t_i}[ob]) = t\}$; i.e., $AccessSet_t$ contains all the operations for which t is responsible.

In nested transactions, when the root commits, its effects are made permanent in the database, whereas when a subtransaction commits, via inheritance, its effects are made visible to its parent transaction. The notion of inheritance used in nested transactions is an instance of delegation. Specifically, when a child transaction t_c commits, t_c delegates to its parent t_p all the operations that it is responsible for

$$(\mathsf{Commit}_{t_c} \in H) \Leftrightarrow (Delegate_{t_c}[t_p, AccessSet_{t_c}] \in H).$$

Delegation need not occur only upon commit or abort but a transaction can delegate any of the operations in its access set to another transaction at any point during its execution. This is the case for Co-Transactions and Reporting Transactions described in [CR91, Chr91].

Delegation can be used not only in controlling the visibility of objects, but also to specify the recovery properties of a transaction model. For instance, if a subset of the effects of a transaction should not be obliterated when the transaction aborts while at the same time they should not be made permanent, the Abort event associated with the transaction can be defined to delegate these effects to the appropriate transaction. In this way, the effects of the delegated operations performed by the delegator on objects are not lost even if the delegator aborts. Instead, the delegatee has the responsibility for committing or aborting these operations.

In cooperative environments, transactions cooperate by having intersecting views, by allowing the effects of other's operations to be visible without producing conflicts, by delegating operations to each other, or by *notifying* each other of their behavior. By being able to capture these aspects of transactions, the ACTA framework is applicable to cooperative environments.

10.3 Characterization of Atomic Transactions

Since the building blocks for a Saga are atomic transactions, we now give a formal characterization of atomic transactions.

Atomic transactions combine the properties of serializability and failure atomicity. These properties ensure that concurrent transactions execute without any interference as though they executed in some serial order, and that either all or none of a transaction's operations are performed.

Let us first define the correctness properties of objects within formal ACTA, starting with the serializability correctness criterion.

DEFINITION

Let $\mathcal{C}$ be a binary relation on transactions, and t_i and t_j be transactions.

$$(t_i \mathcal{C} t_j), t_i \neq t_j \textit{ if}$$
$$\exists ob\ \exists p, q\ (conflict(p_{t_i}[ob], q_{t_j}[ob]) \wedge (p_{t_i}[ob] \rightarrow q_{t_j}[ob]))$$

DEFINITION

Let $\mathcal{C}^*$ be the transitive-closure of $\mathcal{C}$; i.e.,

$$(t_i \mathcal{C}^* t_k) \textit{ if } [(t_i \mathcal{C} t_k) \vee \exists t_j\ (t_i \mathcal{C} t_j \wedge t_j \mathcal{C}^* t_k)].$$

DEFINITION

A set of transactions T is (conflict preserving) serializable *iff*

$$\forall t \in T\ \neg(t \mathcal{C}^* t)$$

DEFINITION

An object ob behaves correctly *iff*

$\forall t_i, t_j, t_i \neq t_j,\ \forall p, q$

$$(\textit{return-value-dependent}(\text{p,q}) \wedge (p_{t_i}[ob] \rightarrow q_{t_j}[ob])) \Rightarrow$$
$$((Abort[p_{t_i}[ob]] \in H^{(ob)}) \Rightarrow (Abort[q_{t_j}[ob]] \in H^{(ob)})).$$

This definition implies that for an object to behave *correctly* it must ensure that when an operation aborts, any return-value dependent operation that follows it must also be aborted. It is not necessary for it to exhibit serial behavior, i.e., it is not necessary for the order in which the operations are executed by different transactions to be serializable. This definition ensures the correct behavior of objects in the presence of failures assuming immediate effects of operations on objects. Similarly, such dependencies can be defined for deferred effects.

DEFINITION

An object ob behaves serializably *iff*

$$\forall t, t_i\ \forall p\ (Commit_{t_i}[p_t[ob]] \in H^{(ob)}) \Rightarrow \neg(t\mathcal{C}^* t).$$

This definition states that the serializable behavior of an object is ensured by preventing transactions from forming cyclic $\mathcal{C}$ relationships.

DEFINITION

An object ob is atomic *if ob behaves* correctly *and* serializably.

DEFINITION

Transaction t is failure atomic *if*

1. $\exists ob\ \exists p\ (Commit_t[p_t[ob]] \in H) \Rightarrow$
   $\forall ob'\ \forall q\ ((q_t[ob'] \in H) \Rightarrow (Commit_t[q_t[ob']] \in H)),$
2. $\exists ob\ \exists p\ (Abort_t[p_t[ob]] \in H) \Rightarrow$
   $\forall ob'\ \forall q\ ((q_t[ob'] \in H) \Rightarrow (Abort_t[q_t[ob']] \in H)),$

As mentioned earlier, failure atomicity implies that all or none of a transaction's operations are executed. In the above definition, the "all" clause is captured by condition 1 which states that if an operation invoked by a transaction t is committed on an object, all the operations invoked by t are committed by t. The "none" clause is captured by condition 2 which states that if an operation invoked by a transaction t is aborted on an object, all the operations invoked by t are aborted by t.

In the same way that serializability and failure atomicity were expressed above, other correctness properties of extended transactions such as *quasi serializability* [DE89], *predicatewise serializability* [KS88] and *quasi-failure atomicity* [Chr91], can be expressed in ACTA [Chr91].

Recall that each transaction model defines a set of significant events that transactions adhering to that model can invoke in addition to the invocation of operations on objects. A transaction is always associated with a set of initiation significant events that can be invoked to initiate the execution of the transaction, and a set of termination significant events that can be invoked to terminate the execution of the transaction. A set of *Fundamental Axioms* which is applicable to all transaction models specifies the relationship between significant events of the same or different type, and between significant events and operations on objects.

DEFINITION

FUNDAMENTAL AXIOMS OF TRANSACTIONS

Let t be a transaction and H^t *the projection of the history H with respect to t.*

I. $\forall \alpha \in \mathrm{IE}_t\ (\alpha \in H^t) \Rightarrow \nexists \beta \in \mathrm{IE}_t\ (\alpha \rightarrow \beta)$

II. $\forall \delta \in \mathrm{TE}_t\ \exists \alpha \in \mathrm{IE}_t\ (\delta \in H^t) \Rightarrow (\alpha \rightarrow \delta)$

III. $\forall \gamma \in \mathrm{TE}_t\ (\gamma \in H^t) \Rightarrow \nexists \delta \in \mathrm{TE}_t\ (\gamma \rightarrow \delta)$

IV. $\forall ob \forall p, (p_t[ob] \in H) \Rightarrow$
$((\exists \alpha \in \mathrm{IE}_t\ (\alpha \rightarrow p_t[ob])) \wedge (\exists \gamma \in \mathrm{TE}_t\ (p_t[ob] \rightarrow \gamma)))$

Axiom I prevents a transaction from being initiated by two different events. Axiom II states that if a transaction has terminated, it must have been previously initiated. Axiom III prevents a transaction from being terminated by two different termination events. The last axiom, Axiom IV, states that only in-progress transactions can invoke operations on objects.

Now let us express in ACTA the basic properties of atomic transactions with a set of axioms.

DEFINITION

AXIOMATIC DEFINITION OF ATOMIC TRANSACTIONS

t denotes an atomic transaction.

1. $SE_t = \{\textsf{Begin, Commit, Abort}\}$
2. $IE_t = \{\textsf{Begin}\}$
3. $TE_t = \{\textsf{Commit, Abort}\}$
4. t satisfies the fundamental Axioms I to IV
5. $View_t = H_{ct}$
6. $ConflictSet_t = \{p_{t'}[ob] \mid t' \neq t, \mathcal{I}nprogress(p_{t'}[ob])\}$
7. $\forall ob\ \exists p\ (p_t[ob] \in H) \Rightarrow (ob\ is\ atomic)$
8. $(\textsf{Commit}_t \in H) \Rightarrow \neg(t\mathcal{C}^*t)$.
9. $\exists ob\ \exists p\ (Commit_t[p_t[ob]] \in H) \Rightarrow (\textsf{Commit}_t \in H)$
10. $(\textsf{Commit}_t \in H) \Rightarrow \forall ob\ \forall p\ ((p_t[ob] \in H) \Rightarrow (Commit_t[p_t[ob]] \in H))$
11. $\exists ob\ \exists p\ (Abort_t[p_t[ob]] \in H) \Rightarrow (\textsf{Abort}_t \in H)$
12. $(\textsf{Abort}_t \in H) \Rightarrow \forall ob\ \forall p\ ((p_t[ob] \in H) \Rightarrow (Abort_t[p_t[ob]] \in H))$

Axiom 1 states that atomic transactions are associated with the three significant events: Begin, Commit and Abort. Axiom 2 specifies that Begin is the initiation event for atomic transactions. Axiom 3 indicates that Commit and Abort are the termination events associated with atomic transactions.

Axiom 4 states that atomic transactions satisfy the fundamental axioms. With respect to the significant events of atomic transactions, the fundamental axioms mean the following:

1. the Begin event can be invoked at most once by a transaction
   $((\textsf{Begin}_t \in H) \Rightarrow \neg(\textsf{Begin}_t \rightarrow \textsf{Begin}_t))$ [Axiom I],

2. only an initiated transaction can commit or abort
   $((\textsf{Commit}_t \in H) \Rightarrow (\textsf{Begin}_t \rightarrow \textsf{Commit}_t)$, and
   $(\textsf{Abort}_t \in H) \Rightarrow (\textsf{Begin}_t \rightarrow \textsf{Abort}_t))$ [Axiom II], and

3. an atomic transaction cannot be committed after it has been aborted
   $((\textsf{Commit}_t \in H) \Rightarrow ((\textsf{Abort}_t \notin H) \wedge \neg(\textsf{Commit}_t \rightarrow \textsf{Commit}_t)))$,
   and vice versa
   $((\textsf{Abort}_t \in H) \Rightarrow ((\textsf{Commit}_t \notin H) \wedge \neg(\textsf{Abort}_t \rightarrow \textsf{Abort}_t)))$ [Axiom III].

Axiom 5 specifies that a transaction sees the current state of the objects in the database. Axiom 6 states that conflicts have to be considered against all in-progress operations performed by different transactions. Axiom 7 specifies that all objects upon which an atomic transaction invokes an operation are atomic objects. That is, they detect conflicts and induce the appropriate dependencies. Axiom 8 states that an atomic transaction can commit only if it is not part of a cycle of $\mathcal{C}$ relations developed through the invocation of conflicting operations. Note that the atomicity property local to individual objects is not sufficient to guarantee serializable execution of concurrent transactions across all objects [Wei84]. Axiom 9 states that if an operation is committed on an object, the invoking transaction must commit, and Axiom 10 states that if a transaction commits, all the operations invoked by the transaction are committed.

Axioms 8, 9 and 10 define the semantics of the Commit event of atomic transactions in terms of the *Commit* operation defined on objects. Similarly, Axioms 11 and 12 define the semantics of the Abort event in terms of the *Abort* operation defined on objects. Axiom 11 states that if an operation is aborted on an object, the invoking transaction must abort, and Axiom 12 states that if a transaction aborts, all the operations invoked by the transaction are aborted.

Based on the above axioms, the failure atomicity and serializability properties of atomic transactions can be shown (see [Chr91]).

10.4 Characterization of Sagas

Sagas have been proposed as a transaction model for long lived activities. A saga is a set of relatively independent (component) transactions T_1, T_2,..., T_n which can interleave in any way with component transactions of other sagas. Component transactions within a saga execute in a predefined order which, in the simplest case, is either sequential or parallel (no order).

Each component transaction T_i $(0 \leq i < n)$ is associated with a compensating transaction CT_i. A compensating transaction CT_i undoes, from a semantic point of view, any effects of T_i, but does not necessarily restore the database to the state that existed when T_i began executing.

Both component and compensating transactions behave like atomic transactions in the sense that they have the ACID[5] properties. However, their

[5] ACID properties are Atomicity (or failure atomicity), Consistency, Isolation (or serializability) and Durability (or permanence).

behavior is constrained by certain dependencies. For example, a compensating transaction can commit only if its corresponding component transaction commits but the saga to which it belongs aborts.

Component transactions can commit without waiting for any other component transactions or the saga to commit. For this reason, sagas do not require a commit protocol as opposed, for example, to nested transactions. Due to their ACID properties, component transactions make their changes to objects effective in the database at their commitment times. Thus, isolation is limited to the component transaction level and sagas may view the partial results of other sagas. This means that each component transaction does not have to observe the same consistent database state produced by committed component transactions belonging to the same saga. Clearly, in sagas, consistency is not based on serializable executions.

A saga commits, i.e., successfully terminates, if all its component transactions commit in the prescribed order. Under sequential execution, the correct execution of a committed saga is:

$$T_1 \; T_2 \cdots \; T_n$$

A saga is not failure atomic but neither can it execute partially. Thus, when a saga aborts, it has to compensate for the committed components by executing their corresponding compensating transactions. Compensating transactions are executed in the reverse order of commitment of the component transactions. Thus, in the sequential case, the correct execution of an aborted saga after the commitment of its kth component transaction, T_k $(1 \leq k < n)$, is:

$$T_1 \; T_2 \; \cdots \; T_k \; CT_k \; CT_{k-1} \; \cdots \; CT_1$$

Note that the commitment of T_n implies the commitment of the whole saga and hence, T_n is not associated with a compensating transaction CT_n.

Now, let us express the basic properties of sagas with a set of axioms. Without loss of generality, let us focus on sagas whose components execute sequentially. As it will become clear below, the axiomatic definitions of sagas with different execution orders differ only in Axiom 18 which specifies the execution order. We will use $pre(e)$ and $post(e)$ to denote the preconditions and postconditions of an operation or a transaction management primitive e respectively.

DEFINITION

AXIOMATIC DEFINITION OF SAGAS

S denotes a saga with n component transactions.
T_i denotes a component transaction.
CT_i denotes a compensating transaction of T_i.
t denotes either a T_i or CT_i.

1. $SE_S = \{\text{Begin, Commit, Abort}\}$
2. $IE_S = \{\text{Begin}\}$
3. $TE_S = \{\text{Commit, Abort}\}$
4. $SE_t = \{\text{Begin, Commit, Abort}\}$
5. $IE_t = \{\text{Begin}\}$
6. $TE_t = \{\text{Commit, Abort}\}$
7. t satisfies the fundamental Axioms I to IV
8. $View_S = \phi$
9. $View_t = H_{ct}$
10. $ConflictSet_S = \phi$
11. $ConflictSet_t = \{p_{t'}[ob] \mid t' \neq t, \mathcal{I}nprogress(p_{t'}[ob])\}$
12. $\exists ob\ \exists p\ (Commit_t[p_t[ob]] \in H) \Rightarrow (\text{Commit}_t \in H)$
13. $(\text{Commit}_t \in H) \Rightarrow \forall ob\ \forall p\ ((p_t[ob] \in H) \Rightarrow (Commit_t[p_t[ob]] \in H))$
14. $\exists ob\ \exists p\ (Abort_t[p_t[ob]] \in H) \Rightarrow (\text{Abort}_t \in H)$
15. $(\text{Abort}_t \in H) \Rightarrow \forall ob\ \forall p\ ((p_t[ob] \in H) \Rightarrow (Abort_t[p_t[ob]] \in H))$
16. $\forall ob\ \exists p\ (p_t[ob] \in H) \Rightarrow (ob\ is\ atomic)$
17. $(\text{Commit}_t \in H) \Rightarrow \neg(t\mathcal{C}^* t)$
18. $post(\text{Begin}_S) \Rightarrow (((T_i\ \mathcal{BCD}\ T_{i-1}) \in DepSet_{ct}) \wedge ((CT_j\ \mathcal{WCD}\ CT_{j+1}) \in DepSet_{ct}) \wedge ((CT_{n-1}\ \mathcal{BAD}\ S) \in DepSet_{ct}))$
    where $1 < i \leq n$, and $1 \leq j < n-1$
19. $post(\text{Begin}_{T_i}) \Rightarrow (((S\ \mathcal{AD}\ T_i) \in DepSet_{ct}) \wedge ((T_i\ \mathcal{WD}\ S) \in DepSet_{ct}) \wedge ((CT_i\ \mathcal{BCD}\ T_i) \in DepSet_{ct}))$
    where $1 \leq i < n$
20. $post(\text{Commit}_{T_i}) \Rightarrow (((CT_i\ \mathcal{CMD}\ S) \in DepSet_{ct}) \wedge ((CT_i\ \mathcal{BAD}\ S) \in DepSet_{ct}))$
    where $1 \leq i < n$
21. $post(\text{Begin}_{T_n}) \Rightarrow ((S\ \mathcal{SCD}\ T_n) \in DepSet_{ct})$

A transaction structure which conforms to a saga transaction model consists of three types of transactions, namely, *saga* transaction, *component transactions* and *compensating transactions.* Axioms 1 and 4 state that each type of transaction is associated with the significant events Begin, Commit and Abort. Axioms 7, 9 and 11–17 capture the fact that component and compensating transactions have semantics similar to atomic transactions.

Saga transactions cannot directly operate on objects in the database [Axiom 8] — saga transactions may execute local operations that do not involve access to the database, e.g., test the outcome and return values of their component transactions[6] — this is the reason for the presence of a saga node, e.g., in Figure 10.3.

Axiom 18 specifies the execution order of the component transactions and their associated compensating transactions. A sequential (total) order is specified by establishing a begin-on-commit dependency $\mathcal{BCD}$ between every pair of component transactions. In a similar way, partial orders may be defined. Clearly, in the case of a parallel execution, Axiom 18 will be absent.

Axioms 19 specifies the relationship between a saga transaction and the component transactions. The composition relationship is captured by an abort dependency $\mathcal{AD}$ of the saga transaction on each of the component transactions and weak-abort dependencies $\mathcal{WD}$ of each component transaction on the saga transaction. This is induced at the time a component transaction begins its execution. The special relationship between a saga transaction and the last component T_n is captured by Axiom 21 in terms of a strong-commit dependency $\mathcal{SCD}$. A saga transaction's strong-commit dependency on T_n ensures that if T_n commits, the whole saga commits.

Axioms 19 and 20 pair component and compensating transactions according to a compensated-for/compensating relationship. This relationship is reflected by a begin-on-commit dependency $\mathcal{BCD}$ of the compensating transaction on its associated component transaction [Axiom 19] and a force-commit-on-abort dependency $\mathcal{CMD}$ and a begin-on-abort dependency $\mathcal{BAD}$ of the compensating transaction on the saga transaction [Axiom 20]. If a component transaction aborts and rolls back, there is no meaning for its compensating transaction to execute. On the other hand, if a component transaction commits, the compensating transaction gives the saga the ability to semantically undo its effects by inducing force-commit-on-abort and begin-on-abort dependencies between the compensating transaction and the saga transaction. The correct execution order of the compensating transactions is ensured by the weak-begin-on-commit dependency $\mathcal{WCD}$ between every pair of compensating transactions [Axiom 18]. The begin-on-abort dependency $\mathcal{BAD}$ of CT_{n-1} on

[6]Saga transactions may also handle the interface to the environment, e.g., users.

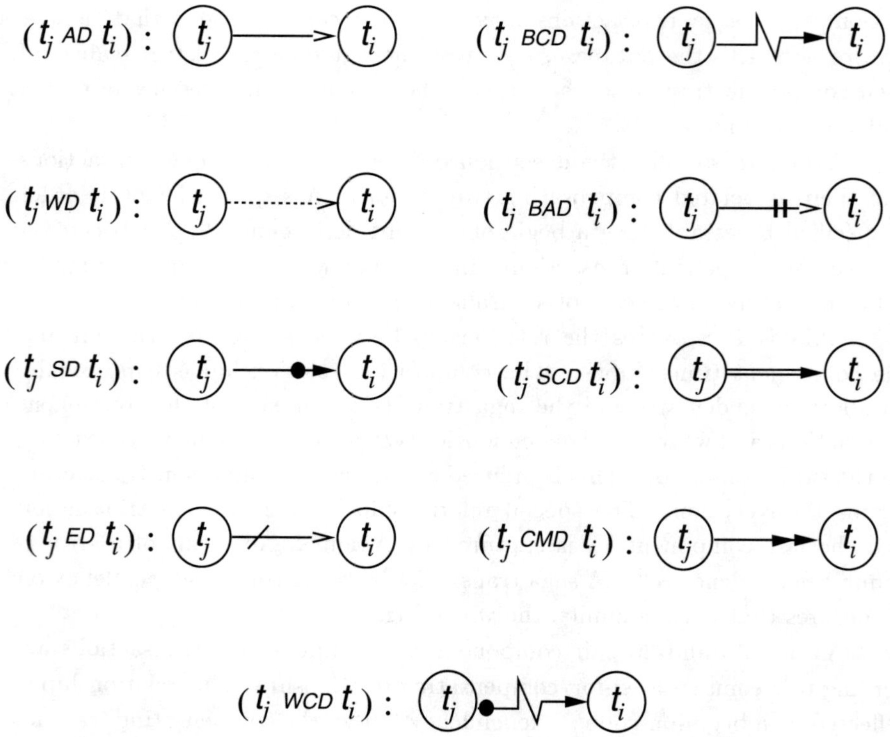

FIGURE 10.2
Dependencies relevant to Sagas

the saga transaction ensures that the compensating transactions do not execute prematurely and concurrently with the component transactions [Axiom 18]. By being the first on the chain of compensating transactions, CT_{n-1}'s outcome need to be considered first for the rest of the compensating transactions to execute.

Figure 10.2 shows the graph representation of the dependencies relevant to sagas. Figures 10.3–10.7 show five snapshots of the evolution of the structure of a saga (dynamics of intra-dependencies): (a) after a saga transaction has invoked begin, (b) when the first component transaction T_1 is in progress, (c) after T_1 commits, (d) when the second component T_2 is in progress and (e) when the last component T_n is in progress and consequently before the commitment of the saga. In these, a shaded node corresponds to a committed transaction.

This axiomatic definition captures the intended behavior of sagas. We now show some of the properties of the saga model using the axioms.

LEMMA 10.1 *Commitment of a Saga*

Let H be a history of a saga S with n component transactions.

$$(\mathsf{Commit}_S \in H) \Rightarrow \forall i, 1 < i \leq n\ (\mathsf{Commit}_{T_{i-1}} \rightarrow \mathsf{Commit}_{T_i})$$

Informally, this lemma states the history in which all component transactions commit in the required order.

PROOF

1. If S commits, T_i $(1 \leq i \leq n)$ must also have committed because of the abort dependency of S on T_i [Axiom 19] and the Fundamental Axiom III which states that a transaction has to either commit or abort [Axiom 7]:

$$\forall i, 1 \leq i \leq n, ((\mathsf{Abort}_{T_i} \in H) \Rightarrow (\mathsf{Abort}_S \in H)) \Leftrightarrow ((\mathsf{Commit}_S \in H) \Rightarrow (\mathsf{Commit}_{T_i} \in H)).$$

2. Given T_i's $(1 < i \leq n)$ begin-on-commit dependency on T_{i-1} [Axiom 18]:

$$\forall i, 1 < i \leq n\ ((\mathsf{Begin}_{T_i} \in H) \Rightarrow (\mathsf{Commit}_{T_{i-1}} \rightarrow \mathsf{Begin}_{T_i})),$$

the Fundamental Axiom II:

$$\forall i, 1 < i \leq n\ ((\mathsf{Commit}_{T_i} \in H) \Rightarrow (\mathsf{Begin}_{T_i} \rightarrow \mathsf{Commit}_{T_i})),$$

and the semantics of the precedence relation, if T_i commits, then T_i commits after T_{i-1} commits:

$$\forall i, 1 < i \leq n\ ((\mathsf{Commit}_{T_i} \in H) \Rightarrow (\mathsf{Commit}_{T_{i-1}} \rightarrow \mathsf{Commit}_{T_i}))$$

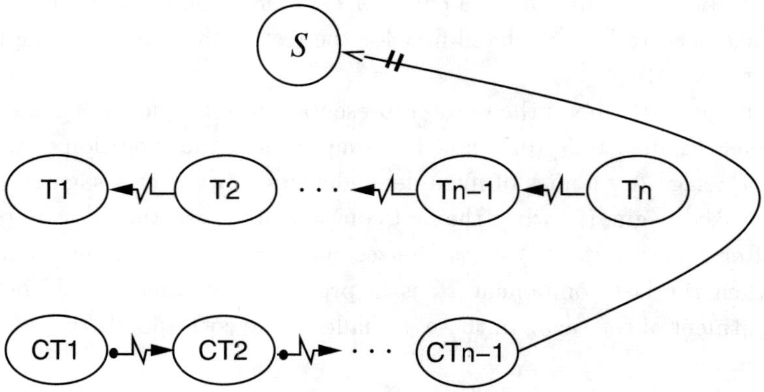

FIGURE 10.3
Structure of a just initiated Saga

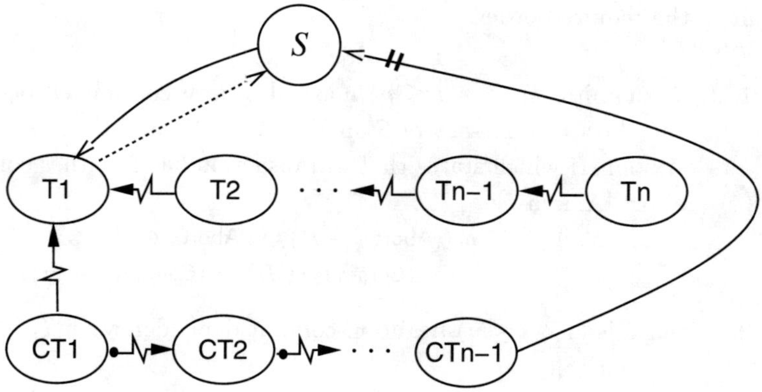

FIGURE 10.4
Structure of a Saga when component T_1 in progress

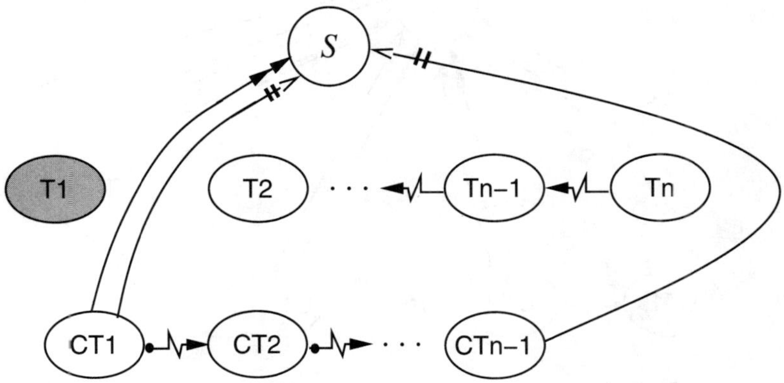

FIGURE 10.5
Structure of a Saga after component T_1 commits

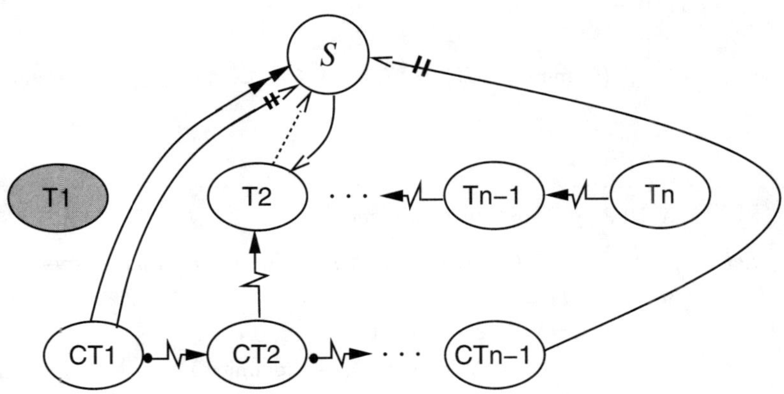

FIGURE 10.6
Structure of a Saga when component T_2 in progress

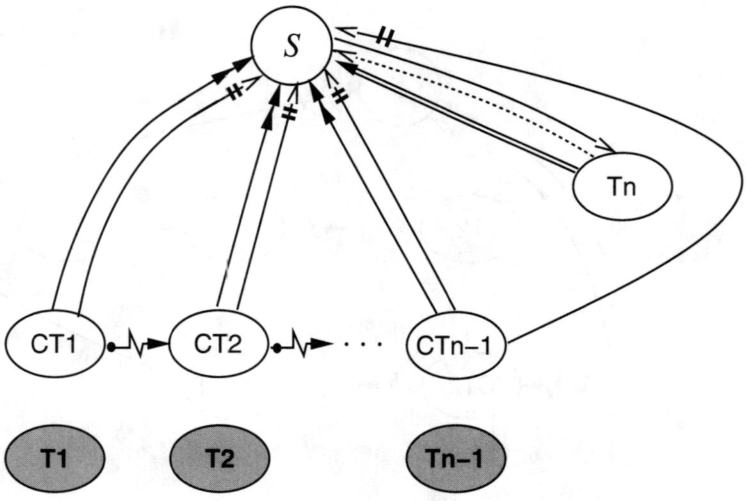

FIGURE 10.7
Structure of a Saga when component T_n in progress

3. Thus, from (1) and (2),

$$(\mathsf{Commit}_S \in H) \Rightarrow \forall i, 1 < i \leq n \ (\mathsf{Commit}_{T_{i-1}} \rightarrow \mathsf{Commit}_{T_i})$$

∎

LEMMA 10.2 *Abortion of a Saga*

Let H be a history of a saga S with n component transactions.

$$\begin{array}{l}(\mathsf{Abort}_S \in H) \Rightarrow \\ \exists k, 1 \leq k \leq n \ \forall i, 1 < i < k-1 \\ \quad (((\mathsf{Abort}_{t_k} \in H) \wedge (\mathsf{Commit}_{T_{i-1}} \rightarrow \mathsf{Commit}_{T_i}) \wedge \\ \quad (\mathsf{Commit}_{T_{k-1}} \rightarrow \mathsf{Commit}_{CT_{k-1}}) \wedge (\mathsf{Commit}_{CT_i} \rightarrow \mathsf{Commit}_{CT_{i-1}})) \vee \\ \exists k, 1 \leq k \leq n \ \forall i, 1 < i < k \\ \quad ((\mathsf{Commit}_{T_{i-1}} \rightarrow \mathsf{Commit}_{T_i}) \wedge \\ \quad (\mathsf{Commit}_{T_k} \rightarrow \mathsf{Commit}_{CT_k}) \wedge (\mathsf{Commit}_{CT_i} \rightarrow \mathsf{Commit}_{CT_{i-1}})))\end{array}$$

Informally, this expresses the history in which for all committed components, their compensating transactions commit in the required order. The first clause corresponds to the case in which a saga aborts while one of its components is in progress whereas the second clause corresponds to the case in which the saga aborts in between the execution of two of its components, i.e., after one of its components has committed and before the next one in order begins executing.

PROOF

Let us first consider the simple case of $k = 1$.

Case 1: If S aborts and T_1 has begun but not yet committed, T_1 is aborted due to the weak-abort dependency of T_1 on S [Axiom 19]. Since CT_1 has a begin-on-commit dependency on T_1 [Axiom 19], CT_1 never executes. This is the trivial case of an aborted saga:

$$(\mathsf{Abort}_S \in H) \Rightarrow (\mathsf{Abort}_{t_1} \in H)$$

Case 2:

1. If S aborts after T_1 commits and before T_2 begins, then CT_1 must commit due to the force-commit-on-abort dependency of CT_1 on S [Axiom 20]:
$$(\mathsf{Abort}_S \in H) \Rightarrow (\mathsf{Commit}_{CT_1} \in H).$$
2. Given the begin-on-commit dependency of CT_1 on T_1, if CT_1 commits, then T_1 must have also committed (see Step 2 of lemma 10.1):
$$(\mathsf{Commit}_{CT_1} \in H) \Rightarrow (\mathsf{Commit}_{T_1} \rightarrow \mathsf{Commit}_{CT_1})$$

Thus, from (1) and (2), $(\mathsf{Abort}_S \in H) \Rightarrow (\mathsf{Commit}_{T_1} \rightarrow \mathsf{Commit}_{CT_1})$.

Now let us consider the general case of $1 < k \leq n$.

Case 3:

3. If S aborts while T_k is in progress, T_k aborts, because of the weak-abort dependency of T_k on S. Consequently, CT_k is never initiated because of its begin-on-commit dependency on T_{k+1}:
$(\mathsf{Abort}_S \in H) \Rightarrow (\mathsf{Abort}_{T_k} \in H))$.

   This also follows, if T_k aborts which causes S to abort due to its abort dependency on T_k.
4. If T_k is in progress, T_j $(1 \leq j < k)$ has committed in the specified order because of the begin-on-commit dependency between

the components:

$$\forall i, 1 < i \leq k-1\ (\mathsf{Commit}_{T_{i-1}} \rightarrow \mathsf{Commit}_{T_i}\cdot$$

5. Given that T_j $(1 \leq j < k)$ have committed, CT_j has a force-commit-on-abort dependency on S. If S aborts, CT_j commits according to force-commit-on-abort dependency:

$$(\mathsf{Abort}_S \in H) \Rightarrow \forall j, 1 < j \leq k\ (\mathsf{Commit}_{CT_j} \in H).$$

6. Given the weak-begin-on-commit dependency of CT_j on CT_{j+1} [Axiom 18], if both CT_j and CT_{j+1} commit, CT_j commits after CT_{j+1} has committed (similar to (2)):

$$(\mathsf{Commit}_{CT_j} \in H) \Rightarrow (\mathsf{Commit}_{CT_{j+1}} \rightarrow \mathsf{Commit}_{CT_j}).$$

From (3), (4), (5) and (6),

$$(\mathsf{Abort}_S \in H) \Rightarrow \exists k, 1 \leq k \leq n\ \forall i, 1 < i < k-1$$
$$((\mathsf{Abort}_{t_k} \in H) \wedge (\mathsf{Commit}_{T_{i-1}} \rightarrow \mathsf{Commit}_{T_i}) \wedge$$
$$(\mathsf{Commit}_{T_{k-1}} \rightarrow \mathsf{Commit}_{CT_{k-1}}) \wedge (\mathsf{Commit}_{CT_i} \rightarrow \mathsf{Commit}_{CT_{i-1}}))$$

Case 4: The other general case in which S aborts after T_k commits and before T_{k+1} begins is similar to Case 3 without the step (3).

■

THEOREM 10.1

The component transactions of a saga produce one of the following committed histories:

1. $\forall i, 1 < i \leq n\ (\mathsf{Commit}_{T_{i-1}} \rightarrow \mathsf{Commit}_{T_i})$
2. $\exists k, 1 \leq k \leq n\ \forall i, 1 < i < k\ ((\mathsf{Commit}_{T_{i-1}} \rightarrow \mathsf{Commit}_{T_i}) \wedge$
   $(\mathsf{Commit}_{T_k} \rightarrow \mathsf{Commit}_{CT_k}) \wedge (\mathsf{Commit}_{CT_i} \rightarrow \mathsf{Commit}_{CT_{i-1}}))$

PROOF

This theorem follows from lemmas 10.1 and 10.2 and the committed projection of the history.

■

10.4.1 A Special Case of Sagas

A special case of sagas is a saga whose transaction structure does not have a saga transaction. The first component transaction T_1 marks the beginning of the saga as if it issues the Begin_S significant event, and the last transaction T_n commits the saga as if it issues the $Commit_S$ significant event.

Here is the axiomatic definition of the special Sagas.

DEFINITION

t denotes either a T_i, a component transaction, or a CT_i, a compensating transaction of T_i.

1. $SE_t = \{\mathsf{Begin}, \mathsf{Commit}, \mathsf{Abort}\}$
2. $IE_t = \{\mathsf{Begin}\}$
3. $TE_t = \{\mathsf{Commit}, \mathsf{Abort}\}$
4. t satisfies the fundamental Axioms I to IV
5. $View_t = H_{ct}$
6. $ConflictSet_t = \{p_{t'}[ob] \mid t' \neq t, \mathcal{I}nprogress(p_{t'}[ob])\}$
7. $\exists ob\ \exists p\ (Commit_t[p_t[ob]] \in H) \Rightarrow (\mathsf{Commit}_t \in H)$
8. $(\mathsf{Commit}_t \in H) \Rightarrow \forall ob\ \forall p\ ((p_t[ob] \in H) \Rightarrow (Commit_t[p_t[ob]] \in H))$
9. $\exists ob\ \exists p\ (Abort_t[p_t[ob]] \in H) \Rightarrow (\mathsf{Abort}_t \in H)$
10. $(\mathsf{Abort}_t \in H) \Rightarrow \forall ob\ \forall p\ ((p_t[ob] \in H) \Rightarrow (Abort_t[p_t[ob]] \in H))$
11. $\forall ob\ \exists p\ (p_t[ob] \in H) \Rightarrow (ob\ is\ atomic)$
12. $(\mathsf{Commit}_t \in H) \Rightarrow \neg(t\mathcal{C}^*t)$
13. $post(\mathsf{Begin}_{T_1}) \Rightarrow (((T_i\ \mathcal{BCD}\ T_{i-1}) \in DepSet_{ct}) \wedge ((CT_j\ \mathcal{WCD}\ CT_{j+1}) \in DepSet_{ct})) \wedge ((CT_{n-1}\ \mathcal{BAD}\ T_n) \in DepSet_{ct})$
   where $1 < i \leq n$ and $1 \leq j < n-1$
14. $post(\mathsf{Begin}_{T_i}) \Rightarrow ((CT_i\ \mathcal{BCD}\ T_i) \in DepSet_{ct})$, where $1 \leq i < n$
15. $post(\mathsf{Commit}_{T_i}) \Rightarrow (((CT_i\ \mathcal{CMD}\ T_{i+1}) \in DepSet_{ct}) \wedge ((CT_i\ \mathcal{CMD}\ T_n) \in DepSet_{ct})$
   where $1 \leq i < n$

Beyond the obvious difference arising from discarding the axioms related to the saga transaction type — Axioms 1–3, 8 and 21, the substantive differences between this axiomatic definition and the original one are:

(a) The Begin_{T_1} event replaces the Begin_S event in all relevant axioms.

(b) Axiom 13 which replaces Axiom 18 of the original definition, substitutes S with T_n.

(c) Axiom 15 which corresponds to Axiom 20 of the original definition, induces an additional force-commit-on-abort dependency $\mathcal{CMD}$ of the compensating transaction CT_i on the component transaction T_{i+1} — the component that executes after CT_i's corresponding component transaction T_i.

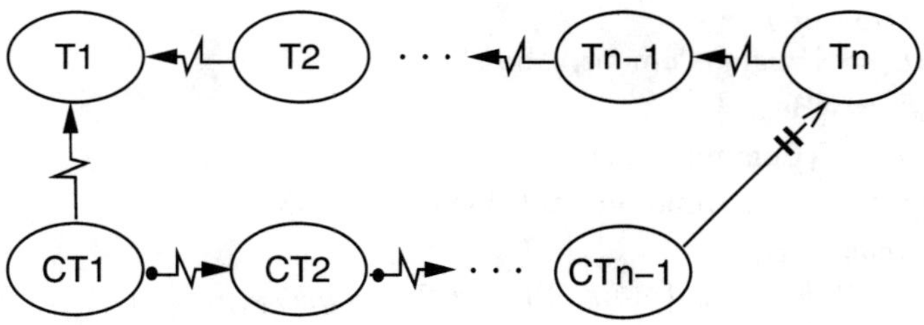

FIGURE 10.8
Structure of a special Saga before component T_1 commits

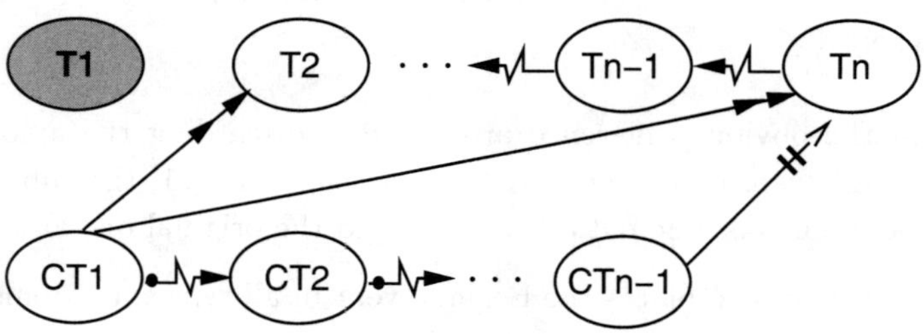

FIGURE 10.9
Structure of a special Saga after component T_1 commits

These differences reflect the fact that, in the special saga, T_1 and T_n carry the control role of the saga transaction, respectively, initiating and terminating the saga.

Figures 10.8 and 10.9 show snapshots of the structure of the special saga before and after the commitment of T_1.

Using these axioms, it is not hard to show that lemmas and theorem similar to lemmas 10.1 and 10.2 and theorem 10.1 hold for the special saga.

10.5 Variations of the Sagas Model

Since serializability and failure atomicity are not associated with a saga, a saga has no notion of commitment control beyond transaction boundaries. However, the commitment of a saga is dependent on the commitment of its components. A failure of a component forces the whole saga to abort. In this respect, sagas do not have the flexibility, e.g., of nested transactions, in being able to retry an aborted component, or to try an alternative component, or even to ignore a failed component.

In the following subsections, we show how sagas can be transformed to exhibit these properties by changing the dependencies defined in the original version of sagas. For the sake of brevity, we focus on the concepts and less on the formal aspects of the transformed sagas model. Where appropriate, we give the new (version of) axioms that formalize the properties of the new model.

10.5.1 Sagas with no Special Relation with Last Component

The original sagas call for a special relationship between a saga transaction and the last component transaction T_n because if T_n succeeds in committing then the saga commits as well. A saga thus lacks the flexibility of aborting after its last component has committed. Aborting a saga is easy and efficient as long as the information needed by the compensating transactions is available and easily accessible in the database. By committing a saga, this information is removed from the system.

To provide sagas with this flexibility, available, for example, in nested transactions, it is sufficient to treat the last component transaction as any other component. This means, first of all, that T_n needs to be associated with

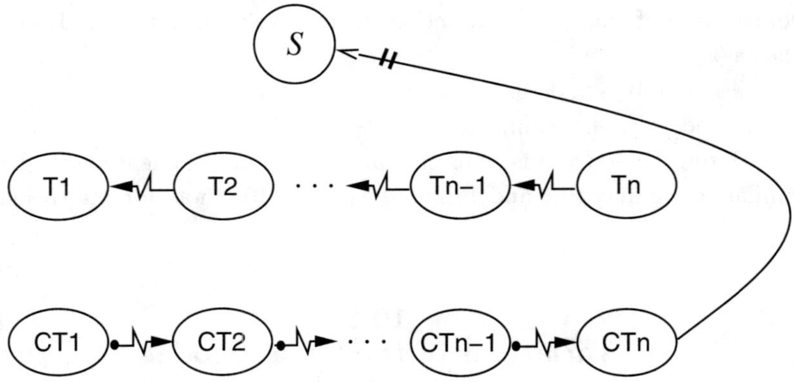

FIGURE 10.10
Structure of a Saga without special relation with T_n

a compensating transaction CT_n. The axiomatic definition of such a saga can be derived from the original axiomatic definition of sagas by dropping the last axiom, Axiom 21, and modifying Axioms 18 and 20 to include T_n. Figure 10.10 shows the structure of such a saga resulting from the modified Axiom 18. This corresponds to Figure 10.3 that represents the structure of the original saga.

10.5.2 Sagas with Vital Components

The relation between the saga and its component transactions is reflected, as stated by Axiom 19, by abort dependencies of the saga transaction on *each* of the component transactions and weak-abort dependencies of *each* of the component transactions on the saga.

Let us consider the case of a saga transaction that has *no* abort dependency on the first component transaction T_1 (see Figure 10.11). Since the abort dependencies of a saga transaction on the component transactions are the only constraints on the completion of a saga, T_1 can abort without preventing the saga from committing. In other words, the saga can ignore T_1 if it aborts (see Figure 10.12. Dotted nodes correspond to aborted transactions and transactions that cannot begin). This is not the case with the rest of the component transactions. Thus, the semantics of the relationship between a saga transaction and the component transactions changes with the removal

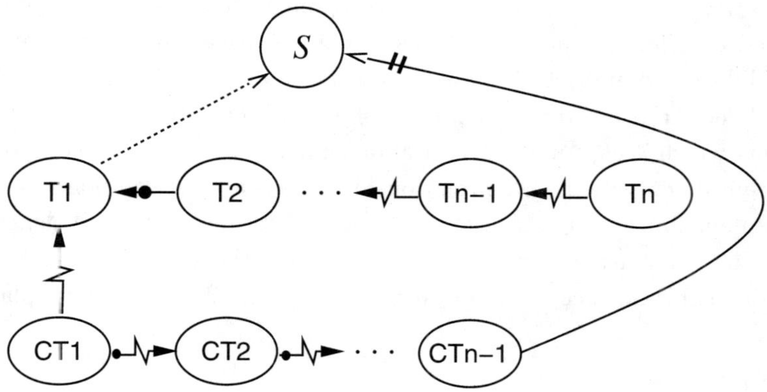

FIGURE 10.11
Structure of a Saga when non-vital component T_1 in progress

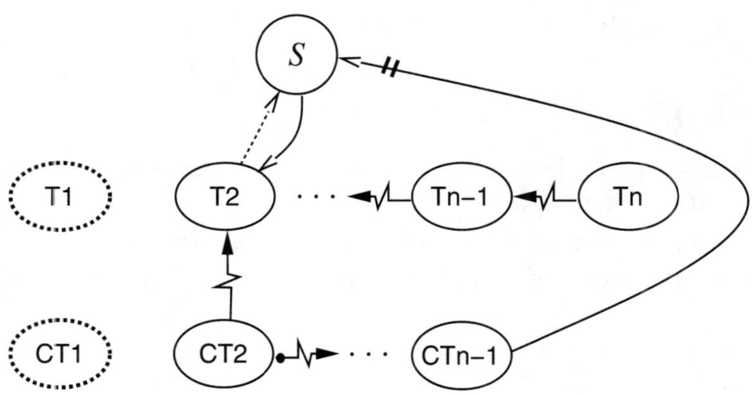

FIGURE 10.12
Structure of a Saga after non-vital component T_1 aborts

of the abort dependency. Specifically, there can be two types of relationships between sagas and its component transactions, namely, a *vital relation* and a *non-vital relation*. Consequently, component transactions can be distinguished as *vital* and *non-vital* transactions. A saga can commit only if its *vital* children commit. In the above case T_1 is not vital.

There is also a different relationship between vital and non-vital components which is captured by a serial dependency $\mathcal{SD}$ of a vital component on a non-vital component. The relationship between vital components remains the same as in the original saga captured by a begin-on-commit dependency.

The axiomatic definition of such a saga is the same as the original axiomatic definition except for Axioms 18 and 19 which need to be replaced by:

1. $VITAL_S = \{T_1\}$
2. $post(\mathsf{Begin}_S) \Rightarrow$
$$(((T_{i-1} \in VITAL_S) \Rightarrow ((T_i \ \mathcal{BCD}\ T_{i-1}) \in DepSet_{ct})) \wedge$$
$$(((T_{i-1} \notin VITAL_S) \Rightarrow ((T_i \ \mathcal{SD}\ T_{i-1}) \in DepSet_{ct})) \wedge$$
$$((CT_j \ \mathcal{WCD}\ CT_{j+1}) \in DepSet_{ct}) \wedge$$
$$((CT_{n-1} \ \mathcal{BAD}\ T_n) \in DepSet_{ct}))$$
where $1 < i \leq n$, and $1 \leq j < n-1$
3. $post(Begin_{T_i}) \Rightarrow ((S \ \mathcal{AD}\ T_i) \in DepSet_{ct})$
where $1 \leq i < n$ and $T_i \notin VITAL$
4. $post(Begin_{T_i}) \Rightarrow (((T_i \ \mathcal{WD}\ S) \in DepSet_{ct}) \wedge$
$$((CT_i \ \mathcal{BCD}\ T_i) \in DepSet_{ct}))$$
where $1 \leq i < n$

and corresponds to the axiomatic definition of the transaction model proposed in [BHMC90, GGK+91].

Using the above modified set of axioms, the correct committed histories of such a saga can be shown in a similar fashion as in Theorem 10.1.

THEOREM 10.2

The component transactions of a saga whose first component is a non-vital *transaction produce one of the following committed histories:*

1. *All component transactions commit in the required order:*
$\forall i, 1 < i \leq n \ (\mathsf{Commit}_{T_{i-1}} \rightarrow \mathsf{Commit}_{T_i})$
2. *All vital component transactions commit in the required order:*
$\forall i, 2 < i \leq n \ (\mathsf{Commit}_{T_{i-1}} \rightarrow \mathsf{Commit}_{T_i})$

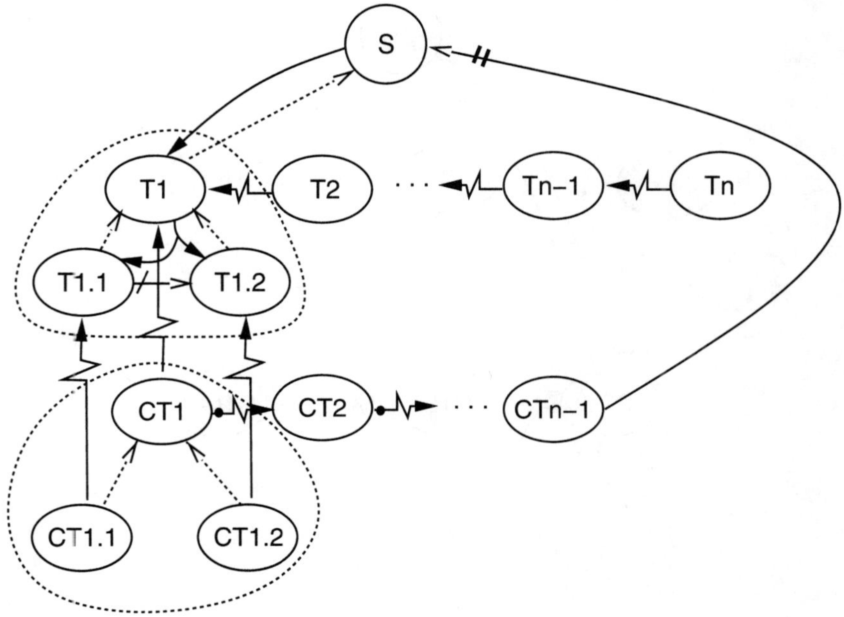

FIGURE 10.13
Saga structure when nested saga component T_1 in-progress

3. *For all committed components, their compensating transactions commit in the required order:*

$$\exists k, 1 \leq k \leq n\ \forall i, 1 < i < k$$
$$((\mathsf{Commit}_{T_{i-1}} \rightarrow \mathsf{Commit}_{T_i}) \wedge$$
$$(\mathsf{Commit}_{T_k} \rightarrow \mathsf{Commit}_{CT_k}) \wedge (\mathsf{Commit}_{CT_i} \rightarrow \mathsf{Commit}_{CT_{i-1}}))$$

10.5.3 Sagas of Sagas

The need for a more flexible transaction model created the concept of sagas. However, as we have already mentioned, sagas lack the flexibility to retry an aborted component, or to try an alternative component or even to ignore a failed component transaction. In the previous section, we saw that, by distinguishing between vital and non-vital transactions, a saga is able to

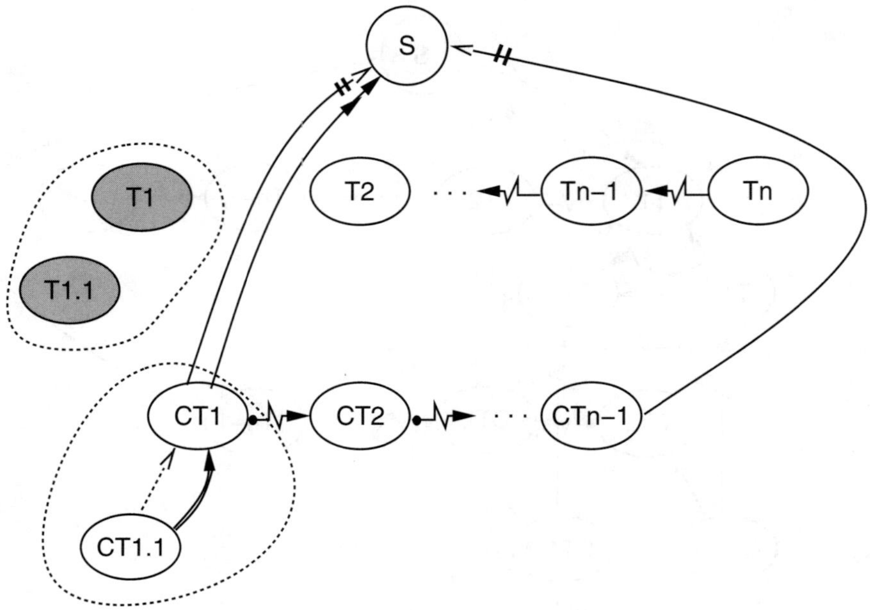

FIGURE 10.14
Saga structure after nested saga component T_1 commits

ignore a failed component. This was achieved fairly easily since the vitality of a component was manifested by the presence of an abort dependency of the saga transaction on the component transactions. Unfortunately, this is not sufficient when alternative transactions [BHMC90, ELLR90] and contingency transactions [BHMC90] are considered. For example, if two components exist where one is an alternative of the other, then both of them have to commit in order for the saga to commit. This contradicts the *at-most-one* semantics of alternative transactions — both alternatives cannot commit. This observation points to the concept of nested sagas[7] which are component transactions of sagas (Figures 10.13 and 10.14).

Dependencies between a nested saga transaction and the components of the nested saga are different from those of a (top) saga transaction on its

[7]Nested Sagas corresponds to a class of sagas with complex structure and hence, it is different from the nested saga model proposed in [GGK+91].

associated components. A nested saga is similar to a saga with non-vital components in the sense that a nested saga can commit even if some of its components abort. However, a nested saga has to abort if all of its component abort. This is captured through a *set-abort dependency* of the nested saga transaction on its associated component transactions:

Set-Abort Dependency (t_j $\mathcal{SAD}$ $\{t_i | 1 \leq i \leq k\}$): if all t_i $(1 \leq i \leq k)$ abort then t_j aborts; i.e., $(\bigwedge_{1 \leq i \leq k}(\mathsf{Abort}_{t_i} \in H)) \Rightarrow (\mathsf{Abort}_{t_j} \in H)$.

In Figure 10.13, set-abort dependency corresponds to an arrow with multiple heads. Set-abort dependency brings out the fact that dependencies may involve more than two transactions.

Each component transaction of a nested saga has a weak-abort dependency $\mathcal{WD}$ on the nested saga transaction. As in the original saga, the weak-abort dependency ensures that if the nested saga aborts while its component transactions are still executing, its component transactions are also aborted.

A nested saga with this structure can exhibit different behaviors depending on the dependencies between its component transactions. In the simplest case, where no dependencies exist between the component transactions, nested sagas exhibit *at-least-one* semantics.

An *exclusion dependency* $\mathcal{ED}$ between the component transactions $T_{1.1}$ and $T_{1.2}$ of a nested saga T_1, as in Figure 10.13, captures the properties of alternative transactions. In particular, alternative transactions execute concurrently while the exclusion dependency ensures the *at-most-one* semantics.

Note that due to the semantics of the exclusion dependency $T_{1.1}$ cannot commit until $T_{1.2}$ aborts. This implies that $T_{1.2}$ is the preferable alternative. A second exclusion dependency from $T_{1.2}$ to $T_{1.1}$ will make both alternatives equally preferable.

Contingency transactions are a special case of alternative transactions in that they cannot execute concurrently. The sequential order of execution of contingency transactions is specified by means of begin-on-abort dependencies. Exclusion dependencies between the contingency transactions ensure the *at-most-one* semantics.

By being a component of a saga, a nested saga must be associated with a compensating transaction. In some special cases, a compensating transaction may be sufficient to compensate for any alternative or contingency transaction of a nested saga. It is often the case, however, that different transactions will need different compensating transactions. For this reason, a nested saga may be associated with a compensating saga whose components are the compensating transactions of the component transactions of the nested saga. Begin-on-commit dependencies pair nested and compensating saga transactions and their associated component transactions (see Figure 10.13) reflecting their compensated-for/compensating relationship. If a component transaction aborts and rolls back, there is no meaning for its compensating transaction to execute. On the other hand, if a component transaction commits, a strong-commit dependency of a component transaction of a compensating saga on the compensating saga transaction propagates the effects of the force-commit-on-abort dependency of the compensating saga transaction on to the top saga transaction.

10.5.4 Sagas with Non-Compensatable Components

Sagas are built on the assumption that all their component transactions can be compensated for. There are many cases of component transaction that cannot be compensated for. There are even more cases of component transactions whose effects on objects can be compensated, but they involve real actions such as messages that cannot be semantically undone. In atomic transactions such actions are deferred until the commit time of the transaction. Since in sagas component transactions commit independently this approach is not directly applicable and hence sagas, as originally defined, are not applicable in such situations.

There are three different ways in which sagas can be extended to include non-compensatable component transactions. Each method is suitable for different situations and allows different levels of concurrency. The first method is applicable for sagas whose non-compensatable components execute concurrently. In such a situation, the weak-abort dependency of the component transaction on the saga transaction can be replaced with an abort-dependency coupling in this way the commitment of the saga with the commitment of the non-compensatable transactions. Thus, real actions are deferred until the saga commits.

Clearly, this method is not applicable for sequential executions because a non-compensatable component transaction T will block the execution of any component transaction which has a begin-on-commit dependency on T. In the second method, a new significant event, e.g., Finish, can be associated with non-compensatable transactions and a new dependency can be defined that relates the Begin and Finish events. (Recall that this is possible in ACTA because ACTA is an open-ended framework allowing the introduction of new dependency relations.) Finish can be invoked by a transaction to terminate its access to shared objects in the database. However, Finish does not commit the operations invoked by a transaction on the shared objects. Thus, Finish does not replace Commit which is still needed to make the changes of a transaction effective in the database.

Defining **begin-on-finish dependency** ($t_j\ \mathcal{BFD}\ t_i$) is straight forward: transaction t_j cannot begin execution until transaction t_i finishes; i.e.,

$(\mathsf{Begin}_{t_j} \in H) \Rightarrow (\mathsf{Finish}_{t_i} \rightarrow \mathsf{Begin}_{t_j})$.

Thus, in this second method, if a component transaction T_i is non-compensatable,

1. $T_{i+1}\ \mathcal{BFD}\ T_i$,
2. $(\mathsf{Finish}_{T_i} \in H) \Rightarrow \not\exists p\ \not\exists ob\ (\mathsf{Finish}_{T_i} \rightarrow p_{T_i}[ob])$
3. T_i can invoke Commit only after invoking Finish:
   $(\mathsf{Commit}_{T_i} \in H) \Rightarrow (\mathsf{Finish}_{T_i} \rightarrow \mathsf{Commit}_{T_i})$,
4. if the saga aborts, T_i aborts after the components that execute following T_i have been compensated:
   $(\mathsf{Abort}_S \in H) \Rightarrow \forall j, i \leq j \leq n\ (\mathsf{Commit}_{CT_j} \rightarrow \mathsf{Abort}_{T_i})$, and
5. the saga commits iff T_i commits:
   $(\mathsf{Commit}_S \in H) \Leftrightarrow (\mathsf{Commit}_{T_i} \in H)$.

The third method does not require any additional significant events or any new dependencies. It simply structures non-compensatable transactions as subtransactions (*a lá* nested transactions) which at commit time delegate all the operations in their AccessSet, i.e., the operations that non-compensatable transactions have performed, to the saga.

Thus, in this last method, if T_i is a non-compensatable component of a saga S:

$$(\mathsf{Commit}_{T_i} \in H) \Leftrightarrow (Delegate_{T_i}[S, AccessSet_{T_i}] \in H).$$

If the saga aborts, all the effects of the operations in its Access Set are rolled back.

Subsection 10.5.1 through 10.5.4 discussed four different extensions to the original saga model and showed how their definitions are mutations of the original definition. Of course, it is possible to conceive of a model for sagas which combines two or more of these extensions. One can fairly easily develop the axiomatic definitions for such combined models given our discussions here. One such combination is a model similar to that of S–Transactions [VE91].

10.6 Conclusions

This paper shows how ACTA captures the (extended) functionality of a transaction model (1) by allowing the specification of significant events beyond commit and abort, (2) by allowing the specification of arbitrary transaction structures in terms of dependencies involving any significant event, (3) by supporting finer grain visibility for objects in the database by associating a view and a conflict set with each transaction and the notion of delegation, (4) and by facilitating object-specific and transaction-specific semantic-based concurrency control.

The application of ACTA to specify the properties of sagas revealed a number of possible variations to the saga model that are of practical interest. These involve (1) permitting a saga to commit even if a (non-vital) subset of the components of a saga aborted; (2) considering the compensatability of a saga component; (3) incorporating the notion of nested sagas within the saga model; and (4) combining alternative and contingency transaction model with the saga model. The ease with which it was possible to consider these variations, once the original Sagas model was characterized, speaks to the modeling capabilities of ACTA. Further, just as it was possible to show the correctness properties of original sagas model, it is possible to specify the correctness requirements of the extended Sagas and show the correctness given the characterizations of these extensions.

Bibliography

[BHG87] Bernstein, P. A., Hadzilacos, V., and Goodman, N. *Concurrency Control and Recovery in Database Systems.* Addison-Wesley, Reading, MA, 1987.

[BHMC90] Buchmann, A., Hornick, M., Markatos, E., and Chronaki, C. Specification of a Transaction Mechanism for a Distributed Active Object System. In *Proceedings of the OOPSLA/ECOOP 90 Workshop on Transactions and Objects*, pages 1–9, 1990.

[BKK85] Bancilhon, F., Kim, W., and Korth, H. A model of CAD Transactions. In *Proceedings of the 11th International Conference on VLDB*, pages 25–33, 1985.

[BR90] Badrinath, B. and Ramamritham, K. Performance Evaluation of Semantics-based Multilevel Concurrency Control Protocols. In *Proceedings of the ACM SIGMOD International Conference on Management of Data*, pages 163–172, 1990.

[Chr91] Chrysanthis, P. K. *ACTA, A Framework for Modeling and Reasoning about Extended Transactions.* PhD thesis, Department of Computer and Information Science, University of Massachusetts, Amherst, Massachusetts, 1991.

[CR90] Chrysanthis, P. K. and Ramamritham, K. ACTA: A Framework for Specifying and Reasoning about Transaction Structure and Behavior. In *Proceedings of the ACM SIGMOD International Conference on Management of Data*, pages 194–203, 1990.

[CR91] Chrysanthis, P. K. and Ramamritham, K. A Unifying Framework for Transactions in Competitive and Cooperative Environments. *IEEE Bulletin on Office and Knowledge Engineering*, 4(1):3–21, 1991.

[CR91b] Chrysanthis, P. K. and Ramamritham, K. A Formalism for Extended Transaction Models. *Proceedings of the 17th International Conference on VLDB*, 1991.

[CRR91] Chrysanthis, P. K., Raghuram, S., and Ramamritham, K. Extracting Concurrency from Objects: A Methodology. In *Proceedings of the 1991 ACM SIGMOD International Conference on Management of Data*, 1991.

[DE89] Du, W. and Elmagarmid, A. K. Quasi Serializability: a Correctness Criterion for Global Concurrency Control in InterBase. In *Proceedings of the 15th International Conference on VLDB*, pages 347–355, 1989.

[DHL90] Dayal, U., Hsu, M., and Ladin, R. Organizing Long-Running Activities with Triggers and Transactions. In *Proceedings of the ACM SIGMOD International Conference on Management of Data*, pages 204–214, 1990.

[EGLT76] Eswaran, K., Gray, J., Lorie, R., and Traiger, I. The Notion of Consistency and Predicate Locks in a Database System. *Communications of the ACM*, 19(11):624–633, 1976.

[ELLR90] Elmagarmid, A., Leu, Y., Litwin, W., and Rusinkiewicz, M. A Multidatabase Transaction Model for InterBase. In *Proceedings of the 16th International Conference on VLDB*, pages 507–518, 1990.

[Elm91] Elmagarmid A. (Issue Editor). Special Issue on Unconventional Transaction Management. *Bulletin of the IEEE Technical Committee on Data Engineering*, 14(1), 1991.

[FZ89] Fernandez, M. and Zdonik, S. Transaction Groups: A Model for Controlling Cooperative Transactions. In *Proceedings of the Workshop on Persistent Object Systems: Their Design, Implementation and Use*, pages 128–138, 1989.

[GGK+91] Garcia-Molina, H., Gawlick, D., Klein, J., Kleissner, K., and Salem, K. Modeling Long-Running Activities as Nested Sagas. *Bulletin of the IEEE Technical Committee on Data Engineering*, 14(1):14–18, 1991.

[Gra81] Gray, J. The Transaction Concept: Virtues and Limitations. In *Proceedings of the 7th International Conference on VLDB*, pages 144–154, 1981.

[GS87] Garcia-Molina, H. and Salem, K. SAGAS. In *Proceedings of the ACM SIGMOD International Conference on Management of Data*, pages 249–259, 1987.

[HW88] Herlihy, M. P. and Weihl, W. Hybrid concurrency control for abstract data types. In *Proceedings of the 7th ACM symposium on Principles of Database Systems*, pages 201–210, 1988.

[KLS90] Korth, H. F., Levy, E., and Silberschatz, A. Compensating Transactions: A New Recovery Paradigm. In *Proceedings of the the 16th VLDB Conference*, pages 95–106, 1990.

[KS88] Korth, H. F. and Speegle, G. Formal Models of Correctness without Serializability. In *Proceedings of the ACM SIGMOD International Conference on Management of Data*, pages 379–386, 1988.

[Mos81] Moss, J. E. B. *Nested Transactions: An approach to reliable distributed computing.* PhD thesis, Massachusetts Institute of Technology, 1981.

[PKH88] Pu, C., Kaiser, G., and Hutchinson, N. Split-Transactions for Open-Ended activities. In *Proceedings of the 14th International Conference on VLDB*, pages 26–37, 1988.

[Ska91] Skarra, A. Localized Correctness Specifications for Cooperating Transactions in an Object-Oriented Database. *IEEE Bulletin on Office and Knowledge Engineering*, 4(1):79–106, 1991.

[SS84] Schwarz, P. M. and Spector, A. Z. Synchronizing Shared Abstract Data Types. *ACM Transactions on Computer Systems*, 2(3):223–250, 1984.

[SZ89] Skarra, A. and Zdonik, S. Concurrency Control and Object-Oriented Databases. In *Object-Oriented Concepts, Databases, and Applications*, pages 395–421. ACM Press, 1989.

[VE91] Veijalaine, J. and Eliassen, F. The S–transaction Model. *Bulletin of the IEEE Technical Committee on Data Engineering*, 14(1):55–59, 1991.

[VRS86] Vinter, S., Ramamritham, K., and Stemple, D. Recoverable Actions in Gutenberg. In *Proceedings of the 6th International Conference on Distributed Computing Systems*, pages 242–249, 1986.

[Wei84] Weihl, W. *Specification and Implementation of Atomic Data Types*. PhD thesis, Massachusetts Institute of Technology, 545 Technology Square, Cambridge, MA, 1984.

[Wei88] Weihl, W. Commutativity-Based concurrency control for abstract data types. *IEEE Transactions on Computers*, 37(12):1488–1505, 1988.

11

A Transaction Manager Development Facility for Non Standard Database Systems

Rainer Unland

Gunter Schlageter

Abstract

Transaction management has been thoroughly investigated in the context of conventional (business data processing) applications. There are relatively few studies, however, that address trans- action management issues of '*advanced database applications*' like, e. g., CAD/CAM, CASE, large AI applications or image and voice processing. The demands on transaction management in such application areas differ substantially from those in traditional database applications; in particular, there is a need to support *'enriched' data models* (which include, e. g., complex objects or version and configuration management), *'synergistic' cooperative work*, and *application* or *user supported consistency*. But, unfortunately, the demands are not only sophisticated but also diversified, which means that different application areas might even place contradictory demands on transaction management. This paper deals with these problems and offers a solution by intro- ducing a flexible and adaptable *tool kit approach for transaction management*. This tool kit enables a database implementor or applications designer to assemble application-specific transaction managers. Each such transaction manager is meant to provide a number of individual, application-specific transaction types. Such transaction types can be constructed by selecting a meaningful subset from a "starter set" of basic constituents. This starter set provides, among others, basic components for concurrency control, recovery, and transaction processing control. In a first step these basic components are assembled and adapted to each other to form a kind of (non executable) "skeleton" transaction. Skeleton transactions can be specialized to more meaningful skeleton transactions. Finally, executable transaction types can be constructed by equipping skeleton transaction with the specific semantics of the transaction model of choice. To be able to emulate each kind of application environment the different transaction types must be executable in any order within a nested transaction hierarchy (no predefined order). For this reason we propose a kind of "meta" (transaction) model. It specifies the constraints and rules which need to be obeyed by each transaction type. Particular emphasis was placed on the integration of flexible and powerful concepts for an adequate support of cooperative work.

11.1 Introduction

One of today's most burning database issues is how to adequately support new classes of database applications that are not well served by relational database systems. For example, CAD/CAM, CASE, large data intensive AI applications, or image and voice processing, place demands on database systems that exceed the capabilities of conventional systems by far. Such 'advanced database applications' differ from traditional database applications in a variety of ways, including their data modelling needs, the types of operations of interest, the storage structures and access methods required for their operations to be efficient, and their considerably extended demands on transaction management. One approach to overcome the weakness of traditional database systems is to provide a **database kernel system** which is meant to be the basis for an arbitrary number of application specific database systems implemented on top of the kernel. This approach is being investigated, e. g., in DASDBS [PSSW87], OMS [FB89], or PRIMA [HMMS87]. A very similar approach is the **tool kit approach** where, in addition to a kernel, an **erector set of modules** is provided to allow a sophisticated applications designer or database implementor (DBI) to put together a customized system. This approach is being taken, for example, in EXODUS [CD87] or GENESIS [Bat88]. Advocates of the tool kit approach argue that requirements from the various application areas differ too much as to be able to identify *one* interface that is appropriate for all of them. The consequence of this understanding is to provide a common storage system (kernel) and, in addition, to offer a tool kit as the basis for the construction of application specific front ends. The assumption is that this architecture not only supports applications in a more appropriate and natural way but, additionally, makes the specifically tailored database systems more efficient. However, it is not sufficient to only provide rich and flexible data modelling facilities together with efficient and adaptable storage structures and access methods. New application areas also make sophisticated demands on transaction management (see, e. g., [ELLR90, Kat84, Kel88, KKB88, KSWU85, LP83, NZ89, US89]. However, the traditional approach to transaction processing only works well as long as transactions are rather short and simple. It indisputably falls short of meeting the much more sophisticated demands of advanced database applications. Some buzzwords in this context are *long-duration, interactive transactions, synergistic cooperative work,* and*application* or*user supported consistency.* A first and rather promising answer to these requirements was an extension of the traditional concept of transactions in the way that the otherwise flat transaction model allows transactions to be executed within other transactions. This kind of transaction is called **nested transaction**. In the commonly known (but not original) approach of Moss [Mos81] a nested transaction recursively consists of a set of children that execute atomically with respect to their parents and their siblings. The main achievements of this approach are the support of **modularity** and **failure handling** since the nesting allows the user to structure and delegate his work and to define more graceful units of recovery (namely subtransactions), and a higher degree of **concurrent work** since subtransactions may be executed concurrently. The nested transaction model is the fundamental basis of all 'advanced transaction models' which are proposed in literature. The difference between the various models consists in the number and meaning of the constraints and rules which they place on the way how (nested) transactions have to look like and how they have to interact with each other. Prominent examples of these constraints and rules are the following:

- Most approaches provide different transaction types. However, these types can only be *nested* in a *special, predefined order*. For example,
  - [KKB85] present a model in which a design transaction consists of a number of project transactions each of which consists of a set of cooperating transactions. Each cooperating transaction, in turn, is a hierarchy of client-subcontractor transactions, each of which is a set of designer's transactions.
  - [KSWU85] define a database transaction to be the basis for a set of user transactions. [US89] add to this model group transactions.
- Some proposals require *all* transactions to run a *strict* two-phase lock protocol (locks cannot be released before end-of-transaction (EOT)), e. g., Moss [Mos81] or Katz [Kat84].
- Almost all proposals restrict children to *commit objects* (or locks) to their *parents* only, e. g., [HR87a, HR87b, KLMP84, KKB85, KSWU85, Mos81, US89].
- Some approaches, e. g., [KLMP84, KKB85, US89], only allow *leaf transactions* to *perform operations* on data. *Non-leaf transactions* only serve as a kind of *database* for their children.

Most of these rules and constraints reflect the individual view of the authors on the requirements and conditions of the application area which is supposed to be the target class of the respective transaction model. Consequently, the transaction model may be suitable for a number of application areas, whereas it may be inappropriate for others.

Another observation is that a large number of approaches to advanced transaction modeling concentrate first of all on modularity, failure handling and parallelism while a support of cooperative work is subordinated to serializability. Mostly, the assumption is still made that (sub)transactions are competitors rather than partners. However, appropriate support of cooperative work can only be achieved if the still predominant rigid concurrency control measures (strict isolation) are weakened, e. g., by moving some responsibility for the integrity of the data from the database management system to the application. Of course, this has to be done in a controlled way and the database management system has to offer as much help as possible.

Finally, it has to be considered that the field of new application areas is diversified to a large extent. Applications may differ substantially in their demands and even in their understanding of consistent operations on data. This has led to a number of different, sometimes even contradictory demands on transaction management.

At the point of time when we started our project we had several basic requirements in mind which we wanted to be fulfilled by our approach. The most important are that our approach should not be suited to a special application area but should be application independent, and that our approach should be capable of intensively supporting synergistic cooperative work. However, as the above discussion already indicates, there are a lot of serious arguments which strongly indicate that *one* given transaction manager can only be a more or less satisfactory compromise (see also [NS89] page 5). This observation led us to the assumption that the most promising solution is an approach very similar to the tool kit approach of database systems: a tool kit for transaction management. This tool kit is meant to be part of the general tool kit (or erector set of modules) of the database (kernel) system; i. e., it serves a sophisticated applications designer or database implementor (DBI) to model 'his' application-specific transaction manager in an appropriate and natural way. An application-specific transaction manager is supposed to provide the application with a comprehensive set of transaction types which are especially suited to the requirements of the application. In our model, transaction types may differ in their structure as well as in their behavior. Different transaction types may run different concurrency control schemes, they may rely on different recovery techniques, or they may or may not support operations like checkout and checkin to mention just a few characteristics which make up different transaction types. Since we do not predefine an order in which transaction types have to be executed within a nested transaction (like design transaction consists of a number of project transactions each of which consists of ...) the different transaction types can be executed in any order. By this all kinds of heterogeneously structured transaction trees can be built up. Within such a transaction tree different concepts as, e. g., strict isolation of (sub)transactions (in the sense of serializability) and non-serializable cooperative work can be applied whenever useful. Of course, to support such an unrestricted nesting of transaction types a fundamental set of basic rules (a kind of "meta" transaction model) need to be defined which must be obeyed by each transaction type.

The remainder of this paper is organized as follows. Section 11.2 summarizes the basic terminology used in this paper. The fundamental set of rules of our approach is presented in section 11.3. The characteristics which make up different transaction types are discussed in section 11.4. Section 11.5 concentrates on lock modes. First, a basic set of lock modes will be introduced. Then it will be shown how a subdivision of a lock into a part which describes the effect for the owner of the lock and another part which describes the effect for competitors can offer a sufficient fine granule for the definition of application specific locks. This subdivision of a lock can especially be exploited within nested transactions to intensively support cooperative work. Furthermore, we will motivate and introduce lock modes which can be linked permanently to objects or temporarily to subjects (instead of temporarily to transactions). By this different version models as well as different object types (e. g. standard or library objects) can be supported. Section 11.6 summarizes the general rules of our transaction model. Section 11.7 gives a brief overview of the structure of the tool kit. Section 11.8 concludes the paper and gives hints for further investigations.

Before we start to discuss our approach some simplifications are to be clarified first:

- The current version of the tool kit concentrates on locks as the means of concurrency control.
- The following discussion focuses on long duration transactions. Other transaction types (e. g., conventional (short) transactions) are not considered.

Finally, we wish to acknowledge that part of this work profited from the fundamental discussion of properties of nested transactions in [HR87a] and [HR87b].

11.2 Transaction types

11.2.1 Conventional transaction management

A transaction is a sequence of reads and writes against a common and shared set of data - the database. Transaction management is concerned with supervising the way in which application programs and / or users share the database. A transaction is usually viewed as both the unit of concurrency and the unit of recovery. More specifically, the notion of transaction is commonly associated with four properties [HR83], namely atomicity, consistency, isolated execution, and durability (persistence).

The **atomicity** property means that the sequence of reads and writes in a transaction is regarded as a single atomic action against the database. This means that atomicity defines a transaction as the unit of recovery. It ensures that a transaction either completes successfully or it has no effect on the database at all. Moreover, the system can always recover to the boundaries of a transaction, such that results of partially completed transactions will not be visible.

Consistency assures that a successfully committed transaction always preserves the consistency of the database.

Isolated execution guarantees that the steps of several transactions can be interleaved so that they will not interfere with each other; i. e., it ensures that a transaction is completely shielded from the effects of any other concurrently executing transactions. The commonly agreed criterion for correct isolation is the **serializability property**. It requires that the effect of concurrent execution of more than one transaction is the same as that of executing the same set of transactions in a serial order. To guarantee serializability a transaction manager employs a concurrency control scheme. The most common scheme is **two-phase locking**. It requires a transaction to be well-formed and two-phase. A transaction is **well-formed** if it always locks an entity in an appropriate lock mode before it works with the entity. It is **(simple) two-phase** if it consists of a **growing-phase** in which objects can only be acquired and a following **shrinking phase** in which objects can only be released [Gra79]. If all objects are acquired (released) at once at begin-of-transaction (BOT) (end-of-transaction (EOT)) the lock protocol is called **two-phase with predeclaring (strict two-phase)**. The lock protocol is called **non two-phase** if it is only well-formed; i. e., objects can be acquired and released in arbitrary order. This protocol is especially important if cooperative work is to be supported.

Finally,**durability** guarantees that once a transaction has been committed successfully its results will survive any subsequent malfunction.

Traditional transaction management was mainly developed for business data processing / administrative applications. In such environments transactions are supposed to be rather short (typically at most a few seconds). Transaction management provides exactly one type of transaction which is flat and works directly on the data of the database. Moreover, it ensures strict isolation with the consequence that transactions are not allowed to exchange data. Consequently, any kind of cooperative work is not within the scope of conventional transaction management.

11.2.2 The concept of nested transactions

The atomicity and serializability properties of transactions have been highly useful for conventional business data processing applications. However, they have some rather undesirable consequences for long-duration transactions, that is, transactions whose duration is much longer than that of conventional transactions. The atomicity property would require a long-duration transaction to back out *all* of the work that has been done if it cannot complete successfully. The serializability property would result in the fact that if a long-duration transaction holds a lock on an object, any other long-duration transaction that must access the same object in a conflicting mode is blocked until the first long-duration transaction completes.

The inability of traditional transaction management to support non-conventional application areas in an appropriate way led to an extension of the traditional concept of transactions in that the originally flat transaction model is allowed to include transactions within transactions. This kind of transaction is called **nested transaction**. The idea of nested transaction seems to have originated with Davies [Dav73] some time ago. He defined a nested transaction hierarchy as a collection of nested spheres of control where the outermost sphere is formed by the top-level transaction (see figure 11.2) which incorporates the interface to the outside world. Reed [Ree78] presented the first comprehensive design of a nested transaction system. This design

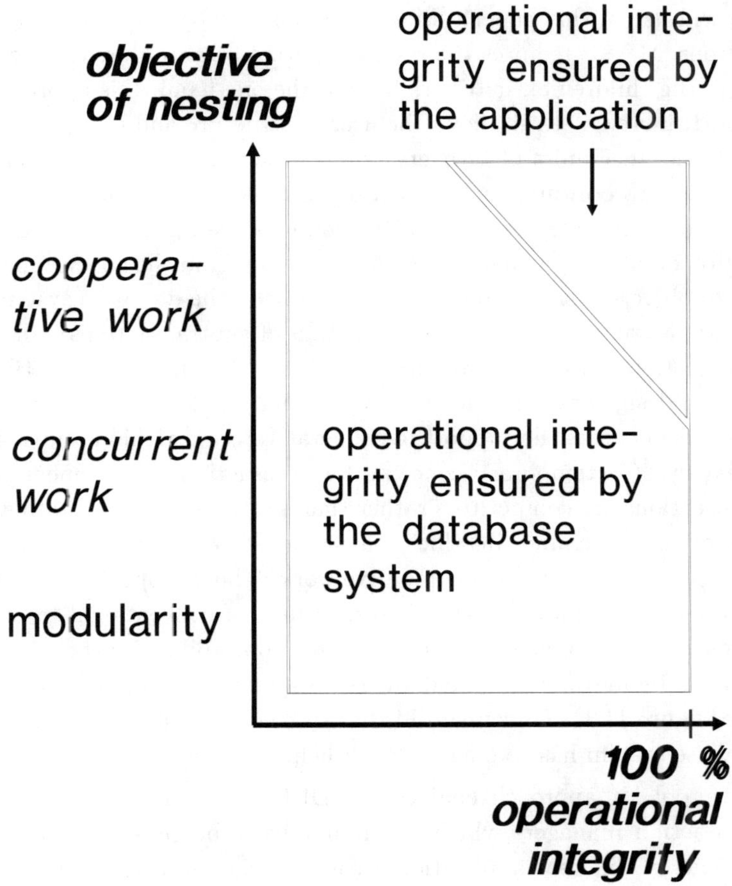

FIGURE 11.1
Motives for the nesting of transactions

uses timestamps for synchronization. It was not before 1981 and the work of Moss [Mos81] that nested transaction attracted greater attention in the database community. Moss defines a **nested transaction** structure to recursively consist of a set of children that execute atomically with respect to their parent and their siblings (figure 11.2 summarizes the 'tree terminology' that we will use in this paper). Moss' commonly known approach to nested transactions [Mos81] requires the results a parent sees from its children to be as though the children execute serially. On the one hand, this approach supports **modularity**; i. e., it allows the user to structure and delegate his work and to define finer units of recovery (subtransactions). On the other hand, it allows users to **concurrently work** on subtasks (within subtransactions). As long as one concentrates on these two features the **operational integrity** (prevention of integrity violation which may result from the concurrent access of users to objects) can still be ensured entirely by the database system since modularity as well as a concurrent execution of subtransactions still permit transactions to be strictly isolated from each other (see figure 11.1). However, especially in design environments this type of nesting is still too restrictive. In such application areas the support of cooperative work within groups of users is mandatory. Contemporary concepts for transaction management assume that transactions are competitors rather than partners. Therefore, they place constraints on the manner in which transactions are allowed to work on the data that prevent any kind of cooperative work. Thus, support of cooperative work can only be achieved if the rigid measures of conventional transaction management can be weakened; i. e., if some responsibility for the integrity of the data can be moved from the database system to the application environment (see figure 11.1). Of course, this has to be done in a controlled way and the database system has to offer as much help as possible.

Our tool kit approach enables the DBI to assemble application specific transaction managers which can individually be suited to the varying requirements of different application areas. Special emphasis was placed on the support of different forms of cooperative work. But, on the other hand, if these concepts are extensively used some burden is placed on the DBI. He has to ensure that the application is 'safe', which means that he has to provide means which allow the application to take on the responsibility for that part of the integrity preservation which was removed from the database system.

Figure 11.2 summarizes the basic 'tree terminology' that will be used in the remainder:

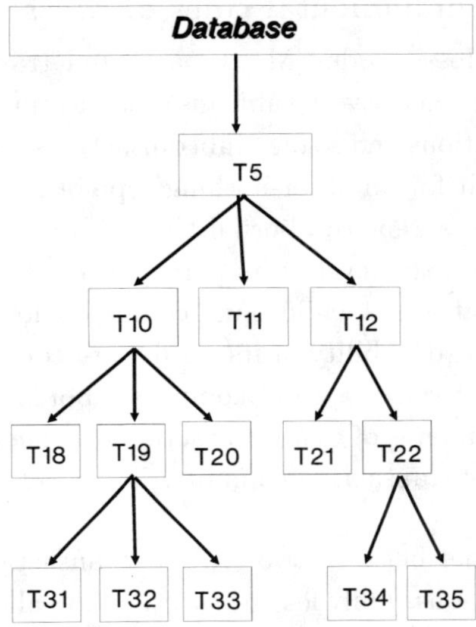

root or top level transaction: root of the transaction hierarchy; here: T5

superior, ancestor: each transaction on the path of a given transaction to the database (ancestor: including the given transaction itself); e. g., T19, T10, T5 form the set of superiors of T31 (ancestor: plus T31 itself)

inferior, descendant: each transaction which is part of the subtransaction hierarchy spanned by a given transaction (descendant: including the given transaction itself); e. g., T21, T22, T34, and T35 form the set of inferiors of T12 (descendant: plus T12 itself)

parent: immediate superior of a transaction; e. g., T5 is the parent of T10 (T11, T12)

child: immediate inferior of a transaction; e. g., T10, T11, T12 are children of T5

sibling: any other child of the parent of a given transaction; e. g., T19, T20 are siblings of T18

leaf transaction: transaction which has no inferior; here: T11, T18, T20, T21, T31 - T35

non-leaf (or inner) transaction: transaction which has at least one inferior; here: T5, T10, T12, T19, T22

ancestor chain: the set of all ancestors of a given transaction (including the database); e. g., the ancestor chain of T34 consists of T34, T22, T12, T5 and the database.

descendant tree (sometimes also called **sphere** of a transaction)**:** the set of all descendants of a given transaction; e. g., the descendant tree of T12 consists of T12, T21, T22, T34, and T35

FIGURE 11.2
Basic tree terminology

11.2.3 Fundamental rules of Moss' approach

According to Moss' model [Mos81] a nested transaction consists of a number of subtransactions. Every subtransaction again may be composed of a number of subtransactions and so on. Subtransactions are the unit of recovery; i. e., they are the unit for an all-or-nothing type of execution. Consequently they do not force the parent to abort if they abort. An aborted child does not leave any marks on the level of its parent; i. e., it leaves the parent as if it had never existed at all. A child must commit before its parent commits. Commit of a child and durability of its results are conditional subject to the fate of its superiors. Even if a child commits, aborting of its superiors will undo its effects. All updates of a subtransaction become permanent only when the enclosing top level transaction commits. These rules are also valid in our approach.

Moss distinguishes between two types of transactions, non-leaf transactions and leaf transactions. Only leaf transactions are allowed to perform operations on objects while non-leaf transactions only serve as a kind of database for their inferiors. With this assumption in mind concurrency control for nested transactions has to obey the following rules:

1. *Meaning of locking*

   For a transaction to perform an operation, the transaction must hold the lock corresponding to that operation.

2. *Strict two-phase locking*

   To avoid rollback propagation a transaction has to be strict two-phase; i. e., no locks can be released until the transaction has either committed or aborted.

3. *Exclusion*

   If a transaction requests a lock, the request can be granted only if all holders of conflicting locks (if any) are ancestors of the requesting transaction.

4. *Release*

   When a transaction succeeds, all its locks are either inherited by its parent or released in case the transaction is top level. When a transaction aborts, all its locks are discarded. If any of its superiors hold a lock on the same object, they continue to do so.

5. *Uniformity*

   All transactions follow these rules.

11.3 Basic concepts and fundamental rules of the tool kit approach

11.3.1 Basic Concepts of the Tool Kit Approach

Most approaches to nested transactions in literature concentrate on modularity and parallelism. Support of cooperative work is only second-rate. However, without question, this feature is a substantial requirement of most non conventional application areas. One essential objective of our approach is to provide such facilities. In this sense our approach is, among others, an extension and enhancement of the concept of nested transactions in the direction of a support of cooperative work.

In this section we will explain the basic terms and concepts of our approach. Moreover, we will compare our approach with Moss' approach to nested transaction and will show how we extended the rules of Moss' model in order to provide more facilities for cooperative work.

The first general concepts of our approach are that we treat a transaction as an abstract data type and that we associate an owner with each transaction:

Object pool

Since in our approach a parent serves as a kind of database for its children we make this explicit by associating with each transaction an object pool. An **object pool** is nothing else but a container for the collection of objects which are associated with the transaction at a given point of time. However, this does not mean that the object pool has to contain each object physically. Instead, it may only manage the object identifiers and the locks imposed on these objects.

The introduction of an object pool points to a substantial difference between Moss' approach and our approach (at least on the conceptual level). In Moss' approach the unit of transfer between transactions is the lock (see figure 11.3). If a transaction acquires a lock it gets the right to perform the corresponding actions on the object (in the database). If transactions want to perform conflicting actions on an object these actions have to be executed one after the other in most approaches to nested transactions. In our approach, if a transaction T acquires a lock it not only gets the lock but also a copy of the object; i. e., the copy of the corresponding object is inserted (at least logically) into the object pool of T. The unit of exchange between transactions is the pair **copy of the object / lock on the object** (see figure 11.4). The reason for this is twofold. First, we want to support the coexistence of

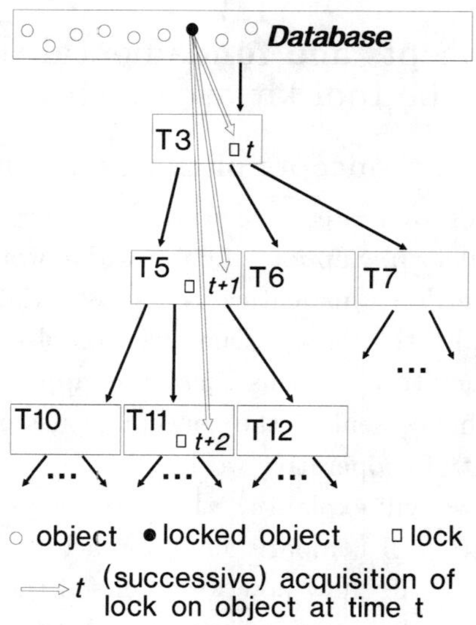

FIGURE 11.3
Transfer unit *lock*

different states of the same object, e. g., during a design process. Different levels within a transaction hierarchy often represent different states of a task. A copy of an object at a higher level of the hierarchy usually represents an older but, as such, "stable" state of the object while a copy at a lower level represents a younger but still "uncertain" state of the object. Secondly, as we will see later, our approach, in order to support cooperative work, permits a controlled concurrent execution of conflicting actions on different copies of the same object. Therefore, it may happen that different copies may exist in the object pools of different transactions. Of course, these different copies need to be integrated to a single, consistent copy at a later point of time.

In the following, if we use the term object or lock (in connection with our approach) we always mean the pair copy of object / (new) lock.

Abstract data type

In our approach a transaction type is seen as an abstract data type; i.e., it is characterized by the operations which come with the type. A number of operations are common to all types; e. g., operations to suspend and continue the transaction, to acquire or release objects, or to commit it. How-

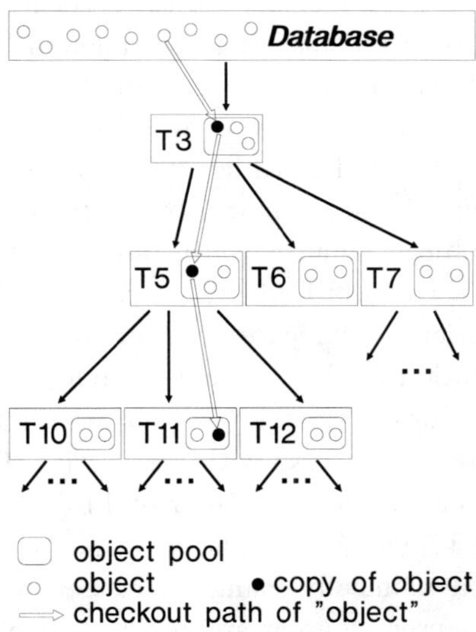

FIGURE 11.4
Transfer unit *copy of object / lock*

ever, these operations may be implemented in different ways (depending on the underlying transaction type). Other operations are only specific to some transaction type since they come with the features by which a transaction type differs from other transaction types. Due to space limitations we will only consider operations in more detail if needed to clarify our concepts. A more comprehensive discussion of the operations can be found in [Unl91].

Owner

Each transaction is associated with an owner who is nothing else but a user or a user group. Only members of the associated user group (in the following called **owners** of a transaction) are allowed to perform operations on the transaction. Moreover, every transaction T can only be active on behalf of one owner at a time. The owner who has control of T can perform any operation associated with T until he explicitly suspends the transaction. An owner may run several transactions at the same time. This enables him to work on different subjects simultaneously, and to use transactions alternatively. However, as an active user U of a transaction T^A, U doesn't have access to objects of a transaction T^B which is not an ancestor of T^A even if U is an owner of T^B (an exception to this rule is an explicit cooperation which will be discussed later on). For example, let us consider the transaction hierarchy of figure 11.3. If U currently works with transaction T10 he is not allowed to acquire objects (in his function as a user of T10) from any transaction of the descendant tree of T7 even if he is also an owner of this transaction. User groups are allowed to dynamically change; i. e., new members can be added to or removed from the user group at any point of time.

Transaction identifier

Each transaction (type) is assigned a unique transaction (type) identifier and a name which has to be established by the user.

11.3.2 Fundamental rules of the tool kit approach

In order to be able to exploit the fundamental semantics of advanced database applications the serializability-based transaction models need to be replaced by models which make it possible to express semantics beyond serializability. Moreover, especially in case of a support of cooperative work, a transaction manager should be able to carefully deal with human or applications involvements in order to ensure correctness of the system as a whole.

With respect to the locking approach there are several ways to achieve these goals, among them the following:

1. By using lock protocols which allow transactions to exchange data or to release data before end-of-transaction (EOT).
2. By providing lock modes which explicitly facilitate a higher degree of concurrent work on data; i. e., which allow the concurrency control component to exploit application-specific semantics.

The second alternative will be discussed in the section about lock modes. In this section we will concentrate on alternative 1. We will start with an example which indicates that an early release of data has to be handled with care.

To avoid rollback propagation most approaches to nested transactions require (sub)transactions to act strictly two-phase. Alternative 1 wants an application, in certain situations, to run (sub)transactions which employ weaker lock protocols, like simple two-phase locking, especially if the application is able to avoid or drastically restrict rollback propagation. However, an early release of objects has to be handled with care since it can violate the two-phase principle as the following discussion will show.

With respect to the acquisition of objects the usual proceeding within nested transactions is that a subtransaction T^S can only acquire objects from its ancestors. To not endanger serializability an object release is treated more restrictively. The commonly applied **object (lock) release rule** requires T^S to upward inherit all its objects (locks) to its parent. While the more restrictive object release rule avoids any consistency problems the more liberal object acquisition rule may lead to consistency problems if subtransactions of a nested transaction are allowed to run other lock protocols than the strict two-phase lock protocol (see figure 11.5; it should be mentioned that some approaches in literature do not treat this problem adequately).

In the given scenario several subtransactions of a nested transaction work, one after the other, on the same object O. First, transaction T5 acquires O from T3 in its growing phase (1), modifies O, and releases the modified object O'. This implies that T5 is now in its shrinking phase. According to the object release rule O must be inherited by the parent of T5, here T3 (2). Next, transaction T6 acquires (3) (this results in the dependency T5 $\longrightarrow$ T6) and modifies O', and releases the modified object O" (4). Again, T3 inherits O". Finally, T12 acquires O" from T3 and modifies it (result: O"').

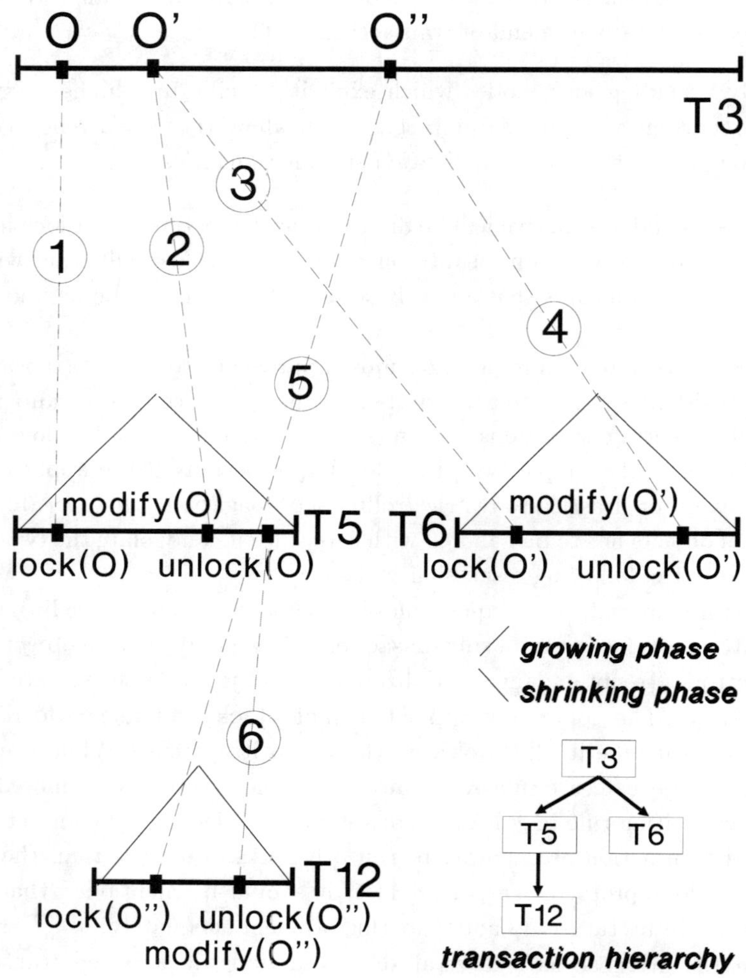

FIGURE 11.5
Example scenario

Since T12 is a child of T5 O"' will be upward inherited to T5 (6). However, T5 is already in its shrinking phase and, therefore, no longer in a position to acquire any object. This situation does not only torpedo the principle of two-phase but it, moreover, violates the principle of strict isolation since T5 gains an insight into the modifications carried out by T6 (which corresponds to the dependency T6 $\longrightarrow$ T5 which, of course, conflicts with the dependency T5 $\longrightarrow$ T6).

Stepwise transfer

If we take a closer look at figure 11.5 it becomes clear that the problem only arises because T12 acquires an object from a superior (different from its parent) without considering the status of its parent T5 (which is already in its shrinking phase). But since T5 inherits all objects from its children it has to be ensured that such a situation cannot occur. The problem can be solved in several ways. One solution is to force each child to consider the status of all transactions in its chain of ancestors up to that transaction from which it wants to acquire an object. Only if the status of each of these transactions permits the acquisition of the object the object can be granted. A more restrictive solution is to only allow a child to acquire objects from its parent. We choose a solution in between which combines the advantages of both approaches. The general principle of our approach is that a transaction T can only acquire objects from its parent. However, if T needs an object O from some other ancestor T^A this is realized by a stepwise check-out of O from the object pool of T^A via the transactions on the path to T (successions of downward check-outs). If, for example, T12 wants to acquire an object O from the parent of T3 such a demand is satisfied by a stepwise check-out of O from the parent of T3 to T3 to T5 to T12. On each level the concurrency control scheme of that level (transaction) is employed to safely transfer O to its destination. The set of objects which is accessible to a transaction is defined by its access view which will be discussed in more detail later on.

In a similar way we define the stepwise check-in of an object O. This means, that we do not require a transaction T to pass O onto its parent. T may transmit O to some other superior T^S if the status (lock protocol) of each transaction on the path to T^S permits such a proceeding (more precisely, if T^S belongs to the release view of T. The release view will be discussed later on).

The installation of the concept of stepwise transfer has the consequence that our approach realizes downward inheritance while most other proposals realize upward inheritance (e. g., [HR87a, HR87b, KLMP84, KKB85, Mos81]. Let us assume that a transaction T wants to acquire an object O from a superior T^S. With **downward inheritance**, O is inserted into the object pool of each transaction on the path from T^S to T *when it moves downward.* With **upward inheritance** the parent inherits the lock on O only after the child has committed; i. e., *when the object (lock) moves upwards.* In both cases O will be added to every object pool on the path from the database to the deepest transaction which has acquired O, with upward inheritance, however, at a later point of time. Downward inheritance has a rather advantageous feature. It guarantees that the object pool of a parent contains all objects of its descendant tree (though, not inevitably the newest status of the object) with the exception of those objects which were newly created by an inferior. Therefore, if a transaction T searches for a special object O it can definitely be concluded that no inferior of the parent of T possesses O if the parent does not. Moreover, if we need to check a lock we only need to consider the ancestor chain up to the first transaction whose object pool contains the object. If, here, the object is not locked in an incompatible mode the lock request can be granted.

Besides the stepwise transfer another fundamental concept of our approach is the two-stage control-sphere.

Two-stage control-sphere

The underlying principle of the **two-stage control-sphere** is that a parent transaction is only responsible for the correct coordination and execution of the work (task) on *its* level. It may define subtasks and start children to deal with these subtasks. Each child, again, is by itself responsible for the correct coordination and execution of its task and, therefore, can decide autonomously, how this task can be executed best. In other words, the characteristics which were established on the level of the parent are only valid for its children. The children, in turn, may establish a different environment for their children (see fig. 11.6). The two-stage control-sphere establishes the foundation for the possibility of executing transactions of different types within one transaction hierarchy.

11.4 Characteristics of transaction types

The various characteristics which make up a transaction can be subdivided into two parts: characteristics which describe the internal representation

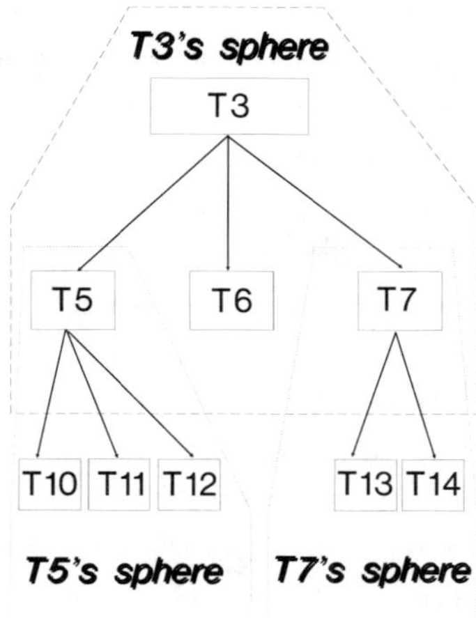

FIGURE 11.6
Two-stage control-sphere

of a type and characteristics which describe its behavior. In this section we will concentrate on the second part. The structure of transaction types will be outlined in section 11.7.

11.4.1 Concurrency control scheme

The two stage control-sphere stands for the possibility that each transaction type T can establish its own concurrency control scheme for its object pool. This means, that each T can independently determine according to which rules descendants of T can acquire objects from T. Such a free choice of concurrency control scheme is possible since the stepwise transfer of objects guarantees that each transaction which is involved in the stepwise transfer needs to use the concurrency control scheme which is required by its parent. For example, in figure 11.7, if transaction T3 wants locks to be used to synchronize access to its object pool its children T5, T6, and T7 need to run a lock protocol if they want to acquire objects from T3. However, each of the children may employ its own type of lock protocol, e. g., T5 may run two-phase locking with predeclaring, T6 simple two-phase locking, and T7 strict two-phase locking (for a discussion of different types of lock protocols see, e. g., [BHG87]. On the other hand, each child may run a different concurrency control scheme for its own object pool. T5, for instance, may run optimistic concurrency control (OCC) [UPS86] with the consequence that the children of T5 (T10, T11, T12) have to run an optimistic concurrency control scheme if they want to acquire objects from T5. For example, if T12 wants to acquire an object O from T3 the stepwise transfer ensures that O is first transferred from the object pool of T3 to the object pool of T5 by using a lock protocol and then from the object pool of T5 to the object pool of T12 by using OCC. To summarize, each transaction T needs to establish two concurrency control schemes. The first scheme lays down according to which rules T can acquire objects from its parent. This scheme must be in accord with the concurrency control scheme which the parent runs on its object pool. The second scheme lays down which concurrency control measures are to be applied to T's own object pool. Here, T is given free hand to install any scheme which is supported by the tool kit.

As already mentioned, the current version of our tool-kit concentrates on the locking approach. It supports all wellknown types of lock protocols (see section 11.2.1), among them *non two-phase locking* and *two-phase locking with extended predeclaring*. **Extended predeclaring** means that objects can be requested as long as no lock was released. If the requested objects are not locked in an incompatible mode they are granted. Otherwise, the lock request is rejected but the transaction is not blocked.

11.4.2 Object visibility (access view and release view)

An **access view** defines the collection of objects which are, in principal, accessible to a transaction T. "In principal" means that an object may not be accessible to T at a given point of time due to the fact that it is being locked by another transaction in an incompatible lock mode.

In the context of this paper we associate with the notion of view the default view provided by the system. No attention is paid to the fact that this view may be restricted by access control mechanisms.

Depending on its position in the transaction hierarchy each transaction T has an individual **access view**. It consists of all objects of the object pools of the chain of ancestors up to the first object pool which is check-out blocked (excluding this object pool) or, if there is none, up to the public database (including the public database). The object pool of the parent T^P

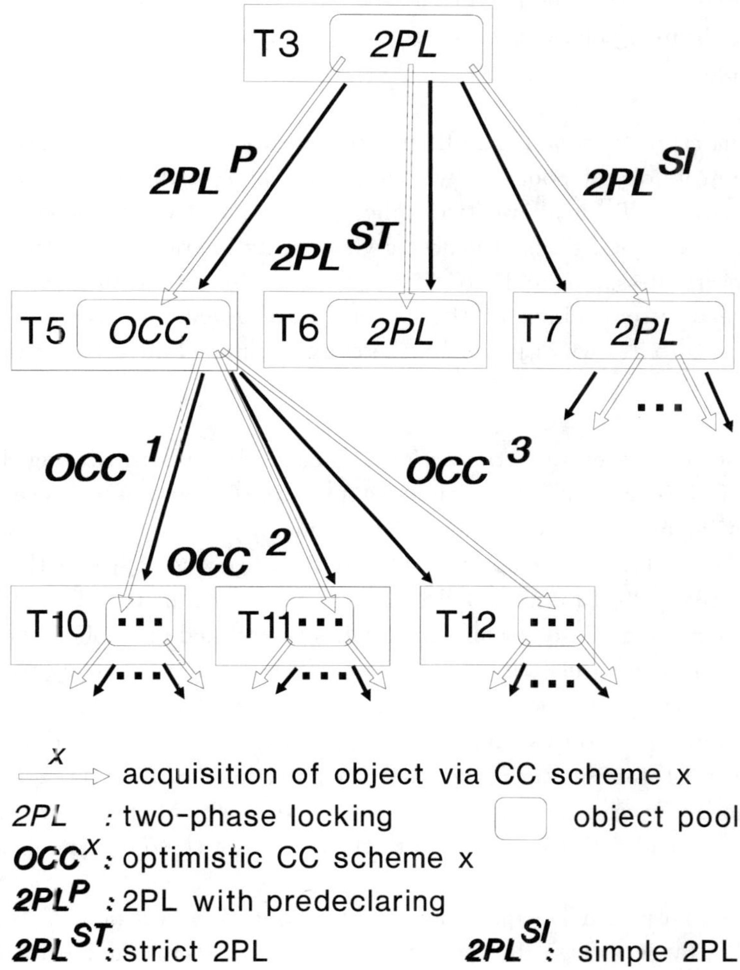

FIGURE 11.7
Use of different CC schemes within a nested transaction

of a transaction T^A is **check-out blocked** if at least one of the following two restrictions is valid:

1. *implicit restriction* T^A runs a two-phase lock protocol and is already in its shrinking phase; i. e., T^A is no longer in a position to acquire objects from T^P.

2. *explicit restriction* T^P explicitly prohibits its inferiors to acquire objects from its object pool or any other object pool of the ancestor chain of T^P; i. e., T^P is allowed to explicitly install a check-out blockade with the consequence that the access views of its inferiors are restricted. If, nevertheless, a child T^C of T^P needs some object O of an object pool of the ancestor chain of T^P this can only be achieved if T^P explicitly transfers O to its own object pool, therefore, making O directly accessible to T^C.

The access view of a transaction T changes dynamically during the lifetime of T since, at any point of time, an ancestor of T may start its shrinking phase or install / remove a check-out blockade.

In figure 11.11 the access view of T38 consists of the objects of the object pools of T38, T26, T15, T8, T4, T1, and the database if neither T4 nor T1 are in their shrinking phase nor an ancestor has established an explicit check-out blockade (T8 cannot be in its shrinking phase since it runs the strict two-phase lock protocol) (please do only concentrate on such features of figure 11.11 which are relevant to this example; other features will be explained later on). As soon as T4 starts its shrinking phase the object pool of T1 and the database are no longer accessible to T38. If T15 installs an explicit check-out blockade the access view of T38 is restricted to the objects of the object pools of T38 and T26.

If a transaction T acquires an object O from an object pool of its access view, O is (at least logically) added to all object pools on the path from the original object pool of O to T. This implies that the access view of T may contain different states of an object (since higher object pools may contain "older" versions of an object). Let us again consider transaction T38 of figure 11.11. If T38 wants to acquire object O from transaction T15, O is also part of the object pools of T8, T4 and T1 (unless O was newly created by some descendant of T15). Since, e. g., T8 may have modified O before it was transferred to T15, different states of O exist within the access view of T38.

This leads to the problem of a "lost update" if T38 acquires O from the object pool of T4. Therefore, by definition, the access view of T38 only contains one instance of O, namely the instance of the first ancestor of T38 whose object pool contains O. In our example this is the instance of the object pool of T15 if O currently doesn't belong to the object pool of T26.

Similar to the notion of access view we define the notion of **release view**. A release view determines the object pool up to which an object of a given transaction T can be released at most (if no other lock on the object prevents this). The release view consists of all object pools of the ancestor chain up to the first ancestor which is check-in blocked (excluding this object pool) or, if there is none, up to the public database (including the public database). An object pool of the parent T^P of a transaction T^B is **check-in blocked**, if at least one of the following two restrictions is valid:

1. *implicit restriction* T^B runs a two-phase lock protocol and is still in its growing phase, i. e., T^B is not allowed to insert objects into the object pool of T^P.

2. *explicit restriction* T^B explicitly prohibits the insertion of objects into the object pool of its parent; i. e., T^B is allowed to explicitly install a check-in blockade. T^B may install a check-in blockade to prevent its inferiors from releasing objects to a superior of it. Due to the nature of check-in and check-out, a check-out blockade works on the level it was defined while a check-in blockade only becomes valid on the level of the parent (since, otherwise, a child would not be able to release any object at all); i. e., in case T^B installs an explicit check-in blockade a child of T^B can still insert an object into the object pool of T^B but not in the object pool of any superior of T^B.

In figure 11.11 the object pool of T1 is check-in blocked for T4 and any inferior of T4 as long as T4 is in its growing phase. The object pool of T8 is check-in blocked for its inferiors since T8 runs the strict two-phase lock protocol. In general, an object pool of a transaction T which obeys a two-phase lock protocol is either check-out blocked (if T is in its shrinking phase) or check-in blocked (if T is in its growing phase).

A transaction can change its parameter value for check-in or check-out blocked at any point of time; i. e., an explicit check-in or check-out blockade can dynamically be established or released.

The implicit version of check-out blocking always propagates from higher levels of the transaction hierarchy to lower levels (an access view can never increase, only decrease) while the implicit version of check-in blocking always propagates in reverse order (since an ancestor can only start its shrinking phase, never a new growing phase). This feature makes it possible to determine, at any point of time, up to which level incorrect objects may have propagated at most; i. e., if an already released object needs to be corrected it is definitely determinable up to which object pool this object may have propagated at most (up to the first object pool which is implicitly check-in blocked (not check-in blocked by an explicit restriction).

11.4.3 Task

Some approaches to nested transactions require work on objects to be exclusively performed in the leaf transactions of the transaction tree. Non-leaf transactions only serve as a kind of database for their children. However, in many applications it is desirable that a non-leaf transactions T can also perform operations on its objects. Of course, in such a case the work of T on its objects has to be synchronized with the work of T's children on these objects. In literature, at least two solutions for this problem are proposed:

1. In [KLMP84, US89] the object pool of a transaction T is subdivided into a part which is only accessible to T (called **private database**) and a part which is accessible to inferiors (called **(semi-)public database**). When T acquires an object it is, by definition, copied into the private object pool. Objects can be made accessible to inferiors by explicitly moving them from the private object pool to the semi-public object pool (see figure 11.8).

2. Härder and Rothermel propose a concept which is based on a releasing (weakening) of lock modes for descendants (they call it **downgrading** a lock) [HR87a]. A transaction T, holding a lock in mode M, can downgrade the lock to a mode M'. By this, descendants are allowed to access the objects in a mode which is compatible to M'. Transactions which do not belong to the descendant tree of T still see the more restrictive lock mode M. Downgrading of locks makes it possible for T to put objects at the disposal of its descendant tree while still protecting them from incompatible access by other transactions (see figure 11.9).

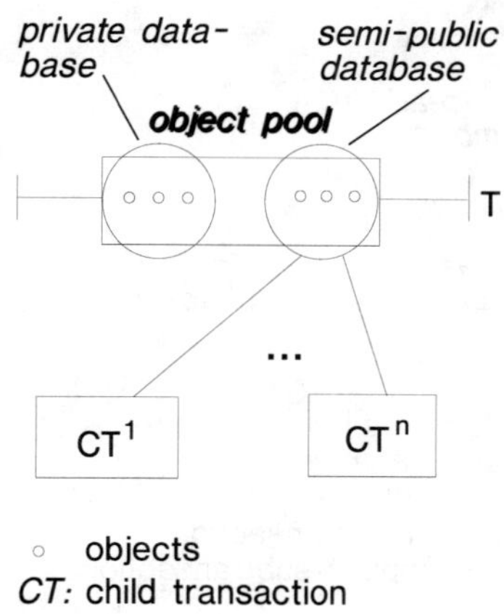

FIGURE 11.8
Private/semipublic database

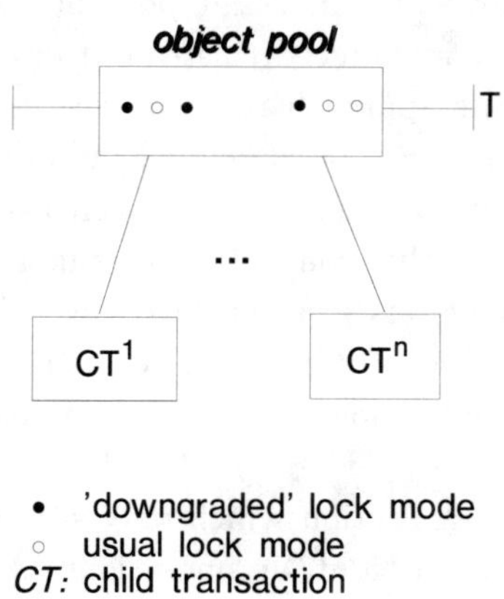

FIGURE 11.9
Downgrading of locks

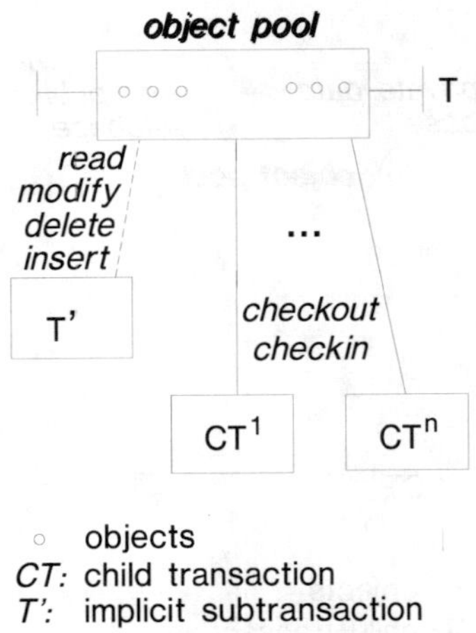

FIGURE 11.10
Implicit subtransaction T'

Although these approaches clearly indicate a solution to the problem we decided to do it in a way which makes it possible to solve the problem by means of concepts already introduced (instead of integrating new concepts). As already mentioned, our approach relies on the concept of abstract data type. Therefore, a transaction type is defined by its behavior. With respect to access operations we strictly separate between two groups of operations. Checkout/-in realize the (only) connection to superiors since they allow a transaction T to *acquire objects from* or *to release objects to* a *superior*. If T wants to manipulate objects it has to use operations like read, modify, delete, insert. Since T is only allowed to manipulate objects of its *own* object pool these operations are only defined on T's object pool. **Aservice transaction** which denotes a transaction which only serves as a database for its children only provides the checkout/-in operations. An **operational transaction** which is a transaction which, additionally, allows its users to operate on the objects of its object pool, additionally provides the second group of operations. However, we don't realize these operations on the level of the operational transaction T itself. Instead, they are associated with an implicit subtransaction T' (invisible for the user) (see figure 11.6). Since T' is treated as a child of T operational integrity is ensured by the usual mechanism (concurrency control algorithm of T). If T runs a lock protocol T', by default, obeys the non two-phase lock protocol. Therefore, a lock can be acquired or released at any point of time. In case of a service transaction the implicit subtransaction is simply not installed.

11.4.4 Concurrent execution of children

A transaction T must define whether its children (including the implicit subtransaction of T in case T is an operational transaction) can execute concurrently. If concurrent execution is prohibited no synchronization measures need to be established on the level of the object pool of T (since no concurrency is possible). Again this characteristic is only valid on the level of T and the children of T. A child may stipulate that its children can execute concurrently.

11.4.5 Explicit cooperation (collaboration)

Our approach supports the possibility of explicitly installing a **direct cooperation** between two or more transactions from different branches of the transaction tree. More specifically, we want to support a controlled lending, transfer, or exchange of objects. A direct cooperation can only be permitted if some conditions are fulfilled. Let us assume that T^A and T^B are two transactions which want to cooperate directly. Let T^R be that transaction of the transaction hierarchy which constitutes the root of the smallest subtree which comprises T^A as well as T^B. A cooperation between T^A and T^B can only be established if the paths from T^A to T^R and from T^B to T^R are neither check-out nor check-in blocked. This means that both transactions, T^A and T^B, are allowed to stepwise check-in objects in the object pool of T^R and, moreover, to stepwise check-out objects from the object pool of T^R to their own object pools (i. e., the object pool of T^R is part of the access and release views of T^A as well as T^B). This situation can only occur if all transactions on the paths from T^B to T^R and T^R to T^B (T^R excluded) support the non two-phase lock protocol. Only in case of a transfer of objects, e. g., from T^A to T^B, can this requirement be diminished to the requirement that the path from T^A to T^R is not check-in blocked and the path from T^R to T^B is not check-out blocked. As long as a cooperation exists none of the involved transactions is allowed to establish a check-out or check-in blockade.

For example, in figure reffig44 a cooperation can be installed between T39 and T42 since all transactions on the paths from T39 to T17 and from

T17 to T42 run the non two-phase lock protocol. On the other hand, a general cooperation between any of the descendants of T8 and T9 cannot be installed since T8 as well as T9 run a (different type of) two-phase lock protocol. However, since T9 is always in its shrinking phase (since it runs the simple two-phase lock protocol with <u>predeclaring</u>) while T8 is always in its growing phase (since it runs the <u>strict</u> two-phase lock protocol) a transfer of objects, e. g., from T42 to T38 is possible (all other transactions on the path from T42 to T4 and from T4 to T38 run the non two-phase lock protocol).

11.4.6 Recovery

To exploit the advantages of nested transactions, recovery has to be refined and adjusted to the demands of the control structure of nested transactions. Moreover, it must be adapted to the requirements of the various applications. In application concurrency control semantic information about the objects and their operations is used in designing specific concurrency control measures to enhance concurrency within objects. Application specific recovery can be designed along the same lines to exploit the semantics of the application in order to minimize the effects of transaction failures. Application specific recovery may reduce the cost of recovery, for example, by tolerating partial failures or by supporting not only backward recovery but also forward recovery (see, e. g., [CR90, RW91]). In the event of failure of transaction components, the failed portions can be isolated, allowing the rest of the transaction to proceed. Failed portions of transaction can be retried, compensated by attempting another alternative, or even ignored (as is indicated in figure 2.5). Nested transactions naturally support user-controlled in-transaction checkpointing since the boundaries of child transactions may act as restart points. Even more flexibility for partial rollback of in-progress transaction can be gained by explicitly establishing savepoints ([GMBL81, KSWU85]). Savepoints allow the transaction to decide which restart point is the best choice in a given situation. However, especially online transaction processing requires a more sophisticated interpretation of savepoints. Users often do not want the complete amount of "new" work to be rolled back to an earlier point of time but only "useless", "faulty", or "unpleasant" portions. Especially, they often want their actual working environment to be left intact if some of their work is to be rolled back. For example, let us consider a travel planning activity. Let us assume that we already did a reservation for a flight and a hotel and just have loaded the information about car rental companies. It happens that one of the car rental companies offers a special discount in case a certain airline is used. Unfortunately, we booked the wrong one and now want to roll back the reservation. In this case we just want the reservation for the flight to be rolled back but not the reservation of the hotel or the loading of the information about the car rental companies. Of course, in this simple case the rollback can easily be done by a compensating action. However, in more complex situations compensation may be a bad idea because it is too complicated, for example, if too many compensating actions have to be performed till the desired state is recovered.

Another problem is, that the system has to clearly advise the user about the state of his application after a rollback was performed so that the user is exactly informed which of his work was undone. For example, if the user is editing a document he needs to know which of his corrections were undone. This requires the recovery component, among others, to be able to support the notion of context and context description.

As a supply to traditional recovery techniques (like before and after images ([Gra79])) compensating transactions (will) play a major role in the field of advanced transaction models. The intention of semantics-based concurrency control is to capture more application specific semantics. Compensating (trans)actions were designed along the same lines. They are a flexible and powerful means to exploit the semantics of the application in order to minimize the effects of transaction failures. They especially relax the all-or-nothing principle since the compensation of an action must not necessarily result in an undo of *all* of the action's effects but may result in an application or even situation specific repair action; i. e., a compensating transaction undoes, according to the *semantics* of the *application*, the effects of the transaction it compensates for. Quite a few advanced transaction models already rely on this technique, like Sagas ([GS87]), *ConTracts* ([WR91]), *multi-level* and *open nested transactions* ([WS91]), or a bunch of transaction models for multidatabase systems, like *Flexible transactions* ([ELLR90]), *Polytransactions* ([RS91]) or *S-transactions* ([VE91]).

Without doubt, compensating (trans)actions are a powerful, flexible, and indispensable recovery concept and, therefore, have to be integrated in our tool kit, too. Since they allow, for example, child transactions to commit and generally release their locks on data (no upward inheritance of locks) data can be released much earlier to the public than by the usual procedure within nested transactions. Especially, compensating transactions seem to be a mandatory feature for the relaxation of the nested (hierarchical) transaction model to more general models. On the other hand, compensating transactions introduce a new dimension of complexity. Especially, their inherent complex and hard to identify influence on other recovery techniques, concurrency control measures and transaction processing control makes it a serious problem to smoothly integrate them into a more general environment like the tool kit.

Since work on recovery aspects is still underway we have to refer the interested reader to forthcoming results [UW9x].

11.4.7 Example

Figure 11.11 gives an example of a heterogeneously structured transaction tree (in which all transactions run a lock protocol). Higher levels of the transaction hierarchy use stricter types of lock protocols (e. g., the first three levels of the nested transaction T1) while lower levels partly provide a more cooperative environment (since they use the non two-phase lock protocol). As already mentioned, it is even possible to use different types of lock protocols on the same level. For example, while T31 and T32 run different types of two-phase lock protocols, T33 runs a non two-phase lock protocol.

The boxes indicate different transaction types. For reasons of simplicity we focus in the figure 11.11 on two characteristics only, namely concurrency control scheme and task. Especially higher level transactions (e. g., T1, T3) only serve as service transactions while the leaf transactions, of course, are always of type operational.

11.5 Lock modes

11.5.1 Motivation of our approach

The data modelling facilities of most non-standard database systems allow the programmer to define complex objects and a rich set of operations on those objects. Since these operations are typically on a semantically higher level than *reads* and *writes* concurrency control mechanisms are needed which allow the programmer to exploit the inherent (application specific) semantics of such operations. A common approach to the integration of application specific semantics into concurrency control is type-specific or semantics-based concurrency control (see, e. g., [BR90, CRR91, HW88, SZ89, SS84, Wei88]). This kind of concurrency control aims at databases modelled in terms of objects; i. e., objects are treated as instances of abstract data types. An abstract data type is characterized by a set of specified operations which describe the only way in which a user is allowed to access and manipulate the instances

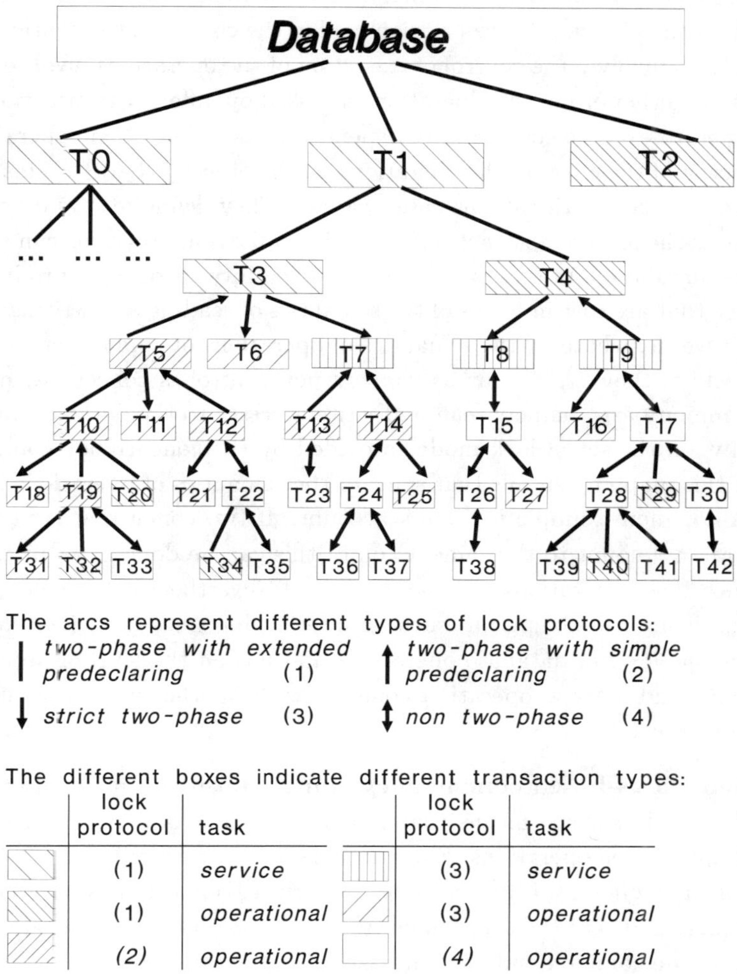

FIGURE 11.11
Heterogeneously structured transaction hierarchy

of that type. Since these operations are treated as part of the database their semantics can be exploited to achieve greater concurrency or to permit non-serializable behavior in specific environments. With semantics-based concurrency control transactions can only invoke operations which are explicitly defined on the objects. Therefore, controlling the concurrent execution of the transactions involves the control of execution of the operations invoked on the objects. Whether or not two operations, invoked by different transactions, can be allowed to execute concurrently depends on the effect of one operation on the other, and the effect of the operations on the object [CRR91]. This stands in contrast to conventional database systems. They define read and write operations as the level of abstraction at which application programs can interact with the database. As a consequence, serializability theory has produced algorithms that are cast in terms of the semantics of reading and writing [SZ89]. In other words, whatever the semantics of operations of application programs on objects is they are, as far as concurrency control is concerned, mapped on a common basis, namely read and write accesses to the database or, more generally, on the set of lock modes provided by the concurrency control. Of course, this mapping entails that some of the semantics of operations may be lost. A common example is a bank account. If two concurrent transactions each add an amount to the same account, this can be done in an interleaved way since these operations are commutative. Nevertheless, the conventional locking scheme will not permit such an interleaving since it decides compatibility on the level of database operations and not on the level of application operations and a write operation conflicts with another write operation on the same object.

Semantics-based concurrency control takes advantage of the operations semantics, which means that concurrency control is performed on the level of application operations. Since application operations are typically on a semantically higher level than reading and writing concurrent work on objects can be increased. On the other hand, this approach has the drawback that it eliminates the common and neutral basis of conventional concurrency control schemes. If, for instance, a new operation is to be integrated which displays all transactions on an account which took place in a given period of time, this operation can't just be mapped on the read operation of the database. Instead, all other operations on the type *Account* need to be considered to decide what kind of concurrency control measures are to be implemented (see figure 11.12). In other words, conventional concurrency control provides a common and static basis (a number of lock modes) on which each operation of an application need to be mapped (see figure 11.12). In semantics-based concurrency control such a common basis is no longer existent. Instead, the compatibility of operations has to be defined on a semantically higher level, namely on the level of the operations. This level is neither static (it may increase or decrease due to the insertion or deletion of new operations) nor is its semantics directly visible to the programmer. Instead, it is hidden in the implementation of the operations of the given type. Therefore, an insertion of a new operation is highly sophisticated and errorprone. An operation like DEPOSIT of transaction T_1 will not conflict with a WITHDRAW operation of a concurrent transaction T_2 as long as both operations are the only operations of T_1 and T_2. But if T_1 also wants to perform a WITHDRAW operation this operation may be rejected since it may violate a constraint (e. g., the balance must not be negative) which would not have been violated had the WITHDRAW operation of T_2 not been permitted to execute in the meantime. The difficulty here comes from the fact that more than one operation is performed within one transaction (instead of treating an operation as an equivalent to a transaction). Without any doubt, semantics-based concurrency control is useful, however, it is hard to design and implement. For the time being, semantics-based concurrency control may be applicable in special environments, but it is not sufficiently understood to be applied as a general approach to concurrency control.

The tool kit approach for concurrency control provides another solution for the inclusion of application specific semantics into concurrency control. It provides a number of elementary concepts from which the relevant can be chosen and put together to properly meet the demands of an application specific concurrency control mechanism. For this reason the tool kit provides a rich set of basic lock modes as the common basis of all operations. These lock modes are not only finer grained but they can also individually be adapted to the requirements of the operations. We have in common with the concept of semantics-based concurrency control that we think of an application layer as a layer which leans on the concept of abstract data type. Therefore, we do not want the user to explicitly handle locks. Instead, we assume that the handling of locks is hidden within the implementation of the operations. Moreover, operations on objects of the database can only be performed within transactions.

Conventional database systems usually provide an exclusive (X-) and a shared (S-) lock mode (hierarchical locks are not considered here). Since transactions in these environments are usually short-lived, the two modes

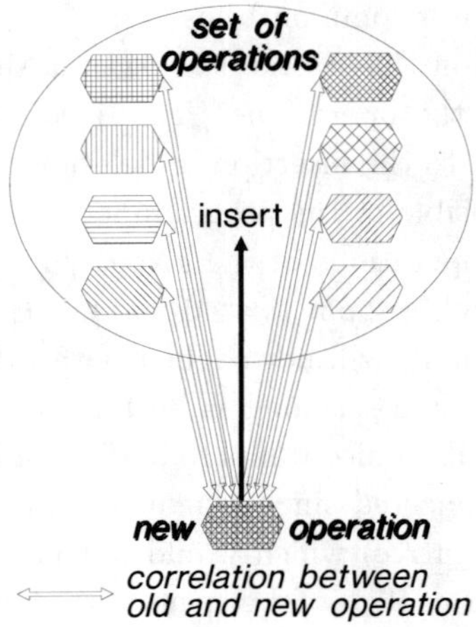

FIGURE 11.12
Semantic-based Concurrency Control

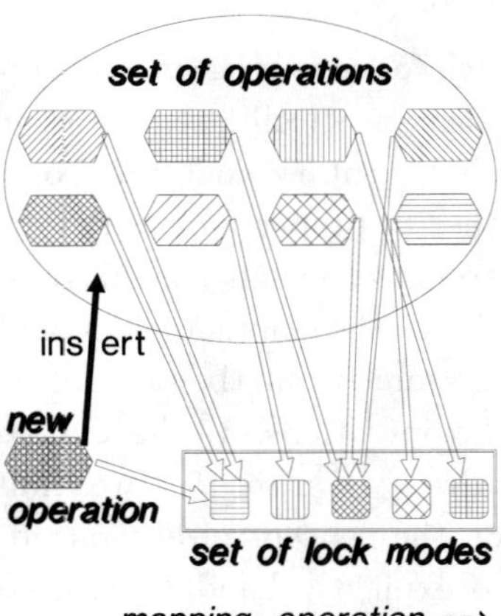

FIGURE 11.13
Traditional Concurrency Control

are sufficient. Advanced database applications, however, behave completely different. Transactions are typically interactive and of long duration which means that objects need to be locked for a substantially longer period of time. Therefore, it is essential that a lock mode fits exactly to the operations that are supposed to be performed on the object.

Example 5.1:

> Let us consider a software engineering environment in which a group of software engineers works on the development of some software. The following situations may occur. A programmer has to implement a module from which he knows that a similar module was implemented by another programmer some time ago. He wants to use this module as a model. Moreover, he needs the currently valid specification of another module since he wants to use it in his program. In both cases he needs to read the object. However, the semantics of the reads are different. In the first case it is of no relevance for the programmer whether the module is currently being modified while in the second case the read needs to be a consistent read.
>
> Another situation might be that some programmers cooperatively work on the implementation of a program. Here it is rather desirable that a programmer of the group is allowed to read any of the commonly used modules even if this module is currently being modified by another programmer. On the other hand, other people (which do not belong to the group) should not be in a position to read a module which is currently being modified.

As the above example clearly indicates, a proper lock technique needs to consider the intention (semantics) of an operation as well as the environment in which the operation is supposed to be executed. In the next sections we will discuss in what way our approach can consider such requirements. To do so, we will first identify a set of useful lock modes. Thereafter, it will be shown how these lock modes can be provided with proper effects on concurrent transactions.

Besides a set of basic lock modes the tool kit offers the ability to not only link locks temporarily to transactions (as in the classical case) but also temporarily to subjects or permanently to objects (the necessity of these concepts will be motivated later).

11.5.2 Basic lock modes of the tool kit approach

In this section we will try to identify a basic set of lock modes which can be regarded as absolutely necessary in the context of most non-standard applications. We assume that updates are not directly performed in the database but that some kind of working on copies is realized.

Of course, the shared (S-) and exclusive (X-) lock will remain useful for all kinds of database application.

shared lock (S-lock): only permits the reading of the object.

exclusive lock (X-lock): permits the reading, modification, and deletion of the object.

Sometimes an application or user is just interested in the existence of an object but not in its concrete realization (description). For example, if a programmer wants to integrate a special, predefined procedure into 'his' software package he often is only interested in the existence of the procedure but not in its actual implementation. Therefore, from the user's point a view it is irrelevant whether the procedure is modified concurrently (at least as long as the modification stays within some limits (e. g., no modification of the procedure interface)). Such a demand can be satisfied if a lock mode is provided which permits the modification of an object but not its deletion. This leads to an update lock (U-lock):

update lock (U-lock): permits the reading and modification of the object.

Another often mentioned requirement is a dirty read (see example 5.1) or browse which allows the user to read an object irrespective of any lock currently granted for that object:

browse lock (B-lock): permits the reading of the object in a dirty mode.

A number of application classes, e. g., design environments, need to handle not only one state per object but several states; i. e., an object is represented by its version graph. In [KSWU85] it was shown that the conventional S-/X-lock scheme is insufficient in such an environment since the derivation of a new version corresponds not only to an insert operation (of the new version of the object) but also to an update operation (the version graph of the object is modified). Thus, it is desirable to enable a transaction to exclude others from simultaneously deriving a new version from a given version v; other transactions may only read v. Therefore, we include a further lock mode:

derivation lock (D-lock): permits the reading of the object and the derivation of a new version of the object.

These five lock modes seem to be a firm basis for the realization of almost all requirements of advanced database applications. However, this basis is still rather coarse. A satisfactory exploitation of application specific semantics is often still impossible. The next section presents a more flexible and convenient solution.

11.5.3 The two effects of a lock

Lock protocols regulate the access to data in a relatively rigid way. As a matter of principle, no transaction has any rights at all to work on data in the database. Such privileges can only be acquired via the assignment of locks. In the remainder, we will distinguish between an **owner of a lock** (**owner** for short) and a **competitor for a lock** (**competitor** for short). An owner already possesses some lock on an object O whereas a competitor is each concurrent transaction, in particular each transaction which competes for a lock on O.

If we analyze the semantics of a lock, it becomes clear that a lock on an object O always has two effects (see figure 11.14):

1. it allows the owner to perform certain operations on O and
2. it restricts competitors in their possibilities to work on O.

This decomposition of the semantics of a lock makes it possible to differentiate between the rights which are assigned to the owner of a lock and the restrictions which are imposed on competitors. From now on, No. 1. will be called the **internal effect** of a lock request while No. 2. will be called the **external effect**.

Example 5.2:

An X-lock has the internal effect in that it allows the owner to read, modify, and delete the locked object. The external effect ensures that no competitor can lock the object in whatever mode.

An S-lock has the same internal and external effect since it allows the owner as well as any competitor to only read the object.

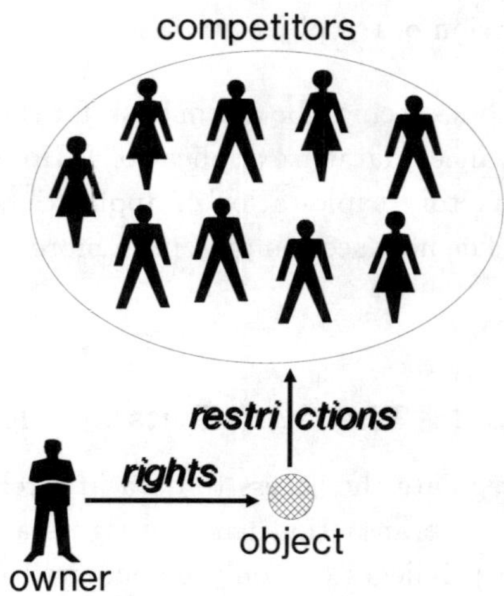

FIGURE 11.14
Two effects of a lock mode

This distinction between the internal and the external effect of a lock makes it possible to determine the rights of an owner without automatically (and simultaneously) stipulating the limitations imposed on competitors. We gain the freedom to determine the external effect of a lock individually.

The lock modes which were discussed in the previous section come with the following internal effects:

exclusive lock (X-lock): permits the reading, derivation of a new version, modification, and deletion of the object.

update lock (U-lock): permits the reading, derivation of a new version, and modification of the object (not its deletion).

derivation lock (D-lock): permits the reading and the derivation of a new version of the object (not its deletion or modification). This lock mode is only useful if the data model supports a version mechanism.

shared lock (S-lock): permits the reading of the object (neither its deletion or modification nor the derivation of a new version).

browse lock (B-lock): permits the reading of the object in a dirty mode (neither the consistent reading, modification, or deletion of the object nor the derivation of a new version).

The examination of the external effect leaves some leeway for further discussion. Conventional database systems enforce the operational integrity to be entirely ensured by the database system. To support advanced database applications, however, it seems to be useful to weaken this rigid view; i. e., to transmit some responsibility for the correct and consistent processing of data from the database system to the application. Especially in design environments users want to work on data in a way which does not automatically guarantee serializability (cooperative work). But, of course, the database system has to ensure that concurrent work on data can preserve consistency as long as the applications take care of their part in consistency control. In this sense, an update and a read operation on the same object may be compatible as long as the reader is aware of the concurrent updater. A simultaneous modification of the same object by different transactions is usually prohibited, at least as long as the data is handled by the system as an atomic unit. However, if the application is capable of mixing the different states of the object to a consistent one before the 'old' version of the object on the next, semantically higher level is replaced by the new one, concurrent updates can also be permitted.

A general mechanism for the definition of lock modes should make it possible to individually combine a given internal effect with any 'meaningful' external effect. The external effects (column) which can be combined with a given internal effect (row) can be inferred from the following compatibility matrix:

In order to be able to precisely describe a lock mode in the remainder it is necessary to specify the internal effect as well as the external effect. Therefore, **X/Y** denotes a lock which combines the internal effect X with the external effect Y.

Table 11.1 lays down which internal effect can be combined with which external effect. + (-) indicates that the corresponding internal / external effect pair can always (never) be combined. * signifies that an uncontrolled granting of such combinations may lead to consistency problems. Therefore, these combinations should only be granted if the application is prepared to accept some responsibility for the consistent processing of data. A ! corresponds to a *, but indicates that this combination should only be used in special environments.

internal effect \ external effect	B	S	D	U	X
B	+	+	+	+	+
S	+	+	*	*	–
D	+	+	*	!	–
U	+	*	!	!	–
X	+	–	–	–	–

+ = permitted * = possible
– = prohibited
! = should only be used in special environments

TABLE 11.1
Compatibility matrix internal/external effects

As a supplement to table 11.1 we need to define lock compatibility.

An **internal effect** is **stronger** (**weaker**) than another one if it concedes the owner more (fewer) rights on the locked object. According to this definition, the internal effect B is the weakest one while X is the strongest one. An **external effect** is **stronger** (**weaker**) than another one if it concedes a competitor fewer (more) rights. Since the external effect X still allows competitors to acquire any lock on the object, it is the weakest one while the external B-mode is the strongest one (it only allows competitors to read the object in a dirty mode).

Two **locks** are **compatible**,

1. if the owner's external effect permits the internal effect of the competitor

2. if the competitor's external effect permits the internal effect of the owner.

A lock L1 is **stronger** (**weaker**) than a lock L2, if

1. the internal effect of L1 is at least (at most) as strong as the internal effect of L2,

2. the external effect of L1 is at least (at most) as strong as the external effect of L2,

3. L1 is different from L2.

Example 5.3:

Let us assume that an S/U-lock is already granted to a user P. If a competitor C wants to acquire a D/S-lock, such a request can be granted since the external effect of P's lock permits the internal effect of C's lock (since D is weaker than U) and the external effect of C's lock does not prohibit the internal effect of P's lock (since both effects are the same). Since the internal effect D is weaker than the internal effect U and the external effects are the same the D/S lock is weaker than the U/S lock.

Dynamic assignment of an external effect

In addition to the possibility of fixing the external effect when the lock is acquired, it is also possible to leave it open for the moment and fix it at a later point of time. In this case, the system assumes the strongest external effect as a default. If, however, a conflict arises which can be solved by a weaker external effect, the owner is asked whether he accepts this weaker external effect. This allows the owner to individually decide whether he wants to accept this kind of concurrent work on the object. Such a decision may depend on the competitor's profile or the current state of the object.

11.5.4 Locks in the context of nested transactions

In this section it will be shown how the decomposition of a lock mode can be exploited by the concurrency control scheme in order to support a more cooperative style of work. Consider the transaction hierarchy of figure 11.15. Let us assume that transaction T5 acquired some object O in lock mode U/B from its parent (not visible) and now wants some work on O to be done by its child T10. To do so, T5 passes the object / lock pair O (U/B) onto transaction T10. This leads to the following situation:

1. O is locked on the level of T5 in lock mode U/B.

2. O is available to the descendant tree of T10 at most in lock mode U/B.

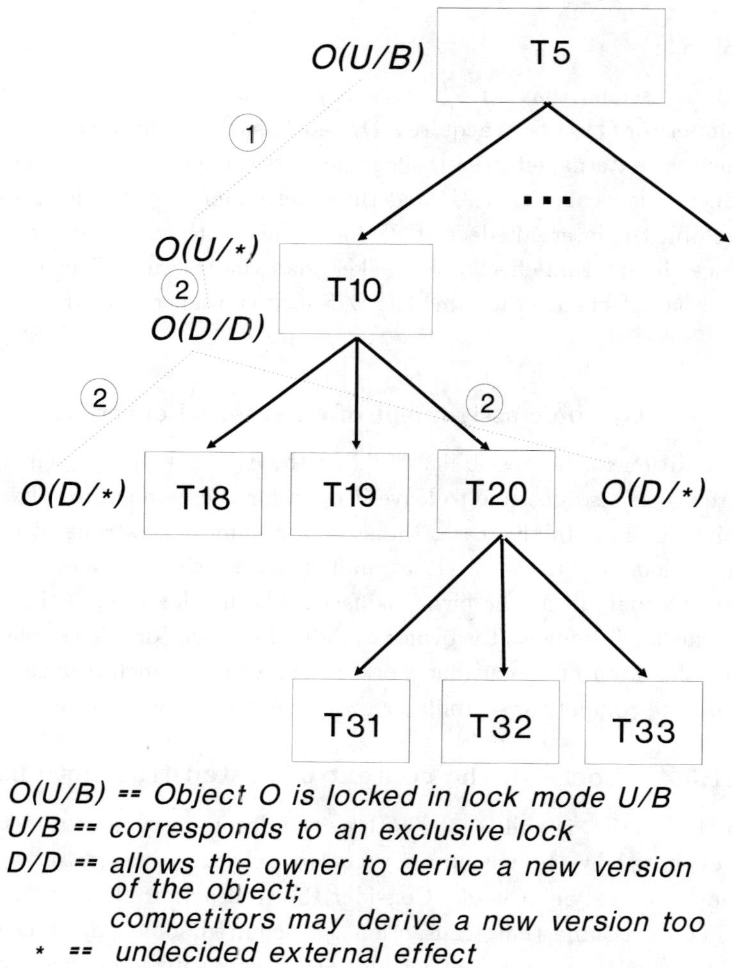

FIGURE 11.15
Acquisition of an object from the parent

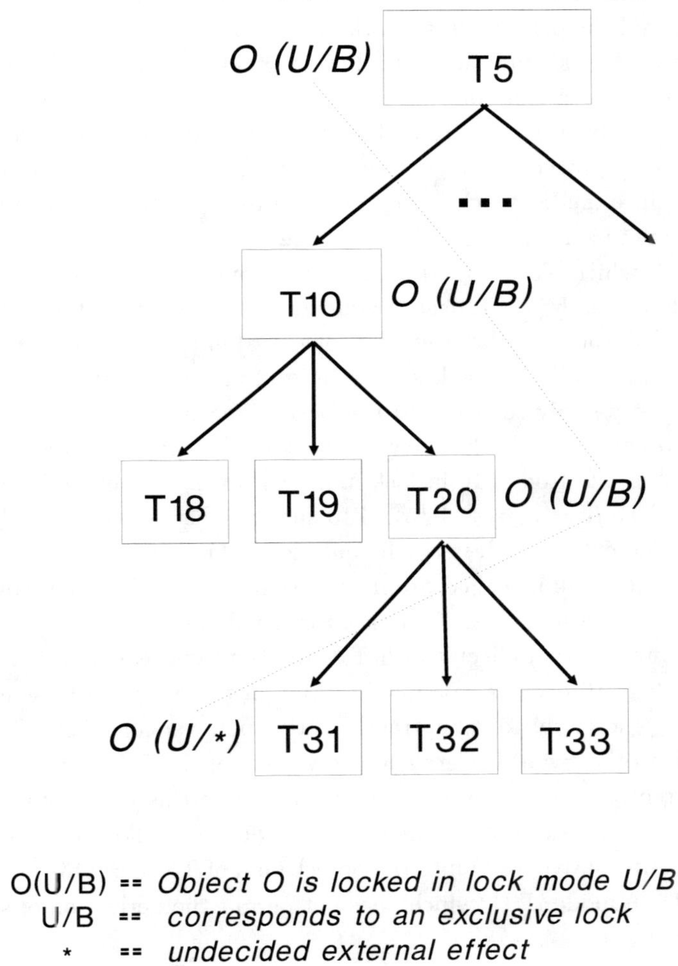

FIGURE 11.16
Acquisition of an object from a superior ($\neq$ the parent)

Feature 1 is a necessary restriction since it prevents other children of T5 (as well as T5 itself) from modifying O. Feature 2, however, is an unnecessary obstacle to the task of T10 for the following reason: T5 is only interested in the results of the work of T10 on O but not in how these results will be achieved. T10 needs O and the permission to work on O in a way which corresponds to its task. However, it should be left to T10 to decide how the work on O can be performed best. For example, if T10 decides to develop several alternatives of O simultaneously, e. g., in T18 and T20, and to afterwards select the best alternative such a proceeding should be permitted. In the scenario above this is prohibited since the U/B lock on O prevents T18 and T20 from concurrently acquiring the necessary locks for O. If we take a closer look at the semantics of the subtask which T5 assigned to T10 it becomes clear that this task is sufficiently described by the object O and the internal effect of the lock on O inherited by T10 from T5. However, the downward inheritance of the external effect of a lock is a useless obstacle since it doesn't mean any advantage for T5. Instead, it unnecessarily restricts T10 in performing its task. Consequently, we decided to only transfer the internal effect to the child. Therefore, if T5 acquires an object O from T10 in lock mode U/B this lock mode is only set on the level of T5 (see figure 11.15). T10 simply inherits the internal effect of the lock. The external effect is left undecided (1). The resulting lock (in our example: U/*) will be called **open lock** from now on. T10 may allow its children to acquire any lock on O with an internal effect equal to or weaker than U and any external effect which T10 wants to concede to its children. In the example, T10 decides to allow its children to concurrently acquire O in D/D mode, therefore, to concurrently derive new versions from O (2) (a D/D lock allows the owner to derive a new version of the object; competitors may (concurrently) derive new versions, too). While this proceeding allows T10 to execute its work on O autonomously, it does not allow T10 to, e. g., insert several alternatives of O into the object-pool of T5 since O is locked on the level of T5 in mode U/B (which does not permit the derivation of several alternatives).

To summarize, in a nested environment a child T^S may acquire an object O in lock mode X/Y from its parent. On the level of the parent O will be locked in mode X/Y. On the level of T^S this mode will be weakened to the mode X/*. T^S may replace * with any permissible external effect. Of course, if T31 wants to acquire an object O in mode U/B from transaction T5 (see figure 11.16) the rule of stepwise transfer requires that the object / lock pair O (U/B) is taken over by each transaction on the path from T5 to T31.

A more detailed discussion of the semantics of lock modes and how they can be upgraded or downgraded is given in [Unl89] and [Unl90].

11.5.5 Object related locks

Usually, locks are bound to transactions. In advanced database applications, however, it seems to be reasonable to think about an extension of this rule in a direction that locks can also be bound to objects. Similar to the life of a human being who is born single and who may, at some later point of time, acquire marriage status (which makes it impossible to return to the status "unmarried"), objects may also go through several states in their lifetime. They may be 'born' without any restrictions on the way in which they can be treated while, during their lifetime, some restrictions come into force (see example 5.4).

Example: 5.4

1. *Version graph*

   In the context of version graphs it is commonly demanded that a non-leaf node (inner node) cannot be modified to prevent the successors of that node from becoming invalid (since the predecessor is no longer the version from which they were created). Here an object is born without any restrictions (leaf) and, later, changes to an object which can no longer be modified (non-leaf node).

2. *Time versions*

   Time versions only permit one version to be valid at each point of time. Therefore, a linear sequence of versions is created. Since time versions only document the sequence of changes to an object any modification of an older (non-leaf) version is prohibited. Again the object is born without any restrictions (leaf). But later on it changes to an object which can neither be modified nor used to derive a new version from it (non-leaf node).

3. *Standard or library objects*

   Many application classes, especially design environments, put standard or library objects at the user's disposal. Such objects can only be read. It is born with the restriction modification prohibited.

The common feature of these three examples is that they define restrictions on the access to data (e. g., updating is prohibited). In principal, these restrictions can be ensured by three mechanisms:

1. access control
2. integrity constraints
3. concurrency control

Of course, none of the alternatives is exactly destined for the desired purpose. However, all of them could be extended in a way that they meet the requirements. We decided to assign the task to the concurrency control component. One reason for this decision is that it is not only elegant but also efficient since the concurrency control mechanism can exploit the additional knowledge about restrictions on the handling of data to increase efficiency and performance. A more detailed argumentation is given in [Unl89].

Our idea is to link locks permanently to objects. This kind of lock will be called **object related lock** (**OR-lock** for short). An OR-lock, once imposed on an object, can neither be weakened nor released, it can only be upgraded. The locks remain valid as long as the object exists. OR-locks behave like conventional locks (locks linked to transactions, called **transaction related locks** in the following (**TR-locks** for short) which only have an internal effect. If an OR-lock is granted, the community of all (potential) transactions can be seen as the owner of the lock. All rights which are captured with the internal effect can still be requested while all other rights can no longer be granted. Since an OR-lock is persistent we will distinguish it from a transaction lock by placing a P in front of the signature.

The following OR-locks can directly be adopted from the set of conventional locks:

PU-Lock: prohibits the deletion of the object. All other operations are permitted.

PD-Lock: prohibits the deletion and modification of the object. All other operations are permitted.

PS-Lock: prohibits the deletion, the modification, and the derivation of a new version of the object. It only permits the read operation.

It is particularly worthwhile to take a closer look at the PD-lock. This lock permits the derivation of a new version of the object locked. However, it is not laid down whether a derivation is permitted only once or more frequently. But such a distinction is extremely useful since it makes it possible to automatically control the observance of the rules of different version models (time versions and version graphs). Due to the great significance of version models, a distinction seems to be reasonable. Therefore, the PD-lock is split into two lock modes:

PSD-lock: only permits the derivation of exactly one new version; i. e., after the first derivation of a new version the lock mode is converted to a PS-lock (forms a sequence of versions).

PMD-lock: permits the derivation of any number of new versions (forms a version graph).

Finally, a PX-lock is introduced as the lock with which every object is 'born':

PX-lock: is a pseudo lock which does not impose any restrictions on the object (needs not to be considered by the concurrency control component).

The introduction of a PB-lock doesn't make any sense since it has the same effect as the PS-lock (if a modification or deletion of an object is prohibited every read is automatically a consistent read).

Table 11.2 describes the compatibility between an OR-lock and (the internal effect of) a conventional lock:

Similar to the external effect of conventional locks, OR-locks increase from PX to PS since each step on this way concedes fewer rights on the object.

As already mentioned with the help of OR-locks concurrency control overhead can be reduced. For instance, with a PS-lock the object has no longer to be considered by the concurrency control component since the only applicable operation is the read operation. A PS-lock is especially favorable if standard objects need to be handled. Let us consider figure 11.17 in which the standard object O2 is a shared subcomponent of several complex objects (CO1, CO2, CO3). If, for example, some transaction T locked CO1 in an exclusive mode (U/B-lock) this lock would prevent each competitor C from locking any of the other complex objects which also include O2 (here CO2 and CO3). However, if a PS-lock is imposed on O2 the lock manager no longer has to consider O2. Therefore, the concurrent access can be granted. Situations like this are rather frequent, especially in design environments.

transaction lock

object lock	B	S	D	U	X
PX	+	+	+	+	+
PU	+	+	+	+	−
PMD	+	+	+	−	−
PSD	+	+	o	−	−
PS	+	+	−	−	−

\+ = *permitted*
− = *prohibited*
o = *single derivation only*

TABLE 11.2
Compatibility matrix object / transaction related locks

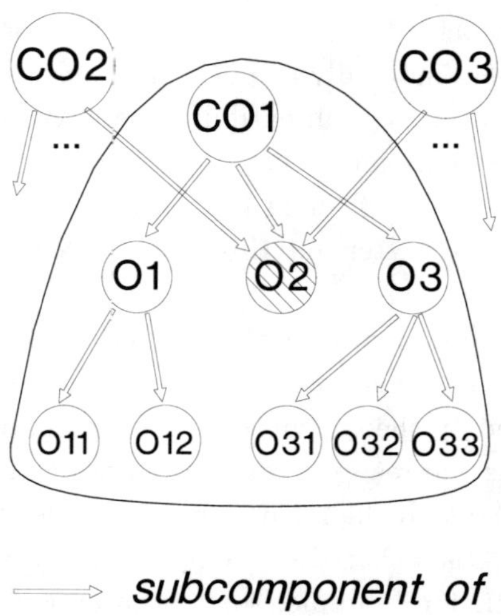

FIGURE 11.17
Standard object O2 as subcomponent of serveral complex objects

In [Kel87] prevention locks were introduced for similar reasons. But these locks were especially designed for CAD databases and versions.

In the appendix an example is presented which demonstrates the different facets of our approach.

11.5.6 Subject related lock

Non-standard applications are usually rather complex in comparison with traditional applications. One frequently finds complex tasks which need to be split into several units of work, each of which, nevertheless, is often still rather long. Since these units of work represent *one* complex task they often have a complex control flow; i. e., some units can be executed concurrently while others need to be executed in succession. Each unit of work touches a (great) number of objects. Some of them are only used within *one* given unit, the, with respect to the task, more central objects are often used within a great number (all) of units of work. This leads to the requirement that objects need to be transferred from one unit of work to the next. If units of work correspond to transactions we need a mechanism which allows an object to be safely transferred from one transaction to the next (see also [Reu89]).

Moreover, a unit of work may consist of several phases each of which works with a few common objects and a number of phase specific objects. If a unit of work corresponds to a transaction the phase specific objects need to be locked for an unnecessary long period of time, therefore, possibly blocking concurrent transactions. To avoid such unfavorable situations, e. g. split transactions were introduced [CKH88]. A split transaction is a long duration transaction which is split into (two) parts in order to be able to release some objects, which are required by a concurrent transaction T^C, at an earlier point of time. Again, to safely transfer the objects to T^C we need some shelter which ensures that the released objects cannot be locked by another competitor before they can be acquired by T^C. To support a safe transfer of objects between transactions the tool kit provides subject related locks. **Subject-related locks** are locks which are assigned to a subject for some period of time. The subject is the owner of the lock and can decide autonomously how to use the locked object (in which transaction or sequence of transactions).

A subject related lock (**SR-lock** for short) corresponds to a transaction related lock (TR-lock) in that it is described by an internal / external effect pair and is bound *temporarily*, however, to a *subject* and not to a transaction. **Asubject** may be anything that can be identified by the transaction manager as such, e. g., an application, a user (group), a named sequence of actions (transactions) etc. Since an SR-lock functions as a placeholder it reserves an object O for (later) use by its owner in one or more (consecutive) transactions. Any subject can acquire an SR-lock at any point of time. The SR-lock can be granted by the lock manager if no incompatible TR-, OR- (object related) or SR-lock on the object is (currently) assigned to any competitor. Here, a competitor is either a transaction (in case of a TR-lock) or a subject (in case of an SR-lock) or an object (in case of an OR-lock). The owner of an SR-lock can hold the lock as long as he wants to hold it; an SR-lock is released by an explicit command of the owner. This can be done at any point of time.

An SR-lock imposes restrictions on the way in which competitors are allowed to work on the locked object. Consequently, the external effect of an SR-lock corresponds to the external effect of a TR-lock. The internal effect determines which TR-lock on the object can be granted at most to a transaction. This means, that in contrast to a TR-lock an SR-lock does not assign any explicit rights to its owner. Rights can only be acquired if the SR-lock is supplemented by a TR-lock within a concrete transaction. However, since the SR-lock is a placeholder it is guaranteed that the lock manager can always grant the corresponding TR-lock immediately, provided that the required TR-lock is not stronger than the SR- lock. If it is stronger, of course, the TR-lock has to compete with all other locks on that object which were already assigned to competitors. In principle, each combination of an internal effect with an external effect which is a valid TR-lock represents a valid SR-lock.

The additional acquisition of the TR-lock is necessary to ensure that the locked object O can only be manipulated within a transaction. Moreover, it guarantees that the owner of the SR-lock cannot improperly exploit his rights, e. g., by using O in an incompatible way in different transactions. The TR-lock ensures that O can only be used in one transaction at a time. Only after the TR-lock on O was released O is, once again, put at the disposal of the owner of the SR-lock and can, therefore, be employed in another transaction. Of course, since O can only be used if a proper TR-lock was acquired an SR-lock can be released at any point of time. Either O is currently not used by some transaction or it is still protected by the additional TR-lock. However, the use of O in a transaction T substantially restricts O's further employment since it causes a dependency from locality. More specifically, the use of O in T1 corresponds to an explicit check-out of O from the database (or some object pool from the ancestor chain) by T1; i. e., O is added to all object pools on the path from the database to T1. Consequently, O can only be used in some other transaction T2 if O can be transferred from T1 to T2 according to the object transfer rule (see the chapter about explicit cooperations).

To differentiate a TR-lock from an SR-lock the latter will be written in italic letters in the following.

Example 5.5:

> Let us assume that a user P has acquired the SR-lock *U/S* on O. Since the external effect of the lock is *S*, O can, at most, be read by any concurrent transaction. If P wants to work on O in transaction T he (the transaction) can directly redeem the SR-lock by any TR-lock which isn't stronger than U/S (e. g., S/S or U/S). If P has acquired some lock on O in T, e. g., a U/S-lock, he cannot acquire an incompatible lock mode on O, e. g., again a U/S-lock, in any other transaction. This is prevented by the TR-lock which was acquired by T.

11.6 General rules of the tool kit approach

This section summarizes the "meta" rules which have to be obeyed by each transaction (type):

1. *Dependency*

   Each transaction strictly depends on a unique parent. The parent can either be the database or another transaction. In the first case the transaction is either the top level transaction of a nested transaction or a flat transaction. In the second case the transaction is a child of another transaction, the parent transaction. Dependency on a parent entails the following effects:

   - A child must commit before its parent commits.
   - Commit of a child and durability of its results are conditional subject to the fate of its superiors. Even if a child commits, aborting of its superiors will undo its effects.
   - A child can only acquire objects from its parent. If it needs an object from another superior the rule of stepwise transfer must be observed.

- A child has to observe the relevant rules and constraints which were defined by its parent with respect to the child (according to the two-stage control-sphere).

2. *Object acquisition and release*

   Each transaction can only acquire objects which belong to its access view. Moreover, it can only insert objects into an object pool of its release view. Only in case of an explicit cooperation may a transaction additionally acquire objects from or release objects into the object pool of another transaction. When a transaction T^C acquires an object from an ancestor T^A the object is duplicated and the copy is inserted into the object pool of T^C. If T^A is not the parent of T^C the object / lock pair is, at least logically, inserted into the object pool of each transaction on the path from T^A to T^C (stepwise transfer). In any case T^C gets the object with an undecided external effect; i. e., T^C is allowed to grant any lock which is compatible with the acquired internal effect. All work of a transaction has to be performed on the objects of its own object pool. If a transaction T^C modifies an object and wants these modifications to become valid T^C has to insert the modified object into the object pool of a superior before EOT (end of transaction). By this, the object version of the superior is replaced by the "new" version of T^C. If the superior is not the parent the object is removed from the object pools of all transactions on the path to the superior (of course, excluding the superior itself).

3. *Concurrency control*

   If children are allowed to concurrently acquire objects from the object pool of their parent the parent needs to run a concurrency control scheme for its object pool. For an operational transaction T to perform an operation on an object of its own object pool, T must observe the concurrency control scheme installed on its object pool.

4. *Exclusion*

   If a transaction requests an object, the request can only be granted if the object is not locked in an incompatible mode (in general, if the appropriate concurrency control scheme agrees to such a request).

5. *Transaction abort or commit*

   When a transaction fails (aborts), its objects are discarded. However, the object versions of its ancestors are left intact. In either case, when a transaction commits or aborts, its locks on the objects in the object-pool of the parent are released.

6. *Uniformity*

   All transactions follow these rules.

11.7 Brief overview of the structure of the tool kit

The tool kit is meant to provide a wide range of different transaction types. This set needs to include conventional (short duration) transactions as well as different types of long duration transactions. This requires that transaction types are made up of different components. For example, while a basic long duration transaction type may hold its own object pool and lock table a more specific transaction type may, additionally, hold its own compatibility matrix for its object pool. By this, access to objects of the object pool can be individually adapted to the requirements of a specific environment. For example, in a more cooperative environment, the compatibility matrix may define lock modes to be compatible which should not be compatible in a more competitive environment.

In this section we will concisely outline how different transaction types can be constructed.

The tool kit can be regarded as a kind of **object-oriented transaction manager development facility** for the following reasons:

- Each component of the tool kit belongs to a **class**; each class represents a different type of component.

- Components are realized as **abstract data types**. This means in particular that transaction types are characterized by the operations which come with them. A number of operations are common to all (long duration) transaction types; e. g., operations to suspend, continue and commit the transaction and to acquire or release objects. However, these operations may be implemented differently for different transaction types (with different semantics or with different implementation part (data structure)). Other operations are only specific to some transaction types since they come with the features by which these transaction types differ from other transaction types. Note, that the concept of abstract data type makes it possible to easily react to changing requirements. If, e. g., in a workstation / server environment the maintenance of an object pool is to be moved from the server to the workstation this can easily be realized due to the locality of such changes. Moreover, this concept leaves some leeway for the implementation of logical structures; e. g., while the logical structure of a transaction type may require a local object pool the actual implementation may lean on a global object pool (a common pool for all transactions).

- The assembly and refinement of transaction types is, among others, realized via (**multiple**) **inheritance**.

A transaction type is developed in the following way: First, the basic constituents are chosen from the set of **basic components** of the tool kit. These constituents are suited to each other (either via multiple inheritance or via aggregation) to form a kind of **skeleton** of a first basic transaction type. For example, in figure 11.18 the skeleton for LONG DURATION TRANSACTION (2) is assembled from the basic components OBJECT POOL and TRANSACTION (1). At this basic level TRANSACTION is nothing more than a frame within which operations can be executed; i. e., no rules or constraints are laid down, no concurrency control or recovery mechanisms are established, etc. A skeleton transaction (or skeleton for short) can be specialized to more specific skeletons by adding more components and / or specializing (refining / extending) existing components. In figure 11.18, LONG DURATION TRANSACTION is specialized to LONG DURATION PESSIMISTIC TRANSACTION (transaction which runs a lock protocol; (4)) by adding the constituents COMPATIBILITY MATRIX and LOCK TABLE (3). A skeleton corresponds to a fundamental transaction type which is not yet executable since it does not obey the specific semantics of some underlying transaction model. For example, a skeleton may already provide a *check-out* operation. However, the rule that objects can only be acquired from an ancestor is not yet laid down; i. e., an instance T of LONG DURATION PESSIMISTIC TRANSACTION can theoretically acquire an object from any other transaction and any other transaction can acquire on object from T (only theoretically since a skeleton transaction is defined to be not executable at all; see above). The rules and constraints of a specific transaction model need to be added

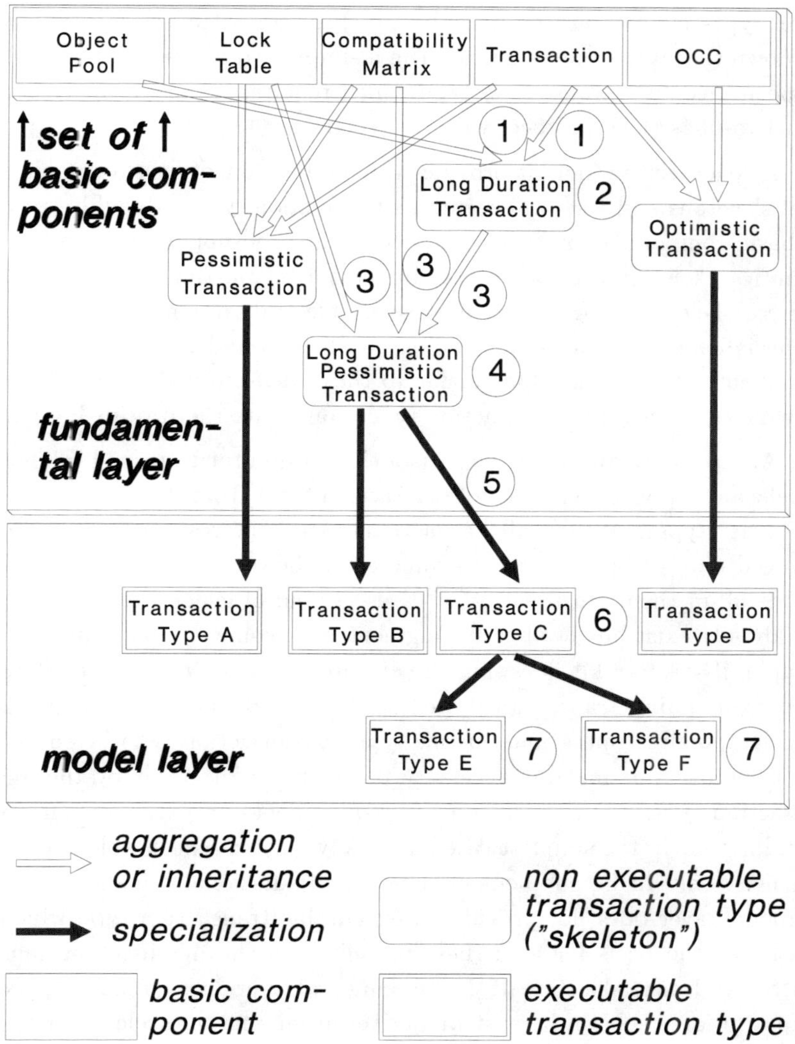

FIGURE 11.18
Structure of the tool kit

in a subsequent phase (this is done within the model layer). Skeletons which are equipped with specific semantics (5) constitute **executable transaction types** (6). Of course, by adding further rules or constraints executable transaction types can be further specialized (7); e. g., a transaction type which lays down that its instances need to run a simple two-phase lock protocol may be specialized to a transaction type which requires its instances to run the strict two-phase lock protocol with predeclaring.

Altogether the tool kit provides three sets, a set of basic components, a set of skeletons and a set of executable transaction types. Roughly speaking, the basic components are general objects which do not provide any specific semantics, skeletons are constructed by recursively putting things (basic components, skeletons) together while executable transaction types are defined by specializing operations and adding constraints and rules, etc. The basic components and the skeletons make up the **fundamental layer** of the tool kit while the executable transaction types constitute the **model layer**.

An **application specific transaction manager** is defined by choosing the relevant (application-specific) transaction types from the set of executable transaction types. At best, all transaction types of interest are already existent and need only to be selected. In some cases, however, the tool kit may not provide all of them. In some other cases, a kind of general transaction type may already exist but need to be augmented by some special semantics. For example, if the tool-kit does not already provide *split transactions* [CKH88] the corresponding transaction types need to be defined (e. g., by adding the corresponding operations) if this type of transaction is to be supported. Situations like this make it necessary to extend the tool kit by the missing transaction types. Dependent on the requirements an extension may affect several layers. In the simplest case an already existent executable transaction type need only to be supplemented by some additional semantics. In case the model layer does not provide an executable transaction type which can be used as the basis for a further specialization the missing type must be constructed from a skeleton. If the fundamental layer does not already provide an appropriate skeleton it must be derived from another skeleton or it must be constructed from the basic set of components. In the worst case, the set of basic components has to be augmented (e. g., by a new concurrency control scheme). Finally, if a different global transaction model is to be installed (e. g., a model which allows a transaction "hierarchy" to be netlike instead of treelike) a new model layer must be developed; i. e., the transaction types of the model layer must be equipped with different semantics. Of course, such a task is rather ambitious and should, therefore, only be performed by a specialist.

11.8
Concluding remarks

We have presented a flexible and adaptable tool kit approach for transaction management. The tool kit allows a sophisticated applications designer or database implementor to develop individual, application specific transaction managers. Much attention was paid to a comprehensive support of different shapes of cooperative work.

The main characteristics of the tool kit are:

1. It supports the definition of a great number of different transaction types. These transaction types are meant to reflect the requirements of different application areas. We presented a basic set of characteristics by which transaction types may differ from each other. However, since the tool kit is extensible this set can be augmented if additional demands need to be met.

2. The different transaction types can be combined with each other in any hierarchical order to form a heterogeneously structured transaction hierarchy which is capable of supporting such different concepts as strict isolation of (sub)transactions (in the sense of serializability) and (non-serializable) cooperative work in one hierarchy. For this reason a general set of rules was proposed which has to be obeyed by each transaction type.

3. The tool kit provides a number of different lock modes. Each lock mode is described by an internal effect and an external effect. This subdivision permits an exact adaptation of the set of lock modes to the requirements of an application area; i. e., application specific semantics can be exploited for reasons of concurrency control. Moreover, it was shown that the subdivision of lock modes can be exploited to comprehensively support cooperative work within a nested transaction.

A first prototype of the tool kit was implemented in Smalltalk on top of the relational DBMS ORACLE and is currently in its test phase. It serves as a testbed for the examination of the weakness and strong points of our approach. We intend, as a second step, to integrate a revised version into the database kernel system OMS [FB89].

Further investigations

An urgent task is the definition of a formal notion of consistency in the context of advanced database applications. Further work has to be invested to integrate concepts which allow a child to become even more independent of its parent, i. e., to support the concept of multi-level or 'open nested' transactions [BSW88]. Moreover, the need that a transaction hierarchy has to form a tree might be too restrictive in same cases (although cooperation makes it possible to evade this principle). We want to support transaction graphs as well.

Another crucial point is the development of an appropriate intelligent interface for the tool kit. Even the current version of our tool kit is rather complex and requires deep knowledge about the characteristics and concepts of transaction management. Therefore, we want the tool kit to provide an intelligent interface which supports a DBI in his task to choose the right components and to combine them in an appropriate way.

At some later point of time we want to extend the tool kit in a way that it also permits the construction of transaction managers for homogeneous / heterogeneous distributed database systems (e. g., multidatabase systems as described in [ED90] and [ELLR90]).

Bibliography

[BR90] B. R. Badrinath, K. Ramamrithan. Performance Evaluation of Semantics-Based Multilevel Concurrency Control Protocols. In *Proc. ACM-SIGMOD Int. Conf. on Management of Data*, Atlantic City, NJ, May 1990.

[Bat88] D. Batory, et. al. GENESIS: An Extensible Database Management System. In *IEEE Transactions on Software Engineering*, Vol. 14, No. 11, Nov. 1988.

[BHG87] P. Bernstein, V. Hadzilacos, N. Goodman. Concurrency Control and Recovery in Database Systems. In *Addison-Wesley Publishing Company*, 1987.

[BSW88] C. Beeri, H.-J. Schek, G. Weikum. Multi-Level Transaction Management: Theoretical Art or Practical Need. In *Proc. Intl. Conference Extending Data Base Technology (EDBT)*, Lecture Notes in Computer Science 303, J. W. Schmidt, S. Ceri, M. Missikoff (Editors), Springer Publishing Company, 1988.

[CD87] M. J. Carey, D. J. DeWitt. An Overview of the EXODUS Project, In *IEEE Database Engineering*, Vol. 10, No. 2, June 1987.

[CKH88] P.Calton, G. E. Kaiser, N. Hutchinson. Split-Transactions for Open-Ended Activities. In *Proc. of the 14th VLDB Conference*, Los Angeles, California, 1989.

[CR90] P. Chrysanthis, K. Ramamrithan. ACTA: A Framework for Specifying and Reasoning about Transactions Structure and Behavior. In *Proc. ACM-SIGMOD Int. Conf. on Management of Data*, Atlantic City, NJ, May 1990.

[CRR91] P. Chrysanthis, S. Raghuram, K. Ramamrithan. Extracting Concurrency from Objects: A Methodology. In *Proc. ACM-SIGMOD Int. Conf. on Management of Data*, Denver, Colorado, May 1991.

[Dav73] C. Davies. Recovery Semantics for a DB/DC System. In *Proc. ACM National Conference*, 28, 1973.

[DJJN88] A. Dennis, F. Joey, L. Jessup, J. Nunamaker, D. Vogel. Information Technology to Support Electronic Meetings. In *MIS Quarterly*, Vol. 12, No. 4, Dec. 1988.

[ED90] A. Elmagarmid, W. Du. A Paradigm for Concurrency Control in Heterogeneous Distributed Database Systems. In *Proc. 6th Int. Conf. on Data Engineering*, Feb. 1990.

[ElGR90] C. Ellis, S. Gibbs, G. Rein. Design and Use of a Group Editor. In *Engineering for Human-Computer Interaction*, G. Cockton (editor), North-Holland, Amsterdam, 1990.

[ElGR91] C. Ellis, S. Gibbs, G. Rein. Groupware: Some Issues and Experiences. In *Communications of the ACM*, Vol. 34, No. 1, Jan. 1991.

[ELLR90] A. Elmagarmid, Y. Leu, W. Litwin, M. Rusinkiewicz. A Multidatabase Transaction Model for InterBase. In *Proc. VLDB*, Brisbane, Australia, Aug. 1990.

[FB89] J. Freitag, T. Bode. A General Manager for Storage Objects as the Basis for the Implementation of Complex Objects in an Object Management System (in German). In *Proc. GI Conference on Database Systems for Office Automation, Engineering, and Scientific Applications*, Zurich, Switzerland, March 1989.

[GS87] H. Garcia-Molina, K. Salem. Sagas. In Proc. ACM-SIGMOD Int. Conf. on Management of Data, San Francisco, California, 1987.

[Gra79] J. Gray. Notes on Data Base Operating Sytems. In *Operating Systems: An Advanced Course*, R. Bayer, M. Graham, G. Seegmüller (editors), Springer Publishing Company, 1979.

[Gre88] I. Greif (editor). Computer-Supported Cooperative Work: A Book of Readings. Morgan Kaufmann, San Mateo, California, 1988.

[GS88] I. Greif, S. Sarin. Data Sharing in Group Work. In *[Grei88]*, 1988.

[GMBL81] J. Gray, P. McJones, M. Blasgen, B. Lindsay, R. Lorie, T. Price, F. Putzolu, I. Traiger. The Recovery Manager of the System R Database Manager. In *ACM Computing Surveys*, Vol. 13, No. 2, 1981.

[HR83] Th. Härder, A. Reuter. Principles of Transaction Oriented Database Recovery. In *ACM Computing Surveys*, Vol. 15, No. 2, June 1983.

[HR87a] Th. Härder, K. Rothermel. Concurrency Control Issues in Nested Transactions. In *IBM Almaden Research Report RJ5803*, San Jose, Aug. 1987.

[HR87b] Th. Härder, K. Rothermel. Concepts for Transaction Recovery in Nested Transactions. *Proc. ACM-SIGMOD*, San Francisco, California, 1987.

[HW88] M. Herlihy, W. Weihl. Hybrid Concurrency Control for Abstract Data Types. In *Proc. ACM Symposium on Principles of Database Systems*, 1988.

[HMMS87] Th. Härder, K. Meyer-Wegener, B. Mitschang, A. Sikeler. PRIMA - a DBMS Prototype Supporting Engineering Applications. In *Proc. VLDB*, Brighton, England, 1987.

[Kat84] R. H. Katz. Transaction Management in the Design Environment. In *New Applications of Data Bases*, G. Gardarin, E. Gelenbe (Editors), Academic Press, 1984.

[Kel87] U. Kelter. Concurrency Control for Design Objects with Versions in CAD Databases. In *Information Systems, Pergamon Journals Ltd.*, Vol. 12, No. 2, 1987.

[Kel88] U. Kelter. Concepts for Transactions in Non Standard Database Systems (in German). In *Informationstechnik it*, R. Oldenbourg Verlag, Vol. 30, No. 1, 1988.

[KLMP84] W. Kim, R. Lorie, D. McNabb, W. Plouffe. A Transaction Mechanism for Engineering Design Databases. In *Proc. VLDB*, Singapore, 1984.

[KKB85] H. F. Korth, W. Kim, F. Bancilhon. A Model of CAD Transactions. In *Proc. VLDB*, Stockholm, Sweden, 1985.

[KKB88] H. F. Korth, W. Kim, F. Bancilhon. On Long Duration CAD Transactions. In *Information Sciences*, 46, pp 73–107, 1988.

[KK88] K. Kraemer, J. King. Computer-based Systems for cooperative work and decision making. In *ACM Computing Surveys*, Vol. 20, No. 2, June 1988.

[KSWU85] P. Klahold, G. Schlageter, W. Wilkes, R. Unland. A Transaction Model Supporting Complex Applications in Integrated Information Systems. In *Proc. ACM-SIGMOD*, Austin, Texas, 1985.

[LP83] R. Lorie, W. Plouffe. Complex Objects and Their Use in Design Transactions. In *Proc. Databases for Engineering Applications, ACM-Database Week*, San Jose, California, 1983.

[Mos81] J. E. B. Moss. Nested Transactions: An Approach to Reliable Computing. In *MIT Report MIT-LCS-TR-260*, Massachusetts Institute of Technology, Laboratory of Computer Science, 1981 and Nested Transactions: An Approach to Reliable Distributed Computing. In *The MIT Press; Research Reports and Notes, Information Systems Series*, M. Lesk (Ed.), 1985.

[NS89] E. Neuhold, M. Stonebraker. Future Directions in DBMS Research. In *SIGMOD Record*, Vol. 18, No. 2, July 1989.

[NZ89] M. Nodine, S. Zdonik. Cooperative Transaction Hierarchies: A Transaction Model to Support Design Applications. In *Proc. VLDB*, Brisbane, Australia, Aug. 1990.

[PSSW87] H.-B. Paul, H. J. Schek, M. Scholl, G. Weikum. Architecture and Implementation of the Darmstadt Database Kernel System. In *Proc. ACM-SIGMOD*, San Francisco, California, 1987.

[Ree78] D. Reed. Naming and Synchronization in a Decentralized Computer System. Ph.D. Thesis, M.I.T. Dept. of Elec. Eng. and Comp. Sci., *Technical Report 205*, Sept. 1978.

[Reu89] A. Reuter. ConTracts: A Means for Extending Control Beyond Transaction Boundaries. In *Proc. 2nd Int. Workshop on High Performance Transaction Systems*, Asilomar, Sept. 1989.

[RW91] A. Reuter, H. Wächter. The ConTract Model (extended abstract). In *IEEE Data Engineering Bulletin*, Vol. 14, No. 1, Special Issue on "Unconventional Transaction Management", March 1991.

[RS91] M. Rusinkiewicz, A. Sheth. Polytransactions for Managing Interdependent Data (extended abstract). In *IEEE Data Engineering Bulletin*, Vol. 14, No. 1, Special Issue on "Unconventional Transaction Management", March 1991.

[SG85] S. Sarin, I. Greif. Computer-Based Real-Time Conferencing Systems, In *IEEE Computer*, Vol. 18, No. 10, Oct. 1985.

[SZ89] A. Skarra, S. Zdonik. Concurrency Control and Object-Oriented Databases. In *Object-Oriented Concepts, Databases, and Applications*, W. Kim, F. Lochovsky, (Editors), Addison-Wesley Publishing Company, 1989.

[SS84] P. Schwarz, A. Spector. Synchronizing Shared Abstract Types. In *ACM TODS*, Vol. 2, No. 3, August 1984.

[Unl89] R. Unland. A General Model for Locking in Non-Standard Database Systems (in German). In *Research-Report*, University of Hagen, Department of Computer Science, 1988 and *Proc. GI 3rd Conf. on Database Systems for Office Automation, Engineering, and Scientific Applications*, Zurich, Switzerland, 1989.

[Unl90] R. Unland. A Flexible and Adaptable Tool Kit Approach for Concurrency Control in Non Standard Database Systems. In *Proc. 3rd Int. Conf. on Database Theory (ICDT)*, Paris, France, Dec. 1990.

[Unl91] R. Unland. Transaction Types for Non-Standard Database Systems. In *Research-Report* (submitted for publication), University of Hagen, Department of Computer Science, 1991.

[UPS86] R. Unland, U. Prädel, G. Schlageter. Redesign of optimistic methods: improving performance and applicability. In *Proc. Int. Conf. on Data Engineering*, Los Angeles, California, Feb. 1986.

[US89] R. Unland, G. Schlageter. A Multi-Level Transaction Model for Engineering Applications. In *Proc. 1st International Symposium on Database Systems for Advanced Applications*, Seoul, South-Korea, April 1989.

[US91] R. Unland, G. Schlageter. A Flexible and Adaptable Tool Kit Approach for Transaction Management in Non Standard Database Systems. In *IEEE Database Engineering Bulletin; Special Issue on "Transaction Models for Advanced Database Applications"*, March 1991.

[UW9x] R. Unland, E. Welker. Recovery Concepts for Non-Standard Database Systems. In *Research-Report* (in preparation), University of Hagen; 199x.

[VE91] J. Veijalainen, F. Eliassen. The S-transaction Model (extended abstract). In *IEEE Data Engineering Bulletin*, Vol. 14, No. 1, Special Issue on "Unconventional Transaction Management", March 1991.

[WR91] H. Wächter, A. Reuter. The ConTract Model. In *Transaction Models for Advanced Database Applications*, A. Elmargarmid (ed.), Morgan Kaufmann Publishers, to appear 1991.

[Wei88] W. Weihl. Commutativity-Based Concurrency Control for Abstract Data Types. In Proc. IEEE 21th Annual Hawaii Int. Conf. on System Sciences (HICSS), Hawaii, Jan. 1988.

[WS91] G. Weikum, H.-J. Schek. Multi-Level Transactions and Open Nested Transactions (extended abstract). In *IEEE Data Engi-*

neering Bulletin, Vol. 14, No. 1, Special Issue on "Unconventional Transaction Management", March 1991.

Appendix: An Example

As already mentioned, the tool kit is designed to offer a basis which allows a sophisticated applications designer or DBI to model his application layer in an appropriate and natural way. To do so he must be in a position to consider operations' semantics in his design. In this section we will demonstrate such an approach by modelling some operations of a simplified software development application. Since we are only interested in concurrency control aspects we will only describe the lock-specific part of the operations in more detail.

Let us assume that our application environment consists of a library which includes standard procedures as well as individual software modules. Standard procedures can be included "as is" in software modules. Software modules consist of standard procedures as well as individual code. A number of software modules can be combined in a software package which, in fact, corresponds to a product, e. g., a word processing system.

Standard procedures

For standard procedures the following rules are valid:

1. Since standard procedures can only be used as is, a programmer is not allowed to modify them.

2. If a standard procedures is to be modified this is only possible by deriving a new version of it.

3. Standard procedures may be implemented in different programming languages. Therefore, different representations of a procedure may exist.

4. Since software environments may slightly differ, variants of a standard procedure can be defined which, e. g., differ in the type of their parameters.

2., 3. and 4. mean that a standard procedure is represented by a version graph which may contain different representations as well as different variants.

The following (informal) operations are defined on standard procedures:

a. *browse_standproc (...)*: Read the complete version graph of a standard procedure (in a dirty mode). This operation needs to acquire a B/X-lock (browse lock).

b. *read_standproc (...)*: Read a specific representation (variant) of a procedure. This operation needs to acquire an S/D (derivation possible) or S/S-lock (derivation not possible).

c. *insert_standproc (...)*: Insert a new standard procedure. This operation needs to impose an (object related) PMD-lock (exclusive derivation) on the object which is to be inserted.

d. *derive_standproc (...)*: Derive a new version (representation, variant) of a standard procedure. This operation needs to acquire a D/S lock for exclusive derivation or a D/D lock for shared derivation. Moreover, it need to establish a PMD-lock on the new version of the object.

The concurrency control component will react as follows:

Every standard procedure is protected by a PMD lock. A PMD lock is only compatible with a B/*, S/* and D/* lock (* can be replaced by any possible external effect). Other locks are prohibited. Therefore, an S/D lock does not have to be considered by the concurrency control component since the PMD lock already excludes every incompatible lock mode. A B/X lock either has not to be considered since it is no lock in the literal sense of the word. Only an S/S, a D/S, and a D/D lock require the concurrency control mechanism to consider them.

Scenario 1: Software packages can't be modified

If software packages can't be modified every modification defines a new version of the package. All versions are arranged in a linear order, since at any point of time only one (unique) version of the software package can be valid, i. e., a time version mechanism needs to be implemented.

In the following we only want to take a closer look at such operations which demonstrate new aspects with regard to concurrency control.

Since at any point of time only one new version of a software package can be derived a PSD lock need to be imposed on each package (by every operation which inserts a new version of a package or a completely new package). A PSD lock only permits the acquisition of a B/*, S/*, or D/S lock from which only an S/S and a D/S lock need to be considered by the concurrency control component. This reduces the overhead for concurrency control substantially.

Let us consider two exemplary operations, a *check-out_softpack (...)* operation which checks out a special software package from the database and a *check-in_softpack (...)* which inserts a new version. The *check-out_softpack* operation needs to request a D/S lock (concurrent transactions are not allowed to modify the package or to derive a new version of it but they are allowed to read the package in S/D mode). The *check-in_softpack* operation has to establish a PSD lock on the new version. Moreover, it may release the D/S lock on the old version. Note, however, that the concurrency control component may delay the release of the lock, e. g., in case the strict two-phase lock protocol is realized till the end of the transaction.

Scenario 2: Software packages can be modified

If we assume that software packages can be updated object related locks need not to be established. In this case we need different check-out operations, one for a check-out to derive a new version and one for a check-out to update. The first check-out operation is similar to the check-out operation of scenario 1. The *check-out_softpack_for_update* has to acquire a U/S lock for the software package which is to be updated. The U/S lock still allows concurrent transactions to read the package (in S/U mode). Now let us assume that a package which is to be updated contains some standard procedures P^S. Since usually these standard procedures will also be locked in U/S mode other transactions are excluded from locking some other software package P which also contains at least one P^S. This reduces concurrency unnecessarily. Since our tool kit supports object related locks, such an unfortunate situation can be avoided since the PMD lock preserves each P^S from being locked in U/S mode. Instead, the concurrency control mechanism needs not to consider any lock on a P^S at all.

12

The S-transaction Model

Jari Veijalainen

Frank Eliassen

Bernhard Holtkamp

12.1 Introduction

The investments on the information technology have increased almost on each sector of the economy and a vast variety of applications already exist, representing a tremendous economical value. This dependence of the society on the information technology on one hand and the emerging possibility of Electronic Data Interchange (EDI) on the other hand are in the wide sense the background of the *semantic transaction model* (S-transaction model) discussed in this chapter. It was initially developed for a large-scale inter-organizational autonomous environment, international banking, in a European project[1], carried out during 1985-1988

The practical goal of the MAP761 project was to develop mechanisms that would help to associate the processing of different banking messages, conveyed through the S.W.I.F.T. II network, and to offer multidatabase services through an open network [MAP86]. Primarily, the S-transaction model supports *computerized cooperation* between organizations, as we call it. The model is, however, more general and can be applied in any environment, where the *autonomy* of the organizations and the corresponding component systems must be preserved.

Autonomy was recognized as an important subject in such inter-organizational environments [VP86, EV87a, VP88, Vei90] and its preservation is pervasive in the S-transaction model. Technically, the initial ideas for the model came from the (hierarchical) transaction models, notably those in [Gra81, BKK85, Mos85], from the notion of objects, and multidatabases [LMR90]. The implementation of the model constitutes the kernel of the developed prototype multidatabase system called MUSE [Ell88, MAP89].

The trend towards computerized cooperation based on EDI is also strong in international trade, as the emerging standards and systems for computer-aided trade show[2]. Therefore, the S-transaction model should find interest in those environments, too.

[1] **Mu**ltidatabase **Se**rvices on ISO/OSI Networks for Transnational Accounting (MUSE), performed by I.N.R.I.A. (France), Gesellschaft für Mathematik und Datenverarbeitung mbH (GMD, Germany), Society for Worldwide Interbank Financial Telecommunications s.c. (S.W.I.F.T., Belgium), and University of Dortmund (Germany), and financed partly by the Commission of the European Communities under contracts MAP761 and MAP761B.

[2] Currently, there exists a standardized grammar with which to define the message types, EDIFACT (Electronic Data Interchange for Administration, Commerce and Transport) standard [ISO9735]. It is part of the Trade Data Interchange Directory, issued and maintained by the United Nation Economic Commission for Europe, UN/ECE. It is used e.g.

From the communication point of view the S-transaction model makes it possible to represent any business or application protocol whose topology is a tree, in a machine executable form. It also incorporates support for overcoming the Heterogeneity within autonomous database environment so that the pertinent data can be accessed. The S-transaction model adopts conventional database transactions with ACID-poperties [HR83] as the basic building blocks, combining them, the "higher level" computation, and data and control flow into distributed hierarchical transactions, S- transactions. To preserve autonomy, isolation among different S-transactions is abandoned and the traditional atomicity is replaced by a probabilistic one. S-transactions are dynamically generated, they preserve local consistency and are exactly as durable as usual transactions they are based on. In S-transactions, the local transactions are the concurrency control units and any sub-S-transaction can be dynamically chosen to become a recovery unit. Backward recovery can be based either on a usual abort mechanism or on compensating transactions. Forward and backward recovery can be dynamically combined within an S-transaction.

We elaborate different aspect of the model as follows. In section 12.2 the autonomy concepts behind the model are reviewed. We identify *organizational (O-)*, *design (D-)*, *management (M-)*, *communication (C-)*, and *execution (E-)autonomy*. We also discuss what basic autonomy and effective autonomy mean.

In section 12.3 we discuss requirements for a transaction model in autonomous environments. The overall architecture and the main software components supporting S-transactions are also presented.

In section 12.4 we first present a formal model for S-transactions and analyze their properties, like atomicity and consistency preservation. The main problem is how to achieve backward recovery based on compensation. In section 12.5 we discuss languages needed in representing S-transaction definitions.

In section 12.6 we discuss the real applications of the model and in section 12.7 further developments of the basic S-transaction model. Section 12.8 concludes this chapter.

---

by car manufacturers and its usage is rapidly increasing in airlines and shipping. Also ISO and CCITT are studying what should be standardized in the computerized cooperation field [EDI91].

12.2 Autonomous environments and their requirements

Autonomy has become lately an issue in distributed systems design. The reason is that distributed information systems have been developed that span several organizations or relatively independent units within an organization. These new environments require understanding what autonomy is and how to cope with it when designing a system. Several aspects that are actually connected to autonomy have been identified during the last 10-15 years. In the communication area the approach stated in the ISO/OSI model [ISO7492] and the standardized protocols developed within its framework, are an important contribution to the understanding of autonomy.

In the database field autonomy was recognized as an issue in the context of distributed databases, notable R* [Sel84], multidatabases [LMR90], and federated databases [HM85]. It was analysed further in Europe mainly by the authors of this chapter [MAP86, VP86, EV87a, EV87b, Hol87, VP88, Hol88]. At the same time, autonomy was addressed within some projects in USA as reported e.g. in [AGS87, GS88, DE89], and in the United Kingdom [ANSA89]. The ACM European Chapter organized a workshop on autonomy in Cambridge in September 1988.

12.2.1 Basic definitions of autonomy

When defining autonomy more accurately we must decide what it is attributed to. Since we need to cope with such different things as organizations, human beings, computers, software modules, databases, etc., we consider autonomy of *entities* in general. An entity is anything that can be separated (by a human being) from its environment. It has a particular *structure* which determines how an entity could behave during its existence. For instance, in a computer system certain hardware and software are required in order it to communicate with other computers or human beings in an "open" way. A lion has organs that enables it to hunt other animals and digest their meat, but it never can fly like a bird because its structure simply does not enable it. In this sense the structure is the "internal limit" of the entity.

When modeling real entities, we view them as capable of *taking actions.* In a formal sense their real structure is thus reduced to a finite number of *possible finite sequences of action types*, called *behavior types*, enabled by the real structure. Some of the actions types are *visible* to the outside world, some are *internal.* The visible actions are the basis for the set of possible *interactions* the entity can take part in within its environment. Some visible actions are *constrained*, meaning that such a visible action is enabled to take place only after some other visible action at some other entity had taken place. Constrained actions model *dependence* of the entity on its environment.

The overall formal structure modeling an entity is a finitely branching, labeled, directed tree with infinite height. Each label is a pair (x, P_i), where x is an action and P_i, $0 < P_i \leq 1$, is the probability with which the action is taken in that situation. It is called *desirability* and the sum of desirabilities on outgoing arcs of any node is one. Each path in the tree, containing an infinite sequence of actions on the arcs, models a *possible future*. The paths together determine what kind of behaviors are potentially possible to an entity by its structure.

Autonomy is the opposite to *controllability* of the possible or actual behaviors of the entity, from the point of view of the entity itself or of the environment. The real self-controlling potential of an entity with respect to its own possible futures is called *self-determination*. An entity having the property that its actually exhibited particular behaviour may deviate from the externally determined criteria, we call *effectively autonomous*. Otherwise we refer to the entity as *externally controllable*.

Let us first look at the self-determination. The *really possible behaviors* are contained in the *really possible futures*, namely those that are left after all futures absolutely impossible within a particular environment have been sorted out. The reason for some behavior B of an entity X to become impossible is that a constrained action v was encountered on the path leading to B, or within B, that could not be taken because the environment did not trigger it. The overall dependence of an entity upon its environment can be measured by a probabilistic measure LA ("loss of autonomy"). It uses a probability of the subtrees, each such probability being the product of the desirabilities on the path from the root of the tree to the root of such a subtree. LA = P(union of subtrees that cannot be freely chosen by X).

The *degree of self-determination* could be measured by 1-LA which is the probability of those really possible infinite futures that can be followed by the entity if it so desires, independently from the actions of its environment. The measure LA can also be defined for any subset of entities in the environment. A more detailed treatment can be found in [Vei90].

The external controllability and effective autonomy can be defined based on clauses of the form (C,B), where C is a condition and B is a behavior. C and B both consists of a finite sequence of actions. The clauses express expectations of form "if C occurs/does not occur then B must/must not/might occur)". If the clause is fulfilled then X is externally controllable, otherwise it is effectively autonomous in that situation for the entity Y that did set up the clause.

The clauses characterizing X's behavior are set up by one entity Y, for each situation separately. This explains why the same or similar behavior B can be considered at the same time effectively autonomous and controllable by different entities. A typical example are two clients at work stations that have different expectations on how quickly the server responds. Further, in two different situations the controlling entity might expect different kind of behavior from the controlled one, even if the interaction was of the same type.

The effective autonomy, as described above makes it possible to understand how external controllability and self-determination can be in effect at the same time. First, self-determination is a concept of potentiality, giving entity X the possibility to behave either as expected by the environment or against it. Second, a clause above might consider all possible and even impossible behaviors of X in that situation as acceptable. In that case X can choose any of the really possible behaviors and be externally controllable. On the other hand, Y might only expect behavior from X that it is not capable of doing by its very structure. In that case the controlled entity is effectively autonomous. For instance, a horse is effectively autonomous for a rider expecting it to run 100 km/h. Similarly, a PC is effectively autonomous towards a user, if it is expected to serve thousands of database requests within one second.

One way of *measuring effective autonomy* is to define how "frequently" an entity exhibits autonomous behavior in different situations. Based on the relative frequency of effectively autonomous instances of behaviors, a fuzzy [Kan86] measure, for instance, can then be defined. Most naturally, it is done for each pair of entities separately. For example, "often" for entity Y might mean the behavior of X is effectively autonomous in more than 20 percent of situations. Using such a measure, the effective autonomy becomes something that an entity X has or does not have, towards another entity Y. For a detailed treatment of these issues, the reader is referred to [Vei90].

The effective autonomy is essential in the real life, since the interactions between entities are often attempts to control the other one and only the really chosen behavior matters, not the possible options. The effective control of X by Y means that Y tries to *enforce* the condition C in a clause and expects then either that X exhibits B (or does not exhibit B, if C is prohibiting condition for B). The attempts are mediated either by actively interacting with the entity X or by refusing to interact with it, or trying the enforcement indirectly, through other entities. The former causes constrained actions, occurring in the condition C, to become possible for X, the latter enforcement causes constrained actions to become impossible for X. Since X can try to control Y and vice versa, the situation is a game. It is possible that both are able to enforce choices at the other, like in communication protocols. Entity Y can also indirectly use other entities Z,W, etc. in order to enforce B at X and vice versa, Z and W might try to use X and Y in their trials of enforcement etc. So, in reality it is a set of very complicated games.

12.2.2 O-autonomy

Computer systems are used by organizations to satisfy their needs. Since organizations are the basis for the existence of computers, *organizational autonomy*, O-autonomy, is the basis for other autonomies. The main entities and interactions in an autonomous database environment are shown in Fig. 12.1. An *organization* consists solely of human beings. The corresponding *overall organization* consists of the *human organization* and *computers and telecommunication facilities* whose usage is solely controlled by it and which support computerized cooperation with other organizations.

Organizational self-determination means that an organization has real alternatives to choose upon in its daily behavior, even if other organizations try to influence it. This influence can be brought to effect through direct interactions as is the case between a negotiating contractor and subcontractor, or indirectly, if companies compete at the market place. There are many different kinds of interactions between organizations and the self-determination must be considered with respect to all of them. We show in Fig. 12.1 only four types of interactions between organizations that are in our case the most interesting from autonomy point of view, namely *negotiations, democratic control, competition*, and *repeated cooperation.*

Effective O-autonomy means that organization X does not behave in a way organization Y expects it to behave in a single interaction or series of interactions, or when Y refuses to interact with X a certain situation.

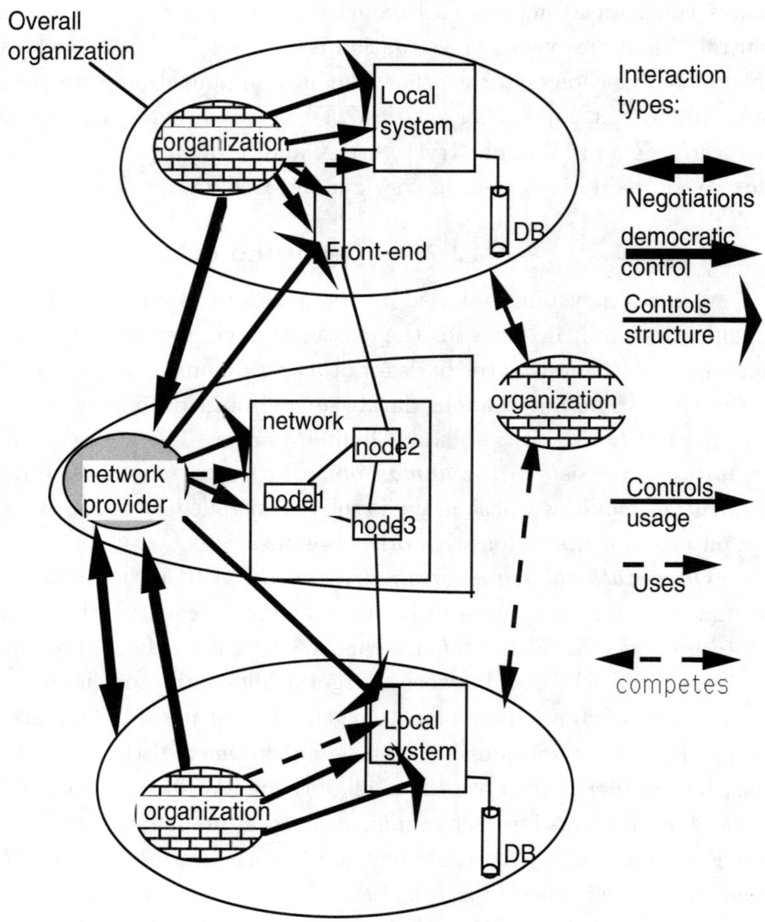

FIGURE 12.1
The main interactions in an autonomous environment

12.2.3 D-and M-autonomy and heterogeneity

Since computers do not have any own intentions they do not start any activities by themselves, but rather, some part of the human organization controls the overall *structure* and *behavior* of computers through two different types of of interactions, namely *controls the usage* and *controls the structure.* These are shown in Fig. 12.1. The former is an interaction type with the help of which the organization decides who is entitled to use the computer system, what rights the users have, how much they must pay for the usage, etc. The other interaction type models the activity where the organization chooses and/or develops the computer systems hardware, software and applications that meet their needs.

The controlling activities might be fully self-determined or effectively controlled by another organization, or something in between. We say that an organization is *M-autonomous* (management autonomous) with respect to a computer system, if it has full organizational self-determination when deciding upon the usage of that system, i.e. with respect to *controls the usage* type of interactions. Usually, M-autonomy[3] precludes that the organization owns or has leased the computer system in question.

Effective M-autonomy means that an organization makes such decisions concerning the usage of its system that are against the expectations of another organization. It is worth noting that the same organization might be effectively M-autonomous towards foreign organizations, but cannot act against the will of the headquarter in this respect.

We say that an organization is *D-autonomous* (design autonomous) with respect to a computer system (or a part of it) if it has full organizational self-determination with respect to controls the structure -type of interactions. In other words, a D-autonomous organization has a number of real alternatives at its disposal when choosing the hardware and software of that system, when developing the conceptual and physical schemata[4] for the database system, when developing databases and other applications, run in that system, and so on.

---

[3]In [Wie87] a bit similar definition was given but the term used was "organizational autonomy". Within Internet one also talks, "for the purpose of routing", about autonomous system , which is "a group of gateways and networks controlled by a single administrative authority" [Com88], p. 166.

[4]Litwin et. al., for instance, discuss four sub-aspects of D-autonomy (name independence, data duplication, data restructuring, value type autonomy) under the name "data definition autonomy" [LMR90].

Note, that an organization may be D-autonomous with respect to one (part of a) system but not with respect to another one, even if it would be M-autonomous with respect to both of them (leased systems). Also note, that an organizational subunit, like an affiliated company, may be D-autonomous with respect to its computer systems, although it might be controlled in some other respects by the headquarter.

When a cooperative system is set up, the *D-autonomy of a system* plays the main role. We say that a (part of a) computer system is D-autonomous with respect to an organization if the organization is *not D-autonomous* with respect to the system. In other words, an organization must be, for some reason, incapable of fully controlling the structure of the D-autonomous system.

Often, the reason for D-autonomy of a particular system with respect to an organization is that there is another organization that is D-autonomous with respect to the same system and refuses to choose or develop such a computer system structure, that another organizations expects from it (in a negotiation). The reason for such a behavior is usually that the expected structures (protocol software or hardware, database system expected, etc.) are not in the *interest* of the D-autonomous organization. Either the latter organization wants to enforce certain solutions in its environment for the benefit of itself, or the required structure is too expensive or even impossible to implement.

D-autonomy of organizations with respect to the local systems managed by them implies that the overall environment is usually *heterogeneous* in all respects (different local hardware and software, database management systems, database schemas, and different consistency constraints embedded in application programs).

For an autonomous environment, like the international banking, the Heterogeneity is likely to be a permanent state of affairs, i.e. organizations will make use of their D-autonomy by constantly developing the systems, structurally controlled by them, as they like. The S-transaction model must consequently cope explicitly with Heterogeneity in order to be applicable for a longer period of time.

12.2.4 C-autonomy

In computerized cooperation the computers are used as a technical means of cooperation. The information exchange needed in cooperation is (partly) implemented by communicating computers of the organizations. A manifestation of effective M-autonomy is that the organization wants to regulate when its system is reachable through the network, when it is detached or shut down. From the network point of view such a system either communicates or does not communicate at all, during a certain period of time.

We say that a system S is *C-autonomous* towards another system S if the latter cannot enforce S to start, stop, or continue communicating[5] with an arbitrary system S". System S is *effectively C-autonomous* towards another system S', if S *sometimes*[6] refuses to respond to communication attempts from S'.

If two systems are not at all willing to communicate at the same real time, they cannot communicate at all, or one or both must adapt their communication behavior. This means actually reduction of C-autonomy (and M-and O-autonomy, which is the actual problem). This can be avoided if at least one system within the network is not effectively C-autonomous within the environment. Such a network, like S.W.I.F.T. I, supports the effective C-autonomy of the participating systems. Supporting C-autonomy requires mechanisms that are designed with this goal. The CCITT X.400 recommendation [X.400] is a good example of such protocols that support maximally C-autonomy of the users. Also, in other ISO/OSI protocols the responding system can always refuse to set up a connection, or brake an existing one, by issuing the corresponding protocol message. The latter are examples of mechanisms supporting effective C-autonomy. The consequences, measures, etc., of C-autonomy are handled more thoroughly in [Vei90].

12.2.5 E-autonomy and erroneous and correct behavior

The cooperative interactions between organizations are structured in a certain way. This structure is reflected into the computer world as an application protocol, sometimes called *business protocol.* Its definition contains protocol message types and their possible orders. An expression of effective O-autonomy (and M-autonomy) is that an organisation does not need to execute all requests carried by messages it receives, in the same way as it does not need to react positively on a letter or telex it receives. We say that a system has *E-autonomy* (execution autonomy) with respect to the corresponding protocol message types if it can choose whether to execute their instances or not and if it can decide itself which other systems should be involved in the execution.

[5] By communication we mean in this context exchange of protocol messages, defined for an OSI layer, between two computers.

[6] This is a fuzzy quantifier, see the discussion in the previous section.

Effective E-autonomy means making use of the possibility not to execute a message. An E-autonomous system can refuse to execute an incoming message for variety of business or technical reasons, like mistrust of the business partner, erroneous information in the message, authorization failure, overload of the system - or because the business protocol does not always require further steps (as e.g. an offer to buy or sell currency). It can also start the execution and even request other systems to completely perform subtasks, but later still come to the decision that it is not possible to execute the message.

The implications of effective E-autonomy become clearer when considering e.g. the 2PC protocol [Gra78]; if a participant system really refuses to execute COMMIT or ABORT message sent by the Coordinator, the protocol does not meet its goals. The 2PC protocol is in autonomous environments not viable, also because the overall banking transactions, for instance, can last hours or even weeks. Blocking pertinent data of an organization for a long period of time blocks the local users using the data, which might substantially reduce the self-determination of the local users, i.e. *local user autonomy*, and M-autonomy.

What is the relationship between "erroneous" and "autonomous" behavior of a computer system? First, if erroneous means qualitative deviation of the system behavior from its overall specification (2+2 =5 type errors, visible protocol errors), then the behavior cannot be accepted by the organization using the system, and the system must be repaired. Other aspect is quantitative. Different values of the same measure might be criteria for the "erroneous" and for the "autonomous" behavior of another system. The fuzzy measure above, for instance, can be used. Then, either it holds that effectively (C- or E-) autonomous behavior is erroneous, or there is a degree up to which it is acceptable, according to these criteria. An example of the latter possibility is statement that "if a system does not communicate for three days it is effectively C-autonomous, but if it does not communicate for a month, then it is erroneous".

The relationships between different aspects of autonomy have been further discussed in [Vei90].

12.3 A gross architecture supporting S-transactions

The S-transaction model was developed for a particular environment, international banking, where all aspects of autonomy are present. The model itself can be used also in other environments, where the requirements are similar, as we show below. We first discuss the general ideas and then deduce the specific requirements for the site architecture, for the overall distributed architecture, and for the necessary communication services and protocols.

12.3.1 Requirements for a transaction model coping with autonomy

Why should there be "transactions" in an autonomous environment and how should they look like? If the different sites have some subtasks that really belong together, then it makes sense to think of "transactions". A transaction then materializes, in a computer executable form, some common task. We call them *S-transactions*, where S stands for "semantical", for reasons explained below.

How are they defined if the environment is heterogeneous and the local database systems D-autonomous towards any global authority? A solution is that there is a machine-executable *homogeneous global transaction language* (e.g. STDL, or FRIL see sections 12.5 - 12.7) with which the global transactions are specified.

Since the environment is heterogeneous and the operational data resides within heterogeneous, D-autonomous database systems, the global language is not yet the whole solution. Preserving D-autonomy of the participating organizations requires that installing the new facilities supporting cooperation should not cause any changes to existing system software or applications. Rather, it should be implementable as an *add-on feature* in the existing environment. For the same reason, those applications that manipulate the operational data of an enterprise should be designed and programmed under its full control, no matter whether they serve inter-organizational cooperation or internal data processing. Thus, those parts of the transaction programs that really access the local data *must be written under the control of the organization having the D- and M-autonomy with respect to the local database system they are run at.* For this purpose the local database (host) language is used. Consequently, the *traditional database transactions* [Gra78] *should be used as the basic building blocks of the S-transaction model.* We call them *local sub-S-transactions.* They should not differ from existing *local transactions* from the point of view of the local database system.

Which overall structures should the S-transactions have? Since many sites can cooperate to perform a common task, and the interaction between them can be arbitrarily complex, the S-transaction model must allow for equally complex *execution structures.* In our case it contains a *spanning tree,* which can be *dynamically generated* during the execution. Thus we have a *root* S-transaction, *superior S-transactions*, and *sub-S-transactions* occurring in the execution structure.

The dynamic generation of the execution structure is guided by the results of the sub-S-transactions and time-outs. One aspect is that if one group of sub-S-transactions fails, the superior can request an other group to perform the missing tasks. The latter group (or transaction) is called *an alternative* (S-transaction). The S-transaction model does *not require* failure propagation upwards in the spanning tree, but rather each superior S-transaction must evaluate failures of it sub-S-transactions and decide on further measures. The global execution mechanism alone cannot do any decisions.

Which further properties should the transaction program executions, i.e. *S-transactions* in the narrower sense, have? A possible answer is that *atomicity, consistency, isolation, durability*, i.e. ACID properties [HR83] are a good goal when considering some program executions to have *transactional* properties.

*D*urability is not a problem, since the local database systems guarantee it.

In an autonomous environment *I*solation is not always desirable and even if it were, it cannot always be enforced without severely reducing local user autonomy and M-autonomy. The reason is that pertinent local data becomes blocked for long periods of time, since the global transactions span several effectively C- and E-autonomous sites and are often *long-living*[7]. Ensuring E-autonomy and autonomy of local users using the data requires, that *local sub-S-transactions are allowed to commit or abort irrespective of the fate of the whole global S-transaction.*

Releasing the updated data for other S-transactions before it is globally committed or aborted, means that the isolation among S-transactions is lost - albeit local isolation might be maintained at each local database system (c.f. each local R-W history is locally rigorous [BHG87]). Abandoning global isolation results in problems with serializability and global recovery. If a superior S-transaction must be rolled back, all its local sub-S-transactions should also be rolled back (failure propagation downwards), otherwise the execution is not *A*tomic. If the local commit is issued only after the global one, then the recovery is achieved by locally aborting the sub-S-transaction. If the local sub-S-transaction was, however, locally committed before the global abort decision, there is no way to roll back it by the recovery facilities offered

[7]In banking, a the overall funds transfer can take several days.

by a usual database system. The rollback must be based on another local, *compensating* sub-S-transaction that is executed to "reverse" or "abolish" the effects of the *normal* sub-S-transaction in the local database.

In E-autonomous environment it is not guaranteed that the compensating sub-S-transaction does not abort. The reason might be technical or semantical. This again jeopardizes global atomicity, that is, *one cannot always guarantee that "an S-transaction either is executed as a whole, or otherwise such a global database state can be achieved as if nothing was executed"*.

S-transactions should also preserve Consistency. In fact, an S-transaction enforces a *semantical constraint*, which can be expressed as a predicate on a collection of state transitions. We handle the issues in section 12.4.

Preserving or abandoning isolation seems to be the key issue for all further considerations: Keeping global isolation by not locally committing a sub-S-transaction before the global commit, might be meaningless in some applications. Combined with effective C- and E-autonomy it easily results in loss of local user autonomy. On the other hand, abandoning global isolation preserves C-, E-, and local user autonomy, but leads maybe to the need of compensating transaction programs. Guaranteeing global atomicity might require violation of local consistency, i.e. this might reduce D-autonomy. *Both approaches should thus be supported by the model*, so that the O-autonomous organization can itself maximize whatever aspects of autonomy it will.

12.3.2 The site architecture

The recurrent cooperations, like an Electronic Funds Transfer (EFT), are all represented as several *interoperable* programs in the environment. Those individual programs that together form an *S-transaction definition* are called *program parts*. They are written with the global transaction language (global program parts) or with some local language usable at a local database system (local program parts). The global program parts are processed by modules that we call *S-transaction Manager* (STM). The STM is at the heart of the site architecture. It controls program part execution and interacts with the other modules that host other program parts belonging to S-transaction definitions. The STM is typically implemented as an "add-on" language interpreter that is able to run many S-transactions in parallel.

How is the global homogeneous transaction language combined with the communication facilities, like message types? The communication support can be arranged fairly independently from other considerations, as long as C-autonomy is supported.

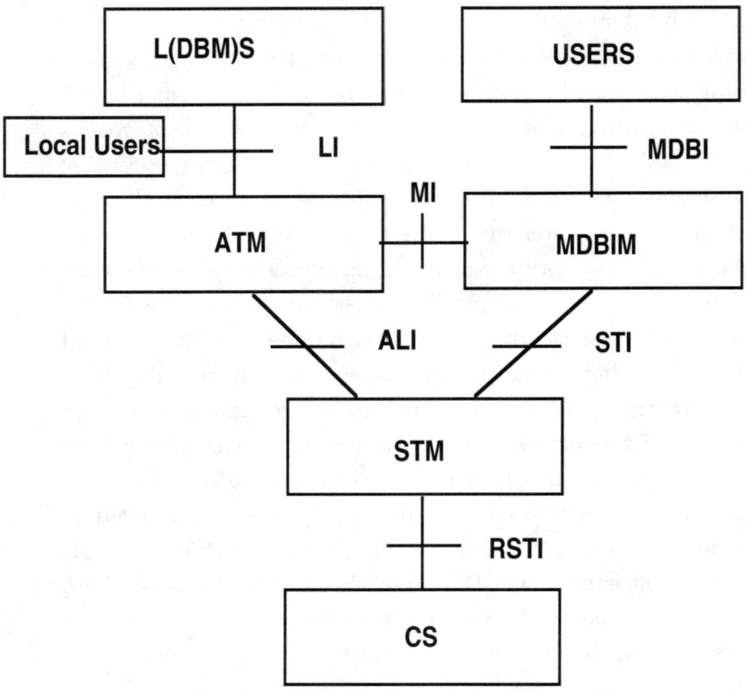

L(DBMS) = Local (Database Management) System
MDBIM = Multidatabase Interface Manager
STM = S-transaction Manager
CS = Communication Server

LI = Local Interface
ALI = Abstract Local Interface
STI = S-transaction Interface
RSTI = Remote S-transaction Interface
MDBI = Multidatabase Interface
MI = Management Interface

FIGURE 12.2
The gross site architecture

Thus in the site architecture of Fig. 12.2 point-to-point communication is taken care of by a *Communication Server* (CS) module, whose functionality is, for instance, that of a X.400 stack (up to the P1 protocol), plus a robust point-to-point protocol (RRA, Request, Response, Abort/Acknowledgement protocol) that replaces the P2 protocol and facilitates message exchanges between a superior S-transaction and one sub-S-transaction at another site.

The next problem is immediately visible; Since the local database systems are heterogeneous, how it possible to identify the local sub-S-transaction programs and instances in a unique way, to cope with the differing parameter data within the programs written in the global homogeneous language? To solve this problem, a module, called *Abstract Transaction Manager* (ATM) must be assumed. It hides the differences of local systems by offering a syntactically homogeneous *Abstract Local Interface* (ALI) to the STM. Each ATM must also be multi-threaded.

An ALI must basically only provide such update and retrieval operations that have a full cooperative application meaning. Retrievals might also be subject to restrictions in a similar way as the updates. We call the operations, offered at an ALI, *abstract local transactions* (ablocal transactions)[8]. They are the only bridge between the local system and the global system. Thus, the exact semantics of each ablocal transaction is crucial for the correct functioning of the global system. It is a non-trivial task of the global *transaction designer*, which is a standardizing committee [Vei90], to agree on it in an autonomous and heterogeneous environment.

An ablocal transaction definition is of form NAME(IN;OUT), where NAME is a globally unique name of an ablocal transaction type, IN is its *input scheme*, OUT its *output scheme*. The schemes contain a (sequence of) relational[9] schema(s) [ISO9075]. Operationally, the data flow from the global part of the multidatabase system into the local system as input parameter instances of different ablocal transactions. They conform syntactically to the corresponding input scheme IN. In the opposite direction the different output parameter instances carry the data, which is structured according to the output scheme.

From the transaction management point of view the ATM can be based on similar structures as a saga manager [GS87], since a local sub-S-transaction

[8]By the ablocal transaction we refer both to the definition and to the execution of them. Sometimes it is explicitly mentioned which aspect is meant but usually it is clear from the context.

[9]The relational model is not the only possibility to describe the schemas, any other model suitable for the application domain will do.

and its compensating transaction can be viewed as a saga [Vei90].

Finally, the multidatabase interface manager (MDBIM) takes care of the interface functions towards global users (USER). It provides global data definition, S-transaction definition, data manipulation, and security facilities to the *global users* at the global interface (MDBI). Management Interface (MI) supports storing definitions of ablocal transactions and authorization information into the ATM module from MDBIM. It is used by the transaction designer.

12.3.3 The overall distributed architecture

The STM-ATM -pairs residing at each site form the heart of the overall architecture. STMs interact with other STMs and the ATM at the same site by way of the RRA protocol that facilitates communication between a superior S-transaction and one sub-S-transaction. An STM executing the superior S-transaction can be seen as a *client* and STM or ATM executing the sub-S-transaction as a *server*. A server STM might become a client if the sub-S-transaction has itself sub-S-transactions.

The *S-transaction protocol* is a collection of RRA associations, bound together by the STMs each one capable of acting both as a client and a server. Each global program part contains a description of how this binding is done.

A client executing the superior S-transaction initiates an RRA association by sending a REQUEST message to the server STM (or ATM). The message contains a unique identification of the program part (or the whole program part) and a list of actual parameters conforming to the formal one. The reception of the REQUEST message causes the server to run up the identified program part as a sub-S-transaction of the superior - or the request is ignored (c.f. effective E-autonomy). After having performed its tasks, maybe thereby launching own sub-S-transactions, choosing alternatives, etc., the sub-S-transaction sends a RESPONSE message to the superior. The message contains "failure", if the sub-S-transaction failed to perform its task, otherwise it contains "success", along with the result data. An incoming RESPONSE message with "failure" is interpreted by the superior to mean that "the sub-S-transaction did not do anything, and I can forget it". Therefore, no further protocol exchanges with it are required, and it is totally on the responsibility of the sub-S-transaction, how and when it propagates the failure downwards. This gives the possibility for maximal parallelism in global recovery.

The superior decides on its own" success" or "failure", based on result data and"success" and "failure" indications of all its sub-S-transactions. If the superior decides to fail then "failure" must be propagated downwards. This is done by issuing ABORT messages to all those sub-S-transactions that have not returned a RESPONSE with "failure".

Since any sub-S-transaction can autonomously decide to fail and failures are propagated downwards, a successful sub-S-transaction must be prepared to issue a ABORT message towards its own sub-S-transactions, as long as not explicitly otherwise stated by its superior. Only the root can decide that the whole S-transaction is successful. In that case it sends to all its direct successful sub-S-transactions an ACK message. This is propagated further down by each superior, until all successful leaves are reached. Operationally, log resources are released and local commits issued, if the policy chosen at the ATM for the ablocal transaction involved was not to issue the local commit before the global one.

On the other hand, all forms of cooperation do not require cancellation (e.g. S-transactions consisting of pure retrievals), and consequently there is no need for ACKs in this case. In certain cases even responses can be omitted, if a component system only wants to inform something to others and does not require any response for the requests it sends. These optimizations can be supported by the RRA protocol. They are described in [EV87b]. We do not handle them here.

Note that the above concepts "success" and "failure" mean that an S-transaction either happens or does not happen, but in the semantical sense. They don't have a simple relationship with e.g. program failures or communication failures. For instance a missing RESPONSE does not mean that no local sub-S-transaction returned "success", i.e. committed locally. Therefore, a superior S-transaction cannot use e.g. time-out to interpret a missing RESPONSE to be the same as value "failure" returned. This fact requires that *the execution mechanism*, consisting of of the STMs and ATMs, is *robust* against all kind of technical failures, like lost messages and crashed program executions. In practice, logs must implemented that record the sub-S-transaction states in an unambiguous way. By this way it is also possible to avoid orphans [Mos85].

12.4 Properties of S-transactions

We have already extensively discussed autonomy, the requirements for the transaction model, and main problems, like atomicity and consistency. In this section we discuss more precisely the properties by using a formal model. We begin by an example.

In Fig. 12.3 we have an example of an S-transaction having sub-S--transactions at four sites. Let site 1 be a travel agency ordering flights for a customer from city A to city C, via city B. The travel agency starts the corresponding S-transaction program at its STM which becomes the *root S-transaction* (T1, an askew striped ball). The root first asks site 2 (an airline) to reserve the entire flight (a *request arc* downwards). The REQUEST message arrives at the STM which runs up the corresponding program part (sub-S--transaction T2, an askew striped ball). T2 first requests an *ablocal transaction* T2a to make the reservations. T2a further issues a *normal local sub-S-transaction* T2b (white ball) to make the reservation at a CODASYL database. T2b finds out that it can only offer a flight from A to B, which is reserved and committed. T2b informs this to T2a (a positive *response arc* upwards), which responds to T2 positively.

T2 then decides to ask site 3 (another airline) for the missing connecting flight from B to C (a request arc from site 2 to site 3). This is handled by T3, T3a, and T3b. T3b finds a late flight which it records a reservation for and T3 responds to T2 positively (thin *response arc* upwards), conveying the reservation information. The flight is too late for the customer, and T2 asks site 4 (yet another airline) for a reservation (request arc from site 2 to site 4). T4, T4a and T4b perform the task, as above. Thereby, T4b records a reservation for a flight starting from B, at a relational database, and T4 responds positively (response arc from T4 to site T2). T2 now chooses this flight and asks the pending T3 to cancel the reservation (dotted *abort arc* downwards). T3 informs T3a and stops. T3a then starts a canceling (compensating) local sub-S-transaction T3c. It aborts locally because of a deadlock problem at a local database (the striped ball). Another attempt T3c' succeeds committing the cancellation (the black ball) and T3a also runs into completion.

Meanwhile, T2 issues a positive response to T1 (response arc upwards) with the complete flight information. T1 (at the travel agency) accepts the reservations and produces the tickets. T1 asks the reservations to be recorded at its local database (T1a, T1b) and acknowledges them (a thin *ack arc* downwards) to pending T2 and T1a. T1 stops. T2 informs T4 that the reservation is in effect (ack arc). T2, T2a, T4 and T4a stop.

The S-transaction above exemplifies several things. The sub-S-transactions T3 and T4 are alternative S-transactions, since they both offer a suitable connecting flight. They could also be started in parallel, since T3 and T4 are neither *data* nor *conditionally dependent* on each other, nor is T2 restricted by T1 (the travel agency) to apply an order among its sub-S-transactions. However, if the first reservation attempt at site 3 did not succeed, T4 would become *failure dependent* on T3. Because a good business practice requires to cancel superfluous reservations, there is an "at most one" dependence between the sub-S-transactions T3 and T4: only one should remain effective. Note that these dependences are only known by T2. As exemplified further by T1, a successful S-transaction can contain sub-S-transactions that have been compensated (above, the entire T3 at site 3). Further, a trial to run a compensating transaction can fail either for semantical reasons or for technical reasons (as above T3c) and it can be repeated (T3c').

12.4.1 A semi-formal model for the S-transactions

In the transaction literature [Lyn83, BHG87, Mos85] a formal transaction usually models one instance of program execution. The program itself remains implicit. Since we want to look at the semantical properties of S-transaction programs, we have to model them both explicitly.

An *S-transaction definition graph* DGi is a finite directed graph, where there is exactly one node Px for each real program part Px occurring in the real S-transaction definition. There is an arc from node Px to node Py if program part Px might issue a REQUEST towards Py, or if Py is a local S-transaction program, which Px might invoke locally. In other words, there is an arc if Py might be executed as a direct sub-S-transaction of Px. There is a *root node* Pi in DGi, from which all other nodes are reachable.

A local S-transaction program in the definition graph is either a *normal* one or a *compensating* one. A compensating node is reachable from the same ablocal node as the normal program, for which the former is a compensating program. Each ablocal node has the out-degree one (only the normal local transaction) or two (the normal and the compensating one) and each local S-transaction program has the out-degree zero, i.e. they cannot invoke sub--S-transactions of their own.

The definition graph DGi contains the structural information for all *formal execution structures* that can be generated from the S-transaction defini-

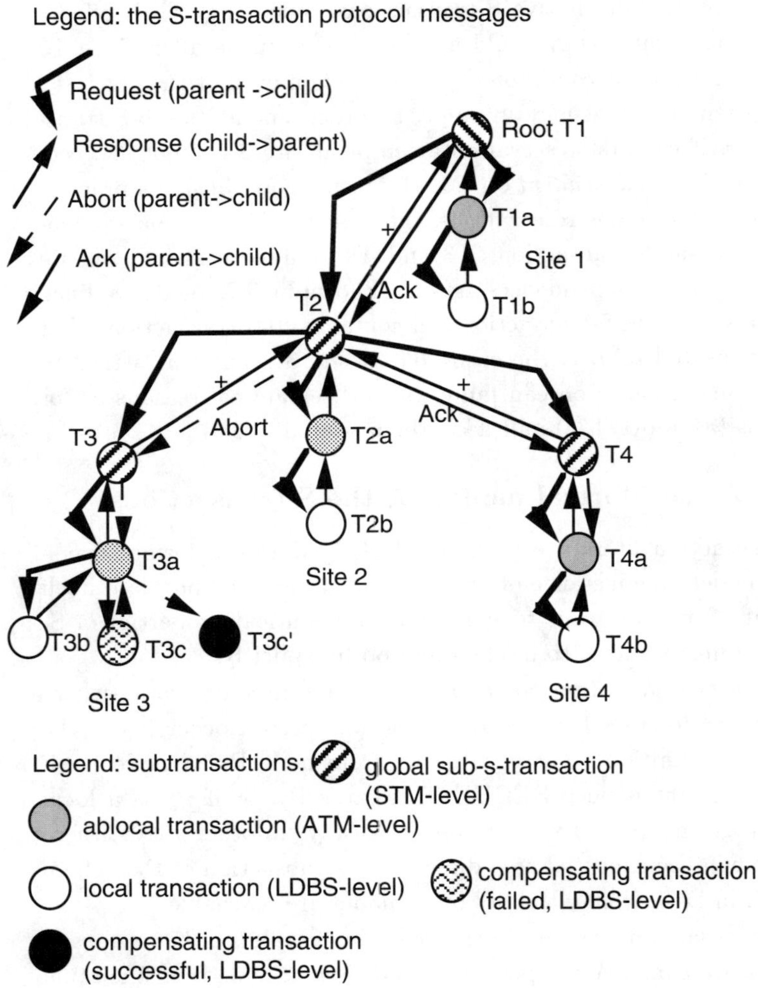

FIGURE 12.3
An example execution structure

tion. An execution structure models one S-transaction, as the one in Fig. 12.3. While a node Px in the definition graph models a program part specification, a node in the execution structure models a program part execution. The execution structure of a cyclic definition graph (i.e. a recursive S-transaction definition) might contain several nodes representing different executions of the same program part. Therefore, the nodes of an execution structure are named by Txj, where x is the program part index whose execution is in question, and j is a unique second index, among the invocations of the same program parts within that S-transaction. The root is simply denoted by Ti.

The arcs in an execution structure model the exchange of (RRA) messages between the real superior and sub-S-transaction. There is a *request arc* (c.f. Fig. 12.3) from Txk to Tyh if Txk invoked Tyh as its sub-S-transaction. There is an *abort arc* if Txk issued ABORT towards Tyh, and *ack arc* if Txk issued ACK towards Tyh. There is *response arc* from Tyh to Txk if the former issued RESPONSE to Txk.

Each node is marked either with "success" (the initial state) or "failure", to model the fate of each sub-S-transaction. For a local sub-S-transaction the state is "success" iff it is not locally aborted, otherwise it is "failure". In a correct node, only the state transition from "success" to "failure" is possible.

What determines which of the execution structures deducible from DGi is generated in a certain situation? We assume that each formal execution structure can be (deterministically) computed by an *evaluator (algorithm)*, from the definition graph, based on the structure and computational semantics of the (deterministic) program parts, the input parameter value *in* of the root transaction, and the overall vector of local source database states $S = (s_1, s_2, \cdots, s_k)$. The evaluator emulates the distributed execution mechanism consisting of real STMs, ATMs, communication facilities, and local database systems. The evaluation result is a particular formal execution structure that contains all sub-S-transactions, the message exchanges between them, input and output values, and the local source and result database states $(s'_1, s'_2, \cdots, s'_k)$, produced during the evaluation.

12.4.2 Syntactical correctness of S-transactions

We view a particular execution of an S-transaction definition as *a sequence of execution structures* generated by the evaluator, i.e. as a sequence of graphs **Ti** = Ti(o), Ti(1), ..., where Ti(o) is the root of the spanning tree of Ti and (x) denotes the number in the sequence. Each graph Ti(x+1) in the sequence contains the previous graph Ti(x) - and thus all previous graphs.

A new graph contains one additional ack, abort, request, or response arc, an additional node, or a new state in a node, as compared to the previous one.

One can characterize many syntactical correctness aspects of the program parts from the sequence **Ti**. First of all, is the sequence finite? If it is not finite, then the S-transaction definition cannot be considered correct. Infiniteness may occur, if for instance a compensating local sub-S-transaction repeatedly fails, or alternatives are tried that do not succeed. A cycle in the definition graph always means a possible infinite recursion which means that the spanning tree has (potentially) an infinite height.

The sequence **Ti** of execution structures contains a full history of S-transaction protocol exchanges and their relative order for a particular S-transaction instance. To guarantee the correct failure propagation properties, one must generally require that in no execution graph Ti(k), the ack arc from a node Tjy(k) may occur, unless an ack arc into the same node already occurs in the preceding graph Ti(k-1). For the same reason, no abort arc may emanate from the node Tjy(k), if an ack arc into the node already occurs in the preceding graph Ti(k-1).

Based on the above syntactical restrictions, one can show that *a node belongs exactly to one of the "failed" subtrees (with state "failure" at the root of that subtree), or to the unique ack tree, emanating from the root Ti.* Further, it follows that no node with state "failure" belongs to the ack tree in any execution structure. Thus, each sub-S-transaction can unambiguously decide whether it fails or succeeds, provided downwards propagation of "failure" and "success" functions in the real execution mechanism and in the evaluator in an analogous way.

We say that an execution structure is *ack complete* if all nodes with the state "success" belong to the ack tree emanating from the root. Note that an ack complete execution structure does not need to be the last in the sequence, since the failure propagation downwards in failed sub-S-transactions can still continue after the ack tree has been constructed. In the above example, for instance, the canceling transaction T3c' might be the last one in the sequence **T1**.

A global node changes its state into "failure" if an abort arc pointing into it emerges. An ablocal node is initially in state "success". It changes its state to "failure" if a negative response arc from its first normal local node emerges (i.e. the normal local sub-S-transaction informs its abort), or if a positive response arc from a compensating local node emerges(i.e. a compensating local sub-S-transaction informs about its commit).

An execution structure is *inconsistent* if there is a node in it, with state "success" and it has an ancestor node in the spanning tree with state "failure", or if an ablocal transaction is in state "success" and all its normal local nodes in state "failure". Otherwise it is *consistent.*

An execution structure is *semantically atomic* if it is consistent and ack complete. The whole S-transaction *fails* (is *successful*) if in the last execution structure Ti(v) in **Ti** the root of Ti(v) is in state "failure" ("success") and Ti(v) is semantically atomic. S-transaction *crashes semantically* if the sequence is infinite or Ti(v) is inconsistent.

12.4.3 Atomicity of S-transactions

Intuitively, an S-transaction that is semantically atomic in the sense defined above either does all what must be done and cancels incomplete attempts in such a way that no "semantically" effective results are left in the databases. This is true in a strong sense if the ablocal transactions are implemented in such a way that the normal local transactions do not commit their results, before the ack or compensate is issued. Whether this is done can be decided by the D-autonomous organization itself. If the local normal transaction commits before it is sure that it belongs to the ack tree, i.e. global isolation is given up, then the results are visible to other local and S-transactions between the normal and compensating transaction. Therefore, the semantic atomicity achieved does not mean that e.g. a failed S-transaction does not have any real effects within the database or in the real world.

When this is is acceptable, is a semantical question. For instance, reserving a flight and canceling it later are a pair of local sub-S-transactions, between which the airline *must* know that the flight reservation was done, since this information guides the capacity planning.

If S-transaction crashes semantically, then it does not halt or it is unable to reproduce (forward recovery in case of unilateral aborts of normal sub-S--transactions) or compensate (backward recovery) some database changes it has made. It means that automatic recovery has reached its limits and a human intervention is usually necessary to rectify the situation. Where the limits are, depends on the semantics of the application and on persistence of the recovery attempts. To decrease the probability of semantical crashes, trying to run local compensating and normal programs several times for recovery purposes should be possible. Then, *renewing failed recovery attempts the probability of reaching semantic atomicity increases.* In this respect semantic atomicity is a fuzzy [Kan86] or probabilistic in nature. It is for further study, how big is the probability of semantical crashes and how factors like idempotence of compensation, program execution time, the interference of local transactions, consistency preservation, etc. influence it. We elaborate only some aspects below.

12.4.4 Consistency preservation of S-transactions

The goal of the execution mechanism is to guarantee that any final execution structure is semantically atomic - which is a purely syntactical characterization of executions. Database consistency is a semantical concept and can only be defined based on the database states. Therefore, to each local node of the formal execution structure there are attached the source s_i, and the result database state s'_i. Each pair expresses a local state transition (s_i, s'_i) caused by the local sub-S-transaction. It should be locally and globally "consistent". We define consistency with the help of state transition relations. *Dynamic consistency* Dev is a binary state transition relation on database states. Dev says which state transitions (s_1, s'_1) are allowed in the database by (complete) transactions. *Static consistency* CS is a predicate on database states saying which states s are consistent, which inconsistent. We have s $\in$ CS iff Dev*($\emptyset$,s), where Dev* is the reflexive transitive closure of Dev. For ith local database there is a local dynamic and static consistency of its own, Dev_i, CS_i.

The global dynamic consistency DEV is relation over all global state vector pairs (S1,S2), where S1 $= (s_1, s_2, \ldots, s_k)$, and S2 $= (s'_1, s'_2, \ldots, s'_k)$. Each such pair contains embedded local state transitions (s_j, s'_j). We have S $\in$ GCS $\equiv$ DEV*($\emptyset$,S). GCS is, as above, the set of *consistent global database states.*

Transaction Ti is *sound* w.r.t. a state transition relation Dev_k (DEV) if it only contains state transitions occurring in Dev_k (DEV). Whether a state transition (s_k, s'_k), attached to a local node of an execution structure is in a unique way "sound" or "inconsistent" depends on whether the global and local consistency are contradictory. Let S $= (s_1, s_2, \ldots, s'_k)$ be a globally consistent state. If there is a locally inconsistent state s'_k within it, then there must be an embedded state transition in DEV, that does not occur in $\text{Dev}_k{}^*$, that is, DEV is not *locally sound.* Thus there are globally seen more consistent states than locally seen. In this case Ti might contain (s_k, s'_k) being globally sound but locally inconsistent.

On the other hand, not all state transitions of a Dev_k need to be embedded in DEV. This means that DEV is not *locally complete.* Consequently, there are locally sound state transitions (s_k, s'_k) that are not globally sound. If Ti now contains (s_k, s'_k) it is globally inconsistent but locally sound. Note that the target state s'_k might in this case be globally inconsistent or consistent with respect to GCS.

It is evident that if the same state transition (s_k, s'_k) occurring in a local node of an execution structure is both sound and inconsistent, then the sub-S-transaction both preserves and violates consistency! This shows that the axiom used e.g. in the serializability theory [BHG87] "a transaction preserves consistency" is not necessarily valid in an autonomous environment. It also means that one must *carefully define which consistency an S-transaction or local transaction preserves.*

Can there be a unique consistency in a D-autonomous environment? In such an environment the local consistency dominates, so no DEV that is not locally sound can be enforced - without changing the local consistency, expressed by $\text{Dev}_j{}^*$, and represented by the local transaction programs. When setting up the global system, reconciling the global and local consistency may be a big task [Vei90].

For the purpose of the subsequent discussion, let us assume that DEV is (after adjusting it or each Dev_j) locally sound and complete. Then there is a unique, albeit trivial, global consistency; Any combination of local state transitions is consistent, and any global state S is consistent iff each local state s_k in it is locally consistent. This means that each local database forms a separate *consistency partition* [Vei90], i.e. there are no permanent value dependencies whatsoever between them.

Let us assume that each local sub-S-transaction Tix preserves local consistency, if run alone, i.e. each state transition (s_i, s'_i) in its execution structure is locally sound. Then, it can be shown by induction on the number of the local transactions in the execution structure that any such S-transaction preserves local dynamic and static consistency at each local database. This result can be extended in an obvious way for any set of interleaved S-transactions and other sound local transactions. The latter result relies on the assumption that each LDBS only allows correct interleaving of the local transactions, i.e. produces view serializable R-W histories [BHG87] among the local transactions and sub-S-transactions hosted by it.

The same line of argument can be extended to trivial global consistency; If any locally sound state transition is considered as globally sound, then a globally sound execution structure only contains globally sound state transitions. Especially, this applies to semantically crashed S-transactions, as well as to incomplete ones. Further, there are no *consistency reasons* for restricting the number of local sub-S-transactions at a site (c.f. the different assumptions - and results - in [GP86]). Of course, this can lead to deadlocks etc., if parallel execution is performed, that must be solved by locally aborting one of the sub-S-transactions. For the same reason, an ablocal transaction definition Pi(IN;OUT) could be implemented through two local programs, the normal and the compensating one. In principle, such a definition can also be implemented using more than one normal local transaction program. For each of them, there should be then a compensating local program. It remains to be seen whether this makes sense in practice.

S-transactions can also be interleaved in an arbitrary serializable order, and still they preserve the global consistency. In a similar proof as above one can use a conceptual "super" S-transaction, whose sub-S-transactions all different S-transactions are. Thus, the STMs (or ATMs) do not need to perform any kind of concurrency control, only the local database systems must find such a serializability for local sub-S-transactions at the site that only allows locally sound state transitions. The class of R-W histories achieved based purely on local concurrency control is a proper superset of quasi-serializable histories [DE89]. It is for further study, whether, and in which cases, it makes sense to prohibit some histories by ordering or aborting sub-S-transactions at STM or ATM level. It is also unclear in general how this could be implemented.

12.4.5 Compensatability of local sub-S-transactions

Semantical crashes exhibited by S-transactions are a new phenomenon that are manifestation of technical problems and E-autonomy but there is still a deeper problem. It might be that canceling an action is simply *semantically meaningless*, because the real action modelled by the normal transaction is *irreversible*. Consequently, there cannot be *any local compensating program* that could model the reversing action, i.e. do the canceling. The other possibility for a failure to compensate is that although it makes sense to cancel the previous normal transactions, and there is the compensating local program, still the compensating sub-S-transaction must be aborted in order to preserve local or global consistency For both reasons, an S-transaction definition is non-compensatable.

Let us elaborate the latter problem. Assume that all S-transactions preserve the above unique trivial consistency, while enforcing dynamically a set of compatible state transitions, i.e. its 'internal global consistency'. Before accessing the global database state, an S-transaction cannot decide whether all the compatible state transitions it wants to perform, are really possible. The problem arises, when not all of them can be performed, for some reason. Then, the already committed state transitions should be reversed - by compensating or by aborting locally. To guarantee global atomicity, a locally not sound state transition might in this case be desirable. An example of this is an electronic funds transfer (EFT), which is the compensating program of itself. If the account of the beneficiary is emptied, by a third EFT, between the normal EFT and the compensating EFT then the latter either aborts ("no funds available") or it moves the database into a locally inconsistent state, where the balance on the account of the beneficiary is negative.

This is a typical trade-off for S-transactions; either the compensation fails and the S-transaction crashes semantically, or the local consistency is violated. Denying aborts of compensating transactions, as in sagas [GS87], saves S-transactions from semantical crashes but jeopardizes the local consistency. Thus, it seems that the trivial global consistency must be in reality replaced by one which also accepts locally inconsistent states as globally consistent, at least if they were achieved when compensating. The avoidance of semantical crashes by inconsistent state transitions leads to other direction of investigation: what really happens if the local database is moved into a locally inconsistent state? Does it cause locally much harm, or is it easy to repair (as is the case in the EFT example)?

There is one additional problem evident; with which parameters the compensating local sub-S-transaction should be issued and where and when should they be generated? For an EFT this is clear, the normal EFT produces them. For a flight reservation system either the reservation can produce the parameter, or the COMPENSATE message can carry it. In general it is, however, not very clear. The reason are again the other local transactions that move the local database into an arbitrary new state between the normal and compensating transaction. In different source states the compensating parameter value needed might be different. This is called *the compensating parameter problem.*

Both latter problems are again totally dependent on the semantics of the applications run at that local database. The further exploration requires a formal analysis of the local and global consistency and the behavior of the local and global transactions. There are some initial results in [Vei90].

```
s_transaction <name>
   input_data
      <set of input data>
   end
   request_data
      <set of request data>
   end
   local_data
      <set of local data>
   end
   continuation_points
      <set of continuation points>
   end
   compensation_points
      <set of compensation points>
   end
end /* of S-transaction <name> */
```

FIGURE 12.4
Basic STDL components in a program part (sub-S-transaction)

12.5 A language supporting S-transactions, STDL

To bring the S-transaction model into practical use, executable S-transaction definition languages have been developed. In this section we will present S-Transaction Definition Language STDL, which was implemented in the MAP761B project. The other language, Functional Transaction Language (FTL) [EV87b], also developed in MAP761B is not presented here. In section 12.7, a language called FRIL, based on FTL and a functional approach to the definition and execution of S-transactions, will be presented.

In STDL an S-transaction is described by its name and a set of different sections [MAP89, HH87]. Fig. 12.4 shows the syntactic framework for the definition of S-transactions. We roughly distinguish between a data definition part (i.e. STDL/DDL) and an operations part (i.e. STDL/DML).

12.5.1 STDL/DDL

As STDL is aimed at being used for the specification of transactions in a dedicated decentralized system, the structure of the data being exchanged between each two interacting sites must be known to both sites. Hence, in the *request data section* the data types and data structures are defined that form a part of the parameter list a REQUEST message to a remote site consists of. The *input data section* contains the data type definitions for the input parameters that have to be filled in when invoking an S-transaction. Internal variables of the program part and intermediate results of an S-transaction are managed in the *local data section.* It also contains the data structures that are shared by different continuation points within the same sub-S-transactions or the root S-transaction.

The data definition features of STDL correspond to those of modern high-level programming languages. STDL provides the primitive data types INTEGER, BOOLEAN, REAL, and STRING. By means of the operators Union, Intersection, Enumeration, and Cartesian Product, more complex data types can be constructed. For the support of relational database systems STDL provides the special constructor Table_of.

For the manipulation of local data and data that are transferred between sites STDL provides a set of built-in functions for boolean operations, arithmetic operations, set operations, and operations on relations.

12.5.2 STDL/DML

A sub-S-transaction provides a service and might request services from remote sites. Therefore, an S-transaction program part is divided into different parts that can be invoked via *continuation points.* The set of continuation points defined in different program parts constitute the *execution plan* for the entire S-transaction. The continuation points denote the entries at which a superior or sub-S-transaction may be activated or may receive results. The special continuation point 'init_cp' is activated at the root S-transaction initiation time when the initiation is requested from a user. The other continuation points can be activated either from remote sites by requesting a service (sending a REQUEST message), provided by that S-transaction type the continuation point belongs to. Submitting results to an already active S-transaction happens by activating, through a RESPONSE message, a suitable continuation point. Thus, from a logical point of view in STDL each active continuation point corresponds to a sub-process.

A continuation point consists of a *unique identification* within a program part, an *input parameter list* and a *path.* The path describes the execution plan of the program part. The path consists of calls to built-in functions and/or requests to continuation points of remote program parts. For these activities an execution order has to be defined and execution constraints may be specified. The order is defined by means of operators indicating a sequential, parallel, or conditional execution. Execution means either calling a built-in function or an ablocal transaction and waiting for a result (like a procedure call), or sending a REQUEST or other message to a remote continuation point. In the latter case the superior or sub-S-transaction has no control over the execution. It isn't possible to wait within the initiating path for a result of another continuation point executed at a different site. This result is sent to another continuation point of the superior S-transaction. It is possible to use local data in the local data section for synchronization.

Within a path, constraints in terms of time conditions or conditions on expected results can be specified. In addition to these conditions, STDL also provides facilities for formulating conditions on communication level. Non-delivery notification of messages, successful execution of sub-S-transactions, sub-S-transaction aborts ("failure"), etc. can be indicated for the superior if they are specified within its path.

12.5.3 Compensation

STDL is aimed at supporting the specification of semantic transactions for distributed systems as well as for decentralized systems. The latter are characterized through the autonomy of their constituents. That implies the need to commit of local sub-S-transactions prior to the termination of their parent transactions. As we are dealing with transactions whose semantics is a priori known we assume that for every sub-S-transaction there usually (see section 12.4) exists a compensating sub-S-transaction that reverses the effects of the normal one. To manage compensation, STDL considers the compensating transaction as forming an integral part of every global and ablocal S-transaction program part.

12.6 Applications of the S-transaction model

The applicability of the S-transaction concept, the corresponding system architecture, and the description formalism has been demonstrated in different application domains. Beside the banking domain S-transactions have originally been developed for, we have also shown their use in Computer Integrated

Manufacturing and in Software Engineering. A complete review of these applications is beyond the scope of this chapter. Nevertheless we give a brief overview of the different application scenarios in order to give the reader a feeling of how the concepts can be used, not only in the above mentioned domains but also in new ones.

12.6.1 Banking

The first application domain for S-transactions has been transnational banking in the context of the S.W.I.F.T. system. This system is maintained by S.W.I.F.T., an organisation that was founded by banks with the main goal of developing and maintaining a communication network for international financial telecommunications. Today about 2500 banks are attached to the S.W.I.F.T. I network. These banks are dispersed all over the world. Consequently, they are in different time zones. A lot of them are only connected to the network during the opening hours. Thus direct access to their databases is not always possible. As a consequence communication has to be based on a store and forward discipline, causing long delays in the execution of financial transactions. Another characteristic feature is the "Heterogeneity" of the banks connected to S.W.I.F.T.. When using the term "Heterogeneity" here, we refer not only to the banks' computing facilities but to banking practice, as well.

A bank can be considered as a server that provides services which may be requested from other banks. The implementation of the services and the execution of requested services is in the banks' responsibility. Thus a bank exhibits autonomy in various respects as discussed in sections 12.2 - 12.3 of this chapter.

In order to enable the cooperation of autonomous, heterogeneous systems S.W.I.F.T. provides standardized message types. Each message has a well-defined syntax and semantics. By these means S.W.I.F.T. supports customer and bank funds transfers, loan and deposit transactions, collections, securities, or documentary credits, for instance.

STDL has been used to define two types of S-transactions: a generic funds transfer and a generalized cash management transaction. Funds transfers make up about 50 percent of the S.W.I.F.T. network activities and are thus of crucial importance.

The following simplified funds transfer transaction example aims at demonstrating the concept of S-transactions applied to a distributed service where multiple sites are involved. The customer payment demonstrated consists of three individual funds transfers, launched by three different message exchanges corresponding to three S.W.I.F.T. message types:

- MT 100 Customer Transfer,
- MT 202 Bank Transfer in Favour of a Third Bank,
- MT 910 Confirmation of Credit (special message).

The ordering customer (O) orders his bank (sending bank - S) to pay a certain amount of money (given in a certain currency) into the beneficiary customer's account (B) with his bank (receiving bank - R). Reimbursement for this customer transfer is through a correspondent bank (C). The sending bank therefore notifies the receiving bank of the funds transfer (MT100) and sends the cover by bank transfer to the correspondent bank (MT202). On receipt, the correspondent bank advises the receiving bank by confirmation of credit (MT910).

The generalised cash management application processes payments where the entire transaction is carried out by S.W.I.F.T. participants, and all transfer instructions and executions are communicated by the S.W.I.F.T. network. A possible example for such an application could look as follows:

```
"Select all my nostros in Belgium, result by 2 p.m.".
"Move funds from one account to another in an optimal way"
```

The cash management application had been chosen to demonstrate the enhanced flexibility of S-transactions compared to the currently used S.W.I.F.T. message types for balance reporting.

The cash management application is a prototype of an 'own account' management system. It collects the account balance data from the correspondent sites of a bank and identifies the necessary actions (such as inter-account transfers, funds to be borrowed, funds available for deposit) that can be taken to use the banks' funds effectively.

The STDL prototype demonstrates the automatic selection of payment types and required messages, the completion, where possible, of missing routing details, the synchronization of advice and instruction prior to execution of instruction, and the various forms of message acknowledgement.

12.6.2 Computer Integrated Manufacturing

Computer Integrated Manufacturing (CIM) subsummarizes a large amount of complex, interacting processes with a priori known semantics. The interactions between these processes take place partly on the communication level in terms of simple message exchanges. Partly it takes place on the interoperation level in terms of partially ordered sequences of actions.

Regarding a CIM environment as a set of autonomous interacting units enables us to apply our system model and thus the concept of S-transactions also to this application domain. In [Hol87] we have described the mapping of a CIM environment into a system architecture that corresponds with the one described in section 12.3 of this chapter.

Every logical unit of the CIM environment may consist of several subordinate units that serve the purpose of the overall logical unit. For example the CAD unit might include different units for mechanical engineering and electrical engineering. The CAM unit could contain different units for NC programming and the control of different machines. The CAQ unit could consist of different units for the evaluation of CAD and of CAM outputs.

By using a flexible manufacturing cell as an example we have demonstrated the use of the S-transaction concept for describing the interoperation of cell components like a floor transport vehicle, a shelf, a tool tower, and a stamping machine as a set of interrelated continuation points in an STDL description of an S-transaction. As the actions performed by the cell component are mostly real actions (e.g. transporting a metal sheet from the shelf to the stamping machine) conventional transactions are not appropriate as the real actions cannot be undone. The compensation concept, inherent to S-transactions, is the more appropriate approach in such a context.

12.6.3 Software Engineering

Software engineering is more and more considered as an application domain in which teams develop software in a distributed environment. For integrated software development environments the term software factory has been coined. A major research effort in this area is the EUREKA Software Factory project [SW90]. In ESF a Software Factory is composed of two parts: *the human part* and the *computerized part.*

The computerized part of a Software Factory is also referred to as Factory Support Environment. In order to obtain an open and extendible Software Factory it is defined as a four stage multi-layer framework for integration. The stages are composed of a number of layers with relationships existing both between adjacent stages and between the layers within a stage:

- the interworking of human users or user groups with other users or user groups of the Software Factory instance;
- the interaction of human users and the ESF User Interaction Compo-

nents, i.e. different roles associated with different people or groups with their respective tools in a Software Factory instance;

- the interoperation of different software platforms, i.e. various constituents like tools in an integrated Software Factory instance;
- the interconnection of different hardware platforms, i.e. different computer sites in a computer network as a distributed instance of a Software Factory. This stage is covered by the ISO/OSI Reference Model.

The computerized part of a software factory, i.e. the Factory Support Environment, consists of a "kernel" and a set of service oriented building blocks. The kernel consists of a factory process engine that executes the software process model (i.e. a set of rules and guide-lines that govern the software development process) and a Software Bus that implements the interconnection and interoperation layers between the service components that are attached to the bus.

The service components are partly developed specifically for an ESF Software Factory and are partly of-the-shelf software development tools. At least the latter exhibit autonomy properties as discussed in section 12.2. As a consequence the interoperation between components in a software factory can or even must be based on S-transactions again because there is no way to weaken the autonomy properties of the third party software development tools. On the other hand, the demand for transaction based cooperation within a development team has been widely discussed in the literature.

The applicability of the S-transaction concept to software factories has been demonstrated at the first international conference on Software Development Environments and Factories, Berlin, May 1989, by describing the interoperations between software developers in STDL and by executing them as S-transactions.

12.7 Further developments

The basic ideas of the S-transaction model can be found in more recently developed transaction models as well. E.g. the transaction model developed for Functional Resource Integration Language (FRIL), [EV88, EK90a] supports the S-transaction model, but does also allow very dynamic implementation of the ablocal and local sub-S-transactions.

12.7.1 FRIL

FRIL is a uniform language format for the definition and "seamless" manipulation of multiple autonomous applications. It is not limited to the original application area of S-transactions (i.e. banking). The architecture supporting the computational model of FRIL is based on the client-server paradigm modelling the distributed environment as interacting client and server entities. Client and server entities are generic *application front ends* (or stubs) allowing an application to act as a client and/or server. The mapping of the site architecture in section 12.3 of this chapter, to the FRIL architecture, is straightforward. An ATM is modeled as a server entity acting as a front-end to an LDBMS application, while an MDBI module is modelled as the combination of a client entity and an application entity where the client entity acts as a front end to the MDBI application. The interface between the server entity and the application corresponds to the LI of the site architecture, while the concept of ALI is modelled as the interface to a server entity.

In FRIL, ablocal transactions correspond to *methods* exported by a server. However, since these methods are functions it makes sense to form larger expressions that combine method symbols with built-in function symbols. Thus in the FRIL architecture server interfaces can be programmable in the sense that a server optionally accepts complete *method expressions* for evaluation. This allows for ad hoc ablocal transactions and reduces the need for giving up isolation between ablocal transactions executed at the same site - since a method expression can be run as a single sub-S-transaction towards the local database and not as separate ones for each method in the method expression (c.f. above).

S-transactions allow both compensatable and non-compensatable sub-S-transactions. The FRIL transaction model allows compensatable sub-S-transactions to commit locally before the global transactions commit, while the commitment of non-compensatable sub-S-transactions is a global decision. A similar approach has been adopted in the transaction model for the Interbase system [ELLR90].

FRIL/SESSL and FRIL/FIOL

FRIL encompasses an interface specification language SESSL (Server Export Schema Specification Language) for specifying interfaces to server entities (i.e. ALIs). A SESSL interface specification consists of a set (abstract) data types (ADT) and a set of derived functions (methods) with signatures based on the set of ADTs. ADTs are in FRIL essentially viewed as abstract definitions for potential objects in a system. SESSL thus models an application as a computational object encapsulating a set of passive (and complex) data objects.

In most database systems, updates are provided through different "non-functional" mechanisms. These mechanisms are clearly in conflict with a functional approach since they rely on side-effects and introduce non-determinism. In FRIL the approach to solve these problems is to distinguish between function level and object level ADTs. For object level ADTs SESSL again distinguishes between *mutable* and *immutable* object types. For mutable objects FRIL has a reflective semantics that supports the notion of in-place or destructive update but introduces non-determinism. The type system applicable for mutable object level ADTs, however, overcomes the problem of non-determinism. It is based on a modification of the concept of linear data types [Wad90]. The linear type system constrains construction of mutable objects to be single-threaded (i.e. linear) and thus can be used to model the update semantics of traditional databases without compromising the functional approach.

FIOL (Functional Interoperation Language) is the second sublanguage of FRIL. This functional language allows for the formulation of programs combining individual methods from *multiple* server interfaces. FIOL is inspired by Backus' FP language [Bac78]. FIOL programs are evaluated on request from clients as distributed S-transactions managed by a set of cooperating *global transaction managers* corresponding to the STM modules of the site architecture in section 12.3.

12.7.2 The computational model of FRIL

The computational model of FRIL is higher level than just message passing. FRIL basically expresses the definition of S-transactions as the functional combination of server methods. The execution of a program part happens by mapping its subexpressions and methods to different STMs and servers (i.e. ATMs), respectively, and subsequently collecting and combining the results of the subexpression and method evaluations.

For the purpose of describing S-transaction support in FRIL, we may assume an S-transaction program ST is transformed into a "canonical form"

$$ST = H\ M_1, ..., M_n$$

before its execution. This form is an abstract representation of the expression tree of ST. $M_1, \ldots, M_n$ are the leaf nodes of the expression tree and denote either different complete method expressions to be mapped to appropriate servers or applications of built-in functions. H denotes the remaining part of the expression tree and can be viewed as a *combinator* denoting the way the results of the methods are functionally combined in ST. From H there can also be deduced the potential different execution orders of $M_1, \ldots, M_n$ (in general a partial order).

During execution, ST is *decomposed* into sub-S-transactions by the STMs. The following (simplified) example illustrates the result of a two level "balanced" decomposition.

$$ST = H' \ (G_1 \ M_1, \ldots, M_k), (G_2 \ M_{k+1}, \ldots, M_i), (G_3 \ M_{i+1}, \ldots, M_n))$$

In the first decomposition, ST is decomposed into three sub-S-transactions. Their execution order and the combination of their results are implied by the combinator H'. The "top level" combinator H has been transformed to H' to reflect that the combination of the results of the sub-S-transactions are now partly done at the next lower level, expressed through the combinators G_1, G_2 and G_3. Each of the sub-S-transactions are mapped to some (other) STM where each method expression is subsequently mapped to some server entity (ATM) in an order implied by the corresponding combinator. Built-in functions are evaluated by the STMs.

Alternative transactions (c.f. section 12.3) are supported by a distributed exception mechanism allowing expressions, in which failure occurs, to be substituted for by *alternative expressions*. The following is a simplified description of this mechanism. The failure of a sub-S-transaction is signalled to the superior S-transaction as a *named return* n. They can be generated by server methods, by the FRIL run time system to signal system errors (i.e. communication failure), or by a special FRIL expression construct ($?n$). Named returns capture the semantics of negative responses in the S-transaction model. A positive response is in FRIL expressed as a normal anonymous function return.

If the sub-S-transaction $T_2 = G_2 \ M_{k+1}, \ldots, M_i$ (say) fails with the named return n for which T_2 has the expression $S_2 = KM_{j_1}, \ldots, M_{j_n}$ as an alternative, ST is transformed to

$$ST' = H'(G_1 M_1, \ldots, M_k), S_2, (G_3 M_{i+1}, \ldots, M_n))$$

i.e. T_2 is substituted for by S_2. We call S_2 a *substitute function* for T_2. S_2 is executed as an alternative sub-S-transaction for T_2 that failed. It is required that the signature of S_2 must conform with the signature of T_2.

If T_2 has no alternative, ST is deemed to fail. The other sub-S-transactions of ST are aborted or compensated as appropriate by sending corresponding ABORT/COMPENSATE messages. A named return is finally signalled to the superior S-transaction of ST. It is assumed that the selection of the means by which compensatable server methods are actually compensated, is a local decision and is generally not visible outside the server entities. Hence the STM only specifiy in the COMPENSATE message *what* need to be compensated, not *how* the compensation should be done. FRIL does not exclude, however, programs that 'compensate' by requesting the execution of some appropriate server method (e.g. compensate a debit method by a credit method). But its success is not 'guaranteed'. It is treated as a normal sub-S-transaction that may fail.

The exception handling mechanism of FRIL is in fact more flexible and general than the mechanism sketched above. Firstly, exception handling can be nested to an arbitrary depth. This means that it is possible to specify alternatives for alternatives, and so on. Secondly, a number of sub-S-transactions can be grouped into an expression called a *substitution context.* A substitution context may have one or more alternative expressions for each of the named returns that subexpressions of the substitution context may produce. Hence, if a sub-S-transaction contained in a particular substitution context fails, the whole group of sub-S-transactions contained in the substitution context is aborted or compensated before the alternative expression is executed (if any). Thus substitution contexts are atomic.

Syntactically a FRIL program consists of a *definition part*, and optionally of a *substitute part* and of a *rules part.* The definition part defines the "primary" S-transaction, including substitution contexts (if any). The substitute part defines the substitute functions associated to substitution contexts in the primary transaction. The definition of each substitute function is again structured into a definition, substitute and rules part. The rules part specifies the rules for function substitution. A rule roughly specifies a substitution context, a named return and a corresponding substitute function. The application of "overlapping" rules is ordered through a set of precedence rules. We refer to [EK90b] for further details.

12.8 Conclusion

We have described in this chapter the S-transaction model. It is intented to be used in environments where autonomy must be preserved.

In section 12.2 the autonomy is analyzed as a general concept. We identify O-, M-, D-, E-, and C-autonomy that have relevance for the system design. We also discuss measures for the self-determination (autonomy potential) and effective autonomy (autonomy manifested to the outside world).

In section 12.3 we discuss the need and requirements for a transaction concept in an autonomous environment and deduce the overall architecture supporting the S-transaction model. It consists of add-on modules. The S--transaction manager (STM) is the heart of the architecture. It is able to execute programs written with a homogeneous transaction language.

To support D-autonomy and to overcome Heterogeneity, the S-transaction definition and execution are divided in the environment into two parts, *the global* and *local* part. For the global part the *abstract local transactions* (shortly *ablocal transactions*), defined at the interface between the local and global system part, form an indivisible basis which they are all composed of. The global permanent data resides at sites conceptually in homogeneous *ablocal databases* that are *virtual* and that are manipulated by the ablocal transactions. The latter are implemented through *local sub-S-transactions* that actually manipulate the *local databases* within the local system part, causing the desired state transitions in the globally visible ablocal databases.

To preserve M-and C-autonomy, local sub-S-transactions are allowed to commit or abort prior to "commit" of the global root. Thus, isolation between different global S-transactions is not required. This causes the need to use compensating local sub-S-transactions for global recovery, assuming that ALI does not enforce isolation. Since compensating local sub-S-transaction might not exist or it might abort for some reason, the S-transactions sometimes "semantically crash", requiring manual intervention for rectifying the end result. In this respect the atomicity of S-transactions is probabilistic or fuzzy ("almost always" atomic). This is closely related to discrepancies between local and global consistency. If the compensating local sub-S-transactions are allowed to violate local consistency, then crashes do not happen (because of consistency preserving), but consistency then becomes a problem. These issues are discussed in section 12.4.

In section 12.5 a language (STDL) is discussed, with which the executable program parts can be represented. Section 12.6 contains three examples of application areas where S-transactions can be used. Section 12.7 discusses another possible transaction language (FRIL) and some further development of the basic model.

The S-transaction model is complete and it has been implemented as part of the MUSE prototype [MAP89]. Still, there are many interesting research problems that require further work, like the compensating parameter problem (i.e. with which parameters should the compensating local S-transaction be invoked and how can they be computed). A high probability of semantically atomic executions are of prime importance for the usability of the model. Therefore, the relationship between consistency and semantical crashes must be further explored. Also, the properties of the vertical mappings between the local database and ablocal database should be understood better.

Acknowledgements. The authors wish to thank the MAP761 project teams for many interesting discussions concerning the model. Especially, the valuable input from the MAP761 steering committee members Prof. Herbert Weber, Prof. Radu Popescu-Zeletin, and Prof. Witold Litwin, is appreciated. The comments of the anonymous refrees and those of Prof. Gerhard Weikum on an earlier draft of this chapter are also appreciated. The financial support of the Commission of the European Communities under contracts MAP761 and MAP761B is also highly appreciated.

Bibliography

[AGS87] Alonso,R., Garcia-Molina,H., Salem,K., Concurrency Control and Recovery for Global Procedures in Federated Database Systems. IEEE Data Engineering Quarterly bulletin (Special Issue on Federated Database Systems) 10(1987),3(Sept.), pp. 5–11.

[ANSA89] Herbert,A.J., The ANSA Project. In: Sape Mullender (ed.) Distributed Systems, ACM Frontier Press, USA 1989, pp. 391–427.

[Bac78] Backus, J., Can Programming Languages be liberated from the von Neumann Style? A functional Style and its Algebra of Programs. Communications of ACM 21(1978),8(Aug.), pp. 613–641.

[BKK85] Bancilhon,F., Kim,W., Korth,H., A Model of CAD Transactions. In: A. Pirotte, Y. Vassiliou (eds.), Proc. of 11th Internat. Confererence on Very Large Databases (VLDB), (Aug. 21-23, 1985, Stockholm). VLDB Endowment, USA 1985, pp. 25– 33.

[BBG89] Beeri,C., Bernstein,P., Goodman,N., A Model for Concurrency in Nested Transaction Systems. Journal of the ACM 36(1989),2(April), pp. 230–269.

[BHG87] Bernstein,P., Hadzilacos,V., Goodman,N., Concurrency Control and Recovery in Database Systems. Addison-Wesley Publishing Company, USA 1987.

[Com88] Comer,D., Interworking with TCP/IP; Principles Protocols, and Architecture. Prentice-Hall International, USA 1988.

[DE89] Du,W., Elmagarmid,A.K., Quasi Serializability: a Correctness Criterion for Global Concurrency Control in Inter-Base. Proc. 15th VLDB Conf., Amster-dam, August 1989, pp. 347–355.

[EDI91] ISO/IEC JTC1/SWG-EDI N222, Report on the Open-EDI Conceptual Model, May 1991.

[EK90a] Eliassen, F., Karlsen, R., Providing Application Interoperability using Functional Programming Concepts, CSR 90-06, University of Tromsø, 1990 (to appear EurOpen'91)

[EK90b] Eliassen, F., Karlsen, R., Distributed Exception Handling for Flexible Transactions, CSR 90-07, University of Tromsø, 1990

[EV87a] Eliassen,F., Veijalainen,J., Support for Multi-database Transactions in a Cooperative, Autonomous Environment. Proc. TENCON 87, 1987 IEEE Region 10 Conference "Computers and Communication Technology Toward 2000", August 25-28, 1987 Seoul. IEEE Computer Society Press, 87CH2423-2, Vol. 1, pp. 277–281.

[EV87b] Eliassen,F., Veijalainen,J., An S-transaction Definition Language and Evaluation Mechanism. Gesellschaft für Mathematik und Datenverarbeitung mbH, Forschungszentrum für Offene Kommunikationssysteme
(FOKUS), Berlin(West). Technical Report "Arbeitspapiere der GMD" Nr. 275/1987, November 1987.

[EV88] Eliassen,F., Veijalainen,J., A Functional Approach to Information System Interoperability. R. Speth(ed.) Proc. of EUTECO'88, Research into Networks and Distributed Applications, EEC, North-Holland, Netherlands 1988, pp. 1121–1135.

[ELLR90] Elmagarmid, A.K., Leu, Y., Litwin, W., Rusinkiewicz, M., A Multidatabase Transaction Model for Interbase, Proc. 16th VLDB, 1990.

[Ell88] Ellinghaus,D., Hallman,M., Holtkamp,B., Kreplin,K.-D., A Multidatabase System for Transnational Accounting. Proc. of EDBT'88, Schmidt and Missikoff (eds.), Lecture Notes in Computer Science Nr. 303, Springer Verlag, Germany 1988, pp. 600–605.

[ElVT88] Eliassen,F., Veijalainen,J., Tirri,H., Aspects of Transaction Modelling for Interoperable Information Systems. R. Speth(ed.) Proc. of EUTECO'88, Research into Networks and Distributed Applications, EEC, North-Holland, Netherlands 1988, pp. 1051–1067.

[Gar83] Garcia-Molina,H., Using Semantic Knowledge for Transaction Processing in a Distributed Database. ACM Transactions on Database Systems 8(1983), 2(June), pp. 186–213.

[GS88] Garcia-Molina,H., Kogan, B., Node Autonomy in Distributed Systems. Proc. of IEEE International Symposium on Databases in Parallel and Distributed Systems (Dec. 1988), IEEE CH2665, USA 1988, pp. 158–166.

[GS87] Garcia-Molina,H., Salem,K., Sagas. Proc. of the ACM-SIGMOD International Conference on Management of Data (May 1987), ACM, USA 1987, pp. 249–259.

[GP86] Gligor,V., Popescu-Zeletin,R., Transaction Management in Distributed Heterogeneous Database Systems. Information Systems 11(1986),4, pp. 287–297.

[Gra78] Gray,J., Notes on Database Operating Systems. In: Bayer,R., Graham,R.M., Seegmüller,H. (eds): Operating Systems, An advanced course. Lecture Notes in Computer Science, No. 60, Springer Verlag, FRG 1978, pp. 393–481.

[Gra81] Gray,J., Transactions Concept: Virtues and Limitations In: Proc of 7th International Conference on Very Large Databases (VLDB '81), Cannes, France, (Sept. 1981), IEEE, USA 1981, pp. 144–154.

[HH87] Hallmann, M. and Holtkamp, B. STDL: A Definition Language for Semantic Transactions Proc. GI Conference "Databases for Software Engineering", Dortmund, Nov. 1987

[HR83] Härder,T., Reuter,A., Principles of Transaction-Oriented Database Recovery. ACM Comp. Surveys, Vol. 15(1983), 4 (Dec.).

[HM85] Heimbigner,D., McLeod,.D., A Federated Architecture for Information Management. ACM Transactions on Office Informa tion Systems, 3(1985), 3(July), pp. 253–278.

[Hol87] Holtkamp,B., Semantic Transactions in CIM Environment. Proc. of International Conference on Data and Knowledge Systems for Manufacturing and Engineering, Oct. 19-20, 1987. IEEE Computer Society Press, Order Nr. 820. pp. 23–29.

[Hol88] Holtkamp,B., Preserving Autonomy in a Heterogeneous Multidatabase System. Proc. of the 12th International Computer Software and Application Conf., COMPSAC '88. IEEE 88CH2611-2, pp. 259–266.

[Hol90] Holtkamp, B., MUSE - A Framework for Decentralized Software Development Environments. Technical Report 40, Computer Science/Software Technology, University of Dortmund, 1989

[ISO7492] ISO/TC97/SC16, Information Processing Systems - Open Systems Interconnection - Basic Reference Model, International Standard IS7492. The International Organization for Standardization, ISO 1983.

[ISO9075] ISO/TC97, Information Processing Systems - Database Language SQL, International Standard ISO 9075:1987 (E). The International Organization for Standardization, ISO 1987.

[ISO9735] ISO/TC154, Electronic Data Interchange for Administration, Commerce and Transport (EDIFACT); Application Level Syntax Rules, International Standard ISO 9735. The International Organization for Standardization, ISO 1988.

[Kan86] Kandel,A., Fuzzy Mathematical Techniques with Applications. Addison-Wesley Publishing Company, Inc. Massachusetts, USA 1986.

[LMR90] Litwin,W., Mark,L., Roussopoulos,N., Interoperability of Multiple Autonomous Databases. ACM Computing Surveys 22(1990),3(Sept.), pp. 267–293.

[Lyn83] Lynch,N., Multilevel Atomicity - A New Correctness Criterion for Database Concurrency Control. ACM Transactions on Database Systems 8(1983), 4(Dec.), pp. 484–502.

[MAP86] Multidatabase Services on ISO/OSI Networks for Transnational Accounting, Final Report, I.N.R.I.A. (ed.)., H.M.I., S.W.I.F.T., University of Dortmund, April 1986. ISBN 2-7261-0442-8, I.N.R.I.A., France 1986.

[MAP89] MAP761B, Multidatabase Services on ISO/OSI Networks for Transnational Accounting, Second phase, Final Report, Edited by S.W.I.F.T., Belgium, April 1989.

[Mos85] Moss,J.E.B., Nested Transactions: An Approach to Reliable Distributed Computing. The MIT Press, Cambridge, Mass., USA 1985.

[SW90] Schaefer, W. and Weber, H. European Software Factory Plan - The ESF Profile in: P.A. Ng and R.T. Yeh (eds.) Modern Software Engineering - Foundations and current perspectives, Chapter 22, Van Nostrand Reinhold, New York, 1990, pp. 613–637,

[Sel84] Selinger,P. et al. The impact of site autonomy on R*. Stocker, P.M., Gray, P.M.D., Atkinson, M.P. (eds.), Databases - Role and Structure. Cambridge Univ. Press., United Kingdom 1984, pp. 151–176.

[Vei90] Veijalainen,J., Transaction Concepts in Autonomous Database Environments. (Ph.D. thesis). GMD-Bericht Nr. 183, R. Oldenbourg Verlag, Munich, Germany 1990, ISBN 3-486-21596-5.

[VP86] Veijalainen,J., Popescu-Zeletin,R., On Multi-database Transactions in a Cooperative, Autonomous Environment. Unpublished Manuscript. Hahn-Meitner-Institut Berlin, December 1986.

[VP88] Veijalainen,J., Popescu-Zeletin,R., Multidatabase Systems in ISO/OSI Environment. In: Malagardis,N., Williams,T., (eds.), Standards in Information Technology and Industrial Control. IFIP, Elsevier Science Publishers (North-Holland), Netherlands 1988, pp. 83–96.

[Wad90] Wadler, P., Linear types can change the world!, Proceedings IFIP WG2.2, 1990, pp. 546–566

[Wie87] Wiederhold,G., File Organization for Dabase Design. ISBN 0-07-070133-4, McGraw-Hill, USA 1987.

[X.400] CCITT Recommendation X.400, Message Handling Systems: Document VIII-66-E, Final Report on the Work of Study Group (Data Communication Networks) during the Study Period 1981-1984. CCITT, June 1984.

13

Concepts and Applications of Multilevel Transactions and Open Nested Transactions

Gerhard Weikum

Hans-J. Schek

13.1 Introduction

This chapter gives an overview on multilevel transactions and its generalization toward open nested transactions. The main features of these transaction models are the following: first, semantic properties of operations can be exploited to relax the isolation of concurrent transactions; second, as a consequence, atomicity is achieved by compensation rather than state-based undo; and third, subtransactions can be made persistent independently of their commit state, that is, global visibility of their updates.

Advanced transaction models and new correctness criteria for transaction executions have been proposed for the following reasons (and possibly further reasons that are not mentioned here):

1. to provide better support for long-lived activities in advanced DBMS applications,
2. to relax the classical ACID paradigm, for example, provide more flexibility as to when updates are made visible to concurrent transactions,
3. to support cooperation between the members of a group of designers (in CAD or CASE),
4. to fit more smoothly with object-oriented data models,
5. to capture more semantics about the operations of advanced DBMS applications,
6. to enhance (inter-transaction) parallelism by exploiting these semantics,
7. to model intra-transaction parallelism,
8. to allow user-defined or system-defined intra-transaction savepoints ("partial rollbacks"),
9. to deal with conversational transactions, and
10. to deal with multiple autonomous subsystems in a federated DBMS environment.

Multilevel transactions and open nesteds meet some of the above demands, namely items 5, 6, 7, 8, 10, and, to a large extent, items 1, 2, and 4. Moreover, open nested transactions can serve as a basic building block in more sophisticated models for cooperative transactions and other long-lived activities.

Unlike many other advanced transaction models, multilevel transactions and open nested transactions preserve two fundamental virtues of the classical transaction concept:

- they are based on a rigorous theoretical foundation that preserves the classical serializability theory as a special case, and
- they can reuse much of the well-proven implementation techniques that account for the high performance of current transaction processing systems.

The main purpose of this chapter is to show that even a relatively moderate extension of the classical transaction concept already provides a fairly powerful model that meets many of the above listed requirements yet stays within a well-defined theoretical framework. The chapter also covers some implementation issues for the following reason. One of the original motivations for multilevel transactions was to model some of the performance tricks of commercial transaction processing systems in a rigorous framework. Once those implementation techniques are clearer understood, they are an important asset in developing more general transaction models.

The rest of the chapter is organized as follows. Section 13.2 reviews the main features of the multilevel transaction model. Based on this simpler and theoretically well-founded model, Section 13.3 discusses the general case of open nesteds, and Section 13.4 discusses in what respect the classical ACID paradigm can be relaxed in these models. Section 13.5 discusses applications of multilevel transactions and open nested transactions in a variety of scenarios. Section 13.6 discusses a particular application in more detail, namely office document filing and retrieval. (Other detailed examples of using open nested transactions for advanced database system applications can be found in [MP90] and [MRKN91].)

13.2 The Multilevel Transaction Model

13.2.1 Concepts of Multilevel Transactions

The idea of open nesteds [Gra81, Tra83] grew out of the seminal work on "spheres of control" by Bjork and Davies [Bj73, Dav73, Dav78]. The special case of multilevel transactions (also known as "layered transactions") is a variant of nested transactions where the nodes in a transaction tree correspond to executions of operations at particular levels of abstraction in a layered system. Thus, all transaction trees have the same height, which is equal to

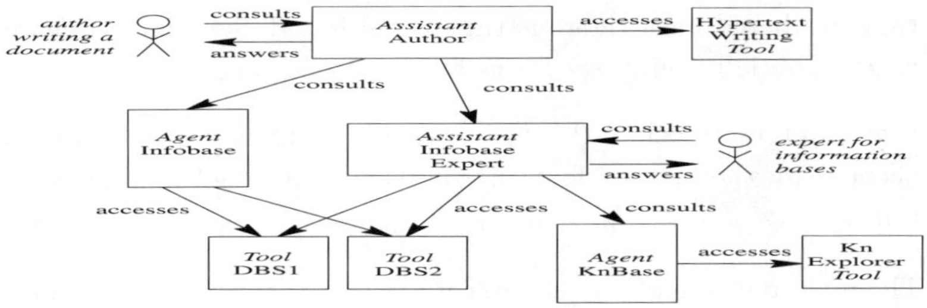

FIGURE 13.1
Concurrent execution of multilevel transactions.

the number of levels in the underlying system architecture, and all leaf nodes in a transaction tree are at the same level. The edges in a transaction tree represent the implementation of an operation that is invoked at level L(i+1) by a sequence of operation executions at the next lower level Li (for i = 0, ..., n-1 in bottom-up order). The implementation of an operation can be state-dependent; that is, an Li operation that is executed in two different transactions may invoke different L(i-1) operations in these two transactions.

The key idea of multilevel concurrency control is to exploit the semantics of operations in **level-specific conflict relations** CON_i that reflect the commutativity (or compatibility [Gar83]; see Section 13.4) of operations. For example, two *Deposit* operations on a bank account are commutative and can therefore be admitted concurrently (e.g., on behalf of two funds transfer transactions).

Conflict relations are defined on operations as specified at a particular level of abstraction rather than operation executions. Two Li operations f and g are considered to be commutative (and therefore conflict-free) iff, for each possible system state σ, the following two conditions hold: 1) the states that result from the execution sequences $f;g$ and $g;f$ applied to σ are not distinguishable by any Li operation, and 2) both f and g have the same return values in both execution sequences. This notion of commutativity of Li operations refers to "abstract" states viewed at level Li rather than "concrete" states. That is, it is acceptable that there are operations at level L(i-1) or lower that can distinguish the state $g(f(\sigma))$ from the state $f(g(\sigma))$.

Figure 13.1 shows a schedule, that is, concurrent execution of two multilevel transactions (with execution order from left to right). Both transactions

T1 and T2 withdraw some money from bank accounts *a* and *b* and deposit the money in account *c*. These high-level operations are implemented by read and write accesses to the underlying records. Suppose that accounts *a* and *b* belong to the same branch of the bank and that *Withdraw* operations automatically update some sort of branch total. Further suppose that this branch total is stored in record *t*.

In terms of the read/write operations at the bottom level L0, the schedule of Figure 13.1 is not correct. It is not (conflict-) serializable with respect to T1 and T2. However, at the higher level L1, one can exploit that the two *Deposit* operations commute, so that the L0 conflict on *c* becomes a **pseudo-conflict**. Therefore, the schedule can be regarded as serializable at the top level L1.

In reasoning that the schedule of Figure 13.1 is "high-level serializable" we make the implicit assumption that each high-level operation such as *Withdraw*(*a*) is executed as if it were indivisible. One way of ensuring this assumption is to execute high-level operations sequentially. However, such a semantic concurrency control method (based on "atomic steps" [Gar83]) would not overlap disk I/O and CPU work, and could not exploit multiple processors in a parallel computer. Therefore, it is crucial to execute (non-conflicting) high-level operations in parallel. In this case, however, pseudo-conflicts at the lower implementation levels need to be dealt with, so as to make **high-level operations appear indivisible**. For this purpose, a concurrency control mechanism is needed at each level Li, where the Li concurrency control treats L(i+1) operations as **subtransactions** (or transactions for i=n-1) and Li operations as the actions that constitute the subtransactions. Intuitively, the goal of the Li concurrency control is to isolate the L(i+1) subtransactions from each other. More precisely, this criterion amounts to providing serializability of the schedule at level Li, where the L(i+1) subtransactions are considered as transactions and CON_i is used as the conflict relation between the Li actions. For example, in Figure 13.1, the shown interleaving between *Withdraw*(*a*) and *Withdraw*(*b*) is admissible, whereas any interleaving of the two *Deposit* operations on account *c* would be incorrect and must therefore be prevented by the L0 concurrency control.

If, in a two-level system, the conflict relation at the higher level is empty, then we arrive at the special case of "sagas" [GS87] (see also [GGKKS91] for nested sagas). Sagas are based on the assumption that all high-level operations (called "steps") are commutative. Therefore, a transaction can in fact be decomposed into a sequence of independent subtransactions. That is, it is sufficient to serialize the resulting subtransactions, and no concurrency control mechanism is needed at the higher level. Presumably, this method of decomposing long transactions is often used in transaction processing systems [GS84]. However, it requires a careful analysis not only of the saga itself but also of the potential interactions with all other transaction types, in order to ensure that "high-level serializability" is still preserved.

Multilevel transaction management allows more concurrency compared to conventional (single-level) concurrency control. On the other hand, transaction aborts can no longer be implemented by restoring the pre-transaction state of the modified L0 objects, since low-level modifications become visible to concurrent transactions at the end of each subtransaction. The solution to this problem is to perform transaction aborts by means of inverse high-level operations that **compensate** complete subtransactions rather than backing them out [BSW88, Gar83, GS87, KLS90, MGG86, MR91, SDP91, VEH91, Wei87, Wei91]. In the scenario of Figure 13.1, for example, aborting transaction T2 after T1 is committed requires two compensating subtransactions $Withdraw(c)$ and $Deposit(b)$.

By viewing the compensating subtransactions as additional regular operations of the transaction that is to be aborted, transaction aborts can be handled within the framework of multilevel concurrency control, too. The resulting correctness criterion is **complete serializability**, that is, multilevel serializability of the schedule in which the compensating subtransactions are explicitly represented [BSW88, Wei87, Wei91]. Complete serializability is an elegant treatment of recoverability in that it does not require a new correctness criterion, but rather extends the scope of serializability to the compensating subtransactions.

13.2.2 Limits of Multilevel Transactions

In the classification of [SZ89], the specification of how semantics can be exploited in multilevel transactions is based on the "data (operation) approach", as opposed to the "transaction (interleaving) approach" that is pursued, for example, in [Gar83, Lyn83, FO89, SZ89]. In the data operation approach, concurrency control is based on a symmetric conflict relation between pairs of operations that can be invoked on instances of abstract data types [SS84, We83, We88]. Read and write accesses to records or pages can be viewed as a special case. Typically, the conflict definition reflects the general (i.e., state-independent) commutativity of operations and considers only

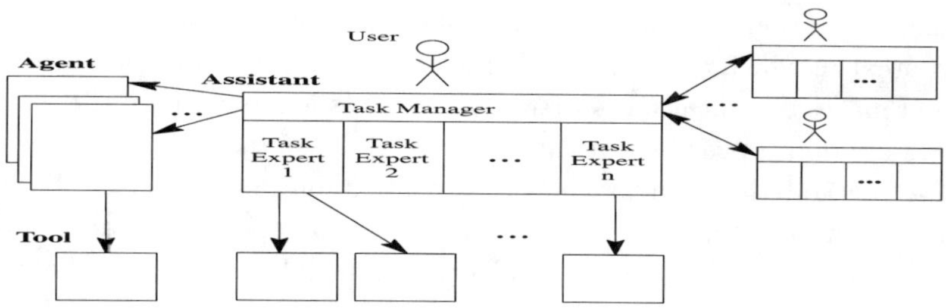

FIGURE 13.2
Concurrent execution based on a transaction interleaving specification.

the name and the input parameters of the operations. In addition, state-dependent commutativity may be exploited, for example, by considering also the return values of operations [GK85, O'N86, We88]. In both cases, the allowable interleavings of transactions are derived from the conflict relation, because (only) commutative pairs of operations can be freely reordered.

In the transaction interleaving approach, on the other hand, the allowable interleavings of transactions are directly specified between all pairs of transaction types. As an example consider a customer report transaction that reports the balance of the checking account and the savings account of a customer. If one assumes that a funds transfer transaction does never access two accounts of the same customer, then one may specify that the two *Balance* operations of a customer report transaction can be freely interleaved with the *Withdraw* and *Deposit* operations of a funds transfer transaction. Further assume that, because of the commutativity of *Deposits*, the high-level steps of two funds transfer transactions can also be interleaved. The execution shown in Figure 13.2 is a correct schedule according to this specification. However, neither *Withdraw* and *Balance* nor *Deposit* and *Balance* are commutative operation pairs, and therefore the schedule of Figure 13.2 cannot be achieved under a multilevel transaction specification.

The example in Figure 13.2 shows that, by considering more context, the transaction interleaving approach seems to be more powerful than the data operation approach because it allows specifications of arbitrary interleavings of transaction trees. On the other hand, the transaction interleaving approach requires considerably more effort to produce a complete and consistent specification, since it considers all pairs of transaction trees. In contrast, the data operation approach considers only pairs of operations, disregarding the context in which an operation is invoked. Because of its modularity, this method makes specifications easier and thus puts less burden on the designer of a transaction processing system.

A method that can exploit some context information while basically staying within the framework of the data operation approach is developed in [VV88]. In this method, the equivalence of schedules and hence the notion of serializability are based on semantically rich axioms that are specified for sequences of operations. Commutativity of operations is subsumed in this model as a special sort of axiom. However, more research is needed to investigate if this model can reconcile the data operation approach with the transaction interleaving approach.

13.2.3 A Summary of the Multilevel Transaction Theory

Multilevel Serializability

The considerations of Subsection 13.2.1 can be cast into a formal model as follows. A layered system architecture is assumed as the basis of the model. Each layer provides a well-defined interface of (abstract) objects and operations, which is referred to as a level. A level is implemented in terms of the objects and operations of the level below. The bottom level is denoted L0; it provides primitive operations that are not further decomposed. A **multilevel transaction** in a system with n levels L0, ..., L(n-1) is formally defined as a tree of height n+1 such that all leaf nodes are at the same level L0. The nodes of a tree are called actions; actions represent executions of level-specific operations. In our examples, actions are labeled by their corresponding operations. The edges between the nodes of level Li and level L(i-1) represent the expansion of Li actions into L(i-1) actions according to the implementation of the Li operations. For technical reasons (i.e., to simplify the formalism), transactions are modeled as if the expansion of actions were not affected by the system state. That is, the tree structure of a transaction remains the same in all equivalent schedules (as in the classical serializability theory).

A **multilevel schedule** is formally defined by a set of transaction trees and an L0 **execution order** $<_0$ between the L0 actions of the executed transactions (i.e., the leaf nodes of the transaction trees). The execution order $<_0$ may be partial; however, we require that L0 action pairs for which the corresponding primitive operations are in (CON_0-) conflict must be ordered. The execution order $<_i$ at higher levels is derived from $<_0$ in the following way. An Li action f precedes an Li action g if and only if all descendants of f at level L0 precede all L0 descendants of g. Otherwise, f and g are concurrent, that is, not $<_i$-related.

The execution order $<_i$ captures the information about the actual ordering of Li actions; the level-specific conflict relation CON_i provides the information on the pairs of Li actions for which the ordering is actually significant. From these two relations we can construct the Li **serialization order** $\lesssim_i$ (called the Li "quasi-order" in [Wei91]) for each level Li as follows. At level L0, $\lesssim_0$ contains all ordered conflict pairs, that is, $\lesssim_0 = <_0 \cap CON_0$. For level L1 and above, $f \lesssim_i g$ holds for two Li actions f and g if and only if they have children f' and g' at level L(i-1) that are in (CON_{i-1}-) conflict and for which $f' \lesssim_{i-1} g'$ holds. For single-level systems where the transaction roots are right above the action level L0, the serialization order $\lesssim_1$ corresponds to the serialization graph as defined in [BHG87]. Thus, the classical serializability theory is preserved as a special case in the multilevel transaction theory.

Now a multilevel schedule is called **multilevel serializable** if and only if, at each level Li ($0 \leq i \leq n$), the relation $\lesssim_i \cup (<_i \cap CON_i)$ is acyclic. The intuition behind this definition is the following. The acyclicity of $\lesssim_i$ is necessary for ensuring that each Li action appears as if it were indivisible. That is, the schedule that is obtained by viewing Li operations as transactions and L(i-1) operations as actions must be serializable. In addition, we must ensure that the low-level serialization of Li actions is compatible with the execution order of the Li actions that are in conflict with respect to CON_i. Otherwise, the execution order of the Li actions would not be a meaningful information for determining the serialization order at the levels above Li.

For the example schedule of Figure 13.1, the only $\lesssim_1$ pair that we obtain is the pair of *Deposit* operations on account c, which results from the read/write and write/write conflicts at level L0. Further assuming that *Withdraw/Withdraw* and *Withdraw/Deposit* on the same bank account are the only conflicting L1 pairs, we obtain an empty $\lesssim_2$ relation. That is, the multilevel schedule of Figure 13.1 is equivalent to both serial executions of the transactions T1 and T2.

A practically important result of the multilevel serializability theory [BBG89, BSW88, HH88, Mar87, MGG86, Wei86a, Wei91] is the following. Suppose that for each pair (f, g) of conflicting L(i+1) operations, there is at least one pair of Li operations among the children of f and g that conflict with respect to CON_i. Under this reasonable assumption, multilevel serializability is already guaranteed by the property of **level-by-level serializability**, that is, by requiring that the serialization graph between each pair of adjacent levels is acyclic. This means that different concurrency control mechanisms can be used at different levels as long as each of them ensures (conflict-) serializability in the classical sense.

Even without the above assumption it is possible to enforce multilevel serializability in a modular way. In general, a sufficient condition for multilevel serializability is **order-preserving serializability between each pair of adjacent levels** [BBG89] (see also [BSW88] for more discussion). This condition allows even a multiversion concurrency control mechanism to be used between levels, provided that the serialization that is achieved by this mechanism preserves the submission order of sequentially executed transactions. Note that order-preservation is essential to make sure that the Li serialization order $\lesssim_i$ is compatible with the execution order $<_i \cap CON_i$ of conflicting Li actions. In the level-by-level serializability approach discussed above, order-preservation is implicitly guaranteed by the stated conflict-mapping condition.

Complete Multilevel Serializability

In this section, we discuss how recovery-related actions may affect multilevel serializability. Generally, little work has been done on the impact of recovery on concurrency control [BSW88, Had88, KLS90, LKS91, MGG86, We89, Wei87, Wei91], compared to the large body of research on concurrency control. Most of the previous approaches introduce additional correctness criteria like strictness [Had88, BHG87], revokability [MGG86], soundness [KLS90], and isolation of recoveries [LKS91], which impose additional constraints on a schedule in order to prevent incorrect behavior (such as cascading aborts that involve transactions that are already committed).

We have developed the simpler criterion of **complete serializability**, which is based on the following two requirements:

- All recovery-related steps must be made explicit actions in the schedule of transaction executions, and are subject to concurrency control.
- The resulting complete schedule must be multilevel serializable in the ordinary sense.

Transaction aborts can be implemented either by 1) state-based undo, that is, restoring all objects in a transaction's writeset to the state as of the

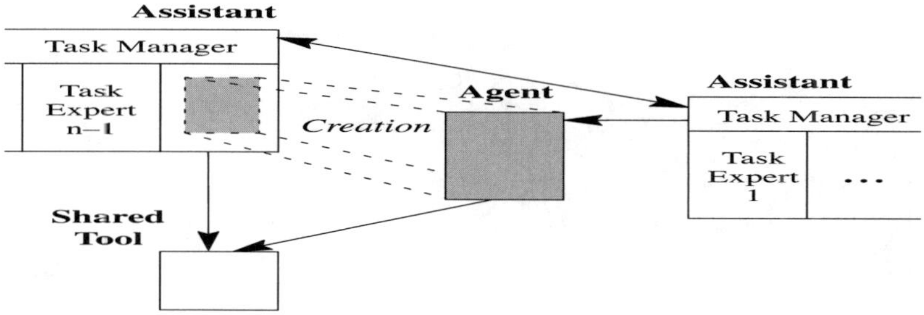

FIGURE 13.3
Multilevel schedule violating complete serializability.

beginning of the transaction, or by 2) invoking compensating subtransactions. In the first case, a transaction abort actually corresponds to a sequence of write accesses, where the order of the transaction's original write operations is reversed. In the second case, the compensating subtransactions are simply additional subtransactions of the aborting transaction, where the order of the transaction's original subtransactions is reversed.

The two implementations of transaction aborts can be represented in a multilevel schedule by attaching the additional operations to the parents of the operations that are undone. Figure 13.3 and Figure 13.4 show examples of each method. The examples are based on the execution of Figure 13.1, now assuming that transaction T2 is aborted. The operations that implement this abort are marked with an overbar. For the sake of simplicity, the updates of the branch total that were shown in Figure 13.1 are omitted here and in all the following examples.

Figure 13.3 shows the state-based undo method, where two additional write actions restore the state of the modified objects b and c as of the beginning of T2. Since the abort is implemented at level L0, the two additional write actions are attached to the L1 subtransaction in which the original writes occurred, that is, to the immediate parents of the actions that are undone. Now that we have a "complete" schedule with all recovery-related actions made explicit, we can use simple serializability arguments. In Figure 13.3, the L0 actions $W(c)$ of T2, $W(c)$ of T1, and $W(c)$ of T2 constitute a cycle in the L1 serialization order $\lesssim 1$. Thus, the schedule cannot be completely multilevel serializable.

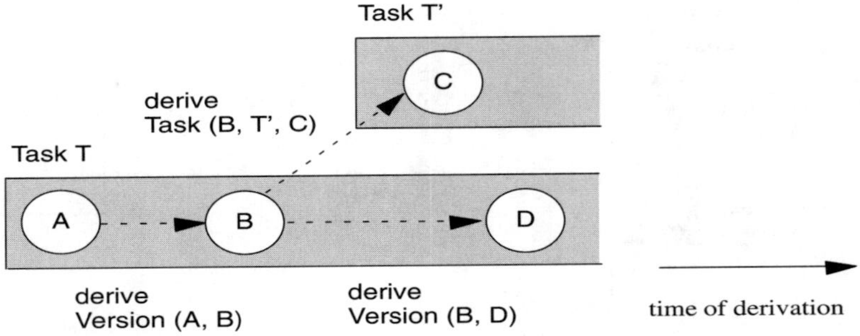

FIGURE 13.4
Completely serializable multilevel schedule.

Figure 13.4 shows the undo method based on compensation. The compensating subtransactions $\underline{Withdraw(c)}$ and $\underline{Deposit(b)}$ are simply additional children of the transaction whose original subtransactions are to be compensated. Now, by using simple serializability arguments, we can obtain a correctness proof for the shown execution as follows. Because of the commutativity of the original two *Deposit* operations and because account b was accessed only by T2, we can rearrange the order of the L1 subtransactions so that the $\underline{Withdraw(c)}$ operation and the $\underline{Deposit(b)}$ operation of transaction T2 appear right after T2's $Deposit(c)$ and $Withdraw(b)$ operations, respectively. With no other operation being interleaved, the *Deposit* and *Withdraw* operations in each of the two pairs nullify each other, and the remaining schedule consists of transaction T1 only.

Undoing a transaction by compensating its completed subtransactions ensures **atomicity**, that is, the "all-or-nothing" property, in the following sense. Suppose that the compensating subtransactions correspond to operations at level Li. Then, no Li operation will ever be affected by the fact that the transaction was partially executed and aborted. In the ideal case, no Li operation will be able to detect the fact that the aborted transaction ever existed; and in no case, the aborted transaction will affect an Li operation's return value or effect on the "abstract" system state as viewed at Li. On the other hand, operations at level L(i-1) or lower may well see some remaining low-level effects of the aborted transaction. This "high-level" or "semantic" notion of atomicity is a consequence of relaxing the strict isolation of transactions by exploiting the semantics of high-level operations.

These considerations show that we can reason about the interaction of concurrency control and recovery steps solely by means of the serializability theory, provided that recovery steps are explicitly represented in a schedule. To ensure complete (multilevel) serializability, the transaction manager simply has to make sure that recovery steps are also subject to the concurrency control protocol that is employed. For example, if the concurrency control protocol is two-phase locking, then all actions that are necessary to undo an aborting transaction must have appropriate locks (see [Wei91] for more detailed discussion). To ensure that the locking protocol is indeed two-phased, no locks can be released at the level at which transaction aborts are implemented before a transaction is really completed (i.e., committed to the user or entirely undone). This condition is uniformly required for both recovery based on state-based undo and recovery based on compensation. The only difference between these two recovery methods is that the first method keeps locks at a low level (e.g., the page level) whereas the second method merely keeps "semantic" high-level locks.

Proof techniques as outlined above can be applied to systems with more than two levels [Wei91], and they can also be used to reason about subtransaction aborts (i.e., partial rollbacks of a transaction) at different levels. In principle, we can also reason about crash recovery methods using the same approach; however, a formal model for multilevel crash recovery is still a research issue.

13.2.4 Implementation Issues

The relationship between the multilevel transaction model and its implementation is twofold. On the one hand, multilevel transactions provide a model for some of the performance tricks used in high performance transaction processing systems. In particular, the multilevel transaction model explains why systems with record locking also need "short" page locks (namely, so as to make record operations appear indivisible). On the other hand, well-proven implementation techniques form a good basis for implementing the multilevel transaction model and open nested transactions in general. Because such efficient implementation techniques are an important asset of the model, we discuss, at a very high level, some implementation issues of multilevel transaction management.

Concurrency Control

Executing high-level operations in parallel requires that a low-level synchronization mechanism takes care of possible low-level conflicts, for example, on indexes or data pages. In relational DBMSs where records do not span pages, this low-level synchronization is usually implemented by page latches, that is, cheap semaphores that are held while a page is accessed. For advanced DBMSs with complex high-level operations that may access many pages in different orders, simple latching is not feasible since it cannot ensure the indivisibility of arbitrary multi-page update operations. Rather, high-level operations must be executed as subtransactions that are dealt with by a general concurrency control mechanism at the lower level.

Without further knowledge about the access characteristics of subtransactions, the best way of implementing the required level-specific concurrency control seems to be two-phase locking at each level. For each level-specific operation a semantic lock mode is introduced, and the (state-independent) commutativity of operations is translated into the compatibility of lock modes [Kor83, SS84]. During the execution of an L(i+1) subtransaction, Li-operation-specific locks are acquired at level Li. These Li locks are held until the end of the L(i+1) subtransaction, thus isolating the subtransaction from concurrent L(i+1) subtransactions. Since the executed Li operations are themselves subtransactions that invoke L(i-1) operations at the level below, the same protocol must be applied to those L(i-1) operations, and so forth. Thus, the lock and unlock calls for the entire transaction tree are subject to a **nested two-phase locking protocol** [BR90, MGG86, WS84, Wei91], where the conflict potential of the locks decreases with higher levels and the lock durations decreases with lower levels.

Note that locks at different levels may be managed by the same lock manager, which is responsible for queue management and deadlock detection. Further note that it is possible to exploit specific knowledge about the object reference pattern of the subtransactions at a particular level. Even though it is usually hard to predict the reference pattern of an entire transaction, such information may be available for subtransactions as they correspond to system-provided operations. For example, a non-two-phase locking protocol may be feasible at a level where all subtransactions have sequential or tree-traversal reference patterns. In the extreme case that each subtransaction accesses only a single object at the level below, we are back to the simple latching method, but latch-based protocols have also been proposed for tree traversals such as index operations [ML89, Moh90].

Recovery

Compensating subtransactions are necessary for both handling transaction aborts and crash recovery after a system failure. An important prerequisite is that both regular subtransactions and compensating subtransactions have to be atomic. Otherwise, the recovery after a crash may be faced with a database state that is not sufficiently consistent to perform the necessary high-level undo steps. For example, the storage structures of a complex object may contain dangling pointers, or some derived data may only partially reflect the primary updates. If a subtransaction modifies multiple pages, a low-level recovery mechanism at the page level is necessary in order to provide subtransaction atomicity. This problem is challenging in that a straightforward implementation of multilevel recovery may cause excessive logging and could thus diminish the benefits of the enhanced concurrency of multilevel transactions. We believe that all advanced transaction models have to address this implementation problem.

Generally, a method for multilevel recovery must satisfy the following requirements:

1. It must ensure that transactions are atomic.

2. It must ensure that transactions are persistent.

3. It must ensure that subtransactions are atomic.

Note that subtransactions need not be persistent before the commitment of their parent. In addition to the above requirements for correctness, the following performance requirement is reasonable in order to guarantee an acceptable recovery time and hence high availability of the DBMS:

4. During a warmstart, redo (of committed transactions) should be performed at the bottom level L0, that is, by reconstructing pages rather than reexecuting potentially resource-intensive high-level operations.

An architecture that meets the above requirements is shown in Figure 13.5. This architecture has in fact been implemented in the DASDBS prototype system [SPSW90]. For requirement 1, undo log records are written at each level. Each of these log records contains information about the compensating subtransaction that is necessary to undo a subtransaction at a particular level. The Li log records of an L(i+1) (sub)transaction are chained together in a backward chain for handling (sub)transaction aborts and for performing transaction undo after a crash. In addition to the level-specific

Object. version Operations	read Version (V')	readLatest TaskVersion (T')	readLatest Version	get VersionNo	deriveVersion (V', D')	deriveTask (V', T', D')
read Version (V)	+	+	+	+	$V \neq D'$	$V \neq D'$
readLatest TaskVersion (T)	+	+	+	+	$D' \notin T$	$T \neq T'$
readLatest Version	+	+	+	+	–	–
get VersionNo	+	+	+	+	–	–
deriveVersion (V, D)	$D \neq V'$	$D \notin T'$	–	–	$D \neq D'$	+
deriveTask (V, T, D)	$D \neq V'$	$T \neq T'$	–	–	+	$T \neq T'$

V, V' Versions
D, D' Derived versions
T, T' Tasks

(shaded) Symmetric condition holds (Corollary 1)

- - - - - Condition for transparent operations holds (Corollary 2)

FIGURE 13.5
Architecture of multilevel transaction management.

operation log records, "end-of-(sub)transaction" log records are written for completed (i.e., committed or aborted) (sub)transactions. For requirements 2 and 4, redo log records are written to an L0 log file.

As mentioned above, requirement 3 is the most difficult one. An efficient way of implementing it is to make sure that the redo log records of a subtransaction (e.g., a set of page after-images) are written atomically to the L0 log. Because redo information is page-oriented and page locks are released early, one has to take care that writing the redo log records of a subtransaction does not violate the atomicity of other subtransactions.

For example, suppose that in the scenario of Figure 13.1, the records a, b, and c are located on the same page p, and that the write operations on these records cause updates to additional pages q, r, s, and t, respectively, containing derived data (e.g., index data). A possible execution including these page accesses is shown in Figure 13.6. Now suppose that transaction T1 is to be committed after having performed all its operations. The commit is

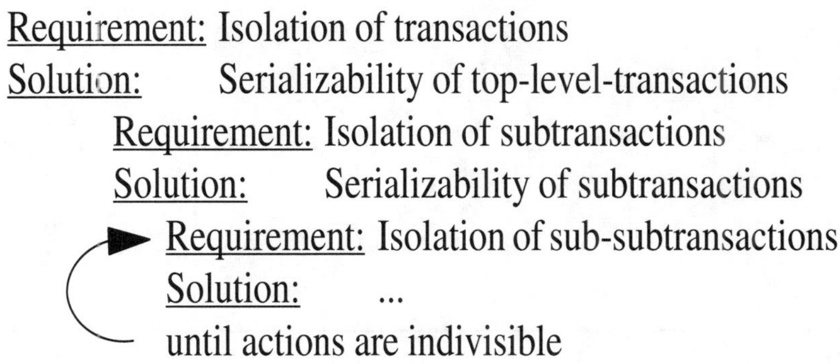

FIGURE 13.6
Multilevel transactions with subtransactions that update multiple pages.

implemented by writing the redo log records for the modified pages p, q, and t to the L0 log file. However, writing these log records may violate the atomicity of the *Deposit*(c) subtransaction of transaction T2. The reason is that the effect of T2's subtransaction is partially reflected in T1's redo log record for page p whereas the updates to page s made by the same subtransaction are not written to the log. A solution to this problem is to combine dynamically the redo information of multiple subtransactions into a **persistence sphere** that is written atomically to the log. Details on this method and further aspects of the implementation of multilevel logging are described in [WHBM90, HW91, WH91].

The described multilevel logging architecture can be implemented with a separate log file for each level or with all level-specific logs physically combined into a single log file. Figure 13.5 depicts both alternatives. During the warmstart after a system crash, the redo log is processed in a forward pass, and, subsequently, the high-level undo logs are processed in a single backward pass. During the undo pass, care must be taken so as not to invoke a compensating subtransaction in a state that does not contain the effects of the original subtransaction that is to be compensated. Methods for dealing with this and other problems during the warmstart of a multilevel transaction system are discussed in [WHBM90, WH91, Moh89].

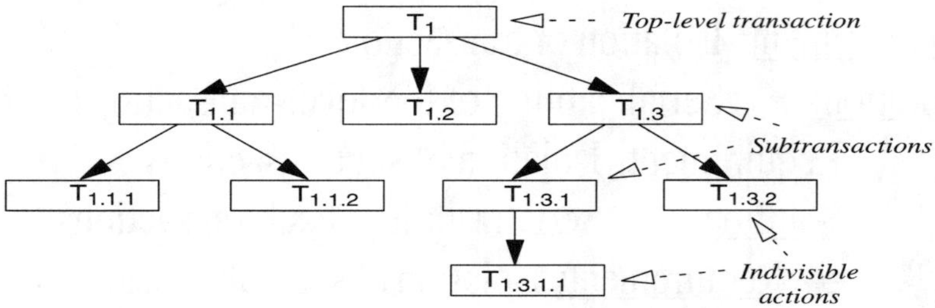

FIGURE 13.7
Concurrent execution of open nested transactions.

13.3 The General Case of Open Nested Transactions

The difference between multilevel transactions and open nesteds is that, in the more general model, the structure of the transaction trees is not restricted to layering; that is, siblings in the transaction tree are allowed to have different nesting depths. Since the leaves of transaction trees always correspond to elementary operations such as page accesses or simple record accesses, one could also say, in "layered terminology", that subtransactions are allowed to bypass one or more layers. This generalization of multilevel transactions is illustrated in the example of Figure 13.7. Compared to Figure 13.1, the example transactions have additional Insert operations that write into an application-managed transaction journal.

Because of the structural limitations of s, the correctness of the concurrent execution shown in Figure 13.7 cannot be proven within our multilevel serializability theory as sketched in Section 13.2.3. However, a rigorous correctness proof can be conducted in the general nested transaction models developed in [BBG89] and [FLMW88, LMWF91]. Note that these models go beyond the conventional notion of nested transactions [Mos85] in that they allow for subtransactions that make updates visible to other top-level transactions before their parents commit.

A proof that the schedule of Figure 13.7 is serializable, based on the model of [BBG89], would run as follows. Because of the commutativity of $Insert(y)$ and $W(c)$, we can exchange the order between these two nodes, thus separating the *Deposit* subtransaction of T1 and the *Insert* action of T2. Next, because the set of nodes labeled *Withdraw*, *Deposit*, or *Insert* now form a front of serial computations, we can reduce the *Withdraw* and *Deposit* subtransactions, that is, prune their descendants. This results in a flat schedule that can be shown to be serializable by commutativity arguments. In general, the serializability proof for a schedule of arbitrarily deep open nesteds involves the alternating application of commutativity and reduction.

13.4 Relaxing the ACID Paradigm

In this section, we discuss in which ways the open nested transaction model is able to relax the so-called ACID paradigm. The ACID paradigm of the classical transaction concept comprises the four properties atomicity, consistency-preservation, isolation, and durability [HR83]. In the classical transaction concept, all four properties are bundled together. Ideally, however, these properties should be orthogonal in the sense that each of them can be waived without affecting the remaining properties (cf. [CCKLLO91, CR91, WR91]). The purpose of this section is to show that, in the open nested transaction model, orthogonality can be achieved to some extent.

13.4.1 Consistency-preservation

In the classical transaction concept, only consistency-preservation can be viewed as orthogonal to the other three properties. Existing transaction managers take care only of atomicity, persistence, and isolation, whereas application programs are responsible for consistency-preservation. This is still true for open nested transactions.

13.4.2 Isolation

The strict isolation of transactions can be relaxed in the following two ways:

- by exploiting the semantics of the operations in the definition of conflicts (as discussed in Section 13.2), and
- by specifying which subtransactions are "open" and which subtransactions are "closed".

The first step toward more semantics is to incorporate general or state-dependent **commutativity** in the conflict definition between operations [O'N86, We88]. For example, two Deposit operations on the same account are generally commutative, and two Withdraw operations are commutative in a state that allows both withdrawals to succeed (i.e., if there are sufficient funds). A more aggressive approach is to substitute commutativity by **compatibility** [Gar83], where two operations can be specified as compatible if their execution order is insignificant from the application point of view. For example, consider a Withdraw operation without overdraft protection, that is, without rejected withdrawals. Suppose that a special penalty of $10 is charged for each withdrawal that results in a negative balance. Clearly, such a Withdraw operation does not commute with a Deposit operation. However, the resulting effects are probably acceptable for both the bank and the customers, and viewing these operations as compatible can improve performance.

Exploiting commutativity or compatibility allows that incomplete transactions can make uncommitted updates visible to those transactions that perform a commutative or compatible operation. Note that this weaker notion of isolation does not leave the solid ground of serializability, since the conflict definition between pairs of operations is essentially a module that is "imported" into serializability theory. Furthermore, exploiting semantics to relax the definition of isolation has no impact on the validity of the other three ACID properties.

The programmer of an open nested can specify which subtransactions do effectively make updates visible to compatible operations. He or she simply attaches one of the attributes "open" or "closed" to each node in the transaction tree (see also [ELLR90, Wal84] for similar approaches). An **"open" node** spawns a new "sphere of control"; that is, all updates of its descendants become visible to other transactions when the node's computation is completed. It is up to the node's parent to take measures that further protect the uncommitted updates, for example, by acquiring a semantically higher lock. A **"closed" node**, on the other hand, simply extends the "sphere of control" of its parent; that is, its updates are still isolated against concurrent transactions as in the conventional model of nested transactions. Note that "sagas" [GS87] correspond to a special case of this model: the restrictions are that the children of a must not have further descendants, and that the operations that correspond to open subtransactions are compatible with all possible operations.

Figure 13.8 shows an example of a nested transaction with both open and closed subtransactions, illustrated by striped and grey patterns, respectively. Suppose a transaction the purpose of which is to pay all monthly bills of a person, using electronic funds transfer rather than mailing checks. The

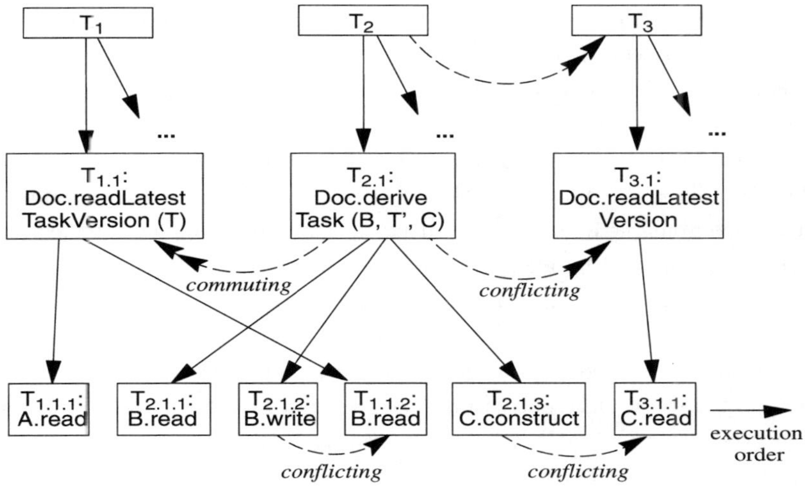

FIGURE 13.8
Open nested transaction with open and closed subtransactions.

Transfer transaction of the previous examples is now used as an operation of the entire transaction, that is, as a subtransaction. Withdraw/Deposit semantics is not exploited here; that is, updates on accounts are modeled as closed subtransactions. Suppose further that withdrawals make an entry in a special journal that is kept for security auditing. This Append operation is executed as an open subtransaction so that its effect becomes immediately visible.

13.4.3 Atomicity

By default, atomicity holds for transactions and subtransactions at all nesting levels. Depending on how much the isolation of transactions is relaxed, the notion of atomicity is interpreted in different ways. The classical interpretation is that atomicity ensures "all-or-nothing" in terms of the low-level details of the system state. The most relaxed interpretation, on the other hand, is that atomicity means masking the existence of aborted transactions or subtransactions to all application transactions that will be subsequently executed. The latter case can still be uniformly interpreted as ensuring the "all-or-nothing" property; however, in this case, the "all-or-nothing" property refers to the "abstract" system state as viewed by the transaction's top-level actions (see also Section 13.2.3).

For failures in closed subtransactions, atomicity is achieved by restoring the old state of the objects that are modified within the subtransaction. To roll back a completed open subtransaction, this state-oriented undo method is not feasible, since the updates of the subtransaction have already become visible to all compatible operations. Rather all completed open subtransactions must be compensated by executing additional "counter-subtransactions". In this sense, an open nested is never really rolled back but always completes successfully, possibly after having compensated its original effects.

A compensating subtransaction need not necessarily be the true inverse of the compensated subtransaction. For example, suppose a subtransaction that inserts a key into a B-tree index. Suppose that a leaf page is split on behalf of this insertion. For the compensation of this subtransaction, it may be sufficient to remove the inserted key; that is, the leaf page split need not be undone [Moh89]. As a second example [KLS90], consider an order entry transaction that causes a restocking of the inventory of one of the ordered items. If the order is later compensated for some reason, the restocking of the inventory would typically not be undone.

There may be operations that cannot be compensated for principal reasons. For example, printing a check or sending a message to a terminal may be considered as non-compensatable operations. Such operations must be deferred until the commit of a transaction [Pau88, BHM90]. Note, however, that this problem and the deferred execution solution are not specific to open nested transactions but must be faced by all advanced transaction models. Further note that deferring an operation may also be useful if compensation is feasible but has unacceptable run-time costs [O'N90].

Note that compensating a completed subtransaction requires that both the forward subtransaction and the compensating subtransaction are atomic. Further note that, like in all nested transaction models, subtransaction failures can be dealt with by undoing and restarting only the failed subtransaction, which provides intra-transaction savepoints. Restarting a failed subtransaction can also mean to invoke an alternate subtransaction that may be provided by the user to handle exceptional situations.

13.4.4 Persistence

In applications such as CASE, it is unacceptable that the work of a long-lived transaction is completely undone if the transaction eventually aborts (e.g., because of a crash). On the other hand, simply modeling a long design session as a sequence of shorter (top-level) transactions may not be an acceptable solution, because this would automatically make the (intermediate) results of each transaction visible to other transactions. The two requirements - long "spheres of control" with respect to isolation and shorter "spheres" with respect to persistence - can be reconciled by allowing the programmer of an open nested to attach a "persistent" attribute to individual subtransactions.

The updates of a persistent subtransaction are made persistent when the subtransaction successfully completes; if the subtransaction aborts before its completion then all its updates are undone. The programmer of an open nested transaction can undo a completed persistent subtransaction only by explicitly invoking a compensating subtransaction. Compensating subtransactions that are implicitly invoked by the system to undo a completed open subtransaction affect only non-persistent subtransactions.

Persistent subtransactions (sometimes called "nested top-level actions" [Moh89]) relax the atomicity of their parents since they survive the abort of a parent. In the example of Figure 13.8, it may be reasonable to specify the Append subtransaction as persistent. That is, an entry in the security journal is not removed if the entire transaction aborts. A persistent subtransaction may have non-persistent as well as persistent descendants. The difference is that the non-persistent descendants are made persistent when their lowest persistent ancestor completes successfully, whereas persistent descendants are made persistent upon their own successful completion.

13.5 Applications of Open Nested Transactions

13.5.1 Extensible Database Systems

A conservative way of extending an existing DBMS is the addition of a preprocessor sitting on top of the DBMS layer and forming, together with the DBMS, the extended database (XDBMS). Examples are preprocessors for geographical data or for document management and retrieval [WS84].

The availability of transactions at the DBMS level enables direct support of XDBMS transactions (XTs) if one XT is mapped to one transaction.

However, since one XDBMS operation is often mapped to many DBMS operations, the resulting XT may become rather long. As a consequence, the degree of concurrency between XTs may be rather low. Often specific indices (e.g., for text retrieval) are implemented on top of the DBMS and are handled by the DBMS as regular user data. This may cause hot spots and leads to a further decrease of the concurrency. Fortunately, multilevel transactions offer an elegant solution by using the transactions of the DBMS as a service for building XTs. A detailed example of such a solution is discussed in Section 13.6.

13.5.2 Federated Database Systems

A federated DBMS (FDBMS) is a collection of DBMSs that cooperate loosely but are not fully integrated. A particular challenge in FDBMSs is the coexistence of global transactions (GTs) that access two or more databases and local transactions (LTs) that operate solely on one database. Under the usual assumption of execution autonomy, each local DBMS (LDBMS) in an FDBMS provides concurrency control and guarantees serializability only for its LTs and the subtransactions of global transactions (GSTs) that are locally processed. In addition, GTs are serialized by a global concurrency control component on top of the underlying LDBMSs. This component cannot directly influence the execution of LTs. (For more detail see [OV91] and the references in it.)

In such an FDBMS architecture, non-serializable schedules of GTs and LTs are possible even though each LDBMS and the global transaction manager provide serializability of the GTs or LTs and GSTs that they deal with, respectively. Quasi-serializability [DE89] has been proposed as a weaker correctness criterion. It can be shown that quasi-serializability can be interpreted as multilevel serializability in a two-level system with a dynamically defined conflict relation at level L1 [SWS91]. In generalizing these ideas, the semantics of the operations of the GTs can be exploited as well.

Consider the example shown in Figure 13.9.The example shows two global Transfer transactions that access data of two LDBMSs (e.g., two different banks). In addition, a local transaction LT3 is executed in LDBMS A. Clearly, both LDBMS schedules are serializable. However, the global schedule is not serializable at level L0. The problem is that because of LT3, there is an indirect dependency from GST11 to GST21, which is incompatible with the dependency from GST22 to GST12. However, by exploiting the semantics of the GSTs, we realize that the dependency between GST22 and GST12

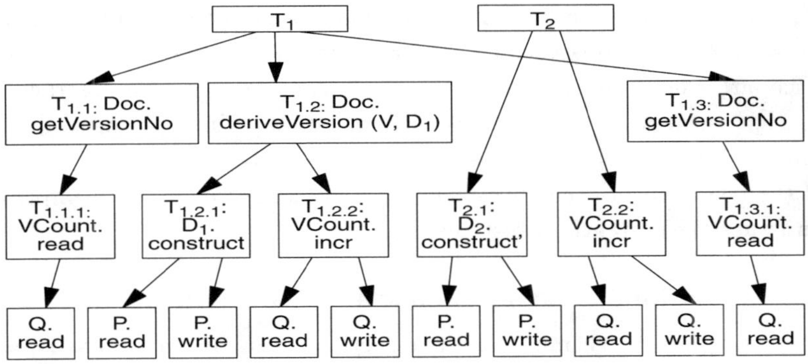

FIGURE 13.9
Multilevel serializable FDBMS schedule.

is actually insignificant, for the two Deposit operations commute. Thus, the entire schedule is in fact serializable from a higher-level point of view.

13.5.3 Exploiting Operating-System Transactions

There is fairly large consensus that future operating systems will provide transaction management facilities [OV91]. Even though OS transactions have been criticized for their inherent inability to exploit semantic knowledge, we believe that it is reasonable to use an OS transaction manager at least as the base layer of a multilevel transaction architecture [Wei86b]. Such an OS transaction manager would have to support atomic and persistent transactions as well as atomic actions, both appearing isolated from concurrent activities. It seems that this would factor out the base services needed by all higher levels. The multilevel transaction approach then is a way for exploiting the application semantics in the higher layers where it is defined.

13.5.4 Object-oriented Database Systems

Transaction management in object-oriented database systems (OO-DBMSs) poses two big challenges: dealing with general object graphs that allow referentially shared (sub-) objects (e.g., [BR88, CF90]), and exploiting the semantics of methods (e.g., [RGN90, SZ89]. The first issue is orthogonal to whether one uses flat or nested transactions; the second issue is obviously related to open nested transactions. By viewing the dynamic method invocation hierarchy of a user-invoked method as an open nested, we can directly exploit semantic properties of methods on a per object basis. This approach is similar to the work on synchronization of abstract data types (e.g., [We88]), except that the latter does not consider implementation hierarchies of abstract data types, that is, nested computations. Of course, applying open nested transactions to OO-DBMSs also raises performance-related issues such as how to avoid the overhead of excessively deep nested transactions. Such implementation issues are currently investigated.

13.5.5 Intra-transaction Parallelism

A nice property of multilevel transactions is modularity, that is, separation of layers with respect to concurrency control and recovery. subtransactions at a lower level are handled uniformly, regardless of whether they belong to different ancestors or to the same ancestor. This property can be exploited to provide the run-time environment for parallel subtransactions within the same top-level transaction [WH91]. Almost no extensions are necessary, neither on the theory nor the implementation side, to deal with such intra-transaction parallelism.

13.6 An Application Study: Office Document Filing and Retrieval

As an application of the multilevel transaction model, we discuss in this section the transaction support for an Office Document Filing and Retrieval Service, shortly DFR [ISO1, ISO2, PSSW87, ZPD90]. This service provides powerful retrieval and update operations on sets of **documents** that are collected in a hierarchy of **folders**. A document consists of a set of descriptive **attributes** such as DocName, CreationDate, or Owner, a potentially long **contents** consisting of text, and a list of **descriptors** for effective document retrieval. A folder contains a set of documents and a set of folders. For the sake of simplicity, we assume that a document can belong to only one folder (even though [ISO1, ISO2] also proposes referentially shared documents). Thus, folders and documents form a tree structure as shown in Figure 13.10. Also shown in Figure 13.10 is a possible mapping of folders and documents onto tables of a relational DBMS that could serve as a platform for implementing the DFR. Note that this may not be the best mapping to a relational DBMS, and that it is actually questionable whether a relational DBMS should be the basis of such a service anyway. However, as far as transaction management is

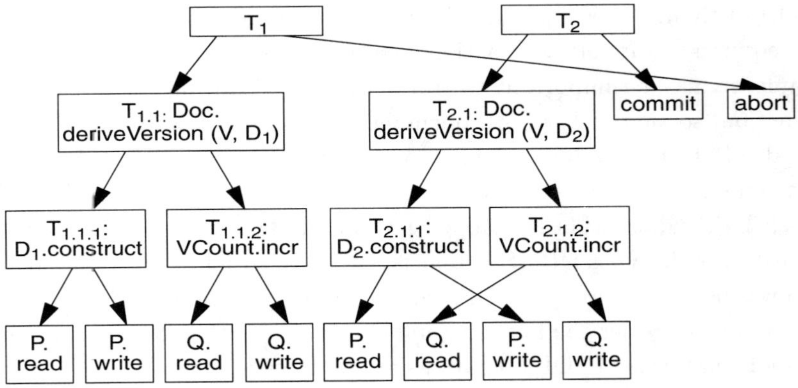

FIGURE 13.10
Object structures of the Office Document Filing and Retrieval Service and their mapping to a relational DBMS.

concerned, the following considerations would also apply to more sophisticated implementations of the DFR.

Example operations provided by the DFR are:

- Store (DId, DocName, ..., Contents, DescrList, ParentFId)
  store a document with given attributes, contents, and descriptor list into a specified folder

- Search (SearchedFId, SearchCondition, DescrList)
  search a specified folder for documents that contain all descriptors of a given descriptor list and satisfy a given search condition on the document attributes (e.g., CreationDate greater than "August-31-1991" and Owner = "Ahmed")

- List (FId)
  list the names and attributes of all documents that are contained in a specified folder or in a subordinate folder

- Archive (FId)
  generate a backup copy of all documents that are contained in a specified folder or in a subordinate folder, and update the ArchivedDate attribute of each processed folder.

Even though these are already quite powerful operations, it is, in addition, required to support transactions that consist of multiple operations. For example, it may be important to store two related documents as an atomic transaction, so that either both documents become visible to other users or none at all. In the simplest case, transactions of the DFR could be directly implemented by the transaction management of the underlying DBMS. That is, each DFR transaction is mapped into one DBMS transaction. However, even if the underlying DBMS supports record and index key-value locking, the powerful operations of the DFR are likely to produce many lock conflicts. For example, consider the following implementation of the *Store* and *Search* operations in terms of SQL operations at the DBMS level.

ALGORITHM **13.1**

Store (DId, DocName, ..., Contents, DescrList, ParentFId)

```
    Insert Into Docs Values (DId, DocName, ..., ParentFId)
    Insert Into Conts Values (DId, Contents)
    for each d ∈ DescrList do
        Insert Into Descr Values (DId, d)
```

ALGORITHM **13.2**

Search (SearchedFId, SearchCondition, DescrList)

```
    Temp1 := Select DId From Descr Where Descriptor = DescrList[1]
    Temp2 := Select DId From Descr Where Descriptor = DescrList[2]
                ⋮
    Result := Select DId From Docs Where
        SearchCondition And
        FId = SearchedFId And
        DId = Select DId From Temp1 And
        DId = Select DId From Temp2 And ...
```

It seems reasonable to assume that an index is defined on the Descriptor column of the Descr table. Further assuming that the SQL query optimizer produces a reasonable access plan, both the *Store* and the *Search* operation make heavy use of this index. Both operations would effectively lock all descriptors in the specified DescrLists. Since these DescrLists may contain between five and more than a hundred (perhaps, automatically generated) descriptors, the probability is quite high that the DescrLists of a *Store* and a *Search* operation are non-disjoint and hence one of the two transactions becomes blocked. The indexed Descr table may thus form a major performance bottleneck.

The described problem is a "classical" example of a pseudo-conflict. From the application point of view, a *Store* and a *Search* operation are non-commutative and hence are conflicting only if all of the following three conditions hold:

1. the folder into which a document is stored is identical to the folder that is searched,
2. the newly stored document satisfies the SearchCondition of the *Search* operation, and
3. the DescrList of the newly stored document contains *all* descriptors that are specified in the DescrList of the *Search* operation.

Note that condition 3 is much stronger than the condition that the DescrLists of the *Store* and *Search* operations are non-disjoint. Assume that k descriptors are specified in the DescrList of the *Search* operation. Further assume that the probability for a descriptor to appear in a document is p. Finally, for the sake of simplicity, assume that descriptors are uniformly distributed and that the distributions of different descriptors are independent. Then, the probability that a newly inserted document is a match to a concurrent *Search* operation and thus causes a (high-level) conflict is p^k. The probability for a pseudo-conflict, on the other hand, is $1 - (1 - p)^k$, which is the probability that the DescrList of the Search operation and that of the inserted document are not disjoint.

The above strawman calculation indicates that a semantic conflict test at the application level would probably eliminate the suspected data-contention bottleneck, yet it ensures serializability with respect to the semantics of the DFR operations. The solution to the performance problem thus is to implement each DFR operation as an open subtransaction of a multilevel transaction. This solution either entails building a multilevel transaction management on top of the DBMSs transaction management, or it requires that the

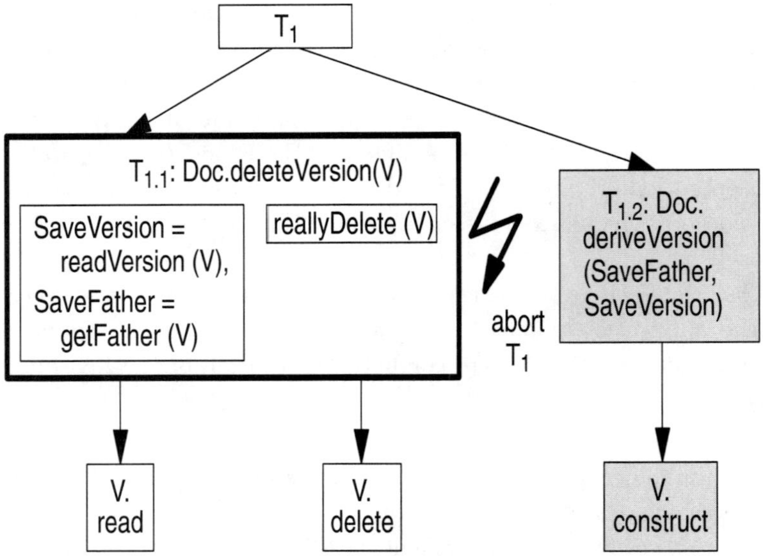

FIGURE 13.11
Multilevel transaction support for the Office Document Filing and Retrieval Service.

underlying DBMS already supports multilevel transactions that are specified by the DBMS's client.

In the following, we assume that client-specified multilevel transactions are supported by the DBMS. An architecture for implementing DFR transactions is depicted in Figure 13.11. In this architecture, the responsibilities are divided among the application system (i.e., the DFR) and the DBMS as follows. The multilevel transaction management of the DBMS takes care of

- managing locks on folders, documents, search predicates, etc., as specified by the application-level conflict test,
- providing isolation of the subtransactions that correspond to DFR operations,
- providing atomicity of the subtransactions that correspond to DFR operations,

- providing persistence of entire DFR transactions by performing redo logging at the page level (see also Section 13.2.4),

- managing all log buffers and log files, and taking responsibility for I/O optimizations such as batching log I/Os, and, finally,

- doing the necessary bookkeeping to ensure that, during a warmstart, compensating subtransactions are invoked only in proper states of the database (see Section 13.2.4).

The application system, on the other hand, has to take the responsibility for

- providing the multilevel transaction manager with a compatibility table for the application-specific lock modes [DPS83], rules for handling lock conversions, etc.,

- providing the contents of the undo log records that are written for the DFR operations, and

- providing the code for the compensating subtransaction that may be invoked for a transaction abort or during crash recovery, using the contents of an undo log record as its input parameter.

The open subtransactions that implement the DFR operations may in turn be decomposed into further subtransactions. For example, each SQL operation that is invoked by an DFR operation could be a closed subtransaction, meaning that its effects are kept isolated until the entire DFR operation completes. This would be the case if the DBMS holds page locks for the duration of an DFR operation. Alternatively, each SQL operation could be implemented as an open subtransaction, meaning that its low-level effects become visible to other operations as soon as the SQL operation returns.

Within an SQL operation, index operations may constitute another level of open subtransactions. Because of the specific page access patterns of such subtransactions, special locking protocols can be employed for isolating index operations [SG88] (see also Section 13.2.4). The protocol itself is encapsulated by the subtransaction; that is, the caller of an index operation simply executes a subtransaction that appears to be indivisible. Thus, the index locking protocol can be easily changed without affecting the correctness of the entire transaction management. Also, novel access path techniques such as advanced signature techniques [CS89] can be added to the DBMS without requiring a redesign of the transaction management.

Structural reorganizations of an access path (e.g., B-tree leaf splits) can be implemented as separate subtransactions with the "persistent" attribute set. That is, a structural reorganization will not be undone even if the entire transaction aborts (see Section 13.4.4). This separation may simplify index concurrency control and recovery [Sha85, ML89].

The described Office Document Filing and Retrieval Service can also benefit from nested transactions as a control structure for intra-transaction parallelism. For example, the Archive operation must traverse a folder and its subordinate folders. This traversal can be easily parallelized by spawning a separate thread of control for each folder that is archived. Since there may be low-level conflicts between these parallel threads (e.g., page conflicts when updating the ArchivedDates of different folders), each thread should be executed as a subtransaction, making sure that the parallelized execution is equivalent to a sequential one. The entire Archive operation forms a transaction tree that reflects the folder hierarchy. This tree of (closed) subtransactions can be used as a subtransaction within a more complex nested transaction, and/or it can be further refined by decomposing the leaves of the tree into further lower-level subtransactions.

13.7 Conclusion

The multilevel transaction model and its generalization toward open nesteds can be viewed as an evolutionary path from the classical transaction concept to more advanced transaction models. While being relatively conservative compared to other models, open nested transactions are yet a fairly powerful instrument that satisfies many of the requirements stated in the introduction. Moreover, the existence of a rigorous theoretical foundation and the knowledge of efficient implementation techniques contribute to the power of the presented transaction models.

Applications of multilevel transactions and open nested transactions benefit especially from the concept of open subtransactions, which improves performance by relaxing the isolation between concurrent transactions. In addition, the modular way that subtransactions are dealt with is especially important for transaction management in the novel areas of extensible database systems, federated database systems, and object-oriented database systems. Further research is needed to investigate the viability of the presented transaction models in such advanced applications.

Acknowledgement

We have benefited from many discussions with colleagues working on the same or related problems. In particular, we would like to thank Catriel Beeri for the fruitful cooperation on multilevel transactions.

Bibliography

[Bj73] Bjork, L.A. Recovery Scenario for a DB/DC System. *ACM Annual Conference*, 1973.

[BBG89] Beeri, C., Bernstein, P.A., Goodman, N. A Model for Concurrency in Nested Transactions Systems. *Journal of the ACM* Vol.36 No.1, 1989.

[BHG87] Bernstein, P.A., Hadzilacos, V., Goodman, N. *Concurrency Control and Recovery in Database Systems.* Addison-Wesley, 1987.

[BHM90] Bernstein, P.A., Hsu, M., Mann, B. Implementing Recoverable Requests Using Queues. *ACM SIGMOD Conf.*, 1990.

[BR88] Badrinath, B.R., Ramamritham, K. Synchronizing Transactions on Objects. *IEEE Transactions on Computers* Vol.37 No.5, 1988.

[BR90] Badrinath, B.R., Ramamritham, K. Performance Evaluation of Semantics-based Multilevel Concurrency Control Protocols. *ACM SIGMOD Conf.*, 1990.

[BSW88] Beeri, C., Schek, H.-J., Weikum, G. Multilevel Transaction Management, Theoretical Art or Practical Need?. *1st Int. Conf. on Extending Database Technology*, Venice, 1988, Springer, LNCS 303.

[CCKLLO91] Cheng, E.C., Chang, E., Klein, J., Lee, D., Lu, E., Lutgardo, A., Obermarck, R. An Open and Extensible Event-based Transaction Manager. *USENIX Summer 1991 Conference.*

[CF90] Cart, M., Ferrie, J. Integrating Concurrency Control into an Object-Oriented Database System. *2nd Int. Conf. on Extending Database Technology*, Venice, 1990, Springer, LNCS 416.

[CR91] Chrysanthis, P.K., Ramamritham, K. ACTA: The SAGA Continues. In: A.K. Elmagarmid (Ed.), *Database Transaction Models for Advanced Applications*, Morgan Kaufmann, San Mateo, CA, 1991.

[CS89] Chang, W.W., Schek, H.-J. A Signature Access Method for the Starburst Database System. *VLDB Conf.*, 1989.

[Dav73] Davies, C.T. Recovery Semantics for a DB/DC System. *ACM Annual Conference*, 1973.

[Dav78] Davies, C.T. Data Processing Spheres of Control. *IBM Systems Journal* Vol.17 No.2, 1978.

[DE89] Du, W., Elmagarmid, A.K. Quasi Serializability: A Correctness Criterion for Global Concurrency Control in InterBase. *VLDB Conf.*, 1989.

[DPS83] Dadam, P., Pistor, P., Schek, H.-J. A Predicate Oriented Locking Approach for Integrated Information Systems. *IFIP Congress*, North-Holland, 1983.

[ELLR90] Elmagarmid, A., Leu,Y., Litwin, W., Rusinkiewicz, M. A Multidatabase Transaction Model for InterBase. *VLDB Conf.*, 1990.

[FLMW88] Fekete, A., Lynch, N., Merritt, M., Weihl, W. Commutativity-Based Locking for Nested Transactions. Technical Report MIT/LCS/TM-370, MIT, Cambridge (Mass.), 1988, to appear in: Journal of Computer and System Sciences.

[FO89] Farrag, A.A., Özsu, M.T. Using Semantic Knowledge of Transactions to Increase Concurrency. *ACM TODS* Vol.14 No.4, 1989.

[Gar83] Garcia-Molina, H. Using Semantic Knowledge for Transaction Processing in a Distributed Database. *ACM TODS* Vol.8 No.2, 1983.

[Gra81] Gray, J. The Transaction Concept: Virtues and Limitations. *VLDB Conf.*, 1981.

[GGKKS91] Garcia-Molina, H., Gawlick, D., Klein, J., Kleissner, K., Salem, K. Modeling Long-Running Activities as Nested Sagas. *IEEE Data Engineering* Vol.14 No.1, 1991.

[GK85] Gawlick, D., Kinkade, D. Varieties of Concurrency Control in IMS/VS Fast Path. *IEEE Database Engineering* Vol.8 No.2, 1985.

[GS84] Gifford, D., Spector, A. The TWA Reservation System. *Communciations of the ACM* Vol.27 No.7, 1984.

[GS87] Garcia-Molina, H., Salem, K. Sagas. *ACM SIGMOD Conf.*, 1987.

[Had88] Hadzilacos, V. A Theory of Reliability in Database Systems. *Journal of the ACM* Vol.35 No.1, 1988.

[HH88] Hadzilacos, T., Hadzilacos, V. Transaction Synchronization in Object Bases. *ACM PODS Conf.*, 1988.

[HR83] Haerder, T., Reuter, A. Principles of Transaction-Oriented Database Recovery. *ACM Computing Surveys* Vol.15 No.4, 1983.

[HW91] Hasse, C., Weikum, G. A Performance Evaluation of Multi-Level Transaction Management. *VLDB Conf.*, 1991.

[ISO1] ISO Draft International Standard ISO/IEC 10166-1. Information Technology - Text and Office Systems - Document Filing and Retrieval (DFR) - Part 1: Abstract Service Definition and Procedures.

[ISO2] ISO Draft International Standard ISO/IEC 10166-2. Information Technology - Text and Office Systems - Document Filing and Retrieval (DFR) - Part 2: Protocol Specification.

[Kor83] Korth, H.F. Locking Primitives in a Database System. *Journal of the ACM* Vol.30 No.1, 1983.

[KLS90] Korth, H.F., Levy, E., Silberschatz, A. Compensating Transactions: A New Recovery Paradigm. *VLDB Conf.*, 1990.

[Lyn83] Lynch, N. Multilevel Atomicity - A New Correctness Criterion for Database Concurrency Control. *ACM TODS* Vol.8 No.4, 1983.

[LKS91] Levy, E., Korth, H.F., Silberschatz, A. A Theory of Relaxed Atomicity. *ACM PODC Conf.*, 1991.

[LMWF91] Lynch, N., Merritt, M., Weihl, W., Fekete, A. *Atomic Transactions*, Morgan Kaufmann, San Mateo, CA, to appear.

[Mar87] Martin, B.E. Modeling Concurrent Activities with Nested Objects. *Int. Conf. on Distributed Computing Systems*, Berlin, 1987.

[Mos85] Moss, J.E.B. *Nested Transactions: An Approach to Reliable Distributed Computing*, MIT Press, 1985.

[Moh89] Mohan, C., Haderle, D., Lindsay, B., Pirahesh, H., Schwarz, P. ARIES: A Transaction Recovery Method Supporting Fine-Granularity Locking and Partial Rollbacks Using Write-Ahead Logging. IBM Research Report RJ6649, San Jose, 1989, to appear in: ACM TODS.

[Moh90] Mohan, C. ARIES/KVL: A Key-Value Locking Method for Concurrency Control of Multiaction Transactions Operating on B-Tree Indexes. *VLDB Conf.*, 1990.

[MGG86] Moss, J.E.B., Griffeth, N.D., Graham, M.H. Abstraction in Recovery Management. *ACM SIGMOD Conf.*, 1986.

[ML89] Mohan, C., Levine, F. ARIES/IM: An Efficient and High Concurrency Index Management Method Using Write-Ahead Logging. IBM Research Report RJ6846, San Jose, 1989.

[MP90] Martin, B.E., Pedersen, C. Long-lived Concurrent Activities. Technical Report HPL-90-178, HP Laboratories, 1990.

[MR91] Muth, P., Rakow, T.C. Atomic Commitment for Integrated Database Systems. *IEEE Data Engineering Conf.*, 1991.

[MRKN91] Muth, P., Rakow, T.C., Klas, W., Neuhold, E.J. A Transaction Model for an Open Publication Environment. In: A.K. Elmagarmid (Ed.), *Database Transaction Models for Advanced Applications*, Morgan Kaufmann, San Mateo, CA, 1991.

[O'N86] O'Neil, P.E. The Escrow Transactional Method. *ACM TODS* Vol.11 No.4, 1986.

[O'N90] O'Neil, P.E. Escrow Promises. Technical Report 90-3, Department of Mathematics and Computer Science, University of Massachusetts, Boston, 1990.

[OV91] Özsu, M.T., Valduriez, P. *Principles of Distributed Database Systems*, Prentice-Hall, 1991.

[Pau88] Pausch, R. Adding Input and Output to the Transaction Model. Ph.D. Thesis, Carnegie Mellon University, 1988.

[PSSW87] Paul, H.-B., Soeder, A., Schek, H.-J., Weikum, G. Supporting the Filing and Retrieval Service by a Database Kernel System (in German). *2nd GI Conf. on Database Systems for Office, Engineering, and Scientific Applications*, Springer, 1987.

[RGN90] Rakow, T.C., Gu, J., Neuhold, E.J. Serializability in Object-Oriented Database Systems. *IEEE Data Engineering Conf.*, 1990.

[Sha85] Shasha, D. What Good Are Concurrent Search Structure Algorithms for Databases Anyway?. *IEEE Database Engineering* Vol.8 No.2, 1985.

[SDP91] Shrivastava, S.K., Dixon, G.N., Parrington, G.D. An Overview of the Arjuna Distributed Programming System. *IEEE Software*, January 1991.

[SG88] Shasha, D., Goodman, N. Concurrent Search Structure Algorithms. *ACM TODS* Vol.13 No.1, 1988.

[SPSW90] Schek, H.-J., Paul, H.-B., Scholl, M.H., Weikum, G. The DASDBS Project: Objectives, Experiences, and Future Prospects. *IEEE Transactions on Knowledge and Data Engineering* Vol.2 No.1, 1990.

[SS84] Schwarz, P.M., Spector, A.Z. Synchronizing Shared Abstract Types. *ACM Transactions on Computer Systems* Vol.2 No.3, 1984.

[SWS91] Schek, H.-J., Weikum, G., Schaad, W. A Multi-Level Transaction Approach to Federated DBMS Transaction Management. *Int. Workshop on Interoperability in Multidatabase Systems*, 1991.

[SZ89] Skarra, A.H., Zdonik, S.B. Concurrency Control and Object-Oriented Databases. In: W. Kim, F.H. Lochovsky (Eds.), *Object-Oriented Concepts, Databases, and Applications*, ACM Press, 1989.

[Tra83] Traiger, I.L. Trends in System Aspects of Database Management. *2nd Int. Conf. on Databases*, Cambridge (UK), Wiley Heyden, 1983.

[VEH91] Veijalainen, J., Eliassen, F., Holtkamp, B. The S-transaction Model. In: A.K. Elmagarmid (Ed.), *Database Transaction Models for Advanced Applications*, Morgan Kaufmann, San Mateo, CA, 1991.

[VV88] Vianu, V., Vossen, G. Conceptual Level Concurrency Control of Relational Update Transactions. *2nd International Conference on Database Theory*, 1988, Springer, LNCS 326.

[Wal84] Walter, B. Nested Transactions with Multiple Commit Points: An Approach to the Structuring of Advanced Database Applications. *VLDB Conf.*, 1984.

[We83] Weihl, W.E. Data-dependent Concurrency Control and Recovery. *ACM Symposium on Principles of Distributed Computing*, 1983.

[We88] Weihl, W.E. Commutativity-based Concurrency Control for Abstract Data Types. *IEEE Transactions on Computers* Vol.37 No.12, 1988.

[We89] Weihl, W.E. The Impact of Recovery on Concurrency Control. *ACM PODS Conf.*, 1989.

[Wei86a] Weikum, G. A Theoretical Foundation of Multilevel Concurrency Control. *ACM PODS Conf.*, 1986.

[Wei86b] Weikum, G. Pros and Cons of Operating System Transactions for Data Base Systems. *ACM/IEEE Fall Joint Computer Conference*, Dallas, November 1986.

[Wei87] Weikum, G. Enhancing Concurrency in Layered Systems. *2nd Int. Workshop on High Performance Transaction Systems*, 1987, Springer, LNCS 359.

[Wei91] Weikum, G. Principles and Realization Strategies of Multilevel Transaction Management. *ACM TODS* Vol.16 No.1, 1991.

[WH91] Weikum, G., Hasse, C. Multilevel Transaction Management for Complex Objects: Implementation, Performance, Parallelism. Technical Report 162, Department of Computer Science, ETH Zurich, 1991.

[WHBM90] Weikum, G., Hasse, C., Broessler, P., Muth, P. Multilevel Recovery. *ACM PODS Conf.*, 1990.

[WR91] Wächter, H., Reuter, A. The ConTract Model. In: A.K. Elmagarmid (Ed.), *Database Transaction Models for Advanced Applications*, Morgan Kaufmann, San Mateo, CA, 1991.

[WS84] Weikum, G., Schek, H.-J. Architectural Issues of Transaction Management in Layered Systems. *VLDB Conf.*, 1984.

[ZPD90] Zabback, P., Paul, H.-B., Deppisch, U. Office Documents on a Database Kernel - Filing, Retrieval, and Archiving. *Int. Conf. on Office Information Systems*, 1990.

14

Using Polytransactions to Manage Interdependent Data

Amit P. Sheth

Marek Rusinkiewicz

George Karabatis

14.1 Introduction

Many large companies use multiple databases to serve the needs of various application systems. One of the significant problems in managing these databases is maintaining the consistency of inter-related data in an environment consisting of multiple semi-autonomous and heterogeneous systems. We use the term *interdependent data* to imply that two or more data items stored in different databases are related through an integrity constraint that specifies the data dependency and the consistency requirements between these data items. Management of such data implies that a certain degree of mutual consistency among the interdependent data is maintained. Therefore, the manipulation (including concurrent updates) of the interdependent data must be controlled.

In the majority of existing applications, the mutual consistency requirements among multiple databases are either ignored, or the consistency of data is maintained by the application programs that perform related updates to all relevant databases. This can be accomplished using various techniques. For example, a message may be sent to another database system managing related data, so that a complementary transaction will be submitted there, or a replica of the data is sent to another system, either electronically or physically (e.g., a tape). However, these approaches have several disadvantages. First, they rely on the application programmer to enforce integrity constraints and to maintain mutual consistency of data, which is not acceptable if the programmer has incomplete knowledge of constraints to be enforced. Secondly, a modification of a part of an application requires changing of other parts of the same or another application to maintain integrity and consistency. Since integrity requirements are specified within an application, they are not written in a declarative way. If we need to identify these requirements, we must extract them from the code, which is a tedious and error prone task.

Alternative approaches to the problem, are based on system supported maintenance of mutual consistency. A possible solution is to enhance the techniques of preserving integrity that were proposed for distributed databases [SV86]. The main limitation of these techniques is that they assume that the consistency between the related data must be restored immediately. However, in loosely-coupled environments we may need to temporarily tolerate inconsistencies among related data. Active databases [MD89] address this problem by allowing evaluation of time constraints, in addition to data-value constraints. They use object oriented techniques to encapsulate the maintenance of consistency inside the methods.

With the current emphasis on data as a corporate asset, whose integrity is of basic importance [Mil89], the management of interdatabase consistency is receiving more attention. Distributed transaction technologies can be used to address some of these problems. Transaction management systems, based on the traditional transaction concept [Gra81, HR83], or its extensions (nested transactions [Mos85], sagas [GMS87], multidatabase transactions [Geo90, GRS91, Reu89]), can be used to preserve database consistency. Transaction technology can assure that all actions needed to preserve the interdatabase dependencies are executed in an atomic way. However, the specification of these actions and, hence, the correctness of the multidatabase updates still rests with the application programmer, who is responsible for the design of the transaction. Also, distributed concurrency control and commitment present serious problems when long-lived transactions span across systems with vastly different capabilities.

In this chapter, we discuss a framework for maintaining consistency among interdependent data stored in multiple databases. Two important features of the proposed framework are: (a) declarative specification of interdependent data and their mutual consistency requirements, and (b) use of the specification to automatically generate related update transactions that manage interdependent data.

The separation of the constraints from the application programs, facilitates the maintenance of data consistency requirements and allows flexibility in their implementation. It also allows investigation of various mechanisms for enforcing the constraints, independently of the application programs. Thus, changes in the application programs can be made independently of the constraints, and vice versa. By grouping the constraints together, we can check their completeness and discover possible contradictions among them.

The chapter is organized as follows. In Section 14.2, we define the data dependency descriptors which are stored in the *Interdatabase Dependency Schema (IDS)*. In Section 14, we introduce the concept of polytransactions. We describe a possible system architecture for management of interdependent data and we specify how polytransactions can be derived from the dependency schema. Section 14.4 provides a more detailed description of the various components of data dependency descriptors and discusses some aspects of correctness of the *IDS*. In Section 14.5 we classify different degrees of consistency among interdependent data. Section 14.6 provides the conclusions.

14.2 Specification of Interdatabase Dependencies

In this section we will discuss briefly the specifications of interdatabase dependencies[1]. They can be used to perform updates in a way that allows us to overcome some of the limitations imposed by traditional transaction management systems. For example, we may allow data to be temporarily inconsistent, within specified limits.

Our framework for specifying interdatabase dependencies consists of three components: data dependency information, mutual consistency requirements, and consistency restoration procedures [RSK91]. While these components have been addressed in the literature separately, in our opinion they represent facets of a single problem that should be considered together. Data dependency conditions are similar to integrity constraints [SV86], although they do not require that full integrity must be maintained at all times. In addition to *immediate consistency*, mutual consistency requirements can be used to specify more relaxed criteria of *eventual and lagging consistency* that have been introduced recently [SK89, RSK91]. Other weak mutual consistency criteria have also been defined (see Section 14.4). Actions to restore consistency between interdependent data were used extensively in active databases [DBB+88, HLM88].

We use *Data Dependency Descriptors* (D^3) to specify the interdatabase dependencies [RSK91]. They can be viewed as an extension of the *identity connection* proposed by Wiederhold and Qian [WQ87]. Each D^3 consists of identification of related objects and a directional relationship defined in terms of three components discussed earlier. A D^3 is a 5-tuple:

$$D^3 = < \mathcal{S}, U, P, C, \mathcal{A} >$$

where:

$\mathcal{S}$ is the set of *source data objects*,

U is the *target data object*,

[1] Before we can specify the interdatabase dependencies, we must eliminate incompatibilities that may exist among related data items in different databases. The corresponding data items in different databases, may have different names, and may be defined using different data types and/or units [DH84, DAT87]. We will not address the problem of resolving data incompatibility in this chapter. Rather, we assume that there is a method [RCE+88], possibly involving the use of a dictionary, thesaurus, knowledge base, and/or an auxiliary database, which may be used to identify the correspondences between the related items and to resolve the incompatibilities among them.

P is a boolean-valued predicate called *interdatabase dependency predicate* (dependency component). It specifies a relationship between the source and target data objects, and evaluates to true if this relationship is satisfied.

C is a boolean-valued predicate, called *mutual consistency predicate* (consistency component). It specifies consistency requirements and defines when P must be satisfied.

$\mathcal{A}$ is a collection of *consistency restoration procedures* (action component). Each procedure, specifies actions that must be taken to restore consistency and to ensure that P is satisfied.

Interdatabase dependency descriptors are uni-directional, from the set of source objects to the target object. While the objects specified in $\mathcal{S}$ and U may belong to the same database, we are particularly interested in those dependencies in which the objects belong to different databases and are managed by independent database management systems.

An operation on either source or target data objects specified in a D^3 may require additional actions to maintain mutual consistency of interdependent data. Consistency predicates involving only operations performed on the source data objects, can be referred to as **push constraints**. In this case, an operation applied to one or more source data objects propagates its effects to the target data object. If a consistency predicate involves only operations on the target data object, we refer to it as **pull constraint**. In this case, the results of earlier updates (if any) to the source data objects are propagated to the target data objects, before the operation specified in the consistency predicate is performed. The implications of push and pull constraints are further discussed in the next section.

D^3s are specified in a declarative fashion and can be viewed as separate schema entities. An *Interdatabase Dependency Schema (IDS)* is a set of all D^3s to be enforced in a multidatabase system. A more detailed discussion of the structure of dependency descriptors is presented in Section 14.4.

14.3 Polytransactions for Managing Interdependent Data

As mentioned earlier, multidatabase transactions can be used to preserve consistency of multiple databases. Multidatabase transaction management addresses the issues of *global* and *local* consistency in such an environment.

However, one problem with the concepts of nested transactions [Mos85] and multidatabase transactions (e.g., "contracts" [Reu89], "flexible transactions" [ELLR90], and "multitransaction activities" [GMGK+90]) is the assumption that all subtransactions, as well as all execution dependencies between them are known in advance. While such assumptions may be realistic in some cases, they limit the applicability of these concepts in environments consisting of interdependent data. This is because the information about all relationships between data stored in multiple data repositories may not be known in advance to the transaction designer. Therefore, in this section we will introduce the concept of *polytransactions* and discuss their use to manage interdependent data. The objective of a polytransaction is to preserve the *mutual* consistency requirements between interdependent data defined in the *IDS*.

14.3.1 System Architecture

A typical multidatabase system architecture assumed in the literature consists of two levels. The local databases comprise the lower level and the global transaction manager acts as a coordinator of global transactions. A multidatabase transaction is decomposed into a collection of subtransactions submitted to the local systems. When all the subtransactions successfully commit, the global transaction succeeds. In contrast, in this chapter we are concerned with the effects that an update operation submitted to a single database may have on the related data. In general, whenever a change occurs in data stored in one database, the interdependent data may have to change. Hence, we view transactions as means to satisfy the dependency and consistency predicates defined in the *IDS*.

A possible system architecture that can be used to maintain interdependent data objects is illustrated in Figure 14.1. Every database participating in a multidatabase environment is augmented with a *Dependency Subsystem (DS)* which acts as an interface between different databases. *DS*s at different sites can communicate with each other. When a transaction is submitted for execution, the *DS* consults the *IDS* to determine whether the data accessed by the transaction are dependent on data in other databases. The *IDS* itself can be either centralized, or distributed over the local sites. In the latter case, only those dependency descriptors that have their source data objects stored locally, may be kept in each fragment.

A transaction submitted to a *DS*, is analyzed before being executed by the local DBMS (*LDBS*). In particular, if the update involves data that are related to data in other databases, a series of related transactions may

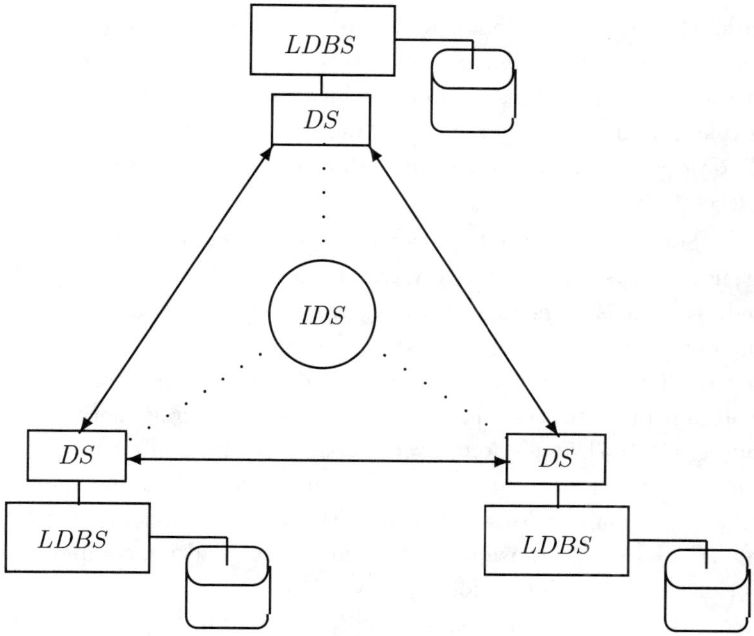

FIGURE 14.1
Architecture of a system for managing interdependent data

be scheduled for execution, to preserve mutual consistency of related data. The initially submitted transaction, and related transactions corresponding to restoration procedures, are submitted to their corresponding *LDBS*s. After the execution of a restoration procedure, the values of the relevant consistency predicates are updated.

14.3.2 The Concept and Properties of Polytransactions

Transactions we are interested in may not have all the *ACID* properties [HR83]. We require that a transaction is correct in a sense defined by the semantics of the application. Depending on the application, requirements other than correctness may optionally be imposed on updates performed on interdependent data.

One such optional properties is *atomicity* which may not be required if some of the operations are *compensable.* In such a case, if it is determined later that the operations should not have been executed, their effects can be "undone" by issuing compensating operations. For example the *flexible transactions* in [ELLR90] allow specification of alternative actions that can be invoked when some actions fail. A multidatabase transaction may accomplish its objectives even if some of its actions (or subtransactions) are not executed successfully.

Sometimes, the interactions of concurrent update transactions require transaction *isolation*. In many traditional applications, such as banking, this requirement is a very natural one. However, this requirement becomes completely impractical in long-lived transactions where an operation may last for several hours and involve multiple data items of large granularity. Enforcing isolation in such cases may mean that no concurrent activities are allowed. *Sagas* [GMS87] divide long-lived transactions into subtransactions, such that each subtransaction can be compensated, if necessary, and the isolation property of the transactions is relaxed. Flexible transactions [ELLR90] may also relax isolation by allowing both compensable and noncompensable subtransactions within a single global transaction.

Another frequent requirement on transactions is *durability*, which states that once the transaction is committed, its results must survive successive system failures. However, durability may not be required for transactions that do not manipulate persistent data.

Earlier in this section, we argued that in a multidatabase environment consisting of multiple autonomous systems, the concept of global (multidatabase) transaction that is composed of a well-defined set of subtransactions may be too restrictive. Therefore, we use the more flexible notion of a *polytransaction* to describe a sequence of related update activities.

A polytransaction (T^+) is a "transitive closure" of a transaction T submitted to an interdependent data management system. The transitive closure is computed with respect to the IDS. A polytransaction can be represented by a tree in which the nodes correspond to its component transactions and the edges define the "coupling" between the parent and children transactions. Given a transaction T, the tree representing its polytransaction T^+ can be determined as follows. For every data dependency descriptor D^3, such that the data item updated by T is among source objects of the D^3, we look at the the dependency and consistency predicates P and C. If they are satisfied, no further transactions will be scheduled. If they are violated, we create a new node corresponding to a (system generated) new transaction T' (child of T) to update the target object of the D^3. T' will restore the consistency of the target object, so that the P and C predicates will be satisfied[2]. Specification of weaker mutual consistency criteria will result in infrequent violations of C. Hence, the restoration procedures (and the corresponding child transaction) will be scheduled less often.

T' corresponds to the restoration procedure (component A) that updates the related target data items specified in the D^3. The above actions correspond to *push* constraints specified in IDS. Similarly, we examine all D^3s, such that the data item read by T, is the target of D^3. If a *pull* constraint involving this data item exists, and P and C are violated, another child transaction is generated to update the affected data item, and a corresponding new node is created in the tree. This process is applied recursively to all children of T.

When a user submits a transaction that updates a data item that is related to other data items through a D^3, this transaction becomes the root of a polytransaction. Subsequently, the system responsible for the management of interdependent data uses the IDS to determine what descendent transactions should be generated and scheduled in order to preserve interdatabase dependency. Execution of a descendent transaction, in turn, can result in generating additional descendent transactions. This process continues until the consistency of the system is restored as specified in the IDS.

The ways by which a child transaction is related to its parent transaction within a polytransaction is specified in D^3, by the *execution mode* of the action component. This relationship is indicated as a label of the edge between each parent and its child in the polytransaction tree. A child transaction is *coupled* if the parent transaction must wait until the child transaction completes before proceeding further. It is *decoupled* if the parent transaction may schedule the execution of a child transaction and proceed without waiting for the child transaction to complete.

If the dependency schema requires immediate consistency, the nested transaction model may be used, in which the descendent transactions are treated as subtransactions which must complete before the parent transaction can commit. Two-phase commit protocol may be used in this case. A coupled transaction can be *vital* in which case the parent transaction must fail if the child fails, or *non-vital* in which case the parent transaction may survive the failure of a child [GMGK+90].

[2] T' can be scheduled either immediately, or its execution can be delayed. The policy of generating and scheduling the child transaction will be discussed in more detail in Section 14.5.

Several new transaction paradigms have been proposed recently in the literature that are based on various degrees of decoupling of the spawned activities from the creator (e.g., [KR88]). Triggers used in active databases [DHL90] are probably the best known mechanism in this group. An application of this idea in the management of interdependent data was discussed in [Mil89]. The authors used a table driven approach to schedule complementary updates whenever a data item involved in a multi-system constraint was updated. The parent transaction would then terminate, without waiting for a chain of complementary actions to take place. The main problem with asynchronous triggers is that the parent transaction has no guarantee that the activity that was triggered will, in fact, complete in time to assure the consistency of the data.

To allow the parent transaction some degree of control over the execution of a child transaction, the concept of a VMS mailbox has been generalized in [GMGK$^+$90]. Similar ideas have been presented in [BHM90], and in [HS90], where the notion of a "persistent pipe" has been introduced. Both generalized mailboxes and persistent pipes allow the parent transaction to send a message to a child process and know that the message will be eventually delivered. If such a guarantee is sufficient, the parent transaction may then commit, without waiting for the completion of the action that were requested. The parent or its descendant may check later if the message has been indeed received and take a complementary or corrective action.

14.3.3 Executing Polytransactions

Most of the work on multidatabase transaction management assume the existence of a *multidatabase management system* (MDBS) which is responsible for the processing of all global transactions. Such MDBS architectures have transactions that are either local (execute at a single database without passing through the MDBS interfaces) or are global. We propose an architecture with a distributed IDS that stores at each site the D^3s involving the interdependent data that can be updated at that site. Using the concept of polytransactions, many of the global transactions can be executed as collections of related single database transactions.

Two approaches to control the execution of multidatabase transactions have been discussed in the literature. Under the first approach, the MDBS controls the scheduling of all subtransactions of a transaction. As we discussed earlier, a disadvantage of this approach is that the set of all subtransactions and the precedence dependencies between them must be known in advance. The second approach is used in active databases and uses triggers to asynchronously schedule subtransactions based on some events, possibly in a decoupled fashion [DHL90].

We propose to schedule the polytransaction activities based on the information in the dependency schema and the database states. We will illustrate this approach using an example.

Example: Consider a collection of telecommunication databases used by applications for planning and establishing new services. Let us consider four databases as follows:

> $DB1$ contains information about each switch (an equipment that establishes circuits and routes telephone calls) and its contents (e.g., what each of its slots contains).
>
> $DB2$ contains summary information about the equipment installed in different switches, for use by a statistical application.
>
> $DB3$ is an operational database containing the status information about each switch.
>
> $DB4$ contains planning information about the switches whose capacities are close to being exhausted.

Figure 14.2 illustrates an example polytransaction on our hypothetical interdependent databases. Let us consider that transaction *T1* submitted to *DB1*, modifies the status of one of the slots in the switch as a result of adding an equipment to the switch. Let us suppose that the interdatabase dependency specifies that database *DB2* should be eventually updated to reflect the changes of the switches. Hence, transaction *T2* will be scheduled to make required changes in *DB2*. Note that due to the eventual consistency requirements, *T2* can be scheduled as a decoupled transaction. Let us further suppose that *DB3* must be updated immediately to reflect the change in the status of the switch. Therefore a transaction *T3* must be scheduled. Because of the immediate consistency requirement, *T3* should be a coupled transaction and *T1* cannot commit until *T3* does. To continue our example, if the change of the status of the switch brings its capacity above a threshold specified in the dependency schema, transaction *T4* will be scheduled to add the relevant switch information to *DB4*. When all transactions resulting from *T1* complete, the polytransaction completes.

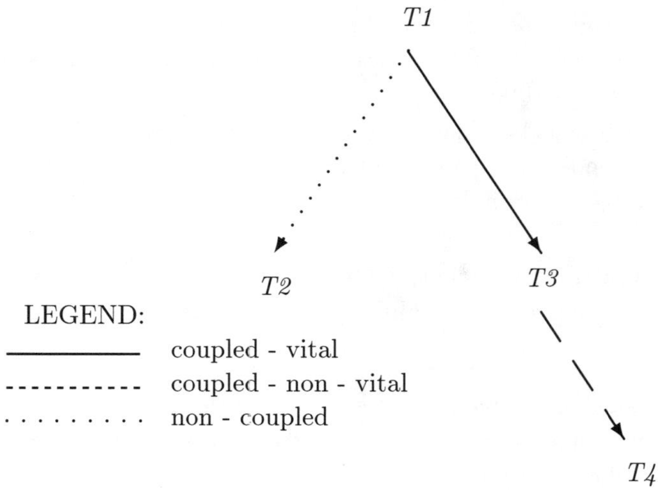

FIGURE 14.2
Generation of a Polytransaction

14.4 Interdatabase Dependency Schema

In this section we will provide a more detailed discussion of the main components of the dependency descriptors. A language or syntax is used for discussing each component. Our specification is extensible. Furthermore, an alternate language or syntax could be used for any of them.

14.4.1 Specification of the Dependency Predicate

The dependency predicate P is a boolean-valued expression specifying the relationship that should hold between the source and target data objects.

Dependency predicates can be specified, using operators of relational algebra (selection, projection, join, union, difference, intersection, etc.). Together with the basic operators, we also use the aggregate operator ξ [Klu82], and the transitive closure operator α [Agr87]. The ξ operator allows specification of aggregate functions such as *sum* or *count* for the whole relation or for groups obtained by partitioning the relation according to the specified attribute. The α operator computes the transitive closure of a single relation R, assuming that the relation is transitive over its first two attributes. Aggregate and grouping operators can be used inside the α operator.

As an example, let us consider relation *EMP* containing the information about individual employees and their salaries that is stored in one database, and another relation *DEPT_SAL* with the summary information about the average salary in each department, that is stored in second database. The *DEPT_SAL* relation is derived by aggregation of the data from the *EMP* relation.

The requirements that each row of the *DEPT_SAL* relation contains the actual average of salaries of all employees in the department can be specified by the following predicate:

$$\xi_{Dnum,Avg(Salary)}(EMP) = \Pi_{Dnum,Avg\_Sal}(DEPT\_SAL)$$

14.4.2 Specification of Mutual Consistency Requirements

In this section, we will discuss the specification of mutual consistency requirements. They will be classified along two dimensions that are to a large degree orthogonal: time and state of data.

A mutual consistency requirement specifies the desired degree of consistency among related data. The requirement that is used usually in the literature is that of *immediate consistency* [SK89] which specifies that as soon as a transaction completes, all related data are also mutually consistent [SLE91]. The immediate consistency can be provided by multi-site transactions that commit updates at multiple sites together. Mutual consistency requirements using timing constraints were introduced in [WQ87, HLM88] and were further explored in [CB$^+$89, SK89, WQ90, SR90]. Also related is the specification of coherency condition used to define "how far" primary copy and quasi-copies can diverge based on time, versions, and arithmetic conditions [ABGM90]. A similar criterion is offered in [PL91].

A mutual consistency criterion called *eventual consistency*, [SK89], [RSK91] specifies that related database objects are made consistent at certain points of time specified by a condition, although they may not be consistent in the interim intervals. The condition is specified as a combination of time and data state (including events/operations). Eventual consistency allows the related objects to diverge during some period, as long as they will be made consistent periodically. **Lagging consistency** [SK89] assumes that the data in one database may be most current while in the other ones the data may not be up-to-date. Updates applied to the first database are always propagated to the related databases. Hence, if all external updates are stopped, the databases will become consistent. Eventual consistency does imply that at some point in time, all databases will be consistent, while lagging consistency does not imply this, because some databases may always lag behind others[3].

The consistency requirement predicate, denoted by C, specifies when (in terms of time and/or data state), the related data must be consistent. Interdependent data objects may be allowed to be inconsistent within certain limits, determined by C. The specification of the consistency predicate can involve multiple boolean valued conditions, each referred to as *consistency terms* and denoted by c_i. Each c_i refers to a mutual consistency requirement involving either time or the state of a data object. Hence, C is a logical expression involving $\vee$, $\wedge$, and $\neg$ operators and consistency terms c_i.

Temporal Consistency Terms

To identify the point in time at which the related data objects must be consistent, we use the following notation. *DD-MMM-YYYY* is used to specify the date (day, month and year) and *hh:mm.ss* to denote time (hour, minute and second). The *on* operator is used in conjunction with date and the @ operator specifies time. The expression *on d* means "on date d", and the expression @*t* translates into "at time t". All time instants are referenced to the international accepted standard of Universal Coordinate Time (UTC). The following consistency requirements involving time may be defined:

At a particular date and/or at a specific point in time. For example,
@ 9:00 means at 9.00 o' clock,
on 27-May-1991 means 'on 27th of May, 1991'.

Before or after a specific instant of time or date. We use the ! operator to denote predicates of this type. The position of the ! is used to distinguish between *before* and *after*. For example,
! 8:00 means before 8 a.m.
25-Aug-1991 ! means after August 25, 1991.

We can specify intervals of time or/and date using the Δ operator[4]. For example,
Δ *(9:00 - 17:00)* means during the whole interval between 9a.m. and 5 p.m.

---

[3]Similar notions of consistency have also been explored within the context of Distributed Directory Services [MD82].

[4]Intervals of time can also be specified by a combination of *before* and *after* operations. For example Δ *(9:00 - 12:00)* is equivalent to *9:00 !* $\wedge$ *! 12:00*

Δ *(10-Jun-1991@17:00 - 11-Jun-1991@8:00)* specifies an overnight interval.

Periodically, when certain amount of time has elapsed. We use the expression ε(*period* @ *t on d*), to specify 'every *period* of time starting at time t and on date d'. The "@ t" and "*on* d" parts of this expression are optional. A period of time, can be specified using

A difference of two times, e.g., $t_2 - t_1$,

One of the keywords *year, month, day, hour, min, immediately,*

A duration of time.

For example,
ε*(day @17:00)* means 'every day at 5 p.m.'.

Data State Consistency Terms

The data state requirements determine "how far" the related data may be allowed to diverge (in terms of data values) before the mutual consistency must be restored [ABGM88, SR90, BGM90]. Consistency terms involving data values, can be specified in the following ways:

By specifying (or limiting) the maximum change in the value of data which is allowed before the consistency must be restored. As an example, let us consider relations *EMP* and *DEPT_SAL* introduced earlier. We may specify that the *DEPT_SAL* relation must be updated whenever salary of an employee is changed by more than 500, using the following condition:

Δ *EMP.Salary* > 500,
where Δ is used to denote the change of value.

By specifying a condition involving data values or an aggregate function on the values of source data items. When this condition is violated, the consistency must be restored. For example, we may specify that the *DEPT_SAL* relation must be updated, whenever the average salary of all employees changes by more than 50, using the following condition:
Δ *AVG (EMP.Salary)* > 50

If a data object is modified by creating new versions, we can specify the maximum allowed discrepancy between version numbers of a given object that can exist in related databases. Once the difference between version numbers exceeds the allowed maximum, the data consistency must be restored. If we assume that relation EMP in database $D1$ has a copy EMP' in database $D2$ we can specify that EMP' can lag no more than 5 versions behind EMP, as follows:
Δ *5 versions (D1.EMP)*
When this requirement is violated, the consistency is restored by updating $D2.EMP'$ relation.

Mutual consistency requirements can be also related to some operations performed on data objects. Such requirements may indicate that consistency should be restored, when a particular operation[5] is performed. These operations can be applied to the source objects, the target object, or on both source and target objects. Several types of consistency terms involving operations can be defined:

We may allow a certain number of updates to be performed on a given source object, before the corresponding changes are made in the target object. As an example of a *push* constraint, the consistency term
10 updates on R_1 where $R_1 \in \mathcal{S}$
specifies that after 10 updates on a source relation R_1, the mutual consistency must be restored.

We may specify that a mutual consistency must be restored before an operation is performed on the target data object (*pull* constraint). This can be specified by the following consistency term:
read on U

By specifying (or limiting) the number of operations allowed on the related data objects before the consistency is restored. For example, we may allow no more than 10 sales transactions before consistency must be restored, using the following term:
10 sales
where *sales* is the transaction name.

[5]The term *operation* is used here to mean any user- or system-defined operation. For example, operation may refer to a particular transaction type defined in the system or an external event.

We can also request the restoration of mutual consistency, *before* or *after* a specific operation is performed. This is specified, by using the **!** symbol placed before or after the operation. For example,
!calculate_payroll_checks
specifies that mutual consistency must be restored before the calculate_payroll_checks transaction is executed. We can also enforce consistency after the execution of an operation or a transaction. In this case, some other updates may be invoked leading to chained updates (triggers fall into this category). For example,
take_inventory!
specifies that after the inventory transaction has been completed, mutual consistency must be restored.

The framework discussed above is adequate for specifying many types of dependencies typically found among data in industry [SK89]. These dependencies can be characterized by the structure of data dependency and its control aspects. The *structural dependencies* may include full or partial replication, overlap of the informational content of the data, vertical or horizontal partitioning, value or existence constraints, etc. It is easy to see that the P predicate can be used to specify this aspect of interdependent data. The *control* aspect specifies the constraints on updating the interdependent data. For example, the derived data may always be extracted or aggregated from one database and stored in another one, that is not directly updatable. In the case of primary-secondary copies, the updates to the primary database are propagated to the secondary databases through a coordinator-subordinate relationship. The directionality of D^3, and the push and pull constraints discussed in this chapter support this aspect.

14.4.3 Specification of consistency restoration procedures

The action component $\mathcal{A}$ of a dependency descriptor is a set of one or more restoration procedures that can be invoked under certain conditions to restore mutual consistency among interdependent data.

As mentioned before, whenever the dependency and consistency predicates, P and C, are not satisfied, inconsistencies between the source and target objects cannot be further tolerated. Hence, we assume the existence of a system that keeps track and controls the updates of all databases. In further discussion we will refer to such a system as the *manager of interdependent data* [SLE91] or the *multidatabase monitor* [Ris89, MD89].

Using the current value of each c_i, the monitor can calculate the value of the consistency predicate C. If the consistency is violated, appropriate actions must be taken to restore it. The action component $\mathcal{A}$, specifies conditional execution of one or more consistency restoration procedures. Conditions in $\mathcal{A}$, denoted by C_R (for restoration condition) can be, but need not be, the same as C. C_R is a logical expression involving $\vee, \wedge$, and $\neg$ operators and the consistency terms.

The syntax of the $\mathcal{A}$ component allows the specification of either single or multiple consistency restoration procedures. $\mathcal{A}$ with single consistency restoration procedure is specified as:

$\mathcal{A}$: *procedure name* [**as** *execution mode*]

Since there may be several ways to restore consistency, more than one consistency restoration procedures can be specified in the action component $\mathcal{A}$. In this case we use the following notation:

when C_{R_1} **do** *procedure name* [**as** *execution mode*]

⋮

when C_{R_n} **do** *procedure name* [**as** *execution mode*]
otherwise *default procedure name* [**as** *execution mode*]

The above specification allows combining the C predicate with one or more of the consistency restoration procedures in a structure similar to a guarded command.

The descriptor D^3 specifies the name of the procedure to be invoked and optionally the *mode* in which it will run. The mode identifies the relationship between the restoration procedure (child) and the transaction that invoked it (parent). The restoration procedures are invoked by the multidatabase monitor.

14.4.4 Correctness of Dependency Specifications

The *IDS* contains semantic information describing the relationships between the participating database objects. In this subsection, we discuss the correctness of dependency predicates, limiting our discussion to D^3s involving singleton source sets.

The *IDS* can be represented by a *dependency graph* consisting of nodes and edges. The nodes correspond to the source and target objects and the edges drawn from the source to the target data objects, are labeled with the corresponding D^3s. Below, we analyze the semantics of the cycles between

D^3s, and examine their validity.

Example: Let us consider the following pair of D^3s:

$S_1 : o_i$
$U_1 : o_j$
$P_1 : o_j = o_i + 2$
$C_1 : \textit{immediately}$
$A_1 : \textit{Update\_o}_j$

$S_2 : o_j$
$U_2 : o_i$
$P_2 : o_i = o_j - 3$
$C_2 : \textit{immediately}$
$A_2 : \textit{Update\_o}_i$

In the example, a cycle exists between objects o_i and o_j. If an update occurs on o_i so that P_1 no longer holds, o_j becomes inconsistent, and must be made current by the restoration procedure *Update_*o_j. After o_j has been updated, the P_2 predicate is violated. That means, o_i is inconsistent, and requires immediate execution of the *Update_*o_i procedure. This will be repeated indefinitely.

The above abnormal behavior is caused by the fact that each P_i predicate of the corresponding D^3s is not the *complement* of the other. If P_2 were $o_i = o_j - 2$ instead of $o_i = o_j - 3$ the cycle would be acceptable since after performing A_2, P_1 and P_2 are both satisfied. Therefore, no more updates will be performed due to restoration procedures. Cycles that do not cause indefinite updates are harmless and are referred to as *stable*.

One way to avoid unstable cycles is to disallow cycles in the IDS. This is undesirable, since there may be applications that require cyclic dependencies. Therefore, we will require that all cycles in the IDS are stable.

To generalize the previous discussion let us assume a cyclic dependency graph as follows:

$$o_1 \xrightarrow{D_1^3} o_2 \xrightarrow{D_2^3} \cdots \xrightarrow{D_{k-1}^3} o_k \xrightarrow{D_k^3} o_1$$

All updates resulting from an update to o_1 can be propagated further, up to o_k. The last dependency D_k^3 introduces a cycle by linking objects o_k and o_1. Let P_i be the dependency predicate of $D_i^3, i = 1, 2 \ldots k$. In order for the cycle to be stable, the last predicate P_k, in general, must be the complement of the composition of all previous predicates, i.e., $P_k = (P_1 \circ P_2 \circ \cdots \circ P_{k-1})^C$. For example, if

$P_1 : o_2 = o_1 + 3,$
$P_2 : o_3 = o_2 - 1,$ then for a stable cycle we must have
$P_3 : o_1 = o_3 - 2.$

All this information can be inferred from the *IDS* and appropriate actions must be taken to ensure that it conforms with the above requirements, i.e., there are only stable cycles. We realize that the correctness of the *IDS* requirements, particularly involving consistency predicates and restoration procedures, is a difficult issue and needs to be explored further.

14.5 Consistency of Interdependent Data

Let us now explore the notion of consistency of interdependent data within the framework presented above.

14.5.1 Definition of Consistency of Interdependent Data

DEFINITION

At any instant of time, the target data object within a given D^3 is defined to be current *with respect to a given D^3, if both the consistency predicate C and the dependency predicate P evaluate to true. The data item is said to be* consistent *if the consistency predicate C evaluates to true, but the dependency predicate P does not. Hence, if a target item is current then its consistency is implied, but the opposite is not true: an object may be consistent and not current. If neither P nor C evaluate to true, the target data object is* inconsistent *and the corresponding D^3 is* violated.

A multidatabase with an IDS is defined to be in a consistent state *if every target data object, is either current or consistent, i.e., $\forall D^3 \in IDS\ D^3.C = true$ (i.e., the C predicates of all descriptors must be satisfied).*

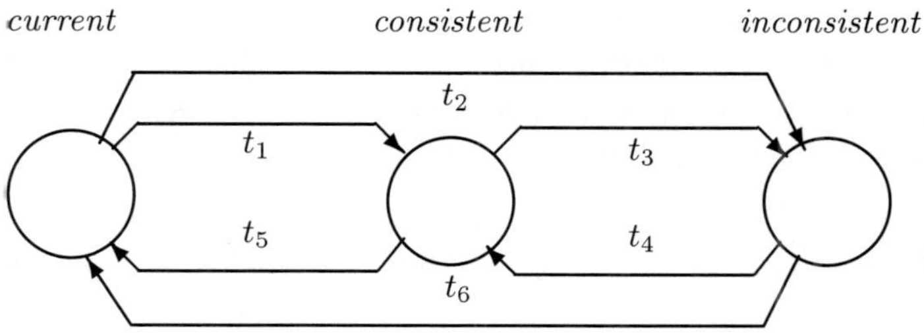

FIGURE 14.3
Transitions of a target data object

Figure 14.3 illustrates the transitions among the three states (current, consistent and inconsistent) of a target data object. These transitions occur as a result of the changes in values of the P and C predicates. The transitions are explained below:

Transition t_1: the state of the target data object changes from current to consistent, as a result of an update to a data item belonging to the source set $\mathcal{S}$. The consistency predicate C continues to be satisfied, although the values of the temporal or data state consistency terms may be changed.

Transition t_2: a current target data object becomes inconsistent as a result of an update on an object in the source set $\mathcal{S}$. Either the data state and/or the temporal terms violate the consistency predicate C.

Transition t_3: a target data object is transformed from the consistent to the inconsistent state, due to a change in the terms of the C predicate.

Transition t_4: the purpose of a restoration procedure is to change the state of a target data object, to either consistent or current. Transition t_4 occurs when we perform a *partial restoration*, so that an inconsistent data object becomes consistent, but not current. Various cost policies may indicate that a partial restoration to a consistent state is more appropriate than a (sometimes more expensive) restoration to a current state.

Transition t_5: this transition occurs when the state of the target data object changes from consistent to current. When the target object is consistent, we have the choice of either doing nothing, or executing a restoration procedure to make the data object current. This choice can be made considering performance parameters, load balancing, etc. Execution of restoration procedures in this manner will be referred to as *eager restoration of current state.*

Transition t_6: an inconsistent data object becomes current, by invoking a restoration procedure in one of the following ways:

(a) the restoration procedure is executed when it is discovered that C is violated. This is referred to as *late restoration of current state.*

(b) the particular data object is marked as inconsistent but no action is taken until an access to the target object is attempted. Then, the restoration procedure is activated before the access is granted. This method is referred to as a *lazy restoration of current state.* This strategy is used in [SLE91].

The main purpose of the IDS is to define when a multidatabase system is inconsistent and how its consistency should be restored. The restoration procedures specify how to upgrade the state of a target data object to consistent or current. The consistency predicate C complemented with the rules specifying eager, late or lazy restoration, determine the policy that maintains the desired level of consistency. Polytransactions provide a possible mechanism for enforcing a desired policy.

14.6 Summary

In this chapter we discussed issues of managing interdependent data. We presented the concept of database dependency descriptor, D^3, that can be used to specify the relationships between data in multiple databases together with the mutual consistency requirements and restoration procedures. Each dependency descriptor consists of three components: dependency predicate, mutual consistency predicate and a set of consistency restoration procedures. Some of the components of a D^3 have been described in the literature separately. However, we believe that the components of the dependency descriptor represent three aspects of a single problem, and must be considered together because of the interactions among them.

The descriptors in a multidatabase system constitute the Interdatabase Dependency Schema. The information stored in the *IDS* can be used to convert a transaction updating a data item in a single database into a polytransaction that spawns various activities needed to maintain the consistency of the interdependent data. The activities constituting a polytransaction, can be either coupled to the parent transaction, or decoupled from it. In the latter case, we can guarantee better response times if the weaker consistency guarantees (e.g., eventual consistency) are sufficient in a given application.

We believe that the polytransaction paradigm provides an attractive alternative to the traditional multitransaction models, since it provides the flexibility needed to support complex interdatabase consistency requirements. Unlike many multidatabase transaction models that require that the subtransactions are known in advance, dependent transactions in a polytransaction need not be known a priori. Like triggers in active databases, the dependent transactions are identified dynamically, using a rather extensive specification of the mutual consistency predicate.

We also discussed the issues of correctness of the dependency between interdependent data using the concept of the dependency graph. We classified various states of consistency of data objects, explained the transitions from one state to another, and identified possible policies that can be used by the polytransaction mechanism to maintain a desired level of consistency among interdependent data. We are currently investigating further the concepts presented in this chapter.

Bibliography

[ABGM88] Rafael Alonso, Daniel Barbara, and Hector Garcia-Molina. Quasi-Copies: Efficient Data Sharing for Information Retrieval Systems. *Proceedings of the Intl. Conf. on Extending Data Base Technology*, 1988.

[ABGM90] Rafael Alonso, Daniel Barbara, and Hector Garcia-Molina. Data Caching Issues in an Information Retrieval System. *ACM-TODS*, 15(3):359–384, September 1990.

[Agr87] R. Agrawal. Alpha: an extension of relational algebra to express a class of recursive queries. *Proceedings of the Third Interna-*

tional Conference on Data Engineering, pages 580–590, February 1987.

[BGM90] Daniel Barbara and Hector Garcia-Molina. The Case for Controlled Inconsistency in Replicated Data (Position Paper). In *Proceedings of the Workshop on the Management of Replicated Data*, Houston, TX, November 1990.

[BHM90] P. Bernstein, M. Hsu, and B. Mann. Implementing Recoverable Requests Using Queues. In *Proceedings of ACM SIGMOD Conference on Management of Data*, 1990.

[CB+89] S. Chakravarthy, B. Blaustein, et al. HiPAC: A Research Project in Active, Time-Constrained Database Management. Technical report, XEROX (XAIT), Cambridge, MA, July 1989.

[DAT87] S.M. Deen, R.R. Amin, and M.C. Taylor. Data Integration in Distributed Databases. *IEEE Transactions on Software Engineering*, SE-13(7):860–864, 1987.

[DBB+88] U. Dayal, B. Blaustein, A. Buchmann, U. Chakravarthy, M. Hsu, R. Ladin, D. McCarthy, A. Rosenthal, S. Sarin, M.J. Carey, M. Linvy, and R. Jauhari. The HiPAC Project: Combining Active Databases and Timing Constraints. *SIGMOD Record*, 17(1), March 1988.

[DH84] U. Dayal and H.Y. Hwang. View Definition and Generalization for Database Integration in a Multidatabase System. *IEEE Transactions on Software Engineering*, SE-10(6):628–644, 1984.

[DHL90] U. Dayal, M. Hsu, and R. Ladin. Organizing Long-Running Activities with Triggers and Transactions. In *Proceedings of ACM SIGMOD Conference on Management of Data*, 1990.

[ELLR90] A. Elmagarmid, Y. Leu, W. Litwin and M. Rusinkiewicz. A Multidatabase Transaction Model for InterBase. In *Proceedings of the 16th International Conference on Very Large Databases*, August 1990.

[Geo90] D. Georgakopoulos. *Transaction Management in Multidatabase Systems*. PhD thesis, University of Houston, Department of Computer Science, 1990.

[GMGK+90] H. Garcia-Molina, D. Gawlick, J. Klein, K. Kleissner, and K. Salem. Coordinating Multi-Transaction Activities. Technical Report CS-TR-247-90, Princeton University, February 1990.

[GMS87] H. Garcia-Molina and K. Salem. SAGAS. In *Proceedings of ACM SIGMOD Conference on Management of Data*, 1987.

[Gra81] J.N. Gray. The transaction concept: Virtues and limitations. In *Proceedings of the 7th International Conference on VLDB*, September 1981.

[GRS91] D. Georgakopoulos, M. Rusinkiewicz, and A. Sheth. On Serializability of Multidatabase Transactions through Forced Local Conflicts. In *Proceedings of the* 7th *IEEE International Conference of Data Engineering*, April 1991. Kobe, Japan.

[HLM88] M. Hsu, R. Ladin, and D. McCarthy. An Execution Model for Active Data Base Management Systems. In *Proceedings of the* 3rd *International Conference on Data and Knowledge Bases*, June 1988.

[HR83] T. Haerder and A. Reuter. Principles of transaction-oriented database recovery. *ACM Computing Surveys*, 15(4), December 1983.

[HS90] M. Hsu and A. Silberschatz. Persistent Transmission and Unilateral Commit- A Position Paper. In *Workshop on Multidatabases and Semantic Interoperability*, Tulsa, OK, October 1990.

[Klu82] A. Klug. Equivalence of Relational Algebra and Relational Calculus Query Languages having Aggregate Functions. *Journal of the Association for Computing Machinery*, 29(3):699–717, July 1982.

[KR88] J. Klein and A. Reuter. Migrating Transactions. In *Future Trends in Distributed Computing Systems in the 90's*, Hong Kong, 1988.

[MD82] J.G. Mitchell and J. Dion. A Comparison of two Network-based File Servers. *Communications of the ACM*, 25(4), April 1982.

[MD89] D. McCarthy and U. Dayal. The Architecture of an Active Data Base Management System. *Proceedings of the ACM SIGMOD Conference on Management of Data*, pages 215–224, 1989.

[Mil89] J. Mills. Semantic Integrity of the Totality of Corporate Data. *Proceedings of the First International Conference on Systems Integration*, pages 482–491, April 1990.

[Mos85] J.E.B Moss. *Nested Transactions: An Approach to Reliable Distributed Computing.* PhD thesis, MIT Press, Cambridge, MA, 1985.

[PL91] C. Pu and A. Leff. Replica Control in Distributed Systems: An Asynchronous Approach. *Proceedings of the 1991 ACM SIGMOD International Conference on Management of Data*, pages 377–386, Denver, May 1991.

[RCE+88] M. Rusinkiewicz, B. Czejdo, R. Elmasri, D. Georgakopoulos, A. Jamoussi, G. Karabatis, Y.Y. Li, and L. Loa. OMNIBASE: Design and Implementation of a Multidatabase System. *Distributed Processing TC Newsletter*, 10(2):20–28, November 1988.

[Reu89] A. Reuter. Contracts: A Means for Extending Control Beyond Transaction Boundaries. In *Third International Workshop on High Performance Systems*, September 1989.

[Ris89] T. Risch. Monitoring Database Objects. In *Proceedings of the 15th International Conference on Very Large Databases*, pages 445–453, 1989.

[RSK91] M. Rusinkiewicz, A. Sheth, and G. Karabatis. A Framework for Specifying Interdependent Data. Technical Report TM-STS-018609/1, Bellcore, May 1991.

[SK89] A. Sheth and P. Krishnamurthy. Redundant Data Management in Bellcore and BBC Databases. Technical Report TM-STS-015011/1, Bellcore, December 1989.

[SLE91] A. Sheth, Y. Leu, and A. Elmagarmid. Maintaining Consistency of Interdependent Data in Multidatabase Systems. Technical Report CSD-TR-91-016, Computer Sciences Department, Purdue University, March 1991.

[SR90] A. Sheth and M. Rusinkiewicz. Management of Interdependent Data: Specifying Dependency and Consistency Requirements. In *Proceedings of the Workshop on the Management of Replicated Data*, Houston, TX, November 1990.

[SV86] E. Simon and P. Valduriez. Integrity Control in Distributed Database Systems. In *Proceedings of the* 20th *Hawaii International Conference on System Sciences*, 1986.

[WQ87] G. Wiederhold and X. Qian. Modeling Asynchrony in Distributed Databases. In *Intl. Conf. on Data Engineering*, February 1987.

[WQ90] G. Wiederhold and X. Qian. Consistency Control of Replicated Data in Federated Databases. In *Proceedings of the Workshop on the Management of Replicated Data*, Houston, TX, November 1990.

Biography

Divyakant Agrawal is currently an Assistant Professor in the Department of Computer Science at the University of California at Santa Barbara. He received his B.E. degree from Birla Institute of Technology and Science, Pilani, India in 1980. He received his M.S. and Ph.D. degrees in computer science from SUNY at Stony Brook in 1984 and 1987. His research interests include design of algorithms for concurrent and fault-tolerant systems.

Dr. Agrawal is a member of the Association for Computing Machinery and the IEEE Computer Society.

Address:
Department of Computer Science
University of California
Santa Barbara, CA 93106, USA

Barbara Blaustein received her B.S. degree from the University of Maryland in 1975 and her Ph.D from Harvard University in 1981. She is a Senior Computer Scientist at Xerox Advanced Information Technology (formerly a part of Computer Corporation of America), involved in research into distributed, object-oriented, time-constrained, and active database management techniques.

Address:
Xerox Advanced Information Technology
Cambridge Massachusetts, USA

Alejandro Buchmann is professor for database management at the Technische Hochschule Darmstadt, where he is conducting research on active, heterogeneous, and time-constrained data management systems. Before joining the T. H. Darmstadt he was associate professor at the National University of Mexico, and held industrial positions with Computer Corporation of America / XAIT, and GTE Laboratories Incorporated.

Address:
GTE Laboratories Incorporated
40 Sylvan Road
Waltham, MA 02254, USA

Omran A. Bukhres is currently the chair of the Computer Science and Information Systems department Moorhead State University, Moorhead, Minnesota. He received his Ph.D in Computer Science from North Dakota State University and has been involved in university research and teaching since 1985, with special interest in multidatabase systems, concurrency control and recovery, knowledge bases, expert systems, and neural networks. In addition to his university duties, Dr. Bukhres serves as an advisor for the local chapter of the Association of Computing Machinery and as a referee for the International data Engineering Conference, the National Science Foundation, and the International Journal of Information Systems. Dr. Bukhres has published several technical papers on his research interests.

Dr. Bukhres is a member of the Association for Computing Machinery and the IEEE Computer Society. He has served on the program committees of many conferences.

Address:
Department of Computer Science and Information Systems
Moohead State University
Moorhead, MN 56563, USA
e-mail: bukhres@plains.nodak.edu

Panos K. Chrysanthis received the B.S. degree in Physics from the University of Athens, Greece, in 1982, and the M.S. and Ph.D. degrees in Computer and Information Sciences from the University of Massachusetts at Amherst, in

1986 and 1991 respectively. Chapter 10 discusses work developed at the University of Massachusetts. Currently he is an Assistant Professor of Computer Science at the University of Pittsburgh.

His research interests lie in the areas of distributed computing, database systems and operating systems. In particular, his research focuses on both formal models and implementation support for transaction processing in complex information systems. In achieving high performance in these typically distributed systems, he investigates methods which exploit semantics information to enhance concurrency and reduce the cost of recovery. His other research activities include support for real-time applications, multiprocessor object-based systems and structuring and controlling of process and interprocess communication.

He is a member of the ACM, the IEEE Computer Society, Sigma Xi the Scientific Research Society and the Greek Computer Society.

Address:
Department of Computer Science
University of Pittsburgh
Pittsburgh, PA 15260, USA
e-mail: panos@cs.pitt.edu

Amr El Abbadi received his B.Eng. in Computer Engineering from Alexandria University, Egypt (1980), and his M.S. (1984) and Ph.D. (1987) in Computer Science from Cornell University. In August 1987 he joined the University of California at Santa Barbara, where he is currently an Assistant Professor. His current interests are in the field of distributed systems and distributed databases. He is especially interested in the design of protocols for highly available fault-tolerant systems.

Dr. El Abbadi is a member of the Association for Computing Machinery SIGACT and the IEEE Computer Society.

Address:
Department of Computer Science
University of California
Santa Barbara, CA 93106, USA

Frank Eliassen is a Professor in Computer Science at the University of Tromsø, Norway, where he is also leading the research group Open Distributed Systems.

Since 1982 he has participated in ISO standardization work in ISO/-TC97/SC16 on the OSI Presentation and Application layers. He is currently active in ISO/IEC JTC1/SC21 working on Open Distributed Processing (ODP). He has worked on several national and international research projects. His international project experience is mainly from participation in the EEC research programs COST 11 bis and ter. From 1986 to 1987 Eliassen visited GMD FOKUS, Berlin, as a guest researcher and worked together with, among others, Veijalainen and Holtkamp on the MUSE multidatabase system. In 1989 he stayed at University of Kent, UK, working with prof. P.F. Linington on issues related to open distributed processing and application integration. Apart from his stays abroad he has had various positions at the University of Tromsø.

Eliassen received the degree of Cand. mag. from the University of Oslo, in 1975, and the degree Cand. real. from the University of Tromsø, 1979, both in computer science. He is a member of ACM and the Norwegian Computer Society (DND). He represents DND in IFIP TC6 (Data Communication). Eliassen has published papers on topics including data communication protocols, CSCW systems, database systems, distributed transaction systems, and tools for information systems interoperability.

Address:
University of Tromsoe
Department of Computer Science
P.O.B. 953, N-9001 Tromsö
Norway
frank@cs.uit.no

Ahmed K. Elmagarmid is an associate professor and executive director of the Indiana Center for Database Systems. He has an assistant professor of Computer Engineering at Pennsylvania State University. Dr. Elmagarmid received a Presidential Young Investigator award had has funding from such companies as: The AT&T Foundation, Bell Northern Research, Tektronix, Mobil Oil; from the State of Indiana through the Indiana Corporation for Science and Technology and from the Federal Government through the National Science Foundation and Department of Defense. He receives support from

Purdue University and the Purdue Research Foundation and is a recipient of a David Ross Fellowship.

Dr. Elmagarmid is the Editor-in-Chief of "Distributed and Parallel Databases: An International Journal". He is associate editor of "Information Sciences" and on the editorial board for the IEEE Transactions on Computers and the IEEE Data Engineering Bulletin.

He was the General Chair for the first International Workshop on Interoperability of Multidatabase Systems (IMS-91), Kyoto, Japan and the Steering Committee Chair for the RIDE Workshop series. He has been a Vice-Chair for the 1990-92 International Conference on Distributed Computing Systems. He will be the Program Co-Chair for the 1993 IEEE Data Engineering Conference. He has served on the program committees of many conferences, workshops and symposia.

Dr. Elmagarmid has an active research program in the area of distributed databases. He has written and edited books, book chapters, journal and conference articles. He is principle investigator of the InterBase project locking into the design and implementation of heterogeneous distributed databases. He has consulted for many companies and has lectured on the subject nationally and internationally. He is an IEEE Distinguished lecturer.

He has been a principle investigator of a project on prototyping a heterogeneous distributed database systems funded by the Software Engineering Research Center (SERC). He has been actively involved with a number of the SERC affiliates performing technology transfer foundations and promoting database technology within these affiliate companies.

Dr. Elmagarmid's research interests focus on the consistency aspects of distributed databases: heterogeneous, federated and multidatabases; transaction management for advanced database applications.

Address:
Department of Computer Sciences
Purdue University
West Lafayette, IN 47907, USA
e-mail: ake@cs.purdue.edu

Dimitrios Georgakopoulos received the B.S. degree in pure mathematics from Aristotelio University of Thessaloniki, Greece, in 1982, and the M.S. and Ph.D. degrees from the University of Houston, Texas, in 1986 and 1990, respectively. He is currently a Member of Technical Staff in the Intelligent Database Systems Department at GTE Labs, where he is responsible for transaction management research in the Distributed Object Management (DOM) project. His research interests include heterogeneous multidatabase systems, object-oriented database systems, and distributed computing systems.

Address:
GTE Laboratories Incorporated
40 Sylvan Road
Waltham, MA 02254, USA

Sara Haradhvala received the MS degree in Computer Science from the University of Wisconsin in 1979. She is currently an independent consultant who specializes in the area of OODBMSs. As a Principal Software Engineer at Xerox Advanced Information Technology, Ms. Faradhvala collaborated on the development of the transaction model described here. Previously, she developed an execution model to support integration of heterogeneous software tools and databases and designed transaction management facilities for an object management system. As a member of the technical staff of Computer Corporation of America, Ms. Haradhvala added the distributed query processing architecture to the Adaplex DBMS and she was also responsible for developing PC database products. Her research interests include Software Engineering Environment (SEEs), support for cooperative work in SEEs, and architectures for federated databases and integration frameworks.

Address:
Xerox Advanced Information Technology
Cambridge Massachusetts, USA

Sandra Heiler is currently a member of the technical staff of GTE Laboratories, where she is working on development of an object model to support integration of distributed, heterogeneous systems and multi-media databases. Previously, while a Senior Computer Scientist at Xerox Advanced Information Technology (formerly part of Computer Corporation of America), Ms. Heiler designed a transaction model to support cooperative work in software engineering environments. She also developed the FUGUE object model and an object management system to support Engineering Information Systems that integrate heterogeneous software tools, DBMSs, and databases. Ms. Heiler has published widely and presented tutorials on integration of heterogeneous databases and on object-oriented systems, including the 1990 Data Engineering Conference tutorial on Object-Oriented Database Management Systems, support for cooperative work, and database management systems for specialized data types, including engineering, and bibliographic data.

Address:
GTE Laboratories
Waltham MA, USA

Bernhard Holtkamp is with the newly founded Frauenhofer Institute for Software and Systems Technology, Berlin, where he is responsible for developing distributed transaction systems and data repositories.

He has worked on several national and international research projects. From 1982 to 1985 he worked as a research scientist in the Operating Systems group on different computer architecture and operating system issues. From 1985 to 1989 he has been with Dortmund's Software Technology group, lead by prof. Herbert Weber, involved in the joint European research project MAP761 that developed the MUSE multidatabase system. From 1989 to 1990 Holtkamp served as an Adjunct Research Professor at the Naval Postgraduate School, Monterey (CA) where he worked with prof. Vincent Y. Lum on a multimedia/multidatabase project. After his return to Dortmund he took over the position as a subproject leader in the EUREKA Software Factory project. The subproject deals with the development of a process-integrated software engineering environment.

Holtkamp received his Diploma and Ph.D. in computer science, both from the University of Dortmund, in 1982 and 1985, respectively. He is a member of the IEEE Computer Society and of the German Gesellschaft für Informatik. His research interests include software engineering, distributed transaction systems, and multimedia systems.

Address:
University of Dortmund
Institut for Software Technology
P.O.B. 500 500,D-4600 Dortmund 50
Germany
holtkamp@udo.informatik.uni-dortmund.de

Mark Hornick is currently a Member of Technical Staff at GTE Laboratories pursuing distributed object database systems research to facilitate interoperability between distributed, heterogeneous systems. As Chief Architect of the Distributed Object Management (DOM) research project, Mark is responsible for prototype design and development. Mark received his Master of Science degree from Brown University and his Bachelors degree from Rutgers University.

Address:
GTE Laboratories Incorporated
40 Sylvan Road
Waltham, MA 02254, USA

Gail E. Kaiser is an Associate Professor of Computer Science at Columbia University and an NSF Presidential Young Investigator in Software Engineering. Prof. Kaiser has published over fifty papers in a wide range of software areas, including software development environments, testing and debugging tools, cooperative transaction models, reusability, application of artificial intelligence technology to software engineering, object-oriented languages and databases, and parallel and distributed systems. Prof. Kaiser received her PhD and MS from Carnegie Mellon University and her ScB from the Massachusetts Institute of Technology. She is a member of AAAI and ACM, and a senior member of IEEE.

Address:
Columbia University
Department of Computer Science
500 West 120th Street
New York, NY 10027, USA
kaiser@cs.columbia.edu, 212-854-3856
Fax: 212-666-0140

George Karabatis received his B.S. degree in Mathematics from Aristotelio University of Thessaloniki, Greece, and his M.S. degree in Computer Science from University of Houston, where he is currently a Ph.D. candidate. His areas of interest include multidatabase systems, interdependent data, and interoperable systems.

Address:

Department of Computer Science
University of Houston
Houston, TX 77204-3475, USA
marek@cs.uh.edu

Wolfgang Klas received his Ph.D. (Dr.-techn.) in computer science in 1990 and his M.Sc. (Dipl.-Ing.) in computer science in 1986 from the Technical University of Vienna. Since 1987 he heads the database research group VODAK at the Integrated Publication and Information Systems Institute (IPSI) of the German National Research Center for Computer Science (GMD) in Darmstadt, FRG, which has developed a prototype of an open, object-oriented database management system. In 1989 and 1990, he has been co-teacher of a course on non-conventional databases at the Technical University of Darmstadt. Currently he is visiting fellow at the International Computer Science Institute (ICSI) at the University of California, Berkeley. During 1989 he was involved in the development of the transaction management for Postgres at the University of California, Berkeley. From 1986 to 1987 he was teaching and research assistant at the Technical University of Vienna. His research interests include database systems, knowledge representation, object-oriented programming and data modeling, and transaction models.

Address:

Integrated Publication and Information Systems Institute (IPSI)
Dolivostraße 15, D-6100 Darmstadt, West Germany
e-mail: klas@darmstadt.gmd.de

Eva Kühn received her M.S. degree in Computer Science in 1983 and the Ph.D. degree in 1989 from the University of Technology in Vienna. In 1990 she received the Heinz-Zemanek research award for her thesis about the implementation of multidatabase systems in Prolog. In the same year she spent the summer at the InterBase Laboratory at Purdue University, Indiana, supported by the Austrian Government (Kurt-Gödel-Stipendium). She is currently working as an assistant professor and lecturer at the Department of Computer Languages at the University of Technology in Vienna. Her research interests include logic programming, parallel programming languages, deductive databases and multidatabase systems. She is the principal investigator on the project "Interoperability of Autonomous Databases" sponsored by the Austrian FWF (Fonds zur Förderung der wissenschaftlichen Forschung).

Address:
University of Technology Vienna
Institute of Computer Languages
Argentinierstr. 8, A-1040 Vienna
Austria, Europe
eva@mips.complang.tuwien.ac.at

Yungho Leu was born in 1957 in Taiwan, Republic of China. He received both B.S. and M.S. degrees in Electrical Engineering from National Taiwan University, Taipei, Taiwan, Republic of China, in 1981 and 1983, respectively, and the Ph.D. degree in Computer Science from Purdue University, West Lafayette, IN, in 1991. His research interests include Distributed Database Systems, Performance Evaluation, Fault Tolerant Computing and Parallel Processing.

Address:
Department of Computer Sciences
Purdue University
West Lafayette, IN 47907, USA
e-mail: yhl@cs.purdue.edu

Frank Manola has a B.S. degree in Civil Engineering from Duke University, and a M.S.E. degree in Computer Science from the University of Pennsylvania. In 1971 he joined the Naval Research Laboratory, Washington, D.C. From 1978 to 1987, he was a Senior Computer Scientist at Computer Corporation of America, where, among other things, he worked on object- oriented and other advanced DBMS technology, and the use of that technology in engineering and geographic applications. He is currently Principal MTS in the Intelligent Database Systems Department of GTE Laboratories, where he is Principal Investigator of the Distributed Object Management project. His research interests include object-oriented database technology, multi-media database applications, and data security. Mr. Manola is a member of several journal editorial boards, has participated in both ANSI and CODASYL standards development activities, and is the author of numerous technical publications.

Address:
GTE Laboratories Incorporated
40 Sylvan Road
Waltham, MA 02254, USA

James G. Mullen is a Graduate Student in the Department of Computer Sciences at Purdue University. He received his M.S. degree in May, 1989 and is currently working on completing his Ph.D. degree requirements. He was awarded a NASA Graduate Student Researchers Program Grant in 1990. His research interests include multidatabase systems and object-oriented database systems He is a member of the ACM and the IEEE Computer Society.

Address:
Department of Computer Sciences
Purdue University
West Lafayette, IN 47907, USA
e-mail: jgm@cs.purdue.edu

Peter Muth received his M.S. degree in computer science (Dipl.-Inform.) in 1989 from the Technical University of Darmstadt, West Germany.

Since 1989, he is a member of the database research group at the Integrated Publication and Information Systems Institute of the German National Research Center for Computer Science (GMD) in Darmstadt. Peter Muth is engaged in the development of a distributed object-oriented database system called VODAK and has published several papers in this area. His research interests include distributed database systems, heterogeneous systems and transaction management.

Address:
Integrated Publication and Information Systems Institute (IPSI)
Dolivostraße 15, D-6100 Darmstadt, West Germany
e-mail: muth@darmstadt.gmd.de

Erich. J. Neuhold is Director of the IPSI research institute of GMD and a Full Professor of Computer Science at the Technical University Darmstadt.

Previously, he was a Professor of Computer Science (Chair of Applied Informatics and Systems Analysis) at the Technical University Vienna, Austria (1984 - 1986). From March 1983 - November 1984, he was Director of the

Information Management Laboratory and later the Systems Software Laboratory of Hewlett Packard Research Laboratories in Palo Alto, USA. From 1972 - 1983, he was a Professor of Computer Science (Chair of Application Software) at the University of Stuttgart. From 1963 - 1972, he worked as a Research Scientist with IBM Corporation. His educational record includes an M.S. in Electronics (Dipl.-Ing.), 1963, and a Ph.D. in Mathematics and Computer Science (Dr.-techn.), 1967, both received at the Technical University of Vienna, Austria.

Prof. Neuhold has done research, taught courses and published papers especially in the field of database systems, expert systems, information and publication systems. He serves as an advisor for various scientific journals and also in committees of national (German Society for Computer Science: Chair of Integrated Publication and Documentation Systems), international (Chair of IFIP WG 2.2), governmental (CEC) organizations and as an advisor for industrial organizations. He was a member and served as a chair of many conference program and organizational committees.

Address:

Integrated Publication and Information Systems Institute (IPSI)
Dolivostraße 15, D-6100 Darmstadt, West Germany
e-mail: neuhold@darmstadt.gmd.de

Marian Nodine is a Graduate Student at Brown University, Providence, RI, where she has been since 1988. Her research interests include advanced transaction models for design databases and heterogeneous multidatabases, parallel applications, and data communications. She has written several papers on transaction models and on communication network monitoring. She also consults and teaches database courses at local corporations.

Mrs. Nodine has been supported since 1990 by an IBM Fellowship. Before starting at Brown, she worked at Bolt, Beranek and Newman from 1981 to 1984 and also from 1985 to 1988. She worked at Sequoia Systems from 1984 to 1985. She received her S.B. and S.M. from MIT in 1981. She is a member of ACM.

Address:

Department of Computer Science
Brown University
Providence, RI 02912, USA
email: mhn@cs.brown.edu

M. Tamer Özsu is an associate professor in the Department of Computing Science at the University of Alberta (Edmonton, Canada), where he leads a research group that investigates distributed databases, distributed multidatabase systems, object-oriented databases, and database operating system design issues. During 1990-91, he was on leave at GTE Laboratories Incorporated doing research on distributed object management issues. He holds B.Sc. and M.Sc. degrees in industrial engineering from the Middle East Technical University (Ankara, Turkey) and M.S. and Ph.D. degrees in computer and information science from Ohio State University. He is the author or coauthor of two books, including Principles of Distributed Database Systems (Prentice Hall, 1991) and of a number of technical papers. He has lectured widely on topics related to his research interests. Dr. Özsu is a member of ACM, IEEE Computer Society and Sigma Xi.

Address:
GTE Laboratories Incorporated
40 Sylvan Road
Waltham, MA 02254, USA

Calton Pu was born in Taiwan, but grew up in Brazil. After receiving his Ph.D. in Computer Science from University of Washington in 1986, he became an assistant professor in the Department of Computer Science at Columbia University. Currently, he is leading two research projects. The Harmony project has two aspects: superdatabases that provide atomic transactions across heterogeneous database boundaries, and asynchronous transaction processing based on epsilon-serializability. The Synthesis project focuses on the design and implementation of a parallel and distributed operating system kernel. It combines an orthogonal high-level kernel interface with efficient execution obtained from dynamic kernel code synthesis. The prototypes of both the Synthesis kernel and an instance of superdatabase are operational. In addition, Prof. Pu also is interested in the measurement of end-to-end application performance over wide-area networks and distributed caching that takes advantage of unused machines in a network to alleviate disk access bottlenecks. Finally, he is also working on extended transaction models for long, open-ended activities and application of kernel code synthesis to distributed software systems. Prof. Pu is a member of IEEE and ACM.

Address:
Columbia University
Department of Computer Science
500 West 120th Street
New York, NY 10027, USA
calton@cs.columbia.edu, 212-854-8110
Fax: 212-666-0140

Franz Puntigam received his M.S. degree in Computer Science in 1989 from the University of Technology in Vienna. He is currently working as a research assistant on the project "Interoperability of Autonomous Databases" sponsored by the Austrian FWF (Fonds zur Förderung der wissenschftlichen Forschung). He plans to finish his Ph.D. thesis by the end of 1991. His work comprises the design, specification, and implementation of the VPL (Vienna Parallel Logic) language and multidatabase transactions in VPL.

Address:
University of Technology Vienna
Institute of Computer Languages
Argentinierstr. 8, A-1040 Vienna
Austria, Europe
franz@mips.complang.tuwien.ac.at

Thomas C. Rakow received his M.S. degree in computer science (Dipl.-Inform.) in 1987 from the Technical University of Braunschweig, West Germany. During the winter semester 1991/92, he is giving a course on non-conventional databases at the Technical University of Darmstadt.

Since 1987, he is a member of the database research group at the Integrated Publication and Information Systems Institute of the German National Research Center for Computer Science (GMD) in Darmstadt. Thomas C. Rakow is engaged in the development of a distributed object-oriented database system called VODAK and has published several papers in this area. His research interests include non-conventional database systems and transaction management.

Address:
Integrated Publication and Information Systems Institute (IPSI)
Dolivostraße 15, D-6100 Darmstadt, West Germany
e-mail: rakow@darmstadt.gmd.de

Krithi Ramamritham received the Ph.D. in Computer Science from the University of Utah in 1981. Since then he has been with the Department of Computer and Information Science at the University of Massachusetts at Amherst where he is currently an associate professor. During 1987-88, he was a Science and Engineering Research Council (U.K.) visiting fellow at the University of Newcastle upon Tyne, U.K. and a visiting professor at the Technical University of Vienna, Austria.

His primary research interests lie in the areas of database systems, real-time systems, and distributed computing. His research activities in the database area deal with enhancing performance and functionality in distributed applications through the use of semantic information about objects and about transactions. The ACTA transaction framework grew out of this work. He also co-directs the Spring project whose goal is to develop scheduling algorithms, operating system support, architectural support, and design strategies for distributed real-time applications.

Dr. Ramamritham is an associate editor of the Real-Time Systems journal and is the co-author of an IEEE tutorial text on hard real-time systems. Dr.Ramamritham is a member of the ACM and the IEEE.

Address:
Department of Computer and Information Science
University of Massachusetts
Amherst, MA 01003, USA

Sridhar Ramaswamy has been a PhD Student at Brown University, Providence, RI since 1989. His research interests include Constraint Query Languages, Query Languages for Object Oriented Systems, and Cooperative Transaction Models.

He got his B. Tech. from the Indian Institute of Technology, Madras, India in 1989. He received his ScM from Brown University in 1991.

Address:
Department of Computer Science
Brown University
Providence, RI 02912, USA
email: sr@cs.brown.edu

Andreas Reuter is a professor of Institute of Parallel and Distributed High Performance Systems at Stuttgart University in Breitwiesenstrasse, Germany. From 1970 to 1979, he was an independent consultant, specializing on the design and implementation of large online information systems. During the period of 1979 - 1981, he was a research associate at Darmstadt University in a project on performance modeling and analysis. Then he joined University of Kaiserslautern as an assistant professor for two years. He worked at IBM Research Laboratory at San Jose as an Visiting Scientist for two years since 1983. He became a full professor for Computer Science at Stuttgart University since 1985. He is director of the Institute of Parallel and Distributed High Performance Systems since 1989.

Address:
Institute of Parallel and Distributed High Performance Systems (IPVR)
Stuttgart University
Breitwiesenstrasse 20-22, W–7000 Stuttgart 80, Germany
email: reuter@ipvr.informatik.uni-stuttgart.dbp.de

Arnon Rosenthal works on massive federated information systems at MITRE Corporation. His research interests include federated databases, query processing, active databases, and database design. Earlier interests included discrete algorithms (especially dynamic programming) and complexity theory with applications to networks and reliability. He was previously employed at Xerox Advanced Information Technology (formerly part of Computer Corporation of America), ETH-Zurich, Sperry Research, and on the faculty of the University of Michigan.

Address:
The MITRE Corporation
Bedford, MA, USA

Marek Rusinkiewicz is an Associate Professor at the Department of Computer Science at the University of Houston. His current research interests include Heterogeneous and Multidatabase Systems.

Address:
Department of Computer Science
University of Houston
Houston, TX 77204-3475, USA
marek@cs.uh.edu

Hans-Joerg Schek received the M.Sc. degree (Dipl.-Math.) in mathematics and the Ph.D. degree (Dr.-Ing.) in civil engineering from the University of Stuttgart, West Germany, in 1968 and 1972, respectively.

Dr. Schek is currently a Professor of Computer Science at the Swiss Federal Institute of Technology (ETH) Zurich, Switzerland, where he is the head of the Database Research Group. From 1983 to 1988 he was a Professor of Computer Science at the University of Darmstadt, West Germany, where he was leading the DASDBS project, an extensible database kernel system for advanced applications. From 1972 to 1983 he was with the IBM Heidelberg Scientific Center, where he started the AIM database research project in 1978. His previous work includes optimization of road designs using digital terrain and thematic map models (1968-1972), the computation of prestressed cable-net roofs for the Munich Olympic Games (1970-1972), and the numeric solution of large sets of linear and nonlinear equations.

Dr. Schek is currently leading the COSMOS project at ETH Zurich, a 15-persons project which encompasses several ambitious subprojects. The overall goal of COSMOS is to develop architectural principles for building interoperable systems that consist of cooperative data management and transaction services. This goal entails object-oriented view management as a means for incremental schema integration, transaction models and transaction management in federated systems, coupling of application systems and extensible database systems, storage management services for hypermedia data, and automatic tuning of data placement, resource management, and parallelism in such services.

Dr. Schek is a member of the Association of Computing Machinery, ACM SIGMOD, IEEE Computer Society, IEEE TC on Data Engineering, GI (German Computer Society), and SI (Swiss Computer Society). He is currently the head of the Institute of Information Systems at ETH Zurich.

Address:
Department of Computer Science
Information Systems - Databases
Swiss Federal Institute of Technology Zurich
CH-8092 Zurich, Switzerland
e-mail: schek@inf.ethz.ch

Amit P. Sheth had his undergraduate education from B.I.T.S., India and received his M.S. and Ph.D. degrees in Computer and Information Science from the Ohio State University, Columbus. Before joining Bell Communication Research as a Member of Technical Staff, he was a Principal Research Scientist at Honeywell, Minneapolis, and a Staff Scientist at Unisys West Coast Research Center, Santa Monica.

Dr. Sheth has led projects on developing a heterogeneous distributed database system, integration of AI systems with database systems, and designing a factory information system. He has also performed research and development on tools for schema integration and view update. Currently he is working on managing interdependent data in multidatabase systems and developing techniques and tools for logical design and integration in federated database systems. His research interests include semantic heterogeneity and transaction management issues in federated information systems.

He has presented tutorials on heterogeneous database integration at most database conferences (incl. Data Engineering, SIGMOD, VLDB), published many papers, and given many invited research seminars in the US and Europe. He is a recipient of two outstanding paper awards and five service recognition awards from IEEE-CS, Federal Computer Conference, and Bellcore. He has served as vice-chair and program committee member for many conferences. Currently, he is the General Chair of the First Intl. Conf. on Parallel and Distributed Information Systems.

Address:
Bellcore, RRC 1J210
444 Hoes Lane
Piscataway, NJ 08854-4182, USA
amit@ctt.bellcore.com

Gunter Schlageter received his Master degree in Electrical Engineering, University of Karlsruhe and his Ph.D. in Computer Science, University of Karlsruhe.

Habilitation 1976, University of Karlsruhe; 1979 Professor at University of Dortmund, since 1980 Full professor of Computer Science at University of Hagen (FernUniversitaet); offers from University of Hamburg, University of Mainz and University of Wien.

More than 70 publications in national and international conferences and journals in the areas of Distributed Systems, Databases, Knowledge-based Systems, Computer-assisted Learning, Object-oriented Systems.

Major functions in various international conferences (Very Large Databases, Data Engineering, etc.), member of the VLDB-Endownment.

Address:
University of Hagen, Department of Computer Science
P.O. Box 940, D-5800 Hagen, Germany

Rainer Unland received M. Sc. (Dipl.-Inform.) in Computer Science from University of Dortmund, Germany, in 1980 and Ph. D. (Dr. rer. nat.) in Computer Science from University of Hagen, Germany, in 1985. He has been working as a research assistant at the University of Hagen since 1980 where he is currently completing his procedure to receive qualification as university lecturer (Habilitation). His research interests include transaction management, computer supported cooperative work, and object- oriented database systems.

Address:
University of Hagen, Department of Computer Science
P.O. Box 940, D-5800 Hagen, Germany

Jari Veijalainen is with the Technical Research Centre of Finland, Laboratory for Information Processing, Helsinki, Finland, where is a senior research scientist. He is mainly responsible for developing advanced transaction facilities for EDI-environments.

He has worked on several national and international research projects. From 1982 to 1985 he worked as a teaching assistant and as a research scientist at the University of Helsinki, Department of Computer Science, taking part in the locally financed projects Distributed Databases and Computer Network

Protocols. During the latter project, he mainly contributed to ISO/OSI standardization work on FTAM in ISO/TC97/SC16/WG5. From 1985 to 1987 he worked as a guest scientist at the Hahn-Meitner-Institut Berlin GmbH, and during 1988 at GMD FOKUS, where he was involved in the joint European research project MAP761. In the course of MAP761, the MUSE multidatabase system and the S-transaction model were developed. During 1983-1989 he also took part in the European COST 11 bis project Distributed Database Management, and in the subsequent COST 11 ter projects Distributed Aspects in Information Systems (DAISY) and Interoperability in Heterogeneous Information Systems (IHIS). Since 1990, he is the Finnish member of the Management Committee of the European COST 14 project on CSCW systems.

Veijalainen received the B.Sc. degree in mathematics in 1978, and M.Sc. degree in computer science in 1983, both from the University of Helsinki, Finland , and the Ph.D. (Dr.-Ing.) degree in computer science, in 1989, from the Technical University of Berlin, Germany. He is a member of ACM and the Finnish computer science association. His research interests include open distributed systems, transaction processing in heterogeneous environment, autonomy in system design, interoperability, formal specification, and CSCW systems.

Address:

Technical Research Centre of Finland (VTT)
Laboratory for Information Processing
Lehtisaarentie 2A, SF-00340 Helsinki
Finland
veijalainen@tik.vtt.fi

Helmut Wächter has studied computer science and business administration at the Stuttgart University, Germany. After acquiring a diploma in computer science he is working as a research assistant at the *Institute of Parallel and Distributed High Performance Systems* since 1988. His research interests are in the field of distributed transaction processing (DTP). Special research activities include (a) the extension of conventional transaction models to support the requirements of large distributed applications adequately and (b) the architecture of future DTP systems and protocols for the reliable execution of long-lived activities on shared resources. At the moment he is preparing his thesis presenting the results of this research and conducts a group of students doing a prototype implementation.

Address:

Institute of Parallel and Distributed High Performance Systems (IPVR)
Stuttgart University
Breitwiesenstrasse 20-22, W–7000 Stuttgart 80, Germany
email: waechter@ipvr.informatik.uni-stuttgart.dbp.de

Gerhard Weikum received the M.Sc. degree (Dipl.-Inform.) and the Ph.D. degree (Dr.-Ing.) both in computer science from the University of Darmstadt, West Germany, in 1982 and 1986, respectively.

Dr. Weikum is currently a Professor of Computer Science at the Swiss Federal Institute of Technology (ETH) Zurich, Switzerland. From 1983 to 1987 he was involved in the DASDBS project, an extensible database kernel system for advanced applications. In particular, he designed and implemented the multilevel transaction management in DASDBS, and developed its underlying theory. From March 1988 to February 1989 he was a visiting scientist at the Microelectronics and Computer Technology Corporation (MCC), Austin, Texas, where he was involved in the prototype development of the highly parallel database machine Bubba.

Dr. Weikum's research interests include database system architecture, high-performance transaction processing, parallelism and distribution, and operating system support for DBMS. He is currently leading the COMFORT project as a part of the COSMOS project at ETH Zurich. The overall goal of COMFORT is to automate tuning decisions in transaction processing and database systems, thus aiming to simplify the tricky job of system administrators and human tuning experts. This goal entails automatic data placement on parallel I/O architectures, intelligent resource management, and the tuning of intra-transaction parallelism in a multi-user environment.

Dr. Weikum is a member of the Association of Computing Machinery, ACM SIGMOD, ACM SIGOPS, IEEE Computer Society, IEEE TC on Data Engineering, GI (German Computer Society), and SI (Swiss Computer Society).

Address:

Department of Computer Science
Information Systems - Databases
Swiss Federal Institute of Technology Zurich
CH-8092 Zurich, Switzerland
e-mail: weikum@inf.ethz.ch

Stanley Zdonik is an Associate Professor of Computer Science at Brown University, Providence, RI, and has been on the faculty there since 1983. He has been a consultant in the area of database management systems to many US corporations.

For the past eight years he has managed the Object-Oriented Database Research Group at Brown University. Through the development of the ENCORE and the ObServer prototypes, this group has pioneered many of the ideas that are currently accepted in the object-oriented database field today. The group is actively engaged in further research into areas such as query processing for object-oriented databases and highly-reliable, high-performance storage servers for object-oriented databases.

Dr. Zdonik has served on many program committees of major conferences in the areas of databases and object-oriented systems, including SIGMOD, VLDB, the International Workshop on Software Engineering, the ACM Conference on Office Information Systems, the International Workshop on Object-Oriented Databases and the ACM Conference on Object-Oriented Programming, Systems, Languages, and Applications. He has served as an Associate Editor of the ACM Transactions on Office Information Systems and is currently an associate editor for IEEE Office Knowledge Engineering, the VLDB Journal, and the Journal of Persistent Object Systems.

He has written numerous papers on object-oriented databases, semantic query optimization, and database interfaces. He is the co-editor of the books "Readings in Object-Oriented Database Systems" (with D. Maier) and "Implementing Persistent Object Bases" (with A. Dearle and G. Shaw), both published by Morgan-Kaufmann. He worked for Bolt, Beranek, and Newman from 1971 to 1976 and at the MIT Laboratory for Computer Science from 1976 to 1983. He received his PhD from MIT in 1983. He was awarded the Office of Naval Research Young Investigator Award in 1986.

Address:
Department of Computer Science
Brown University
Providence, RI 02912, USA
email: sbz@cs.brown.edu

Subject Index

S

T

Author Index